Jack: Documentary Credits

The law and practice of documentary credits including standby credits and demand guarantees

Jack: Documentary Credits

The law and practice of documentary credits including standby credits and demand guarantees

Fourth edition

by

Ali Malek QC
MA (Oxon), BCL
Bencher of Gray's Inn

David Quest
MA (Cantab)
of Gray's Inn, Barrister

with contributions from

Jonathan Davies-Jones, MA (Cantab)
of the Middle Temple, Barrister

Christopher Harris, LLB (Bristol),
LLM (Leiden),
PhD (St. Gallen), MCIArb
of Lincoln's Inn, Barrister

Henry Knox, MA (Edin), PhD (Edin)
of Gray's Inn, Barrister

Benjamin Parker, MA (Oxon)
MA (Cantab)
of the Middle Temple, Barrister

Rajesh Pillai, BA (Oxon), BA (Cantab)
LLM (NYU)
of the Middle Temple, Barrister

David Simpson, BA (Oxon)
of Gray's Inn, Barrister

Tottel
publishing

Tottel Publishing
Maxwelton House
41–43 Boltro Road
Haywards Heath
West Sussex
RH16 1BJ

British Library Cataloguing-in-Publication Data
A CIP Catalogue record for this book is available from the British Library.

ISBN 978 1 84592 347 1

Typeset by Phoenix Photosetting, Chatham, Kent
Printed and bound in Great Britain by Martins the Printers

Acknowledgements

The publishers and authors wish to thank the International Chamber of Commerce for permission to reproduce material from the following sources:

ICC Uniform Customs and Practice for Documentary Credits 600;

ICC Uniform Customs and Practice for Documentary Credits 600E;

ICC Uniform Customs and Practice for Documentary Credits 500;

International Standard Banking Practice 681; and

International Standby Practices – ISP98

All these documents are available from ICC Publishing SA, 38 Cours Albert 1er, 75008 Paris, France or ICC United Kingdom, 12 Grosvenor Place, London SW1X 7HH, www.iccbookshop.com

Five times thirty-nine syllables

The moon is large and yellow
Over the harvest fields.
Upstairs a light shows you are in bed.
Why should I work into the night
When you have put on your light?

●

The sunlight moves over the waving grass
Between the orchard trees.
Only in your indentation is it still,
Pressed like my heart.
So waiting I lie down and take your shape.

●

In this autumn of love tears like leaves
Are blown across my cheeks.
Such aching sadness for this losing
So destroys me that
You do not know me as the one you loved.

●

It is like the tide moving,
Creeping along the creek, whispering its way,
Softly enveloping all it may. So am I
When I awake and thought comes of you.

●

All day we rode, a long column,
Making the climb over the pass,
Then winding down onto the plain.
I sat my horse in silence,
Watching the movement of your hair.

Raymond Jack

Preface to the fourth edition

Although there have been a number of important developments in the case law, the principal impetus for this fourth edition of *Documentary Credits* was the issue by the International Chamber of Commerce of UCP 600, the sixth revision of the Uniform Customs and Practice for Documentary Credits. In the preface to the third edition we noted that if the ICC kept to its historical ten year cycle then UCP 600 should not be expected before 2003; in the event, it was not until July 2007 that UCP 600 came into force, following more than three years of drafting and consultation by the ICC Commission on Banking Technique and Practice.

The UCP has been extensively redrafted in its latest revision. The text has been shortened and simplified, with a reduction from 49 articles to 39; new definitions have been introduced for clarification; controversies raised in the case law have been resolved, including, for example, the decision in *Glencore v Bank of China* (1996) on original documents, and the decision in *Banco Santander v Banque Paribas* (2000) on discounting deferred payment credits. However, the underlying scheme of the UCP has been preserved, as has the fundamental responsibility of banks in documentary credit transactions to examine presentations and to pay, and to pay only, against those which on their face strictly comply with the requirements of the credit.

We have presented the law and practice as it now is under UCP 600, following the same structure and chapter headings as before. In some cases, where there has been a significant or illuminating change in the rules, we have retained the discussion of the former position under UCP 500. In general, however, we took the view that the extent of the changes in drafting would make a detailed comparative analysis of the rules cumbersome and unhelpful. Moreover, Professor James E. Byrne of the Institute of International Banking Law and Practice has produced a comprehensive work on that topic: *The Comparison of UCP 600 and UCP 500*. Whilst there will no doubt continue to be litigation for some time about credits subject to earlier revisions of the UCP (indeed, a 2006 case, *Habib Central Bank v Central Bank of Sudan*, concerned a credit subject to UCP 290, the 1974 revision), the banking practice and legal principles discussed remain of general application. We have included the text of UCP 500 in an appendix, but if a more detailed analysis of a particular article of UCP 500 is required, reference should be made to the third edition of this book.

UCP 600 is not the only important recent publication by the ICC. The ICC's International Standard Banking Practice (ISBP) was first issued in 2003 and was reissued at the same time as UCP 600 in order to 'explain how the practices articulated in UCP 600 are applied by documentary practitioners'. This is a helpful document in clarifying and expanding on the UCP, although its legal status is unclear and it remains to be seen how it will affect the traditional use in English proceedings of expert witness evidence to prove banking practice.

The duties of banks in the examination of documents presented are dealt with in detail, in **Chapter 8**. Despite the frequent statements by the courts and the ICC that banks involved in documentary credit transactions should deal only in documents, the unfortunate practice of parties inserting non-documentary conditions remains prevalent. The difficulties that that can create, and the courts' attempts to balance the parties' freedom of contract with the principle that credits should be operated only by reference to the documents presented, are illustrated in *Korea Exchange Bank v Standard Chartered Bank* (Singapore, 2006) and *Oliver v Dubai Bank Kenya* (2007).

Fraud remains a serious risk for those involved in documentary credit transactions. As fraudsters adapt their methods, banks and others must look for different ways of recovering their losses and different defendants to pursue. Significant recent cases, discussed in **Chapter 9**, include *Solo Industries v Canara Bank* (2001), *Niru Battery Manufacturing v Milestone* (2004) and *Banque Saudi Fransi v Lear Siegler Services* (2006). The possible extension of the fraud exception to cover 'bad faith' calls on credits, a doctrine which began in Singapore but has perhaps gained a foothold in England through *TTI Team Telecom International v Hutchison 3G* (2003), is also discussed.

Whilst Lord Diplock said that fraud was the 'one established exception' to a bank's obligation to pay against conforming documents, the decision in *Mahonia v WestLB* (2004), discussed in **Chapter 13**, gives strong support for a further exception based on illegality of the underlying transaction, although leaving open its scope and limits. The case, which concerned the use of standby credits to implement financial structuring for Enron, is also an illustration of the widespread use of documentary credits outside the field of traditional trade finance. However, the possibility of a 'nullity' exception was ruled out by the Court of Appeal in *Montrod v Grundkotter Fleischvertriebs* (2001).

Demand guarantees, performance bonds and the like, which we refer to as independent guarantees, are sister instruments to documentary credits and share many of their characteristics. But ambiguous drafting continues to create problems in distinguishing them from ordinary instruments of suretyship, as demonstrated by two recent cases in the Court of Appeal: *Marubeni Hong Kong and South China v Government of Mongolia* (2005) and *Gold Coast v Caja de Ahorros del Mediterraneo* (2003). The alleged misuse of an advance payment guarantee was the subject of *Uzinterimpex v Standard Chartered Bank* (2007), a case which raised a number of interesting issues, including whether a bank has a right to recover overpayments. The ICC's Uniform Rules on Demand Guarantees are in the process of being revised; a third draft was circulated for consultation at the beginning of 2009 and the new rules are expected to be issued later in the year.

Conflicts of law and conflicts of jurisdiction, addressed in **Chapter 13**, continue to be important topics and, as previously, documentary credits cases have been at the forefront of the general development of these areas of the law. *PT Pan Indonesia Bank v Marconi Communications* (2007) considered contractual choice of law in documentary credits (for the purpose of determining whether an English court could assume jurisdiction) and the *Trafigura v Kookmin* (2006) litigation considered the law applicable to tortious claims.

We said in the preface to the third edition that the regular use of electronic credits as part of international trade was still a little way off. Despite the lapse of time, it is probably little closer, but at least electronic credits are now catered for in a supplement to the UCP, 'eUCP', which is discussed, together with other developments in this area, in **Chapter 14**.

In preparing this fourth edition, we have had the great advantage of a team of experienced contributors, on whom much of the work has fallen. Benjamin Parker revised Chapters 2, 3 and 4; Jonathan Davies-Jones, Chapters 6 and 7; Henry Knox, Chapters 9 and 10; Christopher Harris, Chapters 11 and 12; Rajesh Pillai, Chapter 13; David Simpson, Chapter 14. All are barristers in commercial practice: Benjamin Parker at 7 King's Bench Walk, the others at 3 Verulam Buildings. We are very grateful for their contribution, without which this edition would not have been possible. We are also grateful to John Turnbull of Sumitomo Mitsui Banking Corporation Europe Limited, co-chair of the ICC Consulting Group for the UCP Revision, for his review of the text and comments. Any opinions expressed in the text are those of the authors.

Sir Raymond Jack, the original author of the book and co-author of the third edition has, through pressure of his judicial duties, been unable to participate on the main text of this edition. He has, however, contributed the poem on **page vi**, which may provide readers with some distraction or solace while studying the UCP.

We express our particular thanks to Sarah Thomas of Tottel Publishing for her support, supervision and patience.

The law is stated as at 1 January 2009.

Ali Malek QC
David Quest

January 2009

Contents

xi

Table of cases

C

Table of statutes

Paragraph references printed in **bold** type indicate where the Act is set out in part or in full.

Chapter 1

Introduction to Documentary Credits and to the Uniforms Customs

A   GENERAL INTRODUCTION

Outline of the chapter

1.1   The object of this chapter is to describe documentary credits, their function and how they are operated in practice, so that Chapter 2 may describe particular kinds of credit and Chapter 3 may begin the sequence of chapters covering specific relationships which arise between the parties to documentary credits. The chapter also introduces the Uniform Customs and Practice for Documentary Credits, referred to in this book as the 'UCP'. These contain provisions governing documentary credits, their operation and the rights and obligations to which they may give rise. The terms 'documentary credit' and 'letter of credit' are both in current use and no distinction need be made between them.

The general concept and function of documentary credits

1.2 In simple transactions of sale, such as may take place in a shop, the buyer pays the seller in exchange for the goods. In commercial transactions where buyer and seller are in different countries and the goods must be transported by sea or road or air by a third party carrier, something more sophisticated is required. The seller may be unwilling to despatch the goods unless he has some security of payment; on the other hand, the buyer may be unwilling to pay for the goods unless he has some security that they will be delivered. A documentary credit is a means of providing payment in a way that addresses, to some extent, both parties' requirements. In essence, it is a promise by a bank of immediate or future payment against specified documents on terms that the bank will be reimbursed by the buyer. Subject to the solvency of the bank, certainty of payment is achieved provided that the seller is able to meet the terms of the credit. However, if the credit specifies payment against the shipping documents for the goods (including, in particular, the transport document), the seller should not be in a position to operate it until the goods have been despatched.

1.3 In addition to providing security of payment, another important function of documentary credits is to facilitate financing of the sale for both buyer and seller. If, rather than providing for immediate payment, a credit provides for deferred payment or payment by way of acceptance by the bank of a bill of exchange, then the buyer will receive the goods but will not have to reimburse the bank which has issued the credit until a date in the future. If the seller nevertheless wants cash immediately – which he may need to pay for the acquisition or manufacture of the goods he is selling – there are a number of options. If a bill of exchange has been used then he can discount the bill either with his own bank or another bank or finance house. Or, if the credit permits it, he can sell the documents to a bank which will pay him immediately and collect payment under the credit at maturity; this is known as negotiation of the credit and is considered in detail in **Chapter 7**. In either case, he will receive a discounted amount reflecting the interest and fees of the bank advancing the money. Credits can also be used, by the mechanism of transfer, to provide for payment to a party from whom the seller is himself acquiring the goods; see **Chapter 10**.

1.4   The transaction whose development was probably the first step towards the documentary credit system is that where the buyer agrees to pay cash against presentation of documents to him by the seller. In a CIF contract the documents to be presented to the buyer would be the invoice, the bills of lading, a policy or certificate of insurance, and such other documents as might be specified in the contract of sale. The feature in common with documentary credits is the promise to pay in return for the transfer of documents of the right description. The main difference from a documentary credit is that the seller has only the promise of the buyer to pay and not that of a bank. The buyer may renege on his promise and refuse to accept the documents because the market or his circumstances have changed, leaving the seller with a claim for damages for breach of contract against a buyer in another country. Or if the documents are accepted but payment is by acceptance of a bill of exchange drawn on the buyer, the seller risks that it will be dishonoured at maturity. The seller will then not receive payment (or if he has discounted the bill he will have to refund the bank or the discount house because he is liable as the drawer of a dishonoured bill[1]) even though he has parted with both goods and documents. A second difference is that to receive payment the seller has to get the documents to the buyer, so there may be a delay before the seller gets paid. But if no bank is involved the banking charges which will be incurred if a credit is used will be saved.

1 Instead of the seller obtaining the buyer's acceptance of the bill prior to his negotiation of it, the seller's bank may be prepared to make an advance to the seller against the price immediately by taking from him the bill drawn on the buyer together with the documents relating to the goods. His bank will then obtain the buyer's acceptance of the bill against the release to him of the documents. Again, if the bill is dishonoured by non-acceptance or by non-payment, the seller will have to reimburse the bank to which he negotiated the bill.

1.5   Although the traditional use of documentary credits is as payment under contracts of sale, they are widely used as security for a range of other obligations. Where the documents to be presented for payment do not include commercial documents relating to goods, the credit is called a 'standby credit'; standby credits are considered in **Chapter 12**.

Parties to the credit

1.6   The party who arranges for the opening of a credit is referred to as the 'applicant'. Where the underlying transaction which gives rise to the need for the credit is one of sale, this will be the buyer. The bank which is requested by the applicant to open the credit is referred to as the 'issuing bank'. The issuing bank takes the risk of reimbursement by the applicant if it pays under the credit and for that reason will usually be the applicant's own bank. The party to whom the undertaking is given is referred to as the 'beneficiary'. This will be the seller where the underlying transaction is one of sale. The simplest form of credit involves only these three parties.

1.7 It is usual, however, for the issuing bank to instruct another bank, which will usually be in the country of the seller or beneficiary, to communicate the terms of the credit, to accept presentation of documents and to effect payment. This enables the beneficiary to deal with a bank in his own country. The bank which performs these functions may be referred to as 'the advising bank' (if it advises the terms of the credit) or 'the correspondent bank' (because it will usually be the issuing bank's correspondent in the country in question). The UCP uses the term 'nominated bank' to mean the bank or banks with which the credit is available, that is, at which the documents may be presented.

1.8 The mere fact that the advising bank advises the credit to the beneficiary does not give the beneficiary rights against it, even if it is the nominated bank, unless it adds its own undertaking to that of the issuing bank. It is most desirable for the beneficiary that it should do so because he then has an enforceable undertaking from a bank in his own country as well as from the issuing bank in the buyer's country. The form which the undertaking of the advising bank then takes is that it 'confirms' the undertaking of the issuing bank or, as it is usually and more shortly put, it 'confirms the credit'. It is then called a 'confirming bank'.

1.9 These relationships can be set out diagrammatically as follows:

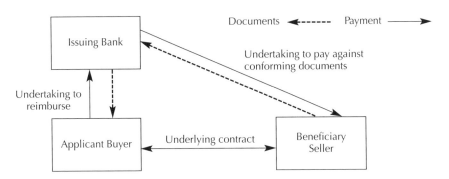

Where the credit is confirmed

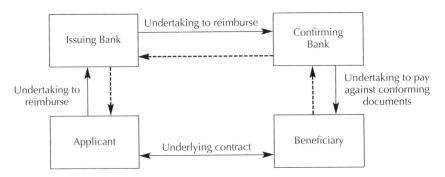

The setting up of a credit and its operation

1.10 Behind every documentary credit there is an underlying transaction (or contract) which has earlier been entered into between the applicant for the credit and the beneficiary. As has been stated, this is most commonly a contract of sale. One term of this underlying contract will be that the credit should be opened. It should specify the type of credit and so far as necessary its terms. It may identify the bank at which documents are to be presented. This contract is the origin of the credit, but it is separate from it and it does not form part of the credit. The credit will be operated in accordance with its own terms and without regard to the terms of the underlying contract or the performance of the underlying contract. This principle, called the 'autonomy of the credit', is central to the law concerning documentary credits and is discussed in para **1.34** below.

1.11 The first stage in relation to the credit itself is the giving of instructions by the applicant (the buyer) to a bank to open the credit in the particular manner which is required. The applicant will usually approach his own bank for this purpose. The second stage will be the instruction by the issuing bank of a correspondent bank, if used, in the beneficiary's country; this will often be by SWIFT, the inter-bank secure electronic telecommunications network. The third stage is the advising of the credit to the beneficiary by the correspondent bank, or where there is no correspondent bank, by the issuing bank itself. As has been mentioned, where the correspondent bank has been so instructed by the issuing bank it will, if it is prepared to, confirm the credit, adding its undertaking to that of the issuing bank. This will be something that the seller/beneficiary is likely to have required when he made his contract with the buyer/applicant. The credit as advised to the beneficiary forms a contract between the issuing bank and the beneficiary, and also between the beneficiary and that correspondent bank if, but only if, the latter has added its confirmation and so become a 'confirming bank'. The issuing and confirming bank charge a fee for their involvement which is typically a percentage of the value of the credit. A bank which acts only as an advising bank will charge a more modest fee.

1.12 Next is the operation of the credit by the beneficiary. When the beneficiary has shipped the goods or done whatever else is necessary to bring into being or obtain the documents which are needed to operate the credit, he presents them to the bank to which presentation under the credit is to be made. The issuing bank may have nominated one or more banks with which the credit is available; if it has not and the buyer has to present the documents to the issuing bank in the buyer's country, he is likely to use his own bank as agent for this purpose. The bank to which documents are presented will check them to see that they comply with the credit and it will also check that presentation has been made as the credit requires. If all is in order, it will pay the beneficiary if that is what the credit provides for. Or it will comply with whatever other payment mechanism the credit provides. If the documents are not in order, it must refuse them. Before the refusal becomes final, at the seller's request it may take instructions from the issuing bank, or from the applicant direct if it is the issuing bank, to see whether the applicant is prepared to accept the documents even though the terms of the credit have not been met.[1] In practice, in very many cases the documents are found not to meet the terms of the credit, and it is common also for buyers to waive the discrepancies which have been notified to them because they want the goods, and the discrepancies are minor.

1 The problems arising in connection with this under UCP Article 16 are considered in paras 5.53 et seq.

1.13 If the credit provides for the documents to be presented to a nominated bank, as is usually the case, and that bank has accepted the documents, it will then remit them to the issuing bank. It will then be the duty of the issuing bank in its turn to check that the documents conform to the credit. If it finds that they do so, it will reimburse the nominated bank what it has paid to the beneficiary. If it considers that they do not do so it will send a notice of refusal to the nominated bank and will return them to it unless the buyer is prepared to waive the discrepancies which have now been found.

1.14 The last step is for the issuing bank to remit the documents to the applicant or buyer. This will be done against payment by the buyer to the bank or in accordance with whatever else may have been agreed between them. If the buyer finds that the banks have accepted documents which do not comply with the credit, he may reject them. When he has obtained the documents, the buyer may use them to obtain possession of the goods; for example, he may need to produce the transport document to the carrier.

A series of contractual relationships

1.15 The relationships established by the setting up of a letter of credit give rise to a number of contracts,[1] and the path down which the documents are passed can be seen as a chain of contracts. When the issuing bank agrees to act on the instructions of the applicant a contract comes into being between them involving rights and obligations on each side. When a correspondent bank agrees to act on the instructions of the issuing bank and to advise the credit and to take on whatever further roles the instructions require, a contract comes into being between the two banks with rights and obligations on each side. The advice of the credit to the beneficiary brings into being a contract between the issuing bank and the beneficiary. If a bank confirms the credit, a contract also comes into being between this confirming bank and the beneficiary. But if the advising bank does not confirm the credit, no contract between it and the beneficiary is created: the beneficiary only has rights against the issuing bank. The majority of disputes which arise in connection with credits are concerned with whether the documents comply with the credit. More complex problems are often to be resolved by considering each contract in turn and spelling out the rights and obligations of the parties to it. Perhaps the most important aspect is the identification of the capacity in which a particular party is acting towards another. The source of the contract will almost always be documentary, and there will very often just be the one document to be examined, such as the applicant's completed form of application to the issuing bank, or the written instructions from the issuing bank to the confirming bank or the credit itself as between the issuing bank and the beneficiary, and as between a confirming bank and the beneficiary.

1 See also para **1.34** below.

1.16 Although contract is the jurisprudential foundation for the obligations contained in the various legal relationships, it is difficult to analyse them satisfactorily without recognising that documentary credits are to some extent of a special nature. The problems in applying general contractual concepts such as consideration and offer and acceptance are discussed below.[1] Courts in different jurisdictions have noted the peculiar nature of documentary credits. In *Bank of Nova Scotia v Angelica-Whitewear Ltd,*[2] the Supreme Court of Canada observed:

> 'There is no doubt that there are important differences between the civil law and the common law concerning the rationale, in contract theory, for the legally enforceable nature of the issuing bank's obligation to the beneficiary under an irrevocable letter of credit. The general opinion appears to be that the obligation is of a sui generis contractual nature for which no completely satisfactory rationale has been found in the established categories of contract theory, but the judicial recognition of its legal enforceability is now beyond dispute.'

And in *Alaska Textile Co v Chase Manhattan Bank*[3] the US Court of Appeals for the 2nd Circuit said:

> 'Letters of credit are sui generis. Virtually unknown at Roman Law, letters of credit were woven into the fabric of the common law, largely under the aegis of Lord Mansfield as he fashioned the law merchant (lex mercatoria) to the needs of the 18th Century Industrial Revolution. Thus, letters of credit are governed by the lex mercatoria, see John F. Dolan, The Law of Letters of Credit 2.02, at 2–5 (2d ed. 1991); Harfield, Letters of Credit, supra, at 1; Rufus J. Trimble, The Law Merchant and the Letter of Credit, 61 Harv. L. Rev. 981 passim (1948), and, in applying this body of law, we are appropriately solicitous of the necessities of commerce and of developments in other jurisdictions.'

1 At para 5.8.
2 [1987] 1 SCR 59 at 82.3.
3 982 F 2d 813 (1992).

The construction of documentary credits and the relevance of banking practice

1.17   Despite their special nature, documentary credits subject to English law should be construed in accordance with the ordinary rules of contractual construction. Where a contract is contained in a document and the meaning is clear, the basic rule is that no evidence in addition to the terms of the document, no extrinsic evidence, is admissible to modify the meaning of the words used. Extrinsic evidence is, however, always admissible to show that words have a particular meaning in their context, which differs from their ordinary meaning. Also, where the meaning is not clear, where there is ambiguity, evidence of the circumstances in which the contract was made is admissible to help to ascertain the meaning of the written words. As Lord Wilberforce stated in *Reardon Smith Line Ltd v Yngvar Hansen-Tangen*:[1]

> 'No contracts are made in a vacuum: there is always a setting in which they have to be placed. The nature of what is legitimate to have regard to is usually described as "the surrounding circumstances" but this phrase is imprecise: it can be illustrated but hardly defined. In a commercial contract it is certainly right that the court should know the commercial purpose of the contract and this in turn presupposes knowledge of the genesis of the transaction, the background, the context, the market in which the parties are operating.'

He went on to refer to the object of ascertaining the intention of the parties in an objective sense. He continued, 'Similarly when one is speaking of aim, object or commercial purpose, one is speaking objectively of what reasonable persons would have in mind in the situation of the parties'. The principles on which contractual documents are construed was restated by Lord Hoffmann in *Investors' Compensation Scheme Ltd v West Bromwich Building Society*.[2]

1 [1976] 1 WLR 989 at 995.
2 [1998] 1 WLR 896 at 912. See also *Charter Reinsurance Co Ltd v Fagan* [1997] AC 313.

1.18   In a commercial context the parties may be presumed to contract in accordance with any custom or usage of the particular trade. Evidence of custom in the trade is admissible to explain the terms used in the contract, and also to clarify ambiguities and to establish matters on which the contract is silent, although proving a sufficiently established custom may be difficult.[1] However, where there is no reliance on a particular custom, evidence on banking practice is not admissible to explain the ordinary terms of the credit or of the UCP. In *Seaconsar Far East Ltd v Bank Markazi Jomhouri Islami Iran*, expert evidence was adduced and relied on to explain the purpose and effect of one of the articles of the UCP. Sir Christopher Staughton said:[2]

> 'It is no part of the function of an expert witness, or for that matter of any other witness, to state his views on the meaning of ordinary English words in a written contract, unless it is sought to prove some custom which is pleaded

and can be supported by appropriate evidence. Expert witnesses are nevertheless often called for that purpose; in our view that is simply a waste of money.'

Certainly, international banking practice cannot override the express effect of the credit or of the UCP.[3] Courts may use their powers under CPR Pt 35 to limit the scope or number of experts, or to appoint a single expert, in order to meet the overriding objectives of the rules.[4] Separately from the construction of the terms of the credit, banking practice is relevant in determining whether there has been a complying presentation. This is considered further in paras **8.11** to **8.14** below.

1 For example, in *Banque de l'Indochine et de Suez SA v JH Rayner (Mincing Lane Ltd)* [1983] QB 711 Parker J said, 'It is clear from the evidence that no uniform banking practice exists either as to the form of the indemnity or guarantee which is used in the case of payment notwithstanding irregularities, nor as to the consequences of a payment being made under reserve'.
2 [1999] 1 Lloyd's Rep 36 at 39.
3 *Glencore International AG v Bank of China* [1996] 1 Lloyd's Rep 135 at 153
4 An application heard under the old Rules of the Supreme Court to adduce expert evidence on banking practice was refused in *Credit Agricole Indosuez v Generale Bank (No 2)* [2000] 1 Lloyd's Rep 123 at 127: a discrepant documents case.

The inclusion of bills of exchange

1.19　It is desirable to state at an early stage that the introduction of bills of exchange, or drafts as they are often called, into the arrangements constituting a documentary credit brings with it a separate group of rights and obligations arising on the bill itself between the parties to it, namely the drawer, the drawee/acceptor, the payee and any indorsers and indorsees. The terms of the credit which have been specified by the applicant pursuant to his agreement with the beneficiary will determine who are to be the parties to the bill and in what capacity. Thus the drawee/acceptor could be the issuing or the confirming bank, or the applicant,[1] or even a third party, as may have been specified and so has become a term of the credit. So the inclusion of a bill of exchange among the documents to be presented adds a complication which requires to be thought through: what is the function of the bill, and what obligations are intended to and will result from it? It is suggested that bills of exchange should not be included among the documents required by a credit without reason. The question of recourse between parties to a bill is of particular importance. This is considered later.[2] It can be stated at this point that issuing and confirming banks do not have a right of recourse against the drawer/beneficiary of the credit in the event of the bill's dishonour by non-acceptance or non-payment.

1 Not permissible under the UCP: see Article 6.c and para **5.21** below.
2 See para **5.94**.

B   THE UNIFORM CUSTOMS AND PRACTICE

History

1.20   The convenience 'if not the necessity' of an international code governing the operation of documentary credits and providing uniformity is obvious given the internationality of credit transactions. By being incorporated into the contracts which come into being in connection with credits, a code can provide a uniformity in the rights and obligations to which those contracts give rise. It can encourage a uniformity of banking practice in relation to credits. It can reduce the differences which might otherwise emerge as a result of differences in national laws relating to credits. In 1933 the International Chamber of Commerce first published *The Uniform Customs and Practice for Documentary Credits*, referred to in this book, as it often is elsewhere, as the UCP.[1] This first code was only adopted by bankers in some European countries. A Revision was published in 1951, which met with greater success, including its adoption by banks in the United States. But it was only the 1962 Revision[2] that secured the approval of banks in the United Kingdom and most Commonwealth countries. This Revision made changes to matters which had previously been objectionable to British banks. The version came close to universal adoption. A third Revision, the 1974 Revision,[3] came into effect in 1975, and was more comprehensive than its predecessors. It was made necessary in particular by the spread of containerisation and the use of combined transport documents. The fourth Revision, known as the 1983 Revision or UCP 400, came into effect on 1 October 1984.[4] The Introduction to the *ICC's Case Studies on Documentary Credits*[5] states that special note was taken for the 1983 Revision of:

> '– the continuing revolution in transport technology, the geographical extension of containerisation and combined transport;
> – the increasing influence of trade facilitation activities on development of new documents and new methods of producing documents;
> – the communications revolution, replacing paper as a means of transmitting information (data) relating to a trading transaction by methods of automated or electronic data processing (ADP/EDP);
> – the development of new types of documentary credits, such as the deferred payment credit and the standby credit;
> – the increasing interest and influence in international trade of nations which are less developed and, therefore, less experienced in this area.'

The same factors lay behind the need for a further fifth Revision, the 1993 Revision or UCP 500,[6] which came into effect on 1 January 1994. In particular it was apparent that further attention was required to the matter of transport documents, the area where once the marine bill of lading once ruled uncontested. A further aim of UCP 500 was to simplify and to clarify. For it appeared that approximately 50% of sets of documents presented under credits were failing to meet the requirements of the credit upon first presentation.

1 'The UCP is an example of a successful international legal initiative. It is a significant legal support for international commerce, enhancing the speed, volume, and ease of international trade transactions': Australian Law Reform Commission, *Legal Risk in International Transactions* (1996) ALRC 80.
2 ICC publication No 222.
3 ICC No 290.
4 ICC No 400.
5 ICC No 459.
6 ICC No 500.

UCP 600

1.21　In May 2003, the ICC authorised the ICC Banking Commission[1] to begin a further revision of the UCP, with the general objective of addressing developments in the banking, transport and insurance industries and generally to review the wording. Concern was also expressed about the high rate at which presentations were still being rejected as discrepant; by then up to approximately 70% on first presentation. The result of the process was UCP 600 which was approved by the ICC Banking Commission on 24–25 October 2006 and came into effect on 1 July 2007. The consultation and drafting exercise is explained in more detail in the Introduction to UCP 600, which is reproduced with the text of UCP 600 in **Appendix 1**. The text has been overhauled and simplified, with consequent renumbering of the articles, and the overall structure has been much improved by the introduction of articles covering definitions (Article 2) and interpretations (Article 3). The underlying concepts, however, remain the same as in previous revisions.

1 See para **1.29** below.

1.22　Unless stated otherwise, references in this book to the UCP are to UCP 600 and the position under earlier revisions is considered only where necessary to explain significant changes of approach in UCP 600. No doubt there will continue to be litigation on historical credits subject to UCP 500; for that purpose reference should be made to the third edition of this book. The Institute of International Banking Law and Practice has published a useful and detailed article-by-article comparison of UCP 600 with UCP 500: *The Comparison of UCP 600 & UCP 500* by Professor James E. Byrne.

The nature and scope of the UCP

1.23　The UCP consist of 39 articles which set out provisions which are intended to regulate many aspects of documentary credit operations. They are promulgated by the ICC and are made effective by their incorporation into credits[1] by the banks of countries whose banking associations have accepted them. They are not intended to be a code having the force of law.[2] For the ICC cannot, and does not purport to, legislate. In this respect they are quite different in nature to the many international conventions, such as those on carriage, which have the force of law in the countries parties to them. In contrast the UCP must rely upon contract, that is, agreement, for their binding effect in each credit contract where they are incorporated. Their contractual nature is fundamental to their understanding. Secondly, although their coverage is growing more comprehensive with each Revision, the UCP do not purport to cover all questions which may arise in connection with credits. The title gives an indication of their nature, 'Uniform Customs and Practice'.[3] They do not purport to be a code setting out the law relating to and governing credits in the way, for example, that the English Sale of Goods Act 1893 and its successors intended to codify and also in some respects to change the English common law relating to sale of goods. Of course the UCP do have to deal with matters which are treated in an English court as matters of law, such as the legal rights and obligations to which credits may give rise. Thus in particular the UCP set out in Articles 7 and 8 the undertakings which are given by issuing and by confirming banks. They are not, however, set out in legal language. Other rights and obligations which may arise in connection with credits are not referred to. Nor are the capacities in which banks act fully considered. Neither are the legal consequences. There is therefore a considerable area which is left to the national courts of whatever country is called upon to decide a dispute. Naturally the framers do take account of legal decisions. There may be one particular reason, in addition to others, why the UCP are not comprehensive, nor intended to be. It is that it is felt that some matters are best left to national courts. An example of this is the effect of fraud or forgery.

1 See para **1.28** below.
2 M *Golodetz & Co Inc v Czarnikow-Rionda Co Inc* [1980] 1 WLR 495 at 509.
3 Up to a point: 'the Uniform Customs and Practice ... like Voltaire's Holy Roman Empire, do not precisely match their name' (per Staughton LJ in *Seaconsar Far East Ltd v Bank Markazi Jomhouri Islami Iran* [1999] 1 Lloyd's Rep 36, referring to Voltaire, *Candide*).

1.24   UCP Article 1 provides:

'**Article 1 Application of UCP**

The Uniform Customs and Practice for Documentary Credits, 2007 Revision, ICC Publication No 600 ("UCP") are rules that apply to any documentary credit ("credit") (including, to the extent to which they may be applicable any standby letter of credit[1]) when the text of the credit expressly indicates that it is subject to these rules. They are binding on all parties thereto unless expressly modified or excluded by the credit.'

A 'credit' is defined in Article 2 as 'any arrangement, however named or described, that is irrevocable and therefore constitutes a definite undertaking of the issuing bank to honour a complying presentation'. It is clear from this definition that the credit is the arrangement (which under English law at least is contractual) between issuing bank and beneficiary. However, the UCP are also relevant to other banks involved in the credit, such as an advising or correspondent bank. While not party to the credit itself (if it has not confirmed it), its relations with the issuing bank are in every practical sense subject to the provisions of the UCP. Similarly, if the applicant has instructed the issuing bank to issue a credit governed by the UCP, then the applicant may be assumed to have accepted that it will be operated in accordance with the UCP, and the UCP contain important provisions which are intended to apply to the applicant. The UCP are thus applicable to a number of relationships or contracts. But they will not apply to the underlying contract between the applicant and the beneficiary, which gives rise to the credit, such as that between a buyer and seller. The application of the UCP would be wholly inappropriate. But the UCP may nonetheless be relevant in determining particular obligations of the buyer regarding the opening of the credit.

1 The function of standby credits is described in **Chapter 12**. In essence they provide for payment on receipt of documents evidencing default under the underlying contract. Sometimes the term 'commercial credit' is used to contrast with standby credits.

1.25 It is to be remarked that Articles 1 and 2 make no reference to the existence of any underlying transaction between the applicant for the credit and the beneficiary, which is usually an essential pre-condition for the coming into being of a credit. Nor is there any reference to the function or purpose of the payment to be made through the credit. These are essential to the understanding of the transaction though not to its definition.

1.26 The effect of Articles 1 and 2 is that the UCP apply to credits as defined in Article 2. So it can at least be argued that, even though a document containing a payment undertaking states that it is subject to the UCP, it is not so subject because the Articles of the UCP only apply to credits as defined by Article 2 and the document falls outside that definition. A way in which the point could quite easily arise is if a credit was issued by a finance house which did not have, or arguably did not have, the status of 'bank'. 'Bank' is not defined by the UCP, and it is probably right that it is not. For the concept of a bank is not easy to define and it varies from one municipal law to another. It is suggested that if a finance house issues a letter of credit which states that it is subject to the UCP, the UCP should be applied to it regardless of whether the finance house is properly to be described as a bank. This would give effect to the intention of the credit.[1] The solution should be the same in any other situations in which the 'credit' states that it is subject to the UCP but falls outside the definitions provided by Article 2.

1 This approach follows the approach of the US Court of Appeals in *Barclays Bank DCO v Mercantile National Bank* [1973] 2 Lloyd's Rep 541 at 544.5 and 481 F 2d 1224.

1.27 The application of the UCP to standby credits and demand guarantees and bonds is considered in Chapter 12. Standby credits sometimes provide for the incorporation of the International Standby Practices 1998, a set of rules designed specifically for standby credits, as an alternative to the UCP.

Incorporation of the UCP

1.28   Parties are free to adopt the UCP or modify or ignore them as they wish. The means by which the UCP are made applicable to credits is by an express term in the credit that it is issued subject to the terms of the UCP.[1] In the unlikely event that there is no express reference to the UCP, an attempt might be made to secure their application by means of a statement issued by an individual bank, or by an association of banks, that all credits issued by the bank, or by members of the association, were issued subject to the UCP. However, there must be serious doubts whether such a notice would be treated as effective, particularly in an international situation, and where it is so very straightforward for a bank's standard form document to carry the wording provided by Article 1 or an equivalent wording. An argument could be put forward for their application on the facts of a particular case if the parties had previously dealt on the basis of the UCP and it appeared that the absence of an express incorporation in the particular instance was through inadvertence. The inference in such a case would probably be that the parties intended that the current revision should apply to the credit even where their previous dealings had been on the basis of an earlier revision. Because the UCP are so universally incorporated, it is likely that even in a case where it cannot be established that they apply, if a point arises which is covered by the UCP, the solution provided by the UCP will be adopted as representing modern banking practice in relation to the principles underlying credits and as to documentary requirements. That would not be so where the terms of the credit in question were actually found to be to contrary effect, nor perhaps where a bank sought to rely on an exclusion of liability in the UCP.[2]

1 Where the credit is advised by SWIFT, as is very often case, the applicable rules (i.e. UCP 600 if that is intended) must be specified in field 40E on form MT700.
2 *Cf Attock Cement Co Ltd v Romanian Bank for Foreign Trade* [1989] 1 WLR 1147 at 1159B.

The ICC Banking Commission and ICC Publications

1.29   The Commission's full name is the ICC Commission on Banking Technique and Practice. It draws its members from countries where the ICC is represented by a National Committee. It meets twice a year, once in Paris and once elsewhere, 'to hear and decide on matters of banking technique and practice including UCP interpretation problems and questions'.[1] From time to time the Commission publishes their decisions or opinions on questions concerning the UCP, most recently *Collected Opinions 1995–2001*.[2] These represent the views of considerable experts, and it is suggested that they should be given substantial weight by a court in accordance with the merits of the particular decision.[3] They are often explanatory of the thinking behind the UCP, and they illustrate banking practice. Official ICC publications are referred to in this book by their publication number, in the form 'ICC No xx'.

1 ICC No 459, p 9.
2 ICC No 632.
3 See *Glencore International AG v Bank of China* [1996] 1 Lloyd's Rep 135 at 145 per Rix J, and *Credit Agricole Indosuez v Credit Suisse First Boston* (unreported 24 January 2001), per Morison J.

The UCP and earlier court decisions

1.30   The first Revision to be accepted by the United Kingdom banks, and therefore incorporated by wording in the credits which they issued, was the 1962 Revision. The subsequent revisions have made substantial changes. In cases decided by an English court prior to 1962 the court will not have been concerned with the UCP. What is the weight of such decisions today, when the UCP will invariably be applicable? The answer is that many of them remain good law, and the same result will often be reached today applying the UCP. This is because in many areas there is little conflict between the law and practice developed in relation to credits in the English cases and the UCP. The approach must now be to examine the UCP to see whether they provide an answer to the point at issue. If they do, that point may help to show the principle, and it may illustrate how it is to be applied. But the case cannot be applied to achieve a result which would be contrary to the relevant provisions of the UCP. Of course, if the UCP are silent on a point, then nothing stands in the way of applying a pre-1962 decision which covers it.

Conflicts between the terms of the credit and the UCP

1.31   One example of a potential conflict is the problem of non-documentary conditions in the credit.[1] The UCP provide that they shall be ignored.[2] This could work to defeat the intention of the parties on a point important to them. Prima facie the parties to the various contracts arising in connection with a credit are free to make the arrangements which they desire, and to include such specific terms as they think appropriate. Article 1 ends 'unless expressly modified or excluded by the credit'. This recognises that the parties may expressly exclude some provisions of the UCP while incorporating the remainder. What is meant by an express provision is a provision expressly stating that, for example, a particular Article is not to apply.[3] In such situations no difficulty will arise, and this is the way in which a potential conflict should be avoided. A difficulty does arise where there is an apparent conflict between a provision of the UCP (which has not been expressly excluded or modified) and a term of the credit. An English court will try first to find a resolution which gives effect to both without doing too much violence to the language of either. An example of this process is given by the *Forestal Mimosa* case.[3]

1 See para **8.22** below.
2 Article 14.h.
3 *Forestal Mimosa Ltd v Oriental Credit Ltd* [1986] 1 WLR 631 at 639C.

1.32 If the conflict cannot be resolved, the general position in English law is that, where an express term of a contract conflicts with a provision of incorporated standard terms, the express term should normally be given effect on the ground that it is a term to which the parties have given their particular attention and so it should override a term which is incorporated only by reference and so is unlikely to have been considered by them. Should a situation arise in which an English court does have to choose between giving effect to a provision of the UCP or to another term of the credit which is in express contradiction of it, the situation is one of real difficulty for the court. For the evidence of banking practice is likely to support the UCP provision, while sound and established principles of construction lead the court the other way. In *Royal Bank of Scotland plc v Cassa di Risparmio delle Provincie Lombarde*[1] Mustill LJ stated:

> 'Nevertheless, whilst not belittling the utility of the UCP, it must be recognized that their terms do not constitute a statutory code. As their title makes clear they contain a formulation of customs and practices, which the parties to a letter of credit transaction can incorporate into their contracts by reference. This being so, it seems to me that the obvious place to start, when searching for a contractual term material to a particular obligation, is the express agreement between the parties. If it is found that the parties have explicitly agreed such a term, then the search need go no further, since any contrary provision in UCP must yield to the parties' expressed intention. If on the other hand the agreement is silent in the material respect, then recourse must be had to UCP, and if a relevant term is found there, that term will govern the case.'

It is suggested that the *Royal Bank of Scotland* case did not present a conflict of the stark nature under consideration here, and so did not in fact give rise to the dilemma.

1 [1992] 1 Bank LR 251 at 256.

International Standard Banking Practice (ISBP)

1.33 The ICC has issued what it described as a 'necessary companion' to the UCP, a publication entitled *International Standard Banking Practice for the Examination of Documents under Documentary Credits*,[1] referred to in this book as ISBP. According to its introduction, the ISBP 'explains how the practices articulated in UCP 600 are applied by documentary practitioners'. The status and effect of the ISBP, and some of its relevant provisions, are discussed in more detail in Chapter 8.[2]

1 ICC No 645.
2 See in particular paras **8.11** to **8.14**.

C THE AUTONOMY OF DOCUMENTARY CREDITS[1]

1.34   In the context of documentary credits 'autonomy' is used to refer to the principle that the credit is to be treated as an independent transaction. In particular it is independent of the terms of the underlying transaction giving rise to it, and its performance is independent of the performance of that transaction. In *United City Merchants (Investments) Ltd v Royal Bank of Canada*[2] Lord Diplock stated[3] in relation to a confirmed credit: 'It is trite law that there are four[4] autonomous though interconnected contractual relationships involved.' In *Themehelp Ltd v West* Evans LJ stated[5] (citing para **9.29** of the second edition of this work), 'Letters of credit, performance bonds and guarantees are all subject to the general principle that they must be treated as autonomous contracts, whose operation is not to be interfered with by the court on grounds extraneous to the credit or guarantee itself.' A useful judicial definition of the principle was given by the Supreme Court of Canada in *Bank of Nova Scotia v Angelica-Whitewear*:[6]

> 'The fundamental principle governing documentary letters of credit and the characteristic which gives them their international commercial utility and efficacy is that the obligation of the issuing bank to honour a draft on a credit when it is accompanied by documents which appear on their face to be in accordance with the terms and conditions of the credit is independent of the performance of the underlying contract for which the credit was issued. Disputes between the parties to the underlying contract concerning its performance cannot as a general rule justify a refusal by an issuing bank to honour a draft which is accompanied by apparently conforming documents. This principle is referred to as the autonomy of documentary credits.'

The principle is fundamental to credit transactions, and it is essential to the continuance of the documentary credit system as the primary means of payment in international trade that it should be scrupulously observed. The principle follows from what is sometimes stated as a second principle, that a documentary credit is a transaction in documents and in documents alone. It is suggested that, although the two principles can be separately stated, they are in reality so closely connected that they cannot be treated independently. Because credits are transactions in documents, if the documents conform to the requirements of the credit, the bank must honour its payment obligations under the credit. This and the fact that the beneficiary of a credit has the promise of a bank give a documentary credit its special value. Transactions which would otherwise be unlikely to take place because the parties cannot trust one another are thereby made possible.

1 See also para **8.17** below.
2 [1983] 1 AC 168.
3 [1983] 1 AC 168 at 182.

4 There are in fact five where the credit is confirmed: Lord Diplock omitted the contract between
  the issuing bank and the beneficiary: thus:
  (i)   buyer/seller (applicant/beneficiary) – the underlying contract;
  (ii) buyer (applicant)/issuing bank;
  (iii) issuing bank/confirming bank;
  (iv) issuing bank/beneficiary;
  (v)   confirming bank/beneficiary.
5 [1996] QB 84 at 89.
6 [1987] SCR 59 at 81 per Le Dain J. See also *Royal Bank of Canada v Gentra Canada
  Investments Inc* (2000) 94 ACWS (3d) 724.

1.35   The immediate and most important consequence of the principle is
that the performance of the contract between the applicant and the
beneficiary which underlies the credit, is irrelevant to the performance of
the credit. It is irrelevant that it may be alleged that the goods are not of the
standard required by the contract. The only exception to this is where there is
fraud on the part of the beneficiary or illegality. Those exceptions and the
principle itself are examined more fully in **Chapter 9** and **Chapter 13**.

1.36   The principle of autonomy is also enshrined in the UCP in articles 4
and 5:

'**Article 4 Credits v. Contracts**

a. A credit by its nature is a separate transaction from the sale or other
contract on which it may be based. Banks are in no way concerned with or
bound by such contract, even if any reference whatsoever to it is included in
the credit. Consequently, the undertaking of a bank to honour, to negotiate or
to fulfil any other obligation under the credit is not subject to claims or
defences by the applicant resulting from its relationships with the issuing
bank or the beneficiary.

A beneficiary can in no case avail itself of the contractual relationships
existing between banks or between the applicant and the issuing bank.

b. An issuing bank should discourage any attempt by the applicant to
include, as an integral part of the credit, copies of the underlying contract,
proforma invoice and the like.

Article 5 Documents v. Goods, Services or Performance

Banks deal with documents and not with goods, services or performance to
which the documents may relate.'

Chapter 2

Types or Categorisations of Documentary Credits

INTRODUCTION

2.1 The rights and obligations created by a credit are to be found in its terms; whether they are or are not typical of a particular type of credit must be treated with caution as a guide to their understanding. For a label may be helpful or it may be misleading if the credit is typical in some respects but not in others. Where, however, a categorisation is established by the UCP, it is important because the rules applying to the category provided by the UCP will apply. This is of particular importance with regard to the distinction between confirmed and unconfirmed credits. The discussion which follows provides a means of further introducing the differing obligations that may be undertaken in connection with credits.

A   REVOCABLE AND IRREVOCABLE CREDITS

2.2   A revocable credit is one which may be cancelled or amended by the bank undertaking to pay, without the beneficiary's consent. An irrevocable credit can be cancelled or amended only with the consent of the applicant, the issuing bank and the beneficiary. UCP 500 distinguished in Article 6 between revocable and irrevocable credits, and provided that in the absence of any clear indication the credit 'shall be deemed to be irrevocable'. By way of contrast, however, revocable credits are entirely excluded from the scheme of the new UCP 600. Irrevocability is now an essential part of the definition of a documentary credit, Article 2 providing that 'Credit means any arrangement, however named or described, that is irrevocable and thereby constitutes a definite undertaking of the issuing bank to honour a complying presentation'. A credit shall be treated as irrevocable even if there is no indication to that effect in its terms: Article 3.

2.3   Given the unsatisfactory nature of a revocable credit,[1] it is right that a credit should be irrevocable in the absence of any contrary indication. The approach of the UCP, that irrevocability is a defining characteristic of a documentary credit, is consistent with the view that an English court would likely take, that an irrevocable credit must be provided where the underlying contract simply provides for payment by letter of credit. This is on the ground that a revocable credit provides no security.[2] In *International Banking Corpn v Barclays Bank Ltd*, Atkin LJ stated in respect of the (admittedly unusual) credit he was there considering: 'And the other matter which I think quite plainly emerges is that a credit so announced is irrevocable unless it appears on the face of it that it is revocable.'[3]

1 See paras **2.6** and **2.7** below.
2 See paras **2.6**, **2.7** and **3.8** below.
3 (1925) 5 Legal Decisions Affecting Bankers 1 at 5.

Revocable credits

2.4   There is no place for revocable credits within the scheme of the UCP 600. Should parties nonetheless wish to create a revocable credit, one way of doing so would be to incorporate the relevant provisions of UCP 500. UCP 500 Article 8 related to revocable credits and provided as follows:

'**Article 8: Revocation of a Credit**
a. A revocable Credit may be amended or cancelled by the Issuing Bank at any moment and without prior notice to the Beneficiary.
b. However, the Issuing Bank must:
   i. reimburse another bank with which a revocable Credit has been made available for sight payment, acceptance or negotiation – for any payment, acceptance or negotiation made by such bank – prior to receipt by it of notice of amendment or cancellation, against documents which appear on their face to be in compliance with the terms and conditions of the Credit;
   ii. reimburse another bank with which a revocable Credit has been made available for deferred payment, if such a bank has, prior to receipt by it of notice of amendment or cancellation, taken up documents which appear on their face to be in compliance with the terms and conditions of the Credit.'

2.5 Although UCP 500 Article 8 may at first sight suggest that a bank can never come under an obligation to a beneficiary in respect of a revocable credit, it is clear that where the credit provides for payment by means of a time draft or for deferred payment (in the sense explained in paragraph **2.16** below) and the beneficiary has presented documents which are accepted by the bank, an obligation will come into being. For Article 8.b assumes that the bank for whose reimbursement it is providing has become obliged to the beneficiary. In any event it would be wholly unacceptable for a bank to be able to reject its payment obligation to the beneficiary after it had accepted the documents and the beneficiary had lost control of them.

2.6 Apart from this very limited protection, a revocable credit provides no undertaking by the issuing bank to the beneficiary at all. For even if the correct documents are presented and the bank has not until then decided to revoke the credit, it may still do so and reject the documents.[1] It might, for instance do that if it thought that the financial circumstances of its customer, the applicant, had deteriorated since the credit was opened. For this reason a confirmed revocable credit would ordinarily be a contradiction in terms, there being no effective undertaking to confirm. A confirmation would mean something, however, where the credit provided for payment to be deferred: then the confirming bank would add its undertaking to that of the issuing bank – which becomes irrevocable after documents have been accepted – that payment will be made in due course.

1 This is confirmed in the commentary on the Article in *Documentary Credits: UCP 500 and 400 Compared*, ICC No 511.

2.7 The serious disadvantage of revocable credits is shown by *Cape Asbestos Co Ltd v Lloyd's Bank Ltd*.[1] There the plaintiffs agreed to sell 30 tons of asbestos to buyers in Warsaw, who opened a revocable credit through Lloyd's Bank in London. Lloyd's informed the plaintiffs: 'This is merely an advice of the opening of the above-mentioned credit, and is not a confirmation of the same.' The first shipment of 17 tons was duly paid for through the credit. The plaintiffs then shipped the remaining 13 tons. Meanwhile, unknown to them, Lloyd's had been informed of the cancellation of the credit. The documents were presented to Lloyd's in London and refused. The action was brought against them on the basis that it was their duty to give reasonable notice of the withdrawal of the credit. The evidence established that it was usual for the defendants to give notice of the withdrawal of credits, but here they had omitted to do so. The court held that there was no legal obligation on the bank to give notice. Thus the credit turned out to be an illusory security, and since the plaintiffs were unable to recover from their buyers they went unpaid. The position where an un-notified amendment took place, for example one involving the addition of a document to those to be presented in order to obtain payment, would be no less galling.

1 [1921] WN 274.

Irrevocable credits

2.8 Almost all credits issued today are irrevocable, and it is only those that will provide the security that the seller has no doubt sought in specifying that payment shall be by letter of credit. As mentioned above, UCP 600 only applies to irrevocable credits. Where a contract specifies payment by letter of credit, an irrevocable credit is required.[1] When a bank issues an irrevocable credit, the bank gives its undertaking that the beneficiary will receive payment as the credit may provide. Article 2 of the UCP uses the term 'honour' to encompass the different methods by which a bank may be required to perform its financial obligations under the credit:

> 'Article 2
> . . .
>
> Honour means:
> a. to pay at sight if the credit is available by sight payment.
> b. to incur a deferred payment undertaking and pay at maturity if the credit is available by deferred payment.
> c. to accept a bill of exchange ("draft") drawn by the beneficiary and pay at maturity if the credit is available by acceptance.
>
> . . .'

Article 7.a of the UCP then spells out the obligations of an issuing bank to honour the credit. In summary, the issuing bank undertakes to pay where the credit provides for sight payment or deferred payment (by itself or by a nominated bank); it undertakes to accept drafts drawn on it, or to be responsible for their acceptance and payment at maturity if they are to be drawn on another bank;[2] where the credit provides for negotiation with another bank, it undertakes to pay if negotiation is not effected by that bank. Article 8.a sets out the equivalent undertakings which are given by a confirming bank to honour or negotiate the credit. These undertakings are further considered in **Chapter 5**.[3] They are at the heart of a documentary credit, and they make the instrument the secure means of payment that it is intended to be. Article 10.a provides that the undertakings cannot be amended or cancelled without the agreement of the issuing bank, the confirming bank (if any), and the beneficiary. Obviously the agreement of the applicant (who has ultimately to fund the operation) is also needed. The amendment of a credit is considered in detail in **Chapter 3**.[4] If the issuing bank purports to revoke the credit unilaterally, then this amounts to a renunciation of the contract with the beneficiary. The beneficiary can elect to accept this renunciation as terminating the contract forthwith and claim damages, but, as with any contract, he must communicate his acceptance clearly and unequivocally to the bank, silence or inactivity generally being insufficient.[5] If the beneficiary does not accept the renunciation, then the contract remains in full effect for the benefit of both parties; in particular if the beneficiary then proceeds to make a non-complying presentation of documents, then the bank has no liability to pay under the credit.

1 See para **3.8** below.
2 The UCP prohibit drafts drawn on the applicant; see para Article 6.c.
3 Paras **5.17** et seq.
4 Paras **3.36** et seq.
5 *Jaks (UK) Ltd v Cera Investment Bank SA* [1998] 2 Lloyd's Rep 89.

2.9 It may be questioned at what point the relevant undertaking becomes binding on the issuing and confirming banks. Clearly the credit must be communicated to the beneficiary, and it is suggested that it becomes binding at that moment. Any previous uncertainties as to the legal position have now been put to rest, at least where UCP 600 applies. This expressly provides in Article 7.b that the issuing bank is irrevocably bound to honour its obligations 'as of the time it issues the credit'. Article 8.b deals with the position of any confirming bank, providing that it is irrevocably bound to honour or negotiate 'as of the time it adds its confirmation to the credit'. This analysis is also confirmed by Article 10.b which provides that an issuing bank is irrevocably bound by an amendment from the moment the amendment is issued (and a confirming bank as of the time when it advises the amendment). There is thus no distinction in this respect between the issue of a credit and the issue of an amendment.

2.10 The contrary analysis (no longer arguable if UCP 600 applies) is that the credit only becomes binding when the seller has acted on it by doing something towards the performance of his contract. This might be the making of an arrangement to ship the goods, or commencing to manufacture or continuing to manufacture them. This was the suggestion of Rowlatt J in *Urquhart, Lindsay & Co Ltd v Eastern Bank Ltd*.[1] But in *Dexters Ltd v Schenker & Co*,[2] Greer J pointed out[3] that on receipt of the credit the seller becomes bound to proceed with the contract (for the provision of the credit is normally a condition precedent to the seller's obligation to ship), and he appeared to consider a bank bound from that moment. These cases are considered further in connection with the consideration for the bank's undertaking.[4]

23

1 [1922] 1 KB 318 at 321, 322.
2 (1923) 14 Ll L Rep 586.
3 (1923) 14 Ll L Rep 586 at 588.
4 See para **5.8** et seq below.

2.11   Where a contract of sale calls for an irrevocable credit to be opened in London, a credit which is advised through a London bank which does not confirm it does not satisfy the contract, since the London bank gives no undertaking: *Enrico Furst & Co v WE Fischer Ltd*.[1] However, the objection must be taken in time by the seller; in *Enrico* a request by the seller for an extension of the credit was held to be a waiver. See paras **3.4** to **3.7** below.

1 [1960] 2 Lloyd's Rep 340.

B   CONFIRMED AND UNCONFIRMED CREDITS

2.12   The use of these terms assumes the existence of an advising bank (also called the correspondent bank), and the distinction depends upon the position taken by that bank. In short, with a confirmed credit the advising bank adds its own undertaking to that of the issuing bank that the credit will be honoured. If the credit is unconfirmed, it does not: the sole undertaking is that of the issuing bank.

Unconfirmed credits

2.13   Where the credit is unconfirmed, the advising bank acts solely as the agent of the issuing bank. It will be instructed by the issuing bank to notify the credit to the seller. The credit is likely to provide for the documents to be presented to the advising or correspondent bank, and it will receive them as agent for the issuing bank. If it is to pay, it will pay simply as the agent of the issuing bank and not because of any obligation existing between it and the seller. The position of the advising bank as agent is considered in greater detail subsequently.[1] The important feature where the credit is unconfirmed is that, if the documents are wrongfully refused by the bank to whom they are presented, the seller has normally a remedy only against the issuing bank, which is usually abroad, and so proceedings may be more difficult than if he had an undertaking from a bank in his own country.

1 See para **6.6**.

Confirmed credits

2.14   Where a credit is confirmed, the advising or correspondent bank adds its own undertaking to that of the issuing bank to honour or negotiate the credit as the case may be. This then gives the beneficiary the advantage of having a paymaster in his own country. The credit will also be an irrevocable credit (see above),[1] and so the beneficiary will have the full benefits that the developed form of documentary credits provides. Article 8 of the UCP sets out the undertaking of a confirming bank (in similar terms as Article 7 sets out the undertaking of the issuing bank) to honour or negotiate the credit, with appropriate changes. Thus, for example, the confirming bank undertakes as appropriate to pay at sight or on a deferred date, to accept bills drawn on itself, and to be responsible for the acceptance of bills drawn on other drawees, and to negotiate without recourse bills drawn by the beneficiary on any drawee apart from itself. Where an advising bank purports to confirm a credit but reserves for itself a right of recourse against the seller, the two are inconsistent and the advising bank is not giving an absolute undertaking. The credit in these circumstances is not to be treated as a confirmed credit: see *Wahbe Tamari & Sons Ltd v Colprogeca*.[2] The position of the confirming banker is further discussed in Chapters 5 and 6.[3] *Silent confirmations* and *confirmations on request* are considered in paras **6.25** and **6.26** below.

1 See para **2.8**.
2 [1969] 2 Lloyd's Rep 18.
3 See **Chapter 5** generally and para **6.22** et seq below.

C   CATEGORISATION OF CREDITS BY PAYMENT OBLIGATION

2.15   UCP Article 6 provides:

> 'Article 6:
> a.   A credit must state the bank with which it is available or whether it is available with any bank. A credit available with a nominated bank is also available with the issuing bank.
> b.   A credit must state whether it is available by sight payment, deferred payment, acceptance or negotiation.'

This provides an important and convenient means of categorising credits in accordance with the type of payment obligation undertaken by the obligated banks. The bank with which the credit is made available, that is, at which the documents may be presented, is known as the 'nominated bank'; see Article 2, which also provides that any bank is a nominated bank if the credit is said to be available at any bank.

Sight credits and deferred payment credits

2.16   A credit may provide for payment on presentation of documents – after allowing time, of course, for them to be examined for compliance with the credit. Then it can be called a *sight payment* or *sight credit*.

2.17   Alternatively, the credit may provide for payment to be made at the conclusion of a period measured from the presentation of documents or, for example, from the date of the transport document. Then the credit is called a *deferred payment credit.* Such a credit has the advantage, for the buyer/applicant, that he need not reimburse the issuing bank until payment has been made and to that extent has the benefit of time to pay. In the UCP, the requirement that a bank should 'honour' the credit includes the obligation 'to incur a deferred payment undertaking and pay at maturity if the credit is available by deferred payment' (Article 2). Where payment is deferred, the beneficiary must wait for his money but has the security of the bank's undertaking; however, if the applicant is in the meantime to receive and to be able to deal with the goods, the bank will have to release the documents to him. The loss of security for the bank which would otherwise occur can be avoided by the use of a trust receipt as described in **Chapter 11**.[1] The risks for a bank which discounts its own deferred payment obligation by early payment, now considerably ameliorated by the UCP 600, are discussed at para **9.43** to **9.47** below.

1 See para **11.11**.

Acceptance credits

2.18   As a further alternative, the credit may provide that it will be honoured not by payment of money by the bank with which it is available but by the acceptance of a bill of exchange drawn by the beneficiary. This is known as an *acceptance credit.* If the bill is what may be called a time draft or a usuance draft and provides for payment after a period from acceptance of the bill, then, unless the credit otherwise provides, payment will only be forthcoming when that time comes. Again, the UCP definition of 'honour' includes the obligation 'to accept a bill of exchange ("draft") drawn by the beneficiary and pay at maturity if the credit is available by acceptance'. The bill must be presented to the party on whom it is drawn for payment to be triggered. This will normally be the bank to which documents are to be presented under the credit and which is to make payment. But if the bill is drawn on the issuing bank or another bank, then, unless the credit otherwise provides, the strict position is that payment is only due on presentation of the bill to the party on whom it is drawn. The issuing bank and any confirming bank are of course obliged to ensure payment, whether or not payment is forthcoming from the party on whom the bill is drawn. The use of a time or usuance draft provides another means of deferring payment under the credit, but with the advantage for the beneficiary that he obtains a negotiable instrument and can obtain payment before maturity by discounting the bill with another bank or finance house. Sometimes credits provide for the acceptance of a sight bill, that is, one payable at sight; those credits are equivalent to sight credits and the bill in that case has no real purpose.

Credits available by negotiation

2.19   Finally, the credit may be *available by negotiation* with a bank nominated in the credit (or with any bank if the credit so provides). UCP Article 2 defines negotiation as follows:

'**Article 2:**
Negotiation means the purchase by the nominated bank of drafts (drawn on a bank other than the nominated bank) and/or documents under a complying presentation, by advancing or agreeing to advance funds to the beneficiary on or before the banking day on which reimbursement is due to the nominated bank.'

The purpose of making a credit available by negotiation is that it enables the beneficiary to get money immediately by negotiating—in effect selling—the documents to the nominated bank. The nominated bank, having negotiated, is then entitled to be reimbursed by the issuing bank in due course. The sum payable to the beneficiary on negotiation will be discounted to reflect the interest accruing between the date of receipt of payment by him and the date on which payment is due from the issuing bank. It is apparent that there will only be need for negotiation where the credit does not provide for immediate payment: if it does, the beneficiary may just as well present the documents to the issuing bank himself either directly or using his own bank as his agent for collection.[1] The term 'negotiation' is sometimes used to refer the acceptance and payment against documents of the full amount of the credit. This is a misuse. Negotiation is better used only when the paying bank pays less than the full amount by reason of a time element, as Article 2 indicates.

Although the UCP envisages that negotiation will take place through the nomination mechanism just described, the cases show that the term is sometimes used in a somewhat different sense to refer to a situation where the undertaking in a credit is extended to third parties as well as the beneficiary, so that any third party covered by the undertaking may purchase the documents and present them to the issuing bank in his own name and his own right. In this book, credits of that type are referred to as 'negotiation credits' (as opposed to credits 'available by negotiation' with a nominated bank) and are discussed in the next section. However, the practice of using negotiation credits in that sense is now very limited and, particularly with the advent of UCP 600, offers little advantage. If, under a credit subject to the UCP, it is intended that the beneficiary should be able to obtain payment by selling the documents to any bank, then the credit should be made freely available by negotiation.

1 Although it is not unusual for credits providing for immediate payment also to be made available by negotiation; this practice is prevalent in relation to credits issued by Chinese banks.

D   STRAIGHT AND NEGOTIATION CREDITS

2.20   A straight credit is one under which the undertaking of the issuing bank, or, if it is a confirmed credit, the undertakings of the issuing and confirming banks, are directed to the named beneficiary alone, and only he may rely on them. With a negotiation credit, by contrast, the undertakings are directed to any bank, or to any bank of a description stated in the credit, which becomes a bona fide holder of any bill of exchange and the other documents which are stipulated by the credit.

2.21   Negotiation by a bank under a negotiation credit may be distinguished from negotiation by a bank which does so as nominated bank under a credit providing for payment to be available from it by negotiation.[1]

1 See para **2.19** above.

2.22   What is necessary to make a credit a negotiation credit, so that its promise may be accepted by any bank of appropriate description that negotiates documents complying with the credit? This is a matter of construing the words of the credit, and if the credit is carefully worded there will be no problem. If it does not appear that the undertaking embodied in the credit is to be construed more widely, the credit must be given effect to as a straight credit. The answer may be provided as a matter of necessary implication, as it was in the old case of *Re Agra and Masterman's Bank, ex p Asiatic Banking Corpn.*[1] There was there an undertaking to honour drafts drawn on the bank, together with this statement 'This credit will remain in force for twelve months and parties negotiating bills under it are requested to indorse particulars on the back hereof.' It was held that this anticipated the negotiation of bills by other parties, and hence that there was an undertaking to them. The credit was not a documentary credit, but was simply a facility to obtain funds by drawing bills. But the logic of the construction was in no way dependent on that and would apply equally to a documentary credit. In *M A Sassoon & Sons Ltd v International Banking Corpn,*[2] a similar argument was presented based on wording that was less clear. The Privy Council merely noted the argument, observing that 'it is a very summary way of converting the terms of a discount offer by one bank into an undertaking applicable to actual discounts by any other bank'. The ground of decision in the case, however, was that the seller had discounted the draft to the plaintiff not on terms that it was a negotiation pursuant to the credit, but on terms that the plaintiff should present the bill and documents to the buyer and so obtain payment. The buyer accepted the bill but later dishonoured it by non-payment, and the plaintiff was held to be entitled to recover from the seller as the drawer of a dishonoured bill.

1 (1867) 2 Ch App 391.
2 [1927] AC 711, PC.

2.23   Suppose that a credit simply states 'negotiation is permitted', and an undertaking is given in these terms: 'We undertake to honour all drafts drawn under and in conformity with the terms of this credit'. Would such wording make the credit generally negotiable? There is no authority on such a wording in English law. A meaning has to be found for the words 'negotiation is permitted'. Their placing and context within the credit will be relevant. It may simply mean negotiation by a bank named in the credit. But if that does not appear possible, then probably the credit should be construed as permitting negotiation by any party.[1,2] What is the position where the credit does not nominate any bank authorised to accept, pay or negotiate, nor allow negotiation by any bank? It is suggested in the ICC's *More Case Studies on Documentary Credits*[3] that it is a normal practice in this event to deem the credit freely negotiable. It is then stated 'However this is not without risk.' It would indeed be a risky assumption to make. For such a credit contains nothing in its wording to suggest that it is freely negotiable and the sounder assumption must be that it is available only with the issuing bank. UCP Article 6.a begins 'A credit must state the bank with which it is available or whether it is available with any bank...'. It does not follow from this drafting that if the credit does not contain any such statement it is presumed to be freely negotiable with any bank.

1   A different position is taken in *Benjamin's Sale of Goods* (7th edn) para 23-063. Whilst it is accepted that without words sufficient to indicate that the credit should be generally negotiable or available it must be construed as a straight credit (see eg *Southern Ocean Shipbuilding Co Pte Ltd v Deutsche Bank AG* [1993] 3 SLR 686), it is suggested that, contrary to the view expressed in *Benjamin*, if the meaning is not obvious, it is a question of construing the words in accordance with international banking practice, and that nowadays there is and should be no tendency in the courts to favour straight credits in cases of uncertainty.
2   See also *Udharam Rapchand (Sons) HK Ltd v Mercantile Bank Ltd* [1985] HKLY 52.
3   ICC No 489, Case 191.

2.24   *European Asian Bank AG v Punjab and Sind Bank (No 2)*[1] demonstrates the difficulties which may arise as well as the principles to be applied in resolving them, and is worth detailed consideration. The Singaporean sellers, Bentrex, sold cloves to the Indian buyers, Jain, c. & f. Bombay. At Jain's request, the Punjab Bank in New Delhi opened a letter of credit through their correspondents in Singapore, the Allgemene Bank, which was advised to Bentrex through the European Asian Bank. The credit was available by Bentrex's drafts at 180 days after bill of lading date. Clause 6 provided 'Letter of credit should be advised through European Asia Bank... and should be divisionable and unrestricted for negotiation'. Clause 9 provided 'We hereby engage with drawers, endorsers and bona fide holders of drafts drawn under and in compliance with the terms of this credit that such drafts will be honoured on presentation and delivery of documents as specified above. Negotiations under this credit are restricted [to Allgemene Bank, Singapore]'. Reimbursement was to be effected from the Irving Trust, New York. Bentrex presented to the European Asian Bank documents and a draft drawn on Jain made payable to the order of the European Asian Bank. The bank sent the documents directly to the Punjab Bank in India, where the draft was accepted by Jain. Jain were then informed that the vessel and cargo had been lost, and claimed on their insurers who repudiated liability: there had been a fraud, and no goods had been shipped at all. Meanwhile Bentrex had been paid by the European Asian Bank who were therefore out of pocket. The Irving Trust were not put in funds. Both the Punjab Bank and the Allgemene Bank (who had confirmed the credit) refused to pay the European Asian Bank. The main points decided by the Court of Appeal were these. It was held first that the European Asian Bank had negotiated the documents[2] and draft and were seeking payment on their own behalf: they were not acting as agents of Bentrex and so were unaffected by the fraud of Bentrex. Secondly, the apparent contradiction between clause 6 and clause 9 was to be resolved as follows. In clause 6 'divisionable' was an error for 'divisible' and the clause meant that the credit was transferable in whole or in part (clause 7 permitted part shipments). 'Unrestricted for negotiation' meant that documents could be presented under the credit by any transferee of the credit. Clause 9 meant that whoever presented the documents (Bentrex or their transferee) could only do so through the Allgemene Bank who would then negotiate the documents as the only authorised negotiator. It was therefore not a negotiation credit, and under the terms of the credit the European Asian Bank had no rights against the Punjab Bank. By reason, however, of the communications between the two banks at the time of the delivery of the documents to the Punjab Bank and Jain's acceptance of the bill, the Punjab Bank was estopped from denying that they were responsible for ensuring payment to the European Asian Bank at maturity. Therefore they were obliged to pay.[3]

1 [1983] 1 WLR 642, [1983] 1 Lloyd's Rep 611.
2 That is, the bank had bought the documents.
3 This may be compared with the view expressed by the ICC Banking Commission, *Opinions* (1984–1986) ICCNo 434 Ref 95, that documents may be presented direct to an issuing bank which must accept them and pay even though it has specified another bank as the negotiating bank in the credit advised to the beneficiary.

2.25   As the *Sassoon* and *European Bank* cases[1] demonstrate, in order to claim under a negotiation credit, the holder of the documents must have acquired them by a negotiation pursuant to the credit and not by other means. The wording of the credit is in any event likely so to provide.

1 See paras **2.22** and **2.24** above.

2.26   Other aspects relating to the position of a negotiating bank are considered subsequently in **Chapter 7**, Part B, and the questions of recourse are referred to in paras **6.32**, **7.7** and **7.9** according to context.

E   TRANSFERABLE AND NON-TRANSFERABLE CREDITS

2.27   Where a credit is designated as transferable, the beneficiary has the right to request the appropriate bank to make the credit available in whole or in part to one or more other parties, and perhaps at some other place. It is important to emphasise at the outset that the right is only a right to request, and the bank is not obliged to accede to the request should it not wish to do so. The credit must be expressly designated as transferable. The object of transfer is to enable the beneficiary nominated in the credit to use the credit to provide a means of payment to a party, or to the parties, from whom he in his turn is buying the goods. He may indeed have contracted to provide them with a credit. He can then satisfy his obligation by the transfer of so much of the credit opened in his favour as is required to pay his seller. He must, however, ensure that the terms of the contract which he has made with the party from whom he is buying will be met by the transfer of the credit for which he has contracted with his buyer. He must also ensure that the documents to which he is entitled from his seller will meet the terms of the contract with his buyer. Where the credit which the beneficiary receives is not designated as transferable, or if the bank does not accede to the request for transfer, the seller has the alternative of arranging a back-to-back credit. UCP Article 38 governs transferable credits, a topic fully discussed in **Chapter 10**.

F   BACK-TO-BACK CREDITS AND COUNTER CREDITS

2.28   A credit may be described as back-to-back when it is intended that the documents which are received through the operation of it may be presented, with substitution of invoices (and possibly other documents), to obtain payment under another credit. Thus a seller of goods, the beneficiary of a credit opened in his favour by his buyer, may approach the bank which has advised the credit to him and request it to open a second credit in favour of his own suppliers, on the security of the first credit. This is likely to be possible only if he is already a customer of that bank. Alternatively he may approach his own bank and request them to do so using the credit already opened in his favour as a 'counter'. In the latter case the second credit may be called a counter credit. In each case the credit that the buyer has secured in favour of his own suppliers is a separate credit for which he is in the position of applicant. When complying documents are presented, he will have to reimburse the bank and take up the documents, regardless of the position between him and his buyer and under the credit of which he is beneficiary. In contrast, if he is able to arrange for transfer of the credit, he will avoid such risk. Back-to-back credits also carry a risk for banks on similar grounds: the bank in the middle of the chain has an obligation to pay the beneficiary of the credit which it has opened, regardless of whether its customer is able to obtain payment under the backing credit. For this reason, banks may prefer to use a transferable credit. It is essential that the documents required under the backing credit will be provided by the second credit. This may be difficult or even impossible where the basis of sale is different, for example, where the bank's customer is buying FOB but selling on CFR or CIF terms and a long sea voyage is involved. Here the second credit is likely to need to be in place before the backing credit is available. There is also room for differences of interpretation where the backing credit and the second credit are payable by different banks; this may create further practical and legal difficulties.

2.29   In *Ian Stach Ltd v Baker Bosley Ltd*[1] Devlin J described the manner in which transferable credits and back-to-back credits may be used to provide payment in a string of sale contracts:

> 'Where, as in the present case, there is a string of merchants' contracts between the manufacturer or stockist and the ultimate user, the normal mechanism for carrying out the various contracts is the familiar one which was intended to be used in this case: the ultimate user, under the terms of his contract of sale, opens a transferable, divisible credit in favour of his seller for his purchase price: his seller in turn transfers so much of the credit as corresponds to his own purchase price to his own seller or, more probably, if his own contract with another merchant also calls for a transferable, divisible credit, procures his own banker to issue a back-to-back credit – that is to say, he lodges the credit in his favour with his own banker, who in his turn issues a transferable, divisible credit for the amount of his purchase price to his own seller; and so on, through the string of merchants, until the banker of the last merchant in the string issues the credit in favour of the actual manufacturer or stockist. The reason why they issue fresh credits is that in banking practice a transferable credit is regarded as transferable once only, and, also as is obvious in this sort of trade, it is desired, naturally enough, by any merchant in the string to conceal from his buyer and his seller who his own customer is. That is the way, as both parties to the present transaction knew, in which this type of business is normally carried on.'[2]

1 [1958] 2 QB 130.
2 [1958] 2 QB 130 at 138.

2.30   It has been suggested[1] that if a credit is not transferable it may be wrong for the advising bank to open a back-to-back credit at the seller's request upon the strength of it. Two reasons are suggested. The first is that the opening of a back-to-back credit is equivalent to transfer, and that, as the first credit is non-transferable, transfer is prohibited. It may be thought more precise to say that transfer is not permitted; it may not be permitted simply because, for reasons of his own, the seller did not contract for a transferable credit. Secondly, it is said that the buyer wants the seller's own goods and not those of a third party; so the bank should not facilitate supply from another source. But often the seller is not a producer of goods, and some goods, such as commodities, may be expected by their nature to be purchased by the seller for the purpose of the contract to which the credit relates. If the buyer requires the seller's own particular goods and no others, he should ensure that the sale contract reflects this: he may also be able to provide that the documents required under the credit also confirm this, which would give further protection. In the absence of any judicial precedent, it is submitted that the practice whereby correspondent banks open back-to-back credits is acceptable in law and in practice.

1 See *Benjamin's Sale of Goods* (7th edn) para 23-082.

2.31   The difficulties which may befall banks who find themselves in what may be termed a *quasi* back-to-back situation, in particular where the object of the transaction is to trade goods between countries that forbid trade with each other, are well illustrated by the case of *Mannesman Handel AG v Kaunlaren Shipping Corpn.*[1] It was held that in the special circumstances of that case it would be contrary to the principle of good faith in Swiss law (the governing law of the documentary credit) for a bank that had received the assigned proceeds of a backing credit nonetheless to refuse to pay out on documents presented in order to claim payment under the credit that it had itself opened – even though there were undoubtedly discrepancies. It remains unclear whether a similar principle will be recognised by English law.

1 [1993] 1 Lloyd's Rep 89.

G   REVOLVING CREDITS

2.32   A revolving credit is one in which the credit limit (that is, the invoice value of the goods in respect of which documents can be presented) is not limited to a fixed overall amount. Rather, the maximum value is restored in a manner provided by the credit. For example, it may stipulate that the limit be restored each time a shipment is made: thus if the limit is £100,000 and a shipment of £95,000 is made, the limit is immediately restored to £100,000, but no single shipment may exceed £100,000. Alternatively the limit may be restored only after an appropriate period of time: there could be a limit of £100,000 per month, which would limit the goods to be shipped in any one month to that figure. Such a revolving credit may be arranged on a cumulative basis, meaning that any sum not utilised during one month is carried forward and will be available subsequently. This is to be contrasted with a non-cumulative instalment credit containing no such provision, which requires a specific shipment each month. In such a case, UCP Article 32 applies to provide that, should any instalment not be drawn in the allowed period, the credit ceases to be available for that and any subsequent instalments (unless the credit provides otherwise: Article 1). As the term 'revolving credit' may mean such different things and as the operation of such a credit can be complicated, it is particularly important that the buyer and seller should spell out in the underlying contract precisely what they intend, and that this should be fully and accurately set out in the credit itself.

H   'RED CLAUSE' AND 'GREEN CLAUSE' CREDITS

2.33   Red clause credits contain a clause traditionally printed in red enabling the seller to draw on the credit in advance of the shipment of the goods. They may be used to finance a seller's own purchase or production of the goods. The buyer may obtain security if the advance is only to be made against documents such as a warehouseman's receipt (although the seller must retain his ability to deal with the goods for the purpose of the shipment, and this of course also enables him to deal with them in other, less desirable, ways). The inclusion of a red clause represents a considerable display of trust by the buyer in his seller. The issuing bank is entitled to be reimbursed by the buyer, whether or not shipment takes place, but it has no right to recover the payment from any other party in the absence of an express repayment guarantee.[1] As to the type of documents which at one time a seller might be required to deposit with the paying bank, see *South African Reserve Bank v Samuel & Co.*[2] The red clause was developed in the Australian, New Zealand and South African wool trades.

1   More Queries and Responses on UCP 500, ICC No 596, Ref 302.
2   (1931) 40 Ll L Rep 291.

2.34   A relatively modern example of a red clause credit is given by *Tukan Timber Ltd v Barclays Bank plc.*[1] Tukan were importers of timber from Brazil and in order to finance the trade they opened a letter of credit in favour of their suppliers which appears to have been a form of revolving credit: it was referred to as an 'umbrella credit'. It contained a 'red clause' which enabled the suppliers to draw on the credit simply by presenting receipts countersigned by one or other of two directors of Tukan. Each advance was to state the lot to which it referred and the amount was to be deducted from the payment made when the lot was shipped and corresponding documents were presented. When a dispute developed between Tukan and their suppliers, the suppliers sought to take advantage of the red clause by presenting receipts which bore the forged signature of a director. The bank did not pay, but Tukan brought proceedings to secure their own position by way of an injunction. The claim failed on the ground that Tukan had not established that there was a sufficient risk of further fraudulent claims being made.

1   [1987] 1 Lloyd's Rep 171. See also, in the United States, *Feinberg v Central Asia Capital Corpn Ltd* F Supp 822 (1997).

2.35   A refinement of the red clause is the 'green clause'. This allows preshipment advances but provides for storage in the name of the bank, and thus should provide the bank with security. Red clause and green clause credits are sometimes called anticipatory credits.

I STANDBY CREDITS[1]

2.36 Documentary credits may be divided under two heads according to their function. The first head covers the traditional function of credits, as has already been described, namely to provide payment to the seller of goods (or less commonly to the seller of services) when he performs his contract by delivering documents to the bank.[2] Standby credits most commonly fulfil the function of providing security against the non-performance of a party to a contract, who may sometimes be a seller, but may sometimes have an entirely different capacity. Standby credits provide for payment to the beneficiary by a bank against delivery of documents to the bank. But it follows from their function that the documents required will be very different from those under a traditional credit: they may comprise only a statement in a specified form that the other party to the underlying contract has failed to fulfil his obligations. Article 1 of the UCP 600 provides for the application of the Uniform Customs to standby credits, but only 'to the extent to which they may be applicable'. The effect of this provision is considered in **Chapter 12**.

1 Standby credits are considered in Part B of **Chapter 12**.
2 Sometimes called commercial credits in contrast with standby credits.
.

Chapter 3

Buyer and Seller (Applicant and Beneficiary)

A   THE OBLIGATION TO OPEN A DOCUMENTARY CREDIT

The origin of the obligation

3.1   A documentary credit comes into being, or is opened, in nearly every case because of the existence of an underlying contract which provides that it should be opened. The most common such contract is one of sale of goods. Hence the title of this chapter, which deals with the relations between the applicant for the credit and its beneficiary. The obligations of the buyer and seller in relation to the credit arise from this underlying contract, and determining their obligations is primarily a matter of construing that contract.

The provisions of the underlying contract

3.2   The underlying contract should spell out with sufficient particularity what the credit should be. It should state the type of credit required, in particular whether it should be revocable or irrevocable (the former being extremely unlikely in modern practice), confirmed or unconfirmed, and whether or not it should be transferable. The amount and currency will normally follow automatically from the price provisions of the sale contract, but if not they too should be specified. The description of the goods, quantity and unit price (if there is one) will also be found in the sale contract. It is advisable to provide where the credit is to be opened and/or where advised and (if applicable) confirmed. It should provide when it is to be opened and the period for which it is to be available. The documents against which the credit is to be honoured should be listed. In a formal contract, the terms of which have been fully considered, these and other matters can be spelt out with precision, leaving no room for uncertainty as to the credit that is required. But in practice this is not often the case. Frequently the term specifying the buyer's payment obligation is very brief: it may be no more than 'Payment by confirmed letter of credit'. What then are the seller's obligations as to the credit that should be opened?

The credit to be opened

3.3   Where the terms of the credit to be opened are not spelt out in the underlying contract, or are not fully spelt out, the choice is either to find them by other means or to hold that the contract is void for uncertainty. Some may be filled in from other provisions in the contract of sale. Custom of the trade, the past dealings of the parties, and considerations of reasonableness may also be relied upon to aid the interpretive process. It may be that the buyer will send to the seller a pre-advice of the credit that he proposes to open: if the seller agrees to the terms, they will become the relevant obligation. Or the buyer may go ahead and open the credit in terms which seem to him appropriate. The seller then has the opportunity to object if he thinks he has grounds for doing so. But if he does not, he may, depending upon his conduct, be held to have accepted the terms of the credit so that they are deemed to satisfy the requirements of the underlying contract. Or he may be held to have waived his right to object. These processes are illustrated by three cases.

3.4   First, in *Soproma SpA v Marine and Animal By-Products Corpn*[1] the contract of sale provided 'Payment: Against letter of credit, confirmed irrevocable, with Marine and Midland Trust Co, New York.' However, the credit opened was not confirmed, and did not cover the whole of the shipment period provided by the contract of sale. The former discrepancy was a contravention of an express term of the payment clause. The latter was in breach of an implied term that the credit should cover the whole of the contractual shipment period. It was also alleged that the credit was defective in that it called for documents not specified in the contract of sale. In respect of this last contention, McNair J stated '... I should not feel disposed to accept this conclusion. It seems to me to be a necessary implication from the use of the words "payment against letters of credit" that the credit itself should set out in detail the specific conditions under which it can be operated including the period of its availability and that so long as these conditions are fair and reasonable and are not inconsistent with the terms of the contract itself no objection can be taken to them by the sellers.'[2] But the sellers had not objected to the credit as opened, and were held to have waived their right to do so.

1 [1966] 1 Lloyd's Rep 367.
2 [1966] 1 Lloyd's Rep 367 at 386.

3.5   In the second case, *Ficom SA v Sociedad Cadex Ltda*,[1] the underlying contract was for the sale of coffee beans. Again the payment provision was shortly stated 'Payment: by immediate irrevocable letter of credit to be opened in favour of the sellers with the Banco Mercantil, La Paz, Bolivia...'. The credit in fact opened required a quality certificate in a particular form. No objection to the credit was taken by the sellers but they did object to one of three amendments proposed to it. Robert Goff J held that there was a binding agreement between the parties as to the form of the credit and that since the sellers were unable to present documents complying with its terms, the buyers were entitled to bring the contract to an end and reject the goods. In an illuminating judgment he examined as a matter of principle the ways in which the correct terms of a credit might become established:

> 'I approach the matter in this way. It is plain on the authorities that parties to a contract of sale, under which payment is to be made by means of a letter of credit, can, by subsequently agreeing to terms of the letter of credit which differ from those specified in the sale contract, thereby vary their contractual obligation under the sale contract: see *W J Alan & Co Ltd v El Nasr Export and Import Co* [1972] 2 QB 189, [1972] Lloyd's Rep 313. A somewhat similar case may arise where the parties do not, in their sale contract, define the terms of the proposed letter of credit. Where that occurs the letter of credit, as subsequently agreed between the parties, may fill the contractual gap and so supplement the terms of the sale contract;[2] if that is not done, for example, where the parties are unable to agree on the terms of a letter of credit to be issued under a contract of sale, then the dispute may have to be resolved by defining where possible, by means of implication or by resort to any approved custom of the trade, the terms upon which the parties must be taken to have agreed that the letter of credit should in due course be issued.

> Now, whether there has, in any particular case, been a binding agreement between the parties either to vary the terms of the original sale contract, or to supplement its express terms, is to be ascertained by asking the question whether the parties intended so to do – their intention to be ascertained objectively in the usual way from their words and actions at the relevant time. Furthermore, in considering whether there has, in any particular case, been any such binding agreement, it is important to bear in mind the possibility that there has been no more than a forbearance by one party, under which he forbears to enforce his strict legal rights under the sale contract, which will at most give rise to no more than an equitable estoppel, and may be capable of withdrawal by him upon giving reasonable notice to the other party.

> In the present case, I am concerned with a contract of sale in which the terms of the letter of credit – and in particular of the documents to be presented under the letter of credit – were undefined in the sale contract. Now, in such a case, it is commonplace that a letter of credit will be opened thereafter – sometimes preceded by a pre-advice by the buyer of the terms of the proposed credit followed by detailed negotiations of the terms so proposed – resulting in a letter of credit being issued in precise terms acceptable to both parties. Often the letter of credit so agreed will take the form which is usually employed in the particular trade. Now, although it is impossible to formulate any general rule, in such a case the terms of the letter of credit so agreed may well become binding contractually upon the parties. If so, and if they depart in any respect from the terms (express or implied) of the original sale contract, they will constitute a binding variation of that contract: if they

simply fill a gap in the original sale contract, then they will operate to supplement that contract. It is of importance to the parties that the terms of the letter of credit, if so agreed by them, should become binding, because on that basis the buyer will enter into a binding arrangement with the issuing bank instructed to issue the letter of credit to the seller, the terms of which will in their turn become binding as between the issuing bank and the seller. An example of a case in which such a binding variation of a sale contract was entered into is the case of *Alan v El Nasr*, to which I have previously referred; I refer in particular to the judgment of Lord Justice Megaw in that case at pp 327 and 217–218 of the respective reports.

Such a case may be contrasted with a case where the letter of credit established departs in some particular respect from the terms required by the sale contract, and the sellers forbear from insisting upon precise compliance with the terms of the sale contract in that particular respect. In such a case, particularly where the contract contemplates deliveries by instalments and therefore drawing on the letter of credit by instalments, such a forbearance may well give rise to no more than equitable estoppel, which the buyers may be able to resile from subsequently by giving reasonable notice to the sellers that they intend to resume their strict legal rights under the contract. Examples of cases of that kind are *Panoutsos v Raymond Hadley Corpn of New York* [1917] 2 KB 473, and *Enrico Furst & Co v W E Fischer Ltd* [1960] 2 Lloyd's Rep 340.

Now what happened in the present case? First of all, we have a sale contract which was silent on the terms upon which the letter of credit was to be opened. It is possible that this gap in the sale contract could, if necessary, have been filled, by implication, by reference to the custom of the trade ... But, be that as it may, I am satisfied, on the special case and the documents exhibited to the case, that the parties by agreement filled the gap in the sale contract. This is not a case where, on the documents before me, there was a pre-advice of the letter of credit terms, followed by negotiation, leading up to an agreement on those terms. But it is plain that the sellers agreed to the letter of credit so opened as being acceptable to them. In reaching that conclusion, I do not rely simply upon the finding of fact in the award that there was no objection to these terms raised on behalf of the sellers. I rely also on the subsequent conduct of the parties, and in particular on the occasion when the buyers subsequently proposed an amendment to that letter of credit relating to the quality certificate, which was rejected by the seller "because it was not agreed initially".[3]

1 [1980] 2 Lloyd's Rep 118.
2 This passage was cited and applied by Bingham J in *Shamsher Jute Mills Ltd v Sethia (London) Ltd* [1987] 1 Lloyd's Rep 388 at 392.
3 [1980] 2 Lloyd's Rep 118 at 131–132.

3.6   In rejecting the submission of counsel that the term in the credit requiring the quality certificate was an unenforceable agreement unsupported by consideration, Robert Goff J stated 'Where, as here, the sale contract is silent as to the terms of the letter of credit contemplated by the sale contract, the definition of those terms is a matter of mutual benefit and acceptance of the terms by each party is therefore supported by consideration moving from the other. In my judgment it is not possible in such a case to isolate one particular facet of the terms so agreed and to argue that that particular term was for the benefit of one party only and so unsupported by consideration moving from the other.'[1]

1 [1980] 2 Lloyd's Rep 118 at 132.

3.7 Finally, in *Glencore Grain Rotterdam BV v Lebanese Organisation for International Commerce*[1] the sellers under an f.o.b. contract objected to a credit which required bills of lading to be marked 'freight pre-paid'. The buyers made some amendments to the credit, but did not change that requirement. The sellers thereafter were silent and made no further reference to the issue. It was held by the Court of Appeal that the sellers' conduct was not sufficiently unequivocal to evince acceptance by them of the terms of the credit.

1 [1997] 2 Lloyd's Rep 386 at 394. See para **3.12** below.

Terms as to revocability and confirmation

3.8 These are matters which should be, and usually are, covered by the underlying contract. If the credit should be confirmed, a revocable credit will not do.[1] Nor will an irrevocable but unconfirmed credit.[2] Where a credit is required to be confirmed and the advising banker purports to confirm it but at the same time reserves a right of recourse against the seller on his bills of exchange, this will not do: for the right of recourse is inconsistent with the concept of a confirmed credit.[3] Where the contract provides for the irrevocable credit to be opened in London, an irrevocable credit advised by a London bank which does not add its confirmation is not an irrevocable credit opened in London because the London bank can resile at any time.[4]

1 *Panoutsos v Raymond Hadley Corpn of New York* [1917] 2 KB 473.
2 *Soproma SpA v Marine and Animal By-Products Corpn* [1966] 1 Lloyd's Rep 367.
3 *Wahbe Tamari & Sons Ltd v Colprogeca* [1969] 2 Lloyd's Rep 18.
4 *Enrico Furst & Co v W E Fischer Ltd* [1960] 2 Lloyd's Rep 340.

3.9 The contract may be silent as to whether the credit is to be revocable or irrevocable, confirmed or unconfirmed. If there is a previous course of dealing between the parties, the court may resolve the question by reference to it. But what if there is not? Because a revocable credit offers no security and because it may be presumed to be the intention of the parties to provide the seller with security, there is a strong argument that the credit must be at least irrevocable. In *Giddens v Anglo–African Produce Co Ltd*[1] the contract called for a credit to be established with the National Bank of South Africa. The credit opened by the bank provided for drafts to be negotiated with recourse. Bailhache J remarked 'How that can be called an established credit in any sense of the word absolutely passes my comprehension'. While this is strictly an authority on the meaning of 'established', it indicates a view of a revocable credit which is likely to be adopted by courts today.

1 (1923) 14 Ll L Rep 230.

3.10   Where the underlying contract does not state that the credit is to be a confirmed credit, prima facie the buyer will fulfil his obligation if he opens an irrevocable credit with his own bank as the issuing bank which is either advised direct to the seller by that bank or is advised to him through a correspondent bank in the seller's country. The seller might argue that he was entitled to a confirmed credit on the grounds that many credits issued in modern international trade are confirmed credits, and that this reflects the very function of a credit as being to give the seller not only the security of a bank undertaking but that of a bank undertaking in his own country. As Denning LJ observed at the beginning of his judgment in *Pavia & Co SpA v Thurmann-Nielsen*: 'The sale of goods across the world is now usually arranged by means of confirmed credits.'[1] Such an argument does not appear yet to have been considered by an English court. Were the point to be taken, it is suggested that it should fail. If the seller requires a confirmed credit, it is for him to say so and have the requirement expressly included in the contract of sale. The seller might adopt a fall-back argument that he was at least entitled to have the credit advised to him by a bank in his own country to which the seller could present documents. He could rely on the fact that in the particular trade in which he is engaged it is rare for a credit to be advised directly to the seller by the issuing bank in another country. (By contrast, in some trades, such as the oil trade, such a practice is common.) It is, he would argue, therefore reasonably to be anticipated that in the ordinary course of his trade a credit will be advised through a local correspondent bank. Such an argument may have a greater chance of success, but also appears untried in English litigation.

1 [1952] 2 QB 84.

Documents to be required

3.11   It is dangerous to generalise because any contract may have its own peculiarities. Obviously with a c.i.f. contract the documents to be presented will include the bills of lading or other transport document, the commercial invoice, and a policy of marine insurance. But what as to documents such as packing lists, certificates of origin, or inspection certificates? In the absence of any prior course of dealing between the parties, one may be thrown back upon what is reasonable as being usual or customary in the trade. A packing list and a certificate of origin may seem innocuous enough – but a requirement for the latter could cause difficulties in some circumstances. Although it will often work to the seller's advantage, implying a requirement for a certificate of inspection by a specified agency is more difficult unless it can be supported by prior dealings between the parties or is usual in the relevant trade. An example of a document which the buyer is clearly not entitled to include among those to be presented under the credit (at least in the absence of a contractual stipulation) is a guarantee that the goods being sold would perform satisfactorily in the future.[1]

1 See *Newman Industries Ltd v Indo-British Industries* [1956] 2 Lloyd's Rep 219 (reversed on other grounds [1957] 1 Lloyd's Rep 211). See also *H & J.M. Bennett Europe Ltd v Agrexco Co Ltd* (6 April 1990, unreported), QBD, where there is a review of the reasonableness of a variety of documents required in respect of a shipment of potatoes.

3.12 The documentary requirements of the credit must not be inconsistent with those of the sale contract. Thus, in *Glencore Grain Rotterdam BV v Lebanese Organisation for International Commerce*[1] the Court of Appeal held that a credit which provided for payment against a freight pre-paid bill of lading was not in conformity with an f.o.b. contract of sale. Under standard (or 'classic') f.o.b. terms, the seller is not responsible for arranging carriage or paying freight, and, in the absence of a special arrangement or guarantee from a third party (not the buyer), the seller cannot be certain that a freight pre-paid bill of lading will be issued on shipment. The credit opened in *Glencore* thus gave no security to the seller that he could obtain payment under the credit on shipment.

1 [1997] 2 Lloyd's Rep 386.

Correcting defects

3.13 If the credit as opened does not comply with the contract, the seller may be able to treat this as a breach entitling him to terminate even though the period for the opening of the credit has not expired, if it is reasonable to deduce that the buyer does not intend to remedy the defect. But, otherwise, if the buyer corrects a defect within the period, the seller must accept the credit. In *Kronman & Co v Steinberger*[1] the sellers tried to take advantage of an obvious mistake in the credit as initially opened which the buyers corrected, and to call the contract off. The court held the sellers liable in damages.

1 (1922) 10 Ll L Rep 39.

The possibility of no enforceable contract

3.14 Where there is no agreement as to the terms of the credit to be opened, it may be held that the parties were never *ad idem*, and so there is no enforceable contract. This occurred in *Schijveshuurder v Canon (Export) Ltd*[1] where the parties were in disagreement as to whether a bill of lading was required to be among the documents to be presented, or whether a goods receipt would be sufficient. Obviously where the parties in their negotiations leading to the alleged contract are in actual disagreement over some feature and this has not been resolved, it is difficult for the court to find a concluded contract. But where the parties to a commercial transaction have intended to bind themselves, the court will be loathe to conclude that they have failed to do so, and will ordinarily find a contract and flesh it out by means of reasonable implication where it is necessary to do so. Thus in *G Scammell & Nephew Ltd v Ouston*[2] Lord Maugham stated:[3] 'In commercial documents connected with dealings in a trade with which the parties are perfectly familiar the court is very willing, if satisfied that the parties thought they had made a binding contract, to imply terms and in particular terms as to the method of carrying out the contract which it would be impossible to supply in other kinds of contract', citing the earlier decision of the House of Lords in *Hillas & Co Ltd v Arcos Ltd*.[4]

1 [1952] 2 Lloyd's Rep 196.
2 [1941] AC 251.
3 [1941] AC 251 at 255.
4 (1931) 40 Ll L Rep 307.

No legal duty to cooperate to finalise the terms of a credit

3.15   It was argued in *Siporex Trade SA v Bank Indosuez*[1] that there is a duty resting on a seller to cooperate with the buyer and perhaps also with the bank in negotiating and finalising the terms of a credit. The case was mainly concerned with a performance bond made payable if no credit were opened. It was held that the bank was bound to pay against an appropriately-worded demand on the bond, and was not concerned with the underlying dispute between the buyers and sellers as to the credit. Hirst J, however, went on to consider the arguments which arose if he was wrong on that primary finding. In doing so he rejected the suggestion of a duty on the part of a seller to cooperate. After referring to *Ficom's* case,[2] he stated:[3]

> 'I shall deal with the buyer's position first. I do not for a moment doubt that in the world of everyday commerce such cooperation frequently occurs, nor do I doubt that it is highly desirable particularly where important matters are left outstanding. But proof of normality of practice, or even of a high degree of desirability, falls far short of establishing the existence of a contractual duty owed by the buyer to be implied as a contractual term. ... In my judgment, under the normal well-established principles of letters of credit, it is for the buyer to establish the letter of credit as required by the contract. If the contract terms are themselves incomplete, and unresolvable by reference to custom, the supposed duty to cooperate would in effect be no more than an agreement to agree, which is not a workable contractual term. Moreover, the scope of the proposed duty in any given case would be impossible to define with the degree of precision required for a workable term...

In these circumstances [the] proposed implied term fails the business efficacy test and I am not prepared to hold that there is any legal duty imposed on the seller to cooperate with the buyer.'

1 [1986] 2 Lloyd's Rep 146.
2 See para **3.5** above.
3 [1986] 2 Lloyd's Rep 146 at 162.

B   THE TIME FOR THE CREDIT TO BE OPENED

General

3.16   A credit must be opened in due time. That must include its communication to the beneficiary. It is not enough for the applicant to instruct a bank within the time. If the credit is to be confirmed, the confirmation must also be communicated in due time. So, in short, the beneficiary must have binding promises from the banks within the appropriate period.[1] The situations relating to that period can be divided into three. First, there are those where the contract of sale makes an express provision as to the date by which the credit is to be opened. This may be done by naming a date or by providing a mechanism for it to be ascertained.[2] Secondly, the contract may have no such provision but it may be of a type, namely a c.i.f. or f.o.b. contract, or one of their variations, where the time can be stated in accordance with principles established in previous cases. These are considered in paras **3.18–3.23** below. Lastly, one may be thrown back upon a test of reasonableness.

1 See *Bunge Corpn v Vegetable Vitamin Foods (Pte) Ltd* [1985] 1 Lloyd's Rep 613 at 617.
2 For a particular point of construction of a contractual term as to when a credit was required to be opened, held to be arguable by the Court of Appeal, see *Sohio Supply Co v Gatoil (USA) Inc* [1989] 1 Lloyd's Rep 588. For a case where the term as to the time for opening the credit gave no difficulty, but which depended for its operation on a clause which did gave rise to a dispute, see *Transpetrol Ltd v Transol Olieprodukten Nederland BV* [1989] 1 Lloyd's Rep 309. The importance of giving effect to what the parties agreed is well illustrated by the decision of the Irish Supreme Court in *Tradax (Ireland) Ltd v Irish Grain Board Ltd* [1984] IR 1.

3.17   Where the contract provides for the credit to be opened immediately, 'that means that the buyer must have such time as is needed by a person of reasonable diligence to get that credit established'.[1] In *Etablissements Chainbaux SARL v Harbormaster Ltd,*[2] Devlin J had to consider the nature of the obligation to provide a credit within a reasonable time.[3] He cited from Lord Watson's speech in *Hick v Raymond and Reid*[4] to the effect that, where the law implies that a contract should be performed within a reasonable time, this 'has invariably been held to mean that the party upon whom it is incumbent duly fulfils his obligation, notwithstanding protracted delay, so long as such delay is attributable to causes beyond his control, and he has neither acted negligently nor unreasonably'. Devlin J went on to hold that only the time taken directly in the arranging of the credit could be considered and not, for example, time taken in obtaining the currency required to enable the credit to be opened.

1 *Garcia v Page & Co Ltd* (1936) 55 Ll L Rep 391 at 392 (Porter J).
2 [1955] 1 Lloyd's Rep 303.
3 [1955] 1 Lloyd's Rep 303 at 311.
4 [1893] AC 22.

C.I.F. contracts

3.18   Where the sale is on c.i.f. terms, frequently nothing will be stipulated as to the time for opening the credit, but invariably a shipment period is stated. It is established in such circumstances that at the latest the credit must be opened by the first possible date for shipment. There is, however, some authority which suggests that it should be opened earlier.

3.19   In *Pavia & Co SpA v Thurmann-Nielsen*[1] the Court of Appeal held that in the case of a c.i.f. contract the credit must be opened for the whole of the shipment period. It had been argued for the buyers that it was sufficient if the credit was opened by the time that the sellers had actually got the documents ready for presentation. The respondent sellers were not called upon to argue in the Court of Appeal: in the court below they had simply argued that the credit must be opened by the start of the shipment period and had not taken the argument to the stage of suggesting that it must be opened a reasonable period before that time.[2]

1 [1952] 2 QB 84.
2 [1951] 2 Lloyd's Rep 328.

3.20   The next case was *Plasticmoda SpA v Davidsons (Manchester) Ltd.*[1] Here there were to be two shipments on c.i.f. terms, 'the first one month from today and the next to follow sixty days later'. Denning LJ began his judgment stating that *Pavia* established that 'when nothing is said the buyer must establish the credit at the beginning of the shipment period. There was in this case no shipment period but only a shipment date. The letter of credit ought no doubt to have been established a reasonable time before that date.'[2] The other judgments (of Singleton and Hudson LJJ) do not refer to the point.

1 [1952] 1 Lloyd's Rep 527.
2 [1952] 1 Lloyd's Rep 527 at 538. The fact that the contract provision as to shipment was in terms of a specific date rather than a period (which gives the seller some leeway) may provide a possible ground for distinguishing *Plasticmoda* from *Pavia*.

3.21   A question similar to that in *Pavia* arose in *Sinason-Teicher Inter-American Grain Corpn v Oilcakes and Oilseeds Trading Co Ltd*[1] where the obligation was to provide not a letter of credit but a bankers' guarantee covering payment. The contest was between the sellers' argument that the guarantee had to be provided as soon as reasonably possible and the buyers' contention that it had to be provided by the first shipment date. Devlin J held that a bank guarantee was to be treated in the same manner as a letter of credit, and that *Pavia* did not decide that the buyer could delay until the first date for shipment before opening the credit. He concluded that the buyers' second argument was correct. But he did not spell out how the reasonable period was to be measured. Is it a reasonable period for the seller to get the goods to the vessel? Does it include time for the seller to do other things to the goods which he may need to do to get them ready for shipment? What if he has substantial work to do to them, or is even to manufacture them? In the Court of Appeal, Denning LJ agreed that *Pavia* does not decide that the buyer can delay right up to the first date for shipment; instead, he stated that the credit must be provided a reasonable time before that date.[2] Birkett LJ did not refer to *Pavia* at all. Morris LJ did: although his judgment is not wholly clear, it tends to uphold the first date of shipment as the date by which a guarantee or letter of credit should be provided.

1 [1954] 1 WLR 935; affd [1954] 1 WLR 1394, [1954] 2 Lloyd's Rep 327.
2 This holding was followed in *H & J.M. Bennett Europe Ltd v Angrexco Co Ltd* (6 April 1990, unreported). On the particular facts, HHJ Humphries held that the credit should have been opened five days before the first date for shipment.

F.O.B. contracts

3.22   The above argument was continued into the field of f.o.b. contracts in the case of *Ian Stach Ltd v Baker Bosley Ltd*.[1] Diplock J held that the f.o.b. contract he had to consider was in 'classic' form and therefore the buyer had the right and responsibility of making arrangements for shipment and choosing the date of shipment. He appears to have held that *Pavia* was a binding authority with regard to c.i.f. contracts and thought that the remarks made about it by Denning LJ in *Sinason-Teicher* were *obiter*. Diplock J rejected the buyers' argument that the credit must be opened a reasonable time before the shipping instructions take effect, and held instead that under a classic f.o.b. contract the credit must be opened at the latest by the earliest date for shipment. He stated that for the purpose of the case before him he need go no further. In *Glencore Grain Rotterdam BV v Lebanese Organisation for International Commerce*,[2] the Court of Appeal observed that the 'prima facie rule' in f.o.b. sales is that the buyer's duty is to open a conforming credit by the beginning of the shipment period.

1 [1958] 2 QB 130.
2 [1997] 2 Lloyd's Rep 386 at 395 (Evans LJ, giving the judgment of the court).

A view

3.23   If there does remain any doubt on the effect of the authorities,[1] it is suggested that the better view is that a buyer's obligation is to open the credit by the first possible date of shipment. If the purpose of the credit extends to enabling the seller to do whatever he has to do to the goods prior to shipment in the knowledge that the credit has been opened, then it might be argued that a credit should be opened 'a reasonable time' before the shipment period. But it cannot be said that this would be the clear intention of both parties. The buyer may well not know what the seller has to do; moreover, he may well not be in a position to judge what a reasonable time would be, particularly in a case where there are special circumstances affecting the seller. He may well consider that it should be sufficient for the seller if the credit is opened prior to the first date for shipment. Further, the introduction of an additional 'reasonable period' prior to the start of the shipment period introduces undesirable uncertainty, something that is particularly inapposite if the timely opening of the credit is a matter where default will or might constitute repudiation of the contract. If an element of reasonable time were to be introduced, time would to that extent cease to be of the essence, and it would be necessary for the seller to serve a notice specifying a particular date by which the credit must be opened before he would be entitled to cancel for default prior to the earliest date for shipment.[2] This last difficulty will not arise if, as may well be the case, time remains of the essence and it remains a condition of the contract that the credit be opened by the reasonable date. The problems which the introduction of an indefinite period of time may introduce have not been considered in the cases, and its introduction is undesirable and potentially inconvenient. If a seller wants the credit to be opened before the time for shipment, he can include a term in the contract of sale providing for that and stating how long before the shipment period it is to be opened.

1 For a contrary view to *Ian Stach*, see *Alexandria Cotton and Trading Co (Sudan) Ltd v Cotton Co of Ethiopia* [1963] 1 Lloyd's Rep 576 at 589 (Roskill J).
2 See para **3.27** below.

Where there is no shipment date

3.24   In the absence of any express provision, it is to be implied that the credit shall be opened within a reasonable time of the contract being made.[1] This is assessed by reference to the expected or likely date of shipment, as well as such other relevant factors as might exist. Thus in *Baltimex Baltic Import and Export Co Ltd v Metallo Chemical Refining Co Ltd*,[2] both parties had anticipated that there might be delays, and the sellers could not complain when they came to pass.

1 As to the assessment of a reasonable time, see para **3.17** above.
2 [1955] 2 Lloyd's Rep 438.

Where the seller lets time go by

3.25   The seller may not cancel the contract when the time for opening the credit is first exceeded: he may continue with the contract in the hope that the buyer will in time perform. What is the position then? Once the seller has done anything to affirm the contract after his right to cancel has accrued, he has waived the right. He may even be treated in appropriate circumstances as having affirmed by silence alone. His position following affirmation is as stated by Devlin J in *Etablissements Chainbaux SARL v Harbormaster Ltd*:[1]

> 'Now, the position of a party who has started out with a contract where time is of the essence and has allowed the time to go by is, I think, quite clearly laid down in the authorities. He has got to make time of the essence of the contract again in the normal case, and that means that he has to give a notice giving the other side what is a reasonable time in all the circumstances to comply with their obligations, and it is only after they fail to do that that he is entitled to cancel the contract.'

He continued:

> '... the notice is not always essential. If the seller...fails to give it, it is still open to him to prove that if he had given a reasonable notice it would have been of no use to the plaintiff.'

Applying these principles, suppose that the contract provides that a credit is to be opened by the beginning of May and shipment is to be in June. The buyer fails to open the credit and the seller urges him to do so. By mid-May he has still not done so. The seller then serves a notice calling upon the buyer to open the credit within seven days. If no credit is provided within that period, the seller may then cancel the contract, provided that seven days was a reasonable time – as *prima facie* it would be. Alternatively the seller may feel that there is now no hope of the buyer providing the credit, so he does not serve notice but simply cancels. So long as he can establish that the further time would not have assisted the buyer, he is within his rights.

1 [1955] 1 Lloyd's Rep 303 at 312. Other examples of cases involving waiver of the time for opening the credit first set by the contract are: *Ian Stach Ltd v Baker Bosley Ltd* [1958] 2 QB 130; *Plasticmoda SpA v Davidsons (Manchester) Ltd* [1952] 1 Lloyd's Rep 527; *Baltimex Baltic Import and Export Co Ltd v Metallo Chemical Refining Co Ltd* [1955] 2 Lloyd's Rep 438; *State Trading Corpn of India Ltd v Compagnie Française* [1983] 2 Lloyd's Rep 679; *Wahbe Tamari & Sons Ltd v Colprogeca* [1969] 2 Lloyd's Rep 18; *Brown Noel Trading Pte Ltd v Donald McArthy Pte Ltd* [1997] 1 SLR 1; and *International Asset Control Ltd v Films sans Frontieres SARL* [1999] EMLR 268.

C THE OPENING OF A CREDIT IS A CONDITION PRECEDENT TO THE SELLER'S OBLIGATION TO SHIP

3.26   The obligation on the buyer to open a credit which conforms to the requirements of the contract of sale is a condition of that contract in the sense that if it is not performed in due time, the seller may accept the buyer's breach of contract as a repudiation of the contract and terminate it. Secondly, the performance of the buyer's duty is a condition precedent to the seller's obligation to ship the goods, in the sense that until it is performed the seller is under no duty to perform his obligation. In *Trans Trust SPRL v Danubia Trading Co*[1] Denning LJ first pointed out that the stipulation for a credit may be a condition precedent to the formation of the contract of sale.[2] It is suggested that, while this is a possible construction, it would be very rare. He continued, however: 'In other cases a contract is concluded and the stipulation for a credit is a condition which is an essential term of the contract. In those cases the provision of the credit is a condition precedent, not to the formation of a contract, but to the obligation of the seller to deliver the goods. If the buyer fails to provide the credit, the seller can treat himself as discharged from any further performance of the contract and can sue the buyer for damages for not providing the credit.' This passage has been cited with approval[3] and is supported by a consistent line of authority.[4] It is submitted that it sets out the usual position.

1 [1952] 2 QB 297.
2 [1952] 2 QB 297 at 304.
3 *A E Lindsay & Co Ltd v Cook* [1953] 1 Lloyd's Rep 328 at 335; *Plasticmoda SpA v Davidsons (Manchester) Ltd* [1952] 1 Lloyd's Rep 527 at 536.
4 *Garcia v Page & Co Ltd* (1936) 55 Ll L Rep 391; *Dix v Grainger* (1922) 10 Ll L Rep 496; *Soproma SpA v Marine and Animal By-Products Corpn* [1966] 1 Lloyd's Rep 367 at 386.

The seller's right to terminate

3.27   It is clear that the seller is not obliged to ship the goods, or indeed to perform any part of the loading operation,[1] until a credit conforming to the contract of sale has been opened. It is clear that where the credit is to be opened by a fixed date (either stipulated expressly by the contract, or determined by its terms), yet it is not opened by that date, the seller may terminate the contract.[2] Time is then 'of the essence', and any failure to meet the obligation entitles cancellation.[3] But it may be that the time for the opening of the credit can only be assessed in terms of what would be a reasonable time.[4] Then the seller can obtain a right to terminate the contract by serving a notice giving the buyer a date by which the credit must be provided, which must not be prior to the expiry of a reasonable time. If the buyer defaults, the seller may then cancel the contract and claim damages. In

British and Commonwealth Holdings plc v Quadrex Holdings Inc,[5] Sir Nicholas Browne-Wilkinson V-C, giving the judgment of the Court of Appeal, stated:[6] '... where, if a time for completion had been specified in the contract, time would have been of the essence, the innocent party can make time of the essence by serving a reasonable notice to complete even though the guilty party has not been guilty of improper or undue delay.' Where the obligation on the buyer is to open the credit within a reasonable time, it must also be open to the seller to terminate the contract where the buyer lets so much time go by without opening the credit that his conduct amounts to a repudiation of the contract.

1 *Kronos Worldwide v Sempra Oil Trading SARL* [2004] 1 All ER (Comm) 915, Court of Appeal. Therefore under the sale contract in that case laytime could not begin to run (and consequently demurrage could not accrue) unless and until a letter of credit was opened.
2 The time for the opening of a credit is considered in paras **3.16–3.25** above.
3 See the cases cited in para **3.26** and *Wahbe Tamari & Sons Ltd v Colprogeca* [1969] 2 Lloyd's Rep 18.
4 See inter alia para **3.24** above.
5 [1989] QB 842.
6 [1989] QB 842 at 858.

Cases where an act by the seller is a pre-condition

3.28   In some instances the buyer's duty to open the credit may not arise until the seller has done some act. In the event of the seller failing so to do, it will be he who is at fault rather than the buyer. Thus in *Knotz v Fairclough Dodd and Jones Ltd,*[1] the contract provided 'Payment by letter of credit for 97% of sellers' provisional invoice...', and it was held that the supply of the provisional invoice was a condition precedent to the buyer's obligation to open the credit. In *Nicolene Ltd v Simmonds,*[2] the buyers had repeatedly offered to open a letter of credit, but the defendants had failed to give any instructions to do so and were held to be the party at fault. This case is also authority (if such be needed) for the proposition that a seller cannot be required to provide a letter from his bank stating that a facility for the credit is available. In *State Trading Corpn of India Ltd v M Golodetz Ltd,*[3] the underlying contract was for the sale of a cargo of sugar. Payment was to be by irrevocable letter of credit in a standard form, which was to be procured by the buyers not later than seven days after the conclusion of the contract and irrespective of the opening of a performance guarantee by the sellers. The performance guarantee was to be provided within seven days of the conclusion of the sale contract. The sellers also undertook to provide a performance guarantee relating to a counter-trade, and this was to be done within seven days of the making of the contract. The sellers opened the performance guarantee but not the counter-trade guarantee. The buyers did not open a letter of credit, arguing that the opening of the counter-trade guarantee was a condition precedent to their obligation to do so. The Court of Appeal rejected this argument and held the buyers liable in damages. The main reason was that the obligation to open a credit was not conditional upon the opening of the performance guarantee, and the counter-trade guarantee was the less important of the two guarantees.

1 [1952] 1 Lloyd's Rep 226.
2 [1952] 2 Lloyd's Rep 419; affirmed [1953] 1 QB 543.
3 [1989] 2 Lloyd's Rep 277.

The buyer's duty to open the credit in due time is absolute

3.29   Subject to such latitude as an obligation to provide a credit within a reasonable time may give him, the buyer's duty to provide a credit in time is absolute. Thus if the communication of the credit is held up by delay on the part of a bank, the buyer is nonetheless responsible: *A E Lindsay & Co Ltd v Book*.[1]

1 [1953] 1 Lloyd's Rep 328.

The seller's remedies against the buyer for damages

3.30   The seller's right to cancel the contract where no conforming credit has been opened by the correct time has already been noted. It has also been stated that where no conforming credit is opened in time, then unless a non-conforming credit is opened which the seller accepts, the seller's obligation to ship or to perform any part of the loading operation never becomes effective. Where the contract is not performed because of the buyer's failure to open a conforming credit, the seller may sue him for damages. Such damages are to be assessed in accordance with the same general principles that apply in any other situation where a buyer repudiates a contract of sale, and reference should be made elsewhere for a full treatment.[1] In brief, the seller's loss will usually be assessed as the difference between the contract price and the market price of the goods, assuming that there is an available market.[2] In *Ian Stach Ltd v Baker Bosley Ltd*,[3] the sellers were entitled to recover the difference between the contract price and the market price (which they had in fact obtained on a re-sale of the goods). If special circumstances were made known to the buyer when the contract was entered into, the seller may recover an alternative measure. Thus in *Trans Trust SPRL v Danubian Trading Co Ltd*,[4] the buyers knew that if they failed to procure the opening of the credit the sellers would be unable to buy in the goods from their own supplier. The sellers were held entitled to recover the actual profit they would have made had the transaction been completed. They were, however, not entitled to be indemnified against liability to their own sellers, because the circumstances giving rise to such liability were not known to the buyers.

1 E.g. *Benjamin's Sale of Goods* (7th edn) paras 16-060 et seq.
2 Sale of Goods Act 1979, s 50(3).
3 [1958] 2 QB 130.
4 [1952] 2 QB 297.

D THE SELLER PROCEEDING AS IF A NON-CONFORMING CREDIT WERE CONFORMING

3.31 Where the credit as opened conforms to the underlying contract, the seller has no right to object to its terms. It may happen in practice that a seller takes no objection to a non-conforming credit and proceeds as though it were conforming. What is the position then? There are three possibilities. First, he may be held to have waived the irregularity. Secondly, he may be held to be estopped from relying on the defects. The cases make little distinction between these two devices but tend to focus on the former. Thirdly, there may be held to have been a variation of the underlying contract to the effect that the credit shall be in the form in which it has in fact been opened. Where there has been a waiver or an estoppel, the seller may in appropriate circumstances give notice to the buyer that despite his previous acceptance of the position he now requires it to be remedied within a reasonable time. In other words, they may have only a suspensory effect on the seller's rights. By contrast, a variation is extinctive in effect, but needs to be supported by consideration. This will often be found in the fact that, for better or worse, both the parties have become bound by the new term.[1]

1 *Cf Ficom SA v Sociedad Cadex Ltda* [1980] 2 Lloyd's Rep 118 at 132and see para **3.5** above.

3.32 A leading case on waiver is *Panoutsos v Raymond Hadley Corpn of New York*.[1] The contract provided for a number of shipments, payment to be by 'confirmed banker's credit'. The credit was not confirmed, but the sellers made some shipments and obtained payments under the credit. They then cancelled the contract, without having given previous notice, on the ground that the credit did not accord with the contractual requirements. The Court of Appeal held that although the seller was entitled to enforce his strict legal rights and cancel the contract, he could only do so on giving the buyer reasonable notice of his intention to cancel, so as to enable the buyer to comply with the requirements of the contract that up until that time had been waived.

1 [1917] 2 KB 473.

3.33 In *Enrico Furst & Co v W E Fischer Ltd*,[1] the credit was required to be an irrevocable credit opened and payable in London. But the London advising bank did not add their confirmation. Nor did the credit provide for a weight certificate as the sale contract required. Nevertheless the sellers treated the credit as valid and asked for an extension of the time provided by the credit for the presentation of documents. Diplock J held that there had been a waiver of the contractual requirements, citing what is now s 11(2) of the Sale of Goods Act 1979.[2]

1 [1960] 2 Lloyd's Rep 340.
2 'Where a contract of sale is subject to a condition to be fulfilled by the seller, the buyer may waive the condition, or may elect to treat the breach of condition as a breach of warranty and not as a ground for treating the contract as repudiated' (formerly s 11(1) of the Sale of Goods Act 1893).

3.34 *WJ Alan & Co Ltd v El Nasr Export and Import Co*[1] concerned the export of coffee from Kenya to Egypt. The contract was priced in Kenyan shillings, but the letter of credit was held to have been opened in sterling. Difficulties arose because the devaluation of sterling caused the credit to be less valuable than it would have been if expressed in Kenyan shillings. This, however, did not occur until after documents had been negotiated in respect of a first shipment and just prior to the presentation of documents for a second shipment. The sellers attempted to recover the difference between the currencies directly from the buyers. Lord Denning MR held that the case was one of waiver. Megaw LJ held that there had been a variation and not a waiver of the obligation in the underlying contract of sale. He held that the sellers had accepted the bank's offer contained in the credit on the buyers' instructions by acting on the credit in presenting documents. So the banks became bound and the credit unalterable, except by the consent of all parties concerned 'all of whose legal rights and liabilities have necessarily been affected by the establishment of the credit'. On this basis the currency of the sale contract was irrevocably altered.[2] Megaw LJ also held that, if there had been no variation, there had nonetheless been a waiver which the sellers could not unilaterally abrogate. Stephenson LJ simply held that the sellers could not now claim against the buyers, because 'they were attempting to assert a liability which, whether by variation or waiver, they had allowed the buyers to alter.'[3]

1 [1972] 2 QB 189.
2 [1972] 2 QB 189 at 218.
3 [1972] 2 QB 189 at 221.

3.35 In *Glencore Grain Rotterdam BV v Lebanese Organisation for International Commerce*,[1] the buyers opened a credit that did not conform to the sale contract because it required the presentation of a freight pre-paid bill of lading. The sellers objected immediately, but when the buyers maintained their position, the sellers did not make any further complaint about the terms of the credit but instead refused to ship the goods unless the price were increased. The Court of Appeal held that the sellers' conduct was not inconsistent with their previous objection and that there had been no unequivocal representation that the sellers had relinquished, or would relinquish, their rights arising out of the buyers' failure to open a conforming letter of credit. The sellers were entitled to justify their refusal to ship on the basis of the buyers' failure, and (on ordinary contractual principles) it did not matter that they had not given this as a reason at the time.

1 [1997] 2 Lloyd's Rep 386; see para 3.7.

E   THE AMENDMENT OF THE CREDIT

Introduction

3.36   The amendment of a credit should be a matter which is instigated by the applicant either with the agreement of the beneficiary or at his request. In that sense it is a matter which arises between them, and is therefore considered in this chapter. The amendment itself is effected between the issuing bank and the beneficiary, probably through an advising bank. So it also involves them and could equally be considered in the chapters concerned with their relations.

The legal position

3.37   A bank undertaking contained in a letter of credit constitutes a binding contract between the bank and the beneficiary. Just as a contract can be amended only by the agreement of all the parties to it, a bank undertaking contained in a documentary credit can be amended only by the agreement of the parties to the undertaking, namely the bank giving the undertaking and the beneficiary. Where the credit is confirmed by the advising bank, its consent is also needed. As the credit is issued on the instructions of the applicant, any amendment of the credit without the agreement of the applicant would constitute a breach of the agreement between the applicant and the issuing bank. In practice the amendment of a credit is initiated by instructions from the applicant to the issuing bank. These instructions may have been preceded by a request for amendment made by the beneficiary. Such a request will be made where the beneficiary considers that the terms of the credit advised to him are inappropriate and should be changed. Alternatively, it may be made subsequently, perhaps to take account of unexpected events, such as a need to extend the shipping period or difficulties in obtaining a certificate in the particular form originally required by the credit. Where the request arises because the terms of the credit as advised to the beneficiary are unacceptable to him, this will in most cases amount to a rejection of the credit. Difficulties arise where the applicant initiates an amendment which is not acceptable to the beneficiary. Then it is clear that the beneficiary is entitled to reject the amendment when advised to him, and the credit remains unchanged.[1]

1 For an example of amendments being accepted and rejected, see *Ficom SA v Sociedad Cadex Ltd* [1980] 2 Lloyd's Rep 118 at 127, and of amendments simply not being accepted, see *United City Merchants (Investments) Ltd v Royal Bank of Canada* [1979] 1 Lloyd's Rep 267 at 275 (Mocatta J). For an example of a case where it was alleged that a credit had been varied, see *Seepoong Engineering Construction Co Ltd v Formula One Management Ltd* [2000] 1 Lloyd's Rep 602.

The UCP

3.38   Articles 7 and 8 of the UCP set out the undertakings which may be given by issuing and confirming banks. Article 10 provides that the undertakings cannot be amended without the consent of the relevant banks and the beneficiary. It states:

'**Article 10:**
a. Except as otherwise provided by article 38,[1] a credit can neither be amended nor cancelled without the agreement of the issuing bank, the confirming bank, if any, and the beneficiary.
b. An issuing bank is irrevocably bound by an amendment as of the time it issues the amendment. A confirming bank may extend its confirmation to an amendment and will be irrevocably bound as of the time it advises the amendment. A confirming bank may, however, choose to advise an amendment without extending its confirmation and, if so, must inform the issuing bank without delay and inform the beneficiary in its advice.
c. The terms and conditions of the original credit (or a credit incorporating previously accepted amendments) will remain in force for the beneficiary until the beneficiary communicates its acceptance of the amendment to the bank that advised such amendment. The beneficiary should give notification of acceptance or rejection of an amendment. If the beneficiary fails to give such notification, a presentation that complies with the credit and to any not yet accepted amendment will be deemed to be notification of acceptance by the beneficiary of such amendment. As of that moment the credit will be amended.
d. A bank that advises an amendment should inform the bank from which it received the amendment of any notification of acceptance or rejection.
e. Partial acceptance of an amendment is not allowed and will be deemed to be notification of rejection of the amendment.
f. A provision in an amendment to the effect that the amendment shall enter into force unless rejected by the beneficiary within a certain time shall be disregarded.'

It will be noticed that the Article refers only to the parties to the credit itself and does not mention the applicant and the need for him to instigate the amendment.[2] In relation to the advice of an amendment, Article 9.d provides:

'**Article 9.d Amendments**
A bank utilizing the services of an advising bank or second advising bank to advise a credit must use the same bank to advise any amendment thereto.'

The consequences of non-compliance are, however, not spelt out, and if the issuing bank were to use the services of a different bank from the first advising bank to advise of an amendment, the English law principles of agency and authority would potentially have room for operation in reaching the appropriate solution.

1 Article 38 relates to transfer.
2 See para **3.36** above.

Problems in practice

3.39   When the issuing bank receives instructions from the applicant to make an amendment, it will, provided that it is content to do so, instruct the advising bank of the amendment, and the amendment will then be advised to the beneficiary, usually in the form of a statement that the credit is thereby amended. This may or may not be accompanied by a request that the beneficiary inform the bank whether the amendment is acceptable. If it is not, it is then for the beneficiary to object to the amendment of his own accord if he so wishes. This, of course, assumes that he is aware of his right to object to unacceptable amendments. It is probable that some beneficiaries do not appreciate that they have any right to refuse an amendment. Even those who do may be fearful that when they present documents which comply with the unamended credit they will be rejected.[1] Where a seller is faced with an amendment to a credit that is unacceptable, he should inform the bank of this and state that he intends to comply with the credit as originally advised, in accordance with Article 10. The bank cannot insist on an amendment, but if it does, the seller is likely to be able to treat that as a repudiation of the credit, entitling him to claim contractual damages from the bank. Alternatively he may prefer to remonstrate with his buyer, insisting that the buyer withdraw the instructions for the amendment. If that is refused, the seller's position will be the clearer against both. Alternatively again, the seller can present documents to the bank that comply with the unamended credit: if the bank refuses these, it will be liable to the seller.[2]

1 As an example of an amendment which beneficiaries felt bound to accept even though it was strongly against their interest to do so, see *Astro Exito Navegacion SA v Southland Enterprise Co Ltd (No 2) (Chase Manhattan Bank NA intervening)* [1983] 2 AC 787.
2 See paras **5.87** et seq below for a discussion of the seller's remedies in these circumstances.

Where the beneficiary is silent following receipt of an amendment

3.40   This position is covered by Article 10.c, which, it is suggested, does not alter the previous position as established by legal principle. If an amendment is advised and the beneficiary does nothing to indicate his acceptance or rejection of it, either by words or conduct, his silence is not to be taken as acceptance. The legal justification is that the advice of the amendment from the bank is to be construed as an offer from the bank to him: unless something can be found which is to be taken as indicating his acceptance of that offer, it remains simply an offer and acquires no contractual force. Article 10.f prohibits the parties circumventing this rule by including in the proposed amendment a term that it shall be deemed to enter into force unless rejected by the beneficiary within a certain period of time: any such provision 'shall be disregarded'. Where the beneficiary remains silent following receipt of an amendment, it will in ordinary circumstances be open to him to present documents complying with the credit as amended, and this will be deemed to be acceptance of the bank's offer of amendment, which takes effect as of the moment of presentation: Article 10.c.

Amendment and the confirming bank

3.41   The first sentence of Article 10.b shows that an issuing bank cannot withdraw an amendment which it has issued even though the credit itself has not yet become amended as a result of the beneficiary's acceptance of the amendment. It is clear from the remainder of Article 10.b that if a confirming bank simply advises of an amendment (which is what happens in the great majority of cases) it will be bound by it. It will not be bound only if it states that it is advising the amendment without extending its confirmation. If it does so, a novel situation arises. Until the amendment is accepted by the beneficiary, the credit remains unamended and the bank remains a confirming bank in respect of it. But once it is accepted, the credit is amended, and the confirming bank ceases to be bound by its confirmation and becomes only an advising bank. In this situation, therefore, the beneficiary has to choose not only whether it wishes the amendment, but also whether it wishes to continue having the benefit of a confirmed documentary credit.

Several amendments in one advice

3.42   It frequently happens that the beneficiary is advised of several amendments in a single advice. Is it open to him to accept those he finds acceptable and to refuse the others? Article 10.e makes it clear that he cannot and that a purported partial acceptance shall be deemed a rejection of all the proposed amendments. The contractual analysis is that the bank's offer to amend is a single offer only capable of acceptance as a whole. The beneficiary's request to accept some but not all of the amendments offered constitutes a counter-offer by him, which the banks in their turn may accept or refuse, but which in any event kills off the original offer and prevents it from being subsequently accepted.

Amendment and transfer

3.43   The problems created by an amendment of a credit which has been transferred are considered in **Chapter 10.**[1]

1 See para **10.28** et seq.

F   THE OPERATION OF THE CREDIT

3.44   Where a credit is opened by the buyer which conforms to the contract of sale or which is accepted by the seller (and the contract of sale is varied to conform with the credit, or the discrepancies are waived), it is the seller's duty to the buyer to ship the goods and present documents to the bank which comply with the terms of the credit. He will then receive payment in accordance with the terms of the credit. If he does not present documents to the bank or if he presents documents which do not accord with the terms of the credit and which are rejected by the bank, he is liable in damages to the buyer for failing to perform his side of the contract.[1] It is necessary to add the qualification 'and which are rejected by the bank' because a high proportion of documents presented under credits are not complying presentations, yet in the great majority of these cases the buyer on being informed of the discrepancies will instruct the bank nonetheless to accept the documents. In such a situation the buyer retains his right to claim damages against the seller for such breaches of the contract of sale as may have occurred by reason of the documents not complying with the contract, but he will receive the goods and the seller will receive the price.

1 See, among other cases, *Soproma SpA v Marine and Animal By-Products Corpn* [1966] 1 Lloyd's Rep 367.

Where the cooperation of the buyer is required

3.45   The operation of the credit may require the co-operation of the buyer. One circumstance in which this arises is if the credit provides that shipment is to be on a vessel nominated by the buyer (as in a 'classic' f.o.b. sale) or contains some similar term.[1] If no vessel is nominated, the seller can neither ship the goods nor claim payment under the credit: but the buyer will be in breach of his contract with the seller by reason of the failure to nominate an effective ship. The credit may provide for the bank to be informed of the nomination by the buyer. This having occurred, if the shipping documents show shipment on the vessel and otherwise comply with the terms of the credit, the bank will be in a position to pay. It may otherwise be necessary for the seller to provide documentary evidence to the bank that the vessel named in the shipping documents has been nominated by the buyer.[2] Another way in which the cooperation of the buyer may be required is in the completion of the documentation to be presented under the credit. Thus the buyer or his representative may be required to sign a certificate of inspection of the goods. If he fails to do so by the time required, he will be in breach of contract with the seller and will have rendered the credit inoperable. In an appropriate case, a mandatory order may be obtained from the court that he complete the document, and in the event of his failure to comply a court official may be empowered to do so in his place.[3]

1 Where the credit is opened in terms that require a further advice, or an amendment, nominating the vessel in order for it to become operative, there is an argument that the bank is in breach of its undertaking if no such advice or amendment is forthcoming, because it has opened an inoperable credit and failed to secure its proper operation. But it is suggested that this argument should be rejected. The credit as opened is only operable if the advice or amendment is forthcoming, and so the bank's undertaking to pay is conditional upon that. The bank gives no express undertaking that the condition will be satisfied. It is also clear that such an undertaking is not to be implied, because it is not within the bank's power to procure its satisfaction; nor will the applicant be liable to the bank for failing to nominate a vessel and satisfy the condition. Yet the applicant will be liable to the beneficiary on the underlying contract of sale, and it is here (and only here) that the remedy lies.

2 Compare the requirement of the credit in *Banque de l'Indochine et de Suez SA v J.H. Rayner (Mincing Lane) Ltd* [1983] QB 711 that 'Shipment to be effected on vessel belonging to Shipping Company that member of an International Shipping Conference'. It was held by Parker J (at 719B) that reasonable documentary proof of this requirement was necessary, a conclusion confirmed by the Court of Appeal: [1983] QB 728 at 729.

3 Pursuant to s 39 of the Supreme Court Act 1981; see *Astro Exito Navegacion SA v Southland Enterprise Co (No 2) (Chase Manhattan Bank NA intervening)* [1983] 2 AC 787 considered in para **9.85** below.

G   THE FAILURE OF THE CREDIT TO PROVIDE PAYMENT

3.46   It may happen that the seller is unable to obtain payment through the credit opened by the buyer even though he presents, or is in a position to present, documents that comply with the terms and conditions of the credit. This may, for example, come about because the bank is insolvent, or because the bank wrongfully refuses to accept the documents. There are a variety of possible situations, not all of which have been considered in the cases. Caution is therefore necessary in stating general legal principles.

Credits as absolute or conditional payment

3.47   It has on occasion been suggested that the provision by the buyer of a letter of credit constitutes absolute payment. This means that once the credit has been provided the buyer has discharged his own obligation to pay, the seller's only right to payment being through the letter of credit, whatever may in practice happen. The alternative analysis is that the credit is provided only as conditional or provisional payment. If a conditional payment, then if the conditions are not (or cease to be) satisfied, the seller has a right to claim payment from the buyer directly. The condition which is most easy to infer is that the relevant bank must be solvent and able to honour the full amount of the credit. A second possible condition is that the bank should accept conforming documents and should honour the credit. It will be appreciated that where a credit provides for immediate payment and the bank fails to honour, the seller's position is very different to situations where the payment undertaking is deferred. In the former situation the seller will be able to retain the documents and also control over the goods. By contrast, where the credit provides for payment at a future date, then (whether or not a bill of exchange is involved) the seller will have parted with his documents on the strength of the bank's promise and the goods are likely to have reached their destination and may have passed into the buyer's possession (although not necessarily ownership). The fact that the buyer has received the goods is likely to be important. The main English authorities and one Australian authority on this area are considered below in chronological order.

3.48 In *Newman Industries Ltd v Indo-British Industries Ltd*,[1] after the credit had been opened the buyers instructed the bank not to pay unless a form of guarantee was provided. Such a guarantee was possibly not required by the letter of credit, and was certainly not required by the contract of sale. The bank rejected the documents. The sellers were not named as the shippers on the bill of lading, nor was it made out to their order. Moreover, they had lost possession of the goods, which had been shipped to Bombay and attracted charges almost equal to their price. Sellers J held that an action for the price lay against the buyers. He said: 'I do not think that there is any evidence to establish, or any inference to be drawn, that the draft under the letter of credit was to be taken in absolute payment. I see no reason why the plaintiffs, in the circumstances which have so unfortunately and unnecessarily arisen, should not look to the defendants, as buyers, for payment.'[2] The letter of credit had been taken in place of a bank guarantee at the request of the buyers and was a confirmed irrevocable credit. It was not decided whether the credit did in fact require presentation of the guarantee the buyers desired, and therefore no finding was made as to whether the bank was right to refuse the documents. The goods conformed to the contract and property had passed to the buyers, although they had not taken up their right to possession. It would seem essential to an analysis of the situation to determine whether the bank had rightly rejected the documents. The point which emerges most clearly from the judgment is that the court considered it right that the sellers should be entitled to recover from the buyers in the circumstances that had arisen.

1 [1956] 2 Lloyd's Rep 219. The decision was reversed by the Court of Appeal on the basis that there was no concluded agreement for the sale of the goods: [1957] 1 Lloyd's Rep 211.
2 [1956] 2 Lloyd's Rep 219 at 236.

3.49 The next decision chronologically was that of the High Court of Australia in *Saffron v Société Minière Cafrika*.[1] The contract here provided for 'payment: by opening a letter of credit with the Banque de l'Indochine ...'. The bank lawfully refused to pay because the tonnage of chromium shipped was below the minimum quantity permissible and because the bill of lading was not indorsed in blank as required. The goods were received by a sub-buyer, but the buyer himself received no payment. The court stated 'It is not reasonable to suppose that the parties here intended that in the unlikely circumstances that the buyer got the chrome but payment therefor against the letter of credit was refused, the seller should not be paid. The trial judge reached the conclusion that the letter of credit was not intended to be the exclusive source of payment, with the assistance by way of analogy of the rules relating to the acceptance of negotiable instruments. This analogy is no doubt useful ...'[2] The trial judge's decision was upheld. The High Court did not need to consider what the position would have been had it been the seller's sole fault that the letter of credit failed as the primary source of payment, since the buyer had been responsible for the format of the bill of lading and had accepted delivery of the tonnage loaded.

1 (1958) 100 CLR 231, applied in *North Western Shipping & Towage Co Pty Ltd v Commonwealth Bank of Australia* (1993) 118 ALR 453.
2 *Saffron v Société Minière Cafrika* (1958) 100 CLR 231 at 244.

3.50 In *Soproma SpA v Marine and Animal By-Products Corpn*,[1] the sellers sued the buyers for damages. The documents had been rejected by the bank as being non-compliant, and the goods (Chilean fishmeal) had been sold for the seller's account on arrival. The documents had also been presented to the buyers direct. McNair J stated:

> 'Under this form of contract, as it seems to me, the buyer performs his obligation as to payment if he provides for the sellers a reliable and solvent paymaster from whom he can obtain payment – if necessary by suit – although it may well be that if the banker fails to pay by reason of his insolvency the buyer would be liable; but in such a case, as at present advised, I think that the basis of the liability must in principle be his failure to provide a proper letter of credit which involves *inter alia* that the obligee under the letter of credit is financially solvent. (This point as to the buyers' liability for the insolvency of the bank was not fully argued before me and I prefer to express no concluded opinion upon it as I understand that it may arise for decision in other cases pending in this Court.) It seems to me to be quite inconsistent with the express terms of a contract such as this to hold that the sellers have an alternative right to obtain payment from the buyers by presenting the documents direct to the buyers. Assuming that a letter of credit has been opened by the buyer for the opening of which the buyer would normally be required to provide the bank either with cash or some form of authority, could the seller at his option disregard the contractual letter of credit and present documents direct to the buyer? As it seems to me, the answer must plainly be in the negative.'

McNair J went on to hold that the credit as opened was not in accordance with the contract of sale but that the discrepancies had been waived by the sellers. He held that the documents presented did not accord with the terms of the credit, and so the sellers were liable in damages. In the light of those findings he did not need to consider the nature of the payment obligation more generally.

1 [1966] 1 Lloyd's Rep 367.

3.51   The decision of the Court of Appeal in *WJ Alan & Co Ltd v El Nasr Export and Import Co*[1] is the leading authority in this area, even though the court's observations as to the nature of the credit as conditional payment were not necessary to the decision and are strictly *obiter*. The underlying contract was for the sale of coffee by Kenyan sellers to Egyptian buyers. The contract provided for payment in Kenyan shillings. A credit was opened which provided for payment in sterling, and the sellers were paid accordingly. But meanwhile sterling had been devalued, and they sued the buyers for the difference between the contract price in Kenyan shillings and the sterling they had received through the credit. It was held that by accepting the sterling credit the sellers had either agreed to a variation of the contractual term for payment in Kenyan currency or had waived it. Thus the question of the nature of the payment provided by the credit did not in fact arise for consideration. But counsel had made submissions on the question of absolute or conditional payment, which led at least Lord Denning MR to make some general statements on this issue. The contract provided for payment by confirmed irrevocable letter of credit and Lord Denning stated: 'In my opinion a letter of credit is not to be regarded as absolute payment unless the seller stipulates, expressly or impliedly, that it should be so. He may do it impliedly if he stipulates for the credit to be issued by a particular banker in such circumstances that it is to be inferred that the seller looks to that particular banker to the exclusion of the buyer.'[2] He concluded that in the ordinary way a contract providing for a confirmed irrevocable credit operates only as a conditional method of payment, and not as an absolute payment.[3] Megaw LJ asked: 'Does the mere establishment of the credit, completed by confirmation, discharge the buyer's liability completely? Or does it discharge it provisionally, and, if so, subject to precisely what provision?' He found that on the simple form of provision for payment in this case, the sellers had no right to require payment other than in accordance with the credit so long as no default was made by the bank in the performance of its obligations.[4] Stephenson LJ stated that if the confirming bank had defaulted the sellers might have been able to sue the buyers, 'For the buyers promise to pay by a letter of credit, not to provide by a letter of credit a source which did not pay.' He agreed that the credit operated only as a conditional payment.[5]

1 [1972] 2 QB 189.
2 [1972] 2 QB 189 at 210.
3 [1972] 2 QB 189 at 212.
4 [1972] 2 QB 189 at 218, 219.
5 [1972] 2 QB 189 at 220, 221.

3.52   *Maran Road Saw Mill v Austin Taylor & Co Ltd*[1] is one of the two reported cases arising from the collapse of Sale & Co, a London merchant bank. The defendants who acted as sellers' agents in London opened a letter of credit through Sale & Co in favour of the plaintiff sellers providing for payment by 90-day drafts. The defendants received payment from the buyers against documents and put Sale & Co in funds. But the bill accepted by Sale & Co under the credit was dishonoured. Ackner J accepted from *WJ Alan & Co v El Nasr*[2] that 'in the ordinary way a letter of credit operates as a conditional payment of the price and not as absolute'[3] and applied the same principle to a letter of credit providing for payment by an agent to his principal. He held the defendants liable, with the result that they had to pay twice.[4]

1 [1975] 1 Lloyd's Rep 156.
2 See para **3.51** above.
3 [1975] 1 Lloyd's Rep 156 at 159.
4 For discussion of another aspect of this case, see para **6.38** below.

3.53   Ackner J had also to decide the next case chronologically, *ED and F Man Ltd v Nigerian Sweets and Confectionery Co Ltd*.[1] Here an irrevocable credit was opened in London by the Nigerian buyers at a bank which was substantially in common ownership with them. Payment was by 90-day drafts. The buyers received the goods, and it appears that they paid the bank. But the bank became insolvent. In holding the buyers liable, Ackner J stated: 'The fact that the sellers have agreed on the identity of the issuing bank is but one of the factors to be taken into account when considering whether there are circumstances from which it can properly be inferred that the sellers look to that particular bank to the exclusion of the buyer. It is in no way conclusive. In this case unlike the United States case of *Ornstein v Hickerson* 40 F Supp 305 (1941) ... there were other circumstances which clearly supported the presumption that the letters of credit were not given as absolute payment but as conditional payment.'[2] The sellers therefore succeeded against the buyers in an action for the price.

1 [1977] 2 Lloyd's Rep 50.
2 [1977] 2 Lloyd's Rep 50 at 56.

3.54   In *Shamsher Jute Mills Ltd v Sethia (London) Ltd*,[1] f.o.b. sellers shipped goods and presented documents, which were rightly rejected by the bank on the basis that they did not comply with the credit. The sellers then sued the buyers directly for the contract price or alternatively damages. It was unclear what had happened to the goods: they had been shipped to Antwerp where they were sold, perhaps in satisfaction of charges, but neither buyer nor seller had benefited. It was argued that if a letter of credit was a conditional payment and if goods conforming to the original contract (which these did) were shipped, the seller could sue the buyer. Bingham J held that by accepting the credit terms the sellers were to be taken as having varied the sale contract or to have waived any right to rely on the earlier contract terms. He held that, as the sellers had failed to comply with the credit terms, they were in breach of the underlying contract of sale and could not recover against the buyers. This case may be contrasted with *Newman Industries Ltd v Indo-British Industries Ltd*.[2] If the two cases are not to be distinguished on their facts, it is suggested that the reasoning of Bingham J in *Shamsher Jute* should be preferred.

1 [1987] 1 Lloyd's Rep 388.
2 [1956] 2 Lloyd's Rep 219: see para **3.48** above.

3.55   The authorities considered above support the following propositions:

(1) The question whether the opening of a letter of credit is an absolute or conditional discharge of the buyer's payment obligation is strictly a question of construction of the contract between the buyer and the seller. The contract will, however, normally be silent and it will be a matter of determining the objective intention of the parties against the relevant factual matrix.[1]

1 *WJ Alan & Co v El Nasr Export and Import* [1972] 2 QB 189; *Newman Industries Ltd v Indo-British Industries Ltd* [1956] 2 Lloyd's Rep 219; *Saffron v Société Minière Cafrika* (1958) 100 CLR 231; *Re Charge Card Services Ltd* [1987] Ch 150 at 165-169 (Millett J) and [1989] Ch 497 at 511, 512 (Court of Appeal).

3.56

(2) In the absence of a clear indication that the seller intended to look to a particular bank to the exclusion of the buyer, the credit will be presumed to be conditional payment only. Such an indication might possibly be found in the express terms of the contract, or more likely in the manner in which the bank or banks and the machinery of payment were chosen.[1]

1 See the cases cited for the first proposition, and also *Soproma SpA v Marine and Animal By-Products Corpn* [1966] 1 Lloyd's Rep 367; *Maran Road Saw Mill v Austin Taylor & Co Ltd* [1975] 1 Lloyd's Rep 156; *ED and F Man Ltd v Nigerian Sweets and Confectionery Co Ltd* [1977] 2 Lloyd's Rep 50; *Chloride Batteries SE Asia Pte Ltd v BPS International plc* (21 March 1996, unreported, Commercial Court).

3.57

(3) Where a credit is absolute payment and is correctly established or is accepted by the seller, the seller will normally have no rights against the buyer if the seller presents conforming documents but nonetheless remains unpaid. His only remedy lies against the bank or banks. There may be two exceptions to this. First, if the buyer induces the banks not to pay, the buyer may be liable for the tort of inducing a breach of contract, depending upon his precise appreciation that a breach was involved. Secondly, if the buyer has received the goods that may give rise to remedies against him, a question considered below.[1] No reported case has touched on the problem of what should happen if the bank fails before the documents can be presented. For then the contractual means of transferring the documents to the buyer have been lost. In such

circumstances the contract might arguably have become frustrated and discharged automatically by operation of law.

1 See para **3.63**.

3.58

(4) If the credit is a conditional payment and the time for payment is deferred but the relevant bank becomes insolvent after documents have been presented, the buyer must pay the seller whether or not he has already paid the bank.[1] Where there is only one bank undertaking to honour the credit, the issuing bank, as in the cases cited, the position is straightforward. But what if the credit is a confirmed credit? If the confirming bank becomes insolvent, the seller can sue[2] the issuing bank to recover payment. It is arguable that the seller is obliged to do so before he can pursue the buyer, on the basis that the buyer's conditional obligation to pay is the last resort for the seller, only to be utilised if the banking machinery fails. The insolvency of the issuing bank will not affect the seller if the credit is confirmed because the confirming bank is obliged to pay him even though its right of recoupment from the issuing bank may be worthless.

1 *Maran Road Saw Mill v Austin Taylor & Co Ltd* [1975] 1 Lloyd's Rep 156; *E D and F Man Ltd v Nigerian Sweets and Confectionery Co Ltd* [1977] 2 Lloyd's Rep 50; *Chloride Batteries SE Asia Pte Ltd v BPS International plc* (21 March 1996, unreported, Commercial Court).
2 *Cf* presentation of documents to the issuing bank, as to which see para **3.61** below. As to the possibility of fresh drafts being drawn where the drawee bank has refused acceptance, see para **5.20** below.

3.59

(5) Where the credit is a conditional payment and the seller has not received payment because the bank has wrongly rejected the documents, can the seller choose to sue the buyer as an alternative to suing the bank, on the basis that a condition of the credit (namely payment by the bank) has failed? No definite answer can be given. A passage in the judgment of McNair J in *Soproma*[1] suggests not. On the other hand, in *Alan v El Nasr*[2] Megaw LJ stated[3] that the seller had no right to claim payment from the buyer 'so long, at any rate, as no default is made by the bank in its performance of the letter of credit obligations'. Stephenson LJ stated that if the confirming bank had defaulted the sellers might have looked to the buyers: 'For the buyers promised to pay by letter of credit, not to provide by a letter of credit a source of payment which did not pay.' If the documents have been rejected, the property in the goods and the control of them is likely to have remained with the seller. In those circumstances it can be argued that it suffices for the seller to have a remedy against a bank, particularly since this is likely to be a confirming bank in his own country. Where the buyer has induced the bank to refuse the documents wrongfully by, for example, by taking some specious point which is to the buyer's advantage, the buyer may be liable in damages for tortiously

inducing a breach of contract. If the buyer has obtained the goods, other considerations may apply, and these are discussed below.[4]

1 [1966] 1 Lloyd's Rep 367 at 386; see para **3.50** above.
2 [1972] 2 QB 189 at 219; see para **3.51** above.
3 [1972] 2 QB 189 at 220.
4 See para **3.63** below.

3.60

(6) Whether the credit is conditional or absolute payment, if the seller presents documents to the bank that do not comply with the credit and are rejected, the seller cannot sue the buyer directly unless the buyer has actually obtained the goods. This is so whether or not the goods conform to the contract. This is the clear outcome of both *Soproma*[1] and *Shamsher Jute.*[2]

1 [1966] 1 Lloyd's Rep 367: see para **3.50** above.
2 [1987] 1 Lloyd's Rep 388: see para **3.54** above.

3.61

(7) A separate point arises where the rejection of the documents is by a confirming bank. Is the buyer bound to re-present them to the issuing bank before pursuing such remedy, if any, that he may have against the buyer? It is suggested that he is not. As between the two banks, the confirming bank acts as the agent of the issuing bank. Further the credit is likely expressly to nominate the confirming bank as the bank with which the credit is available.[1]

1 See para **6.17** below.

3.62

(8) Where the seller does have a claim against the buyer, it may be an action for the price under s 49 of the Sale of Goods Act 1979. Alternatively, it might in substance be for the price but be framed formally as a damages claim for breach of the obligation that the bank should pay. If so, there is no objection in principle to adding a damages claim in respect of the expenses incurred in trying to get the bank to pay. In some circumstances a claim for the price (whether in debt or by way of damages) may be inappropriate, and the claim should instead be framed as one for damages calculated in terms of the seller's loss on the transaction. Reference should be made to the discussion of the seller's remedies against the bank in **Chapter 5** below.[1]

1 See para **5.87**.

Where the buyer has received the goods

3.63 The buyer may receive the goods and yet the seller remain unpaid in two contrasting situations. One is where the credit provides for deferred payment, and the documents are duly processed and taken up by the buyer in order to obtain the goods. The other is where the documents are not accepted, perhaps because the bank rightly rejects them, but the buyer nonetheless obtains the goods. He may, for example, take delivery from the vessel without bills of lading by giving an indemnity to the shipowner. An equivalent result may obtain by reason of a fraudulent scheme devised by the buyer. He may, for example, have ensured that the letter of credit demands a document that the seller is unlikely to be able to provide, or he may have failed to extend the period of the credit to cover a late shipment to which the parties have agreed.

3.64   In the former situation, if the reason why the seller has not been paid is the bank's insolvency and the credit is a conditional payment, then the buyer will be obliged to pay the seller himself, whether or not he had already put the bank in funds.[1] It is suggested that in the rare case of a credit constituting an absolute payment obligation, if the insolvency of the bank terminates the buyer's obligation to put it in funds,[2] the buyer should nonetheless be obliged to pay the seller even though the credit is an absolute payment: otherwise the buyer would receive the goods for nothing. There appears, however, to be no legal authority supporting this proposition and the contrary is certainly arguable.

1 See para **3.58** above.
2 As to which, see *Sale Continuation Ltd v Austin Taylor & Co Ltd* [1968] 2 QB 849, discussed in para **11.14** below.

3.65   Where the documents have not been accepted and yet the buyer has received the goods, one may be confident that the buyer will be held liable for the price. However, the legal basis for reaching this solution may be difficult to predict without knowledge of the precise circumstances. It might be held that by instructing the bank not to pay against the documents because of the discrepancies (the bank will usually request the buyer's instructions), the buyer has waived any right to treat the credit as payment. Where, as is likely, the seller has retained the right to possession of the goods, he has an alternative to his action for the price, which is to sue in the tort of conversion for the value of the goods. The buyer will have converted the goods by taking them if he had no title to them and no right to possession. This remedy is of particular use where the market has risen so that damages may exceed the contract price. In such a situation, if the buyer has himself sold the goods – perhaps for a higher price – the seller may alternatively pursue a restitutionary action to recover the amount received by the buyer as the proceeds of his tort.[1] If the goods have been delivered to the buyer without the buyer having duly presented bills of lading, the seller, if he retains the bills, will have a cause of action against the carrier for misdelivery, in English law for conversion. For an example of such a claim being made against a carrier and admitted by him in exchange for an assignment of the seller's rights under the credit, see *Mannesman Handel AG v Kaunlaran Shipping Corpn.*[2]

1 See Goff & Jones, *The Law of Restitution* (7th edn) ch 36; Virgo, *The Principles of the Law of Restitution* (2nd edn) ch 16.

2 [1993] 1 Lloyd's Rep 89 at 91. See also *The Stone Gemini* [1999] 2 Lloyd's Rep 255, Australia Federal Court.

H   THE BUYER'S CLAIMS AGAINST THE SELLER

3.66   It is beyond the ambit of this book to deal with the rights and obligations of the buyer and seller arising from the contract of sale, save insofar as they relate to the operation of the letter of credit. It may, however, be mentioned that where an international sale contract provides for the seller to deliver both goods and documents (which is classically, but not exclusively, the position in relation to c.i.f. sales), there are separate and successive rights and obligations in relation to each. Both must conform to the contract, so that even if one conforms the seller will be liable if the other does not.[1]

1 See generally *Benjamin's Sale of Goods* (7th edn) paras 19-144 et seq.

I   RESTRAINING THE SELLER FROM OPERATING THE CREDIT

3.67   The buyer may come to believe that the seller has shipped goods which do not accord with the terms of the contract of sale, or even that the seller intends a fraud and has shipped either nothing at all or goods that differ fundamentally from those contracted for. In such circumstances, he may consider the possibility of preventing the seller from presenting documents to the bank in order to obtain payment under the credit, by obtaining a prohibitory injunction or similar court order. This will only be possible if the documents have not yet entered the banking chain. Problems will arise where (as is likely) the seller is in a foreign country. Alternatively the buyer may consider the possibility of obtaining a prohibitory order against the bank directly, in order to prevent it from honouring the credit. The essential rule that governs here has been described under the heading of 'The Autonomy of Documentary Credits' at para **1.34** above, namely that the performance of the underlying contract of sale between applicant and beneficiary is entirely distinct from the operation of the credit and the obligations thereby created. As Articles 4.a and 5 of the Uniform Customs emphasise, the credit is a documentary transaction and allegations concerning the goods or services to which the credit relates are not to be used as a ground for interfering with the operation of the credit. The exceptions to this, arising where there is fraud on the part of the beneficiary or illegality, are considered in detail in **Chapter 9** and **Chapter 13** below.

Chapter 4

The Applicant and the Issuing Bank

A   THE CONTRACT

4.1 When a bank accepts instructions from the applicant to open a documentary credit, a contract comes into being between the applicant and the bank. It is this contract which defines their relations. It is the second of the 'four autonomous though interconnected contractual relationships' referred to by Lord Diplock in *United City Merchants (Investments) Ltd v Royal Bank of Canada,*[1] which he described as follows:

> 'the contract between the buyer and the issuing bank under which the latter agrees to issue the credit and either itself or through a confirming bank to notify the credit to the seller and to make payments to or to the order of the seller (or to pay, accept or negotiate bills of exchange drawn by the seller) against presentation of stipulated documents; and the buyer agrees to reimburse the issuing bank for payments made under the credit. For such reimbursement the stipulated documents, if they include a document of title such as a bill of lading, constitute a security available to the issuing bank.'

1 [1983] 1 AC 168 at 182, 183.

B   THE APPLICATION TO OPEN THE CREDIT

The application

4.2   In accordance with his duty to open a credit arising from his contract with the seller, the buyer will apply to a bank to issue a credit in the appropriate form. It may be that the buyer will have an arrangement with his bank entitling him to open credits through the bank up to a given value at any one time. The documentation relating to such an arrangement is likely to include a right of indemnity in favour of the bank and an authority to debit the applicant's account. If the applicant's business is such that he frequently needs to open credits, such an arrangement is advisable because it may make a formal application on one of the bank's standard application forms unnecessary (an authenticated electronic instruction being more common). Otherwise the applicant will generally be required to complete the bank's application form. If the applicant has not already done so as part of his arrangements with the bank, he is likely also to be required to complete a form of indemnity in favour of the bank and an authority to debit his account.

4.3   If, as is often the case, the underlying contract of sale has been no more specific in its payment provision than, for example, 'Payment by confirmed irrevocable letter of credit', it is at this stage that the buyer must first specify precisely the type of credit that he requires and list the documents against which it is to be honoured. It is essential that the application should set out in clear terms what is wanted. UCP 500 contained an express provision to this effect in Article 5, together with guidance about the form of instructions; the absence of an equivalent provision in UCP 600 does not diminish the importance of the principle. Guidance is given in ISBP Articles 1 and 2:

'The application and issuance of the credit

1) The terms of a credit are independent of the underlying transaction even if a credit expressly refers to that transaction. To avoid unnecessary costs, delays, and disputes in the examination of documents, however, the applicant and beneficiary should carefully consider which documents should be required, by whom they should be produced and the time frame for presentation.

2) The applicant bears the risk of any ambiguity in its instructions to issue or amend a credit. Unless expressly stated otherwise, a request to issue or amend a credit authorizes an issuing bank to supplement or develop the terms in a manner necessary or desirable to permit the use of the credit.'

4.4 The main matters for the applicant to consider in connection with his instructions to the issuing bank are:

(1) whether the UCP should be incorporated (in practice the bank is unlikely to be prepared to issue the credit on any other basis);

(2) whether the credit is to be revocable or irrevocable, confirmed or unconfirmed;

(3) whether the credit is to be transferable;

(4) with which bank or banks the credit will be available, or whether the credit is to be available with any bank (UCP Article 6.a);

(5) whether the credit is to be available by sight payment, deferred payment, acceptance or negotiation (UCP Article 6.b). This involves a decision as to whether the documents to be presented should include a bill of exchange and consideration of the function, if any, that this bill will fulfil;

(6) the sum to be available under the credit, including the required currency and (as appropriate) relevant unit prices;

(7) the identity of the advising (and perhaps also confirming) bank; in practice it is most often left to the issuing bank to choose its own correspondent in the beneficiary's country;

(8) the description of the goods: this will be required to be stated on the commercial invoice – see UCP Article 18.c and para **8.77** below;

(9) the documents to be presented in accordance with the terms and conditions of the credit, the description of the required transport documents being of particular importance;

(10) the latest permissible date for shipment, and the expiry date for the presentation of complying documents (Article 6.d.i);

(11) whether partial and/or instalment shipments are to be allowed;

(12) whether there is any need to prohibit transhipment;[1]

(13) the means of transmission of the credit, and in particular whether by airmail, teletransmission, or electronically pursuant to the provisions of the eUCP the great majority of credits are now transmitted by SWIFT;

(14) whether it is necessary for the parties to exclude or modify any of the Articles of the UCP pursuant to the power to do so granted by Article 1.

---

1 This must be considered in conjunction with the transhipment provisions of the relevant Article among Articles 19–24. As to transhipment, see para **8.100** below.

The bank and its instructions: unclear instructions

4.5 If on checking the application a bank is not happy with the instructions which it has received, it should decline to open the credit until satisfactory instructions have been communicated. The bank should in particular check that the instructions are clear and will not give rise to any difficulties in the operation of the credit, and that there are no contradictory or conflicting terms. There is in practice often an urgency in advising the credit to the seller, and so delay due to the clarification of instructions may give rise to difficulty.

Clarification after issue of the credit

4.6 If the bank finds itself in a situation where it has accepted instructions which are later found to be unclear, it should take further instructions to clarify them, if it is still open to it to do so. But if the credit has been notified to the beneficiary, a contract between the bank and the beneficiary will have come into being, which cannot be modified without the beneficiary's consent. The ambiguity may only have been observed following the presentation of documents by the beneficiary. Suppose the credit as opened can be read as requiring possibly a document of type A among those to be presented, or possibly type B, but it is not immediately clear which. If the 'correct' construction of the credit as notified is that document A is required, it cannot be open to the bank to take instructions from the buyer to clarify the position that it is in fact B that the buyer wants and to refuse to accept documents which include A. In practice, where documents have not been presented, an ambiguity which is observed in good time can often be covered by making an amendment acceptable to the beneficiary (pursuant to the provisions of UCP Article 10).

4.7 A distinction must be drawn between the position of a bank which has issued or confirmed the credit and a bank which has been approached by the beneficiary to negotiate documents. The former is obliged to take up documents from the beneficiary which comply with the credit. This must be determined objectively from the wording of the credit and the applicant's opinion (even if expressed as a 'clarification') is legally irrelevant. The proposed negotiating bank is not, before taking up the documents, party to the credit and has made no commitment to the beneficiary. If it chooses to take up the documents, then it stands in the shoes of the beneficiary when it claims reimbursement. In those circumstances, it is permissible and sensible for the negotiating bank to seek clarification from the issuing bank as to the meaning of a doubtful term in the credit. In *European Asian Bank v Punjab and Sind Bank (No 2)*,[1] where there was a doubt about whether the credit was freely negotiable, the court stated, 'Given this state of affairs, and the obvious nature of this conflict, the proper course of any bank, considering whether to act as negotiating bank, would be to inquire of the issuing bank whether it was intended that negotiation should be regarded as unrestricted.' If clarification is given, then the negotiating bank's right to reimbursement is protected. If, however, no clarification is sought or obtained, then the negotiating bank is entitled to reimbursement if it has acted on its reasonable opinion of the meaning of the credit.

1 [1983] 1 WLR 642 at 656; see para **2.27** above. See also *Patel v Standard Chartered Bank* [2001] Lloyd's Rep Bank 229 (Toulson J, Commercial Court; ambiguity in bank's mandate).

4.8   This issue, and the effect of the *European Asian Bank* decision, arose in *Crédit Agricole Indosuez v Muslim Commercial Bank Ltd.*[1] The credit was poorly worded and did not clearly state whether certain documents referred to in the credit were required to be presented for payment, or whether they were simply to be forwarded after negotiation. Crédit Agricole, which had confirmed the credit, paid without receiving those documents and sought reimbursement from Muslim Commercial Bank, the issuing bank. The Court of Appeal held that there was a genuine doubt about the meaning of the credit and that, having acted on a reasonable construction of it, Crédit Agricole was entitled to be reimbursed. The court rejected the submission made on behalf of Muslim Commercial Bank that, in the light of *European Asian Bank*, Crédit Agricole should have sought clarification before paying. It held that any such 'clarification' could not affect Crédit Agricole's liability to the seller:

> 'If on the true construction of the letter of credit they were obliged to pay the Sellers despite the absence of the two disputed documents, it would be no comfort to have their obligations "clarified" by the Muslim Commercial Bank saying it meant something different. They had bound themselves to the Sellers in the terms of the letter of credit.'

It was therefore unnecessary for Crédit Agricole to seek clarification from the issuing bank as to the meaning of the credit; even if clarification had been forthcoming in time to meet the short deadline provided by the UCP, it would be of no assistance to Crédit Agricole to have Muslim Commercial Bank's opinion on the validity of the presentation, when its liability to the seller depended on the correct and objective construction of the credit, and not on the subjective beliefs of the issuing bank.

1 [2000] 1 Lloyd's Rep 275.

The bank acting on ambiguous instructions

4.9   The principle in *Ireland v Livingston*[1] is that where an agent has received ambiguous instructions he may adopt a reasonable interpretation of them, and it is not then open to his principal to say that he intended something else. *Midland Bank Ltd v Seymour*[2] applied this principle to the position of an issuing bank and referred to the issuing bank as the buyer's agent. As was pointed out in the *European Asian Bank*[3] and *Crédit Agricole Indosuez v Muslim Commercial Bank Ltd*[4] cases, however, this analysis is not strictly correct. In *Commercial Banking Co of Sydney Ltd v Jalsard Pty Ltd*[5] the Privy Council stated:[6]

> 'It is a well-established principle in relation to commercial credits that if the instructions given by the customer to the issuing banker as to the documents to be tendered by the beneficiary are ambiguous or are capable of covering more than one kind of document, the banker is not in default if he acts upon a reasonable meaning of the ambiguous expression or accepts any kind of document which fairly falls within the wide description used: see *Midland Bank Ltd v Seymour* [1955] 2 Lloyd's Rep 147.
>
> There is good reason for this. By issuing the credit, the banker does not only enter into a contractual obligation to his own customer, the buyer, to honour the seller's drafts if they are accompanied by the specified documents. By confirming the credit to the seller through his correspondent at the place of shipment he assumes a contractual obligation to the seller that his drafts on the correspondent bank will be accepted if accompanied by the specified documents, and a contractual obligation to his correspondent bank to reimburse it for accepting the seller's drafts. The banker is not concerned as to whether the documents for which the buyer has stipulated serve any useful commercial purpose or as to why the customer called for tender of a document of a particular description. Both the issuing banker and his correspondent bank have to make quick decisions as to whether a document which has been tendered by the seller complies with the requirements of a credit at the risk of incurring liability to one or other of the parties to the transaction if the decision is wrong. Delay in deciding may in itself result in a breach of his contractual obligations to the buyer or to the seller. This is the reason for the rule that where a banker's instructions from his customer are ambiguous or unclear he commits no breach of his contract with the buyer if he has construed them in a reasonable sense, even though upon the closer consideration which can be given to questions of construction in an action in a court of law, it is possible to say that some other meaning is to be preferred.'

Thus it appears that the bank will be acting correctly and is entitled to be indemnified by the buyer if it accepts documents which accord with the true construction of the credit or which give a reasonable meaning to an ambiguous expression, even if a court might ultimately arrive at a different construction. The same principle applies to a confirming bank seeking reimbursement from the issuer.[7] But, so far as the seller is concerned, if the bank refuses documents on the strength of an ambiguity which it is later found to have misconstrued, the bank will be liable to the seller for refusing documents which were in accordance with the terms of the credit as correctly construed.

1 (1872) LR 5 HL 395.
2 [1955] 2 Lloyd's Rep 147 at 153.
3 [1983] 1 WLR 642 at 656.
4 [2000] 1 Lloyd's Rep 275. Sir Christopher Staughton said at 280, 'It is of course right that there is not *in law* an agency relationship between an issuing bank and a confirming bank. I find it hard to believe that either Devlin J [in *Midland Bank v Seymour* [1955] 2 Lloyd's Rep 147] or

Lord Diplock [in *Commercial Banking Co of Sydney Ltd v Jalsard Pty Ltd* [1973] AC 279; see para **4.24** below] thought that there was. But in terms of commerce the confirming bank is the correspondent of the issuing bank, and acts for the issuing bank in order to do what the issuing bank is not present to do for itself'.

5 [1973] AC 279.
6 [1973] AC 279 at 285, 286.
7 *Crédit Agricole Indosuez v Muslim Commercial Bank Ltd* [2000] 1 Lloyd's Rep 275. See also *Credit Agricole Indosuez v Credit Suisse First Boston*, Zurich, unreported 24 January 2001, where Morison J said it was not uncontroversial that a confirming bank should not to be prejudiced by adopting a reasonable but erroneous interpretation of confused or contradictory provisions in credit. The same approach has been taken in *Singapore in Korea Exchange Bank v Standard Chartered Bank* [2006] 1 SLR 565.

C   THE ISSUING BANK'S DUTIES

4.10   There are three functions which the issuing bank performs and in relation to which it owes duties to the applicant, the buyer:

(1) Following the bank's acceptance of the applicant's instructions, its duty is to arrange that a credit complying with those instructions is duly opened. Depending on the precise instructions, this may be done by the issuing bank itself advising the beneficiary directly of the opening of the credit, or (as is more likely in practice) it will be done by instructing a correspondent bank in the beneficiary's country to advise of the opening of the credit.
(2) It has to receive and examine documents under the credit.
(3) It is obliged to honour the credit in the manner required.

The duty

4.11   The bank must follow its instructions precisely, both in the opening of the credit and in the acceptance or rejection of documents that are presented under it. In that sense, but in that sense alone, it is under an absolute duty.

(a) The nature of the duty in the opening of the credit has not been fully examined by the courts. But it is suggested that it is not absolute, because the bank does not guarantee that it will procure that a credit is opened in accordance with its instructions. Thus, for example, it does not guarantee to procure that the credit will be confirmed. It may be that, unknown to it, the proposed beneficiary is so disreputable that no bank in its own country will be prepared to confirm a credit in its favour. The issuing bank discharges its duty to the applicant if, having taken all reasonable steps to procure a confirmed credit, it informs the applicant that it has been unable to do so. It is difficult to see how something might otherwise go wrong without the fault of the issuing bank or of the advising bank acting as its agent. This suggestion is supported by the decision of the

House of Lords in *Equitable Trust Co of New York v Dawson Partners Ltd.*[1] The provisions of the UCP relevant to an issuing bank's responsibility for the acts or omissions of its correspondent bank are considered below, as are the provisions relevant to errors of transmission.[2]

(b) The nature of the duty in connection with the examination and acceptance or rejection of documents is examined in Chapter 8.[3] It is a duty to examine with reasonable care to ascertain that the documents appear on their face to be a complying presentation.

1 (1926) 27 Ll L Rep 49, and para **4.12** below.
2 Paras **4.16–4.19**.
3 Paras **8.2** et seq.

Equitable Trust Co of New York v Dawson Partners Ltd[1]

4.12   This case is best known for the passage from the speech of Viscount Sumner as to the need for the documents presented to comply strictly with the terms of the credit, an issue considered below at para **8.21**. The facts were that Dawson Partners asked the Equitable Trust Company to open a confirmed credit through their correspondents in Batavia, the Hongkong & Shanghai Bank. The instructions given by Dawson Partners required that payment should be against documents which included 'a certificate of quality to be issued by experts who are sworn brokers, signed by the Chamber of Commerce'. The underlying contract was for the sale of '3000 kilos Java vanilla beans, sound, sweet and of prime quality'. It was alleged that the seller had shipped instead a quantity of sticks, stones and any old iron. Nonetheless documents including a certificate signed by a single sworn broker and countersigned by the institution which performed the functions of the chamber of commerce were presented. They were accepted by the Hongkong & Shanghai Bank, which in turn was reimbursed by the Equitable Trust Company. The latter brought proceedings against Dawson Partners when it refused to pay. The reason why the certificate signed by one broker had been accepted was that the telegraphic codes used by the banks did not distinguish between singular and plural, so that what should have been 'experts' was transcribed mistakenly as 'expert'. The main basis of the House of Lords' decision in favour of Dawson Partners was that they had undertaken to reimburse the bank against documents which included a certificate with the signatures of at least two experts, and that the signature of one would not do: the bank's entitlement to reimbursement was dependent on strict compliance with its instructions. The bank put forward a number of arguments, all of which were rejected. Among them was a submission that, as the buyers had requested the transmission of the credit by cable, the transmission should be at their risk. One conclusive answer to that was that the problem to which the use of the code in question gave rise was both obvious surmountable in practice.[2] Today this aspect of the case would have turned on a consideration of UCP Article 35.[3] It could be argued that this Article is not intended to protect a bank from its own negligence but only from liability arising from transmission faults occurring without the bank's fault, and that in *Equitable Trust* the use of such a code without taking steps to clarify the ambiguity between singular and plural constituted negligence. It is therefore suggested that the Article would have made no difference to the outcome of the case.

1 (1926) 27 LlL Rep 49.
2 (1926) 27 LlL Rep 49 at 53 per Viscount Sumner.
3 Set out at para **4.16** below.

4.13   Most of the cases involving an allegation by the buyer that the issuing bank has failed to comply with instructions involve payment by the bank against documents which were alleged not to comply with the buyer's instructions and the terms of the credit as opened. A rather different example arose in *Midland Bank Ltd v Seymour*,[1] where the credit was to be available in Hong Kong, but the bills drawn on the bank pursuant to it had been passed from Hong Kong to London and accepted there. Devlin J held[2] that if the bank was authorised to pay or accept only in Hong Kong 'then although the place of payment may be commercially immaterial, the bank has exceeded its mandate and cannot recover'. He went on, however, to hold that acceptance in London was in fact also within the bank's mandate.

1 [1955] 2 Lloyd's Rep 147.
2 [1955] 2 Lloyd's Rep 147 at 168.

The consequences of failure

4.14   The consequences of a failure by an issuing bank to comply with its instructions may take two forms. First, it may be liable to the buyer for breach of contract in respect of damages sustained by the buyer as a result of the failure. Thus, if an issuing bank failed to request the advising bank to confirm the credit and in consequence the seller was entitled to and did cancel the contract, the bank would prima facie be liable in damages both to the buyer, its applicant, for his own loss and for what the buyer might himself have to pay the seller in damages. Such a situation is unlikely to arise because the usual course of events would be a complaint by the seller to the buyer that the credit was not confirmed in conformity with the contract between them, and this would lead to the bank's error being corrected. But secondly and more commonly, the consequence of an issuing bank failing to comply with its instructions will be that it is left with documents on its hands in respect of which it has paid the beneficiary or the correspondent bank but which the buyer is not obliged to accept and pay for. That will come about where the credit has been operated in accordance with its own terms but these do not comply with the bank's mandate from its customer, as occurred for example in the *Equitable Trust* case.[1] Alternatively, and this is the most common situation in practice, it comes about where the credit has been correctly opened but the bank is found to have accepted documents which it should have rejected since they do not comply with the terms and conditions of the credit, with the provisions of the UCP, or with international standard banking practice.[2]

1 (1976) 27 Ll L Rep 49.
2 Cf the definition of a 'complying presentation' in Article 2.

Exclusions of liability

General – the bank's own terms

4.15   The application forms provided by banks frequently contain clauses exempting them from liability, and this is unobjectionable where the purpose is to exempt a bank from liability for matters outside its control. But sometimes banks attempt to go further and excuse themselves from errors committed within their own offices. A clause which purported to entitle a bank to be reimbursed against documents which had been accepted through its own negligence and which did not comply with the terms of the credit would be aimed at defeating the very purpose of the documentary credit transaction. Unless such a clause was drafted in the most clear and unambiguous terms it would not be construed as achieving that effect in English law. Reference should be made to the law concerning the construction of exemption clauses in textbooks on the law of contract.[1] A bank might also be prevented from relying on such a clause under s 3 of the Unfair Contract Terms Act 1977 on the basis that it does not satisfy the requirement that it be fair and reasonable.

1 For example, *Chitty on Contracts* (30th edn) chapter 14.

Transmission and translation errors

4.16   UCP Article 35 provides as follows:

'Article 35 Disclaimer on Transmission and Translation:
A bank assumes no liability or responsibility for the consequences arising out of delay, loss in transit, mutilation or other errors arising in the transmission of any messages or delivery of letters or documents, when such messages, letters or documents are transmitted or sent according to the requirements stated in the credit, or when the bank may have taken the initiative in the choice of the delivery service in the absence of such instructions in the credit.

If a nominated bank determines that a presentation is complying and forwards the documents to the issuing bank or confirming bank, whether or not the nominated bank has honoured or negotiated, an issuing bank or confirming bank must honour or negotiate, or reimburse that nominated bank, even when the documents have been lost in transit between the nominated bank and the issuing bank or confirming bank, or between the confirming bank and the issuing bank.

A bank assumes no liability or responsibility for errors in translation or interpretation of technical terms and may transmit credit terms without translating them.'

4.17 The Article covers three distinct issues: the transmission of any messages, letters or documents; the loss of documents in transit between banks; and the translation or interpretation of technical terms, with a general liberty to decline translation. The matters referred to in the first paragraph of the Article are matters which it may be thought will ordinarily arise without an involvement on the part of the bank. There is no suggestion that the purpose is to absolve the bank where it has itself been negligent or otherwise at fault.[1] It is suggested that the Article should not be construed as exempting a bank from liability for its own negligence. This conclusion is supported by the application of the tests contained in the advice of the Privy Council in *Canada Steamship Lines Ltd v R*[2] as to when an exemption clause can be construed as excluding liability for negligence. It may, however, fairly be questioned how far such peculiarly English law tests[3] should be applied to the construction of such an international document using autonomous legal concepts. But in this context it is suggested that they do provide the correct answer and should be applied.

1 See also para **4.15** above.
2 [1952] AC 192 at 208.
3 As to the principles to be applied in the construction of exemption clauses in relation to negligence, see generally *Chitty on Contracts* (30th edn) paras 14-010 to 14-015.

4.18 The second paragraph covers documents presented to a bank under a credit which have to be transmitted to another bank. The beneficiary will usually be entitled to payment by reason of his presentation of the documents to the first, nominated bank. But where this is not the case, and the documents are lost in transit between two banks, the issuing bank or confirming bank must nevertheless honour (or, as the case may be, negotiate) the credit despite the loss, provided only that the nominated bank determined that there had been a complying presentation.

Force majeure

4.19 UCP Article 36 provides:

'**Article 36 Force Majeure:**
A bank assumes no liability or responsibility for the consequences arising out of the interruption of its business by Acts of God, riots, civil commotions,

insurrections, wars, acts or terrorism, or by any strikes or lockouts or any other causes beyond its control.

A bank will not, upon resumption of its business, honour or negotiate under a credit that expired during such interruption of its business.'

Thus an interruption of the bank's business by such a cause may bring about the loss of the benefit of the credit if it expires during the operation of the *force majeure* event. 'Acts of terrorism' has been added in UCP 600, perhaps a sign of the times.

The acts and omissions of the advising bank

4.20   This topic involves first understanding the relationship between the issuing and the advising bank, a topic considered in **Chapter 6**. In essence, so far as the applicant for the credit (the buyer) is concerned, the advising bank is to be treated as the agent of the issuing bank. The acts of the advising bank are therefore attributed to the issuing bank for the purpose of determining any liability which the issuing bank may have to the applicant. Thus if the advising bank fails correctly to perform its function of advising the credit to the beneficiary and the applicant for the credit thereby suffers loss, the issuing bank would be liable on common law principles. It cannot, however, be said that this conclusion is as yet clearly established by case law. It is certainly consistent with the decision of the House of Lords in the *Equitable Trust* case[1] and follows as a matter of principle from the advising bank's position as an agent.[2] It is also theoretically possible for there to be an intermediate position, that an issuing bank should not be automatically liable for the acts of its advising or correspondent bank on the ground that such a bank was its agent, but should be liable only where the issuing bank is itself negligent, for example in its selection or supervision of the advising bank.

The position is now likely to be determined by the application of UCP Article 37, which however is rather unsatisfactorily drafted.

1 (1926) 27 Ll L Rep 49.
2 See para **6.6** below.

4.21   Article 37 provides:

'**Article 37 Disclaimer for Acts of an Instructed Party:**
a.   A bank utilizing the services of another bank for the purpose of giving effect to the instructions of the applicant does so for the account and at the risk of the applicant.
b.   An issuing bank or advising bank assumes no liability or responsibility should the instructions it transmits to another bank not be carried out, even if it has taken the initiative in the choice of that other bank.
c.   A bank instructing another bank to perform services is liable for any commissions, fees, costs or expenses ("charges") incurred by that bank in connection with its instructions.

If a credit states that such charges are for the account of the beneficiary and charges cannot be collected or deducted from proceeds, the issuing bank remains liable for payment of charges.

A credit or amendment should not stipulate that the advising to a beneficiary is conditional upon the receipt by the advising bank or second advising bank of its charges.

d. The applicant shall be bound by and liable to indemnify a bank against all obligations and responsibilities imposed by foreign laws and usages.'

At a first reading the desired effect of this provision appears to be that whatever the advising bank does is done at the risk of the applicant and not of the issuing bank. It is to be remembered that the applicant has no contract with the advising bank, and it is at best doubtful whether any rights lie against it.[1] The most common error made by advising banks is to pay against documents which do not comply with the credit. When that happens, the error should be picked up by the issuing bank when it in turn receives and inspects the documents. The consequence will be that, unless the applicant is prepared to accept the documents and waive any discrepancies, the issuing bank will return them to the advising bank and refuse to reimburse it. If, however, the issuing bank fails to spot the error, the applicant will nonetheless be entitled to refuse the documents when it receives and examines them.

1 See para **6.45** below.

4.22   It cannot be the intention of Article 37 to alter the outcome in either of those situations. It will be noted that they resolve themselves because the bank at fault carries the loss: it honours the credit and yet has no right to reimbursement. Where it is another bank that is to pay, Article 37 can be argued to shift the loss on to an innocent party, the applicant. Where the advising bank advises the credit but commits an error in so doing (for example, by omitting one of the stipulated documents that the applicant required), and the credit provides for payment to be made not by the advising bank but by the issuing bank or another bank nominated by it, the issuing bank will be bound by the advice of the credit. For it will have been made by its agent acting within that agent's ostensible or apparent authority.[1] The beneficiary will then be entitled to payment. Article 37.a appears to have the effect that in such a situation the payment would be 'for the account and at the risk of' the applicant. If so, he would be bound to accept and pay for documents which did not comply with his mandate to the issuing bank, despite the fact that the clear negligence of the correspondent or advising bank as the agent of the issuing bank would give the issuing bank a right of reimbursement against it. Had the issuing bank made such an error itself, the liability would of course rest with it.

1 See paras **6.6** and **6.7** below.

4.23   A similar situation arises where the error by the advising bank is not as to the terms of the credit but in accepting documents which do not in fact comply with the terms as correctly advised, and payment is to be made by another bank. In accepting the documents the advising bank will have acted as the agent of the issuing bank and will bind it, and the beneficiary will be entitled to his payment. Again, Article 37 may be argued to have the effect that the applicant for the credit would be bound to accept and pay for documents which did not comply with his instructions, even though the issuing bank would have a remedy against the bank actually at fault.

4.24 It is surprising if it is the intention of Article 37.a to enable banks to avoid responsibility in these situations. Unless its wording clearly requires that result, it is suggested that it should not be construed as doing so.

4.25 An alternative construction of the Article is that its effect is to prevent an applicant holding an issuing bank liable in damages for any loss caused to the applicant by the action of a bank instructed by the issuing bank: it does not enable the issuing bank to pass on to the applicant liability which would otherwise rest with the banks.[1] The issue is touched on in terms which support this second construction in a very brief decision of the ICC Banking Commission[2] where the Commission stated that the Article's predecessor exonerated the issuing bank for the errors of the advising bank, provided that the issuing bank had not been guilty of negligence itself. The word 'exonerated' does not suggest that the Article enables a bank to require an applicant to accept and pay for documents which do not comply with the applicant's instructions. This confirms that the intended effect is only to prevent the issuing bank from being liable in respect of the errors of a correspondent bank unless the issuing bank has itself been negligent.

1 See also para **6.8**. This statement was approved and applied in *Credit Agricole Indosuez v Generale Bank* [2000] 1 Lloyd's Rep 123. See also *Benjamin's Sale of Goods* (7th edn) para 23-119: '... Article [37] does not preclude the applicant from contesting in a dispute with the issuer the regularity of documents accepted by the correspondent as a regular tender'; and, more generally, Goode, *Commercial Law* (3rd edn) p. 983: 'The disclaimer embodied in art [37] has met with widespread hostility from courts and textbook writers abroad and in practice tends not to be invoked by issuing banks.'
2 *Decisions*, (1975–1979) ICC No 371 Ref 17.

May the bank waive terms appearing to be inserted for its benefit?

4.26 It is a part of the general law of contract that a party may waive compliance with a term in the contract which has been inserted solely for his benefit, and enforce the contract as if the provision had been omitted.[1] In *Guaranty Trust of New York v Van De Berghs Ltd*,[2] the buyer's application for the credit required a bill of lading made out to the bank's order. It was held that the buyer was bound to accept a bill made out to the buyer's order as this was a better document from his point of view. As the provision that the bill be made out to the bank's order was inserted for the bank's benefit, the bank was entitled to waive it. It is suggested, however, that it will often be difficult to be sure that a provision has been inserted solely for the benefit of the bank. Thus although on the particular facts of *Guaranty Trust*[3] the position may have been clear, it is possible to think of situations in which the buyer would have reasons of his own for wanting the bill made out to the bank's order.[4] It may be doubted whether there is room today for this principle of waiver to apply to the documents required under a documentary credit: the buyer should be entitled to precisely those documents which he has stipulated in his application form, and to which the bank has agreed. In any event the principle must be one having a very limited practical application.

1 See *Chitty on Contracts* (30th edn) para 22-046.
2 (1925) 22 Ll L Rep 447.
3 (1925) 22 Ll L Rep 447 at 458 (Sargant LJ).
4 Such as where the buyer is selling the goods on in a different name.

The issuing bank's general duty of care to the buyer in connection with the credit

4.27   If the transaction financed by the credit goes wrong (for example, if the seller were to ship goods of no value whatsoever but nonetheless presented conforming documents and received payment, and then disappeared), the buyer might seek to blame the bank for having failed to advise as to the terms of a credit that would have protected him against such eventualities. For example, it might be alleged that the bank had been negligent in failing to advise the buyer that the documents to be presented under the credit could and should include a certificate of inspection by an independent and reliable agency.

4.28   It is suggested that the validity of such a contention is to be determined by an examination of the particular facts of the case, looking in particular to see what duty the bank has undertaken towards its customer by express agreement or by implication. Thus a bank may well have a greater understanding and knowledge of letters of credit than its customer. If in such a situation the customer specifically seeks advice and the bank gives it and does so without any exclusion of liability, the bank is likely to be liable if it fails to act with the reasonable skill and care to be expected of such a bank. On the other hand if a customer does not seek the bank's advice but simply puts forward its application for a credit, it is unlikely to succeed in an allegation that the bank should have issued a warning or given advice. Two cases are illustrative of the position.

4.29   In *Midland Bank Ltd v Seymour*,[1] Mr Seymour had asked the bank for inquiries to be made about sellers in Hong Kong who were ultimately to ship him rubbish instead of the ducks' feathers he required. The bank made inquiries, passed on the response and suggested that a surveyor's inspection certificate be required, but Mr Seymour thought this unnecessary. The bank then received a further report about the sellers which, however, they failed to pass on. Mr Seymour complained about that, and also alleged that the bank should have made fuller inquiries at an earlier stage. Devlin J held that the bank was acting on a contractual basis in connection with its inquiries. He went on to consider what the bank's duty was. First, it was a duty to take care not to supply misleading information. Secondly he suggested, but did not decide, that there was no duty to pursue its inquiries with due diligence, since it was not being employed as an inquiry agent. He held in any event that on the facts there had been no breach of the duty to pursue inquiries with due diligence (assuming there was such a duty), and that no loss had been occasioned by the bank's breach in failing to pass on the information contained in the further report.[2]

1 [1955] 2 Lloyd's Rep 147.
2 [1955] 2 Lloyd's Rep 147 at 155–160.

4.30   The complaint in *Commercial Banking Co of Sydney v Jalsard Pty Ltd*[1] was that the bank had failed to advise the buyer's representative that the certificate of inspection should cover the checking of the quality or condition of the goods (battery-operated Christmas lights), and not simply that the certifier had inspected them merely visually. In holding that the complaint failed, the Privy Council (on appeal from the Supreme Court of New South Wales) pointed out that there was no request by the representative for advice as to the nature of the certificate and that she had herself decided what form the certificate should take.

1 [1973] AC 279.

4.31   The position may thus be stated in general terms that a bank owes no duty of care to the applicant unless the particular facts show that the bank has undertaken such a duty, usually by means of an assumption of responsibility. The scope and import of any duty will be determined and limited by the particular circumstances of the assumption of responsibility, and the reasonableness of reliance upon the bank's advice or expertise.

D   THE DUTY OF THE BUYER

4.32   It is the duty of the buyer to take up from the issuing bank documents which conform to his instructions and to pay the issuing bank in accordance with the arrangements between them. This may require a cash payment, or may entitle the bank to debit the buyer's account. Those arrangements may also provide for the release of the documents to the buyer upon terms, such as that he execute a trust receipt, a procedure described in **Chapter 11** below.

The bank's security against the buyer

4.33   The question of security is considered in **Chapter 11**. The security of the bank was traditionally the documents against which it paid or undertook a payment obligation. Through them it should have the security of the goods themselves. If it does not, it has only a doubtful security. When the transport document under a letter of credit was almost invariably an ocean bill of lading, there was little difficulty because such a document is a document of title both at common law and under statutory provisions such as the Factors Act 1889. Yet with the increasing use nowadays of other types of transport document, the security of banks in documentary credit transactions has been greatly weakened. Such security has in the past been regarded as one of the essential elements of the transaction. The alternative form of security is security taken directly from the bank's customer, such as a general floating charge over the company's assets, or a guarantee from a holding company. It may well be that in today's trading conditions banks often look to the latter for their security rather than to the documents being presented under the credit.

Charges and costs

4.34   The applicant for the credit is primarily liable for the costs incurred in connection with it. He will have to pay the issuing bank its charges, which are likely to be a small percentage on the amount available under the credit during the period that it is available and a full interest rate on sums advanced for the period until they are recouped from the applicant. He will also have to pay the bank its out-of-pocket expenses in communicating the credit. The charges of the advising bank are usually a matter of agreement. In default they are to be paid by the buyer as the initiator of the arrangement, a position confirmed by Article 37.a and .c quoted above. It should be made a term of the credit that the expenses of the advising bank will be payable by the seller. Then, in practice, they will usually be deducted from the price otherwise payable to him.[1] This raises a problem where the credit is not utilised, or is not utilised through the advising bank. The ICC Banking Commission suggests that a buyer who does not want to be exposed to the charges of a confirming bank should request that the credit be issued on the basis that it is not a confirmed credit until payment of charges by the beneficiary.[2]

---

1   The advising fee and any amendments fees will have been charged at the time of the advice and amendments. But it very commonly happens that they remain unpaid until payment is made under the credit, when they are deducted with the payment fee.

2   *More Queries and Responses on UCP 500*, ICC No 596, Ref 273. The same position would hold good under the UCP 600.

E   THE AUTONOMY OF THE CREDIT: RESTRAINING PAYMENT

4.35   A documentary credit transaction is a transaction in the documents presented pursuant to the credit, and is independent of the underlying transaction in the goods or whatever the subject matter of the underlying contract may be. This principle of the autonomy of the credit has already been introduced in **Chapter 1**.[1] Its consequence is that it is normally no ground for interfering with the operation of the credit, in particular by the grant of a prohibitory injunction against a bank restraining it from paying, that the applicant alleges that the goods do not comply with the terms of the underlying sale contract. There is an exception to this where there is fraud on the part of the beneficiary under the credit. The fraud exception and the question of injunctions are both considered in **Chapter 9**.

1 See para **1.34**.

Chapter 5

The Contracts of the Issuing Bank and the Confirming Bank with the Seller

A   FORMATION OF THE CONTRACT

Issue of the credit

5.1   The nature of an irrevocable credit has been described in **Chapter 2.**[1] An irrevocable credit constitutes a binding contract between the issuing bank and the beneficiary of the credit. Where a credit is confirmed by a second bank, a second and separate contract is established between the confirming bank and the beneficiary. A beneficiary does not obtain a contract with a nominated bank unless the bank adds its confirmation of the credit.

1 Paras **2.8** et seq.

5.2   The requirements of English law that to be enforceable a contract must be supported by consideration moving from the promisee raises a question which is considered shortly.[1] It is, however, clear in English law that enforceable contracts come into being. Indeed this is recognised expressly or implicitly in every documentary credit case involving a bank as defendant and seller or other beneficiary as plaintiff. In *Donald H Scott & Co Ltd v Barclays Bank Ltd*[2] Scrutton LJ stated:[3]

> 'The appellants gave a confirmed credit to the respondents; that is to say that they entered into contractual relations with them from which they could not withdraw except with the consent of the other party . . . .'

Confirmation at the highest level is to be found in Lord Diplock's speech in *United City Merchants (Investments) Ltd v Royal Bank of Canada*[4] where he referred to four contractual relationships which will be involved where there is a confirmed letter of credit.[5]

1 Paras **5.8** et seq.
2 [1923] 2 KB 1.
3 [1923] 2 KB 1 at 14.
4 [1983] 1 AC 168 at 182, 183.
5 He omitted to refer to the contract between the issuing bank and the seller, but referred only to the contract between the confirming bank and the seller. The other three contracts referred to were the underlying contract of sale, the contract between the buyer and the issuing bank and that between the issuing bank and the confirming bank.

5.3   Article 7.b provides that an issuing bank is irrevocably bound to honour as of the time it issues the credit. The UCP does not explain precisely what is required to complete the issue of a credit, but it is suggested that the credit becomes binding on the bank from the moment of receipt of advice of it by the beneficiary; this was the position taken in *Bunge Corp v Vegetable Vitamin Foods (Pte) Ltd*.[1] That does, however, give rise to one problem: what is the position where the beneficiary responds to its receipt by complaining that it does not accord with the underlying contract or otherwise asking for its amendment? If he does that, is the bank nonetheless bound by the credit which it has advised should the beneficiary thereafter change his position and seek to hold the bank to it? The outcome of such a dispute would, no doubt, depend upon the detailed facts, in particular the terms in which the beneficiary had responded to the advice of the credit. It may be thought to be unlikely to arise before the courts. The alternative view, that the credit becomes binding when the beneficiary has done some act in reliance upon it, would introduce an undesirable element of uncertainty.

1   [1985] 1 Lloyd's Rep 613 at 617.

5.4   A statement by a bank that it intends to cancel an irrevocable credit, or conduct which clearly evinces an intention not to honour the credit, amounts to a repudiatory breach of the contract with the beneficiary. The ordinary principles of contract law apply and the beneficiary has a choice whether or not to accept the repudiation as terminating the contract and to claim damages against the bank. But if the bank receives no clear notification of the beneficiary's acceptance of the repudiation, and especially if the beneficiary tenders documents and presses for payment, then the repudiation has no effect on either party's rights and the credit remains in force for the benefit of both.[1]

1   *Jaks (UK) Ltd v Cera Investment Bank SA* [1998] 2 Lloyd's Rep 89.

Pre-advice or preliminary advice

5.5   Sometimes a bank is asked to notify the beneficiary of a forthcoming credit without awaiting its actual issue. The resulting notification may be called a pre-advice or a preliminary advice. If the bank gives such a notification, it is bound to issue a credit in terms not inconsistent with the pre-advice without delay. This may also occur with the notification of amendments. UCP Article 11.b provides:

> '**Article 11: Teletransmitted and Pre-Advised Credits and Amendments**
> b.   A preliminary advice of the issuance of a credit or amendment ("pre-advice") shall only be sent if the issuing bank is prepared to issue the operative credit or amendment. An issuing bank that sends a pre-advice is irrevocably committed to issue the operative credit or amendment, without delay, in terms not inconsistent with the pre-advice.'

Where a confirming bank is involved, the pre-advice may almost certainly come through the confirming bank. Presumably the Article only refers to an issuing bank because of the complications which the involvement of a confirming bank as an obligated party at this stage would involve. A bank which has been asked to notify a pre-advice of a credit which it will in due course confirm will no doubt simply inform the beneficiary of the pre-advice without obligation on its part.

Amendment

5.6   The question of amendment of a credit has been considered in **Chapter 3**.[1] The essential point is that once a credit has been advised to its beneficiary it cannot be amended without his consent. For the advice of the credit brings into being a contract between the beneficiary and the bank or banks and contracts which cannot be unilaterally amended.

1 Para **3.36** et seq.

Revocable credits

5.7   UCP 500 Article 8 made provision for revocable credits. Under a revocable credit, no effective contract[1] comes into being until the beneficiary has presented documents which have been accepted, at which point the beneficiary is entitled to payment in accordance with the terms of the credit.[2] There is no provision for revocable credits in UCP 600, and Article 3 provides:

'A credit is irrevocable even if there is no indication to that effect.'

1 For even if it is right to say that there is a contract, it is a contract which the bank can revoke or amend at any time prior to acceptance of documents.
2 See UCP 500 Article 8.b and para **2.4** above.

Consideration

5.8   It is a requirement of English law that for a contractual promise which is not under seal to be enforceable it must be supported by consideration moving from the promisee. As it is plainly established in English law that the opening of an irrevocable credit establishes a contract between the bank and the beneficiary, it is not important in practice whether there is consideration to be found for the bank's promise or whether the contract is an exception to the general rule as to consideration.

5.9   It is worth first looking at the matter without any preconceptions. How is the communication of the credit to the seller to be seen? It is suggested that it can be described with some accuracy as an offer to the seller from the bank, that if he presents correct documents, payment will follow. This analysis is supported by the dictum of Donaldson J in *Elder Dempster Lines Ltd v Ionic Shipping Agency Inc:*[1]

> 'The best explanation of the legal phenomenon constituted by a banker's letter of credit is that it is an offer which is accepted by being drawn upon.'

1 [1968] 1 Lloyd's Rep 529 at 535.

5.10   But this does not explain as a matter of legal theory why the issuing bank and any confirming bank cannot withdraw the offer made by the opening of the credit at any time prior to the presentation of documents. Once the seller has acted upon the offer by presenting documents to the bank, there is no difficulty in finding consideration. The presentation of documents is a form of executed consideration, just as where a reward is offered and the claimant returns the lost article or provides information as to the crime, that act provides consideration and he has an enforceable right to the reward.[1] The difficulty is to find consideration moving from the beneficiary of the credit in order to establish a binding contract at the time that the credit is first advised to him.[2]

1 See generally, *Chitty on Contracts* (30th edn) paras 2-019 and 2-082.
2 Reference may also be made to the discussion of consideration in relation to performance bonds and guarantees in **Chapter 12**.

5.11   It is suggested that the true position is that irrevocable letters of credit which are governed by English law constitute an exception to the rule of English law as to consideration. The undertakings of the issuing and confirming banks are not supported by consideration moving from the seller, but are binding in law nonetheless.[1] The rationale may be given as 'mercantile usage', meaning that since the first development of irrevocable credits traders and banks have intended and accepted that banks should be bound. In *Hamzeh Malas & Sons v British Imex Industries Ltd*[2] Jenkins LJ stated:[3]

> 'We have been referred to a number of authorities, and it seems to be plain enough that the opening of a confirmed letter of credit constitutes a bargain between the banker and the vendor of the goods, which imposes upon the banker an absolute obligation to pay, irrespective of any dispute there may be between the parties as to whether the goods are up to contract or not. An elaborate commercial system has been built up on the footing that bankers' confirmed credits are of that character, and, in my judgment, it would be wrong for this court in the present case to interfere with that established practice.'

1 That an irrevocable credit is a clear exception to the doctrine of consideration is stated in *Chitty on Contracts* (30th edn) para 2-082.
2 [1958] 2 QB 127.
3 [1958] 2 QB 127 at 129.

5.12   Various arguments have been put forward from time to time in an attempt to find consideration to support the banker's promise, some of which are worth examination.

5.13   In *Dexters Ltd v Schenker & Co*[1] it was pleaded that the undertaking was not supported by consideration. But the plea was withdrawn by counsel at the trial. Greer J stated with reference to the plea:

> 'Now it is clear that, until they got a form of banker's credit which would comply with the terms of the contract, the plaintiffs were not bound to send the goods forward at all; and therefore not having got the banker's credit until there was a substituted arrangement for another credit elsewhere, they were under no obligation to anybody to send forward the goods. Therefore it is quite clear there was full and ample consideration for this undertaking ...'

Where the underlying contract provides for payment by letter of credit the seller's obligation to the buyer to ship the goods and present documents is conditional on the letter of credit being provided.[2] When a credit conforming to the underlying contract is advised to the seller, his obligation towards the buyer becomes unconditional. However, these facts do not establish consideration moving from the seller in relation to the bank's undertaking to him. Consideration need not move towards the promisor: it is sufficient if the promisee suffers some detriment at the promisor's request although no corresponding benefit is conferred on the promisor. But here the promisee, the beneficiary, does nothing: all that happens is that one of the provisions of the contract which the beneficiary has previously made with the applicant for the credit takes effect in accordance with that contract. If something which is relied on as consideration is not given or done in return for the promise in question, but was done before and independently of it, as is the case with the undertakings contained in the contract between the buyer and the seller, it cannot in law amount to consideration for the promise. It is what is called 'past consideration'. It has also to be borne in mind that there is no undertaking from the seller or beneficiary to the bank: the seller never becomes obliged to the bank to present documents conforming to the credit. This fact and the fact that the contract between the buyer and the seller precedes the opening of the credit and the banks are not involved at that stage, lie at the nub of the problem of consideration.

1 (1923) 14 Ll L Rep 586.
2 See para **3.26** above.

5.14   The 'offer and acceptance' theory relies upon the seller's presentation of documents as an acceptance of the bank's offer made by notifying the credit. An example of the application of this theory is *Raiffeisen Zentralbank Osterreich AG v China Marine Bunker (Petrochina) Co Ltd*,[1] where the buyer had issued an irrevocable payment undertaking to the bank financing a sale.

Gloster J rejected the argument that there was no consideration for the undertaking, stating:[1]

> 'In a commercial transaction the courts will be loath to find that an agreement which gives every impression of being a contractual undertaking fails for want of consideration. There are a number of ways of approaching the issue of consideration. One way is to say that the offer was an offer by China Marine to the bank that, if presentation of the documents were made, the payment would be made by China Marine and that, effectively, the consideration was provided by RZB's presentation of the documents [under a credit issued by the bank].'

However, this theory cannot explain how the bank becomes bound prior to the presentation of documents, as is the case save with revocable credits.

1 [2006] EWHC 212 (Comm).
2 At para 31.

5.15   Another theory relies on the buyer being the seller's agent, on the ground that the buyer is to be taken to have the authority of the seller to arrange for the price to be paid by letter of credit as has been agreed between them. It is then apparently suggested that the consideration undoubtedly provided by the buyer to the bank can be taken as provided on behalf of the seller and used to support the contract between the bank and the seller. That suggestion has its own difficulties. But the theory collapses at the start. For the fact that it is the intention of the seller that the buyer should arrange the letter of credit does not make him the seller's agent to do so. It would come as a great surprise to any seller that, in applying to the issuing bank for the credit to be opened, the buyer was acting as his agent, and there is no justification for implying any such agency.

5.16   A further theory relies on the Contracts (Rights of Third Parties) Act 1999.[1] Under this Act a third party can enforce a term of the contract where: (a) the contract expressly provides that he may, or (b) the term purports to confer a benefit on him. In the latter case enforcement is not possible if it appears that the parties did not intend the term to be enforceable by the third party. It is possible, although perhaps unlikely, that the applicant and issuing bank might include an express provision so as to satisfy test (a). Otherwise, the beneficiary could argue that the contract between the issuing bank and the applicant contains a promise to pay against conforming documents and that that term clearly purports to confer a benefit on him. On this analysis the beneficiary would not be enforcing a contract between the bank and himself (which is the contract here under examination), but would be relying on the contract between the applicant and the issuer. That might have unwelcome consequences as to governing law and jurisdiction.

1 See *Chitty on Contracts* (30th edn) paras 18-088 to 18-120.

B   UNDERTAKINGS OF THE ISSUING AND CONFIRMING BANKS

5.17   The main ways in which a credit can be operated have been considered in Chapter 1,[1] and the undertakings which a bank may typically give have been generally described. The undertaking of an issuing bank and a confirming bank are contained, respectively, in UCP Article 7 and Article 8; the term 'honour', which is defined in Article 2, is used to encompass the various types of undertaking.

'**Article 7: Issuing Bank Undertaking**
a.   Provided that the stipulated documents are presented to the nominated bank or to the issuing bank and that they constitute a complying presentation, the issuing bank must honour if the credit is available by:

   i.   sight payment, deferred payment or acceptance with the issuing bank;
   ii.   sight payment with a nominated bank and that nominated bank does not pay;
   iii. deferred payment with a nominated bank and that nominated bank does not incur its deferred payment undertaking or, having incurred its deferred payment undertaking, does not pay at maturity;
   iv.   acceptance with a nominated bank and that nominated bank does not accept a draft drawn on it or, having accepted a draft drawn on it, does not pay at maturity;
   v.   negotiation with a nominated bank and that nominated bank does not negotiate.

b.   An issuing bank is irrevocably bound to honour as of the time it issues the credit.
c.   An issuing bank undertakes to reimburse a nominated bank that has honoured or negotiated a complying presentation and forwarded the documents to the issuing bank. Reimbursement for the amount of a complying presentation under a credit available by acceptance or deferred payment is due at maturity, whether or not the nominated bank prepaid or purchased before maturity. An issuing bank's undertaking to reimburse a nominated bank is independent of the issuing bank's undertaking to the beneficiary.'

'**Article 8: Confirming Bank Undertaking**
a.   Provided that the stipulated documents are presented to the confirming bank or to any other nominated bank and that they constitute a complying presentation, the confirming bank must:
   i.   honour, if the credit is available by
      a.   sight payment, deferred payment or acceptance with the confirming bank;
      b.   sight payment with another nominated bank and that nominated bank does not pay;
      c.   deferred payment with another nominated bank and that nominated bank does not incur its deferred payment

96

undertaking or, having incurred its deferred payment
undertaking, does not pay at maturity;

    d. acceptance with another nominated bank and that nominated
bank does not accept a draft drawn on it or, having accepted a
draft drawn on it, does not pay at maturity;

    e. negotiation with another nominated bank and that nominated
bank does not negotiate.

  ii. negotiate, without recourse, if the credit is available by negotiation
with the confirming bank.

b. A confirming bank is irrevocably bound to honour or negotiate as of the
time it adds its confirmation to the credit.

c. A confirming bank undertakes to reimburse another nominated bank
that has honoured or negotiated a complying presentation and
forwarded the documents to the confirming bank. Reimbursement for
the amount of a complying presentation under a credit available by
acceptance or deferred payment is due at maturity, whether or not
another nominated bank prepaid or purchased before maturity. A
confirming bank's undertaking to reimburse another nominated bank
is independent of the confirming bank's undertaking to the beneficiary.

d. If a bank is authorized or requested by the issuing bank to confirm a
credit but is not prepared to do so, it must inform the issuing bank
without delay and may advise the credit without confirmation.'

1 See para **1.7** et seq.

5.18   If the credit is expressed to be available with a bank other than the
issuing bank – such a bank being a 'nominated bank' in the terminology of
the UCP – then the seller may present the documents to that bank instead of
the issuing bank. Suppose that the nominated bank refuses documents which
conform to the terms of the credit and are presented within time. If, but only
if, the nominated bank has confirmed the credit then the seller has an action
against it to enforce the credit.[1] But the seller can also sue the issuing bank
without the need to present the documents again. The issuing bank's
undertaking under Article 7 is to honour the credit if documents are presented
either to the nominated bank or to the issuing bank. The nominated bank can
be regarded as acting as the issuing bank's agent for receipt of the documents.
This may be important because if the documents were presented to the
nominated bank close to the expiry of the credit then it may be too late to
make a second presentation. Where the credit has been confirmed, the seller
will usually look first for payment to the confirming bank, and in that sense
the issuing bank is the guarantor of the confirming bank rather than the other
way round.

1 See among other cases *United City Merchants (Investments) Ltd v Royal Bank of Canada*
[1983] 1 AC 168.

5.19   In accordance with the definition of 'honour', what is required from
the issuing bank depends on the how the credit is expressed to be available. If
available by sight payment then the issuing bank must make payment on

presentation of documents if the nominated bank does not. If available by deferred payment then, under Article 7.a.iii, the issuing bank must pay at maturity if the nominated bank either refuses to incur a deferred payment undertaking or, having incurred it, does not pay it.

5.20   Where the credit is available by acceptance, the issuing bank's obligation is, under Article 7.a.iv, to honour if the nominated bank does not accept a draft drawn on it or, having accepted a draft drawn on it, does not pay at maturity. The difficulty which arises in that case is that the obligation to honour in an acceptance credit is an obligation to accept a draft drawn by the beneficiary. Does that mean that the beneficiary must draw a fresh draft on the issuing bank in order to establish its liability? A similar difficulty arises if the draft is initially drawn on but not accepted by the issuing bank and the beneficiary wishes to sue a confirming bank. The idea of the beneficiary having to draw fresh drafts on the issuing or confirming bank if the initial draft is not accepted seems an unnecessary complication. It is suggested that the beneficiary must remain entitled simply to demand the money from the issuing or confirming bank at maturity without the need for a second draft. This was the position under UCP 400 and UCP 500;[1] it should also be the position under UCP 600.

1 UCP 500 and 400 Compared, ICC No 511.

5.21   In UCP 400 Articles 10.a.iii and 10.b.iii referred to, and provided for, drafts drawn on the applicant. It has previously been common, in some parts of the world, for credits to involve such drafts but their use can be argued to serve no practical purpose which cannot be better served by a draft drawn on a bank. Further, as credits involve undertakings by banks, it is undesirable to include as part of the operation of the credit a source of obligation between the beneficiary and the applicant by means of a draft drawn by one on the other. It is for such reasons that UCP 600 provides in Article 6.c:

> '**Article 6: Availability, Expiry Date and Place for Presentation**
> c.   A credit must not be issued available by a draft drawn on the applicant.'

However, although the credit must not be *available* by a draft drawn on the applicant, such a draft may be one of the documents stipulated for presentation. This is expressly permitted by ISBP Article 54.[1] Accordingly, if the credit calls for a draft on the applicant (and even if, notwithstanding Article 6.c, the credit is expressed to be available by the draft) the bank should treat it merely as a document to be presented with the other documents called for by the credit and not as playing any part in the mechanism of payment or involving any obligation on the part of the banks.[2]

1 The position was similar under UCP 500, where Articles 9.a.iv and 9.b.iv provided that a credit 'should not' be issued available by a draft drawn on the applicant, but that if it was then the banks should consider the drafts as 'additional documents'.
2 Professor Ellinger therefore identifies Article 6.c as one of the UCP 600's 'imperfect provisions' because of the uncertain consequences of non-compliance with it: [2007] LMCLQ 152, 179.

5.22   In some circumstances it may be necessary for the banks to take further account of the term of the credit providing for drafts on the applicant.[1] Suppose that the credit states that it is 'available by your drafts drawn on the applicant payable 30 days after sight'. Depending on other terms as to the availability of the credit that would probably mean that the credit would provide payment 30 days after the applicant had sight of the draft. In a situation involving a time draft to be drawn on an applicant, the credit cannot be treated as available by immediate payment, because that would defeat the clear intention of the parties. It is probably to be treated as providing for deferred payment 30 days after the documents are presented to the bank where the credit is available. This is a practical but not wholly logical solution to a problem which the Articles create but do not address. The bank would be well advised to seek clarification.

1 *Opinions* (1995–1996) ICC No 565, Ref 205.

5.23   Where, in accordance with the above principles, the seller is entitled to receive payment on the presentation of the documents, if payment is refused he will be able to proceed against the confirming and issuing banks. If he is not entitled to immediate payment but, for example, payment is to be made 80 days after the bill of lading date available by drafts drawn on a bank, if the documents are not accepted by the confirming bank, the seller may proceed against the banks. If the documents are accepted by the banks but the bill is not accepted by the buyers, again the seller may proceed against the banks. Finally, if the bill is accepted but not paid, following the dishonour by non-payment the seller may then proceed against the banks.[1]

1 The right to proceed against a bank where another bank has failed to accept a draft drawn on it gives rise to the problem raised in para **5.20** above as to the need to present a new draft to the bank sought to be held liable. It is there suggested that a new draft is not necessary.

C   PRESENTATION BY THE BENEFICIARY

Place for presentation

5.24   Where should the beneficiary present the documents? UCP Article 6 provides as follows:

'Article 6: Availability, Expiry Date and Place for Presentation
a.   A credit must state the bank with which it is available or whether it is available with any bank. A credit available with a nominated bank is also available with the issuing bank.

...

d.   ii.   The place of the bank with which the credit is available is the place for presentation. The place for presentation under a credit available with any bank is that of any bank. A place for presentation other than that of the issuing bank is in addition to the place of the issuing bank.'

5.25   Under Article 3, branches of a bank in different countries are considered to be separate banks, so documents cannot be presented at a branch of the issuing or nominated bank other than that specified in the credit.

5.26   The identity of the nominated bank will often be obvious as, for example, where the documents are to be presented direct to the confirming bank. But it may be less clear where the documents are to be negotiated through a second bank, as was the case in *European Asian Bank AG v Punjab and Sind Bank (No 2)*.[1] There the credit provided that it was valid for negotiation in Singapore, which in the context meant negotiation at the Algemene Bank to which negotiation was restricted under the terms of the credit.

1 [1983] 1 WLR 642, [1983] 1 Lloyd's Rep 611.

Time for presentation

5.27   There are three periods or dates to be considered. First, the documents must be presented within the period of validity of the credit. Secondly, where a transport document is required, the documents must be presented within a period calculated from the date of shipment. Thirdly, it is likely that shipment itself must be made within a defined period or by a particular date.[1]

1 These must, of course, be considered separately: Case 279 in *More Case Studies on Documentary Credits*, ICC No 489. The beneficiary has only to present the documents by the date: it is, of course, not necessary for him to do so in time to enable the documents to be processed by the bank by the date: Case 275 in *More Case Studies on Documentary Credits* above.

Expiry date

5.28   Article 6 provides:

   '**Article 6: Availability, Expiry Date and Place for Presentation**
   d.   i.   A credit must state an expiry date for presentation. An expiry date stated for honour or negotiation will be deemed to be an expiry date for presentation.

   ...

   e.   Except as provided in sub-article 29 (a), a presentation by or on behalf of the beneficiary must be made on or before the expiry date.'

5.29   Documents cannot be presented once the expiry date has passed,[1] subject only to the possibility of an extension under Article 29.a.[2] The second sentence of Article 6.d.i makes clear that if the credit is available by negotiation then it is the presentation to the nominated bank which must take place by the expiry date and not the presentation following negotiation by the nominated bank to the correspondent bank or issuing bank as it may be.

1 This includes documents which are presented to 'repair discrepancies' as is confirmed by Case 276 in *More Case Studies on Documentary Credits*, ICC No 489.
2 See para **5.32** below.

5.30 The issuing bank is entitled to refuse to take up documents from a confirming or negotiating bank if the documents were presented to that bank out of time. If, as is likely to happen in practice, the issuing bank does not discover this until after it has paid, then it can recover the payment as money paid under a mistake of fact or as damages for breach of an implied representation by the correspondent. Mance J dealt with this point in *Bayerische Vereinsbank Aktiengsellschaft v National Bank of Pakistan*:[1]

> 'The instructions given by an issuing to a confirming bank are, however, limited to taking up documents presented in time under the credit. An issuing bank which was aware that the documents had been presented late could refuse to reimburse a confirming bank which had paid regardless of the late presentation. It appears to me that an issuing bank which reimbursed the confirming bank in ignorance of the late presentation, and later learned of it, could recover the moneys paid on the ground of mistake of fact. Generally speaking, a confirming bank gives to an issuing bank no warranty as to the genuineness or accuracy of documents. However, the time of presentation stands on a different footing. It is a matter within the direct scope of the instructions given to the confirming bank and which it is the duty of that bank to check. If it fails to do so, it must be answerable to the issuing bank. By asking the issuing bank to take up the documents in circumstances where the issuing bank normally has no means of knowing the precise date of presentation, it seems to me that a confirmation bank represents or states implicitly that the presentation was in time.'

1 [1997] 1 Lloyd's Rep 59 at 64; see also *Standard Chartered Bank v Pakistan National Shipping Corpn (No 2)* [2000] 1 Lloyd's Rep 218.

Time from date of issuance of transport documents

5.31 Under a CIF contract it is the duty of the seller to make every reasonable effort to send the documents forward as soon as possible after he has despatched the goods to the buyer.[1] This may have been a source of the practice of banks in connection with letters of credit to reject bills of lading which were 'stale'. But that expression was not normally used to mean that the bills had not been presented as soon as they might have been: it usually meant that they had not been presented in time for the applicant for the credit to deal with the goods on the arrival of the ship, whereby he might have been put to extra expense, for example, by way of storage charges. The practice was unsatisfactory in that certainty as to what was stale and what was not might often be impossible. Article 14.c avoids the difficulty. It provides:

> '**Article 14: Standard for Examination of Documents**
> c.   A presentation including one or more original transport documents subject to articles 19, 20, 21, 22, 23, 24 or 25 must be made by or on behalf of the beneficiary not later than 21 calendar days after the date of shipment as described in these rules, but in any event not later than the expiry date of the credit.'

Article 31.b provides that if the presentation consists of more than one set of transport documents, the latest date of shipment as evidenced on any of the sets of transport documents will be regarded as the date of shipment. Shipment dates are otherwise to be determined in accordance with the provisions of the Articles relating to the different types of transport document, considered in Part C of Chapter 8. The time limit applies to the presentation of transport documents by or on behalf of the beneficiary, so there can be no question of an issuing bank declining documents presented to it by the nominated bank, which were duly presented to the nominated bank by the beneficiary by the required date. Article 14.c applies only to original transport documents, so it does not apply where a standby credit is payable against written notification of non-payment for goods shipped, accompanied by a copy invoice and a copy bill of lading.[2]

1 See *Sanders Bros v Maclean & Co* (1883) 11 QBD 327 and Sassoon *CIF and FOB Contracts* (4th edn) para 242 and the cases there cited.
2 *Opinions* (1987–1988) ICC No 469, Ref 168.

Extension of time when bank closed

5.32   Article 29 extends the time for presentation of documents to the next following business day on which the bank is open where the last day (either the expiry date or the last day for presentation of transport documents, whichever is first) falls on a day on which the bank is closed.

> '**Article 29: Extension of Expiry Date or Last Day for Presentation**
> a.   If the expiry date of a credit or the last day for presentation falls on a day when the bank to which presentation is to be made is closed for reasons other than those referred to in article 36, the expiry date or the last day for presentation, as the case may be, will be extended to the first following banking day.
> b.   If presentation is made on the first following banking day, a nominated bank must provide the issuing bank or confirming bank with a statement on its covering schedule that the presentation was made within the time limits extended in accordance with sub-article 29(a).
> c.   The latest date for shipment will not be extended as a result of sub-article 29(a).'

5.33   The reasons referred to in Article 36 are 'Acts of God, riots, civil commotions, insurrections, wars, acts of terrorism, or by any strikes or lockouts or any other causes beyond its control'. The reason for these to be excluded may be that they are likely to be long-lasting as opposed to the effect of a weekend or public holiday, and it may be undesirable to have credits extended for long and uncertain periods.

Compliance with Article 29.b is not a condition precedent to a confirming bank's right to reimbursement from an issuing bank; failure to provide a statement may, however, give the issuing bank a right to damages in the unlikely event that it suffers any.[1]

1 *Bayerische Vereinsbank Aktiengesellschaft v National Bank of Pakistan* [1997] 1 Lloyd's Rep 59 at 65 (a decision on the UCP 500 Article 44.c, the predecessor to UCP 600 Article 29.b).

Shipment period

5.34   It is likely that the underlying contract of sale will contain a provision as to when shipment should be made. This should be repeated in the credit so that transport documents bearing inappropriate dates will be rejected. An obvious and common example is where the bill of lading shows shipment after the latest date provided in the credit. The UCP contains various provisions for ascertaining the date of shipment under different transport documents:

(a) *Multimodal or combined transport document.* The date of issuance of the transport document will be deemed to be the date of dispatch, taking in charge or shipped on board, and the date of shipment. However, if the transport document indicates, by stamp or notation, a date of dispatch, taking in charge or shipped on board, this date will be deemed to be the date of shipment. (Article 19.a.ii)

(b) *Bill of lading, non-negotiable sea waybill or charter party bill of lading.* The date of issuance of the document will be deemed to be the date of shipment unless it contains an on board notation indicating the date of shipment, in which case the date stated in the on board notation will be deemed to be the date of shipment. If the document contains the indication 'intended vessel' or similar qualification in relation to the name of the vessel, an on board notation indicating the date of shipment and the name of the actual vessel is required. (Articles 20.a.ii, 21.a.ii, 22.a.ii)

(c) *Air transport document.* The date of issuance will be deemed to be the date of shipment unless the document contains a specific notation of the actual date of shipment, in which case the date stated in the notation will be deemed to be the date of shipment. (Article 23.a.iii)

(d) *Road, rail or inland waterway transport document.* Unless the document contains a dated reception stamp, an indication of the date of receipt or a date of shipment, the date of issuance of the transport document will be deemed to be the date of shipment. (Article 24.a.ii).

(e) Courier receipt, post receipt or certificate of posting. The date of pick-up or receipt must be stated and will be deemed to be the date of shipment. (Article 25.a.ii).

Article 3 is also relevant as to the meaning of 'shipment'. It provides:

> 'Article 3: Interpretations
>
> Unless required to be used in a document, words such as 'prompt', 'immediately' or 'as soon as possible' will be disregarded.
>
> The expression 'on or about' or similar will be interpreted as a stipulation that an event is to occur during a period of five calendar days before until five calendar days after the specified date, both start and end dates included.
>
> The words 'to', 'until', 'till', 'from' and 'between' when used to determine a period of shipment include the date or dates mentioned, and the words 'before' and 'after' exclude the date mentioned.'

5.35   Transport documents may indirectly show late shipment, in which case they will be discrepant. For example, if the credit requires presentation of a 21-day notice of readiness for shipment, a notice dated less than 21 days before the latest date for shipment is discrepant: *Credit Agricole Indosuez v Generale Bank.*[1] It has already been noted that no extension of shipping date is obtainable under Article 29, and that, where a credit contains no latest date for shipment, transport documents indicating a date of issue after the expiry date contained in the credit will be rejected even though an extension under the Article is otherwise available.

1 [2000] 1 Lloyd's Rep 123.

Banking hours

5.36   Article 33 provides:

> 'Article 33: Hours of Presentation
>
> A bank has no obligation to accept a presentation outside of its banking hours.'

This leaves it free to a beneficiary in difficulties to make his own arrangements with a bank to accept documents out of hours, if he can.

Where no time for presentation is stipulated

5.37   Very occasionally, and contrary to Article 6.a, there is no statement of the time in which the documents must be presented. It is inconceivable that the parties should intend that the credit should remain open for an unlimited period. So it is to be implied that presentation must take place within a reasonable time of the opening of the credit. There is no English authority supporting this implication, although it is clear as a matter of principle. What such time is will be determined by all the circumstances of the case, in particular the nature of the transaction. They will include the actual circumstances as they arise after the opening of the credit, and not caused or contributed to by the beneficiary.[1] If a bank becomes concerned that the credit with no express time limit remains open, it is open to it to serve a notice on the beneficiary giving the beneficiary a final further period, which must be a reasonable one, in which to present documents, stating that the bank will thereafter treat the credit as expired.[2] Reference may here be made to credits which have what is known as the 'evergreen clause'. This is usually to be found in American performance-related standby credits. The credit has an expiry date but is automatically reinstated unless the issuing bank gives notice that it is to expire. They are also used in standby credits provided by underwriting members of Lloyd's as security for their liabilities.[3]

1 See *Hick v Raymond and Reid* [1893] AC 22 at 29.
2 See *British and Commonwealth Holdings plc v Quadrex Holdings Inc* [1989] QB 842.
3 See *Royal Bank of Canada v Darlington* (1995) 54 ACWS (3d) 738.

Instalments

5.38   A credit may provide for drawings or shipments by instalments within given periods. If it does so, Article 32 applies. It states:

> '**Article 32: Instalment Drawings or Shipments**
> If a drawing or shipment by instalments within given periods is stipulated in the credit and any instalment is not drawn or shipped within the period allowed for that instalment, the credit ceases to be available for that and any subsequent instalment.'

5.39   So the failure to ship or present documents in time will lose the benefit of the credit for subsequent instalments. The position will be the same where documents are presented in time but fail to comply with the credit. For the presentation of non-complying documents is the equivalent of no presentation. The Article may provide a trap where a standby credit is intended to act as a guarantee of more than one payment or obligation. If it is unnecessary to call it on the first occasion, the Article will prevent any further calls thereby defeating the object of the standby credit. Where a standby credit is of this nature, the Article should be excluded from the Credit.[1]

1 See further para **12.30** below.

Partial drawings

5.40   The underlying contract may provide for shipment to be made in instalments, in which case this will be reflected in the credit. The seller should then present documents separately in relation to each instalment. The effect of Article 32 has been already described.[1] It is common also for credits expressly to permit the seller to make partial shipments. He may then present separately documents in respect of each shipment. If the credit is silent, partial drawings and shipments are allowed by Article 31.a, which provides:

> 'Article 31: Partial Drawings or Shipments.
> a.   Partial drawings or shipments are allowed.[2]'

1 See para 5.38.
2 Article 31.a is considered at para 8.130.

D   EXAMINATION AND ACCEPTANCE OR REFUSAL OF DOCUMENTS

Outline

5.41   When documents are presented to a bank under a credit, the bank will, depending upon its role and responsibility in the credit operation, examine them to see whether they comply with the stipulations of the credit. The first bank to do so will commonly not be the issuing bank but a nominated bank, which may be the bank which advised the credit to the beneficiary and may also have confirmed it. If it is satisfied that they conform, it will honour or negotiate. The issuing bank in its turn will then examine the documents. If the documents are discrepant, the applicant may be approached for a waiver of the discrepancies so that the documents can be accepted.[1] Absent a waiver, it is the duty of the bank to refuse the documents and give an appropriate notice in respect of the disposal of the documents. General requirements as to the examination of documents and requirements as to specific documents are considered in Chapter 8 so that the whole subject matter of documents is taken together. This section considers the procedural steps which banks should follow towards the beneficiary, in particular the course to be followed in rejecting documents.

1 As to this practice, see paras 5.53 et seq. Note that Article 16.b refers only to the issuing bank and to its right to approach the applicant.

5.42   The procedure for examination of documents is set out in Article 14 and the procedure for waiver and refusal in Article 16. The relevant parts of those Articles are set out below; as discussed, there are some important differences from their predecessors in UCP 500. Compliance with Article 16 is important because of Article 16.f, which provides:

> 'Article 16: Discrepant Documents, Waiver and Notice
> f.   If an issuing bank or a confirming bank fails to act in accordance with Article 16 then it is precluded from claiming that the documents do not constitute a complying presentation.'

5.43   A bank which fails to act in accordance with Article 16, for example by failing to give a notice of refusal within the prescribed time or in the prescribed form, will be obliged to honour. However, if the documents were in fact discrepant, it will not be entitled to reimbursement, either by the applicant if it is the issuing bank or by the issuing bank if it is a nominated bank which honours or negotiates. So consequences which are very serious for a bank can follow from even a minor non-compliance.

5.44   Article 16.f applies only to an issuing or confirming bank. But in considering the application of Articles 14 and 16 it must be remembered that, in English law at least, a nominated bank which is given the duty under the credit of checking and accepting the documents, and commonly also the function of paying, does so as the agent of the issuing bank.[1] Where the nominated bank also confirms the credit it will act in a dual capacity in performing those functions, namely, so far as the issuing bank is concerned it acts as that bank's agent; and with regard to its own obligations to the seller as the confirming banker it acts as principal. So when a nominated bank comes to examine the documents presented to it, as it is the agent of the issuing bank it must comply with Articles 14 and 16 to secure compliance by the issuing bank with those Articles, as well as its own compliance. If it fails to do so, the effect may be to bar the issuing bank from contending against the beneficiary that the documents do not comply.

This will not matter to the issuing bank if the beneficiary has been paid. For in that situation the outcome will be that the issuing bank will refuse to pay the nominated bank (or, if the nominated bank has been reimbursed prior to the issuing bank's receipt and checking of the documents, it will be obliged to repay the issuing bank). Where it will matter is if, under the terms of the credit, the beneficiary has not been paid following presentation of documents (either because payment has been refused or is deferred under the terms of the credit) and is looking to the issuing bank for payment. Then non-compliance with Articles 14 and 16 by the nominated bank would bar the issuing bank from alleging that the documents were not in order. Should the buyer refuse to waive the discrepancy, the issuing bank could recover its ultimate loss from the advising bank as damages for breach by the advising bank of its duty as the issuing bank's agent.[2]

---

1 See para **6.6** below. Cited, *Bank of Baroda v Vysya Bank* [1994] 2 Lloyd's Rep 87 at 91.1.
2 Reference should also be made to the argument arising from Article 37.a that all acts of the correspondent bank are at the risk of the applicant for the credit, which is considered at para **4.22** above. The matters considered here are a further reason for rejecting that argument.

Examination of documents

5.45   Article 14.a provides:

'**Article 14: Standard for Examination of Documents**
a.   A nominated bank acting on its nomination, a confirming bank, if any, and the issuing bank must examine a presentation to determine on the

> basis of the documents alone, whether or not the documents appear on their face to constitute a complying presentation.'

The documents must appear 'on their face' to constitute a complying presentation. As is provided by Article 5, 'Banks deal with documents and not with goods, services or performance to which the documents may relate.' The bank is not required and not entitled to take account of any information apart from the documents themselves. In particular it may not take account of information relating to the quality of the goods not shown by the documents. This principle, sometimes referred to as the principle of autonomy, has been discussed in **Chapter 1**.[1] The bank's duty in respect of the examination of documents is discussed in more detail in **Chapter 8**.[2]

1 See paras **1.34** et seq.
2 See paras **8.2** et seq.

Time for examination: UCP 600

5.46   In respect of time for examination, Article 14.b provides:

> 'Article 14: Standard for Examination of Documents
> b.   A nominated bank acting on its nomination, a confirming bank, if any, and the issuing bank shall each have a maximum of five banking days following the day of presentation to determine if a presentation is complying. This period is not curtailed or otherwise affected by the occurrence on or after the date of presentation of any expiry date or last day for presentation.'

5.47   In context, the 'day of presentation' must be taken as referring to the day of presentation to the bank carrying out the examination. Where documents are presented by the beneficiary to a nominated or confirming bank, the documents will be examined first by that bank and then, if not refused, by the issuing bank. Although not expressly stated in Article 14.b, it seems clear that a separate period of five banking days applies to the examination by each bank.

5.48   Time for examination is expressly not curtailed or affected by the occurrence on or after the date of presentation of any expiry date under the credit or the last day for presentation. A beneficiary who makes a presentation less than five banking days before expiry has therefore no right to require an expedited examination so as to give himself the opportunity to make a further presentation if his first attempt is refused.

Time for examination: UCP 500

5.49   The introduction of a fixed period of five banking days for examining the presentation and giving notice of refusal is one of the more important changes in UCP 600. Under UCP 500, the bank was given a 'reasonable time not to exceed seven banking days' to examine the documents and decide whether to take them up or refuse them. UCP 500 Article 13 provided:

'[UCP500] **Article 13 Standard for examination of documents**
b   The Issuing Bank, the Confirming Bank, if any, or a Nominated Bank acting on their behalf, shall each have a reasonable time, not to exceed seven banking days following the day of receipt of the documents, to examine the documents and determine whether to take up or refuse the documents and to inform the party from which it received the documents accordingly.'

It must be emphasised that Article 13.b did not allow seven banking days: it allowed a reasonable time up to seven banking days. Moreover, the duty to (a) examine the documents and (b) determine whether to take up or refuse them were regarded as separate obligations and if the bank reached its decision on (a) unusually rapidly it did not excuse a delay in notification.[1] The determination in individual cases of whether a bank had acted within a 'reasonable time' or 'without delay' gave rise to considerable uncertainty and much litigation. The introduction of a fixed period is therefore a welcome development. Since, however, there may continue to be disputes under existing credits subject to UCP 500, a summary of the position under UCP 500 is set out below.

1 *Seaconsar Far East Ltd v Bank Markazi Jomhouri Islami Iran* [1999] 1 Lloyd's Rep 36 at 41, a decision on UCP 400 Article 16.c of the 1983 Revision, the predecessor of UCP 500 Article 13.b.

5.50   Where a contract provides that something is to be done within a reasonable time, in English law this means such time as is reasonable in the circumstances of the particular case. In *Hick v Raymond and Reid*[1] Lord Herschell stated[2] '... there is of course no such thing as a reasonable time in the abstract. It must always depend upon circumstances ... the only sound principle is that "reasonable time" should depend on the circumstances which actually exist'. Those which actually exist as to be contrasted with those that ordinarily exist. But those actually existing are to be excluded in so far as they have been caused or contributed to by the party having the duty to perform within the time. In the same case Lord Watson stated[3] '... the condition of reasonable time has been frequently interpreted; and has invariably been held to mean that the party upon whom it is incumbent duly fulfils his obligation, notwithstanding protracted delay, so long as such delay is attributable to causes beyond his control, and he has neither acted negligently nor unreasonably'. Matters which are obviously to be taken into account will include the numbers of documents to be examined and their complexity, language, and the problems posed in considering any possible discrepancies. It may also be relevant to consider the amount involved and any urgency, for example, caused by the period of time between the tender of the documents to the bank and the arrival of the vessel carrying the goods. A large and experienced bank operating in one of the world's financial centres may be expected to act more quickly than a small bank in an out of the way place.[4] It would be relevant that a bank's checking staff had been severely reduced by an epidemic or that the bank had a sudden and unexpected flood of credit work.

1 [1893] AC 22.
2 [1893] AC 22 at 29.
3 [1893] AC 22 at 32.
4 See *Bankers Trust Co v State Bank of India* [1991] 2 Lloyd's Rep 443 at 455.1 per Farquharson LJ.

5.51   In *Bankers Trust Co v State Bank of India*[1] evidence was given of the practice of the United Kingdom clearing banks to set a three-day time limit, which in general permitted two days for checking and one for taking instructions on any discrepancies found. In that case the bank had checked some 900 pages of documents in three days, but it fell down over the time wrongly allowed to its applicant to check them again.[2] In *Hing Yip Hing Fat Co Ltd v Daiwa Bank*[3] three banking days following receipt of documents was found reasonable to check 19 pages of documents against a four-page credit. Kaplan J referred to the smaller size of the Daiwa Bank, to the fact that checkers in Hong Kong did not have English as their mother tongue and to the business of the particular month. In *Ozalid Group (Export) Ltd v African Continental Bank Ltd*[4] it was common ground that five days should be sufficient. In *Seaconsar Far East Ltd v Bank Markazi*[5] it was conceded that the bank was entitled to five working days. A bank which goes about its task conscientiously should have nothing to fear provided, of course, that exceptional circumstances do not take it out of the seven-day limit,[6] and it may properly be hoped that the courts would not give much weight to criticisms made with hindsight about delays of an hour or two here and there. The *Bankers Trust and Hing Yip* cases, and also the more recent decision of the Hong Court of Appeal in *NV Koninklijke Sphinx Gustavsberg v Cooperatieve Centrale-Raiffeisen-Boerenleenbank*[7] suggest that indeed they will not. The court would have in mind that the success of such an argument will mean that a beneficiary is paid for documents which do not comply with the credit, and the bank may find itself carrying a loss which is quite out of proportion to the fault on its part.

1 [1991] 2 Lloyd's Rep 443.
2 See para 5.52 below.
3 [1991] 2 HKLR 35.
4 [1979] 2 Lloyd's Rep 231.
5 [1993] 1 Lloyd's Rep 236 at 241.2. Cf [1994] 1 AC 438 at 446.
6 In some exceptional circumstances a bank may be able to rely on Article 17, Force Majeure: see para **4.21** above.
7 [2005] 4 HKC 373.

5.52   Under UCP 500, where the issuing bank had to determine whether to refuse the documents within a reasonable time, it was very unwise for the bank to permit the applicant itself to examine the documents for discrepancies. The fact that Bankers Trust had permitted its client to double-check its examination of the documents (which took another three days) was fatal to its claim.[1] In the Court of Appeal it was stated, 'In particular we are agreed that on no view should a bank be allowed time to enable the buyers to examine the documents for the purpose of discovering further discrepancies.'[2] In *Bayerische Vereinsbank Aktiengesellschaft v National Bank of Pakistan*,[3] where the bank acted as a mere 'postbox' for communicating the applicant's decision, Mance J stated:[4]

> 'What is clear, however, is that an issuing bank which (i) hands over to its customer responsibility for determining whether documents are discrepant (as distinct from making up its own mind in the first instance and approaching the customer, if at all, simply to ask whether it is prepared to waive discrepancies identified by the bank), and then (ii) adopts and communicates whatever decision its customer reaches is likely to take in the process more than the "reasonable time" allowed by art. 13(b) and to have failed to act "without delay" as required by art. 14(d) ...'

Under UCP 600, where the issuing bank has a fixed period of five banking days, there is perhaps less risk in involving the applicant, but it cannot be regarded as good practice; it is the job of the bank alone to examine the documents.

1 *Bankers Trust Co v State Bank of India* [1991] 2 Lloyd's Rep 443; applied in *Indian Bank v Union Bank of Switzerland* [1994] 2 SLR 121.
2 [1991] 2 Lloyd's Re 443 at 452.1 per Lloyd LJ. Farquharson LJ said, at 455.1, that it might on rare occasions be permissible for the bank to permit the applicant to examine the documents for the purpose of determining its correct course in the light of discrepancies already found, but only where the discrepancies were of such a nature to require this for the applicant to assess their significance.
3 [1997] 1 Lloyd's Rep 59.
4 [1997] 1 Lloyd's Rep 59 at 69.
5 *Bankers Trust Co v State Bank of India* [1991] 2 Lloyd's Rep 443 at 455.1 per Farquharson LJ.

Refusal or waiver

5.53   Article 16 provides:

> '**Article 16: Discrepant Documents, Waiver and Notice**
> a.   When a nominated bank acting on its nomination, a confirming bank, if any, or the issuing bank determines that a presentation does not comply, it may refuse to honour or negotiate.
> b.   When an issuing bank determines that a presentation does not comply, it may in its sole judgement approach the applicant for a waiver of the discrepancies. This does not, however, extend the period mentioned in sub-article 14 (b).'

5.54   When a bank determines that a presentation does not comply, it has the right to refuse to honour. The issuing bank may also, in its sole judgment, approach the applicant, who is usually its customer, for a waiver of the discrepancies. In many cases the discrepancies are of no commercial significance (they may be trivial) and the applicant still wishes to take up the documents and thereby acquire the goods; in that case, he will be prepared to waive any discrepancies. This practice is very common and has the result that a large number of credit transactions go through which would otherwise fail.[1] The purpose of the approach must be limited to waiver and should not be used to enable a joint decision to be made as to possible discrepancies. Of course, the applicant may have commercial reasons for refusing a waiver, for example if he no longer requires the goods, if he could purchase them elsewhere at a better price, or if the goods have been lost after shipment when at his risk.

1 It has been suggested that in England and America some 60–70% of the documents presented fail to comply on first presentation, and a witness in *Bankers Trust Co v State Bank of India* [1991] 2 Lloyd's Rep 443 stated that in 90% of the cases where the applicant's instructions were sought the instructions were to accept the documents.

5.55 In a documentary sale, the buyer may in practice be able to take possession of the goods shipped even though the documents are discrepant and are refused by the bank. If so, then he will be deemed to have waived any discrepancies in the documents for the purpose of the sale contract but (in another illustration of the autonomy principle) it does not follow that there is also waiver for the purpose of the bank's obligations under the credit. In *Uzinterimpex JSC v Standard Bank plc*,[1] the Court of Appeal rejected the beneficiary's argument that a bank was bound to pay under a demand guarantee because the buyer had persuaded the carrier, in breach of duty, to release the goods to it. Moore-Bick LJ said:[2]

> 'In the case of a documentary sale it is necessary, as that case shows, to distinguish between the seller's right to obtain payment from the bank under the letter of credit and his right to obtain payment from the buyer where for some reason the mechanism provided by the letter of credit fails. As the decision in *Saffron v Société Minière Cafrika* (1958) 100 CLR 231 demonstrates, acceptance of the goods by the buyer may render him liable for the price and may to that extent involve a waiver on his part of discrepancies in the documents that would otherwise have entitled him to reject them, but it is not sufficient to render the bank liable under the letter of credit to pay the seller against documents that do not conform to its requirements.'

1 [2008] 2 Lloyd's Rep 456.
2 At para 29.

5.56 It is to be noted that Article 16.b gives discretion to the issuing bank: 'it may in its sole judgement approach the Applicant'. It has no obligation to do so. No doubt a bank which has an ongoing business relationship with the applicant would ordinarily consult its customer before rejecting the documents, and hence the goods. However, if the applicant is in financial difficulties, the bank is unsecured and there is a risk that the bank will not be reimbursed if it pays the credit, then the bank will be glad of the opportunity to refuse the presentation and will not wish to approach the applicant for a waiver.

5.57   The UCP deals only with the issuing bank's right to seek a waiver. Where documents are not initially presented to the issuing bank but to a nominated or confirming bank, it will be that bank which would have to decide whether to refuse the documents if discrepancies are found. There is no reason in principle why a nominated or confirming bank should not seek a waiver permitting it to pay against the discrepant documents. However, that presents practical difficulties. The nominated bank would need to seek a waiver from the issuing bank, which would in turn need to seek a waiver from the applicant, a process which would be time-consuming and might not be possible within the five banking days permitted for the nominated bank's examination of the documents. Moreover, since the applicant is usually the customer of the issuing bank rather than the nominated or confirming bank, the latter will not usually have any particular interest in whether the underlying transactions succeeds or fails. It is better practice for the nominated bank to promptly refuse the presentation, so that the beneficiary may have an opportunity to put them right within the period of the credit or else send them for collection (see section F below).

5.58   Article 16.b provides that an approach to the applicant for a waiver does not extend the period for examination of the documents, which remains five banking days. UCP 500 Article 14.c similarly provided that an approach did not extend the maximum time period of seven days

Notification of refusal

5.59   Article 16.c provides that when a nominated bank acting on its nomination, a confirming bank (if any) or an issuing bank decides to refuse to honour or negotiate, it must give a single notice to that effect to the presenter.

'Article 16: Discrepant Documents, Waiver and Notice
c.   When a nominated bank acting on its nomination, a confirming bank, if any, or the issuing bank decides to refuse to honour or negotiate, it must give a single notice to that effect to the presenter.

The notice must state:
i.   that the bank is refusing to honour or negotiate; and
ii.   each discrepancy in respect of which the bank refuses to honour or negotiate; and
iii.
    a)   that the bank is holding the documents pending further instructions from the presenter; or
    b)   that the issuing bank is holding the documents until it receives a waiver from the applicant and agrees to accept it, or receives further instructions from the presenter prior to agreeing to accept a waiver; or

> c) that the bank is returning the documents; or
> d) that the bank is acting in accordance with instructions previously received from the presenter.
>
> d. The notice required in sub-article 16 (c) must be given by telecommunication or, if that is not possible, by other expeditious means no later than the close of the fifth banking day following the day of presentation.'

Time for notice

5.60   Does Article 16.d mean that notice must be sent by the close of the fifth banking day, or that it must arrive with the other party before then? There should be no difference where telecommunication is used. The question may be material where telecommunication is not used and there is a delay between the sending and the receipt of the notice. It may well be said that A has not given notice to B until B has received the notice. Nonetheless it is suggested that in the context of Article 16 it is sufficient that the bank refusing the documents should complete the acts which it has itself to carry out to give notice not later than the close of the fifth banking day following the receipt of the documents.

5.61   Under UCP 500, Article 14.d required the bank to give notice of refusal 'without delay'[1] after its decision to refuse the documents.

> 'The words "without delay" mean what they say, and nothing is to be gained by paraphrasing them. Where a decision to reject documents is made at or about the close of business on a Friday, as may have happened in this case, we would expect the obligation to give notice without delay to require that it be given on the Monday, which was the next banking day ... It may well be in other cases the obligation requires notice to be given on the same day as the decision is taken.'[2]

But it is for the party alleging delay, normally the beneficiary, to prove it.[3] The requirement to give notice of the decision without delay is separate from and additional to the obligation to examine the documents within a reasonable time. Thus, if the bank reaches a decision unusually rapidly, it does not excuse any delay in notifying the beneficiary.[3]

1 This was held to mean 'without unreasonable delay' in *Rafsanjan Pistachio Producers Co-operative v Bank Leumi (UK) plc* [1992] 1 Lloyd's Rep 513 at 531.2: *Seaconsar Far East Ltd v Bank Markazi Jomhouri Islami Iran* [1999] 1 Lloyd's Rep 36 at 42 (a decision on UCP 400 Article 16.c).
2 *Seaconsar* at p42.
3 *Seaconsar* at p42.

Form of notice

5.62   Article 16.d requires the use of 'telecommunication or, if that is not possible, by other expeditious means'. 'Telecommunication' includes telephone, telex, fax and email. The ICC Commentary on UCP 400 refers to 'the practice of sometimes advising refusal by a properly authenticated telephone call'. Where authentication is a problem it can be ensured by a follow-up communication. In *Rafsanjan Pistachio Producers Co-operative v Bank Leumi (UK) plc*[1] Hirst J stated 'Moreover in my judgment it would be most undesirable to construe Article 16(d) [now as amended, 14.d] in a manner which obliged a bank to use a particular form of telecommunication. A telephone call might sometimes be the best mode. But I think that a bank might justifiably consider that a rejection message, which is an extremely important step ... should normally be sent in writing by telex; this will also ensure that the message is timed and that the answer-back records receipt, and will thus avoid any subsequent dispute ...' In *Hing Yip Hing Fat Co Ltd v Daiwa Bank*[2] evidence was given that in Hong Kong fax and telex were not used to give notice of refusal because of problems with authentication and verification: advice was sent by mail, courier or messenger, which was found satisfactory given the size of Hong Kong and the propinquity of its banks. Kaplan J held that, if communication by phone, fax or telex was possible, it ought to be used so the beneficiary could know his position as soon as possible, in particular so he could, if he was able, correct the discrepancies before the credit's expiry or consider offering an indemnity. Had this been the only point in the case the bank would have lost by reason of its delay in giving notice. The case emphasises the need for banks to follow the requirements of Article 16 precisely. If a senior representative of the beneficiary is present at the branch of the issuing bank, then the decision can be communicated orally to him, viva voce, and there is no requirement for further notice.[3] The rationale for this is not that an oral communication is a form of telecommunication, which it clearly is not, but because a term permitting such notification can be implied into the documentary credit contract.[4]

1 [1992] 1 Lloyd's Rep 513 at 531.
2 [1991] 2 HKLR 35.
3 *Seaconsar Far East Ltd v Bank Markazi Jomhouri Islami Iran* [1999] 1 Lloyd's Rep 36; discussed by Bennett [1999] LMCLQ 507 at 515–516. Given the importance of the contents of the notice, namely that the bank is prohibited from relying on discrepancies not contained in the notice, it is highly desirable for evidential purposes that there should be a written record. See para **5.65** below.
4 [1999] 1 Lloyd's Rep 36 at 39.

Single notice

5.63   A single notice of refusal must be given, which must cover each of the matters in Article 16.c. Once the bank has given notice that it is refusing to honour or negotiate, then subsequent notices can and should be ignored; this was also the position under UCP 500 even though there was there no express requirement for a 'single notice'.[1]

1 More Queries and Responses on UCP 500, ICC No 596, Ref 27.

5.64 Difficulties may arise in identifying what precisely constitutes the relevant notice. In *Total Energy Asia Ltd v Standard Chartered Bank (Hong Kong) Ltd*,[1] a UCP 500 case, a bank sent to the beneficiary a fax listing discrepancies in the documents. The fax was not in itself a notice of refusal because it did not state that the documents were refused and held at the beneficiary's disposal. However, Stone J held that the bank was entitled to rely on a combination of the fax and a subsequent telephone call as sufficient to constitute a valid notice. Whilst it might be possible for a communication to incorporate by reference the terms of an earlier document (which is what Stone J appeared to have in mind at paragraph 90 of his judgment), it is suggested that very clear words of incorporation would be required. The express requirement in UCP 600 for a 'single notice' makes it even clearer that the matters in Article 16.c should generally be covered in a single communication.

1 [2006] HKCU 2134.

All discrepancies

5.65 Article 16.c.ii provides that the notice must state each discrepancy in respect of which the bank refuses to honour or negotiate. Whilst it does not expressly provide that the bank cannot subsequently rely on a discrepancy not included in its notice (which it might wish to do if it discovered that the original discrepancies were not valid ones), that is clearly the intention of the article.[1] In *Hing Yip Hing Fat Co Ltd v Daiwa Bank*[2] Kaplan J held that a bank was bound by the discrepancies in its notice of refusal and could not later add to them. There are good practical reasons for constructing Article 16 in this way. One object of a speedy notification with grounds of refusal is to enable the beneficiary to rectify the discrepancies within the time limit of the credit: it would be unfair if he were then to be faced with further discrepancies.

1 Accepted as the position in relation to UCP 500 Article 14.d in *Glencore International AG v Bank of China* [1996] 1 Lloyd's Rep 135 at 149.
2 [1991] 2 HKLR 35.

5.66 Is presentation after the expiry of the credit a discrepancy which must be stated in the notice? In *Bayerische Vereinsbank Aktiengesellschaft v National Bank of Pakistan*[1] Mance J gave a provisional view that it was not: 'Articles 13 and 14 [of UCP 500] deal with discrepancies on the face of documents. The precise date of presentation will not, in the usual course, appear upon or upon examination from the face of the documents. Presentation and the right to refuse documents presented late under the credit are matters dealt with separately in UCP 500: cf. arts. 42–45 [now UCP 600 Article 29]. Between the beneficiary and the bank to which the beneficiary presents documents, there is thus much to say for the view that arts. 13 and 14 have no application.'

1 [1997] 1 Lloyd's Rep 59 at 67.

5.67 The position in England at common law apart from the UCP is that a bank would be able to rely on discrepancies which it had not included in its notice of refusal unless the beneficiary was able to show that he had relied on a specific representation or promise made to him by the bank that, if the discrepancies listed were corrected, the bank would accept the documents.[1]

1 *Kydon Compania Naviera SA v National Westminster Bank Ltd, The Lena* [1981] 1 Lloyd's Rep 68; also *Skandinaviska Akt v Barclays Bank* (1925) 22 Ll L Rep 523.

Disposal of documents

5.68 The notice must also state how the bank has or will dispose of the documents. There are four options: (a) the bank is holding the documents pending further instructions from the presenter; or (b) it is holding the documents until it receives a waiver from the applicant and agrees to accept it or receives further instructions from the presenter prior to agreeing to accept a waiver; or (c) it is returning the documents; or (d) it is acting in accordance with instructions previously received from the presenter.

5.69 The options referred to at (a) and (c) above require no further comment. An issuing bank will wish to select option (b) where it has sought a waiver from the applicant but wishes to preserve its right to refuse the documents if a waiver is not forthcoming by the close of the fifth banking day. This is an important change from UCP 500, where a conditional notice of this type was invalid. In *Credit Industriel et Commercial v China Merchants Bank*,[1] the issuing bank gave notice stating, '*We refuse the documents according to Art. 14 UCP no. 500. Should the disc. being accepted by the applicant, we shall release the docs to them without further notice to you unless yr instructions to the contrary received prior to our payment. Documents held at yr risk for yr disposal.*' Steel J held that this was a conditional, and hence invalid, notice because it held open the possibility that the documents could be released to the applicant, within some indefinite period, in the event of the applicant accepting the discrepancies, without any further notice. The notice would have been valid under UCP 600.

1 [2002] 2 All ER (Comm) 427.

5.70 A notice which makes the beneficiary's disposal of the documents conditional on any matter other than the acceptance of a waiver is invalid. In the *Bankers Trust* case[1] Bankers Trust's telex refusing the documents concluded 'Documents held at your risk and will be at your disposal after payment to us.' The bank had paid some US $10 million to the State Bank of India against the State Bank's telex that the documents complied with the

117

credit: it wished to hold the documents (which had rightly been found not to comply) as security for repayment. It might be thought that a bank should be entitled to hold rejected documents as security against repayment but the Court of Appeal unanimously held that this was a non-compliance with UCP 400 Article 16.d; it would also be a non-compliance with UCP 600 Article 16.c.iii.

1 [1991] 2 Lloyd's Rep 443.

5.71   The Bankers Trust case can be contrasted with *The Royan*[1] where the telex of refusal stated 'Please consider these documents at your disposal until we receive our principal's instructions concerning the discrepancies mentioned in your schedules.' In the Court of Appeal it was held that the telex complied with Article 16 of UCP 400: 'The effect of that telex ... was that the documents were being held unconditionally at the disposal of the sellers. The reference to 'until we receive our principal's instructions' was no doubt reflecting the hope that the buyers and sellers might come to some agreement ... I cannot read that expression of hope as meaning that the documents were not at the disposal of the sellers.'[2] In the *Bankers Trust* case the narrow but critical difference was pointed to between documents being at the disposal of the sellers until something happens, and their being at their disposal when (ie after) something happens. The wording in *The Royan* would now be permitted by Article 16.c.iii(b).

1 *Co-operative Centrale v Sumitomo Bank Ltd, The Royan* [1987] 1 Lloyd's Rep 345; on appeal sub nom *Sumitomo Bank Ltd v Co-operative Centrale* [1988] 2 Lloyd's Rep 250.
2 [1988] 2 Lloyd's Rep 250 at 254.1.

5.72   The option to act in accordance with instructions previously received from the presenter in Article 16.c.iii(d) is also new in UCP 600. It covers the possibility that the presenter might have given instructions as to the disposal of the documents at the time of presentation. For example, a beneficiary might instruct the issuing bank that if the documents are refused then they should be sent to the applicant for collection or sent to a broker for sale to an alternative buyer.

5.73   After giving notice pursuant to Article 16.c.iii (a) or (b), the bank may return the documents to the presenter at any time (Article 16.e).

5.74   A credit sometimes provides that one original bill of lading should be sent direct to the buyer or be handed to the captain of the vessel, so the buyer may obtain possession of the goods on the vessel's arrival. If the documents are rejected by the bank as non-conforming, the bank will only be obliged to hold to the presenter's disposal, or to return to him, the documents which it received. They are the documents to which Article 16 relates. If the buyer has taken possession of the goods, he can reject them provided that when he took possession of them he was unaware of the documentary discrepancies and so there is no question of waiver. Alternatively it would seem he can waive the discrepancies and keep the goods: he must then pay for them at the contract price but he is not obliged to do so through the banks involved with the letter of credit provided that machinery has proved inoperative through no fault of his. It is obviously dangerous for a seller to send forward documents of title in this way.

5.75   The bill of lading or other transport documents may be indorsed to the issuing bank. The Banking Commission's opinion is that, if the issuing bank rejects the documents, it is under no obligation to indorse them over to the presenter, even though this may cause difficulties to the presenter in recovering the goods.[1] This might have very harsh consequences; it might be argued on the contrary that a term for re-endorsement could be implied into the issuing bank's contract with the beneficiary.

1 *Opinions* (1995–1996) ICC No 565, Ref 214.

Refusal irreversible

5.76   Once a notice of refusal has been given to a presenter of documents, it can only be withdrawn with the agreement of the presenter. For the documents are then at his disposal and he has the right to them. If the market has risen then he may wish to sell the goods elsewhere and may not be prepared to agree to a withdrawal. If the bank has given a notice in the form of Article 16.c.iii(b) (i.e. that it is holding the documents until it accepts a waiver) then, provided no further instructions have been received from the presenter, it may release the documents to the applicant.

Subsequent presentations

5.77   The fact that a presentation has been made of documents which do not comply with the credit does not prevent the beneficiary presenting fresh sets of documents or documents to replace discrepant documents provided of course that the documents are presented in time. Presentation in time does not simply mean before the expiry of the credit: terms as to date of transport documents and any other terms as to time must be complied with. For this purpose the relevant date must be the date of the presentation of the last document required to complete the set of compliant documents. The process of correcting discrepancies by further presentation is commonplace.[1]

1 For an example taken from a well-known case, see the facts set out in the judgment of Mocatta J in *United City Merchants (Investments) Ltd v Royal Bank of Canada, The American Accord* [1979] 1 Lloyd's Rep 267 at 272.

Waiver by the bank of discrepancies

5.78   It is clear that a bank can waive discrepancies, or become estopped from relying on them, quite apart from the effect of a bank's failure to state them in a notice of refusal given under Article 16. This is made clear by the judgment in *The Lena*,[1] where the elements required, namely a representation by the bank coupled with reliance on it by the beneficiary, are considered. It may arise in two contexts. One is where documents have been delivered to a bank and having examined them the bank represents that the discrepancies which it had referred to are the only ones, or the only ones to which it will take objection, the effect being that, if they are corrected the bank will accept the documents. The other is where it makes a representation as to a discrepancy or possible discrepancy before any documents have been delivered to it. An example of the latter is provided by *Floating Dock Ltd v Hong Kong and Shanghai Banking Corpn*.[2] It was there held that the bank was not able to rely upon non-compliance with one term of the credit because the fact of the certain breach of the term was known to the bank at a time when it reached agreement to amend other terms of the credit so the transaction might go forward. The matter was dealt with on the basis of estoppel.[3] Apart from Article 16.f the position at common law is that failure to reject documents within a reasonable time will amount to an acceptance of them.[4] If, as tentatively suggested by Mance J in *Bayerische Vereinsbank Aktiengesellschaft v National Bank of Pakistan*, late presentation of documents is not a discrepancy of which notice need be given, the issuing bank can still be barred by waiver or ratification from a subsequent objection if it takes up the documents without demur.[5]

1 [1981] 1 Lloyd's Rep 68.
2 [1986] 1 Lloyd's Rep 65.
3 See [1986] 1 Lloyd's Rep 65 at 78.1 and also *Astro Exito Navegacion SA v Chase Manhattan Bank NA, The Messiniaki Tolmi* [1986] 1 Lloyd's Rep 455 at 458, 459 Leggatt J.
4 *Westminster Bank Ltd v Banca Nazionale di Credito* (1928) 31 Ll L Rep 306 at 312.2.
5 [1997] 1 Lloyd's Rep 59 at 67; see para **5.56** above.

Position of the negotiating bank

5.79   A bank which has not confirmed the credit is not obliged to take up and negotiate documents. However, it is suggested that if it chooses to accept documents for examination, then it implicitly agrees to be bound by the credit in accordance with its terms and the UCP and must pay unless it validly rejects the documents within the time prescribed.

Bad faith by the bank

5.80 An exceptional situation arose in *Mannesman Handel AG v Kaunlaren Shipping Corpn*,[1] where Swiss law governed the points at issue. A Swiss bank opened a credit in favour of a German company at the request of a Bermudan company. The bank's position was secured by the assignment of the proceeds of a second credit opened by a Hong Kong bank in favour of an associate company of the Bermudan company. The same goods were intended to be used to perform the contracts underlying each credit. It appears that the overall purpose was to achieve the transfer of pig iron from Russia to China, countries between whom there were difficulties in direct trade. The goods were shipped by the German company. What should have happened was that the documents would have been presented under the credit opened by the Swiss bank and the German company would have been paid. The documents would then have been 'recut' to enable operations of the second credit and presented under it. However, the Bermudan company did not wait for this. It presented documents under the second credit which were accepted. The goods were delivered to the buyers. Meanwhile the German company was pressing for amendments to the first credit which would have shown the Swiss bank that it was unable to present documents conforming to the credit as unamended. In that knowledge and in the knowledge that the Bermuda company had acted dishonestly in connection with the second credit, the Swiss bank claimed and received the proceeds under the second credit as due to it under the assignment. The Bermudan company had become insolvent and the Swiss bank wished to offset the proceeds of the second credit against the debt owed to it by the Bermudan company. Saville J held that in these circumstances, applying Swiss law, the refusal of the Swiss bank to accept and pay for the discrepant documents in due course presented by the German company was contrary to the principle of good faith (les régles de la bonne foi) established by Article 2 of the Swiss Civil Code. So the Swiss bank was not entitled to return the documents and had to pay the German company. Justice requires that the case should have the same outcome under English law: the likely route is by a species of estoppel.

1 [1993] 1 Lloyd's Rep 89. See also *Uzinterimpex JSC v Standard Bank Plc* [2007] 2 Lloyd's Rep 187 at paras 129–132.

E   PAYMENT UNDER RESERVE OR AGAINST INDEMNITY

5.81 It often happens that there is a disagreement between the party presenting documents and the bank receiving them, most often a confirming bank, as to whether the documents comply with the credit. The evidence in the *Banque de l'Indochine* case was that as many as two-thirds of the presentations of documents against confirmed credits in London were thought to deviate from the terms of the credits in some respects; but in the great majority of cases this was overcome by agreement.[1] If there is goodwill between the presenting party and the bank, a solution may be obtained by the bank making payment 'under reserve', or against an indemnity. This will often provide for a satisfactory outcome because the buyer is prepared to accept the documents as tendered. But if he does not, the bank which has paid out will be looking to recover its money. In these circumstances, unless it is clear what the effect of the 'under reserve' arrangement or of the indemnity is, there may be a dispute. There is no provision in the UCP for payment under reserve. If it is simply agreed that the payment shall be 'under reserve', the effect is a matter of construing the term in the circumstances of the particular case. Subject to what is said in the next paragraph no universal answer can be given as to the term's meaning. If there is to be no room for dispute, the intended effect of any 'under reserve' arrangement should be agreed between the parties and recorded in writing. Likewise care must be taken to see that any indemnity agreed to be given is sufficiently and accurately spelt out.

1 *Banque de l'Indochine et de Suez SA v JH Rayner (Mincing Lane) Ltd* [1983] QB 711 at 733F: see para **5.83** below.

5.82   There is no provision in UCP 600 for payment under reserve. It was briefly mentioned in UCP 500 Article 14.f as follows:

[UCP 500] '**Article 14.f:**

If the remitting bank draws the attention of the Issuing Bank and/or Confirming Bank, if any, to any discrepancy(ies) in the document(s) or advises such banks that it has paid, incurred a deferred payment undertaking, accepted Draft(s) or negotiated under reserve or against an indemnity in respect of such discrepancy(ies), the Issuing Bank and/or Confirming Bank, if any, shall not be thereby relieved from any of their obligations under any provision of this Article. Such reserve or indemnity concerns only the relations between the remitting bank and the party towards whom the reserve was made, or from whom, or on whose behalf, the indemnity was obtained.'

In other words any special arrangements bind only the parties to them. Where the remitting bank has accepted documents under such terms, the duty of the issuing bank to examine the documents and to accept or reject them in accordance with the terms of the credit remains unchanged. It is, however, particularly likely that in such situations it will take the instructions of the applicant if it is of the view that there are grounds for rejecting the documents.

5.83   In *Banque de l'Indochine et de Suez SA v J H Rayner (Mincing Lane) Ltd*,[1] a typical payment 'under reserve' situation was considered at first instance and in the Court of Appeal. The facts were that a Djibouti bank opened a credit in favour of the defendant sugar merchants, which was confirmed by the plaintiff bank. Documents were presented and were considered defective by the bank. Following a discussion it was agreed that payment should be made by the bank 'under reserve' owing to specified discrepancies. No consideration was given to the consequences of payment being so made. The Djibouti bank declined the documents as their clients, the buyers, would not agree to accept the documents and so lift the reserve. The plaintiff bank claimed that as the documents had been rejected for the specified discrepancies they were entitled to repayment from the sellers. The sellers argued that the documents conformed to the contract and so they were entitled to retain the money. Parker J found that the sellers were entitled to retain the money unless the documents were bad, which he held that they were. He held that the banking evidence established that there was no uniform practice as to the consequence of a payment being under reserve. He posed two alternatives: did the parties intend that the bank should be entitled to repayment by reason of the rejection of the documents by the Djibouti bank even if the bank were obliged to pay; or did they intend that the bank should only be entitled to repayment if the alleged discrepancies were valid, ie the purpose of the payment being 'under reserve' was solely to prevent the sellers alleging that they had received an unconditional payment. He rejected the former, and held that second meaning accorded with the reality of the situation.[2]

1 [1983] QB 711.
2 [1983] QB 711 at 716.

5.84   The Court of Appeal reached the opposite conclusion, Sir John Donaldson MR holding that the judge had reached a 'lawyer's view' rather than a 'commercial view'. He imputed to the parties an imaginary dialogue as follows:

> 'Merchant: "These documents are sufficient to satisfy the terms of the letter of credit and certainly will be accepted by my buyer. I am entitled to the money and need it."
>
> Bank: "If we thought that the documents satisfied the terms of the letter of credit, we would pay you at once. However, we do not think that they do and we cannot risk paying you and not being paid ourselves. We are not sure that your buyer will authorise payment, but we can of course ask."
>
> Merchant: "But that will take time and meanwhile we shall have a cash flow problem."
>
> Bank: "Well the alternative is for you to sue us and that will also take time."
>
> Merchant: "What about your paying us without prejudice to whether we are entitled to payment and then your seeing what is the reaction of your correspondent bank and our buyer?"
>
> Bank: "That is all right, but if we are told that we should not have paid, how do we get our money back?"
>
> Merchant: "You sue us."
>
> Bank: "Oh no, that would leave us out of our money for a substantial time. Furthermore, it would involve us in facing in two directions. We should not only have to sue you, but also to sue the issuing bank in order to cover the possibility that you may be right. We cannot afford to pay on those terms."
>
> Merchant: "All right. I am quite confident that the issuing bank and my buyer will be content that you should pay, particularly since the documents are in

fact in order. You pay me and if the issuing bank refuses to reimburse you for the same reason that you are unwilling to pay, we will repay you on demand and then sue you. But we do not think that this will happen."

Bank: "We agree. Here is the money 'under reserve'."[1]

Kerr LJ, agreeing, also pointed out that the bank could not have intended to be out of pocket and obliged to sue the seller and the issuing bank to resolve the dispute.[2]

1 [1983] QB 711 at 727, 728.
2 [1983] QB 711 at 733, 734.

5.85   The seller should be watchful. By agreeing to such a payment under reserve he is putting himself into the hands of his buyer. For the buyer can refuse the goods regardless of whether the discrepancies alleged are in fact valid and the seller will have to reimburse the bank, leaving him with the by-now stale documents on his hands and a right to sue the bank to determine the validity of the alleged discrepancies. If the seller refuses to repay the bank contrary to the arrangement between them, the position under English procedure would be that the bank could obtain summary judgment against the seller under CPR Pt 24, leaving the seller's claim against the bank to be determined at a trial in due course. In his judgment in the *Banque de l'Indochine* case Sir John Donaldson MR suggested that the ICC should turn their minds to the meaning of 'payment under reserve' when undertaking the next revision of the Uniform Customs.[1] This was done but without success, because of the difficulty created by the use of the phrase 'under reserve' in other banking contexts.[2] There is no longer any provision for payment under reserve in the UCP.

1 [1983] QB 711 at 727.
2 See UCP 1974/1983 Revisions Compared and Explained, ICC No 411, p 33.

F   PRESENTATION FOR COLLECTION[1, 2]

5.86   Documents which are known not to conform to the credit are sometimes sent to the issuing bank (or, perhaps, to the confirming bank) 'on a collection basis' or 'for collection'. Such phrases are themselves ambiguous, and their meaning must be obtained from the context.[3] The meaning may be that the documents are sent on the basis that they are being presented under the credit with what is in effect a request for the waiver of the discrepancies, such as that they be accepted out of time. In such a case the UCP will apply, and if the documents are accepted all the obligations of the issuing bank and any confirming bank arising under UCP will become effective, including the limits on the time for examination and rejection of the documents by the bank.[4] Or it may be that the documents are being sent on a basis independent of the credit (or, it may be said, outside it), namely for simple collection, the bank probably being made the agent of the party sending them to collect on them from the buyer if the buyer is prepared to take them. In such a case the ICC's Uniform Rules for Collections are likely to apply.[5] It appears that, if the correspondence shows that the presentation is being made under the credit, it will fall into the former category. This was the conclusion reached by Gatehouse J on the facts of the case in *Harlow & Jones Ltd v American Express Bank Ltd*.[6]

1 As to a bank collecting as a beneficiary's agent, see para **6.27** below, and **Chapter 7**.
2 Para **5.86** was cited by the US Court of Appeals (2nd Cir) in *Alaska Textile Co v Chase Manhattan Bank* 982 F 2d 813 (1992) at 818.
3 See *Harlow & Jones Ltd v American Express Bank Ltd* [1990] 2 Lloyd's Rep 343 at 348.1. 'On an approval basis' was held to have the same meaning as 'on a collection basis' in *Alaska Textile* above.
4 See [1990] 2 Lloyd's Rep 343 at 347.2.
5 ICC No 322.
6 The same conclusion was reached, applying *Harlow & Jones*, in *Alaska Textile* (see above) where presentation 'on an approval basis' with a request by the beneficiary for a waiver of discrepancies by the applicant did not displace the Uniform Customs time limits for document examination.

G   BENEFICIARY'S RIGHTS AGAINST A DEFAULTING BANK

Non-payment

5.87   Where a bank wrongly refuses to accept documents under a credit, the seller may sue the bank which has given a payment undertaking claiming the price, provided that the seller remains able to tender the documents to the bank against the bank's payment. Where payment under a credit is to be made through a bill of exchange, the claim will be framed in damages, but will reflect the amount of the bill. It was argued in *Stein v Hambro's Bank of Northern Commerce*[1] that the position was analogous to that where documents were wrongly rejected by a buyer under a CIF contract and the seller is entitled only to damages for loss of his bargain and not to the price because the property has not passed. This argument was rejected, the court stating 'It seems to me that this is clearly a case of a simple contract to pay money upon the fulfilment of conditions which have been fulfilled.'[2] The court gave judgment for the amount of the bill drawn under the credit with interest from the date the bill would have become due. The case went to appeal, but the Court of Appeal did not need to consider this point as it held that the bank was entitled to reject the documents. The seller's right to claim the price does not appear to have been questioned since and is now clearly accepted.[3] It was suggested in *Dexters Ltd v Schenker & Co*[4] that strictly the claim may be for damages for non-payment of money, which would usually be the sum unpaid. This has been held to be the position under Swiss law in an action in England.[5]

The relevance of the point was that the party standing in the position of the buyer might not have suffered damage in the full amount of the price because part had been recovered by the sellers from the carriers who had given up the goods without production of a bill of lading.

1 (1921) 9 Ll L Rep 433 and 507.
2 (1929) 9 Ll L Rep 507.
3 See, inter alia, *British Imex Industries Ltd v Midland Bank Ltd* [1958] 1 QB 542; *United City Merchants (Investments) Ltd v Royal Bank of Canada* [1983] 1 AC 168; *Forestal Mimosa Ltd v Oriental Credit Ltd* [1986] 1 WLR 631 and *Floating Dock Ltd v Hongkong and Shanghai Banking Corp* [1986] 1 Lloyd's Rep 65.
4 (1923) 14 Ll L Rep 586 at 588.
5 *Mannesman Handel AG v Kaunlaren Shipping Corpn* [1993] 1 Lloyd's Rep 89 at 94.1.

5.88   A problem may, however, arise because the goods have been shipped and will arrive in the buyer's country; but the seller retains the documents. Thus in *Belgian Grain and Produce Co Ltd v Cox & Co (France) Ltd*[1] (where the claim against the bank was for the purchase price of a shipment of peas) at the conclusion of the delivery of the Court of Appeal's judgments in favour of the seller the following exchange took place:

> 'Lord Justice Bankes: "What about judgment?"
>
> Mr Claughton Scott: "The amount asked in the writ was £9,495.14s, being the equivalent of 246,888f."
>
> Mr Mackinnon: "What about my peas? I expect they have been sold."
>
> Mr Claughton Scott: I understand they have not been sold. I think they are in the custody of some French authority.
>
> Lord Justice Bankes: "Then it will be judgment for the plaintiffs (appellants) for £9,495.14s in exchange for the documents, with the costs of the appeal and the action. There will be liberty to apply to either party if any trouble arises."'

Had the peas been sold by the plaintiffs and had they been unable to tender the documents, they would not have been able to recover the price but would have had to sue for their loss by way of damages. Where the bank rejects the documents on the ground that they do not conform to the contract, unless the dispute can be quickly resolved the goods will sit in a warehouse collecting substantial charges and possibly deteriorating and at risk to market movement. An interim solution is for them to be sold for the joint account of the parties pending resolution of the dispute. This is easier where the goods are a commodity such as grain than where they are machinery intended for the buyer's use such as a printing press. Another solution is to ask the court for an expedited hearing. In *British Imex Industries v Midland Bank Ltd*[2] the difficulty was avoided by the following litigation timetable: 10 December 1957 – documents presented to bank and rejected; 11 December – action commenced; 19 and 20 December – action heard concluding in judgment for plaintiff sellers. The goods were steel bars. In *Floating Dock Ltd v Hongkong and Shanghai Banking Corpn*[3] the documents were presented on 8 February 1985 and judgment was given on 3 May 1985. The goods were sections of a floating dock. It was ordered that payment be made within seven days in exchange for the documents tendered. In *Glencore International AG v Bank of China*[4] the documents were presented on 5 July 1995, the action was commenced on 15 September, judgment was given on 6 October and an appeal was dismissed by the Court of Appeal on 23 November. The goods were aluminium ingots. In *Forestal Mimosa Ltd v Oriental Credit Ltd*[5] the credit was available by acceptance of the sellers' draft drawn on the buyers at 90 days' sight. It appears that there was some delay before the buyers declined to accept the bills and before it was alleged that the documents did not conform to the credit. The sellers claimed a declaration that the confirming bank was responsible for the acceptance and payment of the bills, and damages. The goods were mimosa extract: it does not appear from the report what had happened to them, or who held the documents. Judgment was given for damages to be assessed. Such damages would appear primarily to have been the amount of the bills, with interest. The sellers also claimed their travel and other costs incurred in trying to overcome the unwarranted objections to the bills. These claims were not considered by the Court of Appeal, but were left over for the assessment of damages.[6] Where under the terms of the credit payment is not due immediately and the documents have been accepted by the bank and there is later a default in payment, either simply because payment is not made or a bill is dishonoured, the seller will have parted with the documents and his claim against the bank will be for the amount due and interest: no problem as to the goods arises. An example of such a claim is *Power Curber International Ltd v National Bank of Kuwait SAK*[7] where the bank failed to pay the balance due a year after shipment because of an injunction granted by its national court obtained by the buyer.

1 (1919) 1 Ll L Rep 256.
2 [1958] 1 QB 542.
3 [1986] 1 Lloyd's Rep 65.
4 [1996] 1 Lloyd's Rep 135.
5 [1986] 1 WLR 631.
6 A petition for leave to appeal to the House of Lords was dismissed: the action settled.
7 [1981] 1 WLR 1233.

5.89   If the bank has refused to pay on a bill as acceptor, s 57(1) of the Bills of Exchange Act 1882 will be directly applicable, providing for the recovery by way of damages of the amount of the bill together with interest.

5.90   It may happen that the bank rejects the documents on the ground that they do not conform to the credit and the seller does not want to run the risk of suing for the price and backing his own judgement of the documents against that of the bank, leaving the goods to accumulate charges in a foreign warehouse in the meanwhile. It is clear as a matter of principle and common sense that the seller can adopt an alternative course. He can accept the bank's refusal of the documents as a repudiation of its obligation to accept conforming documents and to pay as the credit provides, and such acceptance will terminate any on-going contractual obligations on either side. The seller can then use his continuing possession of the documents to resell the goods, thus hopefully recouping at least a substantial part of his money. If the market has risen, he could even make a better profit than under his original bargain. But if he is not so fortunate, his claim against the bank will be for the difference between the resale price and the price due under the credit to which could be added the costs of arranging the resale. It would be open to the bank to argue that the seller had failed to take reasonable steps to mitigate his loss and should have obtained a better resale price. Such an argument becomes unattractive once it is established that the bank should not have rejected the documents, and so it is the bank which is the author of the seller's problems. *Urquhart, Lindsay & Co Ltd v Eastern Bank Ltd*[1] illustrates the above principle in part and applies it to a credit providing for payment in instalments. The underlying contract was to manufacture machinery and ship it in instalments. The bank rejected the documents relating to one instalment. The sellers treated this as a repudiation of the whole contract constituting the credit. They claimed and were awarded damages calculated as the difference between the price which they would have received under the credit and the value of the materials left on their hands together with, it appears, the cost of completing the work.

1 [1922] 1 KB 318. The facts are set out in para **8.18** below.

Delayed payment

5.91   Where a seller has suffered loss through delay in payment, he may recover that loss subject to his satisfying the court that it is recoverable applying the ordinary rules of causation and remoteness of damages. In *Ozalid Group (Export) Ltd v African Continental Bank Ltd*[1] the defendant bank delayed payment of US$125,939 to an English company for some two months, during which the dollar fell against the pound. Under the then existing exchange control requirements the company was obliged to sell its dollars for sterling. It was held that the bank should have been aware of this. The plaintiff sellers recovered the difference between the sterling value of the dollars when they should have been received and when they were in fact received, with interest on the total sum over the period of non-payment, and also their reasonable costs of attempting to collect payment. The correct approach in law to these facts in the light of subsequent authority is shown by *International Minerals and Chemical Corpn v Karl O Helm AG*.[2] Had the exchange regulations not existed, it would nonetheless have been open to the English company to have proved, if it had been the case, that they would have sold the dollars for sterling on or shortly after their receipt, for reasons, for example, of company financial policy, and to justify their loss in that way. This would be likely to satisfy the tests as to remoteness (or likelihood) of damage variously recited in the speeches of the House of Lords in *Koufos v C Czarnikow Ltd*.[3] The position as to claiming interest where the bank pays prior to the commencement of any proceedings but pays late is now governed by the House of Lords' decision in *Sempra Metals Ltd v IRC*.[4] The court has a common law jurisdiction to award compound and simple interest as damages on claims for breach of a contract to pay a debt. Actual interest losses caused by a breach of contract are in principle recoverable, subject to proof of loss, remoteness of damage rules, obligations to mitigate damage and any other relevant rules relating to the recovery of alleged losses.

1 [1979] 2 Lloyd's Rep 231.
2 [1986] 1 Lloyd's Rep 81 at 105.
3 [1969] 1 AC 350.
4 [2007] 3 WLR 754.

Paying an incorrect party

5.92   The bank must ensure that it makes payment to the party entitled to receive it. If it pays another person, its obligation to the party entitled will remain and it will have to pay a second time. This may arise where the bank believes that it is paying an agent of the beneficiary authorised to receive the money on the beneficiary's behalf and is mistaken. An example of such circumstances is provided by *Cleveland Manufacturing Co Ltd v Muslim Commercial Bank Ltd*.[1] There the documents were prepared and presented to the defendant bank by shipping agents instructed by the plaintiffs. The bank paid the shipping agents who did not account to the plaintiffs because they went into liquidation. The shipping agents were not authorised to receive payment, and so the plaintiffs succeeded against the bank.

1 [1981] 2 Lloyd's Rep 646.

H   BANK'S RIGHTS TO RECOURSE AGAINST THE BENEFICIARY

5.93   Circumstances may arise in which an issuing or confirming bank pays a beneficiary and then seeks to recover its payment. Perhaps the most likely situation is where the bank has examined documents and found them acceptable and so it pays, and it is subsequently found that they do not comply with the terms and conditions of the credit so the bank is not entitled to reimbursement from the applicant or the issuing bank as the case may be. Another situation is where the applicant becomes insolvent causing the bank to be unable to recover what it has paid out, and another is where the bank has negotiated documents including a draft drawn on the buyer or some other party, and the draft is later dishonoured. Perhaps the general answer is that an issuing or confirming bank has no such rights of recovery: it is contrary to the intention of documentary credits to provide a certain and secure means of payment that such rights should exist. Particular cases are considered below.

Rights arising in connection with bills of exchange

5.94 A bank which negotiates documents including a bill of exchange, and thereby becomes holder of the bill, would generally have a right of recourse against the drawer (usually the beneficiary) under s 43(2) and s 47(2) of the Bills of Exchange Act 1882 if the bill were subsequently dishonoured by non-acceptance or non-payment.[1] If the bank has also confirmed a credit available by negotiation then Article 8.a.ii provides that it must negotiate without recourse.

1 See para **7.10** below.

5.95 The position of an advising bank which does not negotiate the credit but takes possession of documents to present them to the issuing bank on behalf of the beneficiary, and thus acts as the beneficiary's agent, will usually be that it has not paid the beneficiary and so it will not have become a party to the bill, nor will it have need of recourse. But, if it has paid, it will have a right to recourse.

5.96 Recourse may also be available where transactions involving bills have taken place outside the letter of credit. In *M A Sassoon & Sons Ltd v International Banking Corpn*[1] Sassoon were sellers in Calcutta of goods to buyers in London. The buyers opened a letter of credit with a London bank which was advised to the sellers through the London bank's Calcutta branch which confirmed the credit. Bills drawn on the buyers to which bills of lading were attached were discounted by the sellers with the plaintiff bank. The sellers' memorandum covering the documents to the bank referred to the letter of credit but it stated at its commencement that the drafts were D/A (delivery against acceptance) drafts. This was held by the Board of the Privy Council to be an instruction to the plaintiff bank to present the bills to the buyers for acceptance against delivery of the bills of lading. This having been done, the letter of credit was in effect an irrelevance between the plaintiff bank and the sellers. The bank did not utilise the credit. The sellers were not able to say that, because the bank had not done so, the bank was barred from recourse against the sellers when the bills were dishonoured by non-payment. The sellers were therefore liable.[2] Had the agreement for the discounting of the bills between the bank and the sellers included an instruction to present the documents under the credit and thus designated the letter of credit as the security for the bills, and had the sellers ignored the credit in those circumstances, it appears that they could not have complained thereafter that the bills were dishonoured.[3] Had they in like circumstances attempted to obtain payment through the credit and had they failed through no fault of theirs to do so, it appears that the bank could have recovered its advance from the sellers.

1 [1927] AC 711.
2 [1927] AC 711 at 730.
3 [1927] AC 711 at 729–731.

5.97 If the UCP is not incorporated into a credit, may a confirming bank be entitled to recourse on a bill? It is suggested that the answer must clearly be no, for it is contrary to the whole object of the transaction, namely to provide a certain source of payment by a bank by means of an obligation undertaken by the bank, that there should be any such right of recourse. It was pointed out in the *Sassoon* case[1] that the sellers could not show that, when they discounted the bills, they had bargained that the transaction should be without recourse. This was in the context first that the discounting agreement had not designated the letter of credit as the source of repayment to the discounting bank, and secondly that the bank was not a party to the letter of credit. Where the bank is a party to the letter of credit as the issuing or confirming bank, the circumstances require that it be implied that there shall be no right of recourse where otherwise a right of recourse might arise. The acceptance of the UCP by British banks has simply confirmed this position.

1 [1927] AC 711 at 731.

Mistake as to the documents

5.98 If an issuing or a confirming bank pays against documents presented under the credit which are later found not to conform with the requirements of the credit and are rejected by the buyer, can the bank allege against the beneficiary that the payment was made under a mistake of fact or (following the decision of the House of Lords in *Kleinwort Benson Ltd v Lincoln City Council*[1]) a mistake of law and so is recoverable?
Where the UCP applies, Article 16.f[2] will bar any claim that the documents do not comply with the credit by an issuing bank or confirming bank which has not given notice of rejection of the documents and otherwise followed the requirements of the Article. Such a bank would be unable therefore to put forward a claim based on mistake of fact.

1 [1999] 2 AC 349.
2 See para **5.42** above.

5.99 It is suggested that the answer where the UCP does not apply may be found as follows. Where the buyer of goods under a contract receives them against payment, if he has a remedy in respect of a defect in the goods, it is a remedy for breach of a term of the contract. He may also have a claim for misrepresentation. But except in the most exceptional circumstances he cannot say that when he paid, he paid under a mistake of fact as to the quality of the goods, and that he would like his money back on that ground. The bank is not a purchaser of goods but of documents. The position however must be analogous. It is clear that, at least in the absence of fraud, a party presenting documents to a bank does not make any implied representations as to the documents – in particular that they comply with the terms of the credit. Nor does he give any warranty. So the bank has no remedy. Secondly, it is suggested that once the bank has decided not to reject the documents, it becomes under an obligation to pay for them. That is so whether or not they comply with the terms of the credit. The payment by the bank therefore discharges the bank's obligation to pay which has become effective on its acceptance of the documents. Where money is paid to discharge a genuine legal obligation it cannot be recovered as money paid under a mistake of fact.

Failure of the applicant

5.100   The failure of the applicant to reimburse the issuing bank, or the failure of the issuing bank to reimburse the confirming bank, does not of itself give the bank which finds itself out of pocket, any rights against the beneficiary of the credit. This is so whether or not the failure arises by reason of insolvency.

Fraud[1]

5.101   Where documents are presented to a bank by or on behalf of a party which knows that the documents are not what they purport to be because they are forged or for some other reason, the bank can refuse payment, or, if it has paid before discovering the position, it can recover the payment from a fraudulent beneficiary.[2]

1 As to the effect of the bank's involvement in fraud, see para **5.80** above.
2 See **Chapter 9** below, particularly para **9.48** et seq.

I   SET-OFF

5.102   It will very rarely happen that the factual situation between a paying bank and the beneficiary will be such as to enable the bank to raise a set-off against the beneficiary because there would normally be no commercial relationship outside the credit itself. However, this occurred in *Hongkong and Shanghai Banking Corpn v Kloeckner & Co AG*[1] where there were complicated arrangements between the bank and Kloeckner for the financing of oil trading. These included a standby letter of credit opened by the bank in Kloeckner's favour. Kloeckner made demands under the credit against which the bank sought to set off sums due under related transactions. Hirst J held that the bank was entitled to do so, because the set-off arose from the very transactions in connection with which the credit was opened and the set-off was for a liquidated amount. He held that the bank's obligation to pay, established by the Uniform Customs, had no bearing on the validity of a set-off against that obligation.[2] In *Etablissement Esefka International Anstalt v*

Central Bank of Nigeria[3] it was suggested by Lord Denning MR[4] in the Court of Appeal on applications by the plaintiff beneficiary for a Mareva freezing injunction and by the defendant bank for security for costs, that a bank might set off a claim to recover payments made under a credit in respect of fraudulent shipments against a claim by the beneficiary for payment under the credit in respect of demurrage incurred in relation to other shipments. In *SAFA Ltd v Banque du Caire*[5] the Court of Appeal refused an application for summary judgment under CPR Pt 24 on the grounds, inter alia, that the bank had a counter claim. Waller LJ stated:

'1   'The principle that letters of credit must be treated as cash is an important one, and must be maintained.

2   It is however unusual for a Bank which has opened a letter of credit to be involved in the related transaction to the extent this bank was.

3   When a Bank is involved in the related transaction it may be unjust for that Bank to be forced to pay on a summary judgment where it has a real prospect of succeeding by reference to a claim on the underlying transaction, and particularly if that claim is a liquidated claim, the court should not give summary judgment either because a set-off has a reasonable prospect of success or because there is a compelling reason to have a trial of the letter of credit issue.'

In *Solo Industries UK Ltd v Canara Bank*[6] Mance LJ agreed that there was force to points 2 and 3 in special circumstances such as where the beneficiary and bank are both intimately involved in a wider underlying transaction.

1 [1989] 3 All ER 513, [1989] 2 Lloyd's Rep 323.
2 See [1989] 2 Lloyd's Rep 323 at 330, 331.
3 [1979] 1 Lloyd's Rep 445.
4 [1979] 1 Lloyd's Rep 445 at 448.1 and 449.2.
5 [2000] Lloyd's Rep 600 and see para **9.36** in connection with the fraud exception.
6 [2001] 1 WLR 1800.

Chapter 6

The Correspondent Bank

6.1 Because documentary credits are commonly used to finance international transactions, the issuing bank is normally in a different country to the beneficiary. While the issuing bank may deal directly with the beneficiary abroad, it is more usual for the issuing bank to utilise the services of a bank in the country of the beneficiary, which may be referred to as 'the correspondent bank'. Although the bank may be designated by the applicant pursuant to his arrangements with the intended beneficiary, it is more commonly left to the issuing bank to decide which bank it will use. There will normally be a particular bank (or perhaps more than one) in the country in question, with which it has arrangements under which that bank is prepared to act on the instructions of the issuing bank in connection with documentary credits. Depending on its instructions in the individual matter, such a bank may act in various capacities. Thus, the term 'correspondent bank' is used to refer to a bank, usually in the country of the seller or beneficiary, which deals with the beneficiary concerning the credit in accordance with instructions accepted by it from the issuing bank. The various forms which these relations may take are considered below.

A THE FUNCTIONS WHICH MAY BE ASSUMED BY A CORRESPONDENT BANK

6.2 The function or functions which a correspondent bank performs and consequently its legal position are mainly dependent on the instructions which it receives, although, as will be seen, there are some functions which it may take upon itself independently of its relationship with the issuing bank.

(1) As the advising bank

(a) Role of the advising bank

6.3 UCP Article 2 defines an 'advising bank' as 'the bank that advises the credit at the request of the issuing bank'. Advising the credit involves formal communication both of the fact of the credit's opening and of its terms.

6.4 UCP Article 9.a is expressed in slightly wider terms than the definition contained in Article 2. It provides that a credit and any amendment to it may be advised to a beneficiary through an advising bank. So Article 9.a contemplates the advice of amendments as well as the credit itself and this accords with the way the term 'advising bank' is generally used. Indeed, by Article 9.e a bank using the services of an advising bank to advise a credit must use the same bank to advise any amendment to it. A correspondent bank may obviously choose whether or not to act as an advising bank. But if it chooses not to do so, Article 9.e provides that it must inform the bank from which the credit or amendment was received without delay.

(b)   No undertaking without confirmation

6.5 Unless the correspondent bank is asked to, and does, add its confirmation[1] to the credit, it does not, by advising the credit, undertake any obligation itself to the beneficiary in respect of payment:[2] the sole undertaking in that regard remains that of the issuing bank.[3] It is usual for an advising bank in this situation to make its position clear by expressly stating when advising the credit that no undertaking on its part is included.

1 As to silent confirmations, see para **6.25** below.
2 See UCP Article 9.a.
3 See Article 12.a relating to the 'Nominated Bank'.

(c)   Agency

6.6 Unless the correspondent bank is instructed to issue the credit itself,[1] it will be asked to advise the seller/beneficiary of the opening of the credit by the issuing bank and of its terms. In doing so the correspondent bank, acts as the agent of the issuing bank.[2] In *Bank Melli Iran v Barclays Bank*[3] it was argued for Bank Melli that their relationship with Barclays was that of banker and customer and not that of principal and agent. In rejecting the plea McNair J stated:[4]

> 'In my judgment, both on the constructions of the documents under which the credit was established and in principle, the relationship between Bank Melli, the instructing bank, and Barclays Bank, the confirming bank, was that of principal and agent. This relationship was held to exist in substantially similar circumstances in *Equitable Trust Co of New York v Dawson Partners Ltd* (1927) 27 Ll L Rep 49 (see per Viscount Cave LC, at p 52, Lord Sumner at p 53, and Lord Shaw of Dunfermline at p 57), and the existence of this relationship is implicit in the judgments of the Court of Appeal in *J H Rayner & Co Ltd v Hambro's Bank Ltd* [1943] KB 37. I accept as accurate the statement of Professor Gutteridge KC, in his book on *Bankers' Commercial Credits*, at p 51, that "as between the issuing banker" (in this case Bank Melli) "and the correspondent" (in this case Barclays Bank) "the relationship is, unless otherwise agreed, that of principal and agent..." On the facts of this case I find no agreement to the contrary.'

The facts of the *Equitable Trust* case[5] have been set out at para **4.12** above. It was held that the correspondent and confirming bank, the Hongkong and Shanghai Bank, were the agents of the Equitable Trust Co for the purpose of advising the credit.

1 See para **6.33** below.

2 See, for example, *Gian Singh v Banque de l'Indochine* [1974] 1 WLR 1234, 1238 where Lord
  Diplock referred to the 'notifying bank' as the agent of the issuing bank.
3 [1951] 2 Lloyd's Rep 367.
4 [1951] 2 Lloyd's Rep 367 at 376.
5 (1927) 13 Ll L Rep 49, see para **4.12** above.

6.7   Where a credit is confirmed by a bank other than the correspondent
bank, in advising the confirmation, the correspondent bank also acts as the
agent of the confirming bank.[1]

1 A point canvassed in *Marconi Communications v PT Pan Indonesian Bank* [2007] 2 Lloyd's
  Rep 72.

(d)   Binding the issuing bank as to the terms of the credit

6.8   As the advising bank is authorised to hold itself out to the
seller/beneficiary as authorised on behalf of the issuing bank to pass the
terms of the credit to the seller, the advising bank will bind the issuing bank
even though it deviates from its instructions by, for example, failing to
include in the terms of the credit a document called for by the instructions
from the issuing bank. For the terms of the credit as so advised by the
advising bank will fall within the ostensible authority of the advising bank.[1]
The consequence is that, as regards the beneficiary, the issuing bank will be
obliged to honour the credit as so advised. So, in the example taken, it will
be obliged to pay against documents which do not include that omitted
from the advice of the credit. But it may not have to do so where it is the
advising bank which is to pay the beneficiary (if, for example, the advising
bank had also confirmed the credit). The likely scenario will then be that
the advising bank will pay in accordance with the credit which it has
advised. It will forward the documents to the issuing bank, which will
decline to accept them and to reimburse the advising bank on the ground
that the documents do not comply with its instructions. This assumes that
the advising bank has no defence by reason of UCP Article 35 (transmission
errors).[2] It is suggested that in such circumstances UCP Article 37 would
assist neither the advising nor the issuing bank.[3] The position is more
difficult where it is another bank, the issuing bank or a third bank, which is
to pay the beneficiary. The bank will be obliged to pay in accordance with
the credit as advised. Can the issuing bank then oblige the applicant to
accept and pay for documents which do not accord with his instructions on
the ground that the utilisation of the advising bank was at his risk,
pursuant to Article 37? It is suggested in **Chapter 4**[4] that the issuing bank
cannot: it must pay and recoup its payment from the party at fault, the
advising bank, for breach of the contract between them.

1 See *Bowstead* on Agency (18th edn) article 72.
2 See para **4.16** above.
3 See para **4.22** et seq above.
4 See para **4.23** above.

(e)   Can a beneficiary claim against the advising bank where the latter wrongly advises the credit?

6.9   If the credit provides that payment to the beneficiary is to be made by the issuing bank and the issuing bank declines to accept documents complying with credit as advised by the advising bank on the ground that the advising bank did not advise the credit correctly, can the beneficiary proceed against the advising bank in his own country rather than suing the foreign issuing bank?

6.10   Because the advising bank's advice of the credit will have bound the issuing bank, it is difficult to see how the beneficiary can do so. For the beneficiary received a valid credit. But if, contrary to what is stated above, the issuing bank was in some way not bound by the credit as advised, under English law the advising bank would be liable to the beneficiary for damages for breach of warranty of authority, that is, for breach of the warranty which English law implies that every agent gives that he has the authority of his principal to act as he does. It is suggested that a statement that the credit is advised without any undertaking to honour or negotiate on the part of the advising bank would not avoid this liability: for the intention of that statement is simply to make clear that the advising bank is not joining with the issuing bank in the obligation undertaken by the credit.

6.11   The wording of UCP Article 9.b gives rise to a further possibility (again if, contrary to what is stated above, the issuing bank was in some way not bound by the credit as advised). Article 9.b provides, amongst other things, that, by advising the credit or amendment, the advising bank 'signifies...that the advice accurately reflects the terms and conditions of the credit or amendment received'. This provision was new in UCP 600. The word 'signifies' can probably be taken as a synonym for 'represents'. It strengthens the argument that a beneficiary in the hypothetical position considered above might also have a claim in negligence (under the principles in *Hedley Byrne & Co Ltd v Heller & Partners Ltd*[1]) in addition to the claim for breach of warranty of authority if the advising bank wrongly and negligently advises the credit.

1 [1964] AC 465.

(f)   The authenticity of the credit

6.12   UCP Articles 9.b and 9.f provide:

> '**Article 9: Advising of credits and amendments**
> ...
> b.   By advising the credit or amendment, the advising bank signifies that it has satisfied itself as to the apparent authenticity of the credit or amendment ...

...

f.   If a bank is requested to advise a credit or amendment but cannot satisfy itself as to the apparent authenticity of the credit, the amendment or the advice, it must so inform, without delay, the bank from which the instructions appear to have been received. If the advising bank or second advising bank elects nonetheless to advise the credit or amendment, it must inform the beneficiary or second advising bank that it has not been able to satisfy itself as to the apparent authenticity of the credit, the amendment or the advice.'

These provisions omit any reference to a standard of care by which the advising bank should 'satisfy itself' as to the authenticity of the credit, that is, whether or not it appears to be genuine, namely instructed by the issuing bank which appears to have instructed it and in the terms in which it appears that that has occurred. The corresponding provision in UCP 500 (UCP 500 Article 7.a) made it clear that a bank which chose to act as an advising bank had to exercise reasonable care to check the apparent authenticity of the credit. It is not, however, thought that the omission of any reference to such a standard in UCP 600 was intended to reflect a change in the basis upon which an advising bank is taken to act. If it was intended to impose absolute liability on the advising bank, express words would have been required.

6.13   In most situations, under English law, a bank which advised a credit which it has not in fact been instructed to advise, would be liable for its breach of warranty of authority mentioned in para **6.10** above: for it would be purporting to act with the authority of a principal which it did not have. It is, however, reasonably clear that an advising bank is not to be under any such absolute liability: it will only be liable in respect of a credit which it has advised in respect of which it later turns out that its instructions were not genuine, if it was negligent in checking the authenticity of its instructions. Where the check does not establish the authenticity of the instructions, the advising bank must without delay inform the bank from which they have purported to come, and it may advise the credit nonetheless provided that it informs the beneficiary that it has not been able to establish its authenticity. If it does so, then of course the beneficiary will not be able to rely upon it as authentic until the authenticity is later assured.[1]

1 See generally *Standard Bank London Ltd v Bank of Tokyo Ltd* [1995] 2 Lloyd's Rep 169.

6.14   Most credits are now transmitted by SWIFT. Where a credit is advised by post, the advising bank should check the signature on behalf of the issuing bank against specimen signatures held by it. In the case of teletransmissions, individual test keys may be used (although this is now quite rare), or the mechanism of SWIFT[1] utilised.

1 Society for Worldwide Interbank Financial Telecommunications: see http://www.swift.com.

(g)   Second advising banks

6.15   UCP Article 9.c provides:

> 'c.   An advising bank may utilize the services of another bank ('second advising bank') to advise the credit and any amendment to the beneficiary. By advising the credit or amendment, the second advising bank signifies that it has satisfied itself as to the apparent authenticity of the advice it has received and that the advice accurately reflects the terms and conditions of the credit or amendment received.'

The concept of a 'second advising bank' was introduced by the UCP. The obligations of a second advising bank appear substantially to mirror those of an advising bank (certainly as articulated in the rest of Article 9). Given the authority conferred on an advising bank by Article 9.c to utilize the services of a second advising bank, a second advising bank will be regarded as an agent of the advising bank and as a sub-agent of the issuing bank whom it will bind through any advice it gives (in the same way as an advising bank). Similar issues to those in (d)–(f) above should apply in the context of a second advising bank.

(2)   As the nominated bank

(a)   Definition of 'nominated bank'

6.16   UCP Article 2 defines a 'nominated bank' as 'the bank with which the credit is available or any bank in the case of a credit available with any bank'. Two points arise on that definition:

(a)   The first point is that, read literally, the definition is wide enough to encompass an issuing bank where, for example, the credit specifies the issuing bank as the only bank with which it is available. But the Articles which follow contemplate different banks playing the issuing and nominated bank roles (see, for example, Articles 6, 7, 12, 14, 15 and 16) and the definition of 'nominated bank' needs to be understood accordingly.

(b)   The second point is that the definition is obviously also wide enough to encompass a confirming bank and a confirming bank will always be a nominated bank,[1] notwithstanding the fact that its confirmation imposes obligations upon it which are additional to the consequences of nomination.[2]

1 The case of a bank giving silent confirmations is dealt with in para **6.25** below.
2 Those obligations have been dealt with in **Chapter 5** above.

(b)   Authorisation and invitation to the nominated bank to act

6.17   By nominating a bank as the bank with which the credit is available, an issuing bank invites and authorises the nominated bank to receive and examine documents and to honour or negotiate, as the case may be. UCP Articles 6 and 12 are relevant in this context. UCP Article 6 provides:

> '**Article 6: Availability, expiry date and place for presentation**
> a.   A credit must state the bank with which it is available or whether it is available with any bank. A credit available with a nominated bank is also available with the issuing bank.
> b.   A credit must state whether it is available by sight payment, deferred payment, acceptance or negotiation.
>   …
> d.   i   A credit must state an expiry date for presentation. An expiry date stated for honour or negotiation will be deemed to be an expiry date for presentation.
>   ii   The place of the bank with which the credit is available is the place for presentation. The place for presentation under a credit available with any bank is that of any bank. A place for presentation other than that of the issuing bank is in addition to the place of the issuing bank.
> e.   Except as provided in sub-article 29(a), a presentation by or on behalf of the beneficiary must be made on or before the expiry date.'

So the credit must make clear to which bank(s) the beneficiary is to present documents, that is, which bank(s) will operate the credit so far as the beneficiary is concerned. If, in addition to being available with the issuing bank, the credit is to be available with a nominated bank, it must say so. The credit must also state how it is to be available (by sight payment, deferred payment, acceptance or negotiation), the expiry date for presentation and the place for presentation - being the place of the issuing bank and the place of any nominated bank.

6.18   UCP Article 12 provides:

> '**Article 12: Nomination**
> a.   Unless a nominated bank is the confirming bank, an authorization to honour or negotiate does not impose any obligation on that nominated bank to honour or negotiate, except when expressly agreed to by that nominated bank and so communicated to the beneficiary.
> b.   By nominating a bank to accept a draft or incur a deferred payment undertaking, an issuing bank authorizes that nominated bank to prepay or purchase a draft accepted or a deferred payment undertaking incurred by that nominated bank.
> c.   Receipt or examination and forwarding of documents by a nominated bank that is not a conforming bank, does not make that nominated bank liable to honour or negotiate, nor does it constitute honour or negotiation.'

Article 12.a makes clear that a nomination to act as nominated bank authorises but imposes no obligation on the nominated bank to honour or negotiate the credit, as the case may be. If it acts upon a nomination to honour the credit, it does so as agent of the issuing bank (regardless of whether or not it has also confirmed the credit and has an obligation to honour in its own right) and is sometimes referred to in that capacity as the 'paying bank'. If it acts upon a nomination to negotiate the credit, similarly it does so with the authority of the issuing bank but the process of negotiation also results in a principal to principal contract on the terms of the credit coming into existence between the issuing bank and the negotiating bank.

6.19   UCP Article 12.b had no equivalent in UCP 500. Its effect (taken together with UCP Articles 7.c and 8.c) is to overcome difficulties which the decision in *Banco Santander v Banque Paribas*[1] presented to a nominated bank dealing with a deferred payment credit. The *Banco Santander* decision held that, if a bank, without the authority of the issuing bank, agreed to discount a deferred payment credit by advancing sums against an assignment of the beneficiary's rights, then it was at risk that the issuing bank would decline payment at maturity if a fraud by the beneficiary had come to light in the intervening period. UCP Articles 7.c, 8.c and 12.b make clear that a nominated bank which honours a credit by accepting a draft or incurring a deferred payment obligation and which prepays or purchases the draft accepted or the deferred payment undertaking incurred, acts with the authority of the issuing bank and, provided that the presentation was a complying presentation, can look to the issuing bank or the confirming bank, if any, for reimbursement.

1 [2000] Lloyds Rep Bank 165; see para **9.43** below.

(c)   Examination and reimbursement

6.20   Where a presentation is made to the nominated bank and it chooses to act upon its nomination, it will be its duty to examine the documents to see whether they appear on their face to constitute a complying presentation. The duties of a bank in carrying out such an examination and in connection with acceptance or refusal are considered in Chapter 8. When a nominated bank acting on its nomination determines that a presentation does not comply, it may refuse to honour or negotiate (Article 16.a) and, if it does so, it must notify the presenter (Article 16.b). Conversely, when a nominated bank determines that a presentation is complying and honours or negotiates the credit, it must forward the documents to the issuing bank or the confirming bank, if any (Article 15.). The bank's right to reimbursement and to the payment of commission and other charges will be dependent on the proper performance of these duties.

6.21   UCP Articles 7.c and 8.c provide:

'**Article 7**
c.   An issuing bank undertakes to reimburse a nominated bank that has honoured or negotiated a complying presentation and forwarded the

documents to the issuing bank. Reimbursement for the amount of a complying presentation under a credit available by acceptance or deferred payment is due at maturity, whether or not the nominated bank prepaid or purchased before maturity. An issuing bank's undertaking to reimburse a nominated bank is independent of the issuing bank's undertaking to the beneficiary.'

'**Article 8**

c. A confirming bank undertakes to reimburse another nominated bank that has honoured or negotiated a complying presentation and forwarded the documents to the confirming bank. Reimbursement for the amount of a complying presentation under a credit available by acceptance or deferred payment is due at maturity, whether or not another nominated bank prepaid or purchased before maturity. A confirming bank's undertaking to reimburse another nominated bank is independent of the confirming bank's undertaking to the beneficiary.'

So if the nominated bank honours or negotiates a credit where the presentation was not a complying presentation, it will have no right to reimbursement unless the applicant and the issuing bank are prepared to waive the discrepancies. If reimbursement has already been made to the nominated bank but the issuing bank refuses to honour, or a confirming bank refuses to honour or negotiate, the credit and has given notice to that effect in accordance with UCP Article 16, it shall be entitled to a refund from the nominated bank, with interest, of any reimbursement made (Article 16.f). In such cases, subject to any right of recourse against the beneficiary,[1] the nominated bank will be left with the documents, and hence the goods, on its hands. UCP Article 37 has also to be considered in this context. The position will be no different from that where the advising bank accepts documents which do not comply with the applicant's instructions because it has made an error in advising the credit rather than in examining the documents. It is suggested that Article 37 should not assist the banks in such a context.[2] In performing its task of examining and accepting or refusing the documents the correspondent bank acts so far as the issuing bank is concerned as its agent. In *Gian Singh & Co Ltd v Banque de l'Indochine*[3] Lord Diplock stated[4] '. . . the customer did not succeed in making out any case of negligence against the issuing bank or the notifying bank which acted as its agent, in failing to detect the forgery'. It is suggested that this is so whether or not the correspondent bank has confirmed the credit.[5] If the correspondent bank accepts the documents, as between the issuing bank and the beneficiary, its acceptance will bind the issuing bank, its principal.

1 See paras **6.45** et seq below.
2 See para **6.8** above, and also para **4.22** et seq above.
3 [1974] 1 WLR 1234, [1974] 2 Lloyd's Rep 1.
4 [1974] 1 WLR 1234 at 1239, [1974] 2 Lloyd's Rep 1 at 11, 12.
5 See para **6.24** below.

(3)   As the confirming bank

6.22   The correspondent bank may be authorised or requested by the issuing bank to confirm the credit, that is to add its undertaking 'in addition to that of the issuing bank to honour or negotiate a complying presentation' (UCP Article 2). If it does so, it becomes the confirming bank.

6.23   If it is not prepared to act as confirming bank, Article 8.d provides that it must inform the issuing bank without delay although it may proceed to advise the credit without confirmation.

6.24   The obligations of the confirming bank towards the beneficiary are dealt with in Article 8 and have been considered with those of the issuing bank in **Chapter 5**. The obligation of a confirming bank to pay, or to be responsible for payment if it is not itself to pay, is an obligation which it gives as a principal. This does not prevent it from acting in other respects as the agent of the issuing bank. The credit in the *Equitable Trust* case[1] was a confirmed credit.[2] The position is that in carrying out its functions, where appropriate, it will act in a dual capacity. In so far as its interests as a confirming bank are concerned, it acts as a principal: at the same time as regards the issuing bank it acts as agent. Thus in accepting documents and payment against documents it acts as a principal in relation to its obligations as confirming bank, and it acts as agent for the issuing bank with regard to the obligations of the issuing bank.

1 (1927) 27 Ll L Rep 49.
2 See para **6.6** above.

(a)   'Silent' confirmations

6.25   Even where a beneficiary is prepared to pay the bank charges involved, some foreign banks will refuse requests by applicants to procure that credits opened by them should be confirmed. This may be because they see such a request as an insult to their credit worthiness or to the prestige of their country: in their view their own undertaking should be sufficient. Another reason is that national policy may direct the banks of a country not to request the confirmation of their credits because it utilises valuable and limited lines of credit. In view of the value and utility of a confirmation to the beneficiary, exporters have sought a way round this problem by themselves requesting the confirmation of a credit by the advising bank without the authorisation of the issuing bank. This is referred to as a 'silent' confirmation, something contemplated by the language of UCP Article 12.a. Such a confirmation will, however, fall outside the ambit of UCP Article 8 because that applies to 'confirming banks' – being banks whose confirmations were authorised or requested by the issuing bank. Nonetheless the undertakings to be given by a 'silent' confirmer must follow those set out in the Article. For confirmation of a credit means that the confirmer binds itself that the undertakings constituted by the credit will be met: it guarantees the credit. So, as those obligations which it confirms will be those set out in Article 8, the expression of the silent confirmer's obligations will be found in Article 8 even though the Article does not apply directly.[1] The 'silent' confirming bank will have no rights against the issuing bank arising from its confirmation. Thus, unless it is entitled to be reimbursed because it is also a nominated bank under the credit, if its confirmation leads it to have to pay on the credit, it will not have a right of reimbursement. It will not have a right to object to amendments, and it may be dependent on the beneficiary for knowledge of their terms.

1 The practice of silent confirmations is discussed without disapproval in Cases 176 and 177 in *More Case Studies on Documentary Credits*, ICC No 489.

(b)   Permission to confirm on request

6.26   In contrast, sometimes the instruction to the advising bank will expressly permit it to confirm a credit at the beneficiary's request and expense. Such a situation is encompassed by the definition of a confirming bank in Article 2 – namely, 'the bank that adds its confirmation to a credit upon the issuing bank's *authorization* or request' (emphasis added). It is suggested that such an instruction will bring a confirmation at the beneficiary's request within the express terms of Article 8 as a confirmation by a 'confirming bank' (because it is a confirmation which has been authorised (though not requested) by the issuing bank). In a credit transmitted by SWIFT, the instruction would be given by including 'MAY ADD' in the confirmation field.

(4)   As a collecting bank[1]

6.27   The position of a collecting bank is considered generally in **Chapter 7**. If the correspondent bank's sole duty under the credit is to advise the credit, this having been done it may happen that the beneficiary later presents documents to the correspondent bank and asks the bank to collect on them on its behalf. The correspondent bank then reverses roles and becomes the agent of the beneficiary to present the documents to the issuing bank and to receive payment on the beneficiary's behalf. If the documents are fraudulent to the beneficiary's knowledge, the issuing bank will be entitled to reject them.[2] This position is to be contrasted with that where a bank presents documents to the issuing bank in its own right having acquired them by negotiation, ie purchase, from the beneficiary, where fraud by the beneficiary is irrelevant if it is unknown to the negotiating bank.[3]

1 See also para **5.86** above.

2 See, among other cases, *United City Merchants (Investments) Ltd v Royal Bank of Canada* [1983] 1 AC 168 and *European Asian Bank AG v Punjab Bank (No 2)* [1983] 1 WLR 642 at 652A, [1983] 1 Lloyd's Rep 611 at 615.1.
3 *United City Merchants (Investments) Ltd v Royal Bank of Canada* [1983] 1 AC 168, 187 and *European Asian Bank AG v Punjab Bank (No 2)* [1983] 1 WLR 642 at 657, [1983] 1 Lloyd's Rep 611 at 619. See also para **6.31** and **Chapter 7** below.

(5)   As a negotiation bank

6.28   The position of a negotiation (or negotiating) bank has already been mentioned in the context of a correspondent acting as a nominated bank and is considered generally in **Chapter 7**.[1]

1 See also paras **2.20** et seq.

6.29   Neither of the terms 'negotiation bank' or 'negotiating bank' appears in the UCP, although there is a definition of 'negotiation' in Article 2: 'Negotiation means the purchase by the nominated bank of drafts (drawn on a bank other than the nominated bank) and/or documents under a complying presentation, by advancing or agreeing to advance funds to the beneficiary on or before the banking day on which reimbursement is due to the nominated bank'. That is a narrower definition than the concept of negotiation as sometimes understood. See the discussion of the distinction between credits available by negotiation and negotiation credits in para **2.19** above.

6.30   A correspondent bank may come to negotiate documents in two situations. The first is where it is nominated in the credit to negotiate them and does so. If it has confirmed the credit, it is obliged to do so. This is negotiation within the definition of UCP Article 2. The second situation is where the correspondent bank's instructions cover only the advice of the credit but the credit is a negotiation credit and it is subsequently approached by the beneficiary to negotiate and agrees to do so. As mentioned in para **2.19** above, this second situation is now rarely seen in practice.

6.31   In each case, however, the bank may be described as a negotiation bank. In each case, it will then purchase the documents from the beneficiary and is entitled to present them to the issuing bank in its own right. If it does so, the correspondent bank deals with the documents as principal in its own right, and does so neither as the agent of the issuing bank nor of the beneficiary.[1] The bank is unaffected by the fraud of the beneficiary provided that it had no knowledge of it at the time of negotiation.[2] In addition, in the first, but not the second, of the two situations, the correspondent bank as nominated bank also has a direct right to reimbursement by the issuing bank under UCP Article 7.c and by the confirming bank (if any)) under Article 8.c.[3] If the negotiating bank presents the documents in its own right, it must do so in accordance with the terms of the credit (in particular within the time stipulated for presentation). If, on the other hand the negotiating bank simply seeks reimbursement pursuant to its rights under Articles 7.c or 8.c then, subject to any terms of the credit dealing with reimbursement, it does not have to do so within the time specified for presentation under the credit.

1 See *Maran Road Saw Mill v Austin Taylor & Co Ltd* [1975] 1 Lloyd's Rep 156 at 161.1.
2 *European Asian Bank AG v Punjab Bank (No 2)* [1983] 1 WLR 642, [1983] 1 Lloyd's Rep 611, see para **6.27** above.
3 See para **6.20–6.21** above.

(6)   As a discounter of time drafts

6.32   Where the credit provides for drafts payable at a future date, the correspondent bank may be prepared to discount the drafts, that is to say, to make an immediate payment in purchase of them, the price being reduced by an amount of interest calculated as accruing over the period to the date when the draft becomes due for payment. The situations in which it will do this are:

(a) Where the credit provides that it is available by negotiation by the correspondent bank as nominated bank.
(b) Where the credit is a negotiation credit and the correspondent bank's instructions from the issuing bank are limited to advising the credit, and it subsequently negotiates the documents as described in para **6.28–6.31** above. It will then obtain payment itself when the draft becomes due.
(c) Where the credit does not provide for negotiation in either of the above two ways, but involves time drafts. If documents are presented to it, the correspondent bank may of its own accord at the request of the beneficiary purchase the draft providing the beneficiary with immediate payment. The bank has then to forward the documents to the issuing bank and will receive payment when the draft becomes due.

(7)   As a correspondent issuer

6.33   The correspondent bank may be asked to issue the credit in its own name, that is, so that it rather than the bank from which it receives its instructions will appear as the issuing bank. In such circumstances, even if the credit states that it is issued on the instructions of the bank instructing the correspondent bank, no relationship will come into being between the beneficiary and the instructing bank. As 'correspondent issuer' the correspondent bank is therefore the sole party undertaking liability to the beneficiary. Its position as regards the bank from which it receives its instructions (which cannot in this instance accurately be called 'the issuing banker') is similar to that between an applicant for a credit and an issuing banker.[1] Two early examples are contained in *National Bank of Egypt v Hannevig's Bank Ltd*[2] *and Skandinaviska Akt v Barclays Bank*.[3]

1 See generally **Chapter 4**.
2 (1919) 1 Ll L Rep 69.
3 (1925) 22 Ll L Rep 523.

B ADVICE OF THE CREDIT TO THE CORRESPONDENT BANK, AMENDMENTS

6.34   UCP Article 11.a[1] makes provisions mainly relating to the identification of the operative instrument where teletransmission[2] is used. It provides:

> '**Article 11 Teletransmitted and Pre-Advised Credits and Amendments**
> a.   An authenticated teletransmission of a credit or amendment will be deemed to be the operative credit or amendment, and any subsequent mail confirmation shall be disregarded.
>
> If a teletransmission states 'full details to follow' (or words of similar effect), or states that the mail confirmation is to be the operative credit or amendment, then the teletransmission will not be deemed to be the operative credit or amendment. The issuing bank must then issue the operative credit or amendment without delay in terms not inconsistent with the teletransmission.'

Most credits are now advised through SWIFT,[3,4] the Society for Worldwide Interbank Financial Telecommunications,[5] an organisation which provides secure electronic communication services. SWIFT is owned and controlled by its member banks.

1 Article 11.b relates to pre-advices and is considered in para **5.5** above.
2 It is suggested that teletransmission means instantaneous transmission (tele, from afar) and covers forms of electronic transmission.
3 An example of a SWIFT advice can be found in the appendices.
4 As to authentication and fraud, see *Standard Bank London Ltd v Bank of Tokyo Ltd* [1995] 2 Lloyd's Rep 169.
5 See http: //www.swift.com.

6.35   The question of amendments has been considered generally in **Chapter 3**.[1] Where the correspondent bank confirms the credit, the general position is as there stated, namely that it is bound by the credit as first advised unless amendments to it are agreed by it, the issuing bank and the beneficiary. Paragraph **3.41** above discusses the possibility that a confirming bank may advise an amendment and withhold its confirmation of it, as provided for by Article 10.b. Where the correspondent bank does not confirm the credit, its sole position is as agent for the issuing bank. What should it do if the issuing bank instructs it to advise an amendment to the beneficiary, which the beneficiary rejects but the issuing bank nonetheless then instructs the correspondent bank (as nominated bank) only to accept documents which conform to the credit as it would have been amended? The duty of the nominated bank to its principal and its position as a responsible bank may then appear in conflict. Their relations, however, are governed by the UCP and the issuing bank is obliged to act in accordance with them in its instructions. It is suggested that the nominated bank would be entitled to reject the instructions of the issuing bank as instructions which the issuing bank was not entitled to give. If that is right, it could pay the beneficiary against documents complying with the credit as unamended and would be entitled to be reimbursed by the issuing bank. The alternative argument is that it is bound to follow the instructions of its principal whatever they may be: therefore, as it owes no obligation to the beneficiary, it can and should reject documents not complying with the amendment and leave the beneficiary to his remedy against the issuing bank for breach of the credit. The former course carries the higher risk for the nominated bank because it involves the bank in paying and seeking reimbursement from a bank whose instructions it has declined to follow. In practice it is unlikely that a correspondent bank would pay in these circumstances particularly if it was not in funds.[2]

1 Paras **3.36** et seq.
2 For a different discussion of this problem arriving at the same conclusion by a majority, namely that the correspondent bank should accept documents complying with the credit as unamended, see *Opinions* (1987–1988), ICC No 469, Ref 149.

C   EFFECT OF UNDER RESERVE AND INDEMNITY ARRANGEMENTS

6.36   The effect as between a correspondent bank and a beneficiary of arrangements whereby the bank accepts documents which it considers to be non-conforming has been considered in **Chapter 5**.[1] Article 14.f of UCP 500 made clear that such arrangements had no effect as between the correspondent bank and the issuing bank. So the special arrangement meant that there was no acceptance or rejection by the correspondent bank equivalent to that provided for by UCP 500 Article 14.d. The capacity in which the correspondent bank sent forward the documents to the issuing bank was uncertain. It might have been doing so in a capacity of agent for the beneficiary similar to that of a collecting bank, or it might have been doing so as principal in its own right. When documents were sent forward on such a basis, it was uncertain whether the sender would be entitled to compliance with the machinery provided by UCP 500 Article 14 in connection with the rejection of documents.[2] As has been noted in **Chapter 5**, Article 14.f of UCP 500 finds no equivalent in UCP 600. Despite that, it is suggested that the position remains as before. In particular, any special arrangements bind only the parties to them and the obligation of the issuing bank – to honour against complying documents – remains unchanged.

1 Paras **5.81** et seq.
2 See the American decision, *Alaska Textile Co Inc v Lloyd Williams Fashions Inc* [1992] 1 Bank LR 408.

D   ICC URR 725 AND REIMBURSEMENT OF THE CORRESPONDENT BANK

6.37   UCP Article 7.c obliges an issuing bank to reimburse a nominated bank that has honoured or negotiated a complying presentation.

Traditionally, reimbursement was often effected by the issuing bank direct to the correspondent bank by debiting an account held by the issuing bank with the correspondent. However, it was inconvenient for the issuing bank to maintain an account with every possible correspondent; also it may have been that under the issuing bank's international arrangements funds for the country in question were provided via a different bank in another country or by a branch of the issuing bank in another country. In that situation a third bank, with which the issuing bank holds an account, could act as a 'reimbursing bank' to pay the correspondent. The correspondent in this scheme was known as the 'claiming bank'. For example, a confirming bank in Singapore could be instructed to reimburse itself from a New York bank in respect of a credit issued by an Indian bank: compare the facts in *European Asian Bank AG v Punjab Bank (No 2)*,[1] set out in Chapter 2.[2] There was provision in UCP 500 (UCP 500 Article 19) for this. But on 1 July 1996 the ICC Uniform Rules for Bank-to-Bank Reimbursements under Documentary Credits (known as URR 525) came into effect, providing a complete code for reimbursements. With effect from 1 October 2008, a revised version of URR 525 is in operation, known as URR 725.

Reimbursement is dealt with in UCP 600 by Article 13:

(a) Article 13.a provides that if a credit states that reimbursement is to be obtained by a nominated bank ('claiming bank') claiming on another party ('reimbursing bank'), the credit must state if the reimbursement is subject to the URR in effect on the date of issue of the credit.

(b) Article 13.b provides a set of default rules for reimbursement if the credit is not subject to the URR. The language of Article 13.b mirrors the URR in a number of respects. Whilst Article 13.b is expressed as the only alternative to reimbursement under the URR, there is nothing to prevent the issuing bank and the correspondent bank agreeing their own bespoke arrangements. And the whole of Article 13 is probably qualified by the introductory words to Article 13.a so that it should be understood as applying only where a third party reimbursing bank is contemplated by the credit. In a suitable case, therefore, there is no reason why there could not continue to be direct reimbursement to the correspondent bank simply by debiting an account held by the issuing bank with the correspondent.

(c) Article 13.c provides that an issuing bank shall not be relieved of any of its obligations to provide reimbursement if it is not made by a reimbursing bank on first demand.

1 [1983] 1 WLR 642, [1983] 1 Lloyd's Rep 611.
2 See para **2.24**.

(1)   Reimbursement under the URR

6.38   The procedure for reimbursement is essentially administrative and does not affect at all the rights and obligations between the issuing and correspondent bank and the applicant or beneficiary. For present purposes it is sufficient to note that the reimbursement transaction is entirely separate from the documentary credit. URR Articles 1 and 3 provide:

> '**Article 1 Application of URR**
> The *Uniform Rules for Bank-to-Bank Reimbursement under Documentray Credits* ('rules'), ICC Publication No. 725, shall apply to any bank-to-bank reimbursement when the text of the reimbursement authorization expressly indicates that it is subject to these rules. They are binding on all parties thereto, unless expressly modified or excluded by the reimbursement authorization. The issuing bank is responsible for indicating in the documentary credit ('credit') that reimbursement is subject to these rules ... These rules are not intended to override or change the provisions of the Uniform Customs and Practice for Documentary Credit'

> '**Article 3 Reimbursement Authorisations versus Credits**
> A reimbursement authorisation is separate from the credit to which it refers, and a reimbursing bank is not concerned with or bound by the terms and conditions of the credit, even if any reference whatsoever to it is included in the Reimbursement Authorisation.'

6.39   The reimbursing bank will never see the documents presented – if accepted, they will be passed straight from correspondent to issuing bank – and is not concerned with whether the credit has been operated properly. Reimbursement is made on a simple claim in the form prescribed by the URR (Article 10) without consideration of whether the correspondent is actually entitled to it under UCP Article 7.c.[1] The issuing bank is specifically prohibited from making reimbursement conditional on the provision of a certificate of compliance with the terms and conditions of the credit,[2] and in order to 'guard against confusion and misunderstanding' is also prohibited from sending a copy of the credit to the reimbursing bank.[3] If it transpires that the correspondent has paid against a non-complying presentation, then, provided it has made a compliant claim under the URR, it will receive reimbursement in the first instance. The issuing bank would then have to bring an action to recover the payment (as contemplated by UCP Article 16.g) on the ground that the correspondent was not entitled to it under Article 7.c. The reimbursing bank would not be involved in this dispute. The incidence of charges is dealt with at URR Article 16.

1 See para **6.21** above.
2 URR Article 6.c.
3 URR Article 6.b.i.

(2)   The default rules under UCP Article 13.b

6.40   Where URR is not incorporated, UCP Article 13.b will apply.

'**Article 13 Bank-to Bank Reimbursement Arrangements**

...

b. If a credit does not state that reimbursement is subject to the ICC rules for bank-to-bank reimbursement, the following apply:
   i.   An issuing bank must provide a reimbursing bank with a reimbursement authorization that conforms with the availability stated in the credit. The reimbursement authorization should not be subject to an expiry date.
   ii. A claiming bank shall not be required to supply a reimbursing bank with a certificate of compliance with the terms and conditions of the credit.
   iii. An issuing bank will be responsible for any loss of interest, together with any expenses incurred, if reimbursement is not provided on first demand by a reimbursing bank in accordance with the terms and conditions of the credit.
   iv. A reimbursing bank's charges are for the account of the issuing bank. However, if the charges are for the account of the beneficiary, it is the responsibility of an issuing bank to so indicate in the credit and in the reimbursement authorisation. If a reimbursing bank's charges are for the account of the beneficiary, they shall be deducted from the amount due to a claiming bank when reimbursement is made. If no reimbursement is made, the reimbursing bank's charges remain the obligation of the issuing bank.'

6.41   As the reimbursing bank's role is to pay against demand, it is not relevant whether the documents which give rise to the demand do or do not comply with the credit. So, whether or not there are complying documents, the reimbursing bank is entitled to reimbursement either by retaining funds previously provided by the issuing bank or by payment by the issuing bank. If the documents do not comply, the issuing bank in its turn is entitled to recover the payment from the correspondent bank provided the issuing bank rejects the documents when they are received by it, and provided that it complies with UCP Article 16. There is no privity of contract between the correspondent bank and the reimbursing bank. So, if the reimbursing bank fails to pay – probably because it has not been put in funds by the issuing bank – the correspondent bank has no rights against it: the correspondent bank's rights are against the issuing bank, namely, to recover the principal sum which it has paid out and interest during the delay in payment. UCP Article 13 not only covers the position of a correspondent bank which incurs a payment obligation, but also that of any bank which is entitled to and does negotiate the documents.

6.42   The Court of Appeal had to consider the predecessor of Article 13 of the UCP (Article 21 in UCP 400) in *Royal Bank of Scotland plc v Casa di Risparmio*.[1] The Royal Bank of Scotland wished to sue Italian banks in London for reimbursement under a credit which provided for reimbursement in New York, and relied on what is now Article 13.c to found an alleged obligation to pay in London if repayment was not affected in New York. It was held that for jurisdictional purposes the obligation to reimburse was an obligation to reimburse in New York. The proceedings in England were therefore set aside.

1 [1992] 1 Bank LR 251.

E   RECOURSE BETWEEN AN ISSUING BANK AND ITS CORRESPONDENT

6.43   UCP Article 7.c sets out the principle that, where a correspondent bank acting as nominated bank honours or negotiates a complying presentation and forwards the documents to the issuing bank, it is entitled to reimbursement from the issuing bank. An issuing bank is entitled to reimbursement from its customer, the applicant. If the documents conform, recourse on a draft being contrary to UCP Article 7.a, no question of recourse appears possible. Where the documents do not in fact conform, the question could arise between the two banks if both of them fail to observe the discrepancy and the documents are then refused by the applicant. It is suggested that the issuing bank is not entitled to recourse against the correspondent bank in that situation. Reference is made to Chapter 5 where the question of recourse against the beneficiary on the ground that the documents do not conform is considered as between an issuing or confirming bank and the beneficiary.[1] The further argument has to be met here, that it is the duty of the nominated bank as agent of the issuing bank to check the documents. Can the issuing bank claim against the nominated bank as damages for breach of duty the sum which it has paid to the nominated bank? Three main reasons are suggested as to why it cannot. First, it is also the duty of the issuing bank to check the documents itself: if it had correctly performed that duty, the loss would not have occurred: so the proximate cause of the loss is its own negligence. Secondly, because of the same duty on the part of the issuing bank to check the documents itself, by accepting the documents it is to be taken to have ratified the unauthorised act of the nominated bank in accepting non-conforming documents. Thirdly, if the issuing bank has accepted the documents, UCP Article 16.f will preclude it from claiming subsequently that the documents are not in accordance with the terms and conditions of the credit. This will be the short answer in most cases, and the legal and practical rationale for it is to be found in the first two reasons.

1 See paras **5.93** et seq.

6.44   The position just considered must be distinguished from that where the correspondent bank fails to observe a discrepancy between the documents presented and the terms of the credit and the discrepancy is observed by the issuing bank. If payment has been made by the correspondent bank (acting as nominated bank) it will not be entitled to reimbursement from the issuing bank. If it has already been reimbursed, it is liable to repay the amount reimbursed plus interest. If the credit provides for payment to be deferred, either because it utilises a time draft or because it is a deferred payment credit, the acceptance of the documents by the correspondent bank (acting as nominated bank) will bind the issuing bank because the correspondent bank has acted as its agent to examine and accept or reject the documents. If the applicant refuses the documents because of the discrepancy, and if the correspondent bank does not pay at maturity, the issuing bank will have to pay the beneficiary without a right of reimbursement by the applicant. It will then be entitled to recover its loss from the correspondent bank for breach of its duty to examine the documents with reasonable care. If it has returned the documents to the correspondent bank, its loss will be the amount of its payment to the beneficiary. Otherwise its loss will be the amount of the payment less what it may have been able to recoup as a result of having the security of the documents.

F   RECOURSE BETWEEN THE CORRESPONDENT BANK AND THE BENEFICIARY

6.45   The position where the correspondent bank confirms the credit has already been considered in **Chapter 5**.[1] It is suggested that in the absence of fraud there can be no right of recourse.

1 See paras **5.93** et seq.

6.46   The question of recourse where the correspondent bank does not confirm the credit but acts simply as nominated bank is one on which there is very limited authority. It may arise in a number of situations, some of which are complicated. It is not something which is covered in the UCP. It may be suggested that because the preclusion in Article 16.f applies to an issuing and a confirming bank only, a nominated bank should generally have a right of recourse. Similarly, and in the context of negotiation, the same result may be suggested because the UCP expressly provides for negotiation to be without recourse in the context of a confirming bank – see UCP Article 8.a.ii – but makes no such provision in the context of a nominated bank.[1] But two points must be borne in mind. First, the UCP do not purport to cover all situations. Secondly, the rights and obligations in connection with credits were to be found in the common law and banking practice without reference to the UCP before the situation arose where they are incorporated into, it is believed, all credits coming before the English courts save some standby credits. The common law and banking practice are still the source where the UCP do not cover a situation.

1 The UCP 500 provided for negotiation by both the confirming bank and the issuing bank to be without recourse (Article 9.a.iv and 9.b.iv). The absence of any reference in UCP 600 to negotiation by the issuing bank without recourse is explained by the fact that UCP 600 prohibits a credit being issued by a draft drawn on the applicant and, therefore, no longer envisages any form of negotiation by the issuing bank. It is not a reflection of any change in the basic approach to rights of recourse.

6.47 Where the credit provides for immediate payment by a non-confirming correspondent bank and documents are accepted by that bank and payment is made, the question of recourse by the correspondent bank against the beneficiary will arise if, for example, the issuing bank fails and is unable to reimburse the correspondent bank.[1] It is suggested that these facts would not give the correspondent bank any cause of action against the beneficiary. Would it affect the position if the documents included a sight draft drawn on the issuing bank, which was dishonoured by non-acceptance? The correspondent bank as holder would prima facie have a right of recourse against the beneficiary, the drawer, unless the draft was marked 'without recourse'. It seems unfair to the beneficiary that the probably casual inclusion of the sight draft among the documents should reverse his position. It will have that effect unless an absence of recourse is to be derived from the circumstances of the negotiation as would be the case in respect of an issuing or confirming bank in the absence of the UCP.

1 The problem will be avoided if the timing is such that the correspondent bank can treat its contract with the issuing bank as terminated and arrange with the buyer for the buyer to take up the documents against payment.

6.48 Where immediate payment against documents is made by a non-confirming correspondent bank, the question of recourse will also arise where it is found that the documents do not conform to the credit and so the correspondent bank is not reimbursed by the issuing bank. Can it be asserted against the beneficiary that the payment was made under a mistake of fact that the documents were conforming? Because the bank has no contractual relationship with the beneficiary the analysis must be to some extent different to that in Chapter 5 relating to the position of issuing and confirming banks.[1] The position of the bank is that it has purported to pay and has paid as agent for its principal even though as between it and the principal, the issuing bank, the payment was in breach of the terms of the agency. It is suggested that an agent in such a situation can have no better right of recovery than his principal. The view has been previously expressed that the issuing bank has no right of recovery.[2] But it should not be thought that by reason only of the bank's position as agent it would be barred from suing. In *Colonial Bank v Exchange Bank of Yarmouth, Nova Scotia*[3] it was stated[4] in respect of the plaintiff bank which had paid by mistake 'It seems a perfectly untenable position to say that an agent in that position has not got an interest to recall the money, so that it may be put into the right channel.'[5] It is suggested that in the absence of fraud by the beneficiary or other party presenting the documents, a correspondent bank would have no right of recourse against that party on the ground that it had accepted the documents in the mistaken belief that they complied with the credit whereas in fact they did not. This conclusion may be considered consistent with the commercial function of documentary credits, and with the scheme of Article 16 of the UCP, namely that the buyer/beneficiary should know that once the documents which he has tendered under a credit have been accepted, his right to payment has become absolute.

1 See paras **5.93** et seq.
2 See paras **5.98** and **5.99**.
3 (1885) 11 App Cas 84.
4 (1885) 11 App Cas 84 at 91.
5 See generally *Bowstead on Agency* (18th edn) Article 110.

6.49 The situation considered in the last paragraph may also be complicated by the inclusion of a sight draft among the documents as has been discussed in para **6.47**. The considerations will be similar.

6.50 Where the credit provides for payment to be deferred but does not utilise a time draft, ie it is a deferred payment credit, and the correspondent bank accepts documents presented to it pursuant to the credit which do not conform to the credit,[1] it is suggested that the position is as follows. The acceptance of the documents by the correspondent bank binds the issuing bank so far as the beneficiary is concerned and the beneficiary becomes entitled against the issuing bank to receive payment when the appointed time comes.[2] If the applicant declines to accept the documents the issuing bank then has a claim against the correspondent bank.[3] Can it pass on this claim to the beneficiary? It is suggested that, in the absence of fraud by the beneficiary, it cannot. The claim is not even to recover money paid under a mistake of fact but to recover a sum for which the bank has become liable in damages. The beneficiary does not warrant that the documents which it presents comply with the terms of the credit. It is suggested that no such claim will lie.

1 This makes the assumption, made in para **6.44** above, that the correspondent bank has accepted a duty under the credit to examine the documents. In the circumstances posed it may well not do so. The first examination of the documents will be by the issuing bank.

2 Paras **6.20** and **6.44**.
3 Para **6.44**.

6.51   Where the credit provides for deferment of payment by utilising a time draft among the documents to be presented, if the documents do not conform to the credit but are accepted by the correspondent bank (acting as nominated bank) and then rejected by the buyer or applicant, as between the issuing bank and the beneficiary the documents have been accepted under the credit and the issuing bank is bound to make payment. If the correspondent bank comes to have a claim as the holder of a dishonoured draft, then the question of recourse on the draft will arise. It is to be questioned whether there is any logical reason for distinguishing the position where payment is deferred but no bill is involved. But a correspondent bank that discounts a draft has a right of recourse against the beneficiary in the event of dishonour (except if the bank was acting as confirming bank).

6.52   The last position to be considered is that where the credit provides that it is available by negotiation by the correspondent bank. So the correspondent bank will purchase at a discount for interest the documents which will include a time draft. Here there is authority. In *Maran Road Saw Mill v Austin Taylor & Co Ltd*[1] a credit was opened by Sale & Co available by 90-day drafts drawn on them together with shipping documents as specified, which were to be negotiable by the Bangkok Bank in Kuala Lumpur. It appears that the credit was advised through the latter.[2] Sale & Co failed after the Bangkok Bank had paid on drafts and documents presented to them. The drafts having been dishonoured, the bank claimed repayment from the sellers. The sellers felt obliged to pay and sought to recover the price of the goods from their agents, Austin Taylor, who had arranged the credit as the means of transferring the price to them.[3] Austin Taylor raised the question whether the sellers had been obliged to repay the bank. Ackner J held that they had. After referring to Article 3 of the 1962 Revision of the UCP he stated:[4]

> 'This article makes it clear that a confirming bank may not have recourse. It is otherwise in the case of a non-confirming bank. The reason is that whereas the latter is the agent of the issuing bank for the purpose of advising the credit, it acts as principal vis-à-vis the beneficiary. He is under no duty to negotiate and if it does so, it may make whatever conditions it likes as to a pre-requisite to doing so. It follows that if the credit is available by "time" draft, the negotiating bank may have recourse on the draft if this is ultimately unpaid. The fact of advising places no responsibility on the negotiating bank, no greater responsibility than if it were not the advising bank; and it makes no difference that negotiations may be restricted to that bank. (See Gutteridge & Megrah *The Law of Bankers' Commercial Credits* (4th ed) p 73.)'

The statement '... whereas the latter[5] is the agent of the issuing bank for the purpose of advising the credit, it acts as principal vis-à-vis the beneficiary' is somewhat compressed. The meaning appears to be that in negotiating the documents and draft the correspondent bank acts as principal. If so, an advising bank nominated to negotiate documents is in the same position as a third party bank which negotiates documents under a negotiation credit, and there is a contrast with the position where the correspondent bank receives documents under credits containing other forms of undertaking (or, adopting the language of UCP 600, that is in contrast with the position where the nominated bank honours a credit). Having negotiated the draft and documents as principal, it is entitled to present them to the issuing bank and provided they conform it is entitled to payment as the credit may provide. Therefore, like a negotiation bank[6] it is entitled to recourse against the beneficiary on the bill should it not be honoured.

1 [1975] 1 Lloyd's Rep 156.
2 See [1975] 1 Lloyd's Rep 156 at 161.1, line 21.
3 See para **3.52** above.
4 [1975] 1 Lloyd's Rep 156 at 161.1.
5 The non-confirming bank.
6 See para **7.10** below.

G THE CORRESPONDENT BANK AND THE APPLICANT OR BUYER

6.53 Whatever functions the correspondent bank fulfils there is no contract between it and the applicant for the credit. It was accepted by the Court of Appeal in *United Trading Corpn SA v Allied Arab Bank Ltd*[1] that it was arguable that a bank at one end of a performance bond chain owed a duty of care to the account party at the other end not to pay a fraudulent demand made by the beneficiary. This was questioned by the Court of Appeal in *GKN Contractors Ltd v Lloyds Bank plc*.[2] It is at least as difficult to see how a correspondent bank might owe such a duty. Where a tender of documents is made to the correspondent bank and discrepancies are found which are advised to the buyer through the issuing bank, the buyer may give instructions to take up the documents. If it is later found that there are other discrepancies in addition, the buyer will not be obliged to take up the documents unless he is willing to waive them also. They will be left on the hands of the bank.

1 [1985] 2 Lloyd's Rep 554n at 560.
2 (1985) 30 BLR 48 at 62 see para **9.73**.

H CHARGES OF THE CORRESPONDENT BANK

6.54 UCP Article 37.a provides that the utilisation by one bank of another to give effect to the instructions of the applicant is done for the account of the applicant. It may of course be arranged between the applicant and the issuing bank that the charges of the advising bank shall be for the account of the beneficiary, this being a provision of the underlying contract of sale. The credit will then include a term that the charges of the correspondent bank are for the account of the beneficiary. The correspondent will usually request that they be paid in advance, but if this does not happen then the charges will be deducted from the payment due to the beneficiary when conforming documents are presented.[1] If they are not presented, under Article 37.c the correspondent bank will be entitled to recover its charges for advising the credit from the issuing bank.

1 The advising fee and any amendments fees will have been charged at the time of the advice and amendments. But it very commonly happens that they remain unpaid until payment is made under the credit, when they are deducted with the payment fee.

6.55 Where the correspondent bank's sole initial role is that of advising bank and it subsequently acts as a collecting bank for the beneficiary, or negotiates the documents from the beneficiary and presents them in its own right, it will deduct its charges from what it would otherwise pay the beneficiary. It is the general rule of agency law that an agent is accountable to his principal for any profits above his entitled remuneration from his principal. It is suggested that an attempt to use this rule to require a correspondent bank to pay over these charges to its principal, the issuing bank, would be doomed to failure. For there is nothing improper in a correspondent bank acting in this way; nor are the charges to be attributed to its employment as agent.

Chapter 7

The Collecting Bank and the Negotiation Bank

ADVISING BANKS ACTING AS COLLECTING OR NEGOTIATION BANKS

7.1   An advising bank whose instructions are limited to the advice of the credit may on occasion act as a collecting bank or as a negotiation bank. Its functions in such a situation have been considered in the previous chapter. But a bank may obviously also act as a collecting bank or as a negotiation bank without having acted as an advising bank.

A   COLLECTING BANKS

General

7.2   A collecting bank is a bank which is requested by the beneficiary to present the documents under the credit on the beneficiary's behalf. It may come to act as collecting bank for two rather different reasons. First, the beneficiary may find it convenient to use its services in this way. For example, the beneficiary may prefer to use its own bank to forward the documents where they have to be presented abroad rather than forwarding them itself. It may also want to have the documents checked by the bank for compliance with the credit. If there are discrepancies, a bank may be in a better position to request their waiver than the beneficiary itself. Secondly, the beneficiary may have been financed by the bank to obtain the goods which are the object of the transaction underlying the credit, either by way of a general overdraft arrangement or by a specific advance. In either case the bank may well require that the documents be presented through it, so that it has control of the documents in the event that the transaction goes wrong. Where a credit is a straight credit, that is to say, is not a negotiation credit, the only way in which the beneficiary's bank can involve itself with the documents to be presented under the credit is to act as agent for collection unless, of course, the credit has been advised through it.

The collecting bank as agent

7.3   A collecting bank acts as the agent of the beneficiary for the purposes of presentation and receiving payment.[1] This has the consequence that, if the documents are fraudulent to the beneficiary's knowledge, there will be no obligation to pay the collecting bank.[2] So if the collecting bank makes an advance to the beneficiary in anticipation of the collection, it will be at risk. In cases of fraud it will be important, therefore, to determine whether the bank is collecting in its own right having negotiated, ie purchased, the documents from the beneficiary, or whether it is collecting as the beneficiary's agent. This may involve a careful examination of the relations between the bank and the beneficiary and of the relevant documents, particularly as to at what stage, if it did, the bank credited the beneficiary with the sum in question.[3]

1 See, for example, the role performed by SCB in *Marconi Communications v PT Pan Indonesia Bank* [2007] 2 Lloyds Rep 72 at 75.2.
2 See, among other cases, *United City Merchants (Investments) Ltd v Royal Bank of Canada* [1983] 1 AC 168 and *European Asian Bank AG v Punjab Bank (No 2)* [1983] 1 WLR 642 at 652A, [1983] 1 Lloyd's Rep 611 at 615.1.
3 See *European Asian Bank AG v Punjab Bank (No 2)* [1983] 1 WLR 642 at 657, [1983] 1 Lloyd's Rep 611 at 618, 619. For reference to the cases relating specifically to discount and collection of bills of exchange see *Benjamin's Sale of Goods* (7th edn) paras 22-067 et seq.

Recourse and fraud

7.4   If payment has been obtained fraudulently, then the paying bank has a restitutionary claim against the beneficiary[1]. If the money is still in the hands of the collecting bank, or has been handed over to the beneficiary by the collecting bank acting other than in good faith or acting with knowledge of the paying bank's claim, then a restitutionary claim may also lie against the collecting bank.[2]

1 See para **9.48** below.
2 See para **9.50** below and the discussion of the scope of the change of position defence to restitutionary claims in *Niru Battery Manufacturing Co v Milestone Trading Ltd* [2004] QB 985 at paras 143–172 and 191–192.

B   NEGOTIATION BANKS

General

7.5   As mentioned in **Chapter 6**, the term 'negotiation bank' does not appear in the UCP. It is used here to refer to a bank which has negotiated (ie purchased) documents in its own right to be presented by it as a principal under a letter of credit which is a negotiation credit. Straight and negotiation credits have been considered in **Chapter 2**.[1] The difference between credits available by negotiation and negotiation credits has been described in para **2.19**. In short, a negotiation credit in this sense is one where the undertaking given by the credit is addressed to all bona fide holders of the documents, or to banks generally or to banks of a particular description. It is open to such parties to negotiate, that is, to buy, the documents and to present them under the credit in their own right. In contrast, the undertaking contained in a straight credit is directed only to the beneficiary, and no other party can obtain rights under the credit save by transfer (if it is transferable) or by assignment. A bank which purchases the documents under a negotiation credit may be called a negotiation bank. The essential distinction between a negotiation bank and a collecting bank is that a negotiation bank holds the documents in its own right, whereas a collecting bank holds them as agent for the beneficiary.

1 See para **2.20**.

The contract

7.6   A negotiation bank becomes a contracting party to the credit, and, if the undertaking contained in the credit is not honoured, it may sue the issuing bank and any confirming bank. The contract probably comes into being when the bank acquires the documents in reliance on the credit. The alternative is that it comes into being when the documents are presented by it. The former appears more consistent with the likely position between the issuing bank and the beneficiary, which is that the contract comes into being on the advice of the credit to the beneficiary.[1] A bank may acquire documents without reliance on, and without intending to utilise, the letter of credit.[2] If it does so, it may be that it cannot then operate the credit. This appears to be the position in the United States.[3] If it is the case that the contract between a negotiation bank and the issuing bank comes into being when the negotiation bank acquires the documents, it would follow that no contract would then come into being if the negotiation bank acquires the documents with a different intention. But this need not prevent a contract coming into being subsequently if the intention changes, at any rate by the time documents are actually presented. It is to be pointed out that the paying bank will not know in what circumstances and with what intention the negotiation bank acquired the documents and so, if that were relevant, it would not know whether or not it was bound to accept them. It is therefore suggested that the more practical view is that a bank which acquires documents without the intention of presenting them under the credit, may later change its intention and do so. There is, however, no authority in English law.

1 See para **5.3** above.
2 See the facts in *M A Sassoon & Sons v International Banking Corpn* [1927] AC 711 set out at para **5.96**.
3 See *Banco Nacional Ultramarino v First National Bank of Boston* 289 F 169 (1923).

Recourse against a negotiation bank

7.7   A negotiation bank is in the same position as the beneficiary of a credit so far as any question of recourse by an issuing or confirming bank is concerned. Subject to para **7.8** below, it is suggested that there is, therefore, no right of recourse for the reasons discussed in **Chapter 5** and **Chapter 6**.[1]

1 Paras **5.93** et seq and **6.45** et seq.

Fraud

7.8   The right of a negotiation bank to operate the credit is not defeated by the fact that the beneficiary or a third party has been fraudulent, provided that it takes the documents in good faith. The negotiation bank is not responsible for the genuineness of the documents.[1] There can, however, be recourse against a negotiation bank if there was fraud by the beneficiary and the negotiation bank did not take the documents in good faith or if there was independent fraud by the negotiation bank itself. Formerly, the position was different for a bank which was not a negotiation bank but a bank which had agreed to discount a deferred payment credit by taking an assignment of the beneficiary's rights. That distinction, however, is no longer the case.[2]

1 See *Guaranty Trust Co of New York v Hannay & Co* [1918] 2 KB 623, *European Asian Bank AG v Punjab Bank (No 2)* 1[1983] 1 WLR 642 at 652 and 658 and more generally *United City Merchants (Investments) Ltd v Royal Bank of Canada* [1983] 1 AC 168 and **Chapter 9** below.
2 See para **6.19** above.

Recourse by negotiation bank

7.9   The bank will undertake to negotiate the documents upon terms which may be found in the bank's form completed by the beneficiary requesting the bank to negotiate the documents, or the terms may be found in other documents. It is essential to examine the relevant documents to see what the terms are. Generally the position may be stated as follows. Whereas an issuing bank can look only to the applicant for reimbursement and if the documents which it has accepted do not conform to the credit it is at risk, and a confirming bank can only look to the issuing bank and is similarly at risk, a negotiation bank is free to agree rights of recourse against the beneficiary. The negotiation bank's position is closely allied to that of the beneficiary and unlike an issuing and a confirming bank, will ordinarily have recourse against the beneficiary if the credit fails to provide payment, as is discussed in the next two paragraphs.

(a)   Bills of exchange

7.10   Where, as is usually the case, a negotiation bank buys documents which include drafts, if these are dishonoured the bank has the right of recourse of a holder against the beneficiary as the drawer of the draft.[1] The negotiation bank will only lose this right of recourse on the bill if it is expressly agreed that it shall not have such a right, either as part of the terms on which the bill is discounted, or by the beneficiary marking the bill when he draws it 'without recourse' or with some other wording so as to exclude his liability under it to a holder.[2] Such a wording, however, would not exclude recourse where the beneficiary was fraudulent, although, as the negotiation bank if bona fide would take the documents free of the fraud and be able to present under the credit, recourse should not then be necessary (assuming the documents were otherwise compliant).[3] Even where the bill is drawn without recourse, the negotiation bank may perhaps have a right of recourse arising not on the bill but separately from the negotiation transaction itself.[4] But it is more likely that the drawing of the bill 'without recourse' negates any such right. In short, the negotiation bank will normally be entitled to recover from the beneficiary what it has paid with interest in the event that the bill is dishonoured because the documents are rejected as not complying with the credit, or for any other reason not the fault of the negotiation bank.

1 Bills of Exchange Act 1882, s 55(1).
2 See Bills of Exchange Act 1882, s 16(1).
3 See also Bills of Exchange Act 1882, s 29(1) and 38(2). In *KBC Bank v Industrial Steel (UK) Ltd* [2001] 1 Lloyds Rep 370 the negotiation bank's claim in deceit against the beneficiary succeeded despite having negotiated 'without recourse'. The documents negotiated were discrepant as well as fraudulent and it was, therefore, common ground that the issuing bank had been entitled to reject them.
4 See Case 11 in *Case Studies on Documentary Credits*, ICC No 459.

(b)   Without bills

7.11   It is thought that in the past it was unusual for a negotiation bank to purchase documents which did not include a bill of exchange. The position is changing with the growth of deferred payment credits (which do not utilise a time draft but achieve the same effect). Drafts may also not be used to avoid the heavy stamp duty payable on them in some countries. In the event that this occurs the negotiation bank should agree as one of the terms whereby it undertakes the negotiation that, in the event of the failure of the letter of credit to provide payment, the negotiation bank should be entitled to return the documents to the beneficiary against reimbursement. In the absence of any express term it is suggested that the position would be uncertain. It would as always depend on the facts and circumstances of the particular case. As the beneficiary provides the documents to the negotiation bank on the basis that the credit provides a secure means of payment and that the documents will enable that payment to be obtained, it is suggested that the tendency should be to provide the bank with recourse against the beneficiary in the event that, through no fault of the bank, payment is not available by means of the credit.

Chapter 8

The Documents and their Examination

INTRODUCTION

8.1 When a bank examines documents presented to it under a credit, questions may arise as to the extent of the bank's duty in conducting the examination. Questions may also arise as to what the credit requires in the documents themselves, which is what the bank should be checking in its examination. Those requirements may be requirements which apply to all types of documents, or they may be peculiar to particular types, such as bills of lading or the insurance documents. This chapter therefore divides into three sections: the bank's duty, general requirements as to documents and requirements as to particular documents.

A   A BANK'S DUTY IN THE EXAMINATION OF DOCUMENTS

The duty

8.2 The purpose of a bank's examination of documents is to see whether the documents presented meet the requirements of the credit. Under UCP 600, this duty is contained in Article 14, which provides:

> '**Article 14 Standard for Examination of Documents**
> a.   A nominated bank acting on its nomination, a confirming bank, if any, and the issuing bank must examine a presentation to determine, on the basis of the documents alone, whether or not the documents appear on their face to constitute a complying presentation.'

This article must be read with the definition of 'complying presentation' in Article 2; it is:

> '. . . a presentation that is in accordance with the terms and conditions of the credit, the applicable provisions of these rules and international standard banking practice.'

There is also a requirement of consistency: the documents must be consistent in the sense that the data in each document must not conflict with other data in the same document or in other documents in the presentation. This requirement is found in Article 14.d:

'Article 14 Standard for Examination of Documents

d.   Data in a document, when read in context with the credit, the document itself and international standard banking practice, need not be identical to, but must not conflict with, data in that document, any other stipulated document or the credit.'

8.3   Article 14 represents a significant change from its predecessor, UCP 500 Article 13.a. In UCP 500, the bank's duty was to 'examine all documents stipulated in the Credit *with reasonable care* to ascertain whether or not they appear, on their face, to be in compliance with the terms and conditions of the Credit' (emphasis added). It was never very clear precisely what was added by the 'reasonable care' qualification[1] since, if documents were non-compliant on their face (having regard to international standard banking practice), any reasonably careful examination ought to have detected the discrepancy. If not redundant, it appeared to envisage the possibility of an exceptional case where a discrepancy on the face of the documents might not be discovered despite the exercise of reasonable care. However, as discussed in para 8.4 of the third edition of this book, that gave rise to an apparent inconsistency with UCP 500 Article 14.a which provided for reimbursement of an issuing bank which had paid against documents compliant on their face without any reference to the exercise of reasonable care by that bank.

1   Some guidance as to what was required can be found in a dictum of Evans LJ in *Kredietbank Antwerp v Midland Bank plc* [1999] Lloyd's Rep Bank 219 at 222: 'The professional expertise of a trading bank includes knowledge of the UCP rules and of their practical application. This necessarily involves a degree of judgment, and for this reason the administrative task of checking whether documents conform with the requirements of the credit is supervised by experienced senior managers to whom problems are taken and by whom decisions are made.'

8.4   Under UCP 600, the standard of the bank's examination is set solely by reference to the question of whether the documents appear on their face to constitute a complying presentation. Where there is an issue about compliance not determined by the provisions of the UCP or the credit itself, it is to be resolved by reference to 'international standard banking practice', a concept discussed below. Whilst the content of that practice will no doubt reflect what a reasonable and careful bank would do, there is no longer a separate express obligation for a bank to exercise reasonable care in examining documents. The omission of any reference to reasonable care should be regarded as intended to clarify, rather than amend, the duties of a bank.

8.5   In *Gian Singh & Co Ltd v Banque de l'Indochine* Lord Diplock stated that the relevant provision of the UCP (there the 1962 Revision, but unchanged in UCP 400 and substantially reproduced by UCP 500 Article 13.a) did no more than state the duty of a bank at common law. If the changes in UCP 600 Article 14.a are intended to clarify the position then this is still the case.

1   [1974] 1 WLR 1234 at 1238, [1974] 2 Lloyd's Rep 1 at 11.

8.6   In summary, Articles 14.a and 14.d establish three principles:

(1) that the duty is to examine a presentation to determine, on the basis of the documents alone, whether or not the documents appear on their face to constitute a complying presentation;
(2) that compliance is to be determined by the terms and conditions of the credit, the applicable provisions of the UCP and international standard banking practice;
(3) that documents appearing inconsistent, in the sense described above, will be considered not to comply.

The first and second are considered in this Part, while the third is considered in Part B below.[1]

1 Para **8.42** below.

8.7   Article 14.g provides

'**Article 14 Standard for Examination of Documents**
...
g   A document presented but not required by the credit will be disregarded and may be returned to the presenter.'

This may seem to state the obvious, but it is directed at avoiding any problem arising from a discrepancy in a document not called for by the credit, such as an inconsistency in the description of the goods. Because such a document is not to be examined, such a discrepancy is of no relevance and must be ignored.

8.8   The following Articles are also relevant to the appreciation of a bank's duty:

'**Article 4 Credits v. Contracts**
a.   A credit by its nature is a separate transaction from the sale or other contract on which it may be based. Banks are in no way concerned with or bound by such contract, even if any reference whatsoever to it is included in the credit. Consequently, the undertaking of a bank to honour, to negotiate or to fulfil any other obligation under the credit is not subject to claims or defences by the applicant resulting from its relationships with the issuing bank or the beneficiary. A beneficiary can in no case avail itself of the contractual relationships existing between banks or between the applicant and the issuing bank.
b.   An issuing bank should discourage any attempt by the applicant to include, as an integral part of the credit, copies of the underlying contract, proforma invoice and the like.'

'**Article 5 Documents v. Goods, Services or Performance**
Banks deal with documents and not with goods, services or performance to which the documents may relate.'

'**Article 34 Disclaimer on Effectiveness of Documents**
A bank assumes no liability or responsibility for the form, sufficiency, accuracy, genuineness, falsification or legal effect of any document, or for the

general or particular conditions stipulated in a document or superimposed thereon; nor does it assume any liability or responsibility for the description, quantity, weight, quality, condition, packing, delivery, value or existence of the goods, services or other performance represented by any document, or for the good faith or acts or omissions, solvency, performance or standing of the consignor, the carrier, the forwarder, the consignee or the insurer of the goods or any other person.'

8.9 Article 4.b, which is new to UCP 600, appears to be intended to discourage the practice, which is sometimes seen, of annexing the underlying contract, or related documents, to the credit and purporting to make it part of the credit, although it is unclear what effect parties intend by that. The practice is contrary to the principle, expressed in Article 4.a, that the credit and the underlying contract are autonomous. Article 4.b does not indicate what the bank is supposed to do by way of discouragement or how in practice the provision could be enforced.[1] There is no good reason for a credit bank to purport to 'include' the underlying contact, and a bank should simply refuse to issue or confirm a credit on those terms.

1 Along similar lines, UCP 500 Article 5(a) directed banks to discourage attempts to include excessive detail in the credit 'to avoid confusion or misunderstanding'.

8.10 Article 5 may be seen as restating Article 4 in terms of documents and goods rather than transactions and contracts. Article 34 may be seen as setting out some of the particular consequences of Articles 4 and 5.

International standard banking practice

8.11 In January 2003, during the currency of UCP 500, the ICC issued *International Standard Banking Practice for the Examination of Documents under Documentary Credits* (ISBP).[1] It was the product of extensive work by a task force of the ICC Banking Commission and was approved in October 2002 by the full ICC Commission. In the foreword, it described itself as follows:

> 'The ISBP … is a practical complement to UCP 500, ICC's universally used rules on documentary credits. The ISBP does not amend the UCP. It explains, in explicit detail, how the rules are to be applied on a day-to-day basis. As such, it fills a needed gap between the general principles announced in the rules and the daily work of the documentary credit practitioner.'

However, the absence of any reference to the ISBP in UCP 500 (which predated it by ten years) or any other direct relationship with UCP 500 gave rise to some uncertainty about the status of ISBP. There are no reported decisions referring to or relying on ISBP. Despite the care taken in its compilation, having no contractual effect, it was no more than an important but non-binding source of good banking practice.

1 ICC No 645.

8.12   In 2007, following the publication of UCP 600, a new version of ISBP was published. Although not formally incorporated into UCP 600, it is intended to be integrated with it. The introduction to UCP 600 states:

> 'During the revision process, notice was taken of the considerable work that had been completed in creating the International Standard Banking Practice for the Examination of Documents under Documentary Credits (ISBP), ICC Publication 645. This publication has evolved into a necessary companion to the UCP for determining compliance of documents with the terms of letters of credit. It is the expectation of the Drafting Group and the Banking Commission that the application of the principles contained in the ISBP, including subsequent revisions thereof, will continue during the time UCP 600 is in force. At the time UCP 600 is implemented, there will be an updated version of the ISBP to bring its contents in line with the substance and style of the new rules.'

In turn, the introduction to the 2007 version of ISBP, after quoting the passage above, states:

> 'The international standard banking practices documented in this publication are consistent with UCP 600 and the Opinions and Decisions of the ICC Banking Commission. This document does not amend UCP 600. It explains how the practices articulated in UCP 600 are applied by documentary practitioners. This publication and the UCP should be read in their entirety and not in isolation. It is, of course, recognized that the law in some countries may compel a different practice than those stated here.

> No single publication can anticipate all the terms or the documents that may be used in connection with documentary credits or their interpretation under UCP 600 and the standard practice it reflects. However, the Task Force that prepared Publication 645 endeavoured to cover terms commonly seen on a day-to-day basis and the documents most often presented under documentary credits. The Drafting Group have reviewed and updated this publication to conform with UCP 600.

> It should be noted that any term in a documentary credit which modifies or excludes the applicability of a provision of UCP 600 may also have an impact on international standard banking practice. Therefore, in considering the practices described in this publication, parties must take into account any term in a documentary credit that expressly modifies or excludes a rule contained in UCP 600. This principle is implicit throughout this publication. Where examples are given, these are solely for the purpose of illustration and are not exhaustive.

> This publication reflects international standard banking practice for all parties to a documentary credit. Since applicants' obligations, rights and remedies depend upon their undertaking with the issuing bank, the performance of the underlying transaction and the timeliness of any objection under applicable law and practice, applicants should not assume that they

may rely on these provisions in order to excuse their obligations to reimburse the issuing bank. The incorporation of this publication into the terms of a documentary credit should be discouraged, as the requirement to follow agreed practices is implicit in UCP 600.'

8.13   The intention seems to be that the 'international standard banking practice' referred to in Article 2 comprises, or at least includes, that contained in the ISBP. There are clear practical advantages in having a single authoritative statement of relevant practice. As was pointed out in the Preface to the first edition of this book there are difficulties in looking to the practices of banks as a source of documentary credit obligation. To quote one sentence 'A number of Opinions of the ICC Banking Commission show the differences that can exist on important questions.' It may be difficult for a checker in one bank in one country to know whether a practice of which he is aware is indeed 'international standard banking practice'. Traditionally, in disputed cases, expert evidence was called on both sides to support rival contentions as to suggested established banking practice. The outcome was often difficult to predict: sometimes there was no established practice.

8.14   If that is the intention, however, it is unfortunate that UCP 600 does not expressly say as much in the body of the rules. Despite the importance attached to ISBP by the ICC in the introductory texts, there remains a question as to whether it should be regarded as either definitive or exhaustive, or whether disputed questions of banking practice should continue be treated by the courts as matters on which expert evidence may also be admissible.

'Small print' clauses

8.15   Bills of lading and other transport documents frequently contain numerous detailed provisions, usually on their reverse. How far is a bank obliged to study such terms and their effect to see if they may contain something that would make the document objectionable? This has been touched on in two dicta in English cases, but there has been no specific determination of such a question in a reported case. In *National Bank of Egypt v Hannevig's Bank*[1] Scrutton LJ stated:

> 'In some cases, the obligation of a banker, under such a credit, may need very careful examination. I only say at present that to assume that for one-sixteenth per cent of the amount he advances, a bank is bound carefully to read through all bills of lading presented to it in ridiculously minute type and full of exceptions, to read through the policies and to exercise a judgment as to whether the legal effect of the bill of lading and the policy is, on the whole, favourable to their clients, is an obligation which I should require to investigate considerably before I accepted it in that unhesitating form.'

In *British Imex Industries Ltd v Midland Bank Ltd* Salmon J expressed the same sentiments:[2]

'The defendant bank contends that inasmuch as the bills of lading do not contain on their face an express acknowledgement that the goods have been marked in accordance with the provisions of Additional Clause B, then either they are not clean bills of lading – I have dealt with that point – or that they are so seriously defective that the bank is entitled to refuse payment. It is to be observed that the letter of credit did not call for bills of lading to be indorsed with any acknowledgement that the provisions of Additional Clause B had been complied with. I do not consider that the bank has any right to insist on such an acknowledgement before payment. According to their case, it was their duty, for the remuneration of £18, to read through the multifarious clauses in minute print on the back of these bills of lading, and, having observed Additional Clause B, to consider its legal effect, and then to call for an acknowledgement that it had been complied with. I respectfully share the doubt that Lord Justice Scrutton expressed in *National Bank of Egypt v Hannevig's Bank* as to whether any such duty is cast upon the Bank. I doubt whether they are under any greater duty to their correspondents than to satisfy themselves that the correct documents are presented to them, and that the bills of lading bear no indorsement or clausing by the shipowners or shippers which could reasonably mean that there was or might be some defect in the goods, or in their packing.'

This can be read as suggesting that a bank may wholly ignore the small print. That may seem a somewhat bold view. However, if the bank is not bound to study it in detail, can it be that, if its duty is only to look at it cursorily, its cursory examination may be held to have been negligent? That would invite a contradiction in terms. The practice of banks is generally not to examine such provisions.[3] This practice is confirmed in the transport document provisions of UCP 600. For example Article 20.a.v provides that in respect of bills of lading banks will not examine the contents of the terms and conditions of carriage.

1 (1919) 3 LDAB 213 (the case is also reported in 1 Ll L Rep 69 but Scrutton LJ is simply reported as having given a judgment concurring with that of Bankes LJ).
2 [1958] 1 QB 542 at 551.
3 Cited in *Homburg Houtimport BV v Agrosin Private Ltd, The Starsin* [2004] 1 AC 715 at para 17.

The burden of proof

8.16   In *Gian Singh & Co Ltd v Banque de l'Indochine*, Lord Diplock held that the bank's customer bore the burden of proving that the bank had failed to exercise reasonable care in examining the documents.[1] That must be correct. It does not follow, however, that it is not for the bank which seeks reimbursement to establish at least a prima facie case that the documents which it has examined and accepted do conform to the credit. If it fails in that, it will of course lose the case. But it will otherwise win unless the defendant applicant, or issuing bank, succeeds in establishing a discrepancy or discrepancies and that the bank seeking reimbursement should have discovered them. In practical terms the burden will therefore be on the party alleging the discrepancy to establish it.

1 [1974] 1 WLR 1234 at 1239, [1974] 2 Lloyd's Rep 1 at 11.

The autonomy of the credit: extraneous matters

8.17   The bank should not take account of any matters other than the terms of the credit and the documents which are presented to it. This is subject to the possible exception considered under the next heading[1] and to the exceptions of established fraud and illegality which are covered in **Chapter 9** and **Chapter 13**. This principle, referred to as the principal of autonomy of the credit has been introduced in **Chapter 1**.[2] Its observation is essential to the viability of documentary credits as a means of secured payment under international contracts. The principle is enshrined in UCP Articles 4 and 5. The leading English authority is *United City Merchants (Investments) Ltd v Royal Bank of Canada*[3] where Lord Diplock stated:

> 'If, on their face, the documents presented to the confirming bank by the seller conform with the requirements of the credit as notified to him by the confirming bank, the bank is under a contractual obligation to the seller to honour the credit, notwithstanding that the bank has knowledge that the seller at the time of presentation of the conforming documents is alleged by the buyer to have, and in fact has already, committed a breach of his contract with the buyer for the sale of the goods to which the documents appear on their face to relate, that would have entitled the buyer to treat the contract of sale as rescinded and to reject the goods and refuse to pay the seller the purchase price. The whole commercial purpose for which the system of confirmed irrevocable documentary credits has been developed in international trade is to give to the seller an assured right to be paid before he parts with control of the goods that does not permit of any dispute with the buyer as to the performance of the contract of sale being used as a ground for non-payment or reduction or deferment of payment.'

1 See para **8.22**.
2 See para **1.34**.
3 [1983] 1 AC 168 at 183.

8.18   An early illustration is the case of *Urquhart, Lindsay & Co Ltd v Eastern Bank Ltd*.[1] The claimant sellers had entered a contract with buyers in Calcutta to ship machinery in instalments at agreed prices subject to a term that if the cost of labour increased, the price should be correspondingly increased. A confirmed irrevocable credit was opened by the defendant bank with a limit of £70,000, the documents to include 'signed invoices in duplicate'. Two shipments were made and paid for. The buyers then found that the invoices had included an element on account of increased costs and directed the bank to decline to pay more than the original prices. The bank accepted, and acted on, the buyer's direction. So the claimants refused to part with their documents. They cancelled the contract and sued the bank for damages, being the loss of material thrown on their hands and loss of profit. It was argued for the defendants that the letter of credit should be taken to incorporate the contract between the parties and that under it any price increases were to be dealt with outside the letter of credit. Rowlatt J stated:[2] 'The answer to this is that the defendants [the bank] undertook to pay the amount of invoices for machinery without qualification, the basis of this form of banking facility being that the buyer is taken for the purposes of all questions between himself and his banker or between his banker and the seller to be content to accept the invoices of the seller as correct.' The claimants succeeded against the bank, and it is to be hoped that the bank was able to obtain an indemnity from its clients whose instructions it had accepted, but should have refused.

1 [1922] 1 KB 318.
2 [1922] 1 KB 318 at 322, 323.

8.19 In *Westpac Banking Corpn v South Carolina National Bank*[1] the Privy Council held that the court below had erred in speculating how a bill of lading came to be issued rather than considering only the documents. Lord Goff of Chieveley stated:

> 'Their Lordships approach the matter as follows. First, they are unable to accept the proposition that the words "Shipped on Board" make the bill internally inconsistent. True it is that the bill is on a "received for shipment" form and for that reason refers to *Columbus America* as the intended vessel; but there is nothing inconsistent in a document which states that the specified goods have been received for shipment on board a named vessel and have in fact been shipped on board that vessel. Their Lordships feel bound to say, with all respect, that the majority of the Court of Appeal fell into error in their approach to the construction of the bill of lading. For, as appears from the judgment of Mr Justice Priestly, he went beyond the terms of the document itself and sought to draw inferences of fact as to what had occurred at the time when the document was issued. In particular, he inferred that the bill of lading was in fact the receipt which was issued for the goods received at Sydney, and that it was in fact so issued at the time when those goods were so received. In their Lordships' view there was no sufficient basis for either inference. Some other more informal receipt may have been provided by the agents at Sydney at the time when the goods were received there, to be replaced later by the bill of lading issued at Newcastle; and in any event the bill of lading may have been signed and issued at Newcastle at some date after the date of the receipt of the goods at Sydney. Be that as it may, it is well settled that a bank which issues a letter of credit is concerned with the form of the documents presented to it, and not with the underlying facts. It forms no part of the bank's function, when considering whether to pay against the documents presented to it, to speculate about the underlying facts. For that reason, the Court of Appeal erred in approaching the problem by seeking to draw the inferences of fact to which their Lordships have referred.'[2]

In short a bank should not speculate as to facts which may lie behind the documents.

1 [1986] 1 Lloyd's Rep 311 at 315.
2 See further para **8.91** below.

8.20   In *J H Rayner & Co Ltd v Hambro's Bank Ltd*[1] the judge at first instance had heard evidence that there was a trade usage that 'coromandel groundnuts' were the same as 'machine-shelled groundnut kernels', these being respectively the terms employed in the credit itself, and in the bills of lading, and he held that the bank was not obliged to reject the documents in the light of this. The Court of Appeal dismissed the usage as irrelevant. The terms of the bank's mandate were to pay against documents relating to coromandel groundnuts, and it paid against any other documents at its peril.[2]

1 [1943] KB 37.
2 As to trade usage, see also para **8.45** below.

8.21   Despite this, it must be recognised that the bank's duty is not to engage in a merely mechanical proof-reading exercise but to use its judgment, banking experience and general knowledge to test compliance. For example, a credit may call for documents evidencing shipment to 'any European port'. A bank can safely accept a bill of lading showing goods consigned to Rotterdam and safely reject one showing goods consigned to Singapore without requiring documentary proof of the fact that the former port is in Europe and the latter is not.[1] Other cases may be less clear-cut and there must remain some doubt as to where exactly the dividing line falls between a fact which a bank can be expected to know, or to look up in an atlas, and one which it is not required to investigate.

1 See More Queries and Responses on UCP500 ICC No 596, Ref 261: 'It can fall within the scope of a nominated and/or issuing bank to satisfy itself that the ports mentioned on the bills of lading ... are either those specifically stated in the credit, or are located in the country or region that are specified in the credit. If in the course of this investigation it transpires that one or both of the mentioned "ports" are not actually ports, then the nominated and/or issuing bank has the right to highlight the anomaly as a discrepancy.'

Non-documentary conditions: the inclusion of 'facts' among the requirements of the credit

8.22   It sometimes happens that the credit requires that the bank shall be satisfied of a fact before it accepts documents, or it contains a provision which has that effect. Two examples may be given. In the *Gian Singh & Co Ltd v Banque de l'Indochine*,[1] one of the documents required was a certificate signed by Balwant Singh, holder of a passport of a particular number. This meant that the passport had to be presented with the documents so the bank could compare the signatures to see if that on the passport corresponded with that on the certificate. The passport was not a document which would be retained by the bank after payment and passed with the other documents to the applicant. After checking it would be returned to the person who presented the documents. It appears that in this case by their agreement that the credit should take this form the buyer and seller had imposed on the bank a duty which fell outside its duty as foreseen by the UCP. The bank's duty was still a documentary one and by agreeing to open a credit in such terms it was indicating that it was prepared to undertake the duty. In *Banque de l'Indochine v J H Rayner (Mincing Lane) Ltd*[2] under the heading 'Special Conditions' the credit stated 'Shipment to be effected on vessel belonging to shipping company that member of an International Shipping Conference'. Parker J held[3] that, although no specific documentary proof was called for, as parties to credits deal only in documents, the beneficiaries were obliged to provide reasonable documentary proof. Thus the absence of a certificate to the required effect would have given the bank reason to refuse payment. In the Court of Appeal Sir John Donaldson MR stated:[4]

> 'This is an unfortunate condition to include in a documentary credit because it breaks the first rule of such a transaction, namely, that the parties are dealing in documents, not facts. The condition required a state of fact to exist. What the letter of credit should have done was to call for a specific document which was acceptable to the buyer and his bank evidencing the fact that the vessel was owned by a member of a conference. It did not do so and as, accordingly, the confirming bank had to be satisfied of the fact, it was entitled to call for any evidence establishing that fact. All sorts of interesting questions could have arisen as to what evidence could have been called for and what would have been the position if, contrary to that evidence, the vessel was not owned by a conference member. In fact it was so owned and merchants produced the evidence required by the bank before the expiry of the credit. Accordingly no such questions arise.'[5]

1 [1974] 1 WLR 1234, [1974] 2 Lloyd's Rep 1.
2 [1983] QB 711.
3 [1983] QB 711 at 719B–C.
4 [1983] QB 711 at 728G–H.
5 See also *Astro Exito Navegacion SA v Chase Manhattan Bank NA, The Messiniaki Tolmi* [1986] 1 Lloyd's Rep 455 at 461–464.

8.23   The problem of non-documentary conditions is addressed in the UCP by Article 14.h. It provides:

'Article 14 Standard for Examination of Documents
h.   If a credit contains a condition without stipulating the document to indicate compliance with the condition, banks will deem such condition as not stated and will disregard it.'

The alternative which was considered and rejected when the rule was first introduced, as UCP 500 Article 13.c, was that a bank might accept any documentary proof which it deemed sufficient where there was a non-documentary condition. The problem of non-documentary conditions is a real one, to which the Article may provide a solution. The only satisfactory solution, however, is that banks should not accept instructions to issue or to confirm credits containing non-documentary conditions. Article 14.h may give rise to two difficulties. The first can be illustrated on the facts of the

Banque de l'Indochine case and of the *Gian Singh* case, which have been considered in the previous paragraph. In the *Banque de l'Indochine* case, if Article 14.h had been applied, there would have been no need for any confirmation that the vessel belonged to an International Shipping Conference. In the *Gian Singh* case, if applied, it would probably have had the result that the bank could have ignored the requirement to compare the signatures. The former confirmation as to the vessel may not have been of fundamental importance: but the latter verification of signature was intended as an essential step to prevent fraud. Is it right that a bank can accept such instructions and then by reliance on the UCP be entitled to disregard them? It could well be argued that a bank was in breach of its duty to the applicant/customer in accepting such instructions without pointing out that, once incorporated in the credit, they would have to be ignored. It is advisable that if a bank accepts instructions in relation to a credit which contains a condition which is not meant to be complied with by means of a document then Article 14.h should be excluded. If the condition can be complied with in documentary form, it should be expressed in a documentary form.

8.24   The second problem arises in connection with the construction of a credit which contains a non-documentary condition and incorporates Article 14.h.[1] It arises because the parties to a contract are free to make their own bargain within the limits of the law, and the UCP do not have the force of statute. It is clear that, if a credit expressly provided that Article 14.h should not apply, it would not. It can be strongly argued that the same result can be achieved by implication in appropriate circumstances. For the inclusion of a term in the credit that payment is only to be made if a non-documentary condition is satisfied is an expression of the parties' intention which is specific to that credit and to which it may be assumed from the circumstances that the parties have directed their attention. It is a principle of English law relating to the construction of contracts that, where there is a conflict between an express term of the contract and a standard incorporated term, the express term should be given preference on the ground that it is a term to which the parties have given their attention.[2] Where a credit is issued containing a non-documentary condition among those to be satisfied before payment, it can certainly be argued that it is Article 14.h which must give way. The strength of the argument will be increased the greater the importance of the condition to the working of the credit. If the argument was accepted, a further difficulty might arise because the court might find that Article 14.h had been excluded as between the applicant and the issuing bank but not as between the issuing bank and the beneficiary. The bank might then find itself in the most unfortunate position of being obliged to take up the documents but unable to pass them on if there was a non-documentary discrepancy. It is suggested that in the absence of an express exclusion an English court will seek to uphold the scheme of the UCP by requiring all effective conditions to be documentary.

1 The exclusion of Article 14.h from the credit would make plain the parties' intention that the credit should be operated in accordance with its terms.
2 See *Chitty on Contracts* (30th edn) para 12-079.

8.25   The issues discussed in the preceding paragraphs were considered by the Singapore Court in *Korea Exchange Bank v Standard Chartered Bank*.[1] Korea Exchange Bank issued credits in the amount of US$800,000 to cover a purchase of gas oil but subject to an express condition that the amount payable would automatically fluctuate according to a price clause, which set the price of the gas oil by reference to the market. Conditions of this type are not uncommon in commodity sales. Standard Chartered Bank negotiated the credits, paying a sum significantly in excess of US$800,000 because the market price of gas oil had risen. However, Korea Exchange refused to reimburse Standard Chartered in full arguing, amongst other things, that the price fluctuation clause was non-documentary and therefore had to be disregarded under UCP 500 Article 13.c, the predecessor to Article 14.h. Andrew Ang J rejected that argument for two reasons. First, he observed that the purpose of Article 13.c was to protect a negotiating bank or confirming bank (or, presumably, a beneficiary) against the issuing bank, referring to the statement in *Documentary Credits: UCP 500 & 400 Compared* that the onus was on the applicant and issuing bank to issue the credit properly and to determine the documents required. He said that Korea Exchange was 'turning Article 13.c on its head' by attempting to use it to renege on its obligations under the credit.[2] Second, he said that the credit would be unworkable without the express fluctuation provision because the price of gasoil was not fixed. Therefore, even if non-documentary, effect should be given to it in priority to Article 13.c.[3]

1 [2006] 1 SLR 565.
2 [2006] 1 SLR 565 at para 30.
3 [2006] 1 SLR 565 at para 33.

8.26   The problem with non-documentary conditions is that the bank examining a presentation has no means of determining whether they have been satisfied without reference to extraneous material, and it has only a limited time to refuse a non-compliant presentation.[1] One way of avoiding the problem is to require the presentation of a suitable certificate or statement by the beneficiary. For example, if the parties wish the amount payable under the credit to fluctuate according to the market price, as in *Korea Exchange Bank*, then the credit could stipulate for the presentation of a statement of the price. The issuing bank can then make payment by reference to the statement without any need to investigate the market itself. If the applicant or issuing bank is concerned that this leaves too much to the beneficiary, then the credit could require a statement from a trusted third party.

1 See para 5.59. The problem does not seem to have arisen in *Korea Exchange Bank* because there was no issue as to the relevant price of gas oil.

8.27   In *Oliver v Dubai Bank Kenya Ltd*[1] a standby credit was used to secure payment under a share sale agreement. It was payable against presentation of, amongst other documents, an authenticated Swift message or tested telex issued by the *issuing* bank confirming the beneficiary's fulfilment of their commitments under the share sale agreement. By agreeing those terms, the beneficiary fell into the trap of making payment conditional on presentation of a document which it had no power itself to obtain. The beneficiary sought to extricate himself from this trap by arguing that the relevant condition should be disregarded because it required the bank to concern itself with the underlying agreement in deciding whether to issue the telex. Andrew Smith J said that if the credit made the obligation to pay conditional upon anything other than a documentary condition then the court might have to consider whether the general words that incorporate the UCP into the credit should prevail over the parties' express stipulation. However, the relevant condition did not expressly oblige the bank to decide whether the Swift or telex should be issued, and no obligation to that effect could be implied if the consequence would be that the condition itself would then have to be disregarded as non-documentary.[2] He added:[3]

> 'I am not dissuaded from this conclusion by the claimants' observation that this in effect puts it within the bank's sole power to prevent the letter of credit becoming payable. After all, the claimants' interpretation would put it within their sole power to ensure that the letter becomes payable in any circumstances: it would, in the United States language referred to by Jack, cit sup, at para. 12.10,[4] be a "suicide credit".'

1 [2007] EWHC 2165 (Comm)
2 At para 15.
3 At para 16
4 See now para **12.11**.

8.28   It will generally not be possible to imply a term which is non-documentary in nature. In *Uzinterimpex JSC v Standard Bank plc*,[1] the defendant, Standard Bank, had financed advance payments on behalf of its customer, who was purchasing consignments of cotton from the claimant, Uzinterimpex. Standard Bank was the beneficiary of a demand guarantee from the National Bank of Uzbekistan in the amount of the advance payments, with the intention that Standard Bank could recover the payments if the goods were not delivered. The advance payment guarantee was subsequently called by Standard Bank, even though some of the goods had in fact been received by its customer and the proceeds banked with Standard Bank. Uzinterimpex (which had taken an assignment of NBU's position, having presumably had to reimburse NBU) argued that Standard Bank had made a double recovery and that it had an implied obligation to account to the NBU 'in circumstances where the bank had received both the proceeds of the guarantee and the proceeds of the cotton to which it related'. The Court of Appeal rejected the argument. Moore-Bick LJ emphasised that banks have the obligation to consider whether documents conform *on their face* and said:[2]

> 'Banks cannot be expected to be aware of, or to implement, terms that do not appear on the face of the documents. The implied term for which Uzinterimpex contends would have the potential effect of imposing on the Bank a liability which could not be identified from the face of the document and which would be very uncertain in its effect, since as pleaded the term

leaves it wholly unclear when or by whom the demand is to be found to have exceeded the loss sustained by AMJ or might otherwise be found to be excessive.'

1 [2008] 2 Lloyd's Rep 456.
2 [2008] 2 Lloyd's Rep 456 at para 23.

The bank is not concerned with 'why?'

8.29   It is a bank's duty to construe its instructions which have become the terms of the credit, and to consider the documents presented to it, without speculating on what may have been in its customer's mind. In *Commercial Banking Co of Sydney Ltd v Jalsard Pty Ltd*,[1] Lord Diplock stated:[2]

'The banker is not concerned as to whether the documents for which the buyer has stipulated serve any useful commercial purpose or as to why the customer called for tender of a document of a particular description.'

But this must not be taken too far. The commercial purpose of most documents is clear, and, should it need to, a bank is entitled to have that purpose in mind in considering whether a tendered document satisfies the credit. An example of this is *Kredietbank Antwerp v Midland Bank plc*.[3] The credit required presentation of a 'draft survey report' which, it was argued by the buyer, must be a report containing measurements of the drafts of the vessel. The document presented was entitled 'draft surveyor report' and stated only the weight of the goods loaded as measured by the draft surveyor. Evans LJ held that the document was conformant, observing in support of his holding that what the buyer was interested in was the weight of the cargo and the draft measurements, and thus the contents of a 'draft survey report' would have been of no concern to him.[4] However, what the bank is not entitled to do is to say 'I do not see the point of this, so I will not bother about it'. It is not for a bank to reason why.[5]

1 [1973] AC 279, PC.
2 [1973] AC 279 at 286.
3 [1999] Lloyd's Rep Bank 219.
4 [1999] Lloyd's Rep Bank 219 at 230.
5 See per Devlin J in *Midland Bank Ltd v Seymour* [1955] 2 Lloyd's Rep 147 at 151.2 and *Seaconsar Far East Ltd v Bank Markazi Jomhouri Islami Iran* [1993] 1 Lloyd's Rep 236 at 239.

Ambiguity

8.30   Where the terms of the credit are ambiguous in the sense that it is unclear what is called for, or unclear whether A or B is called for, a bank may be entitled to act on its own interpretation of the terms provided that it is reasonable. This and the opposing concept that in this time of often almost instantaneous communications a bank should seek instructions to clarify the ambiguity have been considered in **Chapter 4.**[1]

1 Paras **4.5–4.9.**

B   GENERAL REQUIREMENTS AS TO DOCUMENTS

Strict compliance

8.31   The documents must comply strictly with the requirements of the credit. As stated by Viscount Sumner in *Equitable Trust Co of New York v Dawson Partners Ltd*:[1]

> 'It is both common ground and common sense that in such a transaction the accepting bank can only claim indemnity if the conditions on which it is authorised to accept are in the matter of the accompanying documents strictly observed. There is no room for documents which are almost the same, or which will do just as well. Business could not proceed securely on any other lines. The bank's branch abroad, which knows nothing officially of the details of the transaction thus financed, cannot take upon itself to decide what will do well enough and what will not. If it does as it is told, it is safe; if it declines to do anything else, it is safe; if it departs from the conditions laid down, it acts at its own risk.'

Quoting this passage in the *Gian Singh* case[2] Lord Diplock stated:[3] 'This oft-cited[4] passage has never been questioned or improved upon.' The issue in the *Equitable Trust* case was whether a requirement of 'a certificate of quality to be issued by experts who are sworn brokers' was satisfied by a certificate signed by one such broker.[5] It was held by the House of Lords that it was not. Reference may also be made to the dictum of Bailhache J in *English, Scottish and Australian Bank Ltd v Bank of South Africa*[6] which has also often been referred to:

> 'It is elementary to say that a person who ships in reliance on a letter of credit must do so in exact compliance with its terms. It is also elementary to say that a bank is not bound or indeed entitled to honour drafts presented to it under a letter of credit unless those drafts with the accompanying documents are in strict accord with the credit as opened.'

Despite the 'common sense' and 'elementary' nature of the rule of strict compliance (a rule which is not expressly stated in the UCP or ISBP) there has been much debate and litigation over just how strict or exact the compliance must be. It is clear from the passages cited that it is no part of the bank's role to consider the materiality of discrepancies to the parties or whether they affect the value or effect of the documents. On the other hand, as mentioned above, document examination requires judgment by the bank and is not simply a mechanical exercise of comparison. The doctrine of strict compliance is not to be applied in a literal or robotic manner[7] and does not require the presentation of documents the contents of which exactly duplicate the relevant parts of the credit.[8] Various aspects of the doctrine are considered with examples in the following paragraphs.

1 (1926) 27 Ll L Rep 49 at 52.
2 [1974] 1 WLR 1234.
3 [1974] 1 WLR 1234 at 1239, 1240.
4 See, eg, *J H Rayner & Co Ltd v Hambros Bank Ltd* [1943] KB 37 at 40; *Bank Melli Iran v Barclays Bank* [1951] 2 Lloyd's Rep 367 at 374; *Moralice (London) Ltd v E D and F Man* [1954] 2 Lloyd's Rep 526 at 532; *Banque de l'Indochine v J H Rayner Ltd* [1983] QB 711 at 730; *Glencore International AG v Bank of China* [1996] 1 Lloyd's Rep 135 at 146.
5 Whether the sellers could have produced a certificate signed by two or more 'experts who were sworn brokers' to cover what was said to be 'a quantity of sticks, stones and old iron' instead of '3000 kilos Java vanilla beans, sound, sweet and of prime quality' is unknown.
6 (1922) 13 Ll L Rep 21 at 24.
7 Ellinger, *The Doctrine of Strict Compliance: Its Development and Current Construction*, in Francis Rose (ed), *Lex Mercatoria*.
8 Ie what is sometimes referred to as 'mirror image' (eg in *UCP 500 and 400 Compared* ICC No 511, at p 39; *Kredietbank Antwerp v Midland Bank plc* [1998] 2 Lloyd's Rep Bank 173), although a pedant might observe that a mirror image is precisely the reverse of what is intended.

(a) Technicalities

8.32 A discrepancy may not affect the value or merchantability of the goods, and may thus appear merely technical. A bank is nonetheless obliged to take the point unless it is instructed by its customer, the buyer, that the documents are acceptable.[1] The buyer's reason for not wanting to take up the documents is almost always unrelated to the discrepancy, for example the market may have moved against him or he may suspect that the goods do not comply with the contract. In *Glencore International AG v Bank of China*[2] Sir Thomas Bingham MR observed, 'The Judge described the Bank of China's argument as "very technical" and observed that it might appear to lack merit. Both comments are apt. But a rule of strict compliance gives little scope for recognizing the merits.' Because so many sets of documents are presented which do not comply with the terms and conditions of the credit,[3] a technical discrepancy may be the buyer's best chance of avoiding paying for the goods.

1 *Glencore International AG v Bank of China* [1996] 1 Lloyd's Rep 135.
2 [1996] 1 Lloyd's Rep 135 at 153.
3 See *Banque de l'Indochine v J H Rayner Ltd* [1983] QB 711 at 733F.

(b) No application of the de minimis rule

8.33 In *Moralice (London) Ltd v E D and F Man*[1] the documents were required to evidence the shipment of 500 metric tons of sugar in bags of 100 kgs net weight each. The shipment was three bags short (0.06%). It was held that because it was a letter of credit transaction the maxim *de minimis non curat lex*, or the rule of insignificance, could not be relied upon, and the bank was entitled to reject the documents. (This case would today be decided differently by reason of UCP Article 30.b, which allows a tolerance of 5%.[2]) Among the several points taken in *Soproma SpA v Marine and Animal By-Products Corpn*[3] it was argued that the bills of lading did not comply with the credit because they stated that at the moment of loading the temperature of the fish meal did not exceed 100°F, whereas the credit referred to 37.5°C. The difference was a matter of 0.5°C. F. McNair J who had also decided the *Moralice* case[4] stated:[5] 'Seeing that the de minimis rule does not apply to the tender of documents under a letter of credit (see the [*Moralice* case] I suppose that in strict law I should give effect to this objection, but I confess I should be reluctant to do so if it stood alone.' There were other valid objections to the documents so the point was unimportant. The case indicates the reluctance of judges to take the principle of strict compliance to absurd lengths. It may well be that had the temperature point been the sole point in the case the court would have found a way round it, perhaps by concluding that to the nearest degree 100° F was the Fahrenheit equivalent of 37.5° C. The point also illustrates the desirability of following the terms of the credit precisely: if the document had been expressed in Celsius, no point should have arisen. This aspect of the strict compliance principle is relevant where there are very small numerical discrepancies. Because Article 30.b gives a tolerance of 5%, the principle will seldom apply where the quantity shipped is in question. It will be relevant in the case of other divergences. When it can be plainly seen that the divergence is of no possible importance, the court may look for a way round, or ignore it where it is almost imperceptible.[6] But otherwise, a set of documents which does not precisely meet the terms of the credit must be rejected.

1 [1954] 2 Lloyd's Rep 526.
2 See paras **8.70** et seq.
3 [1966] 1 Lloyd's Rep 367.
4 Above.
5 [1966] 1 Lloyd's Rep 367 at 390.
6 See *Astro Exito Navegacion SA v Chase Manhattan Bank NA* [1986] 1 Lloyd's Rep 455 at 461, Leggatt J; affirmed on other grounds [1998] 2 Lloyd's Rep 217.

(c)   Exact literal compliance

8.34   Notwithstanding the rejection of the *de minimis* principle, insignificant or trivial differences such as typographical errors in names are not regarded as discrepancies. 'While the English and Canadian courts have not adopted a rule of substantial documentary compliance there has apparently been recognition that there must be some latitude for minor variations or discrepancies that are not sufficiently material to justify a refusal of payment.'[1] Of course this begs the question of what is immaterial, insignificant or trivial.[2] In *Seaconsar Far East Ltd v Bank Markazi Jomhouri Islami Iran*[3] Lloyd LJ said:[4]

> 'Mr. Clarke relies on the observation of Mr. Justice Parker in the *Banque de l'Indochine* case [1982] 2 Lloyd's Rep 476 at 482; p 721:
>
>> "I accept ... that Lord Sumner's statement[5] cannot be taken as requiring rigid meticulous fulfilment of precise wording in all cases. Some margin must and can be allowed ..."
>
> He argues that the absence of the letter of credit number and the buyer's name was an entirely trivial feature of the document. I do not agree. I cannot regard as trivial something which, whatever may be the reason, the credit specifically requires. It would not, I think, help to attempt to define the sort of discrepancy which can properly be regarded as trivial. But one might take, by way of example, *Bankers Trust Co v State Bank of India*, [1991] 2 Lloyd's Rep 443 where one of the documents gave the buyer's telex number as 931310 instead of 981310. The discrepancy in the present case is not of that order.'

1 *Bank of Nova Scotia v Angelica-Whitewear Ltd* [1987] 1 SCR 59 at 67.
2 If the test, as suggested in Seaconsar, is that 'trivial' errors can be ignored, then one has the possibility of the parties arguing over whether a particular error is trifling (de minimis: 'minimus' least, smallest, trifling), when the document must be rejected, or merely trivial, when it must be accepted.
3 [1993] 1 Lloyd's Rep 236.
4 [1993] 1 Lloyd's Rep 236 at 240.
5 See para **8.31** above.

8.35 In *Hing Hip Hing Fat Co Ltd v Daiwa Bank Ltd*,[1] the credit was applied for by Cheergoal Industries Limited, and this name appeared on the credit. But the presenting bank 'presented the letter of credit on a document which showed the drawee as Cheergoal Industrial Limited'.[2] Kaplan J referred to a passage from *Gutteridge & Megrah*[3] to the effect that strict compliance did not extend to the dotting of 'i's and the crossing of 't's or obvious typographical errors, concluding that it was impossible to generalise: each case had to be considered on its own merits. He held that the reference to 'Industrial' was an obvious typographical error, had caused no confusion and could not be relied upon as a discrepancy.

1 [1991] 2 HKLR 35 (Hong Kong).
2 It is not clear which document or documents required by the credit was discrepant.
3 *The Law of Bankers' Commercial Credits* (7th edn) p 120.

8.36 In *United Bank Ltd v Banque Nationale de Paris*,[1] in Singapore, it was held that a bank was entitled to reject documents in the name of a company called 'Pan Associated Pte Ltd' when the letter of credit was issued in favour of 'Pan Associated Ltd', even though there was evidence that under Singapore company law there could not be two different companies with those names and therefore the difference was 'commercially insignificant'. Chao Hick Tin J said that 'any discrepancy, other than obviously typographical errors, will entitle either the negotiating or the issuing bank to reject'.

1 [1992] 2 SLR 64. Other Commonwealth and United States decisions on this point include: *Royal Bank of Canada v Ohannesyan* [1994] OJ No 1728 (Canada), name '*Gary* Ohannesyan' acceptable tender for '*Garo* Ohannesyan' in credit; *Voest-Alpine Trading USA Corp v Bank of China* (2000) US Dist LEXIS 8223 (USA), port name 'Zhangjiag*ng*' acceptable tender for 'Zhangjiag*ang*'; *Hanil Bank v PT Bank Negara Indonesia* (2000) US Dist LEXIS 2444 (USA), name 'Sung Jun Electronics Co' not acceptable for 'Sung Jin Electronics Co' (and note that this was the issuing bank's mistake in the drafting of the credit, not that of the beneficiary). ICC Banking Commission *Opinions*: error in postal code acceptable; name 'Chai' not acceptable for 'Chan'; address 'Industrial Parl' acceptable for 'Industrial Park' (all ICC No 565, Ref 209); goods description 'raygn' not acceptable for 'rayon' (ICC No 613, Ref 345). This last *Opinion* is doubtful, as is the Commission's view that the bank has a discretion to waive the error without express consent of the applicant.

8.37 In *Kredietbank Antwerp v Midland Bank plc*,[1] Evans LJ, after reviewing *Seaconsar* and other cases concluded that:

> 'the requirement of strict compliance is not equivalent to a test of exact literal compliance in all circumstances and as regards all documents. To some extent, therefore, the banker must exercise his own judgment whether the requirement is satisfied by the documents presented to him.'

The Court of Appeal there held that a 'draft surveyor report' signed by 'Daniel C. Griffith (Holland) BV ... member of the worldwide inspectorate' conformed with the requirement to tender a 'draft survey report issued by Griffith Inspectorate'. This represents a loosening of the rule of strict compliance which, it is suggested, may go too far. It is conceivable that the buyer in Kredietbank might have had a good reason for requiring a certificate from 'Griffith Inspectorate' rather than 'Daniel C. Griffith (Holland) BV inspectorate'. Many international firms of professionals have affiliates or subsidiaries which have very similar names but which do not necessarily have the legal identity, reputation or liability insurance. Documents may need to be passed on to sub-buyers, customs authorities or official bodies who require exact compliance. It is not for a bank to speculate or investigate why the certificate was required in that form.[2]

1 [1999] Lloyd's Rep Bank 219 at 223. See Ellinger, The Doctrine of Strict Compliance: Its Development and Current Construction, in Francis Rose (ed), *Lex Mercatoria*.
2 See para **8.29** above.

8.38 It is suggested that the correct approach is that a document containing an error in a name or similar should be rejected unless the nature of the error is such that it is unmistakably typographical and that the document could not reasonably be referring to a person or organisation different from the one specified in the credit. In assessing this, the bank should look only at the context in which the name appears in the document and not judge it against the facts of the underlying transaction. This is consistent with the position in the United States; as shown by *Beyene v Irving Trust Co*.[1] There the name 'Sofan' was misspelled as 'Soran'. The Court of Appeals (2nd Cir) stated:

> 'While some variations in a bill of lading might be so insignificant as not to relieve the issuing or confirming bank of its obligation to pay, see, e.g., H.

Harfield, *Bank Credits and Acceptances* 75–78, we agree with the district court that the misspelling in the bill of lading of Sofan's name as "Soran" was a material discrepancy that entitled Irving to refuse to honor the letter of credit. First, this is not a case where the name intended is unmistakably clear despite what is obviously a typographical error, as might be the case if, for example, "Smith" were misspelled "Smithh." Nor have appellants claimed that in the Middle East "Soran" would obviously be recognized as an inadvertent misspelling of the surname "Sofan".'

It is also the approach taken in the ISBP, which provides at para 25:

> '**Misspellings or typing errors**
> 25) A misspelling or typing error that does not affect the meaning of a word or the sentence in which it occurs, does not make a document discrepant. For example, a description of the merchandise as "mashine" instead of "machine", "fountan pen" instead of "fountain pen" or "modle" instead of "model" would not make the document discrepant. However, a description as "model 123" instead of "model 321" would not be regarded as a typing error and would constitute a discrepancy.'

1 762 F 2d 4 (US Ct of Apps (2nd Cir) (1985). It is submitted that this approach is preferable to that taken in other United States authorities where there has been consideration of what detriment would or might be caused to the paying bank by the error. See *Bank of Cochin Ltd v Manufacturers Hanover Trust* Co 612 F Supp 1533 (SDNY, 1985).

(d)   Abbreviations

8.39   The ISBP permits the use of abbreviations as follows:

> '**Abbreviations**
> 6) The use of generally accepted abbreviations, for example "Ltd." instead of "Limited", "Int'l" instead of "International", "Co." instead of "Company", "kgs" or "kos". Instead of "kilos", "Ind" instead of "Industry", "mfr" instead of "manufacturer" or "mt" instead of "metric tons" – or vice versa – does not make a document discrepant.
> 7) Virgules (slash marks "/") may have different meanings, and unless apparent in the context used, should not be used as a substitute for a word.'

Combined documents

8.40   All documents must be tendered. In *Donald H Scott & Co v Barclays Bank Ltd*[1] Bankes LJ stated:[2] 'A tender of two bills of lading and understanding to produce the third, or of two bills of lading and an indemnity, is not a compliance with a condition requiring production of a full set.' That much is straightforward. A credit may call for a certificate as to quality and a certificate of weight. What if the two certificates are combined in one? Or if the certificate of weight is written on the face of the invoice? It can be argued that there is a document which is a certificate of weight, although it is also a certificate of quality or an invoice as the facts may be. The credit, however, is likely to contain a list of documents from which it can reasonably be deduced that a specific number of documents is required. The combination of the document into one would be inconsistent with that.[3] There may also be good practical reasons why a buyer would not want combined documents. Thus if he was selling on the documents he would not want to include the invoice addressed to him as a certificate of weight to his own buyer and indeed his buyer might be able to refuse such a certificate.

1 [1923] 2 KB 1.
2 [1923] 2 KB 1 at 11.
3 This view is supported by Case 227 in *More Case Studies on Documentary Credits*, ICC No 489. In the Hong Kong case of *Netherlands Trading Society v Wayne and Haylit* (1952) 36 HKLR 109; (1952) 6 LDAB 320 it was held combined certificates of weight and certificates by the jute mill were acceptable. The credit does not appear to have been subject to the UCP and evidence was called that it was usual to combine the two certificates. Neither does there appear to have been any commercial objection to the combination on the facts of the case.

8.41   The possibility of combined documents is not addressed in UCP 600[1] but the ISBP provides that, in general, that documents listed in a credit should be presented as separate documents (para 42). However, two exceptions are permitted:

> If a credit requires a packing list and a weight list, such requirement will be satisfied by two original copies of a combined packing and weight list, provided such document states both packing and weight details (para 42).
>
> A certification, declaration or the like may be contained within another document. If it appears in another document which is signed and dated, no separate signature or date is required on the certification or declaration if it appears to have been given by the same entity that issued and signed the document (para 8).

1 UCP 500 Article 38 provided that an attestation of certification of weight may be superimposed on the transport document (other than one by sea) unless the credit specifically stipulates a separate document.

Consistency

8.42   UCP 600 Article 14.d provides, 'Data in a document, when read in context with the credit, the document itself and international standard banking practice, need not be identical to, but must not conflict with, data in that document, any other stipulated document or the credit'. This is a significant change in wording from the predecessor to Article 14.d, UCP 500 Article 13.a, which provided, 'Documents which appear on their face to be inconsistent with one another will be considered as not appearing on their face to be in compliance with the terms and conditions of the Credit.' The ICC felt that 'not conflict with' is a narrower definition than the previous formulation.[1] Professor Byrne suggests that the best interpretation of Article 14.d 'is that it applies only to situations where there is a true as opposed to an apparent conflict and only to situations where the "conflict" is substantive in its impact on the document and not superficial and irrelevant to the role of the document and the data (if any) in the letter of credit'.[2] In the third edition of this book,[3] the view was expressed that UCP 500 Article 13.a should simply be taken as meaning that documents which contained contradictions were unacceptable; this appears still to be the case under UCP 600.

1 ICC No 680, p 23.
2 *The Comparison of UCP 600 & UCP 500*, p 136.
3 At para 8.30.

8.43   An example of a presentation unacceptable because of inconsistency which is sometimes given is found in *Soproma SpA v Marine and Animal By-Products Corpn.*[1] The credit stated that the documents were to cover 'Chilean Fish Fullmeal 70% Protein . . .'. An invoice from the shippers included in error among the documents presented referred to 'minimum 67% protein'. The certificate of quality gave the analysis as 'Protein 67 per cent minimum'. The analysis certificate stated 'Protein 69.7 per cent'. The last two documents were held to be a bad tender. This could be justified on the straightforward basis that neither showed protein of 70%. The two documents are probably also inconsistent in that one suggests protein at 69.7%, and the other a lower percentage going down to not less than 67%. An example of inconsistency between documents which did not involve an inconsistency between the documents and the term of the credit would be where goods were sold ex-warehouse in Singapore and the documents showed two warehouse addresses for the goods in relation to the same day.

1 [1966] 1 Lloyd's Rep 367.

Description

8.44   In relation to the description, the UCP provide:

'**Article 18 Commercial Invoice**
c.   The description of the goods, services or performance in a commercial invoice must correspond with that appearing in the credit.'

and

'**Article 14 Standard for Examination of Documents**
e.   In documents other than the commercial invoice, the description of the goods, services or performance, if stated, may be in general terms not conflicting with their description in the credit.'

8.45   The principle of the Article may be illustrated with the facts relating to one aspect of *Banque de l'Indochine v J H Rayner Ltd.*[1] The description of the goods given in the credit was '200 (two hundred) metric tons up to 5% more or less EEC white crystal sugar category no 2 minimum polarisation 99.8 degrees, Moisture Maximum 0.08 per cent'. It appears that this was set out on the invoice. It was sufficient if the other documents such as the bills of lading or certificates of origin gave a simpler description such as 'sugar' provided that it was not inconsistent.[2] If they had referred to a type of sugar other than 'white crystal' or stated a polarisation of less than 99.8 degrees, there would have been an inconsistency between the document and the term of the credit. Such an inconsistency was among the problems which arose in *Bank Melli Iran v Barclays Bank*,[3] a case which did not involve the UCP. The description of the goods in the credit was 'sixty new Chevrolet trucks'. The delivery order described the trucks as 'new-good'. McNair J stated[4] 'In my judgment this description, like the description "new, good" or "in new condition" is not the same as "new".' *J H Rayner & Co Ltd v Hambro's Bank Ltd*[5] is an earlier illustration of the difficulties with description. It likewise was not a UCP case. The credit referred to a cargo of 'Coromandel groundnuts'. The documents presented included a bill of lading for 'machine-shelled groundnut kernels' and an invoice for 'Coromandel groundnuts'. The Court of Appeal held that the bill of lading was objectionable and that it was nothing to the point that there was evidence that machine-shelled groundnut kernels meant Coromandels in the trade. The court probably considered that the bill of lading had to refer to the description of the goods given in the credit. The case would be likely to be decided with the same outcome today on the ground that the two descriptions were inconsistent as a matter of words and any special meaning in the trade was something which the bank was neither bound nor entitled to take into account.

1 [1983] QB 711.
2 The case was decided under UCP 400, which contained in Article 41.c similar provisions to Articles 18.c and 14.e, except that the phrase 'not inconsistent with' was used in place of 'not conflicting with'.
3 [1951] 2 Lloyd's Rep 367.
4 [1951] 2 Lloyd's Rep 367 at 375.
5 [1943] KB 37.

8.46   Correspondence between the description and the words of the document need not be identical. A document is acceptable even if it contains words supplementing the description of the goods in the credit, provided of course that there is no conflict. In *Glencore International AG v Bank of China*[1] the Court of Appeal held that a commercial invoice which described the goods as 'Origin: Any Western brand – Indonesia (Inalum brand)' conformed with a requirement that the goods be 'Any Western brand'. The additional reference to Indonesia was not sufficient to invite litigation or call for further inquiry.

1 [1996] 1 Lloyd's Rep 135 at 154.

8.47   It is also unnecessary for each document to contain full particulars or a complete description of the goods. This arose in *Midland Bank Ltd v*

Seymour[1] where Devlin J stated:[2]

> 'The set of documents must contain all the particulars and, of course, they
> must be consistent between themselves, otherwise they would not be a good
> set of shipping documents. But here you have a set of documents which is not
> only consistent with itself, but also incorporates to some extent the
> particulars that are given in the other – the shipping mark on the bill of lading
> leading to the invoice that bears the same shipping mark and which would be
> tendered at the same time, which sets out the full description of the goods.'[3]

Although this case was not decided under the UCP, the rule is also applicable
to credits governed by the UCP.[4] Indeed, in providing that the description of
the goods etc '*if stated*, may be in general terms not conflicting with their
description in the credit', Article 14.e makes it clear that it is not mandatory
for a description to be contained in any document other than the commercial
invoice. Although the qualification 'if stated' did not appear in UCP 500 or
earlier revisions, it is a clarification rather than a modification: the ICC
Banking Commission has previously said that 'there is no specific requirement
for a goods description to appear on any document other than the commercial
invoice'.[5]

1 [1955] 2 Lloyd's Rep 147.
2 [1955] 2 Lloyd's Rep 147 at 153.
3 See also [1955] 2 Lloyd's Rep 147 at 155.1.
4 *Glencore International AG v Bank of China* [1996] 1 Lloyd's Rep 135 at 155.
5 *Collected Opinions 1995–2001*, ICC No 632, §228, R364.

Linkage

8.48   In addition to the issue of description, there is a separate issue as to the
extent to which each document must identify the goods shipped. The
inclusion of a transport document among the documents to be presented will
identify the goods in respect of which payment is being sought as the goods
shipped under that document. But it is also important that other documents
which are required should be capable of being related to the goods shipped.
For example, a certificate of the quality of the goods is of no value, even if it
describes the goods, unless it is clear that its subject matter is the goods for
which payment is sought, namely those covered by the transport document.

8.49   In order to assess the present position under the UCP it is helpful to see
how it has developed historically. In *Banque de l'Indochine v J H Rayner Ltd*,
after considering whether the documents adequately described the goods, Sir
John Donaldson MR stated:[1]

> 'So far so good from the point of view of the merchants. But there is another
> obstacle in their way. There is, in my judgment, a real distinction between an
> identification of "the goods," the subject matter of the transaction, and a
> description of those goods. The second sentence of article 32 (c) [now Article

14.e] gives latitude in description, but not in identification. For example, the E.U.R. certificate or certificate of origin could identify "the goods" by reference to marks on the bags or by reference to a hold in the vessel which they occupied provided that no other goods were in the hold. Having so identified "the goods" they could then describe them as "sugar" simpliciter since this description is not inconsistent with "E.E.C. White Crystal Sugar Category No. 2, Minimum Polarisation 99.8 degrees Moisture Maximum 0.08 per cent." But however general the description, the identification must, in my judgment, be unequivocal. Linkage between the documents is not, as such, necessary, provided that each directly or indirectly refers unequivocally to "the goods." This seems to me to be the proper and inevitable construction to place upon article 32(c) if the specified documents are to have any value at all. It is here that the merchants are in difficulties.'

The court rejected an argument (based on the absence of any reference to linkage in the UCP, then in the 1974 Revision) that the documents need not be linked through identification of the goods, provided that they were not inconsistent with each other. In the *Banque de l'Indochine* case, the bill of lading showed that the goods had been loaded on the *Markhor* at Antwerp bound for Djibouti in transit for the Yemen. One quality certificate related to sugar loaded on the 'MV Markhor or substitute'. That could have been a different vessel and so a different parcel of sugar. One certificate of origin was similarly worded. The other referred to 'Transport mixtes à destination Djibouti Port in Transit Yemen'. Each could have referred to different parcels of sugar. The three EUR1 certificates gave no means of relating the sugar to which they referred to the sugar shipped on the *Markhor*. It seems that, had the documents referred to the correct quantities and named the *Markhor*, that would have been sufficient. It may be that some other means of identification would also have been adequate, such as references to the markings on the bags. For the difficulty arose at least in part because the certificates were prepared prior to loading on the vessel. At the end of the relevant passage in his judgment Sir John Donaldson MR stated 'Clearly these certificates could relate to the goods, but they do not necessarily do so. This will not do.' The judgment does not refer to the commercial invoice save to note that no complaint was made by the bank about it.[2] The thought process in the judgment was clearly to identify the goods sold as the shipment of sugar on the *Markhor* and to require the sugar referred to in the certificates to be related to that. It is unclear how far the necessity of relationship referred to by Sir John Donaldson is to be taken. It is possible, for example, that sugar described in a certificate as loaded on the *Markhor* could have been loaded on a voyage subsequent to that covered by the bill of lading and so be a different parcel of sugar. If that may seem fanciful, it is less so where the connecting factor is the marking on the bags, particularly if that is a simple one, such as a single letter. Perhaps 'necessarily' in the passage quoted from the judgment of the Master of the Rolls should have been 'with reasonable certainty'.

1 [1983] QB 711 at 731–732.
2 [1983] QB 711 at 731B.

8.50   UCP 600 does not (nor did UCP 500 or any of its predecessors) make any express provision for linkage. As mentioned above, there is no requirement that the goods etc be described in documents other than the commercial invoice. In respect of the data content of such documents, UCP 600 provides as follows:[1]

'**Article 14 Standard for Examination of Documents**
f.   If a credit requires presentation of a document other than a transport document, insurance document or commercial invoice, without stipulating by whom the document is to be issued or its data content, banks will accept the document as presented if its content appears to fulfil the function of the required document and otherwise complies with sub-article 14 (d).'

It might be argued that, absent any express requirement in the UCP, it is not necessary that goods referred to in a certificate should be referrable to those in the invoice, only that, because of the reference to Article 14.d, there should be no conflict. If so, certificates etc need not be capable of being positively related to, or identified with, the goods for which payment is sought. That would be an invitation to fraud and would greatly detract from the security which the inclusion of such documents is aimed to provide. It is to be hoped that banks will continue the practice in accordance with the position as it was held to be at the time of the *Banque de l'Indochine* case of requiring that documents sufficiently identify the goods to which they relate. A second approach to the same end is to treat the concept of linkage as incorporated in the requirement for consistency between documents which is stated in Article 14.d. It is suggested that this is to stretch the ordinary meaning of consistent and inconsistent. A third approach would be to say that the requirement for identification arises under the common law, since the UCP are silent on the point.[2] The safe course is for the applicant to ensure that the position is covered by the express wording of the credit: issuing banks need to be alive to the point.

1 This is a slight change from UCP 500 Article 21 which read: 'When documents other than transport documents, insurance documents and commercial invoices are called for, the Credit should stipulate by whom such documents are to be issued and their wording or data content. If the Credit does not so stipulate, banks will accept such documents as presented, provided that their data content is not inconsistent with any other stipulated document presented.'
2 *Glencore International AG v Bank of China* [1996] 1 Lloyd's Rep 135 at 145.

8.51   In *Glencore International AG v Bank of China*,[1] the packing lists tendered under the credit gave the lots, bundles and weights making up the cargo of aluminium and identified the shipper but did not identify the shipment or the commercial invoice. Rix J referred to the discussion in the previous paragraph and considered the extent of the identification required by the UCP and the common law.[2] However, he found it unnecessary to reach a concluded view because looking at the documents as a whole and the correspondence between them, the goods described in the packing list were 'unequivocally, albeit indirectly' identified with both the letter of credit goods and the goods shipped. He also held that Bank of China had waived any right to rely on the point because its notice of rejection had raised only the issue of the description of the goods, not their identification. The Court of Appeal agreed with Rix J, holding that the bank was bound to look at the documents tendered as a whole. Sir Thomas Bingham MR stated:[3]

'This objection [by the issuing bank] loses any force it might otherwise have if it is permissible to look at the packing lists alongside the certificates of weight and quantity, in which the commodity is identified as aluminium ingots and the name of the vessel on which the cargo was shipped is given. The correspondence between the packing lists and certificates of weight and quantity are, as the Judge demonstrated in his judgment, comprehensive and exact. There is, furthermore, a close correspondence between the packing lists and the certificates of weight and quantity and the bills of lading. The Bank of China's objection is accordingly one that can in my view prevail only if law or practice requires a document, in the absence of any stipulation to that effect, to be read and considered in isolation from other documents tendered with it at the same time. We do not understand this to be the law.'

Since the linkage between the packing lists and the other documents was 'clear, exact and devoid of discrepancy'[4] the documents were acceptable.

1 [1996] 1 Lloyd's Rep 135.
2 [1996] 1 Lloyd's Rep 135 at 143–146.
3 [1996] 1 Lloyd's Rep 135 at 154.
4 [1996] 1 Lloyd's Rep 135 at 155.

Regular on their face, not inviting further inquiry, current in the trade

8.52   There are dicta in various cases which support the propositions that the documents must be regular on their face, should not be such as to invite further inquiry, and should be such as are current in the trade in question. But examination of the cases suggests that a bank would do well to avoid reliance on such general principles and seek to identify specific defects in the documents, which defects entitle rejection.

8.53   A famous passage is contained in the speech of Lord Sumner in *Hansson v Hamel and Horley Ltd*:[1]

'When documents are to be taken up the buyer is entitled to documents which substantially confer protective rights throughout. He is not buying a litigation, as Lord Trevethin (then AT Lawrence J) says in the *General Trading Co's Case* (1911) 16 Com Cas 95 at 101. These documents have to be handled by banks, they have to be taken up or rejected promptly and without opportunity for prolonged inquiry, they have to be such as can be re-tendered to sub-purchasers, and it is essential that they should so conform to the accustomed shipping documents as to be reasonably and readily fit to pass current in commerce. I am quite sure that, under the circumstances of this case, this ocean bill of lading does not satisfy these conditions. It bears notice of its insufficiency and ambiguity on its face: for, though called a through bill of lading, it is not really so. It is the contract of the subsequent carrier only, without any complementary promises to bind the prior carriers in the through transit.'

The contract in question was a sale c. and f. Norway to Japan and did not involve a letter of credit. The goods were first shipped in several shipments to Hamburg where bills of lading were issued. It was held that the Hamburg bills were not through bills as they gave no protection to the buyers on the voyage from Norway to Hamburg and so did not satisfy the conditions of the contract. Secondly, the contract of carriage had not been procured, as was necessary, on shipment, and the bills issued 13 days later in another country were also defective for that reason.

1 [1922] 2 AC 36 at 46.

8.54 The central passage from the above extract was quoted by both Donaldson J and the Court of Appeal in *M Golodetz & Co Inc v Czarnikow-Rionda Co Inc*.[1] The problem in that case was that when the sugar, the subject of the c. and f. contract, was partly loaded fire broke out on the vessel and 200 tons were damaged by the fire and by water used to extinguish it. The 200 tons had to be unloaded and became subject to general average. A separate bill of lading was issued in respect of it which bore a typed notation to the effect that the cargo it covered had been discharged at the port of loading due to fire and/or water damage. The question was whether the sellers were entitled to tender this bill to the buyers and be paid the price. Donaldson J and the Court of Appeal held that they were. The arbitrators (who first heard the case and determined the facts) had not found that the bills of lading were not acceptable in the trade in this form, and it was held that they were clean bills in the sense they contained nothing to qualify the ship's admission that the goods were in apparent good order and condition at the time of shipment.

1 [1980] 1 WLR 495.

8.55 *Golodetz* was not a documentary credit case. But suppose that a bank were to find such a bill of lading among the documents when it came to check them against the terms and conditions of a letter of credit. The checker might say 'Well, the goods were shipped in good order and that is the sellers' duty, so we must take up the documents and leave it to the buyer to claim on the insurance which he should have taken out.' He would be right. But one may wonder whether a bank is obliged to take such a bold line where there is a bill of lading with such an unusual notation, and whether the bank might not say, 'This bill reeks of trouble; it is not our job to be legal experts, and we are not going to accept.'

8.56 Where the point at issue is one of what is acceptable in a particular trade, if the bill is claused in a way to raise doubt about its acceptability, there is a distinction between a merchant who has to determine whether to pay against documents and a bank. For it is reasonable to assume that a merchant is familiar with his particular trade, and there is no reason to attribute the same knowledge to a bank. In *J H Rayner & Co Ltd v Hambro's Bank Ltd*[1] it was held that trade usage was irrelevant. Admittedly this was in part on the ground that the contract there involved shipment from India to Denmark, and the evidence of usage was as to the business usages of Mincing Lane. But Mackinnon LJ continued[2], 'Moreover, quite apart from these considerations, it is quite impossible to suggest that a banker is to be affected with knowledge of customs and customary terms of every one of the thousands of trades for whose dealings he may issue letters of credit.' Goddard LJ likewise stated that trade practice is irrelevant. There may be a distinction to be drawn between the customs of a particular trade of which a bank is not required to have knowledge and which it should ignore, and matters of general commercial custom such as those pertaining to bills of lading, of which a bank should take notice. The latter, however, will often come to points which a judge will feel competent to decide as matters of law. In the *Golodetz* case,[3] not a letter of credit case, the court relied on the fact that the arbitrators had not found the claused bill of lading to be unusual in the trade. But a bank has no time to seek the views of trade arbitrators. It must act on what it sees before it, and, if what it sees raises problems which cannot be answered readily, it should be entitled and obliged to reject the documents. The proposition which is here advanced may be said not to give sufficient weight to the early decision of the Court of Appeal in *National Bank of Egypt v Hannevig's Bank*.[4] Here the plaintiff bank paid out against documents as the bank which had opened the credit on the instructions of the defendant bank. The latter bank refused to pay because the bills of lading were marked 'several bags torn and re-sewn' and so were not 'clean'. The case was actually decided on the basis that the defendants had authorised the plaintiffs to pay against claused bills. But the court queried whether clean bills were in fact required in view of the difficult conditions affecting the Egyptian onion trade in wartime, and attributed knowledge of this to the paying bank. In view of the actual decision, that is to be treated as obiter dicta, and was advanced as a matter of uncertainty rather than the concluded view of the court.

1 [1943] KB 37.
2 [1943] KB 37 at 41.
3 *M Golodetz & Co Inc v Czarnikow-Rionda Co Inc* [1980] 1 WLR 495.
4 (1919) 1 Ll L Rep 69 and see 3 LDAB 213.

8.57 A letter of credit was at issue in *National Bank of South Africa v Banca Italiana di Sconto*[1] and it was alleged and held that the bills of lading presented were not in usual form.[2] The bill was in a form which left it unclear whether it was to shipper's order or to the order of the consignee – who had not indorsed it. It was held to be a bad tender. This case shows that where a document raises on its face some uncertainty, which cannot readily be resolved by the bank, the bank is entitled to reject the documents. The statement of Lord Sumner quoted above[3] and contained in a judgment delivered on the same day (16 March 1922) is directly applicable.

1 (1922) 10 Ll L Rep 531.
2 (1922) 10 Ll L Rep 531 at 535.1 and 536.2.
3 See para **8.53**.

8.58   A document which is or has become ineffective and illegal at the time of presentation to the bank is a bad tender. In *Arnhold Karberg & Co v Blythe Green Jourdain & Co*[1] sellers under a CIF contract tendered a bill of lading evidencing shipment on the enemy vessel. As, on the outbreak of war, the bill had become void and unenforceable as regards any obligations, this was held to have been a bad tender.

1 [1916] 1 KB 495.

Dating of documents

8.59   Transport documents and insurance documents must be dated.[1] There is no requirement for other types of documents to be dated. If a document is dated, then Article 14.i provides that it may be dated prior to the issuance date of the credit, but must not be dated later than its date of presentation.[2]

1 UCP Article 19.a.ii (multimodal transport), Article 20.a.ii (bills of lading) Article 21.a.ii (sea waybill), Article 22.a.ii (charter party bills of lading), Article 23.a.iii (air transport), Article 24.a.ii (road, rail and inland waterway transport), Article 25.a.ii (courier or post receipt), Article 28.e (insurance).
2 This is an improvement on its predecessor, UCP 500 Article 22, which provided that '… banks will accept…' documents dated prior to the issuance date of the credit. As suggested in the third edition of this book, para 8.47, this should not to be read as meaning that banks *must* accept such documents however old they are by the time of presentation, just as it is not to be read as obliging banks to accept documents so dated which contain other defects.

8.60   Article 3 contains provisions as to the application of a number of terms which may be used in connection with dates. It includes the following provisions:

> The expression 'on or about' or similar will be interpreted as a stipulation that an event is to occur during a period of five calendar days before until five calendar days after the specified date, both start and end dates included.
>
> The words 'to', 'until', 'till', 'from' and 'between' when used to determine a period of shipment include the date or dates mentioned, and the words 'before' and 'after' exclude the date mentioned.
>
> The words 'from'" and 'after' when used to determine a maturity date exclude the date mentioned.
>
> The terms 'first half' and 'second half' of a month shall be construed respectively as the 1st to the 15th and the 16th to the last day of the month,[1] all dates inclusive.
>
> The terms 'beginning', 'middle' and 'end' of a month shall be construed respectively as the 1st to the 10th, the 11th to the 20th and the 21st to the last day of the month, all dates inclusive.

It should be noted that, unlike in UCP 500 where the equivalent provisions, in UCP 500 Article 47, applied only to dates referring to shipment, these provisions apply to all dates.

1 Perhaps not what the parties would expect if the month is February.

Stale or out-of-date documents

8.61   The position in respect of transport documents, in particular the requirement of UCP Article 14.c that they be presented within 21 days of date of shipment, is considered in **Chapter 5**[1] as part of the discussion of when documents must be presented. The reason for requiring transport documents to be presented within a period is to ensure that they are available to enable the applicant for the credit to take possession of the goods.

1 See paras **5.31** et seq.

8.62   There is no equivalent provision relating to other classes of documents, nor is it usual for credits in practice to provide such a period. Such classes of document may also become out-of-date in a different manner from delay in presentation. Thus inspection certificates which pre-dated the bill of lading by any substantial amount might be thought unacceptable. To take two examples, this would be true of a certificate which covered the presence of weevils or other pests; it would be true of a certificate covering the polarisation and moisture content of samples from a cargo of sugar. This problem should be avoided by the credit prescribing when and perhaps where the inspection is to take place. If it is not, in most cases a bank is likely to rely upon Article 14.f (considered and set out in para **8.50**) and 14.i as entitling it to accept the documents regardless of their date. It is suggested that in all but clear cases a bank should take the position that it is for the applicant to include an appropriate provision in the credit and, if he fails to do so, the bank will accept documents as presented. But in a case where it is clear that a document such as a certificate is out-of-date in the sense that it cannot be relied upon as informative of the condition of the goods at date of shipment, it should be rejected.[1]

1 This view is supported by Case 230 in *More Case Studies on Documentary Credits*, ICC No 489.

Originality

8.63   The basic rule is and has always been that original documents are required.[1] Thus, the UCP provides at article 17:

> 'Article 17 Original Documents and Copies
> a.   At least one original of each document stipulated in the credit must be presented.'

The use of carbon copy bills of lading might appear to be an exception, but these are better regarded as a series of identical documents each with the status of an original.

1 Cited *Glencore International AG v Bank of China* [1996] 1 Lloyd's Rep 135 at 151; a decision under UCP 500, when the requirement was not explicit.

8.64   However, modern methods of document production have given rise to problems as to when a bank is entitled to reject a tendered document because it is not (or appears not to be) an original, and as to what is meant by an 'original' document. These problems arose in two cases in the Court of Appeal: *Glencore International AG v Bank of China*[1] and *Kredietbank Antwerp v Midland Bank plc*[2] and prompted the issue of a policy statement by the ICC Banking Commission.

1 [1996] 1 Lloyd's Rep 135.
2 [1999] Lloyd's Rep Bank 219.

8.65   Any discussion of what is meant by an original document quickly becomes mired in technical and even philosophical debate. A handwritten or typed document would normally be considered as an original, and a photocopy or fax as a copy. But what about a document which is generated electronically, faxed or emailed from a computer and printed only by the recipient? Moreover, a document can be an original for one purpose but a copy for another. For example, if a draft contract is photocopied and the copy is signed then the signed copy is the legally operative document and is an 'original' in that sense. It is important to keep in mind the purpose behind the requirement for the presentation of original documents, namely that the original has or may have a particular commercial, legal or evidential value in giving the holder rights against the issuer or counterparty. As Evans LJ explained in *Kredietbank*:[2]

> 'The kind of insurance document which the bank is entitled to demand under Article 34 is the one which enables the holder of the document to establish a claim against insurers, if the need arises to do so. This means the actual document whose existence renders the insurers liable, usually but not necessarily by reason of their signature appearing upon it. No copy of that document is acceptable, by whatever means the copy may have been produced, and so the word original is used here in contrast to copies of any kind.'

1 In its Policy Statement (see para **8.69** below) the ICC Banking Commission seems to regard the question as turning on the intention of the person producing the document. For a detailed discussion of the concept of 'originalness' (sic), see Byrne, *The Original Documents Controversy*.
2 [1999] Lloyd's Rep Bank 219 at 226.

8.66   A bank, however, should not need to be concerned with the niceties of how a document has been produced or what its legal or commercial effect is. Just as with other tests of discrepancy, in carrying out its duty to examine the documents for compliance the bank looks only at their appearance and form. The relevant question is therefore not whether a tendered document is in fact an original or a copy, a matter outside the bank's knowledge and responsibility, but whether it has a sufficient *appearance* of originality to be an acceptable tender under the credit. If the document is on its face clearly original, then the bank is entitled and obliged to accept it without further inquiry.[1] In that respect, UCP Article 17 provides as follows:[2]

'**Article 17 Original Documents and Copies**

b. A bank shall treat as an original any document bearing an apparently original signature, mark, stamp, or label of the issuer of the document, unless the document itself indicates that it is not an original.

c. Unless a document indicates otherwise, a bank will also accept a document as original if it:

   i.   appears to be written, typed, perforated or stamped by the document issuer's hand; or

   ii. appears to be on the document issuer's original stationery; or

   iii. states that it is original, unless the statement appears not to apply to the document presented.

d. If a credit requires presentation of copies of documents, presentation of either originals or copies is permitted.'

1 Verification of actual originality will become increasingly difficult as document reproduction technology continues to improve and colour copying becomes commonplace. It may become impossible to be sure that any document is an original, even if it has a coloured or embossed logo or appears to be partly handwritten.

2 See for further guidance paras 28–33 of the ISBP.

8.67   UCP 500 did not contain provisions similar to UCP 500 Article 17; the only guidance was in Article 20.b as follows:

'**UCP 500 Article 20 Ambiguity as to the Issuers of Documents**

b. Unless otherwise stipulated in the Credit, banks will also accept as an original document(s), a document(s) produced or appearing to have been produced:

   i.   by reprographic, automated or computerised systems;

   ii. as carbon copies;

   provided that it is marked as original and, where necessary, appears to be signed.

   A document may be signed by handwriting, by facsimile signature, by perforated signature, by stamp, by symbol, or by an other mechanical or electronic method of authentication.'

8.68   This article gave rise to the controversial decision in *Glencore v Bank of China*.[1] In that case, the beneficiary presented a certificate which (it was assumed) had been generated by photocopying an original page laser-printed off a word processor. The photocopy was hand signed, although signature was not a requirement of the credit. The Court of Appeal held that the issuing bank, Bank of China, was entitled to reject the certificate on the ground that it had been produced by reprographic means and under Article 20.b was unacceptable unless 'marked as original'.

'As argument before us amply demonstrated, there is abundant room to debate what, in the context of modern technology, is an original. A handwritten or typed document plainly is, but other documents can also be plausibly said to be so. Article 20(b) is, as it seems to us, designed to circumvent this argument by providing a clear rule to apply in the case of documents produced by reprographic, automated or computerized systems. The sub-article requires documents produced in a certain way (whether "original" or not) to be treated in a certain way. It is understandable that those framing these rules should have wished to relieve issuing bankers of the need to make difficult and fallible judgments on the technical means by which documents were produced. The beneficiary's certificates in this case may, in one sense, have been originals; but it is plain on the evidence that they were produced by one or other of the listed means and so were subject to the rule.

Even if it is true that the certificates did not appear to have been produced by one or other of these means (which must, we think, be very doubtful) that makes no difference if in fact they were: the sub-article is clear in its reference to "document(s) produced or appearing to have been produced...".'[2]

This seemed to set a firm rule that *any* document appearing to be produced by reprographic, automated or computerised means must be marked as original, whether or not it is actually original. Moreover, the fact that the certificate was manually signed did not help *Glencore*:

'The original signature was of course a means of authenticating the certificates, and they were not required to be signed. But a signature on a copy does not make an original, it makes an authenticated copy; and art. 20(b) does not treat a signature as a substitute for a marking as "original", merely as an additional requirement in some cases.'[3]

1 [1996] 1 Lloyd's Rep 135.
2 [1996] 1 Lloyd's Rep 135 at 153.
3 [1996] 1 Lloyd's Rep 135 at 153.

8.69   *Glencore* was distinguished in both *Kredietbank Antwerp v Midland Bank plc*1 and *Credit Industriel et Commercial v China Merchants Bank*;[2] in the latter case David Steel J said that its ratio 'was directed to the treatment of documents appearing or known to be copies or, in some analogous respect, of a class not prior thereto treated as originals'.[3] *Glencore* also prompted the ICC to issue a Policy Statement dated 12 July 1999 which 'does not amend sub-Article 20(b) of UCP 500 in any way, but merely indicates the correct interpretation thereof which has been adopted unanimously by the ICC Commission on Banking Technique and Practice on 12 July 1999'. The Policy Statement was essentially in the terms of what is now UCP 600 Article 17.c, and also noted:

'Banks treat as original any document that appears to be hand signed by the issuer of the document. For example, a hand signed draft or commercial invoice is treated as an original document, whether or not some or all other constituents of the document are preprinted, carbon copied, or produced by reprographic, automated, or computerized systems...

Banks treat as non-original any document that appears to be a photocopy of another document. If, however, a photocopy appears to have been completed by the document issuer's hand marking the photocopy, then... the resulting document is treated as an original document unless it indicates otherwise.'

For credits governed by UCP 600 the controversy raised by *Glencore* has now been laid to rest; for a fuller discussion of the position under UCP 500 the reader should refer to the third edition of this book.[4]

1 [1999] Lloyd's Rep Bank 219.
2 [2002] 2 All ER (Comm) 427.
3 At para 57.
4 At paras 8.48 et seq.

The amount of the credit, the quantity, the unit price

8.70 UCP Article 30 provides:

> 'Article 30 Tolerance in Credit Amount, Quantity and Unit Prices
> a. The words 'about' or 'approximately' used in connection with the amount of the credit or the quantity or the unit price stated in the credit are to be construed as allowing a tolerance not to exceed 10% more or 10% less than the amount, the quantity or the unit price to which they refer.
> b. A tolerance not to exceed 5% more or 5% less than the quantity of the goods is allowed, provided the credit does not state the quantity in terms of a stipulated number of packing units or individual items and the total amount of the drawings does not exceed the amount of the credit.
> c. Even when partial shipments are not allowed, a tolerance not to exceed 5% less than the amount of the credit is allowed, provided that the quantity of the goods, if stated in the credit, is shipped in full and a unit price, if stated in the credit, is not reduced or that sub-article 30 (b) is not applicable. This tolerance does not apply when the credit stipulates a specific tolerance or uses the expressions referred to in sub-article 30 (a).'

Article 30.a permits a variation of up to 10% in the amount of the credit or the quantity to be supplied, or the unit price, where in the credit the relevant amount is preceded by the word 'about' or 'approximately'. It should be noted that this is slightly more restrictive that its predecessor, UCP 500 Article 39.a, which referred to the use of 'about', 'approximately', 'circa' or a similar expression. The amount of the credit means the sum of money available under the credit. This cannot be exceeded by reason, for example, of the quantity being exceeded within the 10% margin unless the amount too is preceded by a word such as 'about' entitling the beneficiary to a 10% margin in respect of it.[1]

1 See *Opinions* (1998–1999) ICC No 613, Ref 365.

8.71 In contrast Article 30.b does not need words such as 'about' for it to apply. It relates only to the quantity of the goods. If the quantity is intended to be precisely adhered to, the credit must say so. Otherwise a tolerance of 5% will be permitted, provided, of course, that the amount of the proposed drawing does not exceed the amount of the credit. The tolerance does not apply where the credit stipulates the quantity in terms of a number of packing units or individual items. The sphere of its application therefore appears to be where the quantity is given by weight or by volume. Thus a credit which gave the quantity as 1,000 metric tons would permit a 5% tolerance, whereas one which gave it as 10,000 bags of 100 kilos each would not. So the decision in *Moralice (London) Ltd v E D and F Man*[1] would today have been in favour of the shipper had the UCP applied because the documents were to evidence 'shipment of the following goods: … 500 metric tons Tate & Lyle granulated sugar of UK manufacture, packed in heavy single bags, each bag of 100 kgs nett weight …'. To take another example from a decided case, it does not apply to the tonnage of a vessel being sold, because the tonnage is part of the description of the vessel, and is not a quantity, just as with the phrase 'about 100 planks of sawn timber about 30 foot long and about 18 inches wide', the quantity is about 100 and the measurements are part of the description of the planks.[2] Where a credit covers '116 mt net (six isotanks)', the 5% tolerance may be applied to the tonnage.[3] Where a credit provides for 'up to 3400 long tons', there is no limitation on the minimum amount of 5% as provided by Article 30.b.[4] The Article is of particular relevance in considering the application of the de minimis rule to quantities, which is discussed in para **8.33** above.

1 [1954] 2 Lloyd's Rep 526. See para **8.33** above.
2 See *Kydon Compania Naviera SA v National Westminster Bank* [1981] 1 Lloyd's Rep 68 at 76.1.
3 See Case 272 in *More Case Studies on Documentary Credits*, ICC No 489.
4 See Case 270 in *More Case Studies on Documentary Credits*, ICC No 489.

8.72   The tolerance permitted by Article 30.b cannot be used as a means of increasing the amount of the credit. So if the amount of the credit is stated as the multiple of the stated quantity and the stated unit price and is not preceded by any word such as 'about', the 5% tolerance cannot be used to recover the price in respect of a shipment over the stated quantity but within 5% of it. The position would then be governed by Article 18.b.[1] Unless the credit otherwise provides, the nominated bank is given an option to accept a commercial invoice issued for an amount in excess of the amount permitted by the credit. But the bank may not honour or negotiate in an amount in excess of that amount. So the seller would not be paid through the credit for the extra amount that he had shipped. He would need to proceed against the buyer for the balance, and in that he might face some difficulty if they did not have good relations.

1 See para **8.81** below.

8.73   Where it applies, Article 30.c allows a tolerance of 5% less in the amount drawn (ie money value) whereas, where Article 30.b applies, it allows a tolerance of 5% more or less in quantity (eg tonnage). Article 30.c requires that if the credit states a quantity it is shipped in full and that any unit price is not to be reduced. Its practical sphere of operation would appear to be credits where the unit price underlying the transaction may turn out to be less than allowed for because insurance or freight charges turn out to be less than anticipated, or where the credit amount results from a rounding up of unit price and quantity.

8.74 Subject to these points it is of course essential that the correct quantity should be evidenced by the documents as the *Moralice* case[1] demonstrates. And it is also obvious that the documents must evidence that quantity and not a quantity in some other unit which cannot be related to it. Thus in *London and Foreign Trading Corp v British and Northern European Bank*[2] the credit described the goods as 500 tons South African maize meal CIF Liverpool. The bill of lading simply stated a quantity of 5,895 bags of maize meal. The invoice gave the same number of bags and the weight of the bags as 190 lbs, which gave 500 tons. The bank was held not to have been entitled to pay against such a bill because it gave the buyer no rights against the ship in respect of any particular tonnage without establishing the weight of the bags, which the buyer might or might not be able to do. In fact the number of bags was found to be correct, but there was a shortfall in weight.

1 See para **8.33** above.
2 (1921) 9 Ll L Rep 116.

Terms as to issuers of documents

8.75 There is a temptation for an applicant for a credit to seek to strengthen his position by requiring documents to be issued by parties who are described with adjectives which sound well but are incapable of any precise application, such as 'first class' or 'official' to take two examples. Whilst UCP 600 does not proscribe the use of such terms, as UCP 500 did in Article 20.a, Article 3 deprives those terms of any real significance. The Article states:

> 'Terms such as "first class", "well known", "qualified", "independent", "official", "competent" or "local" used to describe the issuer of a document allow any issuer except the beneficiary to issue that document.'

C REQUIREMENTS AS TO PARTICULAR DOCUMENTS

(1) The commercial invoice

Name of applicant

8.76 UCP Article 18.a provides:

> 'Article 18 Commercial Invoice
> a. A commercial invoice:
>   i. must appear to have been issued by the beneficiary (except as provided in article 38);

ii.   must be made out in the name of the applicant (except as provided in sub-article 38 (g));
iii.   must be made out in the same currency as the credit; and
iv.   need not be signed.'

This is simply to say that, where the underlying contract is one of sale, the invoice must be made out in the name of the seller[1] and must be addressed to the buyer. The exception to this is where the credit has been transferred, and there is a second beneficiary in relation to whom the first (or original) beneficiary stands as applicant. Article 38 covers transfer and is considered in Chapter 10 below. The requirement that the invoice should be made out in the same currency as the credit is new to UCP 600 and was not in UCP 500 Article 37, the predecessor to UCP 600 Article 18.a.

1 Compare Article 14.k which permits the naming of the consignor as a party other than the beneficiary.

Description

8.77   The invoice should set out a description of the goods which fully and accurately follows the description in the credit. As has been noted above,[1] the relevant provisions are as follows:

'**Article 18 Commercial Invoice**
c.   The description of the goods, services or performance in a commercial invoice must correspond with that appearing in the credit.'

and

'**Article 14 Standard for Examination of Documents**
e.   In documents other than the commercial invoice, the description of the goods, services or performance, if stated, may be in general terms not conflicting with their description in the credit.'

The words 'must correspond' do not mean that they must be precisely the same. But there should be no differences in the descriptive words themselves. The safe course is to follow the wording of the credit precisely. This may be illustrated by one aspect of *Kydon Compania Naviera SA v National Westminster Bank Ltd, The Lena*.[2] The underlying contract was for the sale of a vessel described in the credit as:

'one Greek flag motor vessel "LENA", built January 1951 of about 11250 tons gross register 6857 tons net register and about 5790 long tons light displacement "as built", with all equipment outfit and gear belonging to her on board, as per M.O.A.[3] dated 2nd July 1974'.

It may be thought that this was not a well-considered wording. The wording of the invoices (three were required, signed, with a certificate that the vessel was as per the Memorandum of Agreement) stated:

'To net sale price of "LENA"…(US$4953,771.00). We hereby certify that the mt "LENA" registered under the Greek Flag under official number 3723 of 11,123.89 tons gross and 6,297.41 tons net is as per Memorandum of Agreement dated 2nd July 1974…'

It will be seen that:

(1) Both gross[4] and net register tonnages were different.[5]
(2) The year of construction was not mentioned.
(3) The light displacement tonnage 'as built' was not mentioned.
(4) It was not stated that all equipment and gear belonging to her was on board.

In an attempt to avoid these great difficulties it was argued that all that was required was a certificate that the vessel complied with the agreement, and that it would have been sufficient 'description' merely to refer to the vessel '*Lena*'. It was held that the certification requirement was an additional requirement and did not obviate the need that the description in the invoice should correspond with that in the credit. Parker J stated:[6]

'Unless otherwise specified in the credit, the beneficiary must follow the words of the credit and this is so even where he uses an expression which, although different from the words of the credit, has, as between buyers and sellers, the same meaning as such words. It is important that this principle should be strictly adhered to. An example of its operation is to be found in *J H Rayner & Co Ltd v Hambro's Bank Ltd* (1943) 74 Ll L Rep 10, [1943] KB 37. Departure from the principle would involve banks in just those sort of uncertainties which it is essential for the proper operation of the credit system should be avoided. Mr Tugendhat's overall answer to the discrepancies that the specific provisions as to invoices on the continuation sheet of the credit calls merely for … Signed invoices … certifying the vessel is as per Memorandum of Agreement dated the 2nd July 1974 … and the invoices in fact provided did so certify and that they were therefore sufficient cannot in my judgment succeed. The specific requirement for certification was an additional requirement. The obligation was still to provide an invoice in accordance with the terms of UCP. The description of the vessel in the invoice must therefore correspond with the description in the credit. On the face of it, it does not. It may be that the year of building, light displacement tonnage "as built" and so on as set out in the letter of credit do appear in the memorandum of agreement so that the certificate incorporates them, but this is not a matter which is of any concern to the bank. For all it knows the year of building, et cetera, may have been contained in some separate documents. If specific items of description are included in the credit they must also be included in the invoice. The certification may no doubt incorporate this and a lot more detail besides, but all of these are nothing to do with the bank.'

However, additional or supplementary wording, provided that there is no inconsistency, do not make the document discrepant.[7]

1 See para **8.44**.
2 [1981] 1 Lloyd's Rep 68.
3 Memorandum of Agreement.
4 It may be suggested that 11,123.89 tons gross corresponds with 'about 11,250 tons gross'.

5 As to the inapplicability of Article 30 (or its predecessors), see para **8.71** above.
6 [1981] 1 Lloyd's Rep 68 at 76.
7 *Glencore International AG v Bank of China* [1996] 1 Lloyd's Rep 135 discussed at para **8.46** above.

8.78   The problem as to the invoice which faced Leggatt J in *Astro Exito Navegacion SA v Chase Manhattan Bank NA*[1] involved considering first the precision with which the description had to be followed and second what constituted the description. The credit was not well drawn in this respect. The underlying contract was for the sale of a vessel, and the credit required among the documents a copy of the notice of readiness covering:

'… a Greek flag motor tanker, Messiniaki Tolmi ex Berger Pilot of about 20,150 long tonnes displacement with one bronze working propeller, one spare tail end shaft to arrive under own power at Kaohsiung, Taiwan, on or before September 30th 1980 as is and always safely afloat and substantially intact as per memorandum of agreement dated July 2nd 1980.'

Having referred to Article 32(c) of UCP 290, the predecessor of UCP 600 Article 18.c and 14.e, the judge continued:[2]

'The reference in the article itself to a "description in general terms not inconsistent with the description in the credit" suggests that correspondence in description requires all the elements in the description to be present, although the article does not say that the description in the invoice must be the same as that in the credit. As to the expressions "ex Berger Pilot" and "previous name Berger Pilot", between which a distinction has been sought to be drawn, I hold that in this context "ex" means "previous" name. There therefore was correspondence in that respect. The remaining question is whether "as is and always safely afloat and substantially intact" is part of the description. It does not seem to matter whether the words "as per MOA" governs those words or the words "to arrive" (with or without some part of what follows), since the "as is" clause is already reproduced verbatim from the memorandum of agreement. The clause is obviously a vital element in the condition of the vessel, but is it part of the description, even if not part of the particulars required by par. 2 of the letter of credit? I have come to the conclusion that it is not. The words from "to arrive" to the end of the paragraph relate merely to the condition of the vessel when the notice of readiness is issued. They do not form part of the description of the particular vessel being sold.'

These cases demonstrate the importance of the description of the goods being clearly identifiable as the description in the credit, and of keeping it simple.

1 [1986] 1 Lloyd's Rep 455.
2 [1986] 1 Lloyd's Rep 455 at 458.

8.79   In *Chailease Finance Corpn v Credit Agricole Indosuez*, the credit required documents 'covering vessel MV "Mandarin" sale agreement dated July 31, 1998 for delivery in Taipei during August 17–20, 1998'. The judge held that the delivery date was not part of the description; the Court of Appeal agreed, albeit obiter.[1]

1 [2000] 1 Lloyd's Rep 348 at 358.

8.80   A problem of a different nature is considered in *Opinions* (1987–88) Ref 166.[1] The credit was transmitted by SWIFT MT 700 and the description of the physical goods was followed by 'FOB Keelung as per Incoterms 1980 Edition'. The invoice presented stated 'FOB Keelung' only. The Commission considered that the reference to Incoterms was part of the description. This was reinforced by the fact that it had been transmitted in field 45 of MT 700, which was set aside for the description of the goods.

1 ICC No 469. See also *Opinions* (1998–1999) ICC No 613, Ref 362 where it was considered that an invoice stating 'CFR Vancouver WA' was not discrepant when the credit described the goods as 'CFR Vancouver WA USA port'. The ICC Banking Commission pointed out that UCP 500 Article 37.c, the predecessor to UCP 600 Article 18.c, does not require exact compliance.

Amount

8.81   The total amount of the invoice should not exceed the amount of the credit. If it does, then the bank may accept the documents against payment of the maximum amount of the credit, unless the credit provides otherwise. This is the effect of Article 18.b, which states:

'**Article 18 Commercial Invoice**
b.   A nominated bank acting on its nomination, a confirming bank, if any, or the issuing bank may accept a commercial invoice issued for an amount in excess of the amount permitted by the credit, and its decision will be binding upon all parties, provided the bank in question has not honoured or negotiated for an amount in excess of that permitted by the credit.'

(2)   Transport documents

Introduction

8.82   A transport document is issued by the carrier when the goods are consigned. In the documentary credit transaction it performs three main functions:

(1)   It evidences receipt of the goods in the charge of the carrier for delivery as specified in the document. This gives the bank and the buyer an assurance when paying against the document that the goods have been despatched.
(2)   In the case of a negotiable marine bill of lading (and, possibly, certain other transport documents) it acts as what can loosely be described as a document of title giving rights of ownership or possession to the holder.[1] This provides a security to the bank holding the bill of lading which can be realised by the possession and sale of the goods.[2]
(3)   It evidences the existence and terms of the contract of carriage between the consignor and the carrier. Rights under that contract may be vested in the buyer or bank under the Carriage of Goods by Sea Act 1992.

Historically, the usual form of transport document was a marine bill of lading, and this is the form with which most of the reported decisions of the courts have been concerned. Modern developments in commerce and transport have given rise to new forms of document. The growth of containerised transportation has involved the appearance of container freight stations, which are often inland, where containers are assembled and may be filled (or 'stuffed') with the goods of different consignors (or shippers), and of container ports specialising in the handling of containers and of container vessels. Typically more than one carrier and more than one mode of carriage (by road, rail, river, ocean etc) is involved. Often a multimodal transport operator arranges or coordinates the route and issues a multimodal transport document. Fast sea crossings and air freight mean that fully negotiable bills of lading are cumbersome and unnecessary, and goods are usually shipped under a non-negotiable waybill on these routes. And goods shipped in bulk, such as oil or grain, are usually sold for payment against a delivery order. This situation led to major changes in the UCP in successive revisions. The changes in both UCP 400 and UCP 500 involved a complete re-organisation and re-drafting of the section covering transport documents; they have been further redrafted in UCP 600.

1   It is not an entirely accurate characterisation because the passage of property is governed by the contract of sale and may not always pass with the bill of lading.
2   See **Chapter 11**.

8.83   The scheme of the UCP is to make separate provision in Articles 19–25 for each of several specific types of document. If the credit calls for or permits a document which does not fall within any of Articles 19–25 then it will be covered by Article 14.d and 14.f: banks will accept the document as presented if its content appears to fulfil the function of the required document provided that the data in the document does not conflict with data in any other stipulated document or the credit.

Bills of lading

8.84   UCP Article 20 sets out provisions which relate specifically to bills of lading. It provides:

'**Article 20 Bill of Lading**
a.   A bill of lading, however named, must appear to:
  i.   indicate the name of the carrier and be signed by:
    •   the carrier or a named agent for or on behalf of the carrier, or
    •   the master or a named agent for or on behalf of the master.

      Any signature by the carrier, master or agent must be identified as that of the carrier, master or agent.

      Any signature by an agent must indicate whether the agent has signed for or on behalf of the carrier or for or on behalf of the master.

    ii.   indicate that the goods have been shipped on board a named vessel at the port of loading stated in the credit by:
- pre-printed wording, or
- an on board notation indicating the date on which the goods have been shipped on board.

> The date of issuance of the bill of lading will be deemed to be the date of shipment unless the bill of lading contains an on board notation indicating the date of shipment, in which case the date stated in the on board notation will be deemed to be the date of shipment.
>
> If the bill of lading contains the indication "intended vessel" or similar qualification in relation to the name of the vessel, an on board notation indicating the date of shipment and the name of the actual vessel is required.

    iii.   indicate shipment from the port of loading to the port of discharge stated in the credit.

> If the bill of lading does not indicate the port of loading stated in the credit as the port of loading, or if it contains the indication "intended" or similar qualification in relation to the port of loading, an on board notation indicating the port of loading as stated in the credit, the date of shipment and the name of the vessel is required. This provision applies even when loading on board or shipment on a named vessel is indicated by preprinted wording on the bill of lading.

    iv.   be the sole original bill of lading or, if issued in more than one original, be the full set as indicated on the bill of lading.

    v.   contain terms and conditions of carriage or make reference to another source containing the terms and conditions of carriage (short form or blank back bill of lading). Contents of terms and conditions of carriage will not be examined.

    vi.   contain no indication that it is subject to a charter party.

  b. For the purpose of this article, transhipment means unloading from one vessel and reloading to another vessel during the carriage from the port of loading to the port of discharge stated in the credit.

  c. i.   A bill of lading may indicate that the goods will or may be transshipped provided that the entire carriage is covered by one and the same bill of lading.

    ii.   A bill of lading indicating that transhipment will or may take place is acceptable, even if the credit prohibits transhipment, if the goods have been shipped in a container, trailer or LASH barge as evidenced by the bill of lading.

  d. Clauses in a bill of lading stating that the carrier reserves the right to tranship will be disregarded.'

8.85 UCP 500 Article 23, the predecessor to Article 20, was entitled Marine/Ocean Bill of Lading and expressly applied where 'a bill of lading covering a port-to-port' shipment was called for. The use of marine or ocean was intended to distinguish inland waterway bills.[1] The references to "marine" or "ocean" bills of lading and port-to-port shipment have been removed in UCP 600. However, the ISBP provides at para 92 that Article 20 is applicable to "a bill of lading ('marine', 'ocean' or 'port-to-port' or similar) covering sea shipment only". This suggests that there was no intention to extend the scope of Article 20 to inland waterway bills, which are covered separately by Article 25.

1 Case 85 Case Studies on Documentary Credits, ICC No 459.

8.86 If the transport document does not refer exclusively to a carriage by sea but combines it with other carriage such as a carriage by land, it will be a form of multimodal or combined transport document which will fall within Article 19 and not Article 20. The document may nonetheless show places of taking in charge and final destination different from the ports of loading and discharge respectively, as is permitted by Article 19.a.iii, and these need not be ports.[1] Article 20.a states that a document meeting the requirements of the article is acceptable 'however named'. For example, a document which is in the form of a standard form combined transport bill will nonetheless be a good tender against a credit requiring a marine bill of lading if it is completed so that it relates exclusively to sea carriage and otherwise meets the requirements of Article 20, in particular is notated to show receipt on board a named vessel. A negotiable FIATA Combined Transport Bill of Lading, a document in very common use, can be acceptable under Article 20, if it meets the requirements of that article.[2]

1 More Queries and Responses on UCP 500, ICC No 596, Ref 280.
2 *Opinions* (1995–1996) ICC No 565, Ref 219.

8.87 A brief consideration of what is a bill of lading is appropriate. *Sassoon CIF and FOB Contracts*[1] states:

'A bill of lading is a document which is signed by the carrier or his agent acknowledging that goods have been shipped on board a particular vessel bound for a particular destination and stating the terms on which the goods so received are to be carried.'

Scrutton on Charterparties[2] gives an expanded statement and refers to the uncertain position of some 'through' bills of lading:

'After goods are shipped, a document called a bill of lading is issued, which serves as a receipt by the shipowner, acknowledging that the goods have been delivered to him for carriage.

Besides acting as a receipt for the goods, the bill of lading serves also as:

(1) Evidence of the contract of affreightment between the shipper and the carrier.
(2) A document of title, by the indorsement of which the property in the goods for which it is a receipt may be transferred, or the goods pledged or mortgaged as security for an advance.

By the Carriage of Goods by Sea Act 1992, the lawful holder of the bill of lading acquires all rights of suit and may become subject to all the liabilities under the contract of carriage as if he had been a party to that contract.

> It has become increasingly common for liner companies and others to issue documents called through bills of lading, which may evidence a contract for carriage by land or air as well as by water. Such documents present special problems, and it is doubtful to what extent they share the characteristics of the conventional bill of lading.'

The three characteristics of a bill of lading are therefore (1) as a receipt, (2) as a contract of carriage, and (3) as a document of title. The Carriage of Goods by Sea Act 1992 provides for the ability of the holder of a bill of lading to sue on the contract of carriage, and makes equivalent provisions in respect of sea waybills and ship's delivery orders.

1 (4th edn) para 132.
2 (21st edn) p 2, cited in its earlier edition by Sassoon.

Name of carrier

8.88   A bill of lading is acceptable which appears to indicate the name of the carrier who is undertaking the carriage. As a bill of lading evidences a contract of carriage it is fundamental that it should indicate who the carrier is. The carrier named need not be the vessel owner nor have the right to the vessel whether by charter or otherwise provided that he has identified himself in the document as carrier.[1,2]

1 See *Opinions* (1984–1986), ICC No 434, Ref 121. The introduction to the *Opinion* refers to a definition of 'carrier' which appeared in a draft for the 1983 Revision [Document 470/391] which probably did not cover non-vessel-owning operators. See also Case 87 in *Case Studies on Documentary Credits*, ICC No 459.
2 And it seems that the word 'carrier' must be used: *Southland Rubber Co Ltd v Bank of China* [1997] 2 HKC 569.

Signature or authentication

8.89   The bills of lading must be signed or authenticated by the carrier or the master, or by an agent of one of them. UCP Article 3 provides that a document may be signed by handwriting, facsimile signature, perforated signature, stamp, symbol or any other mechanical or electronic method of authentication. The Article does not require that when the master signs he signs on behalf of the carrier: it is enough if the carrier is named on the bills and they are signed by the master. This may be presumed to be because it is within the ordinary authority of a master to issue bills of lading on behalf of the party who has the right to the use of the vessel. The carrier will almost always be a company and so cannot provide a signature save by an agent, whether that agent be an employee of the carrier or of another company which is acting as the agent of the carrier. Where the signature or authentication is by an agent, the agent must indicate the name and capacity of the party (carrier or master) on whose behalf he is acting.

Loaded on board or shipped on a named vessel

8.90   The bills of lading must indicate that the goods have been shipped on board a named vessel.[1] It is not enough that the goods have been received for shipment; the buyer is entitled to the carrier's assurance that the goods have actually been taken on board. This is in accordance with the decisions of the English courts that received-for-shipment bills are not a good tender under a CIF contract.[2] Article 20.a.ii provides for this to be done in two ways.

1 'Shipped in apparent good order', 'Laden on board', 'Clean on board' or other phrases incorporating words such as 'shipped' or 'on board' have the same effect as 'Shipped on board': ISBP para 97.
2 See *Diamond Alkali Export Corpn v Bourgeois* [1921] 3 KB 443 and *Yelo v SM Machado & Co Ltd* [1952] 1 Lloyd's Rep 183 at 192.

Pre-printed shipped bills

8.91   The first is where the bills have pre-printed wording showing that the goods have been shipped on a named vessel. This does not require the name of the vessel to be printed: but the printed bills must be in a shipped form rather than in a received-for-shipment form. Even though it may have been on the bill when issued, an annotation to that effect, that is, anything which does not form part of the original printed bill, makes the bills of the received-for-shipment type and must be completed in the second way.[1] If the bills indicate a place of receipt different from the port of loading, a notation is required as described next even if the bills are printed in a loaded-on-board form.

1 Compare *Westpac Banking Corpn and Commonwealth Steel Co Ltd v South Carolina National Bank* [1986] 1 Lloyd's Rep 311, Privy Council, which would now be decided differently: see Case 106 in *Case Studies on Documentary Credits*, ICC Publication No 459. Banks should not be, and now are not, required to try to ascertain when a notation was placed on a bill.

Notations

8.92   In all other cases loading or shipment on board a named vessel must be established by a notation on the bills of lading, that is, by something that does not form part of the printed part of the bills. So bills which are printed in a received-for-shipment form may be stamped 'Shipped' or 'Loaded on board'. The date of the notation must be added but there is no requirement that the notation should be signed or initialled by the carrier or his agent.

Intended vessels

8.93   Where the bills as originally drawn name the vessel as an intended vessel, or use words to like effect,[1] the on-board notation must include the date of shipment and the name of the actual vessel on which they are loaded (even where it is the same as the intended vessel). Where the bills as originally drawn name a vessel without qualification but are in the received-for-shipment form, need the notation repeat the vessel's name? The relevant part of Article 20.a.ii refers only to bills using the indication 'intended vessel' or a similar qualification, and so would not apply in this case.

1 A bill of lading sometimes contains on its face a statement that the goods are carried 'on the named vessel or any substitute at carrier's option'. This qualification, even though pre-printed in standard form, renders the bill of lading unacceptable without a sufficient on-board notation. See *More Queries on UCP 500*, ICC No 596, Ref 283.

8.94   Where a credit permits transhipment and the bill of lading indicates that carriage will be effected in two journeys, the bill should acknowledge loading on board the first vessel. This is so even if the division of the voyages indicates that the first ship is of the nature of a feeder vessel.[1]

1 *Opinions* (1984–1986) ICC No 434, Ref 118; *Opinions* (1998–99) ICC No 613, Ref 350.

Ports of loading and discharge

8.95   Article 20.a.iii provides that the bills of lading must indicate shipment from the port of loading[1] to the port of discharge stated in the credit required by the credit. If it does not (for example, if the goods are containerised and have been received by the carrier for transport to the port for loading on a vessel), or if the port of loading is qualified as 'intended' or similar, then there must be an on-board notation giving the port of loading, the date of shipment and the name of the vessel. This apples even when loading on board or shipment on a named vessel is indicated by pre-printed wording.

1 The credit may not mention a port of loading. For example, if the underlying contact is for sale of wheat CIF Antwerp, the port of loading is likely to be at the choice of the seller and will not be referred to in the credit.

Date of shipment

8.96   Where the bills are pre-printed in the loaded-on-board form, the date of issue of the bills is deemed to be the date of shipment. Where there is an on-board notation, the date of the notation is deemed to be the date of shipment.

All original bills

8.97   Article 20.a.iv requires the full set of original bills of lading as issued or the sole original bill if only one was issued. The origin of the practice of issuing bills of lading in sets (usually of three) lies in the earlier difficulties of transport when bills were dispatched separately by different routes to the buyer for safety. Each bill is effective to pass the property, and any one may be presented to the vessel to obtain delivery of the goods. So under the old wording bills were often expressed to be 'of even tenor, the one being accomplished, the others to stand void'. Such a system presents opportunities for fraud. Thus it was usual for credits to require that the full set of bills of lading should be presented to obtain payment, as was the case in *Donald H Scott & Co Ltd v Barclays Bank Ltd*[1] where it was held that two out of three bills would not do. The UCP now make this the requirement unless it is otherwise stipulated in the credit. The bills presented must be originals (unless otherwise stipulated). As the bank has to be satisfied that it has the full set, the bills of lading must indicate how many the set consists of. The shipper or consignor need not be the beneficiary unless the credit so provides: see Article 14.k.[2]

1 [1923] 2 KB 1.
2 See para **8.119** below.

Short form bills

8.98   Article 20.a.v requires either the bills of lading to contain all the terms and conditions of carriage, or to do so by incorporating them from another document. When the latter is done, the bills are called short form or blank back bills (because the back is devoid of all the usual small print). Banks are not required to examine the terms and conditions of carriage, whether or not they are contained in the bills themselves.

Subject to a charterparty

8.99   Article 20.a.vi requires that the bills of lading should contain no indication that they are subject to a charterparty. This may of course be expressly allowed by a term of the credit. Charterparty bills are considered under Article 25 at para **8.108**.

Transhipment

8.100   Articles 20.b–d relate to transhipment. Article 20.b defines transhipment as 'unloading from one vessel and reloading to another vessel during the carriage from the port of loading to the port of discharge stated in the credit'. The Article is intended to reflect the realities of container transport and also to take account of the fact that a prohibition on transhipment will often be inserted into a credit even though it is unrealistic. Article 20.c.i provides that bills of lading are acceptable which indicate that the goods will be transhipped provided that the entire carriage is covered by one bill of lading.[1] Even if transhipment is expressly prohibited by the credit, Article 20.c.ii provides that, where the goods are shown by the bills of lading to be shipped in containers, trailers or LASH barges, the bills may show that transhipment will take place (although not spelled out in the Article, this is presumably also subject to the entire carriage being covered by one bill of lading). Lastly Article 20.d ensures that a bill of lading which only reserves a right to tranship is acceptable. The position at common law is that a bill of lading which permits transhipment is permissible provided, first, that the bill of lading does give rights in respect of the entire carriage[2] and, secondly, that transhipment is not prohibited by the terms of the credit.[3]

1 See para **8.101** below.
2 See para **8.101** below.
3 See *The Marlborough Hill* [1921] 1 AC 444 at 452; *Holland Colombo Trading Society Ltd v Alawdeen* [1954] 2 Lloyd's Rep 45 at 53.2.

Through bills: to cover the whole carriage

8.101   Article 20.a.iii refers to bills of lading covering port-to-port shipment, and the transhipment provisions emphasise the need for one bill (or set of bills), that is one contract of carriage, to cover the entire carriage. The underlying rule is that the bills of lading must evidence a contract of carriage covering the whole of the journey from the port of shipment to the port of discharge. This is the general common law rule subject to the proof of custom to the contrary: see *Hansson v Hamel and Horley Ltd*[1] and *Arnold Otto Meyer NV v Aune*.[2] The credit may specify the port of shipment as well as the port of discharge, in which case the bill must cover the whole voyage to comply with that express provision. If the credit is silent as to the port of shipment, the reason for requiring a bill of lading which covers the whole of the sea journey from the actual port of shipment is that the buyer is entitled to have a document giving him rights covering all the journey so that he is properly covered in the event of loss or damage to the goods. It must be emphasised that a liberty to tranship, whether arising from the express terms of the credit or by reason of Article 20, does not affect the principle that the transport document must cover the whole voyage. Thus a document issued by a carrier which covers transport by more than one carrier, is acceptable only if the issuing carrier undertakes liability in respect of the whole voyage. If he accepts liability only in respect of that part carried out by him and acts as agent in respect of carriage by vessels owned by other carriers, the document is unacceptable unless the credit expressly permits this. It is particularly important here not to be guided by the title of the document: it is necessary to examine its terms and conditions to see what liability the issuing carrier is undertaking.

1 [1922] 2 AC 36; see the quotation in para **8.53** above.
2 [1939] 3 All ER 168.

8.102   Where a bill of lading gives a liberty to tranship in its small print which may, if exercised, mean that the carrier will no longer be contractually responsible for part of the voyage, the position at common law is more uncertain: the answer may be that at least if the liberty is unexercised, the bill is not objectionable. In *Soproma SpA v Marine and Animal By-Products Corpn*[1] McNair J stated:[2]

> 'As at present advised I should not be disposed to hold that a bill of lading otherwise unobjectionable in form which did in fact cover the whole transit actually performed would be a bad tender merely because it contained a liberty not in fact exercised, but which, if exercised, would not have given the buyers continuing cover for the portion of the voyage not performed by the vessel named in the bill of lading.'

If that is the correct approach, it would appear to involve the bank possibly taking account of a fact which would not be apparent from the face of the documents presented to it, namely whether there had been a transhipment. This would breach the rule as to the autonomy of the credit. If the terms of the credit prohibit transhipment, a bill with such a clause can nonetheless be argued to be permitted by Article 20.d despite the fact the bills will give no cover if transhipment occurs, because the Article makes no reference to this situation. The contrary argument would rely on the underlying principle that the bills must give complete cover. But a bank is not obliged to look at the terms and conditions at the back of a transport document to see whether there is such a right to tranship: see para **8.15** above.

1 [1966] 1 Lloyd's Rep 367.
2 [1966] 1 Lloyd's Rep 367 at 388.2.

Issued on shipment

8.103   The bill of lading should be issued 'on shipment'. In *Hansson v Hamel and Horley Ltd*[1] Lord Sumner stated:[2]

> 'I do not understand this proposition as meaning that the bill of lading would be bad, unless it was signed contemporaneously with the actual placing of the goods on board. "On shipment" is an expression of some latitude. Bills of lading are constantly signed after the loading is complete and, in some cases, after the ship has sailed. I do not think that they thereby necessarily cease to be procured "on shipment", nor do I suppose that the learned judge so intended his words. It may also be that the expression would be satisfied, even though some local carriage on inland waters, or by canal, or in an estuary or barge or otherwise preceded the shipment on the ocean steamer, provided that the steamer's bill of lading covered that prior carriage by effectual words of contract. "On shipment" is referable both to time and place ... I am quite sure that a bill of lading only issued thirteen days after the original shipment, at another port in another country many hundreds of miles away, is not duly procured "on shipment".'

1 [1922] 2 AC 36.
2 [1922] 2 AC 36 at 47.

8.104 In *M Golodetz & Co Inc v Czarnikow-Rionda Co Inc*[1] it was argued before Donaldson J but not before the Court of Appeal that the bill of lading was stale in this particular sense because it was issued on 6 April when loading was complete on 24 March. This was probably caused by the fact that the parcel in question was loaded early in the vessel's loading which continued over a period and it was intended to issue one bill covering all the cargo covered by the contract, not only the cargo which became fire damaged. The judge stated 'it was issued as soon as reasonably practicable after the completion of the loading of the whole parcel and at or about the time when the ship sailed'. The objection failed.

1 [1980] 1 WLR 495.

To order blank indorsed

8.105 This means that the bill of lading must provide for deliver 'to order', that is, that there is no named consignee, and 'to order' is written in the space for the name of the consignee. It means to order of the shipper. The buyer or his bank may be nominated as the 'notify' party. 'Blank indorsed' means that the shipper is, as it were, to give his order by indorsing the bills in blank, that is to say they are simply to be indorsed with his signature[1] on the bill. The bill can then be transferred without further indorsement by mere delivery. A bill which is not made out to order but is made out to a named consignee is not negotiable unless it contains words indicating transferability and has been indorsed by the consignee. In *Skandinaviska Akt v Barclays Bank*[2] blank indorsed bills were called for by the credit. The 'to order' bills did not name a shipper and so it was unclear who was entitled to indorse them: they were a bad tender. In *Soproma SpA v Marine and Animal By-Products Corpn*[3] the bills of lading were bad because, inter alia, they were straight bills made out to the consignees instead of being issued to order and blank indorsed.[4] Where it is uncertain whether a bill of lading is to be construed as a bill to shipper's order or to the order of the consignee the bill is to be rejected: *National Bank of South Africa v Banca Italiana di Sconto*.[5]

1 Ie the company name with the signature of an authorised person in the case of a company.
2 (1925) 22 Ll L Rep 523.
3 [1966] 1 Lloyd's Rep 367.
4 See [1966] 1 Lloyd's Rep at 388.1.
5 (1922) 10 Ll L Rep 531.

Non-negotiable sea waybills

8.106 The waybill concept has been long established in rail transport and later in air transport. It has more recently been applied to sea carriage, partly to overcome the problem that, while goods now arrive more rapidly, the postal services relied on to convey bills of lading have deteriorated. It achieves this by providing that the goods shall be delivered to the consignee named in the waybill upon proof of identity, rather than to the holder of the document. It shares the characteristics of bills of lading in that it is both a receipt for goods and a contract of carriage. It is not however a document of title nor is it negotiable: its transfer cannot be used to transfer the ownership of the goods to which it relates. This may make it unsuitable where it is intended to resell goods afloat.[1] Important provisions relating to waybills are made by the Carriage of Goods by Sea Act 1992 (which likewise apply to bills of lading). The nature of a waybill has two consequences which are important in documentary credits:

(a) Unless the seller/consignor gives up the right, he will have the right to vary his instruction to the carrier at any time up to the consignor's identification of himself and request for the goods. It is important that the consignor should not be able in this way to direct delivery to a third party while the documents are going through the credit. This may be done by the inclusion of a *non-disposal clause* in the waybill (often called a NODISP clause), whereby the consignor irrevocably gives up the right to vary the identity of the consignee during transit. But while such a clause protects the buyer, it leaves the seller in an impossible position if the documents are rejected under the credit. A solution (whose success may depend upon the timing of events) is for the clause to provide for the seller to give up his right to vary the identity of the consignee upon the acceptance of the waybill under a documentary credit and the confirmation of that acceptance by the accepting bank to the carrier.

(b) As the consignee is entitled to the delivery of the goods without the production of the waybill, he will be able to obtain delivery of them without the documents having come to him through the credit. He may do this with the result of defrauding the seller who has not been paid under the credit, or with the result of defrauding the bank which has paid under the credit but which has not been reimbursed by him. The seller can prevent the former, if time allows and if he is aware of the need to do so, by changing his delivery instructions to the carrier. If he does so and the carrier nonetheless delivers to the buyer, the carrier will be liable for misdelivery. The carrier would not be liable in the absence of a change of instructions. Whereas, with a bill of lading, if the seller remained entitled to the bills and hence to the possession of the goods, the carrier would be liable for misdelivery because he had delivered up the goods without production of a bill of lading even though there had been no change of instructions. A bank can prevent a buyer taking possession of the goods without having settled with the bank, by requiring itself to be named in the waybill as the consignee and the buyer as the notify party. It can then assign its rights as consignee to the buyer on receipt of settlement from the buyer, and will then notify the carrier enabling the buyer to obtain delivery. If the bank takes this course it will become a party to the contract of carriage, and so liable under it. Nonetheless many third world countries insist on this procedure to seek to control their foreign exchange position. An alternative is for the bank to require that the waybill be indorsed with a clause to the effect that the bank has a lien on the goods and that delivery was only to be made against written authority from the bank.

1 The end result may be achieved by the consignee taking a delivery order from the carrier and indorsing the order to the sub-purchaser, who can then present the delivery order to claim the goods from the carrier.

8.107 Article 21 governs the position where the credit calls for a non-negotiable sea waybill covering port-to-port shipment. The Article then follows precisely the wording of Article 20 with the substitution of 'non-negotiable sea waybill' for 'bill of lading'.

Charterparty bills of lading

8.108 Charterparty bills of lading are marine bills of lading which are issued subject to the terms of a charterparty. These are not acceptable unless the credit expressly so provides. This is the effect of Article 20.a.vi. This follows the practice of banks as established in the case of *Enrico Furst & Co v W E Fischer Ltd*.[1] Charterparty bills are provided for by Article 22:

'**Article 22 Charter Party Bill of Lading**
a. A bill of lading, however named, containing an indication that it is subject to a charter party (charter party bill of lading), must appear to:
    i.   be signed by:
        •   the master or a named agent for or on behalf of the master, or
        •   the owner or a named agent for or on behalf of the owner, or
        •   the charterer or a named agent for or on behalf of the charterer.

        Any signature by the master, owner, charterer or agent must be identified as that of the master, owner, charterer or agent.

        Any signature by an agent must indicate whether the agent has signed foror on behalf of the master, owner or charterer.

        An agent signing for or on behalf of the owner or charterer must indicatethe name of the owner or charterer.

    ii. indicate that the goods have been shipped on board a named vessel atthe port of loading stated in the credit by:
        •   pre-printed wording, or
        •   an on board notation indicating the date on which the goods have been shipped on board.

        The date of issuance of the charter party bill of lading will be deemed to be the date of shipment unless the charter party bill of lading contains an on board notation indicating the date of shipment, in which case the date stated in the on board notation will be deemed to be the date of shipment.

    iii. indicate shipment from the port of loading to the port of discharge stated in the credit. The port of discharge may also be shown as a range of ports or a geographical area, as stated in the credit.

    iv.   be the sole original charter party bill of lading or, if issued in more than one original, be the full set as indicated on the charter party bill of lading.
  b. A bank will not examine charter party contracts, even if they are required to be presented by the terms of the credit.'

1 [1960] 2 Lloyd's Rep 340 at 345, 346.

8.109　The UCP might have dealt with charterparty bills of lading by modification of Article 20. Article 22 takes the longer but probably clearer route of starting afresh. The Article follows Article 23 with these exceptions:

(a) The bills need not name the carrier. It is common for charterparty bills not to do so.
(b) Signature or authentication of the bills must be by or on behalf of the master or owner (the owner does not appear in Article 20).
(c) The 'intended vessel' provisions in Article 20 are omitted, presumably on the basis that if the bills are subject to a charterparty it follows that the vessel must have been identified.
(d) The bills must indicate the port of loading and the port of discharge stipulated in the credit. The passages in Article 20 covering 'intended' ports are omitted.
(e) The port of discharge may be shown as a range of ports or a geographical area as stated in the credit.
(f) The reference to short form/blank back bills is omitted: for a charterparty bill is by definition just such a bill.
(g) The provisions relating to transhipment are omitted: for a bill which is subject to a charterparty supposes the one vessel.
(h) Article 22.b precludes banks from examining the charterparty even if it is a document which the credit requires to be presented.

Although it is not indicated in the Article, just as with bills of lading which are not subject to a charterparty, charterparty bills must cover the whole of the carriage. Paragraph **8.101** above therefore applies. But in the context in which charterparty bills are issued this should not be a problem.

Multimodal/combined transport documents

8.110　Multimodal or combined transport documents are documents which cover at least two different modes of transport, for example, rail and sea, or road and air. Article 19 applies when the credit calls for such a document:

'**Article 19 Transport Document Covering at Least Two Different Modes of Transport**
  a. A transport document covering at least two different modes of transport (multimodal or combined transport document), however named, must appear to:

    i.   indicate the name of the carrier and be signed by:
- the carrier or a named agent for or on behalf of the carrier, or
- the master or a named agent for or on behalf of the master.

            Any signature by the carrier, master or agent must be identified as that of the carrier, master or agent.

            Any signature by an agent must indicate whether the agent has signed for or on behalf of the carrier or for or on behalf of the master.

    ii.   indicate that the goods have been dispatched, taken in charge or shipped on board at the place stated in the credit, by:
- pre-printed wording, or
- a stamp or notation indicating the date on which the goods have been dispatched, taken in charge or shipped on board.

            The date of issuance of the transport document will be deemed to be the date of dispatch, taking in charge or shipped on board, and the date of shipment. However, if the transport document indicates, by stamp or notation, a date of dispatch, taking in charge or shipped on board, this date will be deemed to be the date of shipment.

    iii.   indicate the place of dispatch, taking in charge or shipment and the place of final destination stated in the credit, even if:

        a.   the transport document states, in addition, a different place of dispatch, taking in charge or shipment or place of final destination,

            or

        b.   the transport document contains the indication "intended" or similar qualification in relation to the vessel, port of loading or port of discharge.

    iv.   be the sole original transport document or, if issued in more than one original, be the full set as indicated on the transport document.

    v.   contain terms and conditions of carriage or make reference to another source containing the terms and conditions of carriage (short form or blank back transport document). Contents of terms and conditions of carriage will not be examined.

    vi.   contain no indication that it is subject to a charter party.

b.   For the purpose of this article, transhipment means unloading from one means of conveyance and reloading to another means of conveyance (whether or not in different modes of transport) during the carriage from the place of dispatch, taking in charge or shipment to the place of final destination stated in the credit.

c.   i.   A transport document may indicate that the goods will or may be transhipped provided that the entire carriage is covered by one and the same transport document.

        ii.   A transport document indicating that transhipment will or may take place is acceptable, even if the credit prohibits transhipment.'

8.111   Article 19 follows the same form as Article 20, and so having commented fully on Article 23 it is again convenient to compare the two:

(a) Article 19 applies where the credit calls for a transport document covering at least two different modes of transport.
(b) The document must indicate the name of the carrier, sometimes called the multimodal transport operator. They must sign or authenticate it. Alternatively it may be signed by the master, or a named agent for them or the master. The agent must indicate the name and capacity of the party he is acting for, in the same way, mutatis mutandis, as is provided by Article 20.
(c) The documents must indicate that the goods have been dispatched, taken in charge or shipped on board. Where the document shows a date of dispatch etc by a stamp or otherwise, that date is to be taken as the date of shipment: otherwise the date of issue of the document is to be taken as the date of shipment (Article 19.a.i).
(d) It must indicate the place of taking in charge and the place of final destination stipulated in the credit. These may be different from the ports, airports or places of loading and unloading respectively (Article 19.a.iii.a).
(e) Any vessel and the port of loading and of discharge may be qualified as 'intended' or similarly (Article 19.a.iii.b).
(f) It must not indicate that it is subject to a charterparty (Article 19.a.vi).
(g) Even where the credit prohibits transhipment, the document may show that transhipment will or may take place, provided that the entire carriage is covered by the one document[1] (Article 19.c).

1 See para **8.101** above.

Air transport documents

8.112 Air transport documents usually take the form of an air waybill. International carriage by air is covered by international Conventions, in particular by the Hague–Warsaw–Montreal Convention.[1] An air waybill is a document made out in three original parts by the consignor. One part is designated for the carrier and is signed by the consignor. One part is designated for the consignee: it is signed by the consignor and the carrier and accompanies the cargo. The third is designated for the consignor: it is signed by the carrier and is handed to the consignor after the acceptance of the cargo. On the arrival of the cargo at destination the consignee is entitled to have the second original handed to him. It will be seen that the only original available to the consignor and therefore which the consignor/beneficiary can present under a credit is the third original signed by the carrier.

1 Made part of English law by the Carriage by Air Act 1961 which sets out the Convention as the First Schedule.

8.113 Article 23 provides as follows:

'**Article 23 Air Transport Document**
a.   An air transport document, however named, must appear to:
　　i.   indicate the name of the carrier and be signed by:
　　　　•   the carrier, or
　　　　•   a named agent for or on behalf of the carrier.
　　　　　Any signature by the carrier or agent must be identified as that of the carrier or agent.
　　　　　Any signature by an agent must indicate that the agent has signed for or on behalf of the carrier.
　　ii.   indicate that the goods have been accepted for carriage.
　　iii.   indicate the date of issuance. This date will be deemed to be the date of shipment unless the air transport document contains a specific notation of the actual date of shipment, in which case the date stated in the notation will be deemed to be the date of shipment.
　　　　　Any other information appearing on the air transport document relative to the flight number and date will not be considered in determining the date of shipment.
　　iv.   indicate the airport of departure and the airport of destination stated in the credit.
　　v.   be the original for consignor or shipper, even if the credit stipulates a full set of originals.
　　vi.   contain terms and conditions of carriage or make reference to another source containing the terms and conditions of carriage. Contents of terms and conditions of carriage will not be examined.
b.   For the purpose of this article, transhipment means unloading from one aircraft and reloading to another aircraft during the carriage from the airport of departure to the airport of destination stated in the credit.
c.   i.   An air transport document may indicate that the goods will or may be transhipped, provided that the entire carriage is covered by one and the same air transport document.
　　ii.   An air transport document indicating that transhipment will or may take place is acceptable, even if the credit prohibits transhipment.'

8.114　It will be seen that:

(a)　Article 23.a.i requires the name of the carrier to appear and the document to be signed or authenticated by the carrier or on his behalf. These provisions broadly follow those of Article 20.a.i, which have been considered in para **8.84** above.

(b)　Article 23.a.v requires the document to be the original for the consignor/shipper, thus identifying it as the third original referred to in para **8.112** above. Any reference in the credit to a full set of originals may be ignored: it is inappropriate – air waybills are not issued in sets to the consignor like bills of lading but as have been described.

(c)　It must show that the goods have been accepted for carriage (Article 23.a.ii).

(d)　It must indicate the date of issuance, which will be deemed to be the date of shipment unless the document contains a specific notation of the actual date of shipment (Article 23.a.iii). Such a requirement is not satisfied by the appearance of a flight number and date in the box on the document marked 'For carrier use only' or with a similar expression: a separate notification is required.

(f) It must show the airport of departure and of destination (Article 23.a.iv).

(g) It must either show all the terms and conditions of carriage itself or show them by reference to another source: but banks will not examine them (Article 23.a.vi).

(h) Transhipment as defined by Article 23.b is permissible even though the credit prohibits it, provided that the entire carriage is covered by the one document. This takes account of the realities of air transport and the non-availability of direct flights between many airports.

8.115 'House air waybills' are air waybills issued not by an airline but by freight forwarders or consolidators. If the credit states that a house air waybill or freight forwarder's air waybill is acceptable, or uses similar phrasing, then the air transport document may be signed by the freight forwarder without any need to identify itself as carrier or agent for a carrier and the document need not show the name of the carrier: see ISBP para 138.

Road, rail or inland waterway transport documents

8.116 A provision in a credit for a road, rail or inland waterway transport document will be governed by Article 24, which therefore covers some disparate transport forms. The Article provides:

'**Article 24 Road, Rail or Inland Waterway Transport Documents**
a. A road, rail or inland waterway transport document, however named, must appear to:
   i. indicate the name of the carrier and:
   • be signed by the carrier or a named agent for or on behalf of the carrier, or
   • indicate receipt of the goods by signature, stamp or notation by the carrier or a named agent for or on behalf of the carrier.

   Any signature, stamp or notation of receipt of the goods by the carrier or agent must be identified as that of the carrier or agent.

   Any signature, stamp or notation of receipt of the goods by the agent must indicate that the agent has signed or acted for or on behalf of the carrier.

   If a rail transport document does not identify the carrier, any signature or stamp of the railway company will be accepted as evidence of the document being signed by the carrier.

   ii. indicate the date of shipment or the date the goods have been received for shipment, dispatch or carriage at the place stated in the

227

            credit. Unless the transport document contains a dated reception stamp, an indication of the date of receipt or a date of shipment, the date of issuance of the transport document will be deemed to be the date of shipment.

      iii.   indicate the place of shipment and the place of destination stated in the credit.

   b.   i.   A road transport document must appear to be the original for consignor or shipper or bear no marking indicating for whom the document has been prepared.

      ii.   A rail transport document marked "duplicate" will be accepted as an original.

      iii.   A rail or inland waterway transport document will be accepted as an original whether marked as an original or not.

   c.   In the absence of an indication on the transport document as to the number of originals issued, the number presented will be deemed to constitute a full set.

   d.   For the purpose of this article, transhipment means unloading from one means of conveyance and reloading to another means of conveyance, within the same mode of transport, during the carriage from the place of shipment, dispatch or carriage to the place of destination stated in the credit.

   e.   i.   A road, rail or inland waterway transport document may indicate that the goods will or may be transhipped provided that the entire carriage is covered by one and the same transport document.

      ii.   A road, rail or inland waterway transport document indicating that transhipment will or may take place is acceptable, even if the credit prohibits transhipment.'

The features provided for by the Article are:

(a) It must give the name of the carrier and be signed or authenticated by or on behalf of the carrier, as is required also by Article 20. If a rail transport document does not identify the carrier, any signature or stamp of the railway company will be accepted as evidence of the cdocument being signed by the carrier,

(b) It must show that the goods[1] have been received for shipment etc. The date of issue is deemed the date of shipment unless there is a reception stamp (whose date is then deemed the date of shipment).

(c) It must show the places of shipment and destination stipulated in the credit.

(d) A full set of documents must be presented. However, unless the numbers on the documents presented indicate otherwise, the documents presented will be accepted as a full set.

(e) Even if prohibited by the credit, transhipment is acceptable provided that the entire carriage is covered by the one document and is within the same mode of transport. So, if more than one mode of transport is to be utilised, the credit should provide for a multimodal transport document as set out in Article 19.

---

1 As to the non-acceptability of a groupage rail waybill, see para **8.133**, n 4.

Courier and post receipts

8.117   Article 25, which is self-explanatory, states:

'**Article 25 Courier Receipt, Post Receipt or Certificate of Posting**
a.   A courier receipt, however named, evidencing receipt of goods for transport, must appear to:
  i.   indicate the name of the courier service and be stamped or signed by the named courier service at the place from which the credit states the goods are to be shipped; and
  ii.   indicate a date of pick-up or of receipt or wording to this effect. This date will be deemed to be the date of shipment.
b.   A requirement that courier charges are to be paid or prepaid may be satisfied by a transport document issued by a courier service evidencing that courier charges are for the account of a party other than the consignee.
c.   A post receipt or certificate of posting, however named, evidencing receipt of goods for transport, must appear to be stamped or signed and dated at the place from which the credit states the goods are to be shipped. This date will be deemed to be the date of shipment.'

Transport documents issued by freight forwarders

8.118   UCP 500 Article 30 provided that transport documents issued by freight forwarders were not acceptable unless the name of the forwarder appeared as carrier or as agent for the carrier. That exclusion of freight forwarder bills was in accordance with banking practice as it was found by Diplock J in *Enrico Furst & Co v W E Fischer Ltd*.[1]

1 [1960] 2 Lloyd's Rep 340 at 345, 346.

8.119   There is no equivalent provision in UCP 600. Instead, Article 14.l provides:

'**Article 14 Standard for Examination of Documents**
l.   A transport document may be issued by any party other than a carrier, owner, master or charterer provided that the transport document meets the requirements of articles 19, 20, 21, 22, 23 or 24 of these rules.'

Articles 19 to 24 still require the transport document to be signed by the carrier or by a named agent on the carrier's behalf. However, ISBP provides in relation to multimodal transport documents (para 72), bills of lading (para 95) and air waybills (para 138) that if the credit states that a freight forwarder transport document is acceptable then the document may be signed by the freight forwarder without the need to identify itself as carrier or agent for the carrier and the document need not show the name of the carrier.

Carriage on deck

8.120 Unless the credit provides otherwise, where the credit includes carriage by sea, a positive statement in a transport document that goods will be carried on deck makes the document unacceptable. One which refers to the possibility only is acceptable. Article 26.a provides:

> 'Article 26 "On Deck", "Shipper's Load and Count", "Said by Shipper to Contain" and "Charges Additional to Freight"
> a.   A transport document must not indicate that the goods are or will be loaded on deck. A clause on a transport document stating that the goods may be loaded on deck is acceptable.'

8.121 It has always been the practice of banks to refuse bills showing stowage on deck because of the additional likelihood of damage to goods so stowed. In view of the construction of many container vessels whereby the containers are stacked several high on a low deck, the situation is today rather altered. Article 26.a does not state what the position is if the credit specifically prohibits loading on deck, or calls for under-deck loading but it is suggested that in that case a document indicating that goods may be loaded on deck would be unacceptable.

'Shipper's load and count'

8.122 A transport document which is claused 'shipper's load and count' or 'said by shipper to contain' or such like is acceptable unless the credit provides otherwise. Article 26.b provides:

> 'Article 26 "On Deck", "Shipper's Load and Count", "Said by Shipper to Contain" and "Charges Additional to Freight"
> b.   A transport document bearing a clause such as 'shipper's load and count' and 'said by shipper to contain' is acceptable.'

The effect of such clausing is that the carrier is not bound by the quantity or weight declared to him by the consignor and which he would otherwise acknowledge by the bill of lading. The need to be able to clause bills in this way is greatly increased by the use of containers: unless the carrier has put the goods into the container himself it is only in exceptional circumstances that he will check the contents. Bills of lading frequently contain a printed clause stating 'weight, measure, quantity, contents and value unknown'. This does not render the bill unclean. Nor does it qualify an acknowledgement of apparent condition.[1]

1 See *M Golodetz & Co Inc v Czarnikow-Rionda Co Inc* [1980] 1 WLR 495 at 512 per Donaldson J whose decision was not taken to appeal on this point.

Name of consignor

8.123 The credit may stipulate who should be the consignor or shipper of the goods named in the transport document. If it does not, the consignor so named need not be the beneficiary under the credit, ie the seller. This takes account of the possibility that the beneficiary may well be a purchaser in a string or otherwise from a third party who has shipped the goods. Article 14.k thus provides that the shipper or consignor of the goods indicated on any document need not be the beneficiary of the credit.

Clean transport documents[1]

8.124 It is usual for credits to state expressly that bills of lading or other transport documents must be clean. Under the UCP, clean transport documents are required unless the credit expressly stipulates the clauses or notations which may be accepted. At common law, in nearly all circumstances clean bills would be required even if the credit was silent on the point. In *British Imex Industries Ltd v Midland Bank Ltd*[2] Salmon J stated:[3]

> 'The letter of credit stipulated that payment would be made against bills of lading without qualification. The plaintiffs suggest that this does not necessarily mean clean bills of lading. In my judgment, when a credit calls for bills of lading, in normal circumstances it means clean bills of lading. I think that in normal circumstances the ordinary business man who undertakes to pay against the presentation of bills of lading means clean bills of lading: and he would probably consider that that was so obvious to any other business man that it was hardly necessary to state it. That seems to have been the view taken by Bailhache J in *National Bank of Egypt v Hannevig's Bank*. I entirely agree with it. No doubt, as was pointed out by the Court of Appeal in that case, (1919) 1 Ll L Rep 69 and 3 Legal Decisions Affecting Bankers 213 there may be circumstances where, for instance, business has been disorganized by war, in which a credit against bills of lading is not necessarily a credit against clean bills of lading. That is a point which it is unnecessary to decide in this case, for here there are no special circumstances, and I read 'bills of lading' in the letter of credit as meaning clean bills of lading. A 'clean bill of lading' has never been exhaustively defined, and I certainly do not propose to attempt that task now. I incline to the view, however, that a clean bill of lading is one that does not contain any reservation as to the apparent good order or condition of the goods or the packing. In my judgment, the bills of lading in this case are plainly clean bills of lading. They contain no reservation by way of endorsement, clausing or otherwise, to suggest that the goods or the packing are or may be defective in any respect.'

Reference may also be made to *Hannevig's* case (where the Court of Appeal's doubt that in the particular circumstances clean bills would have been required even in the absence of a direction to accept claused bills was no doubt influenced by the need to encourage trade in wartime and the very fact of that direction) and to *Westminster Bank v Banca Nazionale di Credito*[4] where Roche J commented on the conflict in *Hannevig's* case between the view of Bailhache J and that of the Court of Appeal arising on the particular facts of the case.[5] In *M Golodetz & Co Inc v Czarnikow-Rionda Co Inc*[6] Donaldson J held and it was accepted in the Court of Appeal that in the context of a CIF contract a 'clean bill' is one in which there is nothing to qualify the admission by the carrier that the goods were in apparent good order and condition at the time of shipment. It was accepted by the buyers in the Court of Appeal that the bill (which was claused to the effect that the goods had been damaged by fire after shipment and had had to be discharged) was clean in that sense. A wider argument was advanced that the bill was not 'clean' in the sense that it was not a document that would ordinarily and properly have been accepted in the trade as being an appropriate document, citing the dictum of Lord Sumner from *Hanssen v Hamel and Horley Ltd.*[7] The Court of Appeal held that as the arbitrators had not found that the bill was not reasonably and readily fit to pass current in commerce, the bill was 'clean' in the wider sense.[8] (It may be helpful to point out that the loss of the goods subsequent to loading does not entitle the buyer under a CIF contract not to take up the documents: he must take up the documents and pay for them, and his remedy is against the carrier or on the insurance. Thus in *Manbre Saccharine Co Ltd v Corn Products Co Ltd*[9] the vessel was sunk on 12 March 1917 and the sellers were held entitled to make a good tender on 14 March despite their knowledge of the loss. The argument in *Golodetz* was not based on the loss of the cargo but on the clausing of the bill.)

1 The ICC publishes a pamphlet entitled 'Clean Transport Documents', ICC No 473.
2 [1958] 1 QB 542.
3 [1958] 1 QB 542 at 551.
4 (1928) 31 Ll L Rep 306.
5 (1928) 31 Ll L Rep 306 at 311.
6 [1980] 1 WLR 495; see para **8.54** above.
7 [1922] 2 AC 36 at 46.
8 For a discussion of this conclusion, see paras **8.54** and **8.56** above.
9 [1919] 1 KB 198.

8.125   The UCP define a clean transport document in Article 27, which states:

> '**Article 27 Clean Transport Document**
> A bank will only accept a clean transport document. A clean transport document is one bearing no clause or notation expressly declaring a defective condition of the goods or their packaging. The word "clean" need not appear on a transport document, even if a credit has a requirement for that transport document to be "clean on board".'

It will be seen that:

(1) Even where a credit expressly calls for 'clean on board' bills of lading, or bills marked 'clean on board', it is not necessary for the words 'clean on board' to appear.
(2) The definition is confined to the narrow sense of 'clean' (see the discussion of *Golodetz* in para **8.124** above) and follows the common law

view as expressed in the *British Imex* and *Golodetz* cases. It is suggested that the wider objection to a bill which was sought to be advanced in *Golodetz* that, because of a clausing or notation, it would not be fit to pass current in the trade, is unaffected by the Article, which is not seeking to deal with that situation.

(3) The Article does not refer to the time to which any clause or notation should relate. As Donaldson J remarked in *Golodetz* the crucial time as between the shipowner and shipper including those who claim through the shipper as holders of the bill of lading is the time of shipment. It is to this time that the clause or notation must relate. It is perhaps surprising that after the problems in *Golodetz* the UCP still do not make this clear.

Further guidance is given in ISBP paras 106–107. Clauses or notations which do not expressly declare a defective condition of the goods or packaging (the example is given of a notation 'packaging may not be sufficient for the sea journey') do not render the bill unclean.

Clean bills of lading given against indemnity

8.126   Where a carrier is minded to clause a transport document with a notation which would render it unclean, the shipper may attempt to avoid this by offering the carrier, in return for the issue of a clean transport document, an indemnity against liability asserted against him on the ground that the bill was clean. This is a dangerous and highly undesirable practice. The document so produced may well be considered to be a fraud on the transferee of the bill who will take delivery of the goods. As the indemnity is a part of the fraud and is against the consequences of fraud, it will be unenforceable.[1] A bank which gives the indemnity, or which is involved in its preparation, may be held party to the fraud.

1 *Brown, Jenkinson & Co Ltd v Percy Dalton (London) Ltd* [1957] 2 QB 621; *Standard Chartered Bank v Pakistan National Shipping Corpn (No 2)* [2000] 1 Lloyd's Rep 218 at 221.

Freight and other charges

8.127   Under a CIF contract the general rule is that a seller has an option: he can pay the freight and provide pre-paid bills of lading, or he can provide what are called freight collect bills and invoice the CIF price less freight (freight collect bills are bills under which the freight is payable by the receiver of the goods).[1] This is, of course, subject to any relevant provision of the particular contract. The position under a letter of credit is the same. The seller has a choice unless the credit provides that the freight must be pre-paid. In *Soproma SpA v Marine and Animal By-Products Corpn*[2] the credit required

'Full set clean on board ocean B/L issued to the order and blank endorsed; destination Sarona, marked "freight pre-paid"'. The bills of lading rendered were marked 'freight collect'. McNair J referred to the arbitrators' finding that freight collect bills were commonly regarded as a good tender provided freight was either deducted from the invoice or shown to have been paid by the freight receipt. He continued:

> 'If this finding means more than that it commonly happens that buyers do not take the objection that a bill of lading in this form is not a valid tender if either the freight is deducted from the price in the invoice or a receipt for freight is tendered, it would, as it seems to me, be a finding which could not be sustainable in law since on the hypothesis stated the documents would be mutually inconsistent.'

It is not clear what documents he was referring to as being inconsistent. If freight was deducted from the invoice, this would not be inconsistent with the bill of lading being marked 'freight collect'. Nor would it be clear that a freight collect bill was inconsistent with a receipt. He must have meant that the marking on the bill of lading was inconsistent with the express provision of the credit, which is surely the point.

1 See Sassoon *CIF and FOB Contracts* (4th edn) paras 104–107 and *The Pantanassa* [1970] 1 All ER 848 at 855.
2 [1966] 1 Lloyd's Rep 367.

8.128 UCP 500 Article 33 provided that, unless otherwise stipulated in the credit or inconsistent with any of the documents presented under the Credit, banks would accept transport documents stating that freight or transportation charges have still to be paid. There is no equivalent provision in UCP 600. Instead, the ISBP provides, in relation to bills of lading, as follows:

111) If a credit requires that a bill of lading show that freight has been paid or is payable at destination, the bill of lading must be marked accordingly.

112) Applicants and issuing banks should be specific in stating the requirements of the documents to show whether freight is to be prepaid or collected.

113) If a credit states that costs additional to freight are not acceptable, a bill of lading must not indicate that costs additional to the freight have been or will be incurred. Such indication may be by express reference to additional costs or by the use of shipment terms which refer to costs associated with the loading or unloading of goods, such as Free In (FI), Free Out (FO), Free In and Out (FIO) and Free In and Out Stowed (FIOS). A reference in the transport document to costs which may be levied as a result of a delay in unloading the goods or after the goods have been unloaded, e.g., costs covering the late return of containers, is not considered to be an indication of additional costs in this context.

There are equivalent provisions for other types of transport documents. This appears to leave open the question of whether a freight collect transport document is acceptable if, contrary to ISBP para 112, the credit is silent. It is suggested that in that case, as under UCP 500, the beneficiary should be entitled to present either a freight prepaid or a freight collect transport document.

8.129   Article 26.c provides that a transport document may bear a reference, by stamp or otherwise, to charges additional to the freight. Such charges might, for example, cover loading or unloading costs.

Partial shipments

8.130   The credit may prohibit partial shipments. If it does not, they are allowed. Article 31 provides for this and also provides that certain shipments are not to be regarded as partial shipments and therefore as caught by any prohibition. It states:

'**Article 31 Partial Drawings or Shipments**
a.   Partial drawings or shipments are allowed.
b.   A presentation consisting of more than one set of transport documents evidencing shipment commencing on the same means of conveyance and for the same journey, provided they indicate the same destination, will not be regarded as covering a partial shipment, even if they indicate different dates of shipment or different ports of loading, places of taking in charge or dispatch. If the presentation consists of more than one set of transport documents, the latest date of shipment as evidenced on any of the sets of transport documents will be regarded as the date of shipment.

A presentation consisting of one or more sets of transport documents evidencing shipment on more than one means of conveyance within the same mode of transport will be regarded as covering a partial shipment, even if the means of conveyance leave on the same day for the same destination.

c.   A presentation consisting of more than one courier receipt, post receipt or certificate of posting will not be regarded as a partial shipment if the courier receipts, post receipts or certificates of posting appear to have been stamped or signed by the same courier or postal service at the same place and date and for the same destination.'

8.131   Where the credit provides for drawings and/or shipments within given periods, failure to ship or draw within one period means that the credit ceases to be available for that and any subsequent instalments: see Article 32.

Date of shipment and presentation

8.132   The Articles relating to specific types of transport document contain provisions to identify the date of shipment or of dispatch. The date may be relevant in three respects:

(1) The credit may well provide a period for shipment or a latest date for shipment. Bills of lading or other transport documents not adhering to the provision will be rejected: see para **5.29** above.
(2) Bills of lading and other transport documents must be issued on shipment. This is considered at para **8.103** above.
(3) Presentation must be made not later than 21 calendar days after the date of shipment: Article 14.c.

Description and identification of goods in transport documents

8.133   Transport documents must indicate receipt or shipment of 'the goods'. So they must show that there is a contract of carriage relating to 'the goods' and that 'the goods' have been placed with the carrier. 'The goods' must be the goods for which the applicant is being invoiced. The quantity must be stated in the same terms as the invoice or in a manner which can be directly related to the invoice quantity as being the same: see, for an example of where this could not be done, *London and Foreign Trading Corpn v British and Northern European Bank*.[1] Another example is given in Case 250 in the ICC's *More Case Studies on Documentary Credits*.[2] There the bill of lading referred to 25 containers with their numbers. The invoice referred to 25 containers but did not give their numbers. The majority view of the group of experts was that because the documents were consistent in a number of respects (same letter of credit reference, same description of goods, number of containers and net weight) they complied with the requirements of the credit: it was unnecessary for the container numbers to be shown on the invoice. It is suggested that this is indeed correct. On the other hand the transport document must not cover additional goods: if it does it is unacceptable.[3] This may well happen in situations where there has been 'groupage' of the relevant goods with other goods.

1 (1921) 9 Ll L Rep 116, considered more fully in para **8.74** above.
2 ICC No 489.
3 Bills of lading, see *Decisions* (1975–1979) ICC No 371, Ref 65; groupage rail waybill, see Case 233 in *More Case Studies on Documentary Credits*, ICC No 489.

(3)   Insurance documents

Instructions and the risks to be covered

8.134   Article 28 provides:

'**Article 28 Insurance Document and Coverage**
a.   An insurance document, such as an insurance policy, an insurance certificate or a declaration under an open cover, must appear to be issued and signed by an insurance company, an underwriter or their agents or their proxies.

Any signature by an agent or proxy must indicate whether the agent or proxy has signed for or on behalf of the insurance company or underwriter.

b.   When the insurance document indicates that it has been issued in more than oneoriginal, all originals must be presented.
c.   Cover notes will not be accepted.
d.   An insurance policy is acceptable in lieu of an insurance certificate or a declaration under an open cover.
e.   The date of the insurance document must be no later than the date of shipment, unless it appears from the insurance document that the cover is effective from a date not later than the date of shipment.
f.   i.   The insurance document must indicate the amount of insurance coverage and be in the same currency as the credit.
    ii.   A requirement in the credit for insurance coverage to be for a percentage of the value of the goods, of the invoice value or similar is deemed to be the minimum amount of coverage required.

        If there is no indication in the credit of the insurance coverage required, the amount of insurance coverage must be at least 110% of the CIF or CIP value of the goods.

        When the CIF or CIP value cannot be determined from the documents, the amount of insurance coverage must be calculated on the basis of the amount for which honour or negotiation is requested or the gross value of the goods as shown on the invoice, whichever is greater.

    iii.   The insurance document must indicate that risks are covered at least between the place of taking in charge or shipment and the place of discharge or final destination as stated in the credit.

g.   A credit should state the type of insurance required and, if any, the additional risks to be covered. An insurance document will be accepted without regard to any risks that are not covered if the credit uses imprecise terms such as "usual risks" or "customary risks".
h.   When a credit requires insurance against "all risks" and an insurance document is presented containing any "all risks" notation or clause, whether or not bearing the heading "all risks", the insurance document will be accepted without regard to any risks stated to be excluded.
i.   An insurance document may contain reference to any exclusion clause.
j.   An insurance document may indicate that the cover is subject to a franchise or excess (deductible).'

237

8.135   In most cases, the trade being one in which the buyer is experienced, the buyer will have no difficulty in specifying the cover that he requires. In other cases it is important that he should give appropriate consideration and seek advice as necessary. The terms to be used in specifying terms of insurance cover can be highly technical. In such cases the requirement should be stated in the credit with precision but without undue complexity.

All risks

8.136   The expression 'all risks' is often used and its meaning has been the subject of a number of decisions. The difficulties which it poses are substantially avoided by Article 28.h. The insurance document need not have an 'all risks' heading and it does not matter that certain risks are excluded, provided that the document contains an 'all risks' notation or clause. The Article does not contain words to make its effect subject to any provisions of the credit. But obviously this must be so. There must also be some limit to the risks that can be excluded. It is suggested that this is a matter for the bank to consider. If the cover provided is so cut down by the exclusions that it would clearly fall short of the cover to be reasonably expected for the transaction in question, it should be rejected.

The documents to be issued

8.137   Article 28.c prohibits cover notes. A cover note is commonly issued by the broker as his own indication that he has arranged cover. It is not issued with the authority of the insurer. Where a broker has that authority and so acts as agent of the insurer, the position is different. The unacceptability of a broker's cover note was considered, probably obiter, in the early case of *Wilson, Holgate & Co Ltd v Belgian Grain and Produce Co Ltd.*[1]

1 [1920] 2 KB 1.

Open covers

8.138   An open cover is a policy issued by an insurer which enables a named party, perhaps a broker or an underwriting agent or, less often, a party through whose hands goods pass, to make declarations under it of risks which fall within the risks permitted by the cover. A declaration under an open cover is acceptable under Article 28.a.

8.139   A problem arising with certificates or declarations issued under open covers is that they do not usually set out the full terms of the insurance. It is suggested that where by reason of the Article an open cover document is acceptable, it will not be defective simply because it refers to the terms of the policy itself which will be unknown to the bank and which cannot be examined by the bank. Nonetheless it must contain sufficient information to show that the terms of the credit as to insurance have been complied with. It is suggested that the position is different in this respect to that without the Article. In the early case of *Donald H Scott & Co Ltd v Barclays Bank Ltd*[1] the document tendered was a certificate of insurance that the goods were insured under a policy having a particular number. As Bankes LJ stated[2] 'That only indicates that a policy has been issued by this company; but the terms of that policy, the risks insured against, and the conditions imposed by the policy respecting shipment can only be ascertained by reference to some document which did not accompany the certificate and of which [the bank] could know nothing.'[3]

1 [1923] 2 KB 1.
2 [1923] 2 KB 1 at 12.
3 See also *Diamond Alkali Export Corpn v Bourgeois* [1921] 3 KB 443 and *Malmberg v HJ Evans & Co* (1924) 41 TLR 38.

8.140   Article 28.d also provides that where the credit calls for a certificate or declaration under an open cover, a policy will be acceptable. However, it is suggested that the reverse is not the case: if a policy is called for, a declaration under an open cover cannot be substituted.

Period of cover

8.141   By the transport document the carrier usually acknowledges the acceptance of the goods in apparent good order and condition. The insurance should cover the goods from the moment of taking in charge by the carrier to that of delivery at destination. This is addressed in Article 28.f.iii and is also reflected in Article 28.e which provides that the date of the insurance document must be no later than the date of shipment.

Currency

8.142   If a policy is expressed in a currency different to that of the credit there may be a problem in evaluating the cover provided, and, more importantly, fluctuations in exchange rate could cause the devaluation of the policy. Article 28.f.i provides that it must be in the same currency as the credit.

8.143   The fact that the policy is issued abroad should not make it objectionable.

Amount

8.144   The insurance document must indicate the amount of the insurance coverage. Absent any indication of the required coverage, there must be coverage for at least 110% of the CIF or CIP value of the goods. The purpose of the insurance is to cover the goods for their full value under the contract, which is in effect their arrived value, which is why freight and the cost of insurance during the carriage are added. If the CIF/CIP value cannot be determined from the documents, there must be cover for 110% of the invoice value or the amount demanded under the credit, whichever is the greater.

8.145   A franchise (Article 28.j) is an amount or percentage stated in a policy which must be reached before any claim is payable. If it is reached, then the claim is payable in full. The words which are customarily used to indicate that there is to be no franchise provision are 'irrespective of percentage'. In foreign insurance 'franchise' may be used to mean what in English insurances is termed an 'excess' or a 'deductible'. An excess or deductible is similar to a franchise save that after the amount or percentage is reached only the amount in excess of it is recoverable. Unfortunately, the Article says nothing about the level of the excess and therefore it is not clear whether a bank could reject a document showing an unusually large excess or franchise.

(4)   Certificates etc

8.146   The buyer may require the inclusion of other documents in addition to the ordinary CIF documents (invoice, bills of lading, insurance document) with the object of obtaining greater control as to what is shipped, and documents included with that aim will usually fall under the general description of certificate. Certificates of weight, certificates of origin, certificates of quality and certificates of analysis fall into this category.

Instructions

8.147   There are three points to be borne in mind by the seller in instructing the bank as to the requirements of the credit in this respect: who is to be the certifier; what is he to cover in his certificate (which should include setting out that he has done what he was intended to do); the need to relate the goods certified to the goods shipped. Care must be taken not to use general adjectives which cannot be precisely applied in describing the certifier, such as 'first class', independent etc. These add nothing and will be ignored by a bank; see Article 3.

8.148   An example of a case where the buyer wanted protection through a certificate of inspection, but failed to obtain it, is *Commercial Banking Co of Sydney Ltd v Jalsard Pty Ltd*[1] (which was not a case under the UCP). All the credit required in accordance with the buyer's instructions was 'Certificate of Inspection'. The goods were battery-operated Christmas lights to be shipped from Taiwan to Sydney. Two certificates were provided from surveying companies in Taipei in substantially the same form and they certified that the surveyor had checked the quantity and condition of the goods. It was apparent from the certificates, although they did not expressly so state, that the surveyors had found no defects in their goods or their packing. The buyers argued that the certificates were required to state that the goods were of acceptable standard and condition (which would have involved electrical testing as opposed to a merely visual inspection). This argument was rejected. The Board of the Privy Council stated:[2]

> '"Certificate of Inspection" is a term capable of covering documents which contain a wide variety of information as to the nature and the results of the inspection which had been undertaken. The minimum requirement implicit in the ordinary meaning of the words is that the goods the subject-matter of the inspection have been inspected, at any rate visually, by the person issuing the certificate. If it is intended that a particular method of inspection should be adopted or that particular information as to the result of the inspection should be recorded, this, in their Lordships' view, would not be implicit in the words "Certificate of Inspection" by themselves, but would need to be expressly stated.'

Had the buyer named the inspection agency to be used, and specified that the certificate should certify that the goods had been inspected visually and that samples chosen in a particular manner had been tested electrically, the shipment of defective goods might have been avoided.[3] It may be important to provide for the inclusion in the credit as to how samples are to be drawn. Thus in *Basse and Selve v Bank of Australasia*[4] the analysis was genuine but the certificate was not required to cover the drawing of the sample and it was here that the fraud by the seller arose.

1 [1973] AC 279, PC.
2 [1973] AC 279 at 285.
3 The failure of the buyer's alternative case against the bank for alleged negligence in advising as to the terms of the credit is discussed at para **4.31** above.
4 (1904) 90 LT 618.

Relation to the goods

8.149   It is essential that any certificate or other document of like nature should relate to the goods which have been shipped and not to some other goods of acceptable quality which have been examined and certified but not shipped. The possibility of fraud is obvious. It is suggested in para **8.48** above that banks should require documents to be capable of being related to the goods invoiced and shipped. It is preferable that buyers ensure that the terms of credits expressly require that any certificates should be sufficiently linked to the goods shown to have been shipped. Cases preceding the UCP but illustrating the previous need for certificates to be capable of being related to the goods shown to have been shipped include *Bank Melli Iran v Barclays Bank*[1] where the certificate failed on this count among others, and the old case of *Re Reinhold & Co and Hansloh's Arbitration*[2] where the certificate might have applied to any 1,000 tons of maize on the vessel rather than to all of it: so it was unclear whether the buyer would get maize that had been examined and certified.

1 [1951] 2 Lloyd's Rep 367 at 375.2.
2 (1896) 12 TLR 422.

Several certificates

8.150 It is suggested that generally fractional certificates can be used, that is to say, certificates each covering part of the shipment and together covering the whole, and a single global certificate is not usually required. No objection was taken on this ground in the *Banque de l'Indochine* case,[1] and with large quantity commodity contracts it is common practice.

1 [1983] QB 711.

Certificates requiring the buyer's cooperation

8.151 Perhaps the strongest protection that the buyer can seek is that the documents to be presented should include a certificate signed by the buyer or his agent that he has inspected the goods on or prior to shipment and found them to comply with the contract. Sometimes the certifier is named as the holder of a particular passport number, which appears to require the bank to verify the signature on the certificate against that on the passport: see *Gian Singh Ltd v Banque de l'Indochine*.[1] But as that case shows, even these expedients can be defeated by the seller bent on fraud. They can also be abused by the buyer. For if the transaction becomes unattractive to him, he can refuse to cooperate. In the event of fraud, swift action may find a way round this in s 39 of the Supreme Court Act 1981, as is considered in the next chapter.[2] However, as shown by the decision in *Oliver v Dubai Bank Kenya*,[3] absent fraud, it will not generally be possible to imply an obligation of cooperation.

1 [1974] 1 WLR 1234, see para **8.22** above.
2 See para **9.85**.
3 [2007] EWHC 2165 (Comm), see para **8.27** above.

Liability of the certifier

8.152   Although it is the buyer who is relying on the certificate for protection, the certifier is usually instructed by the seller and has no contractual relationship with the buyer. Does the buyer have a remedy if he suffers loss through the certifier's negligence? This issue arose in *Niru Battery Manufacturing Co v Milestone Trading Ltd.*[1] A buyer of a consignment of lead for shipment to Iran had arranged for the issue of a credit payable against presentation of documents including an inspection certificate confirming, amongst other things, that the goods had been loaded. The certifier was persuaded by the fraudulent seller to issue a certificate without actually witnessing the loading of the goods; the seller used the certificate, together with a fraudulent bill of lading, to obtain payment under the credit without ever shipping the goods. The Court of Appeal held that the certifier owed a tortious duty of care to the buyer and had breached that duty by issuing the certificate negligently. It was therefore liable for the loss suffered by the buyer, which had to reimburse its bank but never received the goods.

1 [2004] 1 Lloyd's Rep 344.

(5)   Drafts – bills of exchange

8.153   In some transactions where the credit called for a draft, the draft may seem of little importance as, for example, where a sight draft drawn on the issuing or the confirming bank is required. Even in these instances the draft must comply with any specific requirements of the credits and, as discussed in **Chapter 4,**[1] the bank may not waive those requirements even if inserted for its own benefit. An argument that a draft was unnecessary because it was of no importance was advanced in *Kydon Compania Naviera SA v National Westminster Bank Ltd, The Lena,*[2] in relation to a requirement for a sight draft drawn on the purchasers and was rejected.[3] The draft presented must comply with the relevant terms of the credit. Thus it must be drawn by the correct party or parties – (see *Elder Dempster Lines Ltd v Ionic Shipping Agency Inc*[4]) and on the correct party (*The Lena*).[5]

1 See para **4.27**.
2 [1981] 1 Lloyd's Rep 68.
3 [1981] 1 Lloyd's Rep 68 at 75.1. See also *Astro Exito Navegacion SA v Chase Manhattan Bank NA, The Messiniaki Tolmi* [1986] 1 Lloyd's Rep 455 at 457.2; *Computer Place Services Pte Ltd v Malayan Banking Bhd* [1996] 3 SLR 287 (Singapore).
4 [1968] 1 Lloyd's Rep 529.
5 [1981] 1 Lloyd's Rep 68.

8.154   The draft must have the correct time for payment, ie at sight, a period after sight, or after bill of lading date, etc. Sections 14(2) and (3) of the Bills of Exchange Act 1882 provide:

'(2) Where a bill is payable at a fixed period after date, after sight or after the happening of a specified event, the time of payment is determined by excluding the day from which the time is to begin to run and by including the date of payment.

(3) Where a bill is payable at a fixed period after sight, the time begins to run from the date of the acceptance if the bill is accepted, and from the date of noting or protest if the bill be noted or protested for non-acceptance, or for non-delivery.'

8.155 It is common although not essential for credits to require that drafts should be noted as drawn under the credit and marked with the number and date of the credit and the name of the issuing bank.

8.156 For the purpose of any general stipulations in the credit as to the form of documents, drafts may be treated as being in a separate category from the other commercial documents (eg the transport document, invoice etc) presented under the credit. In *Credit Industriel et Commercial v China Merchants Bank*,[1] the credit provided as a special condition that all documents should be in English; however, the beneficiary had presented a draft in French. David Steel J held that, properly construed, the special condition did not extend to the drafts and accordingly the presentation was not discrepant. Although the issuing bank was not bound to accept the draft (in the sense of incurring liability on it) it was bound to take up the documents from the negotiating bank and pay the credit at maturity. He said:[2]

'This approach reflects the function of the drafts. They were not part of the commercial documentation, which, following negotiation, was to be passed on to the applicant Jiangsu. They were simply part of the process whereby [the issuing bank] CMB's obligations to pay could be put in a form in which they could be readily discounted. Non-acceptance of the draft would not relieve CMB of its obligation to pay at maturity. It merely deprived [the negotiating bank] CIC of the opportunity of going into the market.'

1 [2002] 2 All ER (Comm) 427.
2 Para 34.

Chapter 9

Fraud and Injunctions

TWO RELATED TOPICS

9.1   Fraud in connection with documentary credits represents a significant risk to the banks and buyers involved. Cresswell J described antedated and false bills of lading as 'a cancer in international trade'.[1] This chapter deals with two topics: first the effect of fraud on the substantive rights of the parties to the documentary credit transaction; and secondly the availability of injunctions and other interlocutory relief intended to prevent losses due to fraud. The question of the effect of fraud, or an allegation of fraud, on a documentary credit transaction arises mainly in the following situations:

(1) Where documents have been presented but the paying bank has refused to pay, and is being sued by the beneficiary/seller and is resisting payment on the ground of fraud.
(2) Where the paying bank has not yet paid and the applicant for the credit desires to prevent it paying, or to prevent the beneficiary/seller from presenting documents, because the applicant believes that the beneficiary/seller is fraudulent.
(3) Where the paying bank has paid but the applicant is resisting reimbursement on the ground that the bank should not have paid because of fraud.
(4) Where the paying bank has paid and recovery of the payment is sought by it from the beneficiary/seller on the ground that the presentation of documents involved fraud.

In the second situation the applicant may seek an injunction to prevent the bank from paying. This is the reason why the topic of injunctions is included in this chapter.

---

1 *Standard Chartered Bank v Pakistan National Shipping Corpn (No 2)* [1998] 1 Lloyd's Rep 684 at 686; the passage was indorsed by Evans LJ on appeal at [2000] 1 Lloyd's Rep 221, and also by Longmore J in *Shinhan Bank Ltd v Sea Containers Ltd* [2000] 2 Lloyd's Rep 406.

A FRAUD

What is the exception?

9.2 Fraud is an exception to the principle of autonomy,[1] which requires the credit to be treated as a transaction independent from the underlying contract between applicant and beneficiary and unaffected by disputes on that contract. For the purpose of establishing fraud, the court may, contrary to the general rule,[2] take into account extraneous evidence, that is, evidence apart from the terms of the credit and the contents of the documents themselves. The evidence might relate to the goods, for example that bottles of water have been shipped rather than bottles of gin as per contract, or it might relate to a document, for example that a date has been falsified or a signature on an inspection certificate forged. Fraud is also an exception to the rule that a bank deals in documents alone and is obliged to pay against documents which are conformant on their face without regard to their accuracy or genuineness.[3]

1 See paras **1.34** et seq above.
2 Paras **8.17** et seq above.
3 UCP Articles 5, 7, 8, 34.

Source of the exception

9.3 In England the fraud exception is part of the common law and applies despite the fact that the UCP contain no provision for an exception.[1] The policy of the ICC is instead to leave questions of fraud to the relevant municipal law and for determination by the courts.

1 *Montrod Ltd v Grundkotter Fleischvertriebs Gmbh* [2001] EWCA Civ 1954; [2002] 1 WLR 1975 at para 40.

9.4 The leading case on the exception is *United City Merchants (Investments) Ltd v Royal Bank of Canada*,[1] in the House of Lords, which was itself based on the US case, *Sztejn v J Henry Schroder Banking Corp*.[2]

1 [1983] 1 AC 168: see below.
2 31 NYS 2d 631 (1941).

9.5 For the purposes of the fraud exception, cases relating to performance bonds or guarantees have been treated by the English courts as involving the same principles as documentary credits.

9.6 Important cases on the fraud exception since the third edition of this book include: *Solo Industries UK Ltd v Canara Bank*,[1] *Montrod Ltd v Grundkotter Fleischvertriebs Gmbh*,[2] *Mahonia Limited v JPMorgan Chase*

Bank,[3] *TTI Team Telecom International Ltd v Hutchison 3G UK Ltd*,[4] *Sirius Insurance Co v FAI General Insurance Ltd*,[5] *Banque Saudi Fransi v Lear Siegler Services Inc*.[6]

1 [2001] EWCA Civ 1059; [2001] 1 WLR 1800.
2 [2001] EWCA Civ 1954; [2002] 1 WLR 1975.
3 [2003] EWHC 1927 (Comm); [2003] 2 Lloyd's Rep 911.
4 [2003] EWHC 762 (TCC); [2003] 1 All ER (Comm) 914.
5 [2003] EWCA Civ 470; [2003] 1 WLR 2214.
6 [2006] EWCA Civ 1130; [2007] 2 Lloyd's Rep. 47.

Sztejn v J Henry Schroder Banking Corp

9.7   The foundation stone of English law in this area is a United States case, *Sztejn v J Henry Schroder Banking Corp*.[1] In this action the applicant for a credit claimed an injunction against the issuing bank to prevent the issuing bank paying on the documents which had been presented. The credit had been advised to the seller in India by the issuing bank's correspondent in India. The correspondent had not confirmed the credit. The applicant alleged that what had been shipped was rubbish rather than any resemblance of the goods contracted for. The bank applied to dismiss the claim for an injunction on the ground that there was no cause of action. For the purpose of hearing that motion the court assumed the facts alleged by the buyer to be true, and thus the buyer did not face the difficulty (which has caused great problems for buyers in subsequent English cases) of establishing the fraud which he alleged with sufficient certainty to satisfy the court. Having set out the principle that normally complaints about the goods are no ground for a court demanding or even permitting a bank to delay payment, Shientag J stated:

> 'However, I believe that a different situation is presented in the instant action. This is not a controversy between the buyer and seller concerning a mere breach of warranty regarding the quality of the merchandise; on the present motion, it must be assumed that the seller has intentionally failed to ship any goods ordered by the buyer. In such a situation, where the seller's fraud has been called to the bank's attention before the drafts and documents have been presented for payment, the principle of the independence of the bank's obligation under the letter of credit should not be extended to protect the unscrupulous seller. It is true that even though the documents are forged or fraudulent, if the issuing bank has already paid the draft before receiving notice of the seller's fraud, it will be protected if it exercised reasonable diligence before making such payment. (Citations.) However, in the instant action Schroder has received notice of Transea's active fraud before it accepted or paid the draft. The Chartered Bank, which under the allegations of the complaint stands in no better position than Transea, should not be heard to complain because Schroder is not forced to pay the draft accompanied by documents covering a transaction which it has reason to believe is fraudulent.
>
> Although our courts have used broad language to the effect that a letter of credit is independent of the primary contract between the buyer and seller,

248

that language was used in cases concerning alleged breaches of warranty; no case has been brought to my attention on this point involving an intentional fraud[2] on the part of the seller which was brought to the bank's notice with the request that it withhold payment of the draft on this account. The distinction between a breach of warranty and active fraud on the part of the seller is supported by authority and reason. As one court has stated: "Obviously, when the issuer of a letter of credit knows that a document, although correct in form, is, in point of fact, false or illegal, he cannot be called upon to recognise such a document as complying with the terms of the letter of credit." (Citations.)

No hardship will be caused by permitting the bank to refuse payment where fraud is claimed, where the merchandise is not merely inferior in quality but consists of worthless rubbish, where the draft and the accompanying documents are in the hands of one who stands in the same position as the fraudulent seller, where the bank has been given notice of the fraud before being presented with the drafts and documents for payment, and where the bank itself does not wish to pay pending an adjudication of the rights and obligations of the other parties. While the primary factor in the issuance of the letter of credit is the credit standing of the buyer, the security afforded by the merchandise is also taken into account. In fact, the letter of credit requires a bill of lading made out to the order of the bank and not the buyer. Although the bank is not interested in the exact detailed performance of the sales contract it is vitally interested in assuring itself that there are some goods represented by the documents. (Citations.)

On this motion only the complaint is before me and I am bound by its allegation that the Chartered Bank is not a holder in due course but is a mere agent for collection for the account of the seller charged with fraud. Therefore, the Chartered Bank's motion to dismiss the complaint must be denied. If it had appeared from the face of the complaint that the bank presenting the draft for payment was a holder in due course, its claim against the bank issuing the letter of credit would not be defeated even though the primary transaction was tainted with fraud.'

So the case is authority that the court may interfere to prevent a bank with whom the party applying to the court is in contractual relations paying against documents which have been presented by, or on behalf of, a party whose fraud has been called to the bank's attention. It must follow that the same fraud would entitle the bank of its own motion to refuse to pay, and provide it also with a defence to any action subsequently brought against it to enforce payment.

1 31 NYS 2d 631 (1941). See *Asbury Park & Ocean Grove Bank v National City Bank of New York* 35 NYS 2d 985 (1942), also a decision of Shientag J; *Discount Records Ltd v Barclays Bank Ltd* [1975] 1 WLR 315 at 318; *Edward Owen Engineering Ltd v Barclays Bank International Ltd* [1978] QB 159 at 169; *United City Merchants (Investments) Ltd v Royal Bank of Canada* [1983] 1 AC 168 at 183; *Czarnikow-Rionda v Standard Bank* [1999] 2 Lloyd's Rep 187 at 198–199.

2 United States courts often add the gloss 'intentional fraud' or 'outright fraudulent practice' (eg *Semetex Corp v UBAF Arab American Bank* 853 F Supp 759 (1994)), but these terms do not seem to add anything to the definition of fraud discussed below.

United City Merchant (Investments) Ltd v Royal Bank of Canada[1]

9.8 This is the leading English case on fraud and also on illegality.

1 [1983] 1 AC 168, HL; [1982] QB 208, CA; [1979] 1 Lloyd's Rep 267 and [1979] 2 Lloyd's Rep 498, Mocatta J.

(a) The facts

9.9 The facts which were relevant to fraud were as follows. The documents were presented for payment to the defendants, the confirming bank, who refused to pay and were sued by the assignees of the beneficiary/sellers. The ground on which the bank supported its refusal to pay was that the documents contained a material misstatement, namely that the bill of lading showed that shipment had been made on 15 December 1976, when it had in fact been made on 16 December 1976, the last date for shipment provided by the credit being 15 December. The date was inserted by an employee of the loading brokers to the carriers. He acted fraudulently in that he knew that the date he inserted was a false one. The judge held that neither the sellers nor their merchant bankers (to whom they had assigned their interest under the credit) were privy to the brokers' employee's fraud: they believed that the statement that the goods had been loaded on 15 December was true. The goods which had been shipped were a glass-fibre forming plant, and the fact that it was shipped a day late would seem to have made very little difference in practical terms. But had the true date been shown on the bill of lading, the sellers could not have obtained payment under the credit unless the buyers were prepared to waive the discrepancy. Although the goods arrived in Peru, the buyers did not take delivery of them.[1]

1 See [1982] QB 208 at 218A/B.

(b) The decision of the judge[1]

9.10 Mocatta J held:[2]

'The question remains of the effect, if any, upon the plaintiffs' claim of what I have found to be the fraudulent misrepresentations of Mr Baker in relation to the date the goods were shown on the bills of lading to have been on board. I have found that Mr Baker was not the plaintiffs' agent for making out the bills of lading and that there was no fraud on the part of the plaintiffs in presenting them. The case is, therefore, vitally different from the *Sztejn v Schroder* case[3] approved by the Court of Appeal in the recent *Edward Owen v Barclays Bank* case.[4] Where there has been personal fraud or unscrupulous conduct by the seller presenting the documents under the letter of credit, it is right that a bank should be entitled to refuse payment against apparently conforming documents on the principle *ex turpi causa non oritur actio*. But here I have held that there was no fraud on the part of the plaintiffs, nor can I, as a matter of fact, find that they knew the date on the bills of lading to be false when they presented the documents. Further, there is no plea either by way of an implied term or by way of a warranty imposed by the law that the presenter of documents under a letter of credit warrants their accuracy. Accordingly, I take the view, on the principle so recently affirmed by the Court of Appeal, that the plaintiffs are, on the matters which have so far been argued before the Court, entitled to succeed.'

1 [1979] 1 Lloyd's Rep 267.
2 [1979] 1 Lloyd's Rep 267 at 278.
3 31 NYS 2d 631 (1941): see para **9.7** above.
4 [1978] QB 159.

(c)   The decision of the Court of Appeal[1]

9.11   The Court of Appeal held that because the bill of lading had been fraudulently completed (in the sense that the employee had misstated the date with intention to deceive), even though the sellers were not party to this fraud, the bank was entitled to refuse to pay. This made it unnecessary for the court to consider the main argument which had been addressed to it, that any inaccurate and material statement in a document was a ground for a bank to refuse to pay. The main strand of the court's reasoning was that a document which was a nullity because it was forged could be rejected by a bank, even though it was forged other than by the beneficiary, and there was no reason for distinguishing from a document which was a nullity, one which was in any way false to the knowledge of a third person.[2]

1 [1982] QB 208.
2 See [1982] QB 208 at 239D, 247F/H and 255B/C.

(d)   The decision of the House of Lords[1]

9.12   The leading speech was given by Lord Diplock. He had delivered the judgment of the Privy Council in *Gian Singh & Co Ltd v Banque de l'Indochine*,[2] which affirmed that a bank was entitled to be reimbursed by its customer against documents which included a forged certificate, the documents having been examined with due care and the forgery not having been detected. Lord Diplock began with a description of the autonomous contracts which may arise in connection with letters of credit, and emphasised that disputes as to the goods are irrelevant to the seller's rights to payment. He continued:[3]

'To this general statement of principle as to the contractual obligations of the confirming bank to the seller, there is one established exception: that is, where

251

the seller, for the purpose of drawing on the credit, fraudulently presents to the confirming bank documents that contain, expressly or by implication, material representations of fact that to his knowledge are untrue.'

After referring to the *Sztejn* case[4] he went on:

'The exception for fraud on the part of the beneficiary seeking to avail himself of the credit is a clear application of the maxim ex turpi causa non oritur actio or, if plain English is to be preferred, "fraud unravels all".[5] The courts will not allow their process to be used by a dishonest person to carry out a fraud.'

The argument against the sellers had been 'that a confirming bank is not under any obligation legally enforceable against it by the seller/beneficiary of a documentary credit, to pay to him the sum stipulated in the credit against presentation of documents, if the documents presented, although conforming on their face with the terms of the credit, nevertheless contain some statement of material fact that is not accurate'.[6] As Lord Diplock pointed out[7] this would render the fraud exception to the autonomy rule superfluous. He held that such a rule would undermine the whole system of credits by destroying their autonomy. He then came to the proposition of the Court of Appeal, categorised as a 'half-way house' because it was half-way between the fraud exception as stated by Lord Diplock and the main argument on behalf of the bank. Lord Diplock held that his rejection of the main argument also entitled the rejection of the argument relating to material representation of fact false to the knowledge of the persons issuing (in contrast with presenting) the document; for if documents containing a material misrepresentation of fact were not to be rejected, what difference could it make if unknown to the seller the misstatement was made fraudulently rather than by mistake? Lord Diplock referred to the Court of Appeal's reliance upon the position as stated by it in relation to forged documents. He stated:[8]

'I would not wish to be taken as accepting that the premise as to forged documents is correct, even where the fact that the document is forged deprives it of all legal effect and makes it a nullity, and so worthless to the confirming bank as security for its advances to the buyer. This is certainly not so under the Uniform Commercial Code as against a person who has taken a draft drawn under the credit in circumstances that would make him a holder in due course, and I see no reason why, and there is nothing in the Uniform Commercial Code to suggest that, a seller/beneficiary who is ignorant of the forgery should be in any worse position because he has not negotiated the draft before presentation. I would prefer to leave open the question of the rights of an innocent seller/beneficiary against the confirming bank when a document presented by him is a nullity because unknown to him it was forged by some third party; for that question does not arise in the instant case. The bill of lading with the wrong date of loading placed on it by the carrier's agent was far from being a nullity. It was a valid transferable receipt for the goods giving the holder a right to claim them at their destination, Callao, and was evidence of the terms of the contract under which they were being carried.'

1 [1983] 1 AC 168.

2 [1974] 1 WLR 1234.
3 [1983] 1 AC 168 at 183G.
4 31 NYS 2d 631 (1941): see para **9.7** above.
5 A more accurate translation, and one which better reflects the rationale of the fraud exception in English law, is 'an action does not arise from a base cause'. 'Fraud unravels all' is the translation of a different maxim, *fraus omnia vitiat* (or *corrumpit*), which forms the basis for the fraud exception in civil law, see Stoufflet *Le Crédit Documentaire* (1957) p 327, cited in *Bank of Nova Scotia v Angelica-Whitewear Ltd* [1987] 1 SCR 59 at 82.
6 See [1983] 1 AC 168 at 184.
7 [1983] 1 AC 168 at 184.
8 [1983] 1 AC 168 at 187H.

Legal basis of the fraud exception

9.13　Lord Diplock stated that the basis for the exception is that the courts will not allow their process to be used by a dishonest person to carry out a fraud, relying on the doctrine *ex turpi causa non oritur*. For the obtaining of payment through the credit by means of dishonest documents is the essence of the fraud, which the court would be assisting if they did not recognise the exception. Therefore, the bank is released from, or the beneficiary cannot enforce, the obligation to pay against documents which are conformant on their face.

9.14　An alternative or supplementary basis for the exception might be that there is an implied term of the contract between paying bank and beneficiary that the documents presented do not to the presenter's knowledge make any statements of fact which are false, and that the documents are not being presented as part of a fraud against the bank or the buyer. Breach of the term would entitle the bank to reject the documents. This has support from Rix J in *Czarnikow-Rionda v Standard Bank*, who said that Lord Diplock's reference to the *ex turpi causa* principle 'may appropriately be viewed as an authoritative expression of the source in law of the implied limitation on a bank's mandate'.[1] The term could be implied as necessary for the proper working of the contract or as a matter of obvious inference.[2] Whilst there is no direct authority for such a term in English law, it does seem to be an implied term of the contract between the bank and the applicant that the bank will not make payment where there is an obvious fraud. In *Tukan Timber Ltd v Barclays Bank plc*[3] Hirst J said that an applicant would have a 'cast-iron claim' for damages for breach of contract against a bank which paid in the face of a fraud; there should be no difficulty in implying a corresponding term into the contract between the bank and the beneficiary.

1 [1999] 2 Lloyd's Rep 187 at 203.
2 As to the basis on which a term will be implied into a contract governed by English law, see *Liverpool City Council v Irwin* [1977] AC 239.
3 [1987] 1 Lloyd's Rep 171 at 177.

Scope of the exception and the meaning of 'fraud'

9.15   In stating the exception[1] Lord Diplock referred to 'documents that contain, expressly or by implication, material representations of fact that to his knowledge are untrue'. This suggests that the exception is confined to fraud in the documents themselves. Whether and if so to what extent it also applies to wider fraud in the underlying transaction is an important but open question.

1 [1983] 1 AC 168 at 183G.

(a)   Fraud in the documents

9.16   Lord Diplock's formulation is very close to a statement of the elements of fraudulent misrepresentation which constitute the tort of deceit. But there are crucial distinctions. For the bank has not acted on any misrepresentation. It made the contract with the beneficiary by advising the credit.[1] It is refusing to perform that contract because of the fraud, rather than being duped by the fraud.[2] Nonetheless the heart of the exception is a misrepresentation of fact known to be untrue by the party putting the document forward.[3] Thus, although the judge did not, and did not need to, analyse the facts in this manner, in the *Sztejn* case[4] the bills of lading presumably stated that the goods on board were bristles which was what the contract of sale provided, and, as the buyer alleged, was false to the knowledge of the seller. In the performance bond or guarantee cases such as *Edward Owen Engineering Ltd v Barclays Bank International Ltd*[5] the maker of the demand represents by making it that he honestly believes that the event on which the bond becomes payable has occurred.[6]

1 See **Chapter 5** above.
2 See *Rafsanjan Pistachio Producers Co-operative v Bank Leumi (UK) plc* [1992] 1 Lloyd's Rep 513 at 542.1.
3 [1992] 1 Lloyd's Rep 513 at 540.1 and 2.
4 31 NYS 2d 631 (1941): see para **9.7** above.
5 [1978] QB 159.
6 See *United Trading Corp SA v Allied Arab Bank Ltd* [1985] 2 Lloyd's Rep 554n at 559.1 where Ackner LJ cited the dictum of Lord Denning MR from *State Trading Corpn of India Ltd v E D & F Man (Sugar) Ltd* [1981] Com LR 235 and *GKN Contractors Ltd v Lloyds Bank plc* (1985) 30 BLR 48 at 63.

9.17   The representation must be 'material'. It is suggested that this must mean material to the bank's duty to pay, so that if the document stated the truth the bank would be obliged and entitled to reject the documents. For example, if the bill of lading and invoice in the *Sztejn* case[1] had stated that the shipment consisted of 'cowhair and rubbish purporting to be bristles', they would not have conformed. And, in the *United City Merchants* case[2] itself, if the bill of lading had had the correct date of shipment, it would have been outside the credit period. It does not mean 'material' in the sense of being of concern to the bank, for example because it affects its security.[3] A fraud which did not affect the bank's obligation to pay might be regarded as immaterial, for example a bill of lading which was falsely dated but where the true date was still within the shipping period.

1 31 NYS 2d 631 (1941): see para **9.7** above.
2 *United City Merchants (Investments) Ltd v Royal Bank of Canada* [1983] 1 AC 168, HL: see paras **9.8**–**9.12** above.
3 *Rafsanjan Pistachio Producers Co-operative v Bank Leumi (UK) Ltd* [1992] 1 Lloyd's Rep 513 at 541.2.

9.18 The representation must be untrue to the knowledge of the presenter of the documents. What may be covered by 'knowledge'? Actual knowledge is the state of mind that is primarily to be considered. But it may be that something less will do. In the tort of deceit the following states of mind are sufficient: (1) knowing the representation to be false; (2) without belief in its truth; or (3) recklessly, careless whether it be true or false.[1] It may well be that where the party presenting the documents has some serious ground for suspicion of a document so that if he gave proper consideration to it he would realise that it most likely contained a false statement but shuts his eyes to that, this would be sufficient. Proof, however, might be very difficult. A bank is not under any duty to investigate any allegation. The fact that a reasonable person would have appreciated that the documents he was presenting were false would not by itself be sufficient. But the beneficiary must have acquired knowledge of the falsity of the documents before presentation. In *Group Josi Re v Walbrook Insurance Co Ltd* Staughton LJ said, 'it is nothing to the point that at the time of trial the beneficiary knows, and the bank knows, that the documents presented under the letter of credit were not truthful in a material respect. It is the time of presentation that is critical.'[2]

1 See generally *Clerk and Lindsell on Tort* (19th edn) para 18-17.
2 [1996] 1 WLR 1152 at 1161 relying on the dictum of Lord Diplock in *United City Merchants (Investments) Ltd v Royal Bank of Canada* [1983] 1 AC 168 at 183. See also *Montrod Ltd v Grundkotter Fleischvertriebs GmbH* [2001] EWCA Civ 1954; [2002] 1 WLR 1975 at [42].

9.19 Lord Diplock refers simply to the seller. If the party presenting the documents is a collecting bank and is therefore the seller's agent, the bank will be in no better position than the seller. It is also possible but unlikely that a bank collecting on its own behalf such as a negotiation bank could have knowledge of the fraud. If so, it would be unable to collect. In *GKN Contractors Ltd v Lloyds Bank plc*.[1] Parker LJ postulated the case of a bank receiving a demand which it appreciated was mistaken, then passing it on as genuine, which could be resisted on the ground of fraud.[2]

1 (1985) 30 BLR 48.
2 (1985) 30 BLR 48 at 63. Indeed, those were essentially the facts in *Standard Chartered Bank v Pakistan National Shipping Corpn (No 2)* [2000] 1 Lloyd's Rep 218, although the presentation was rejected for other discrepancies. Even though its fraud was unsuccessful, the deceitful bank was not prevented from recovering the payment it had made to the fraudulent beneficiary.

(b)   Fraud of the applicant

9.20   The credit may be tainted with fraud from the start in that it has been opened by the bank in reliance upon a fraudulent misrepresentation made by the applicant in the application to open the credit, for example, as to the facts concerning the goods which it is intended should form the subject matter of the credit. If at the start the beneficiary is party to this fraud, it will bar him from any entitlement to payment.[1] The bank would be entitled to refuse payment on the grounds that the instrument is invalid due to fraudulent misrepresentation. So in *Solo Industries UK Ltd v Canara Bank*[2] the Court of Appeal declined to grant summary judgment against a bank which had shown a real prospect that a performance guarantee or bond was procured by and had been validly avoided by the bank on account of fraudulent conspiracy and fraudulent misrepresentation by the applicant in conjunction with the beneficiary. If the beneficiary discovers the applicant's fraud subsequently, he will be barred from operating the credit unless he has given consideration (or acted to his detriment) prior to his discovery.[3] In any situation where the beneficiary is party to a fraud by the applicant, it seems factually unlikely that the beneficiary will not also be guilty of fraud by presenting documents which he knows are in some way false.[4]

1   *Rafsanjan Pistachio Producers Co-operative v Bank Leumi (UK) plc* [1992] 1 Lloyd's Rep 513 at 535–539.
2   [2001] EWCA Civ 1059; [2001] 1 WLR 1800.
3   This appears to be the reasoning in *Rafsanjan Pistachio Producers Co-operative v Bank Leumi (UK) plc* [1992] I Lloyd's Rep 513 at 539.
4   See *Standard Bank London Ltd v Canara Bank* [2002] EWHC 1574 (Comm) Moore-Bick J at para 72.

(c)   Documents which are a 'nullity'

9.21   Lord Diplock said that he would 'prefer to leave open the question of the rights of an innocent seller/beneficiary against the confirming bank when a document presented by him is a nullity because unknown to him it was forged by some third party'.[1] A document will be a nullity if it is forged or fraudulent in such a way as to destroy its essence.[2] Typically, this will be because it is a document purporting to be issued by a third party but where the issuing party is fictitious or his signature has been forged. For example, a bill of lading evidences a contract of affreightment and is utilised to enable the holder to obtain possession of the goods shipped. If a bill is purportedly made out on behalf of the shipping line whose name appears on it by some third party having no authority to do so, or is made out on behalf of a line which does not exist, it will evidence nothing nor will it give any rights to the holder. It will mean that a bank which has paid out against it and is unable to obtain reimbursement through the credit chain will be in possession of a valueless security and will have lost its money (if it cannot recover it from the party to whom it was paid). A buyer who has paid the issuing bank will receive documents of no value. Such a bill is to be contrasted with the bill of lading in the *United City Merchants* case.[3] The bill there was not a nullity: all that was false was the date, and there were valuable goods which had been shipped and to which the bill could give the right of possession.[4] A second example of a document which would be a nullity is a certificate of inspection which is required to be made out by a named certification agency and is made out by someone who has no connection with the agency. As a certificate it is wholly without effect, and the fact that it has been brought into existence and tendered is likely to mean that the goods are far from what they are meant to be.

1 *United City Merchants (Investments) Ltd v Royal Bank of Canada* [1983] 1 AC 168 at 187H, quoted at para **9.12** above.
2 Cited, *Lambias (Importers & Exporters) Co Pte Ltd v Hongkong & Shanghai Banking Corpn* [1993] 2 SLR 751 (Singapore).
3 [1983] 1 AC 168 at 187H.
4 See also *Kwei Tek Chao v British Traders and Shippers Ltd* [1954] 2 QB 459 at 475, 476.

9.22   So the question that was posed but not answered by Lord Diplock is in effect whether 'nullities' represent a separate type of exception so that the bank can reject a nullity even though the presenting party is not involved in wrongdoing. It is to be remembered that the beneficiary himself may be a purchaser of the documents if he is in a string of contracts and may be acting in good faith. The basis on which a bank might reject a document as a nullity where the party presenting it has no knowledge of any fraud, cannot be the *ex turpi causa* rule.[1] If such documents can be rejected, it must surely be on the basis that a document which is forged so as to be a nullity and waste- paper is simply not a 'bill of lading' or a 'certificate of inspection' as required by the credit even though on its face it appears to be.

1 See paragraph **9.13** above. See per Ackner LJ in *United City Merchants (Investments) Ltd v Royal Bank of Canada* [1982] QB 208 at 246, CA.

9.23   The question was eventually answered in *Montrod Ltd v Grundkotter Fleischvertriebs GmbH*[1] by Potter LJ who held that there was no general nullity exception based upon the concept of a document being fraudulent in itself or devoid of commercial value. So a demanding party was not disentitled to payment where a document presented, which conformed on its face with the terms of the letter of credit, was fraudulent *in itself* independently of the knowledge and bona fides of the demanding party. In that case, it had been argued that the nullity exception referred to by Lord Diplock should extend to a document presented which was not forged (ie fraudulently produced) but was signed by the creator in honest error as to his authority but Potter LJ declined to recognise such an exception.[2] He held that there were sound policy reasons for not extending the law by creation of a general nullity exception:

> 'Most documentary credits issued in the United Kingdom incorporate the UCP by reference. Various revisions of the UCP have been widely adopted in the USA and by United Kingdom and Commonwealth banks. They are intended to embody international banking practice and to create certainty

in an area of law where the need for precision and certainty are paramount. The creation of a general nullity exception, the formulation of which does not seem to me susceptible of precision, involves making undesirable inroads into the principles of autonomy and negotiability universally recognised in relation to letter of credit transactions. In the context of the fraud exception, the courts have made clear how difficult it is to invoke the exception and have been at pains to point out that banks deal in documents and questions of apparent conformity. In that context they have made clear that it is not for a bank to make its own enquiries about allegations of fraud brought to its notice; if a party wishes to establish that a demand is fraudulent it must place before the bank evidence of clear and obvious fraud (see *Edward Owen v Barclays Bank International Ltd* [1978] QB 159 c.f. *Turkiye Is Bankasi A.S. v Bank of China* [1996] 2 Lloyd's Rep 611 per Waller J at 617). If a general nullity exception were to be introduced as part of English law it would place banks in a further dilemma as to the necessity to investigate facts which they are not competent to do and from which UCP 500 is plainly concerned to exempt them. Further such an exception would be likely to act unfairly upon beneficiaries participating in a chain of contracts in cases where their good faith is not in question. Such a development would thus undermine the system of financing international trade by means of documentary credits.'

It may seem startling that a bank can be compelled to purchase worthless paper which passes down the credit chain to the buyer who is left to sue the seller on the contract of sale if he can. But it is suggested that it is the better rule that a party innocent of any fraud should be entitled to reimbursement against documents which appear on their face to accord with the terms and conditions of the credit. Such a rule will assist the integrity of the system of documentary credits as a means of financing international transactions, whereas any widening of the fraud exception will detract from it. In any case the bank should not be concerned with the 'worth' of the document; a document can still be worthless even if it is not a nullity, eg if it is discovered that the cargo has perished before loading. It is inherent in documentary contracts that, along a string of innocent parties, the ultimate buyer bears the risk associated with documents which are apparently conformant but actually worthless.[3]

1 [2001] EWCA Civ 1954; [2002] 1 WLR 1975.
2 See at paras 56–57.
3 *Manbre Saccharine Co Ltd v Corn Products Co Ltd* [1919] 1 KB 198: bill of lading was a good tender under a CIF contract even though the parties were aware that the cargo had already been lost.

(d)   Forged documents

9.24   A document may be fraudulent without being forged, and a document may contain a forgery without being a nullity. It is suggested that whether or not a document is correctly described as being forged is a question which is irrelevant to the application of the fraud exception as established by the

United City Merchants case.[1] A document is unlikely to be a nullity unless it is forged, but forgery is not determinative of that question.

1 *United City Merchants (Investments) Ltd v Royal Bank of Canada* [1983] 1AC 186, see paras 9.8–9.12 above. See also *Gian Singh & Co Ltd v Banque de L'Indochine* [1974] 1 WLR 1234 per Lord Diplock at 1238.

(e) Fraud in the transaction

9.25   Recent cases support an extension of the exception to a situation where the documents presented are truthful but there is fraud in the underlying transaction. In *Themehelp v West*[1] the buyer of a business alleged that the purchase had been induced by the fraud of the seller and successfully applied for an injunction restraining payment on a performance guarantee securing the purchase price. In *Czarnikow-Rionda v Standard Bank*[2] the applicant relied on an allegation that the opening of the credit had been induced by the beneficiary's fraud. There was no suggestion by the parties or the court that such a fraud would fall outside the scope of the exception. In *Solo Industries Ltd v Canara Bank*[3] the Court of Appeal declined to grant the beneficiary of a performance bond summary judgment against a bank which had purported to avoid the bond on the ground that its issue was induced by a fraudulent conspiracy and/or misrepresentation to which the beneficiary was party.

1 [1996] QB 84.
2 [1999] 2 Lloyd's Rep 187.
3 [2001] EWCA Civ 1059; [2001] 1 WLR 1800.

9.26   In the United States the Uniform Commercial Code expressly covers both forged or fraudulent documents and situations where 'honor of the presentation would facilitate a material fraud by the beneficiary on the issuer or the applicant',[1] and New York law recognises fraud in the transaction as a defence to credits governed by the UCP.[2] In Canada the Supreme Court has also endorsed the wider scope of the exception. In *Bank of Nova Scotia v Angelica-Whitewear Ltd*[3] Le Dain J held:

> 'In my opinion the fraud exception to the autonomy of documentary letters of credit should not be confined to cases of fraud in the tendered documents but should include fraud in the underlying transaction of such a character as to make the demand for payment under the credit a fraudulent one. The *Sztejn* and *Cambridge Sporting Goods* cases, to which reference has been made, illustrate the difficulty of distinguishing in some cases between a case of false documents and a case of fraudulent shipment covered by documents which accurately describe the goods called for. Yet the English decisions, in which the fraud exception has been stated in terms of documentary fraud (cf. *Etablissement Esefka International Anstalt v Central Bank of Nigeria*, [1979] 1 Lloyd's Rep 445 (CA), at 447–448), clearly assume that the situation in *Sztejn* falls within the fraud exception as they have adopted it, in reliance on that case. Moreover, the words of Lord Denning MR in *Edward Owen*

Engineering – "the request for payment is made fraudulently in circumstances when there is no right to payment" – suggest that it was not intended to limit the fraud exception to documentary fraud, strictly speaking. In my view the fraud exception to the autonomy of a documentary credit should extend to any act of the beneficiary of a credit the effect of which would be to permit the beneficiary to obtain the benefit of the credit as a result of fraud.'

It is suggested that the extension is an appropriate one which accords with the rationale that the court will not permit a beneficiary to obtain payment in reliance on his own wrongdoing. On this basis, it would be odd if the bank were obliged to pay an obviously fraudulent beneficiary only because the fraud did not manifest itself in false documents. There may be difficulties in practice in determining how close the connection must be between the fraud and the issue of the credit in order to justify refusal of payment.

1 §5–109(a).
2 *United Bank Ltd v Cambridge Sporting Goods Corp* 392 NYS 2d 265 at 269 (1976); *Semetex Corpn v UBAF Arab American Bank* 853 F Supp 759 (1994).
3 [1987] 1 SCR 59 at 83.

(f) Unconscionability

9.27   In Singapore there has been an extension of the doctrine to cover unconscionable, as distinct from fraudulent, calls on bonds. Under Singaporean law, unconscionability on the part of the beneficiary in calling for payment on a performance guarantee is a separate and distinct ground from fraud for seeking injunctive relief.[1] See *Dauphin Offshore Engineering & Trading Pte Ltd v HRH Sheikh Sultan bin Khalifa bin Zayed Al Nahyan*[2] where the Singapore Court of Appeal, following its earlier decision in *GHL Pte Ltd v Unitrack Building Construction Pte Ltd*,[3] affirmed the extension as a 'conscious departure' from English law, although with its genesis in a dictum of Eveleigh LJ in *Potton Homes Homes Ltd v Coleman Contractors (Overseas) Ltd*.[4] If applicable, there should be no difference between the position of bonds and credits. Whilst giving some examples of unconscionability, the court said in *Dauphin*:[5]

'We do not think it is possible to define "unconscionability" other than to give some very broad indications such as lack of bona fides. What kind of situation would constitute unconscionability would have to depend on the facts of each case. This is a question which the court has to consider on each occasion where its jurisdiction is invoked. There is no pre-determined categorisation.'

There has also been an inconclusive judicial debate in Australia about the relevance of unconscionability.[6]

1 See eg *Samwoh Ltd v Sum Chung Ltd* [2002] BLR 459, CA of Singapore; *McConnell Dowell Construction (Aust) Pty Ltd v Sembcorp Engineering and Constructions Pte Ltd* [2002] BLR 450, High Court, Singapore.
2 [2000] 1 SLR 657.

3 [1999] 4 SLR 604. The principle seems to have first arisen in *Bocotra Construction Pte Ltd v A-G (No 2)* [1995] 2 SLR 733.
4 (1984) 28 BLR 19 at 28.
5 [2000] 1 SLR 657 at para 42.
6 *Olex Focas Pty Ltd v Skodaexport Co Ltd* [1998] 3 V.R.380, Batt J; *Hortico (Australia) Pty Ltd v Energy Equipment Co (Australia) Pty Ltd* (1985) 1 NSWLR 545 at 554.

9.28 In England, the possibility of an extension of the doctrine to cover unscrupulous conduct by the beneficiary not amounting to fraud was considered but left open by Potter LJ in *Montrod Ltd v GrundKotter Fleishvertriebs GmbH*.[1] With reference to Lord Diplock's reservation in relation to a document forged by a third party, he stated as follows:

> 'I would not seek to exclude the possibility that, in an individual case, the conduct of a beneficiary in connection with the creation and/or presentation of a document forged by a third party might, though itself not amounting to fraud, be of such character as not to deserve the protection available to a holder in due course. In this connection, I note the reference by Mocatta J in the *United City Merchants* case to 'personal fraud' or *'unscrupulous conduct'* on the part of the seller presenting documents for payment, a remark upon which Lord Diplock made no adverse comment when approving the original judgment on the documentary credit point. In this connection, we have had brought to our attention the decision of the High Court of Singapore in *Lambias (Importers and Exporters) Co PTE Limited v Hong Kong & Shanghai Banking Corporation* (1993) 2 SLR 751, in which the defendant bank rejected documents tendered under a letter of credit which included a quality and weight inspection certificate required to be countersigned by a named individual. The court held that the certificate contained discrepancies which entitled the bank to refuse the documents tendered and went on to find that the inspection certificate was in any event a nullity in that, not only did it fail to state the particulars of the goods and their quality and weight, but that, having been issued by the beneficiary instead of the applicant, it had been countersigned by an impostor. Having considered the observations, and in particular the reservation, of Lord Diplock in the *United City Merchants* case and the particular facts before the court in relation to the plaintiffs, who had themselves introduced the countersignatory to the bank as the person named, the court observed:
>
>> "The law cannot condone actions which, although not amounting to fraud per se, are of such recklessness and haste that the documents produced as a result are clearly not in conformity with the requirements of the credit. The plaintiffs in the present case are not guilty of fraud, but they were unknowingly responsible for having aided in the perpetration of the fraud. In such a case, where the fraud was discovered even before all other documents were tendered, I think it is right and proper that the plaintiffs should not be permitted to claim under the letter of credit."
>
> While such a finding was not necessary to the outcome of the case, it fell within the reservation of Lord Diplock in the *United City Merchants* case and has certain attractions. However, it is not necessary for us to decide in this case whether it is correct.'

1 [2001] EWCA Civ 1954; [2002] 1 WLR 1975 at paras 59–60.

9.29   In the context of performance bonds or guarantees, there has been recognition that 'breach of faith' on the part of the beneficiary might be a ground for restraining a beneficiary from calling on a bond or from receiving the product of a call. In the case of *TTI Team Telecom International Ltd v Hutchison 3G UK Ltd*[1] HHJ Thornton QC (sitting in the Technology and Construction Court) applied the case of *Elian and Rabbath v Matsas*[2] to hold that under English law 'lack of good faith' provided a basis to restrain a beneficiary from calling a bond or guarantee, although the bad faith required had to be both 'significant' and 'clearly established'.[3] Drawing on the approach taken by the Singaporean Courts the Judge gave examples of a lack or breach of faith by the beneficiary in threatening a call that could justify restraining a beneficiary from calling on a bond or from receiving the product of a call:[4]

> 'The basis for a contention of breach of faith must be established by clear evidence even for the purposes of interim relief. A breach of faith can arise in such situations as: a failure by the beneficiary to provide an essential element of the underlying contract on which the bond depends;[5] a misuse by the beneficiary of the guarantee by failing to act in accordance with the purpose for which it was given; a total failure of consideration in the underlying contract; a threatened call by the beneficiary for an unconscionable ulterior motive; or a lack of honest or bona fide belief by the beneficiary that the circumstances, such as poor performance, against which a performance bond had been provided actually exist.'

1 [2003] EWHC 762 (TCC); [2003] 1 All ER (Comm) 914.
2 [1966] 2 Lloyd's Rep. 495.
3 [2003] EWHC 762 (TCC); [2003] 1 All ER (Comm) 914 at paras 34, 37, 46.
4 [2003] EWHC 762 (TCC); [2003] 1 All ER (Comm) 914 at para 46.
5 This particular example appears to have derived partly from the following *dicta* of Eveleigh LJ in *Potton Homes Ltd v Coleman Contractors Ltd* (1984) 28 BLR 19, 29: 'For a large construction project the employer may agree to provide finance (perhaps by way of advance payments) to enable the contractor to undertake the works. The contractor will almost certainly be asked to provide a performance bond. If the contractor was unable to perform because the employer failed to provide the finance, it would seem wrong to me if the court was not entitled to have regard to the terms of the underlying contract and could be prevented from considering the question whether or not to restrain the employer from the mere assertion that a performance bond is like a letter of credit.'

9.30   There are a number of problems with recognizing 'breach of faith' as an exception to the autonomy of credit. Firstly, it is of broad but uncertain ambit and difficult to define. Secondly, it would tend to reduce confidence in the system of credits and impose a further duty on banks to investigate facts or consider investigating facts when the scheme of the UCP is to ensure that banks deal in documents alone and are obliged to pay against documents which are conformant on their face. The same policy reasons given by the Court of Appeal in the *Montrod* case[1] (which was not cited by the judge) against recognising a general nullity exception would apply equally to a 'breach of faith' exception. Thirdly, it is doubtful that the *Elian and Rabbath v Matsas*[2] case relied on in support of the exception does in fact support such a broad exception to the autonomy of credit. In that case the Court of Appeal upheld an injunction restraining shipowners from calling on a guarantee which had been procured by sellers of goods on the understanding that the shipowners would release certain goods and not impose a further lien. However, in breach of that understanding the shipowners imposed a further lien. The shipowners later sought to enforce the guarantee and the sellers claimed for a declaration that the guarantee was not a valid contract and an injunction to restrain the shipowners or their agent claiming or receiving from the bank the money under the guarantee. Denning LJ said it was a 'special case' in which an injunction should be granted because when the shipowners imposed a further lien in breach of the understanding between the parties they were 'disabled from acting on the guarantee'. Danckwerts LJ (who thought the guarantee should properly be called an undertaking) stated:

> 'It seems to me that if the shipowners were entitled immediately after obtaining the undertaking to claim a fresh lien and use it for the purpose of the undertaking it would amount at least to a breach of faith in regard to the arrangement between the parties. Whatever may be the final result of the case, it seems to me this is an instance where the Court should interfere and prevent what might be an irretrievable injustice being done to the plaintiffs in the circumstances.'

The precise basis for this decision is difficult to follow. The Court of Appeal granted the injunction without any apparent consideration of the sellers' cause of action. The case may not have concerned a performance or on-demand bond or guarantee at all but merely an ordinary guarantee.[3] It may be regarded as an early example of the exercise of the Mareva jurisdiction, 10 years before its time. It may also be significant that the validity of the contract was disputed and so the decision gives no support to the proposition that the beneficiary can be restrained when the validity of the contract and therefore the beneficiary's entitlement to exercise his contractual rights is not in issue.[4] In the case of *Howe Richardson Scale Co Ltd v Polimex-Cekop*[5] the Court of Appeal declined to follow *Elian and Rabbath v Matsas* stating that the decision should be regarded as very special and one which went further than subsequent cases. Since then there have been repeated statements by the Court of Appeal in *Edward Owen* and subsequent cases that the only recognized exception to the autonomy of credit is the case of fraud.[6] In the *Edward Owen* case,[7] one of the members of the Court of Appeal in *Elian and Rabbath v Matsas* (Lord Denning MR) himself said that that a bank must honour a performance guarantee according to its terms and pay according to its guarantee, on demand, if so stipulated, without proof or conditions. 'The only exception is when there is clear fraud of which the bank has notice'.

---

1 *Montrod Ltd v Grundkotter Fleischvertriebs Gmbh* [2001] EWCA Civ 1954; [2002] 1 WLR 1975.
2 [1966] 2 Lloyd's Rep 495.
3 See the remarks by Staughton LJ in *Group Josi Re v Walbook Insurance Co Ltd* [1996] 1 WLR 1152 at 1159 G–H.
4 See the remarks of Evans LJ in *Themehelp Ltd v West* [1996] QB 84 at 104.
5 [1978] 1 Lloyd's Rep 161.
6 See, for example: *GKN Contractors Ltd v Lloyds Bank plc* (1985) 30 BLR 53 per Parker LJ at 63 and the cases cited; *Themehelp Ltd v West* [1996] QB 84 per Waite LJ at 89; *Turkiye Is*

Bankasi AS v Bank of China [1998] 1 Lloyd's Rep 250 per Hirst LJ at 251 col 2; *Balfour Beatty Civil Engineering v Technical & General Guarantee Co Ltd* (1999) Con LR 180; *Solo Industries UK Ltd v Canara Bank* [2001] EWCA Civ 1059; [2001] 1 WLR 1800 per Mance LJ at para 6; *Sirius Insurance Co v FAI General Insurance Ltd* [2003] EWCA Civ 470; [2003] 1 WLR 2214 per May LJ at para 26; *Banque Saudi Fransi v Lear Siegler Services Inc* [2006] EWCA Civ 1130; [2007] 2 Lloyd's Rep 47 per Arden LJ at para 11. See also *Montrod Ltd v Grundkotter Fleischvertriebs Gmbh* [2001] EWCA Civ 1954; [2002] 1 WLR 1975 per Potter LJ at para 56: 'The fraud exception to the autonomy principle recognized in English law has hitherto been restricted to, and it is in my view desirable that it should remain based upon, the fraud or knowledge of fraud on the part of the beneficiary or other party seeking payment under and in accordance with the terms of the letter of credit.'

7 *Edward Owen Engineering Ltd v Barclays Bank Ltd* [1978] QB 159 per Denning LJ at 169D–171A.

Consequences where the exception applies

9.31   As indicated at the start of this chapter, the effect of the exception is fourfold. First, it provides a bank with a ground for refusing to pay and with a defence should it be sued by the fraudulent beneficiary or other party presenting the documents. Secondly, if the bank has paid, then the applicant may resist reimbursement, arguing that the bank should have refused to pay on the ground of fraud. Thirdly, it entitles the bank to recover the payment from the beneficiary, if the beneficiary has not disappeared with the money or become insolvent. Fourthly, on occasions, which it is suggested will be very rare, the effect of the exception may also be to enable an applicant/buyer to prevent by injunction a bank from paying on fraudulent documents. This is considered below in Part B.

(a)   Paying bank's right to refuse payment

9.32   If the bank decides not to pay, it will then have to establish the fraud at a trial if it is sued by the beneficiary. Actual fraud must be demonstrated, it is not sufficient for the bank merely to prove that there is material which would lead a reasonable banker to infer fraud by the beneficiary.[1] The civil burden of proof where fraud is alleged is that applicable in civil actions generally, namely proof on the balance of probabilities, but it has often been said that the court will require 'cogent evidence' in order to be satisfied that it is appropriate to make a finding of dishonesty.[2] As Lord Nicholls pointed out in *In re H (Minors)* [1996] AC 563 at pages 586–587:

> ' ... the court will have in mind as a factor, to whatever extent is appropriate in the particular case, that the more serious the allegation the less likely it is that the event occurred and, hence, the stronger should be the evidence before the court concludes that the allegation is established on the balance of probability.'

1 *Society of Lloyd's v Canadian Imperial Bank of Commerce* [1993] 2 Lloyd's Rep 579.

2 See for example the documentary credit case of *Niru Battery Manufacturing Company v Milestone Trading Limited* [2002] EWHC 1425 (Comm); [2002] 2 All ER (Comm) 705. In *Rafsanjan Pistachio Producers Co-operative v Bank Leumi (UK) plc* [1992] 1 Lloyd's Rep 513, another documentary credit case, Hirst J referred to the need to establish the case 'to the highest level of probability', citing *Hornal v Neuberger Products Ltd* [1957] 1 QB 247, CA, though the phrase is not there used.

9.33   It is likely that the alleged facts relating to the fraud will have been supplied to it by the buyer, and the bank will effectively be looking to the buyer to provide the necessary evidence. But the bank should always bear in mind that it has undertaken an independent legal obligation to the beneficiary under the documentary credit and it must make its own decision as to whether the evidence of fraud is sufficient to affect that obligation. It should not reach a decision simply as an accommodation to its customer.[1] Of course the bank also runs a risk of damage to its financial reputation if payment is refused.

1 *Bank of Montreal v Mitchell*, (1997) 143 DLR (4th) 697 Ont. Gen. Div. per Farley J.

Summary judgment where fraud alleged

9.34   Since the purpose of a credit is to ensure prompt payment, a disappointed beneficiary will want to obtain a swift remedy against a bank and will often seek summary judgment. Under CPR Pt 24.2, the court may give summary judgment against a defendant on the whole of a claim if it considers that the defendant has no real prospect of successfully defending the claim or issue and that there is no other reason why the case or issue should be disposed of at a trial. This raises the important question as to the circumstances in which a bank can resist judgment by alleging that the demand is fraudulent. The unusual position where the bank can rely on a counterclaim based on a related transaction with the beneficiary is discussed in para **5.102** above.

9.35   In *Balfour Beatty Civil Engineering v Technical & General Guarantee Co Ltd*,[1] a case decided under the old RSC Ord 14, it was argued by a surety under a performance bond that it need only show an arguable case of fraud to avoid summary judgment. This would have had the effect of keeping the beneficiary out of the proceeds of the credit until after what could well be a lengthy and complex fraud trial. In his analysis, Waller LJ (with whom the rest of the Court of Appeal agreed) posed a series of questions:

'1.   When the demand was made did the surety or the Bank have clear evidence from which the only inference to be drawn is fraud? If the answer is no then prima facie the beneficiary is entitled to judgment.

2.   What, on the information now available [ie at the summary judgment hearing], is the strength of the surety's case that the demand was fraudulent?

   (a)   If the evidence is now clear, then no judgment will be given in favour of the beneficiary because of the fact that the surety would be entitled to a judgment for the equivalent sum.

(b)   If the evidence is powerful but not quite sufficient to enable Order 14 judgment to be entered in favour of the surety on the basis that the demand was fraudulent, then either judgment would be entered with a stay of execution or probably no judgment would entered at all until what is in effect the counterclaim had been fought out.

(c)   If the evidence is less than powerful, judgment will be entered in favour of the beneficiary, and the surety will be left either to pursue his remedy against the customer or pursue a claim or counterclaim for reimbursement if so advised.'

The court held that there was no arguable evidence of fraud and granted judgment. However, there are a number of difficulties with the analysis. First, it supposes that the beneficiary may, in theory, be entitled to judgment on the credit even if there is clear evidence of fraud at the date of the summary hearing, albeit that it will not be given summarily because the bank has a matching judgment for recovery of the money. As discussed below, it is suggested that the court should not give judgment on a fraudulent claim even if the evidence of the fraud does not come to light until after the demand for payment.[2] Fraud gives the bank a defence to payment, not merely a counterclaim or set-off. Secondly, the analysis appears to draw a new distinction between 'clear', 'powerful' and 'less than powerful' evidence of fraud. This may introduce some doubt into an area where certainty is essential. Suppose a bank believes that there is powerful, but not clear, evidence of fraud. Should it decline payment, knowing that the beneficiary will not be able to obtain judgment until there has been a full trial at which all of the facts will come out, possibly demonstrating the fraud? Thirdly, where there is a related counterclaim the court has a discretion to refuse summary judgment or grant a stay of execution – and one which has arguably been broadened under the CPR[3] – which is at odds with the commercial requirement of promptness and certainty.

1 (1999) 68 Con LR 180.
2 See para **9.53** below.
3 See CPR Pt 24..

9.36   The position under the CPR was considered by the Court of Appeal in *SAFA Ltd v Banque du Caire*.[1] Waller LJ again gave the leading judgment. The facts were complex and unusual and it was emphasised that the relationship between the bank and the beneficiary were, unusually, not governed only by the terms of the credit because other arrangements had been made between all of the parties. Waller LJ referred to *Balfour Beatty Civil Engineering v Technical & General Guarantee Co.* He said that under the CPR the requirement for 'powerful evidence' should be equated with 'real prospect of success' and, so far as it applied to allegations of fraud in the demand, reformulated the test as follows:

'If a Bank can establish a claim with a real prospect of success, either that the demand was fraudulent even if it had no clear evidence of fraud at the time of the demand, or that there was a misrepresentation by the beneficiary directed at persuading the bank to enter into the letter of credit, it may also be unjust to enter summary judgment against the Bank either because the Bank has a reasonable prospect of succeeding in a defence of set-off or because there is a compelling reason for trial of the letter of credit issue.'

1 [2000] Lloyd's Rep 600, see also para **5.102**.

9.37   This test was considered by the Court of Appeal in *Solo Industries UK Ltd v Canara Bank*.[1] Mance LJ (with whom the other members of the Court agreed) distinguished between the two situations referred to by Waller LJ:

(1) where the bank has a claim with a real prospect of success that the demand was fraudulent, even if it had no clear evidence of fraud at the time of the demand; and
(2) where the bank has a claim with a real prospect of success that there was a misrepresentation by the beneficiary directed at persuading the bank to enter into the letter of credit.

Mance LJ doubted that the 'low test' of a 'real prospect' of establishing fraud could justify permission to defend a summary judgment application on the basis of an allegedly fraudulent demand (situation 1). He emphasised that:

'the cash principle means that (short of established fraud) any claim that a bank may acquire against a beneficiary making a fraudulent demand must be pursued separately and subsequent to payment , and cannot normally be used as a defence or set off to avoid payment'.[2]

In the light of the *Harbottle*[3] and *Edward Owen*[4] cases Mance LJ doubted whether, by analogy with the rules for obtaining an injunction set out in the *United Trading* case[5], a bank should be able to resist an application by the beneficiary for summary judgment where the bank had a real prospect of proving that on the material available the only realistic inference is that the beneficiary could not honestly have believed in the validity of its demand:[6]

'If instruments such as letters of credit and performance bonds are to be treated as cash, they must be paid as cash by banks to beneficiaries. The courts in *Harbottle* and *Edward Owen* emphasised this and, in my view, set a higher standard than "a real prospect of success" in relation to all these situations. Short of "established fraud", a bank will not normally be allowed to raise any defence or set-off based on alleged impropriety affecting the demand … 'The courts in *Harbottle* and *Edward Owen* were concerned with the interlocutory stage. The test that they stated was undiluted by any reference to "arguable case". The defence that they and later authorities identify, of established fraud known to the bank, is, by its nature, one which, if it is good at all, must be capable of being established with clarity at the interlocutory stage. If and in so far as that defence is limited to the time when the demand was or payment should have been made, but the court will still refuse judgment if by the time of judgment fraud is established, again there would seem to be little room for considering whether there is an "arguable case" or "real prospect" of establishing fraud. On any view … the court should be careful not to allow too extensive a dilution of the presumption in favour of the fulfilment of independent banking commitments.'

1 [2001] EWCA Civ 1059; [2001] 1 WLR 1800.
2 See at paras 31, 35.
3 [1978] 1 QB 146.
4 [1978] 1 QB 159, 171.
5 [1985] 2 Lloyd's Rep. 554 (note).
6 See [2001] EWCA Civ 1059; [2001] 1 WLR 1800 at para 32.

9.38   Where however, the challenge was to the validity of the instrument itself (as in situation 2), Mance LJ said this fell outside the principles in *Harbottle* and *Edward Owen*. A bank was permitted to raise a defence with a real prospect of success based on a challenge to the validity of the instrument. Accordingly, summary judgment was not awarded against the bank in favour of the beneficiary where the bank had shown a real prospect that the relevant instrument was procured by and had been validly avoided by the bank on account of fraudulent conspiracy and fraudulent misrepresentation by the applicant in conjunction with the beneficiary. Similarly in the case of forgery a bank would be able to advance a defence with a real prospect of success that an instrument relied upon by the beneficiary is a forgery.[1]

1 See [2001] EWCA Civ 1059; [2001] 1 WLR 1800 at paras 33, 36, 41.

9.39   Mance LJ's analysis of the appropriate test to justify permission to defend a summary judgment application on the basis of an allegedly fraudulent demand was cited with approval by the Court of Appeal in the recent case of *Banque Saudi Fransi v Lear Siegler Services Inc.*[1] So it appears that on a summary judgment application against a bank under a letter of credit or performance bond a higher test than that laid down by Part 24 will apply to a claim by the bank to rely on an alleged fraudulent demand on an otherwise valid instrument.[2] But where the bank's defence goes to the validity of the instrument itself (eg that the instrument was procured by a misrepresentation on the part of the beneficiary), it is sufficient for the bank to satisfy the court that there is a real prospect of establishing that defence at trial.

1 [2006] EWCA Civ 1130; [2007] 2 Lloyd's Rep. 47 at para 15.
2 See *Banque Saudi Fransi v Lear Siegler Services Inc* [2006] EWCA Civ 1130; [2007] 2 Lloyd's Rep 47 at para 16.

(b)   Paying bank's right to reimbursement

9.40   If the bank has clear evidence of fraud then it should not pay against the documents and will not be entitled to reimbursement from the applicant or other instructing party if it does.[1] However, unless the fraud is clearly established so that the bank is satisfied of it and is not able to give any reason of substance for remaining doubtful of the position, the court will uphold the bank's right to be reimbursed if the bank determines to accept the documents and pay against them. One course which is open to it is to invite the buyer to seek an injunction against it to prevent it from paying. If the court grants the injunction, the bank may well feel that this will protect its reputation when it does not pay. If the injunction is refused on the grounds of insufficient evidence of fraud, the bank can safely pay and it will be entitled to be reimbursed by the buyer. Clearly there is a considerable attraction to the issuing bank, as well as the applicant, in having, in effect, an interim decision by the court on the strength of the evidence. This method may become less effective if, as discussed below,[2] the courts adopt the approach in *Czarnikow-Rionda v Standard Bank* of refusing injunctions on the balance of convenience and irrespective of the strength of the evidence. If no application is made, or no ruling is made on the evidence, then the bank should pay unless the fraud is clear and obvious.[3] See *Bank of Nova Scotia v Angelica-Whitewear Ltd*:[4]

> 'Where, however, no such application [for an injunction] was made and the issuing bank has had to exercise its own judgment as to whether or not to honour a draft, the test in my opinion should be the one laid down in *Edward Owen Engineering*[5] – whether fraud was so established to the knowledge of the issuing bank before payment of the draft as to make the fraud clear or obvious to the bank. The justification for this distinction, in my view, is the difficulty of the position of the issuing bank, in so far as fraud is concerned, by comparison with that of a court on an application for an interlocutory injunction. In view of the strict obligation of the issuing bank to honour a draft that is accompanied by apparently conforming documents, the fact that the decision as to whether or not to pay must as a general rule be made fairly promptly, and the difficulty in many cases of forming an opinion, on which one would hazard a lawsuit, as to whether there has been fraud by the beneficiary of the credit, it would in my view be unfair and unreasonable to require anything less of the customer in the way of demonstration of an alleged fraud.'

The bank need not and should not carry out any investigation into the merits of the allegation if it is not obvious. In *Turkiye Is Bankasi AS v Bank of China*, Waller J said:[6]

> 'It is simply not for a bank to make enquiries about the allegations that are being made by one side against the other. If one side wishes to establish that a demand is fraudulent it must put the irrefutable evidence in front of the bank. It must not simply make allegations and expect the bank to check whether those allegations are founded or not.'

1 'I do not see how payment in the face of fraud can be a mere matter of discretion by a bank: it must be either within its mandate or not, and either a matter of obligation or not': *Czarnikow-Rionda v Standard Bank* [1999] 2 Lloyd's Rep 187 at 203 per Rix J. Contrast the United States Uniform Commercial Code §5-109(a), see para **9.61** below, where the issuer has an option whether to pay, albeit one which must be exercised in good faith.
2 See para **9.74** below.
3 See para **9.67** below on the standard of proof required.
4 [1987] 1 SCR 59 at 84.
5 [1978] QB 159 at 171C.
6 [1996] 2 Lloyd's Rep 611 at 617. The passage was approved in the Court of Appeal at [1998] 1 Lloyd's Rep 250 at 253 where Hirst LJ said, 'I am quite satisfied that ... the Judge applied the correct test throughout, and that the use of the adjective "irrefutable" was intended to do no more than epitomize the [*Edward Owen*] test, which Mr Bueno himself in his opening

argument characterized as requiring "an irresistible inference", though he backed away from that form of words in his reply'.

9.41 The bank's claim for reimbursement from the applicant or other instructing party will succeed unless the defendant can show clear evidence that the beneficiary had made a fraudulent demand of which the bank was aware at the time of payment.[1] It appears from the decision of the Court of Appeal in *Banque Saudi Fransi v Lear Siegler Services Inc*[2] that on an application for summary judgment by the bank it is sufficient for the defendant to establish that such a defence has a real prospect of success. The defendant does not have to satisfy what the Court of Appeal described as 'the higher test' considered in *Solo Industries UK Ltd v Canara Bank* that would apply to a defence by the bank relying on an alleged fraudulent demand by a beneficiary.[3]

1 *Crédit Agricole Indosuez v Generale Bank* [1999] 2 All ER (Comm) 1009 at 1015.
2 [2006] EWCA Civ 1130; [2007] 2 Lloyd's Rep. 47.
3 See para **9.37** above.

9.42 The *Banque Saudi* case concerned what must be shown by a defendant, against whom an application for summary judgment is made under a counter-indemnity in respect of the obligations of the party at whose request the claimant bank has issued a performance bond. The defendant alleged that the beneficiary of the performance bond had made a dishonest request for payment under it and at the time of payment the claimant bank knew or must have known this. The Court of Appeal held that it was sufficient for the defendant to establish that there is a real prospect of proving by clear evidence the fraud exception at trial. The Court of Appeal described this as a 'high hurdle' and held that it was one which the defendant was unable to meet on the facts of the case. Nevertheless it appears to follow from the decision of *Banque Saudi* that banks may not obtain summary judgment on counter-indemnities at the same as judgment is given against them on letter of credit and performance bonds.[1]

1 The Court of Appeal appeared to acknowledge and accept this result (see at para 18) would follow from its distinguishing the earlier case of *Solo Industries UK Ltd v Canara Bank* [2001] EWCA Civ 1059; [2001] 1 WLR 1800 at para 31 where the Court of Appeal had rejected the 'low test' of a 'real prospect' of establishing fraud in the context of claims by the bank to be entitled to withhold payment on the grounds of a fraudulent demand. See also para **9.37** above.

Discounting of deferred payments before maturity

9.43 Where the credit provides for deferred payment,[1] the issuing or confirming bank which has undertaken the deferred payment obligation may choose to discount its obligation to the beneficiary, that is, it may at the request of the beneficiary choose to make payment immediately but in a reduced amount to reflect the advantage of early receipt to the beneficiary. The bank will then seek reimbursement of the full amount of the credit at maturity from the applicant or, if the bank is a confirming bank, from the issuer. For letters of credit subject to UCP 500, as a result of the decision in *Banco Santander SA v Banque Paribas*,[2] unless such an arrangement was expressly permitted by the applicant or under the terms of the credit, then the bank took the risk that it would lose its entitlement to reimbursement if a fraud by the beneficiary was discovered before maturity. If no fraud was established at the maturity date, then the confirming bank could at that point be treated as having complied with its instructions and became entitled to reimbursement.

1 See para **2.17** above.
2 [2000] Lloyd's Rep Bank 165.

9.44 The facts in *Banco Santander* were as follows. Bayfern Ltd was the beneficiary of a 180-day deferred payment credit issued by Banque Paribas and confirmed by Banco Santander. Documents which appeared to be conformant were presented by Bayfern to Santander on 15 June 1998 and, in accordance with the credit, Santander would have been obliged to make payment in the sum of US$20.3 million on 27 November 1998. However, Santander agreed to discount the credit by paying US$19.7 million on 17 June 1998. One week later, Santander was informed that the documents were forged, and it was assumed for the purpose of the preliminary issue before the court the evidence of fraud was sufficient to trigger the exception. Therefore, had Santander not already paid, it would have been entitled to refuse payment at maturity. Santander argued, however, that it had discharged its obligations as confirming bank without notice of the fraud and was therefore entitled to reimbursement from Paribas under Article 14.a of UCP 500.

9.45 The Court of Appeal held that Santander's right to reimbursement from the issuing bank arose only when it had validly discharged its obligation under the credit to Bayfern. However, in making an early payment, Santander's intention was not to discharge that obligation but to keep it alive until maturity and to take an assignment of the benefit of it from Bayfern.[1] This resulted in a situation where Santander was the assignee of a claim against itself.[2] As soon as the fraud came to light, there was no valid claim by the beneficiary on the confirming bank and, therefore, no claim for reimbursement from the issuer. As assignee, Santander could be in no better position than Bayfern whose established fraud would prevent it recovering against Santander or Paribas. Therefore, Santander was not entitled to reimbursement. The Court of Appeal rejected Santander's argument that because the practice of discounting in this way had become prevalent a bank which took an assignment in good faith should not, contrary to the general law, be affected by the fraud of the assignor. If commercial parties wish to take an assignment free of this risk of fraud or other prior equities, then they can provide for the use of a negotiable instrument such as a bill of exchange which gives the special statutory protection of the Bills of Exchange Act 1882 when it is discounted to a holder in due course or they can provide by the terms of the trade or the express terms of the instrument itself the protection for assignees that a negotiable instrument would provide.[3]

1 This analysis was supported by the fact that Santander's claim was not for reimbursement of the discounted sum paid out but for the full US$20.3 million which would have been due to Bayfern under the credit at maturity and, more obviously, that the documents executed by Bayfern referred in terms to an assignment.
2 There is no reason why a debtor cannot take an assignment of his creditor's claim, see *Re Bank of Credit and Commerce International SA (No 8)* [1998] AC 214.
3 If rather than making early payment, Santander had accepted a 180-day bill of exchange (as it would, had the credit been an acceptance credit) and discounted its own bill in good faith, then its claim would be based on a right as holder in due course which would not be affected by the fraud of Bayfern. The court was told that the purpose of discounting deferred payment obligations, rather than using time drafts, may have developed in order to avoid stamp duty payable in some jurisdictions on negotiable instruments.

9.46   The Court of Appeal also held that even if Santander had validly discharged its obligation as confirming bank by its early payment, it was still not entitled to reimbursement. The right to reimbursement under Articles 10.d and 14 of the UCP 500 arose only if the paying bank had acted in accordance with its instructions as set out in the credit. Whilst it was not a breach of mandate to discount the deferred payment, neither was it in accordance with Santander's instructions. In such circumstances, the confirming bank acted at the risk that the beneficiary may at maturity not have been entitled to payment. If no fraud was established at the maturity date, then the confirming bank could at that point be treated as having complied with its instructions and becomes entitled to reimbursement. Waller LJ said:[1]

> 'In my view [Santander] cannot argue simply from the fact that to do something is not a breach of mandate to the position that what was done was authorised by the principal so as to produce a right of reimbursement. An agent may be entitled to go off and do something on his own account without being in breach of his mandate from the principal, but it does not follow that when he does do something on his own account, because he is not in breach of the mandate, the principal must indemnify him in relation to that which he has done. In my view the position is that Santander had no authority to negotiate from Paribas to discount, and did not seek it. It was something they were entitled to do on their own account. If they had not chosen to discount and had waited until 27th November, they would have had a defence, and it is in those circumstances not open to them to claim reimbursement from Paribas.'

1 [2000] Lloyd's Rep Bank 165 at 172.

9.47   For credits subject to UCP 600, this latter part of the analysis in *Banco Santander* no longer applies. Under Article 12.b, a nominated bank is expressly authorised by the issuing bank to make prepayment under a deferred payment credit. Further, there is no longer any need for a confirming bank which has discounted a deferred payment obligation to take an assignment (and risk the result in *Banco Santander*) in order to claim reimbursement of the full amount of the credit at maturity. Under Article 7.c the issuing bank undertakes to reimburse a nominated bank that has honoured or negotiated a complying presentation and forwarded the documents to the issuing bank. Reimbursement is due for the amount of a complying presentation under a credit available by deferred payment 'at maturity, whether or not the nominated bank prepaid or purchased before maturity'. The article also makes clear that such undertaking is independent of the issuing bank's undertaking to the beneficiary. Article 8.c imposes a similar obligation on a confirming bank and again makes clear that this is independent of the confirming bank's undertaking to the beneficiary. So a bank has the right to obtain reimbursement at maturity where it prepays or purchases an acceptance or deferred payment undertaking regardless of any fraud by the beneficiary discovered prior to maturity.

(c) Paying bank's right to recovery from the beneficiary

9.48 If the paying bank is unable to obtain reimbursement from the applicant, for example if the applicant is insolvent, or if it is found that the bank should not have paid because the fraud was apparent or the documents were discrepant, then it can attempt to recover its payment from the recipient. The claim is for restitution for payment by mistake. In *Bank Russo-Iran v Gordon Woodroffe & Co Ltd*,[1] quoted with approval by Lord Denning MR in *Edward Owen Engineering Ltd v Barclays Bank International Ltd*[2] and *Etablissement Esefka International Anstalt v Central Bank of Nigeria*[3], Browne J stated: 'In my judgment, if the documents are presented by the beneficiary himself, and are forged or fraudulent, the bank is entitled to refuse payment if it finds out before payment, and is entitled to recover the money as paid under a mistake of fact if it finds out after payment.' In *Bank Russo-Iran* the bank had issued in Teheran a letter of credit payable in London in favour of the defendant company for goods invoiced for some £229,000; in fact the goods had been acquired for £9,000 and the sale was a sham. In *Bank Tejarat v HSBC*,[4] where Bank Tejarat paid against forged shipping documents, Tuckey J noted that it was 'common ground that a bank which has paid under a letter of credit as a result of fraud, does so under a mistake of fact and is entitled to recover the money so paid as money had and received'.

1 (1972) 116 Sol Jo 921, (1972) Times, 4 October (but nowhere adequately reported).
2 [1978] QB 159 at 169.
3 [1979] 1 Lloyd's Rep 445 at 447.2, 448.1.
4 [1995] 1 Lloyd's Rep 239 at 244.

9.49 If a bank would be entitled to refuse to pay on the ground of fraud it seems plainly right that it should be entitled to recover a payment if the fraud is discovered later. However, the exact nature of the actionable mistake is difficult to identify and has not been the subject of analysis in the cases. It cannot simply be a mistaken belief by the bank that the documents are accurate, because the bank does not have the same right of recovery if the beneficiary innocently or negligently presents false documents, and a mistaken belief that the beneficiary is acting honestly seems artificial. Perhaps it is enough to say that one who obtains a benefit *ex turpi causa* has been unjustly enriched and is liable to restore it. At any rate, the restitutionary claim where there is fraud is well established in the authorities.[1]

1 In *Niru Battery Manufacturing Company v Milestone Trading Limited* [2002] EWHC 1425 (Comm), [2002] 2 All ER (Comm) 705 and [2003] EWCA Civ 1446, [2004] QB 985 it was common ground that a bank which had paid under a letter of credit as a result of fraud by the beneficiary had a claim in restitution against the recipient bank for money paid under a mistake of fact, subject to the defence of change of position.

9.50   Since the claim is restitutionary it can in principle be pursued against any party into whose hands the money can be traced, for example a collecting bank or other agent of the beneficiary. However, it is a defence if the agent has paid over the money to his principal in good faith and without notice of the claim.[1] A recipient who had or thought he had good reason to believe that payment under a letter of credit had been made to him by mistake failed to act in good faith if he paid the money away without making inquiries of the payer. This was the position in *Niru Battery Manufacturing Company v Milestone Trading Limited*,[2] where the issuing bank paid against a fraudulent presentation. The beneficiary's bank, although not party to the fraud, knew that the underlying cargo had already been disposed of and, therefore, that the payment might have been mistaken. However, rather than contacting the issuing bank for confirmation, it paid over the money to the fraudster. It was held liable to make restitution of the money which it had received, even though it no longer had it.

1 *Continental Caoutchouc v Kleinwort Sons & Co* (1904) 9 Com Cas 240; *Bank Tejarat v HSBC* [1995] 1 Lloyd's Rep 239; *Bowstead on Agency* (18th edn) Article 111(2)(c).
2 [2003] EWCA Civ 1446, [2004] QB 985.

9.51   An alternative ground for recovery by the bank against the beneficiary is a claim for damages for deceit on the ground that by presenting the documents the beneficiary represents that they are truthful. The Court of Appeal may have had this in mind in *Balfour Beatty Civil Engineering v Technical & General Guarantee Co Ltd*,[1] a performance bond case, where Waller LJ said:

'It is clear that simply because after demand on a bond it turns out that no sum was due from the customer to his contractor, that does not lead to the Bank or surety having any remedy against the beneficiary of the bond. The customer who of course must indemnify the Bank or surety may have a right as against the beneficiary under their contract but that is all. If however the beneficiary has made a fraudulent representation to the Bank in order to obtain money under the bond, I cannot see why in addition to any remedy that the Bank's customer may have (if the customer has been forced to indemnify the Bank), the Bank does not have its own remedy directly against the beneficiary. That may be very important in the context of a case such as the present in which the customer of the surety or the Bank has gone into liquidation.'

The analysis is straightforward where the beneficiary has presented documents knowing them to be false, and banks have successfully claimed in deceit against the beneficiary and others responsible for procuring the fraudulent presentation of documents to the bank.[2] The analysis is more difficult where the documents themselves are truthful but there is fraud in the underlying transaction.

1 (1999) 68 Con LR 180, CA.
2 See *KBC Bank v Industrial Steels (UK) Limited* [2001] 1 All ER (Comm) 409; *Komercni Banka A.S v Stone and Rolls Limited* [2002] EWHC 2263 (Comm), [2003] 1 Lloyd's Rep 383; *Niru Battery Manufacturing Company v Milestone Trading Limited* [2002] EWHC 1425 (Comm), [2002] 2 All ER (Comm) 705.

9.52   The bank may be able to make a recovery from the beneficiary even where it is itself guilty of fraudulent conduct, provided that it does not have to rely on that conduct in support of its claim. In *Standard Chartered Bank v Pakistan National Shipping Corpn (No 2)*,[1] the beneficiary presented to Standard Chartered Bank (SCB), as confirming bank, documents which were forged and false. SCB was not aware of the inaccuracies in the documents; however, it was aware that some of the necessary documents were presented out of time and it would, therefore, have been entitled to reject the presentation. SCB nevertheless accepted the documents and passed them to Incombank, the issuing bank, under cover of a letter which stated that the documents had been presented in time. SCB knew that this statement was false. In the event, Incombank, unaware of either SCB's or the beneficiary's fraud, properly declined to indemnify SCB on the ground of unrelated discrepancies in the documents. Despite its own conduct, SCB was not prevented by the *ex turpi causa* rule from pursuing the beneficiary to get its money back. But Evans LJ said:[2]

> 'The result, however, to my mind is profoundly unsatisfactory, if SCB is entitled to recover full damages from the appellants, because they were deceitful, when its own deceitful conduct was in part responsible for its loss. The pot calls the kettle black, and the law prevents the kettle from answering back, except in extreme cases. In the interests of condemning the deceitful defendant, the law is prepared to countenance and overlook deceitful conduct by the claimant which is incidental to but not wholly removed from his loss, and partly causative of it.'

Further, where the bank is entitled to damages for fraudulent misrepresentation there will be no reduction in the bank's damages to reflect its own negligence. So even though SCB made payment partly in reliance on the negligent and mistaken belief that it could obtain reimbursement from the issuing bank, the damages it suffered as a result of being induced to make payment in reliance on the false documents did not fall to be apportioned under the Law Reform (Contributory Negligence) Act 1945. [3]

1 [2000] 1 Lloyd's Rep 218.
2 [2000] 1 Lloyd's Rep 218 at 230.
3 [2002] UKHL 43; [2003] 1 AC 959.

Time at which fraud must be apparent

9.53   At what time must the fraud be apparent to the bank? This question arises in two different situations: first, if the bank has already paid on the credit and the applicant (or other instructing party) is resisting reimbursement;[1] secondly, if the bank has not paid and is resisting proceedings by the beneficiary for payment under the credit.[2]

1 See para **9.40**.
2 See para **9.32**.

9.54   In the first situation, if the bank pays in accordance with the terms of the credit, then it is entitled to reimbursement unless there was clear evidence of fraud at the time of payment.[1] The bank has a strictly limited period to consider the documents and cannot and should not engage in prolonged inquiries of the sort which might be carried out at a full trial between beneficiary and applicant. It is not open to the applicant objecting to the bank's decision to rely on evidence not made available to the bank at the time of payment. See *United Trading Corpn SA v Allied Arab Bank Ltd*:[2]

> **'The relevant date for establishing knowledge of fraud**
> It seems to us clear that, where payment has in fact been made, the bank's knowledge that the demand made by the beneficiary on the performance bond was fraudulent must exist prior to the actual payment to the beneficiary and that its knowledge at that date must be proved. Accordingly, if all a plaintiff can establish is such knowledge *after* payment, then he has failed to establish his cause of action. The bank would not have been in breach of any duty in making the payment without the requisite knowledge. We doubt that this is really open to contest.'

1 *Crédit Agricole Indosuez v Generale Bank* [1999] 2 All ER (Comm) 1009 at 1015.
2 [1985] 2 Lloyd's Rep 554n at 560.

9.55   In the second situation, if fraud is apparent at the time payment is due, then the bank must not pay and has a defence to a claim by the beneficiary. Suppose, however, that the bank rejects documents for alleged discrepancies or for alleged fraud but that decision is subsequently held (or conceded) to be wrong based on the material available at the time payment was due, can the bank defend proceedings relying on new evidence of fraud which came to light after the date for payment but before the trial? As discussed above, in *Balfour Beatty Civil Engineering v Technical & General Guarantee Co Ltd*[1] Waller LJ identified the 'absurdity' that would result if a court, having heard evidence on an application for summary judgment, felt bound to give judgment because it concluded that, although fraud was now sufficiently established, it had not been sufficiently established and known to the bank at the time when the demand was made under the relevant instrument. The key to avoiding this absurdity lay in his view in recognising that the bank would, in this situation, have a cause of action against the beneficiary for fraudulent misrepresentation, on which it could obtain summary judgment which it could then use to extinguish its liability on the instrument. In a case where the fraudulent misrepresentation was so clear as itself to justify summary judgment, no difficulty arose. The parties' established rights to judgment would simply cancel out and preclude any judgment on the claim. In other cases, if the evidence of fraud was 'powerful' the bank could either seek a stay of execution in respect of its liability on the instrument or a deferral of any judgment on the instrument until after trial of its counterclaim. If the evidence was less than powerful, the bank would simply be left to pursue a counterclaim against the beneficiary for reimbursement or its remedy against its customer.[2]

1 (1999) 68 Con LR 180, see para **9.35** above.
2 In this context 'powerful evidence' is similar to 'real prospect of success'. See *Safa Ltd v Banque du Caire* [2000] 2 Lloyd's Rep. 600.

9.56 However, in the later case of *Safa Ltd v Banque du Caire*[1] Waller LJ accepted that a claim by a bank that is being sued on what it alleges is a fraudulent demand is something the bank can raise by way of defence or set-off and not simply by counterclaim. In *Solo Industries UK Ltd v Canara Bank*[2] Mance LJ (with whom the other members of the Court of Appeal agreed) considered Waller LJ's analysis in *Balfour* and held that:

> 'Another way of reaching the same conclusion in cases where there is, *by* although not before the time of the hearing, established fraud, (and probably also in case where there is, by the same time "powerful" evidence of fraud) may be by applying Lord Diplock's underlying principle that the court should not lend its process to assist fraud and that "fraud unravels all". No question arises in this context of the grant of injunctive relief or of any requirement for that purpose to have a cause of action. It would affront good sense, and probably general principles relating to illegality, if courts were obliged to give judgment in favour of a beneficiary now shown to be acting fraudulently.'

1 [2000] 2 Lloyd's Rep 600.
2 [2001] EWCA Civ 1059; [2001] 1 WLR 1800 at [21].

9.57 In *Mahonia Ltd v JP Morgan Chase Bank*,[1] Colman J expressed the view that it was unnecessary to confine the bank's position to one founded on a counterclaim for damages or circuity or potential circuity of action: 'as long as there is before the court evidence which establishes fraud by the beneficiary there is evidence sufficient to establish a straight defence based on ex turpi causa'. For this purpose Colman J agreed with Waller LJ 's analysis in the *Balfour Beatty* case that the strength of the fraud case has to be tested on the evidence available at the hearing as distinct from the time of demand. He reasoned that just as the bank's entitlement to withhold payment was based, according to the *United City Merchants* case, on clear evidence of fraud and therefore of an ex turpi causa defence at the time when the demand is made and payment would otherwise be due, so also the bank should have a direct defence on the basis of ex turpi causa at whatever stage in the proceedings prior to the hearing it can adduce the evidence necessary to establish fraud. The availability of the defence could not depend on whether evidence of fraud becomes available before or after demand is made and payment is otherwise due.[2]

1 [2003] EWHC 1927 (Comm); [2003] 2 Lloyd's Rep 911 at paras 45–47.
2 At the subsequent trial Cooke J agreed with Colman J's conclusions on this issue. See *Mahonia Ltd v JP Morgan Chase Bank* [2004] EWHC 1938 (Comm) at para 209.

9.58   The same conclusion should be reached if, as considered in para **9.14** above, the basis of the exception is a limitation in the bank's mandate, for in common with the general rule in contractual disputes the bank should be entitled to justify retrospectively its refusal to perform its obligations using any reasons known at trial.[1] Article 16.f prevents the bank doing this in respect of discrepancies if they have not been notified to the beneficiary, but the fraud exception is governed by common law and not by the UCP and there is no equivalent provision which prevents the bank from relying on late evidence in support of a fraud defence. Therefore, although the bank's initial decision to reject should be based on clear evidence of fraud at that time, it is suggested that if that decision should be wrong the bank should be entitled to justify its rejection using all facts known at the time the matter is tried, whether on an application for summary judgment or at a full trial. It is conceivable that a bank might abuse such a rule by declining payment in a borderline fraud case, taking a chance that further material will come to light before trial. Of course it is then taking a risk with its reputation as well as its liability and it is doubtless for that reason that the reported cases mostly concern attempts by applicants to restrain payment rather than attempts by banks to avoid payment.

1 This is the general rule in contractual disputes: *Chitty on Contracts* (30th edn) para 24-014.

Other materials on fraud

9.59   For comparison purposes, set out below are the relevant extracts relating to fraudulent or abusive drawings in International Standby Practices 1998 (ISP98) (a set of rules for standby credits), the United States Uniform Commercial Code and the United Nations Convention on Independent Guarantees and Standby Letters of Credit. None of these is directly applicable to the English law on the fraud exception.

(a)   Fraud and ISP98[1]

9.60   Like the Uniform Customs, ISP98 does not make provision for fraud, but contains an express reservation:

> 'Rule 1.05: Exclusion of Matters Related to Due Issuance and Fraudulent or Abusive Drawing
> These Rules do not define or otherwise provide for: . . .
>
> c.   defenses to honour based on fraud, abuse, or similar matters. These matters are left to applicable law.'

1 See para **12.34** below.

(b)   *Fraud and the United States Uniform Commercial Code*

9.61   The United States Uniform Commercial Code (UCC) applies to credits governed by United States state law and not, of course, to those governed by English law. The UCC is also displaced, so far as it is inconsistent, by the provisions of the UCP where they are expressly incorporated into a credit. However, it is a useful illustration of how the exception can be codified.

'UCC §5–109 Fraud and Forgery:

(a)   If a presentation is made that appears on its face strictly to comply with the terms and conditions of the letter of credit, but a required document is forged or materially fraudulent, or honor of the presentation would facilitate a material fraud by the beneficiary on the issuer or applicant:

(1)   the issuer shall honor the presentation, if honor is demanded by

(i)   a nominated person who has given value in good faith and without notice of forgery or material fraud,

(ii)   a confirmer who has honored its confirmation in good faith,

(iii)   a holder in due course of a draft drawn under the letter of credit which was taken after acceptance by the issuer or nominated person, or

(iv)   an assignee of the issuer's or nominated person's deferred obligation that was taken for value and without notice of forgery or material fraud after the obligation was incurred by the issuer or nominated person; and

(2)   the issuer, acting in good faith, may honor or dishonor the presentation in any other case.'

(c)   *Fraud and the United Nations Convention on Independent Guarantees and Standby Letters of Credit*

9.62   The Convention entitles but does not impose a duty on the guarantor/issuer, as against the beneficiary, to refuse payment when confronted with fraudulent or abusive demands for payment. The Convention has not been ratified by the United Kingdom, United States or any Commonwealth country or European Union member state.[1] However, it provides another codification of the exception. The Explanatory Note to the Convention[2] states that 'a main purpose of the Convention is to establish greater uniformity internationally in the manner in which guarantor/issuers and courts respond to allegations of fraud or abuse in demands for payment under independent guarantees and stand-by letters of credit ... That difficulty and the resulting uncertainty have been compounded further because of the divergent notions and ways with which such allegations have been treated both by guarantor/issuers and by courts approached for provisional measures to block payment. The Convention helps to ameliorate the problem by providing an internationally agreed general definition of the types of situation in which an exception to the obligation to pay against a facially compliant demand would be justified'.

'Article 19 Exception to payment obligation:
(1) If it is manifest and clear that:
    (a) Any document is not genuine or has been falsified;
    (b) No payment is due on the basis asserted in the demand and the supporting documents; or
    (c) Judging by the type and purpose of the undertaking, the demand has no conceivable basis, the guarantor/issuer, acting in good faith, has a right, as against the beneficiary, to withhold payment.
(2) For the purposes of subparagraph (c) of paragraph (1) of this article, the following are types of situations in which a demand has no conceivable basis:
    (a) The contingency or risk against which the undertaking was designed to secure the beneficiary has undoubtedly not materialized;
    (b) The underlying obligation of the principal/applicant has been declared invalid by a court or arbitral tribunal, unless the undertaking indicates that such contingency falls within the risk to be covered by the undertaking;
    (c) The underlying obligation has undoubtedly been fulfilled to the satisfaction of the beneficiary;
    (d) Fulfilment of the underlying obligation has clearly been prevented by wilful misconduct of the beneficiary;
    (e) In the case of a demand under a counter-guarantee, the beneficiary of the counter-guarantee has made payment in bad faith as guarantor/issuer of the undertaking to which the counter-guarantee relates.'

1 The Convention has been ratified or acceded to by Belarus, Ecuador, El Salvador, Gabon, Kuwait, Liberia, Panama and Tunisia.
2 See paras 45 and 46 of the Explanatory Note by the UNICTRAL secretariat.

B INJUNCTIONS

Introduction

9.63 Where the applicant for a documentary credit or a performance bond considers that the beneficiary is going to make or has made a presentation under the credit or bond which he should not make and which should not be met with payment by the paying bank, he may seek to prevent the presentation or payment or both by applying for injunctions against relevant parties. Such an application will meet a number of difficulties. Injunctions have been upheld in three cases: *Themehelp Ltd v West*;[1] *Kvaerner John Brown Ltd v Midland Bank plc*[2] (both in reliance on the fraud exception and criticised in *Czarnikow-Rionda v Standard Bank*);[3] and *Lorne Stewart plc v Hermes Kreditversicherungs AG*[4] (where a performance bond was found not to be payable according to its terms). The general principles to be applied in applications for interlocutory injunctions were set out in the speech of Lord Diplock in *American Cyanamid Co v Ethicon Ltd*,[5] but caution must be exercised in drawing too close parallels with those general principles because of the special factors which apply to letters of credit, and the public policy in not obstructing the flow of the 'lifeblood of commerce'.[6] A claimant faces two difficulties in particular. First, he must show that he has a good arguable claim against the party he is seeking to injunct. This will involve him establishing a case of fraud to the knowledge of the party to be injuncted (otherwise the court will not interfere with the operation of the credit), and he must establish a duty owed to him by that party, either in contract or in tort. Secondly, it must appear that the grant of an injunction is the correct exercise of the court's discretion after considering the balance of convenience. So, even if a case as to fraud is sufficiently established, the case is likely to fail where the party sought to be injuncted is a bank because damages will be a sufficient remedy for any breach of duty by the bank. These principles as developed in connection with documentary credit and performance bond or guarantee cases are considered below.

1 [1996] QB 84.
2 [1998] CLC 446. The balance of convenience was not explicitly considered by the court.
3 [1999] 2 Lloyd's Rep 187 at 190.2.
4 (Unreported, 22 October 2001) Garland J.
5 [1975] AC 396.
6 *Group Josi Re v Walbrook Insurance Co Ltd* [1996] 1 WLR 1152 at 1161.

The basic rule – the autonomy of the credit[1]

9.64   The basic rule is that the court will not interfere to prevent the operation of a credit on the ground of matters which are extraneous to the credit itself. This is but one aspect of the autonomy principle. In *Hamzeh Malas & Sons v British Imex Industries Ltd*[2] the plaintiff buyers considered that the goods supplied as the first instalment under a two-instalment contract were seriously defective and sought to prevent the defendant sellers from presenting documents in respect of the second instalment under the confirmed credit which the buyers had arranged to be opened as the means of payment. The injunction was refused. In giving the leading judgment in the Court of Appeal, Jenkins LJ stated:[3]

'We have been referred to a number of authorities, and it seems to be plain enough that the opening of a confirmed letter of credit constitutes a bargain between the banker and the vendor of the goods, which imposes upon the banker an absolute obligation to pay, irrespective of any dispute there may be between the parties as to whether the goods are up to contract or not. An elaborate commercial system has been built up on the footing that bankers' confirmed credits are of that character, and, in my judgment, it would be wrong for this court in the present case to interfere with that established practice.

There is this to be remembered, too. A vendor of goods selling against a confirmed letter of credit is selling under the assurance that nothing will prevent him from receiving the price. That is of no mean advantage when goods manufactured in one country are being sold in another. It is, furthermore, to be observed that vendors are often reselling goods bought from third parties. When they are doing that, and when they are being paid by a confirmed letter of credit, their practice is – and I think it was followed by the defendants in this case – to finance the payments necessary to be made to their suppliers against the letter of credit. That system of financing these operations, as I see it, would break down completely if a dispute as between the vendor and the purchaser was to have the effect of "freezing", if I may use that expression, the sum in respect of which the letter of credit was opened.'

1 Cited, *Themehelp Ltd v West* [1996] QB 84, CA.
2 [1958] 2 QB 127.
3 See [1958] 2 QB at 129.

9.65   In *Howe Richardson Scale Co Ltd v Polimex-Cekop*[1] the claimant sellers had arranged for a performance bond or guarantee to be given by the second defendant bank in respect of the deposit paid to them by the buyers (who were the first defendants), the deposit to be repaid by the bank on the buyer's first demand if the goods were not delivered by a date. Problems arose in the performance of the contract, in particular as to the opening by the buyers of a letter of credit. The sellers contended that in any event the goods were delivered to warehouse by the date. The buyers made a demand on the bond and the bank informed the sellers that it felt bound to pay. The sellers initially sought injunctions against the buyers and the bank, but did not pursue the latter on appeal. The buyers did not take part in resisting the application, the case being argued by the bank. The Court of Appeal declined to follow *Elian and Rabbath v Matsas*[2] where an injunction restraining a party from calling a guarantee was granted, stating that that decision should be regarded as very special.[3] Roskill LJ stated:[4]

'The bank, in principle, is in a position not identical with but very similar to the position of a bank which has opened a confirmed irrevocable letter of credit. Whether the obligation arises under a letter of credit or under a guarantee, the obligation of the bank is to perform that which it is required to perform by that particular contract, and that obligation does not in the ordinary way depend on the correct resolution of a dispute as to the sufficiency of performance by the seller to the buyer or by the buyer to the seller as the case may be under the sale and purchase contract; the bank here is simply concerned to see whether the event has happened upon which its obligation to pay has arisen. The bank takes the view that that time has come and that it is compelled to pay; and in my view it would be quite wrong for the Court to interfere with Polimex's apparent right under this guarantee to seek payment from the bank, because to do so would involve putting upon the bank an obligation to inquire whether or not there had been timeous performance of the sellers' obligations under the sale contract.'

1 [1978] 1 Lloyd's Rep 161.
2 [1966] 2 Lloyd's Rep 495.
3 See [1978] 1 Lloyd's Rep at 165.1.
4 [1978] 1 Lloyd's Rep at 165.2.

9.66   Lastly, it is worth quoting an often-referred-to passage from the judgment of Kerr J in *R D Harbottle (Mercantile) Ltd v National Westminster Bank Ltd*.[1] He stated:

> 'It is only in exceptional cases that the courts will interfere with the machinery of irrevocable obligations assumed by banks. They are the life-blood of international commerce. Such obligations are regarded as collateral to the underlying rights and obligations between the merchants at either end of the banking chain. Except possibly in clear cases of fraud of which the banks have notice, the courts will leave the merchants to settle their disputes under the contracts by litigation or arbitration ... The courts are not concerned with their difficulties to enforce such claims; these are risks which the merchants take. In this case the plaintiffs took the risk of the unconditional wording of the guarantees. The machinery and commitments of banks are on a different level. They must be allowed to be honoured, free from interference by the courts. Otherwise, trust in international commerce could be irreparably damaged.'

1 [1978] QB 146 at 155H–156A.

The fraud exception and proof

9.67   The autonomous nature of letters of credit means that absent fraud by the seller presenting documents to the confirming bank seeking payment, the court will not restrain a bank from paying a letter of credit which is payable according to its terms, nor a beneficiary from seeking payment. Nor, again, absent fraud, will the court restrain a beneficiary from drawing on a letter of credit which is payable in accordance with its terms on the application of a buyer who is in dispute with the seller as to whether the underlying sale contract has been broken.[1] The exception has been considered specifically in relation to injunctions in a number of cases.[2] It has been emphasised in all of them that the fraud and the knowledge of the bank must be clearly established. Thus in the *Edward Owen* case[3] Lord Denning MR stated[4] 'The only exception is where there is a clear fraud of which the bank had notice' and Browne LJ stated:[5] 'But it is certainly not enough to allege fraud: it must be "established" and in such circumstances I should say very clearly established.' Geoffrey Lane LJ referred[6] to 'if it had been clear and obvious to the bank that the buyers had been guilty of fraud'. With this in mind, at the termination of the judgment of the Court of Appeal in *Bolivinter Oil SA v Chase Manhattan Bank*[7] the court gave general guidance as to the granting of ex parte injunctions in relation to credits and bonds. The court stated:[8]

> 'Before leaving this appeal, we should like to add a word about the circumstances in which an *ex parte* injunction should be issued which prohibits a bank from paying under an irrevocable letter of credit or a purchase bond or guarantee. The unique value of such a letter, bond or guarantee is that the beneficiary can be completely satisfied that whatever disputes may thereafter arise between him and the bank's customer in relation

to the performance or indeed existence of the underlying contract, the bank is personally undertaking to pay him provided that the specified conditions are met. In requesting his bank to issue such a letter, bond or guarantee, the customer is seeking to take advantage of this unique characteristic. If, save in the most exceptional cases, he is to be allowed to derogate from the bank's personal and irrevocable undertaking, given be it again noted at his request, by obtaining an injunction restraining the bank from honouring that undertaking, he will undermine what is the bank's greatest asset, however large and rich it may be, namely its reputation for financial and contractual probity. Furthermore, if this happens at all frequently, the value of the irrevocable letters of credit and performance bonds and guarantees will be undermined.

Judges who are asked, often at short notice and *ex parte*, to issue an injunction restraining payment by a bank under an irrevocable letter of credit or performance bond or guarantee should ask whether there is any challenge to the validity of the letter, bond or guarantee itself. If there is not or if the challenge is not substantial, *prima facie* no injunction should be granted and the bank should be left free to honour its contractual obligation, although restrictions may well be imposed upon the freedom of the beneficiary to deal with the money after he has received it. The wholly exceptional case where an injunction may be granted is where it is proved that the bank knows that any demand for payment already made or which may thereafter be made will clearly be fraudulent. But the evidence must be clear, both as to the fact of fraud and as to the bank's knowledge. It would certainly not normally be sufficient that this rests upon the uncorroborated statement of the customer, for irreparable damage can be done to a bank's credit in the relatively brief time which must elapse between the granting of such an injunction and an application by the bank to have it discharged. The appeal will be dismissed.'

1 *Group Josi Re v Walbrook Insurance Co Ltd* [1996] 1 WLR 1152, 1160-1162; *Sirius Insurance Co v FAI General Insurance Ltd* [2003] EWCA Civ 470; [2003] 1 WLR 2214.
2 *Discount Records Ltd v Barclays Bank Ltd* [1975] 1 WLR 315; *R D Harbottle (Mercantile) Ltd v National Westminster Bank Ltd* [1978] QB 146; *Edward Owen Engineering Ltd v Barclays Bank International Ltd* [1978] QB 159; *Bolivinter Oil SA v Chase Manhattan Bank* [1984] 1 Lloyd's Rep 251, also reported in part at [1984] 1 All ER 351n, [1984] 1 WLR 392; *United Trading Corpn SA v Allied Arab Bank Ltd* [1985] 2 Lloyd's Rep 554n; *Tukan Timber Ltd v Barclays Bank plc* [1987] 1 Lloyd's Rep 171; *Themehelp Ltd v West* [1996] QB 84; *Czarnikow-Rionda v Standard Bank* [1999] 2 Lloyd's Rep 187. See also *Society of Lloyd's v Canadian Imperial Bank of Commerce* [1993] 2 Lloyd's Rep 579 and *Group Josi Re v Walbrook Insurance Co Ltd* [1996] 1 WLR 1152.
3 *Edward Owen Engineering Ltd v Barclays Bank International Ltd.* [1978] QB 159.
4 [1978] QB 159 at 171C.
5 [1978] QB 159 at 173A.
6 [1978] QB 159 at 175.
7 [1984] 1 Lloyd's Rep 251.
8 [1984] 1 Lloyd's Rep at 251, [1984] 1 WLR at 393, [1984] 1 All ER at 352.

9.68 In *United Trading Corpn SA v Allied Arab Bank*[1] the Court of Appeal had to consider an argument that every possibility of an innocent explanation had to be excluded by the applicant for the injunction. In rejecting this as an over-statement of the burden of proof the court entered upon a detailed examination of what must be shown and concluded that it was sufficient that it established as seriously arguable that, on the material available, the only realistic inference was that the beneficiary was guilty of fraud. Ackner LJ stated:[2]

> 'The evidence of fraud must be clear, both as to the fact of fraud and as to the bank's knowledge. The mere assertion of allegation of fraud would not be sufficient (see *Bolivinter Oil SA v Chase Manhattan Bank* [1984] 1 Lloyd's Rep 251 per Sir John Donaldson MR at p 257). We would expect the Court to require strong corroborative evidence of the allegation, usually in the form of contemporary documents, particularly those emanating from the buyer. In general, for the evidence of fraud to be clear, we would also expect the buyer to have been given an opportunity to answer the allegation and to have failed to provide any, or any adequate answer in circumstances where one could properly be expected. If the Court considers that on the material before it the only realistic inference to draw is that of fraud, then the seller would have made out a sufficient case of fraud.
>
> While accepting that letters of credit and performance bonds are part of the essential machinery of international commerce (and to delay payment under such documents strikes not only at the proper working of international commerce but also at the reputation and standing of the international banking community), the strength of this proposition can be over-emphasised. As Mr Justice Neill observed in the judgment under appeal, it cannot be in the interests of international commerce or of the banking community as a whole that this important machinery that is provided for traders should be misused for the purposes of fraud. It is interesting to observe that in America, where concern to avoid irreparable damage to international commerce is hardly likely to be lacking, interlocutory relief appears to be more easily obtainable. A temporary restraining order is made essentially on the basis of suspicion of fraud, followed some months later by a further hearing, during which time the applicant has an opportunity of adding to the material which he first put before the Court. Moreover, their conception of fraud is far wider than ours and would appear to include ordinary breach of contract. (See *Dynamics Corp of America v Citizens and Southern National Bank* 356 F Supp 991 (1973); *Harris Corp v NIRT* 691 F 2d 1344 (1982); and *Itek Corp v F N Bank of Boston* 566 F Supp 1210 (1983)). These cases appear to indicate that, for the purpose of obtaining relief in such cases, it is not necessary for an American plaintiff to demonstrate a cause of action against a bank, whereas it is as previously stated, common ground that a plaintiff must in this country show a cause of action. There is no suggestion that this more liberal approach has resulted in the commercial dislocation which has, by implication at least, been suggested would result from rejecting the respondent's submissions as to the standard of proof required from the plaintiffs. Moreover, we would find it an unsatisfactory position if, having established an important exception to what had previously been thought an absolute rule, the Courts in practice were to adopt so restrictive an approach to the evidence required as to prevent themselves from intervening. Were this to be the case, impressive and high-sounding phrases such as 'fraud unravels all' would become meaningless.
>
> The learned Judge concluded that the test to be applied by the Courts is the standard of the hypothetical reasonable banker in possession of all the relevant facts. Unless he can say "this is plainly fraudulent; there cannot be any other explanation", the Courts cannot intervene. We respectfully disagree. The corroborated evidence of a plaintiff and the unexplained failure

of a beneficiary to respond to the attack, although given a fair and proper opportunity, may well make the only realistic inference that of fraud, although the possibility that he may ultimately come forward with an explanation cannot be ruled out. The claim before us is a claim for an interlocutory judgment. The first question is therefore – following the principles laid down in *American Cyanamid Co v Ethicon Ltd* [1975] AC 396 – Have the plaintiffs established that it is seriously arguable that, on the material available, the only realistic inference is that Agromark could not honestly have believed in the validity of its demands on the performance bonds?'

It was held that on the evidence before the court the claimant had not met that test. An important point was that the failure of Agromark, the beneficiary, to explain its defence to the charge of fraud was explicable by the fact that Agromark was contesting the jurisdiction of the English court and so would be wary of taking any steps which might be said to be a submission to the jurisdiction. However, the Court of Appeal in *Turkiye Is Bankasi AS v Bank of China*[3] emphasized that in *United Trading Corp* Lord Justice Ackner was in no way diluting the test in *Edward Owen*, which was firmly established as the proper criterion in a case of alleged fraud.

1 [1985] 2 Lloyd's Rep 554n.
2 [1985] 2 Lloyd's Rep at 861. See also *Group Josi Re v Walbrook Insurance Co Ltd* [1996] 1 WLR 1152 at 1161,*Kvaerner John Brown Ltd v Midland Bank plc* [1998] CLC 446 and *Consolidated Oil Ltd v American Express Bank Ltd* [2002] CLC 488.
3 [1998] 1 Lloyd's Rep 250 at 253.

9.69 The claimant has succeeded in establishing fraud to the satisfaction of the court only in a handful of cases. The fraud in the *Tukan Timber* case[1] involved the forgery of signatures, which in the particular circumstances was capable of clear proof, and indeed the bank did not argue otherwise. The injunction was refused on the ground that the bank had already declined to pay against the documents presented under the credit to date, and in the circumstances an injunction against it was unnecessary. An injunction was granted in *Kvaerner John Brown Ltd v Midland Bank plc*,[2] where the beneficiary under a performance bond presented a certificate that written notice of default had been served on the applicant when it was common ground that it had not. An injunction was also granted in *Themehelp Ltd v West*[3] on evidence that the sellers of a company withheld financial information in their possession from the buyers.

1 [1987] 1 Lloyd's Rep 171.
2 [1998] CLC 446.
3 [1996] QB 84.

Parties and cause of action

9.70 If the beneficiary has not yet presented documents or made a claim under the credit or bond, then the applicant may seek an injunction against him.¹ If it is too late for that, then the applicant will seek an injunction against the bank which is to pay the credit or bond. The bank which must be prevented from paying is the first bank to pay because, once it has paid, its right to be indemnified will arise, with which the court is even less likely to interfere.

1 See further para **9.76** below.

9.71   Under the principle explained in *The Siskina*,¹ an injunction is generally only granted in support of a substantive cause of action against the person restrained.² It was suggested in *Group Josi Re v Walbrook Insurance Co Ltd*³ that letters of credit may be an exception to this rule. However, in *Czarnikow-Rionda v Standard Bank* Rix J rejected an argument that a cause of action was unnecessary because the court could rely on a more general power to intervene where necessary to prevent fraud.⁴

1 [1979] AC 210.
2 On the scope of the principle explained in *The Siskina*, see generally *Fourie v Le Roux* [2007] UK HL 1; [2007] 1 WLR 320; *Masri v Consolidated Contractors* [2008] EWCA Civ 625.
3 [1996] 1 WLR 1152 at 1160.
4 [1999] 2 Lloyd's Rep 187 at 203.

9.72   If the beneficiary has not yet presented documents or made demand, there should be no difficulty in finding a cause of action against him, whether on an actual or quia timet (threatened) basis. The underlying contract may be governed by a foreign law, and may contain an arbitration or foreign jurisdiction clause. But these may be no bar to interlocutory relief by way of injunction in England.

9.73   Where the target of the injunction is the issuing bank (that is, there is no correspondent bank who pays), the applicant has a contract with that bank and no problem as to finding a legal right on which to found the claim arises. Likewise where the paying bank is the advising bank and has not confirmed the credit, the paying bank will act simply as the agent of the issuing bank¹ and an injunction against the issuing bank from paying by itself or by its agents should prevent payment. A confirming bank has in addition given its own undertaking to pay, and so an injunction directly against it is likely to be necessary as it is entitled to make up its own mind how to perform its obligation. The applicant has no contract with it, and so any legal right has to be based in tort on a duty of care. It was recognised as arguable that such a duty existed in a similar situation involving a performance bond in the *United Trading* case.² The situation with a performance bond is usually that the original bond is given by a bank in the beneficiary's country which is backed by a counter-guarantee from the applicant's bank which is in turn backed by a counter-guarantee from the applicant; and there may be further intermediary banks and counter-guarantees. So there is no possibility of any relationship as the agent of a party contracting with the applicant's own bank. In the *United Trading* case it was accepted by the banks as arguable that a bank contemplating payment against an allegedly fraudulent demand by the beneficiary under a performance bond owed a duty of care to the party ultimately liable at the end of the chain. That was in 1984 since when the tendency has been to restrict the ambit of claims in negligence after some years of unpruned growth. In *GKN Contractors Ltd v Lloyds Bank plc*[3] Parker LJ felt bound to follow *United Trading* in this but in terms which suggest that if the point were fully argued no duty would be found. Rix J also expressed doubts about a tortious cause of action in *Czarnikow*.[4] Lastly, with regard to foreign parties, it is necessary for the applicant, as always where foreign entitles are involved, to find a basis for the jurisdiction of the English court over them.[5]

1 See para **6.6** above.
2 *United Trading Corpn SA v Allied Arab Bank Ltd* [1985] 2 Lloyd's Rep 554n at 560.1.
3 (1985) 30 BLR 48 at 62.
4 *Czarnikow-Rionda v Standard Bank* [1999] 2 Lloyd's Rep 187 at 200. See para **12.82** below where it is suggested that no duty of care arises.
5 See **Chapter 13**.

The balance of convenience

9.74 This is likely to raise a further considerable, if not insuperable, difficulty in the way of a claimant. A question which arises on every application for an interim injunction (that is an injunction pending the full trial of the action) is whether the balance of convenience favours the grant or refusal of the injunction. If damages would be a sufficient remedy no injunction will ordinarily be granted.[1] That apart, it will be considered whether more harm will be done by granting or refusing the injunction.[1] Thus in *Harbottle (Mercantile) Ltd v National Westminster Bank Ltd* Kerr J stated:[2]

'The plaintiffs then still face what seems to me to be an insuperable difficulty. They are seeking to prevent the bank from paying and debiting their account. It must then follow that if the bank pays and debits the plaintiffs' account, it is either entitled to do so or not entitled to do so. To do so would either be in accordance with the bank's contract, then the plaintiffs have no cause of action against the bank and, as it seems to me, no possible basis for an injunction against it. Alternatively, if the threatened payment is in breach of contract, which the plaintiffs' writs do not even allege and as to which they claim no declaratory relief, then the plaintiffs would have good claims for damages against the bank. In that event the injunctions would be inappropriate, because they interfere with the bank's obligations to the Egyptian banks, because they might cause greater damage to the bank than the plaintiffs could pay on their undertaking as to damages and because the plaintiffs would then have an adequate remedy in damages. The balance of convenience would in that event be hopelessly weighted against the plaintiffs.'

This was also seen to be an insuperable difficulty in the way of the grant of an injunction in *GKN Contractors v Lloyds Bank*[3] where the plaintiff's dilemma was emphasised: if there is no breach by the bank, there is no case for an injunction; if there is or may be a breach, the bank will be well able to pay such damage as may be suffered, so there is no need for the injunction.

1 For the origin of the modern law, see *American Cyanamid Co v Ethicon Ltd* [1975] AC 396.
2 [1978] QB 146 at 155, cited with approval by the Court of Appeal in *United Trading Corpn SA v Allied Arab Bank Ltd* [1985] 2 Lloyd's Rep 554n at 565.
3 (1985) 30 BLR 48 at 64, 65. And see *Consolidated Oil Ltd v American Express Bank Ltd*, [2002] CLC 488, a performance bond case.

9.75   The factors affecting balance of convenience are normally similar from case to case and ought therefore to result in predictable decisions by the court. The beneficiary (if represented) will usually argue that the whole basis of a documentary credit is that it irrevocably guarantees payment; the bank will argue that if it cannot pay its reputation in the market may be irretrievably damaged (although it is questionable how realistic this is if the bank is simply obeying an order of the court); the applicant will argue that if there is a fraud then it is unlikely that any payment will ever be recovered from the beneficiary at trial. Rix J considered the application of the balance of convenience as a matter of principle in *Czarnikow-Rionda v Standard Bank*,[1] where the bank argued that, even assuming clear fraud, on the balance of convenience an application for an injunction should always fail, and the applicant argued that it should always succeed. He summarised the relevant factors as follows:[2]

> 'In other words, the competing interests become the importance to international trade of the integrity and autonomy of banking commitments on the one hand, and the demands of the allegedly defrauded claimant, assisted as he is by the protection of *Mareva* relief,[3] on the other hand. I say "allegedly defrauded" because, first, ex hypothesi what the claimant alleges to have been a clear case of fraud has not been accepted as such by his bank, and secondly, the matter has to be dealt with at a pre-trial stage.'

Following Kerr J in *Harbottle (Mercantile) Ltd v National Westminster Bank Ltd*[4] and refusing the injunction on the ground of balance of convenience, Rix J concluded:[5]

> 'I do not know that it can be affirmatively stated that a Court would never, as a matter of balance of convenience, injunct a bank from making payment under its letter of credit or performance guarantee obligations in circumstances where a good claim within the fraud exception was accepted by the Court at a pre-trial stage. I do not regard Mr. Justice Kerr and the other Courts which have approved or applied the logic of his "insuperable difficulty" as necessarily saying that it could *never* be done. It is perhaps wise to expect the unexpected, even the presently unforeseeable. All that can be said is that the circumstances in which it should be done have not so far presented themselves, and that it would of necessity take extraordinary facts to surmount this difficulty.'

It is submitted that this approach must be correct. If the evidence of fraud is clear, then the applicant can expect that the issuing bank will not pay; if it does pay despite the evidence then the applicant will not be required to reimburse it, or will have a 'cast-iron' claim for damages.[6] If there is any doubt about the evidence, or the matter requires further investigation, then the beneficiary is entitled to payment and the applicant must be left to pursue him for damages under the sales contract. Whilst this may raise all sorts of problems for the applicant in making a recovery, these are inherent in the transaction when the parties agree to use an irrevocable documentary credit, and the adverse consequences can be mitigated by the availability of freezing orders as discussed below.

1 [1999] 2 Lloyd's Rep 187.
2 [1992] 2 Lloyd's Rep 187 at 204.
3 Rix J regarded the availability of Mareva relief to the applicant as a highly important consideration in the balance of convenience, see para **9.79** below.
4 [1978] QB 146.
5 [1999] 2 Lloyd's Rep 187 at 204.
6 *Tukan Timber Ltd v Barclays Bank plc* [1987] 1 Lloyd's Rep 171 at 177.

Injunctions against the beneficiary

9.76   In the *Harbottle* case the claim was for declarations against the English and Egyptian banks that the beneficiaries were not entitled to claim under the guarantee, and for injunctions restraining the banks from paying under it. The position in the *United Trading* case was similar. In each the beneficiary had made its claim under the guarantee, and the question therefore was whether the banks should be permitted to pay against it. However, if the beneficiary has not yet made a claim, the applicant may seek a quia timet injunction. This may become particularly important in standby credits governed by ISP98 where the bank is not required to notify the applicant that a presentation has been made.[1] There should be no difference in the court's approach to injunctions, whether the applicant is seeking an injunction against paying bank or beneficiary since, as Staughton LJ noted in *Group Josi Re v Walbrook Insurance Co Ltd*:[2]

> 'the effect on the life blood of commerce will be precisely the same whether the bank is restrained from paying or the beneficiary is restrained from asking for payment. That was the view of Sir John Donaldson MR in *Bolivinter Oil SA v Chase Manhattan Bank NA Practice Note* [1984] 1 Lloyd's Rep 251, 254, of Donaldson LJ in *Intraco Ltd v Notis Shipping Corp* [1981] 2 Lloyd's Rep 256, of Lloyd LJ in the *Dong J in Metal* case, 13 July 1993, and of both Clarke and Phillips JJ in the present case.'

It must be remembered also that if the beneficiary is not permitted to claim (or to present documents in the case of a credit) he will lose his opportunity to do so when the expiry date passes. So the effect of an injunction will be to deprive the beneficiary wholly and finally of the benefit for which he contracted.[3]

1 See para **12.38** below.
2 [1996] 1 WLR 1152 at 1161. The position in the United States is the same: *Ground Air Transfer Inc v Westate Airlines Inc* 899 F2d 1269 (1st Cir, 1990).

3 The court has no power to order an extension of the expiry date but in *Themehelp v West* [1996] QB 84 the injunction was made subject to confirmation (which was duly given) by the guarantor that an extension would be allowed.

9.77   However, a different view was taken in *Themehelp Ltd v West*,[1] one of the very rare cases in which an injunction was allowed. There a seller had obtained a guarantee to secure payment of the purchase price. The guarantor was obliged to pay on notice from the seller and would then be indemnified by the buyer. The buyer sought an injunction restraining the seller from making demand on the guarantee for the final instalment on the ground that the contract of sale had been obtained by fraudulent misrepresentation. The majority (Waite LJ and Balcombe LJ) upheld the injunction, considering that different principles should apply when an injunction is sought to restrain the beneficiary without involving the guarantor.[2] Waite LJ said:[3]

'In a case where fraud is raised as between the parties to the main transaction at an early stage, before any question of the enforcement of the guarantee, as between the beneficiary and the guarantor, has yet arisen at all, it does not seem to me that the slightest threat is involved to the autonomy of the performance guarantee if the beneficiary is injuncted from enforcing it in proceedings to which the guarantor is not a party. One can imagine, certainly, circumstances where the guarantor might feel moved to express alarm, or even resentment, if the buyer should obtain, in proceedings to which the guarantor is not a party, injunctive relief placing a restriction on the beneficiary's rights of enforcement. But in truth the guarantor has nothing to fear. There is no risk to the integrity of the performance guarantee, and therefore no occasion for involving the guarantor at that stage in any question as to whether or not fraud is established.'

In both legal and commercial terms it is difficult to support this distinction. There could be no clearer undermining of the autonomy of the credit than an order preventing the beneficiary from drawing on it at the request of the party who instructed it to be opened. Evans LJ, dissenting, said:[4]

'We were informed that there have in fact been close relations between the buyers and their banks, through their respective solicitors, and that these have continued. So the position is this. The banks have felt unable or unwilling to rely upon the "fraud exception" defence. If they are entitled to do so, no injunction against the sellers is necessary. The buyers have attempted a pre-emptive strike which, if the injunction is granted, relieves them of the need to decide whether to rescind their agreement or not, thus retaining the business whilst disputing their liability to pay for it ... The commercial advantages of taking this alternative course for the bank and its customer are obvious. If the injunction is granted, they obtain at least temporary relief from the bank's obligation to pay in a situation where the bank cannot or may not be able to rely upon its own "fraud exception" defence. A bank could (I do not say that these banks have) encourage the customer to undertake the lighter burden of proving merely that the underlying contract could arguably be, or have been, rescinded, not necessarily for fraud. The integrity of the bank's separate undertaking in such a case would be undermined.'

It is suggested that this is the better view.[5]

1 [1996] QB 84.
2 Staughton LJ regarded this holding as 'not essential to the decision': *Group Josi Re v Walbrook Insurance Co Ltd* [1996] 1 WLR 1152 at 1161. See also the comments by Rix J in *Czarnikow-Rionda Sugar Trading Inc v Standard Bank London Ltd* [1999] 2 Lloyd's Rep 187, 202 and Peter Lever QC in *Britten Norman Ltd v State Ownership Fund of Romania* [2000] 1 Lloyd's Rep Bank 315. But see *Kvaerner Singapore Pte Ltd v UDL Shipbuilding (Singapore) Pte Ltd* [1993] 3 SLR 350: the principle in *Edward Owen Engineering Ltd v Barclays Bank International Ltd* [1978] QB 159 has 'no application where the injunction is sought against a party to the underlying contract who seeks to take advantage of the performance guarantee …'.
3 [1996] QB 84 at 98–99.
4 [1996] QB 84 at 102.
5 In *Sirius Insurance Co v FAI General Insurance Ltd* [2003] EWCA Civ 470; [2003] 1 WLR 2214 the Court of Appeal described the majority decision in the *Themehelp* case as 'questionable': See at para 31 per May LJ, with whom Carnwarth LJ agreed at para 34.

9.78 In recent cases English courts have recognised that there are circumstances besides the fraud exception where it may be appropriate to grant interim injunctive relief restraining a beneficiary from calling on a performance bond or guarantee or receiving the product of a call or drawing on a letter of credit.

In the case of *Lorne Stewart Plc v Hermes Kreditversicherungs AG*[1], Garland J granted an injunction restraining the bondsman from paying and the beneficiary from receiving a sum demanded by the beneficiary pursuant to a performance bond on the grounds that the demand was invalid. It should be noted that the bondsman in that case was not a bank and adopted a neutral stance, seeing no commercial mischief in the grant of injunctive relief since the issue depended on the construction of the terms of the bond. The judge held that the terms of the bond required a payment demand to be made before the termination date as defined in the underlying contract but the demand was dated one day after that date. In those circumstances the judge concluded that the position was the same as if no requirement for payment had been made.[2] The claimant had guaranteed the surety's liability under the bond and on those grounds the judge held that the surety clearly owed a duty to the claimant not to expose it to liability under the guarantee.[3] The judge held that in the circumstances the balance of convenience was in favour of granting the injunction (rather than leaving the bondsman free to make payment in the knowledge that the judge had determined that no payment was due) as this would preserve the status quo rather than provoke further litigation between the parties.

In *TTI Team Telecom International Ltd v Hutchison 3G UK Ltd*[4]. HHJ Thornton QC also concluded that a court would intervene on behalf of third party to restrain an 'invalid call':

> 'Examples are where a condition precedent to a call has not yet been fulfilled; where the bond is a "see to it" bond necessitating prior proof of loss by the beneficiary or poor performance by the third party which has not been established;[5] or where the demand or the supporting documents show that the demand does not conform to the requirements imposed by the bond for a valid demand'.

The judge also held that under English law a third party could seek to restrain a beneficiary from calling a bond or receiving the product of a call not only where there has been fraud in setting up or calling the bond but also ' where there is a lack or breach of faith by the beneficiary in threatening a call'. On the facts of the case he declined to grant an injunction on the grounds of breach of faith because he found the allegations of bad faith were 'mere speculation without any factual basis'.[6]

In the unusual case of *Sirius Insurance Co v FAI General Insurance Ltd*[7] the Court of Appeal held that the principle of autonomy of letters of credit did not mean that a beneficiary could draw on a letter of credit when he had expressly agreed with the applicant not to do so unless certain conditions were fulfilled and they had not been fulfilled. In that case there was a related agreement regulating as between the applicant and the beneficiary the terms on which the letter of credit would be established which included express contractual restrictions on the circumstances in which the beneficiary would be entitled to draw on the letter of credit. The Court of Appeal held that to that extent the letter of credit was less than the equivalent of cash and the beneficiary's security was correspondingly restricted. Although those restrictions were not terms of the letter of credit, and although the bank would have been obliged and entitled to honour a request to pay which fulfilled its terms, that did not mean that as between himself and the applicant the beneficiary was entitled to draw on the letter of credit if the express conditions of the underlying agreement were not fulfilled.[8] May LJ was also strongly of the opinion that, had it been necessary to do so on the facts of the case, the court would have granted an injunction restraining the beneficiary from drawing on the letter of credit in breach of express conditions of the agreement with the applicant. He emphasised that the 'unusual' underlying contract and the express terms restricting the circumstances in which the beneficiary was entitled to draw on the letter of credit took the case outside the more typical case where absent fraud, the court would not restrain a beneficiary from drawing on a letter of credit that was payable in accordance with its terms.[9] The House of Lords reversed the decision of the Court of Appeal on other grounds and found it unnecessary to deal with arguments about the autonomy principle.[10]

1 (Unreported, 22 October 2001).
2 See at para 25. See also at para 32: 'A demand made out of time is not a demand at all'.
3 Relying on dicta by Parker LJ in *GKN Contractors v Lloyds Bank plc* (1985) 30 BLR 48 at 64 and 65.
4 [2003] EWHC 762 (TCC); [2003] 1 All ER (Comm) 914.
5 The reference to 'see to it' bonds derives from the distinction drawn by the English courts between, on the one hand, performance or on demand bonds or guarantees which may be called without proof of loss and, on the other, 'see to it guarantees' which require such proof as a precondition of call: See *Trafalgar House Construction (Regions) Ltd v General Surety and Guarantee Co Ltd* [1996] AC 199.The judge said there was little doubt that in the case of the latter a court would restrain the beneficiary from calling the bond where there was no prior proof of loss.
6 [2003] EWHC 762 (TCC); [2003] 1 All ER (Comm) 914 at paras 34, 37, 46, 94-96. On the difficulties with this approach see para **9.30** above.
7 [2003] EWCA Civ 470; [2003] 1 WLR 2214.
8 [2003] EWCA Civ 470; [2003] 1 WLR 2214 at para 27.
9 [2003] EWCA Civ 470; [2003] 1 WLR 2214 at para 29.
10 [2004] UKHL 54; [2004] 1 WLR 325.

Freezing/*Mareva* injunctions

9.79   A freezing injunction, formerly known as a *Mareva* injunction,[1] restrains a defendant from removing his moneys or other assets out of the jurisdiction, or otherwise dealing with them within or without the jurisdiction subject to a limitation in amount, which is usually the amount of the claimant's claim together with an allowance for his likely costs. It is available only where the claimant can establish that there is a risk of the assets being removed or otherwise dissipated. Ordinarily those assets must be in England. Because a freezing injunction is of the nature that it is and is not a preservation order it is an imperfect weapon, though it is often effective to achieve what a claimant requires. In *Z Ltd v A-Z and AA-LL*[2] Lord Denning MR stated of a *Mareva* injunction:

> 'The injunction does not prevent payment under letter of credit or under a bank guarantee (...[citations]...); but it may apply to the proceeds as and when received by or for the defendant.'

Similarly, in the passage quoted from *Bolivinter*[3] the court made the caveat 'although restrictions may well be imposed on the freedom of the beneficiary to deal with the money after he has received it'.

1 So called from case of *Mareva Cia Naviera SA v International Bulkcarriers SA* [1980] 1 All ER 213n, [1975] 2 Lloyd's Rep 509. See now CPR Pt 25.1(f) which uses the new terminology of 'freezing injunction'.
2 [1982] QB 558 at 574.
3 *Bolivinter Oil SA v Chase Manhattan Bank* [1984] 1 Lloyd's Rep 251: see para **9.67** above.

9.80   A buyer who suspects his seller of fraud or simply of providing goods which do not fully accord with the contract of sale, may not fancy his chances of enforcing his claim against the seller if the credit is operated and the seller receives the price and is free to do what he likes with it. For the seller may be in a jurisdiction where proceedings against him will be difficult, or he may become insolvent, or disappear. Instead of trying to prevent the bank paying, which even in the case of fraud will face the great difficulties already discussed, the buyer may consider an application for a freezing injunction. Because the order does not interfere with the operation of the credit, but restrains the use of the proceeds of its operation, the buyer does not have to bring himself within the fraud exception to the autonomy rule to claim a freezing injunction. The claim for a freezing injunction may be supported by a simple claim by the buyer against the seller for breach of contract. A freezing injunction is ordinarily drafted to affect only assets within the jurisdiction of the English court. Where it is served upon a bank the order should be confined by its terms to the defendant's bank accounts themselves and should not extend to the defendant's assets as may be comprised by a documentary credit itself. The bank must be free to honour such credit in accordance with its terms.[1] Although worldwide freezing injunctions may be made in exceptional circumstances[2] it is thought unlikely that circumstances will arise in which an English court would make an order affecting money paid under a letter of credit by a bank abroad.[3] Similarly, an order requiring a bank to pay the money into an account in England would be an unjustified interference in the operation of the credit if the credit was payable abroad.[4] So an order will only be of use where a credit is payable within the jurisdiction. Then, if the other requirements for an order are satisfied, the beneficiary can be restrained from disposing of money within the jurisdiction (this assumes, of course, the only asset within the jurisdiction will be the proceeds of sale received from the credit: if there are other assets, these will introduce fresh considerations and ease the buyer's situation).

1 *Themehelp v West* [1996] QB 84 at 103 (dissenting judgment of Evans LJ); *Britten Norman Ltd v State Ownership Fund of Romania* [2000] 1 Lloyd's Rep Bank 315.
2 *Z Ltd v A-Z and AA-LL* [1982] QB 558 at 591.
3 See *Derby & Co Ltd v Weldon (No 3 and 4)* [1990] Ch 65.
4 *Britten Norman Ltd v State Ownership Fund of Romania* [2000] 1 Lloyd's Rep Bank 315.

9.81   The position is illustrated by the case of *Intraco Ltd v Notis Shipping Corpn, The Bhoja Trader*.[1] The defendants sold their vessel, the *Bhoja Trader*, to the claimants who provided a bank guarantee for part of the price. The vessel was delivered but shortly afterwards it was arrested and the claimants had to pay money to secure its release and suffered losses due to cargo cancellations. The sellers had no assets in England other than their rights under the guarantee. An ex parte injunction was granted restraining them from calling on the guarantee. This was discharged on the basis that such an injunction should not be granted unless there was fraud. But an injunction was granted in its place restraining the sellers from removing from the jurisdiction or otherwise disposing of their assets, in particular the proceeds of the guarantee, save in so far as they exceeded a nominated sum. In the Court of Appeal it was established that the guarantee was payable in Greece and not in London and so the court discharged the injunction, stating 'If this guarantee is to be treated as cash it must be treated as cash in Greece.' In its judgment the court referred to the rule that in the absence of fraud an injunction would not be granted to interfere with a seller's right to call on a bank to make payment under a letter of credit or a bank guarantee. It continued:[2]

> 'The learned Judge went on to say that this did not prevent the Court, in an appropriate case, from imposing a *Mareva* injunction upon the fruits of the letter of credit or guarantee. Again we agree. It is the natural corollary of the proposition that a letter of credit or bank guarantee is to be treated as cash that when the bank pays and cash is received by the beneficiary, it should be subject to the same restraints as any other of his cash assets. Enjoining the beneficiary from removing the cash asset from the jurisdiction is not the same as taking action, whether by injunction or an order staying execution, which will prevent him obtaining the cash (see *Montecchi v Shimco (UK) Ltd* [1980] 1 Lloyd's Rep 50, [1979] 1 WLR 1180).
>
> If therefore this bank guarantee had provided for payment in London, we should have agreed wholly with the learned Judge's judgment, . . .'

The court reserved the position where the beneficiary of a guarantee could, at his option, call for payment within or without the jurisdiction. It is suggested that in those circumstances he could not be forced to exercise his option by calling for payment in England. For there would be no grounds on which to do so, and it is established by the cases referred to that the court will not prevent a beneficiary calling a bank guarantee. If the beneficiary then called for payment abroad, the situation would be covered by the decision in the *Intraco* case.

1 [1981] 2 Lloyd's Rep 256.
2 [1981] 2 Lloyd's Rep 256 at 258.

9.82   The availability of a freezing injunction as alternative protection for the buyer is an important factor in persuading the court *not* to grant on order restraining payment by the bank. See Rix J in *Czarnikow-Rionda v Standard Bank*:[1]

'…where the balance of convenience is being considered, it seems to me that the availability of the protection of *Mareva* relief to a claimant must be a highly important consideration and goes very far to undermine [the buyer's] complaint about the difficulties of his position if the credit is drawn upon.'

In *Themehelp*, Evans LJ, dissenting, would have refused an injunction restraining payment under the performance guarantee, but said that the case 'cries out for *Mareva* relief…' and the injunction sought by the applicant against the bank was 'an unwarranted extension of the *Mareva* jurisdiction'.[2]

1 [1999] 2 Lloyd's Rep 187 at 203.
2 *Themehelp Ltd v West* [1996] QB 84 at 103.

Potton Homes Ltd v Coleman Contractors (Overseas) Ltd[1]

9.83   Here both parties were English companies. The plaintiffs agreed to supply prefabricated homes to the defendants in Libya. The defendants were in arrears with their payments but alleged defects in the houses delivered. The plaintiffs had given a performance bond. The judge at first instance gave judgment for the plaintiffs for £89,621 but stayed execution on the ground that the defendants had a counterclaim which they were entitled to set off against it. A call had been made by the defendants on the bond for £68,816. The judge held that following authority he was not able to prevent the call. Nor, he held, were the facts such that in reliance on *The Bhoja Trader*,[2] he was justified in granting a Mareva order restraining dealing with the proceeds of the call. Nonetheless he considered that the proceeds should be frozen and that he had power to do so under RSC Ord 29, r 2(1) (which relates to the preservation of property involved in an action). This was set aside by the Court of Appeal. Eveleigh LJ took the view that documentary credits and performance bonds were not necessarily to be treated in the same way, particularly so far as the buyer and seller were concerned. He stated:

> 'As between buyer and seller the underlying contract cannot be disregarded so readily. If the seller has lawfully avoided the contract *prima facie*, it seems to me he should be entitled to restrain the buyer from making use of the performance bond. Moreover, in principle I do not think it possible to say that in no circumstances whatsoever, apart from fraud, will the court restrain the buyer. The facts of each case must be considered. If the contract is avoided or if there is a failure of consideration between buyer and seller for which the seller undertook to procure the issue of the performance bond, I do not see why, as between seller and buyer, the seller should not [?] be unable to prevent a call upon the bond by the mere assertion that the bond is to be treated as cash in hand. It is true that in *Edward Owen Ltd v Barclays Bank* it was unsuccessfully submitted that the failure of the buyer to procure a letter of credit in accordance with the contract terms should entitle the plaintiffs to an injunction against the bank. That case, however, was not concerned with the position as between buyer and seller, ...
>
> For a large construction project the employer may agree to provide finance (perhaps by way of advance payments) to enable the contractor to undertake the works. The contractor will almost certainly be asked to provide a performance bond. If the contractor were unable to perform because the employer failed to provide the finance, it would seem wrong to me if the court was not entitled to have regard to the terms of the underlying contract and could be prevented from considering the question whether or not to restrain the employer by the mere assertion that a performance bond is like a letter of credit.
>
> There are differences between a performance bond and a letter of credit. They operate from different directions. When a bank pays under a letter of credit upon receipt of the documents, those documents provide some security, namely, title to the goods themselves. There is no such security in the case of the performance bond.
>
> I have made these observations in order to sound a note of caution. I would not wish in these interlocutory proceedings to say more than is necessary for the purpose of deciding the matter with which we have to deal. I particularly would not wish to add to the entrenched status of the bond beyond the limits set in the decided cases. I would wish at least to leave it open for consideration how far the bond is to be treated as cash in hand as between buyer and seller.'

He went on to hold that as the judge had found that there were no grounds for a *Mareva* injunction the court should not interfere with the bargain which the parties had made by restraining the ability of the defendants to obtain the money which the bond provided on call. The other member of the court, May LJ, held that, as the judge had found that the facts did not justify a *Mareva* order, he had been wrong to make any order freezing the proceeds of the call. Both Lords Justice held that the court had no power under RSC Ord 29 r 2(1) in the circumstances. This was not a case where the demand was alleged to be fraudulent. The remarks of Eveleigh LJ relating to the position of the buyer and seller are, it is suggested, in conflict with the statement of Donaldson LJ in *The Bhoja Trader*[3] 'In refusing to interfere with the sellers' right to call upon the bank to make payment under its guarantee, the learned judge acted in conformity with the well-established principle that the Court will not grant such an injunction unless fraud is involved' and also with those of Staughton LJ in *Group Josi Re v Walbrook Insurance Co Ltd*.[4] The Court of Appeal of Hong Kong declined in *Guangdong Transport Ltd v Ancora Transport NV*[5] to apply the dictum of Eveleigh LJ and declined to hold that the position between buyer and seller was any different.

1 (1984) 28 BLR 19.
2 *Intraco Ltd v Notis Shipping Corpn, The Bhoja Trader* [1981] 2 Lloyd's Rep 256.
3 [1981] 2 Lloyd's Rep 256 at 257.2.
4 [1996] 1 WLR 1152 at 1161.
5 [1987] HKLR 923.

The appointment of a receiver

9.84　Where a credit is payable in England, there may be a possibility for a buyer who suspects his seller of fraud or simply of providing goods which do not accord with the contract of sale, of applying to the court for the appointment of a receiver and for an order that the payment under the credit be made not to the seller, but to the receiver pending the resolution of the dispute between the buyer and the seller.[1] This would have the advantage of putting the money into the hands of an independent third party whereas the effect of a freezing injunction is only to prevent the seller dissipating it. It is understood that one such application has been successfully made.[2] So the jurisdiction and practice in relation to the appointment of receivers and payments under letters of credit have yet to be established. The appointment of a receiver has much the same effect as the sequestration effected by order of the Swiss courts in *Camilla Cotton Oil Co v Granadex SA*,[3] where the buyers paid through the letter of credit and then, on the ground of claims against the sellers on other contracts, sequestrated the payment before it could be transferred to the sellers. The difficulty with the jurisdiction may be that although an order can be framed so that the receiver takes the payment on behalf of the sellers, his intervention does in reality prevent the seller taking possession of the money due under the credit, which is at least contrary to the spirit of the *Edward Owen* line of cases, and is probably contrary to the ratio of the decision of the Court of Appeal in the *Potton Homes* case.[4] A freezing injunction, on the other hand, permits the seller to have possession, but seeks to tie his hands thereafter.

1 The jurisdiction to appoint a receiver is given in wide terms by the Supreme Court Act 1981, s 37: see, generally, Gee *Commercial Injunctions* (5th edn) ch 16.
2 The judgment was given in chambers and is therefore not public.
3 [1976] 2 Lloyd's Rep 10, HL; reversing [1975] 1 Lloyd's Rep 470, CA, see the facts at 472.2.
4 See para 9.83.

Where the operation of the credit requires the cooperation of the buyer: orders under the Supreme Court Act 1981, s 39

9.85   Some credits include among the documents which are to be presented to obtain payment a document which is to be executed by the buyer or his agent. Such a provision is inserted by the buyer to obtain protection for himself, for example, by enabling him to certify that he has inspected the goods to be shipped. But it also enables him to frustrate the credit by refusing to provide the document when he should. In appropriate circumstances the court will order the buyer to execute the document so that it can be presented to the bank and payment obtained, and on default it can order a third party (who is likely to be an officer of the court) to execute the document on the buyer's behalf. This course was followed in *Astro Exito Navegacion SA v Southland Enterprise Co Ltd (No 2) (Chase Manhattan Bank NA intervening)*.[1] The underlying contract was for the sale of a ship. Payment was by letter of credit confirmed by a London bank. By an amendment to the credit accepted by the seller under protest it was provided that the notice of readiness was to be signed and accepted by the buyers' agents. The buyers refused to accept the notice of readiness. The letter of credit would expire on 30 October. The judge made an order that the buyers by their agents sign the notice of readiness by noon on 28 October, failing which a master of the Supreme Court was to sign the order on behalf of the buyers under s 47 of the Supreme Court of Judicature (Consolidation) Act 1925 (now s 39 of the Supreme Court Act 1981). He also ordered the buyers to instruct the issuing bank in Taiwan to instruct the confirming bank in London to release the full amount of the letter of credit. The proceeds were to be paid into an interest-bearing account in the joint names of the buyers' and the sellers' solicitors. The sellers presented the documents to the bank including the notice of readiness signed by a master of the Supreme Court. But the bank refused to pay. The House of Lords held that the order of the judge was within the ambit of s 47 and was properly made.[2] The facts in this case may be compared with those in *Elder Dempster Lines Ltd v Ionic Shipping Agency Inc and Midland Bank*.[3] There the claimants agreed to sell a vessel to the first defendants. The deposit was guaranteed by a letter of credit issued by the second defendants payable against a bill drawn by the plaintiffs and first defendants jointly. The claimants obtained an order that the first defendants join with them in drawing a bill. But the first defendants did not comply with the order and the credit expired, no order having been obtained under s 47 of the 1925 Act. The claimants' claim against the bank failed. The power under s 39 of the 1981 Act may be a useful power where documents are to be presented under a credit in England and one of the documents requires the cooperation of the buyer.

1 [1983] 2 AC 787.
2 When the sellers' action against the bank for non-payment came to trial their claim failed because it was held that the documents did not appear on their face to accord with the credit:

in particular there was nothing to show that the gas free certificate had the approval of the Harbour Bureau of Kaohsiung: *Astro Exito Navegacion SA v Chase Manhattan Bank NA, The Messiniaki Tolmi* [1986] 1 Lloyd's Rep 455 discussed at para **8.78** in relation to the description of the vessel on the invoice.
3 [1968] 1 Lloyd's Rep 529.

Duty of full disclosure

9.86 Applications for injunctions restraining payment or freezing the proceeds on grounds of fraud are often made in the first instance without notice to the beneficiary,[1] and sometimes without notice to the bank. On applications without notice the applicant and its lawyers have a duty to make full and frank disclosure of all material facts to the court. The court may discharge the injunction subsequently if it is discovered that inadequate disclosure was made.[2] Where an applicant seeks to restrain the issuing bank from paying, the bank may, for the reasons explained above,[3] tacitly support the application; if so, then anything which might be regarded as cooperation or collusive non-opposition should be disclosed.[4]

1 Governed by CPR Pt 23, Practice Direction – Applications, para 3.
2 This rule is not invariable but will be applied to meet the justice of the case: *Memory Corporate plc v Sidhu (No 2)* [2000] 1 WLR 1443; *Arena Corps Ltd v Schroeder* [2003] EWHC 1089 (Ch).
3 See para **9.40**.
4 *Czarnikow-Rionda v Standard Bank* [1999] 2 Lloyd's Rep 187 at 206–207.

Future development

9.87 It may be thought that, with their emphasis on the individual contracts and on the high standard of proof which is required, the English courts have taken a course which is unduly favourable to the beneficiary whose good faith is in dispute. This may be particularly the case where dubious demands are made under standby credits or demand guarantees (eg performance bonds) in situations where, once the money has been paid by the bank or banks within the jurisdiction of the English court, there is little realistic chance of its recovery whatever the merits of the account party's position. The sums involved are often very large. If English law is to develop further in this area, the way forward must be towards establishing a process whereby, in appropriate cases, rights under credits and guarantees can be held in abeyance while the underlying dispute is investigated. This, of course, would be directly contrary to the principle of autonomy and great care would be needed. But the principle should not be allowed to become a cause of injustice.

9.88 The United Nations Convention on Independent Guarantees and Standby Letters of Credit, which is not in force in England, illustrates a possible international approach. Article 20 of the Convention sets out the criteria for the grant of 'provisional measures' where fraud has been established:

'**Article 20 Provisional court measures:**

(1) Where, on an application by the principal/applicant or the instructing party, it is shown that there is a high probability that, with regard to a demand made, or expected to be made, by the beneficiary, one of the circumstances referred to in subparagraphs (a), (b) and (c) of paragraph (1) of article 19 is present,[1] the court, on the basis of immediately available strong evidence, may:

(a) Issue a provisional order to the effect that the beneficiary does not receive payment, including an order that the guarantor/issuer hold the amount of the undertaking, or

(b) Issue a provisional order to the effect that the proceeds of the undertaking paid to the beneficiary are blocked, taking into account whether in the absence of such an order the principal/applicant would be likely to suffer serious harm.'

Note the test: it must be shown 'that there is a high probability' of fraud based on 'immediately available strong evidence'.

1 See para **9.62** above.

Chapter 10

Transfer and Assignment

A TRANSFER

Introduction

10.1   The transfer of credits is a well-established practice which is now regulated by Article 38 of the UCP. Article 38 restates in simplified form the rules regarding transfer in UCP 500 Article 48. The principal addition is a requirement that the second beneficiary make presentation to the transferring bank.

Function

10.2   Where the seller in a transaction in respect of which payment is to be provided through a credit is buying the goods from a third party, he may use the transfer of the credit to pay the party selling to him. When the credit has been transferred to the third party (who is called the second beneficiary), the third party can present documents under the credit including his own invoice and will receive payment. Where the seller is buying from more than one third party he may transfer an appropriate part of the credit to each of his sellers. Assuming of course that the price the second beneficiary receives is lower than that provided for by the credit as between the buyer and the original seller, the seller (called the first beneficiary) can present his own invoice to the bank and receive in payment the difference in price between his invoice and what has already been invoiced by the second beneficiary. In this way he receives his profit on the transaction. The bank then substitutes his invoice for that of the second beneficiary and the documents are passed on and will reach the buyer. The buyer will know from the fact that the party selling to him has asked for the credit to be transferable that the seller is acting as a middleman (if that was not already known to him) but he will not know who the third party is unless this is revealed by other documents such as the transport documents which might name the third party seller as the consignor.[1] Even then he will not know the profit which the first beneficiary is making on the transaction. The importance of the first beneficiary's ability to conceal the name of the party selling to him lies in the fact that otherwise the buyer might cut him out on future transactions dealing directly and more cheaply with the third party seller. An alternative means to this end, which may be more effective for these purposes, is to use a back-to-back credit as considered in **Chapter 2**.[2]

1 UCP Article 14.k permits acceptance of transport documents which indicate as the consignor of the goods a party other than the beneficiary of the credit.
2 See para **2.28**.

10.3   In *Jackson v Royal Bank of Scotland*[1] it was said that a transferable letter of credit had three functions:

(1) to provide a secure source of payment, not only for the seller of the goods but also for the first beneficiary as the middleman;
(2) to enable the first beneficiary to conceal the identity of the seller of the goods from the applicant; and
(3) to enable the first beneficiary to keep confidential from the applicant the profit which he is making on the transaction.

Lord Hope commented as follows:[2]

> 'The duty of confidence arises from the acknowledged need for the issuing bank to protect its customer from disclosure of his level of profit and from the danger that if that level of profit is disclosed his purchaser will go instead direct to the customer's own supplier … the right of the first beneficiary to substitute his own invoice for that of the second beneficiary and draw on the credit according to its pre-transfer terms is an important part of the transfer regime. It enables the first beneficiary to keep confidential from the applicant the amount of his profit from the transaction. For sound commercial reasons he is entitled to keep the amount of that profit secret. The information is confidential to the first beneficiary. It is the duty of the issuing bank to protect that confidentiality'

In that case the bank inadvertently sent to the applicant (rather than to the first beneficiary) a copy of the second beneficiary's invoice and thereby disclosed to the applicant the amount of the first beneficiary's profit with the consequence that the applicant decided for the future to deal directly with the second beneficiary. It was held that the bank owed a duty of confidentiality to the first beneficiary in respect of the second beneficiary's prices and that the first beneficiary was entitled to damages for lost profit arising from their disclosure to the applicant. In the absence of any provision in the letter of credit limiting or excluding liability for loss of repeat business the only limit was the point in time beyond which it became too speculative to say whether any loss had been sustained, which on the facts represented a period of about four years.

1 [2005] 1 WLR 377.
2 [2005] 1 WLR 377 at para 27.

Transferability – a trap

10.4 Where a seller wishes to transfer a credit to provide the means of payment to his own seller, he will agree with his buyer that the credit shall be transferable, and the credit will be designated as transferable when it is issued. This will not, however, give him a right to require transfer. It will only give him a right to request transfer, at least where the UCP apply. The bank to which the request is made may refuse it outright or it may only agree to it to such extent and in such manner as it will accept. The Privy Council so held in respect of Article 46 of the 1974 Revision of the Uniform Customs in *Bank Negara Indonesia 1946 v Lariza (Singapore) Pte*

Ltd,[1] and Article 38 of UCP 600 is in even clearer terms. The first two paragraphs of Article 38 provide:

> **'Article 38 Transferable Credits:**
> a. A bank is under no obligation to transfer a credit except to the extent and in the manner expressly consented to by that bank.
> b. For the purpose of this article:
>   Transferable credit means a credit that specifically states it is "transferable". A transferable credit may be made available in whole or in part to another beneficiary ("second beneficiary") at the request of the beneficiary ("first beneficiary").'

1 [1988] AC 583.

10.5 The unhappy story in the *Bank Negara* case was as follows. Lariza were commodity dealers and agreed to sell palm oil to Bakrie, and they contracted to purchase the oil from Ban Lee. On Bakrie's application, a credit which was designated as transferable was issued by Bank Negara and advised through the Bank of Canton, Lariza's own bankers. Lariza requested the Bank of Canton and then Bank Negara to transfer the credit to Ban Lee. Both refused, the Bank of Canton on the grounds that the credit was badly drafted and that in any event they were only the advising bank. So no credit was opened in favour of Ban Lee who sued Lariza and obtained judgment. Bakrie had become insolvent and had gone into liquidation. Lariza tried to recover its loss from Bank Negara for breach of its alleged undertaking to transfer the credit. The Privy Council held that before a bank was obliged to effect a transfer under the terms of Article 46 of the 1974 Revision the bank must have consented to the particular transfer requested. In overruling the Court of Appeal of Singapore the Board held that the consent of a bank requested to transfer a credit was not to be found in its agreement to designate the credit as transferable: a separate consent to the particular transfer was required. The Board also stated:

> 'The Court of Appeal was concerned that, unless the beneficiary had not only a right to instruct the issuing bank to effect a transfer, but also a right to have his instructions complied with, the whole purpose of his having a transferable letter of credit could readily be defeated. That may be so, although, without expert evidence on the relevant banking practice, it is not possible to estimate the likelihood of this happening at all frequently.'[1]

1 [1988] AC 583 at 599H.

10.6 What Lariza might have done was to open a new credit through the Bank of Canton on a back-to-back basis but avoiding the unsatisfactory drafting of the first credit. This would not have been possible if the Bank of Canton were not prepared to open a new credit because they would only do so on the strength of a satisfactory and workable credit which would back the new one: they presumably felt that the first credit's operation was likely to give rise to problems and the documents might be refused.

10.7 It might be thought desirable that, if banks are to have the right to refuse to transfer transferable credits, there should at least be some limit on the exercise of that right. It is suggested in *Benjamin's Sale of Goods*[1] that a bank should only be entitled to refuse to transfer a transferable credit on reasonable grounds, drawing an analogy with the limited right of a landlord to refuse to grant his consent to the transfer of a lease (although it is noted that the basis of the limitation there is statutory). If this were the case, it would cause uncertainty which would be undesirable, in particular as the beneficiary might not know the reasons for the refusal. But in any event there seems no basis on which to imply such a limitation; if it were intended, it could easily have been stated in the UCP.

1 (7th edn) para 23-078.

10.8 The fact that a transferable credit can only be transferred if the bank to whom request is made agrees to it is something of a contradiction in terms. If the arrangements resulting from transfer were always simple, there would be a strong argument for saying that it was undesirable that there should be such a right of refusal. But they are not always simple, and it is understandable that banks should wish to keep the right to say no where they anticipate that a transfer may lead to difficulties for them and the parties with whom they deal. If they are to have that right, it is probably correct that they should have an unfettered right, subject to acting in good faith, leaving it to their good sense in each case to determine whether there are objections to a transfer, rather than attempting to impose limitations which might lead to uncertainties and disputes.

Which bank should effect transfer?

10.9 Article 38.b defines 'Transferring bank' as follows:

> 'a nominated bank that transfers the credit or, in a credit available with any bank, a bank that is specifically authorized by the issuing bank to transfer and that transfers the credit. An issuing bank may be a transferring bank'.

'Nominated bank' is defined in Article 2 as meaning 'the bank with which the credit is available or any bank in the case of a credit available with any bank'.

10.10 In the case of a credit available with any bank, the terms of Article 38 provide for an issuing bank to authorise a bank as the transferring bank. The equivalent Article in UCP 500, Article 48, provided that request may be made to the bank specifically authorised 'in the Credit as a transferring bank'. The normal practice would be to specify the transferring bank in the credit itself, but the change in wording in UCP

600 appears to permit the issuing bank to authorise a transferring bank subsequent to the issue of the credit. The consequences of the issuing bank being the transferring bank have not been followed through in Article 38.i, which assumes that the transferring bank will be presenting documents to the issuing bank.[1]

1 If it is a negotiating bank, it may well be presenting documents to a correspondent bank.
2 See paras **10.28** et seq.

Mechanics: substitution of invoice and drafts

10.11   The procedure of transfer has already been outlined in the preceding paragraphs. Article 38.h refers to the first beneficiary's right to substitute his own invoice and draft (if called for by the credit) for those of the second beneficiary. This enables him to provide the documents which the credit as issued requires and thus to make effective his own right to be paid. Article 38.h provides:

> 'h   The first beneficiary has the right to substitute its own invoice and draft, if any for those of a second beneficiary for an amount not in excess of that stipulated in the credit, and upon such substitution the first beneficiary can draw under the credit for the difference, if any, between his invoice and the invoice of a second beneficiary.'

An example of transfer where credit freely available

10.12   Let it be supposed that the Alpha Bank issues a transferable credit which is advised and confirmed by the Beta Bank to Export Ltd, the beneficiary. The credit provides for deferred payment 60 days after bill of lading date, and is 'a credit available with any bank'. The credit names Beta Bank as the transferring bank. Export Ltd is buying the goods from Sources SA, which banks with Gamma Bank. Export will request Beta Bank to transfer to Sources so much of the credit as will pay to Sources the price payable to Sources by Export. Beta Bank will then advise Sources of the credit as transferred. Sources can then approach his bank, Gamma bank, to ask if it will act as a nominated bank under the transferred credit, which is freely available, and provide a deferred payment undertaking and then prepay or discount that undertaking. If it agrees, on receipt of documents Gamma Bank will check them against the credit, and if they comply will buy them from Sources, crediting Sources with the discounted value, that is, less a discount to take account of the delay in payment under the credit. Gamma Bank will pass the documents to Beta Bank which will check them in its turn. It will substitute for the invoice of Sources the invoice which Export will supply to it and pass the documents to Alpha Bank. Alpha Bank will check them again and will then deal with them in accordance with its arrangements with its customer, the buyer/applicant. Sixty days after bill of lading date Alpha Bank is bound to pay Beta Bank the full amount of the invoice of Export.[1] Beta Bank will pay to Gamma Bank the amount of Sources' invoice, and the difference to Export.

1 This is subject to the reimbursement arrangements between them.

Transfer of parts of a credit: no second transfer

10.13   As has been indicated a beneficiary will usually only wish to transfer such part of the credit as will enable him to pay his supplier, leaving a portion to himself representing his profit. He may also be using more than one supplier. He will then want to transfer part of the credit to one and part to another, while still retaining a balance for himself. In the past credits frequently stated that they were 'transferable and divisible' or used a similar wording. This concept should now be incorporated by the use of the single word 'transferable'. This is the effect of Article 38.b and 38.d.[1] Article 38.d also prohibits second transfers at the request of second beneficiary to a subsequent beneficiary (but not re-transfers to the first beneficiary). Article 38.d provides:

> 'd.   A credit may be transferred in part to more than one second beneficiary provided partial drawings or shipments are allowed. A transferred credit cannot be transferred at the request of a second beneficiary to any subsequent beneficiary. The first beneficiary is not considered to be a subsequent beneficiary.'

1 UCP 500 Article 48.b stated that terms such as 'divisible', 'factionable', 'assignable' and 'transmissable' did not render a credit transferable and were to be disregarded if present. Although this rule has not been replicated in UCP 600, these terms should continue to be disregarded.

Terms of the credit as transferred

10.14   Article 38.g provides:

> 'g.   The transferred credit must accurately reflect the terms and conditions of the credit, including confirmation, if any, with the exception of:
> (i)   the amount of the credit,
> (ii)   any unit price stated therein,
> (iii)   the expiry date,
> (iv)   the period for presentation, or,
> (v)   the latest shipment date or given period for shipment,
>
> any or all of which may be reduced or curtailed.

> The percentage for which insurance cover must be effected may be increased in such a way as to provide the amount of cover stipulated in the credit, or these articles.
>
> The name of the first beneficiary may be substituted for that of the applicant in the credit.
>
> If the name of the applicant is specifically required by the credit to appear in any document other than the invoice, such requirement must be reflected in the transferred credit.'

Accordingly, the matters that can be varied are:

(1) The amount of the credit, and any unit prices. This enables the first beneficiary to receive his profit on the transaction and to pay to the second beneficiary or beneficiaries what is due to them.

(2) The expiry date. It might be thought that the purpose of this was to enable the first beneficiary to shorten the periods so he could be sure of being able to present his own invoice within the periods limited by the credit. However, it appears from Article 38.i and 38.j[1] that he need not do so. Article 38.i institutes a procedure whereby the transferring bank may demand the invoice (and draft) from the first beneficiary and if he fails to supply them 'on first demand' the bank can deliver the documents to the issuing bank with the second beneficiary's invoice and drafts. This suggests that the time limits are irrelevant to the first beneficiary's performance of the contract. Secondly, the wording of Article 38.j shows that the second beneficiary may have the full period of the credit in which to present documents. These provisions are considered further below.[2] Although it might be expected that it would be more prominently stated, this makes it clear that the time limits which would apply to presentation under the original credit do not apply to the first beneficiary once the credit has been transferred. The only purpose in curtailing the periods as permitted by Article 38.g would appear to be to enable the credit as transferred to match the contract of sale between the first and second beneficiaries where this sets a stricter timetable.

(3) The period for presentation. Article 14.c relates to the period after shipment within which presentation must be made. The points are to be made as in the previous paragraph.

(4) The latest shipment date or period for shipment. This is of a different nature because it does not directly affect the time for presentation of documents. But the purpose for which it is permitted appears to be the same.

(5) The percentage for which insurance cover must be effected. This enables the first beneficiary to ensure that the cover provided by the second beneficiary will be sufficient to enable the first beneficiary to be paid under the credit as he will have to provide a certificate which fully covers the value of the cargo to the applicant. Thus, if the credit requires insurance to the CIF value of the goods which is £110,000, and the CIF price payable to the second beneficiary is £98,000, the credit as transferred should be amended to require insurance for 112.25% of CIF

value as per the documents to be presented by the second beneficiary. This will mean that the first beneficiary's level of profit is disclosed, which is a disadvantage of transfer.

(6) The name of the first beneficiary can be substituted for that of the original applicant but if the applicant's name is to appear in any document other than the invoice it must appear. The invoice will of course be substituted. If the name of the applicant does have to appear, this will destroy part of the confidentiality which the system of transfer is designed to maintain.

(7) Drafts. Drafts are not referred to in Article 38.g and it would appear from this provision by itself that any term of the credit relating to drafts cannot be varied. As considered in the next paragraph Article 38.i and j show otherwise.

1 Article 38.j: para **10.17** below.
2 See para **10.16** below.

Drafts

10.15   If the credit requires drafts, they will almost certainly be the drafts of the first beneficiary. Article 38.g does not include any provision as to drafts among the terms which exceptionally may be varied. However Article 38.h refers to the right of the first beneficiary 'to substitute his own invoice and draft for those of a second beneficiary'. So if the credit as originally drawn requires sight drafts drawn on the issuing bank it would appear that the credit as transferred should require drafts so drawn by the second beneficiary. The first beneficiary will in due course substitute his draft for the full amount to be drawn under the credit.

Date for presentation of substituted documents by first beneficiary

10.16   It has been observed that the terms of the credit as transferred relating to the expiry date, the period for presentation of documents and the latest shipment date or period for shipment may be reduced or curtailed.[1] In connection with this it was pointed out that it follows from Article 38.i and .j, particularly the latter, that the first beneficiary need not provide his invoices (and drafts) for substitution within the period limited by the credit either originally or as transferred.[2] He may provide them to the transferring bank[3] in advance of the presentation of documents by the second beneficiary to await their arrival. That is the prudent course. Or he may wait until the bank demands them from him, when he must provide them 'on first demand'. 'On demand' means that the party shall have a reasonable time to respond to the demand according to the nature of the thing to be done.[4] The addition of the word 'first' simply emphasises that the bank need not give the first beneficiary a reminder, though no doubt it would be courteous and perhaps avoid a dispute if the bank did check with the first beneficiary what the position was. Thus there is to be permitted a reasonable time for the provision of the documents to the bank, after which the bank may send the documents received by it from the second beneficiary to the issuing bank. This is a drastic step because the first beneficiary then loses his right to payment. Although the UCP do not expressly say so, it is to be inferred that the issuing bank is entitled to be paid in its turn by the applicant against the second beneficiary's documents.

1 See para **10.14** above.
2 This is confirmed by *Opinions* (1980–1981), ICC No 399, Ref 83. See also Case 286 in *More Case Studies on Documentary Credits*, ICC No 489.
3 Where the transferring bank is the issuing bank because it is the accepting bank – see above, he will provide them through the advising bank.
4 See *Toms v Wilson* (1862) 32 LJQB 33 at 37 per Blackburn J (affd at 32 LJQB 382).

Transfer to another place (bank)

10.17　Article 38.j makes it clear that the credit can be transferred so that the second beneficiary can receive payment at a bank to which the credit is transferred as the paying or negotiating bank. It provides:

'j.　The first beneficiary may, in its request for transfer, indicate that honour or negotiation is to be effected to a second beneficiary at the place to which the credit has been transferred up to and including the expiry date of the credit. This is without prejudice to the right of the first beneficiary in accordance with sub-article 38(h).'

The reference to 'honour or negotiation is to be effected to a second beneficiary at the place to which the credit has been transferred' can only be taken as referring to a branch of a bank, although it is odd that it is not made more clear. This bank is then likely to become the advising bank for advising the credit to the second beneficiary. If requested by the transferring bank it could, it is thought, add its confirmation, or it could do so without engagement on its part. Transferable credits may sometimes indicate to which countries transfer may be effected rather than leaving it to the discretion of the bank to whom the request for transfer is to be made.

10.18　A credit which is stated to be transferable may also state that it is available at a stated banker's counters. It is the view of the ICC Banking Commission that this does not prevent transfer to another bank in the country of the second beneficiary.[1]

1 See *Opinions* (1984–1986) ICC No 434, Ref 139, and *Opinions* (1987–1988) ICC No 469, Ref 172.

10.19   Article 38.k provides:

> 'k.   Presentation of documents by or on behalf of a second beneficiary must be made to the transferring bank.'

So where a nominated bank acts as transferring bank, it would appear that presentation must be made to that bank and not the issuing bank. This contrasts with the general position under the UCP which is that a credit is always available for presentation at the issuing bank.[1]

1 See Article 6.d.iii.

The legal analysis

10.20   Article 38 does not indicate the legal nature of the transactions for which it provides, and there have been no reported decisions in English law touching on it. It is suggested that the matter must be approached on the basis of ordinary contractual principles, and that there are two situations which must be treated separately. The first is that where the transfer is effected by a bank involved with the original credit such as the confirming bank, and the second is that where it is effected by another nominated bank.

10.21   (a) Take first the case where the transferring bank is the correspondent or advising bank which is also the paying bank (and which may or may not also confirm the credit), and take the simple case where the terms of the credit as transferred are advised to the second beneficiary by that bank and the transferred credit is not made payable at another bank as provided for in Article 38.j. It is suggested that the relationships of the banks with the second beneficiary are exactly the same as those between them and the first beneficiary save that the terms of the credit as transferred, in particular as to amount, are likely to be different as permitted under Article 38.g. The undertakings provided for by Articles 7 and 8 of the UCP will apply to the credit as transferred, and thus the second beneficiary has the issuing bank's undertaking that payment will be made (if the credit provides for payment) and it has a confirming bank's undertaking to pay.[1]

1 A different analysis is suggested in Gutteridge & Megrah *The Law of Bankers' Commercial Credits* (8th edn) p 126. Having referred to the contract between the issuing bank and the first beneficiary it is then stated: 'When a transferee is introduced a fresh contract is set up between the first beneficiary, the second beneficiary, the issuing bank and (when the credit is confirmed), the confirming bank. That contract depends both on the terms on which the transfer is made and the provisions of article 48 [now 38]. The issuing bank is not in privity with the transferee.' This analysis is not accepted.

10.22   (b) Take next the case which is the same as that considered at (a) but assume that the transferred credit is advised to the second beneficiary by, and is made available at, a third bank which may or may not be in the same

313

country as the original correspondent bank. It is suggested that with regard to the relationships of the second beneficiary with the issuing bank and with the correspondent bank, the position is unchanged: the second beneficiary will have the Article 7 and 8 undertakings as appropriate. The third bank is in the position of an advising bank and acts as the agent of the bank from which it received its instructions, namely, the transferring bank. Its position as regards advising the credit, examining documents, payment and its right to reimbursement following payment is the same as any other advising bank. If it is asked to confirm the credit and is prepared to do so, it will give the appropriate undertaking to the second beneficiary as provided for by Article 8. In appropriate circumstances a bank to whom a credit is transferred may be prepared to confirm the credit: if it is, it considerably increases the value of transfer to the transferee.

10.23   (c) In the situations considered it is suggested that the contracts between the issuing bank and the confirming bank (if any) and the first beneficiary remain unchanged in their nature. But their performance is affected by the transfer. For by asking for the transfer the first beneficiary accepts that he will only be able to collect the difference between the value of his invoice and the second beneficiary's invoice. Even where there will be no balance for him to draw, he will retain an interest in the performance of the contract and will need to substitute his own invoice: he does not drop out. When his request for transfer is accepted by the bank, this acts as a variation of the contracts with him in that respect. It is uncertain whether the issuing and confirming banks undertake to him that documents will be accepted from the second beneficiary, and the second beneficiary will be paid, in accordance with the transferred credit. But it is suggested that this should be the case. An analogy may be drawn with the situation where A agrees to buy goods from B for £100 and then agrees to accept goods from C in performance paying £80 to C and £20 to B. A is contractually bound to B to accept the goods from C and to pay C. A is in the position of a bank which has given an undertaking under a credit and later agreed to its transfer.

10.24   (d) Where the credit transferred is available by negotiation and the request for transfer is made to a bank which is simply a bank entitled to negotiate the credit, by acceding to the request for transfer it is arguable that the negotiating bank must be taken also to have agreed with the first beneficiary to negotiate documents which conform to the credit when they are presented in due course. For although prior to its agreement to the request the bank had no obligations in relation to the credit, it would be nonsensical if an agreement to transfer did not also carry with it agreement to negotiate the documents in due course. Nothing in the UCP imposes such an obligation, and the matter is not covered by authority, but if this were not so, it would mean that the negotiating bank could subsequently decline to negotiate documents from the second beneficiary and decline to pay the first beneficiary on substitution of its invoice and draft. It follows that, by its agreement to transfer the credit, unless it specifies the terms on which it is acting, the negotiating bank may put itself into a position similar to that of an issuing bank, and broadly its position as regards the first and second beneficiaries and any bank through which the transferred credit is advised to the second beneficiary would be as discussed at (a) to (c) above. But the fee that a negotiation bank usually takes is a small one. It is therefore very likely to make it a term of the transfer that it does so without engagement on its part: it will negotiate with recourse.

10.25 (e) Where the transfer is effected by a negotiating bank the first beneficiary retains his remedies against the issuing bank and any confirming bank, as discussed at (c) above. The second beneficiary's position against them is as discussed at (a), namely, in relation to the transferred credit it has the benefit of the undertakings provided by Articles 7 and 8.

10.26 The position may be summarised as follows. A transferable credit embodies a contract or contracts with the first beneficiary which the credit foresees may be varied on transfer. On transfer variation of the contract or contracts with the first beneficiary takes place, and contracts also then come into being between the issuing bank and any confirming bank with the second beneficiary.

Other views

10.27 Other views have been expressed as to the legal nature of a transfer. One is that it is an equitable assignment of the benefit of the credit. It is doubtful whether the transaction can properly be described as an assignment, particularly as the second beneficiary can only obtain the benefits by performance on his part, that is, by presenting conforming documents. It certainly does not appear to assist in understanding the transaction to consider it in this way. It has secondly been suggested that there is a novation. A 'novation takes place where the two contracting parties agree that a third shall stand in the relation to either of them to the other. There is a new contract and it is therefore essential that the consent of all parties shall be obtained.'[1] As in nearly all cases the first beneficiary will remain entitled to claim the balance due to him after payment of the second beneficiary and in any event retains an interest in the performance of the contract and will need to insert his own invoice; this analysis is unsatisfactory. Neither does it throw light on the nature of the transaction.

1 *Chitty on Contracts* (30th edn) para 19-086.

Amendments

10.28 The amendment of a transferred credit gives rise to serious practical and theoretical difficulties. Article 10.a provides 'Except as otherwise provided by Article 38[1] a credit can neither be amended nor cancelled without the agreement of the issuing bank, the confirming bank, if any, and the beneficiary'. This simply reflects the legal position that when a contract has been made it can only be amended with the agreement of the parties to it.[2] Where a credit has been transferred there are two parallel contracts or sets of contracts, namely those between the first beneficiary and the issuing and any confirming bank, and those between the second beneficiary and the banks.[3]

1 Article 38 relates to transfer.
2 See **Chapter 3** above.
3 If the analysis put forward in paras **10.20** et seq is correct.

10.29   UCP Article 38 deals with the amendment of transferred credits in these terms:

'e.   Any request for transfer must indicate if and under what conditions amendments may be advised to the second beneficiary. The transferred credit must clearly indicate those conditions.

f.   If a credit is transferred to more than one second beneficiary, rejection of an amendment by one or more second beneficiary does not invalidate the acceptance by the other second beneficiary with respect to whom the transferred credit will be amended accordingly. For any second beneficiary that rejected the amendment, the transferred credit will remain unamended.'

10.30   Article 38.e provides either expressly or by implication that:

(1)   The first beneficiary has a right to refuse to allow the transferring bank to pass amendments on to the second beneficiary. One would expect those amendments to concern items other than those identified in Article 38.g such as unit price because there is no requirement for those items to be the same in the original and the transferred portion of the credit.

(2)   He may only exercise this right if he instructs the transferring bank, when he requests the transfer, that he is retaining the right to refuse.

(3)   The transferring bank may take his retention or non-retention of the right into account in deciding whether to consent to the transfer.

(4)   The transferred credit must clearly indicate the conditions under which amendments may be advised to the second beneficiary.

(5)   When a credit has been transferred to a second beneficiary and the right to refuse advice of amendments to him has been retained by the first beneficiary, the first beneficiary may, or may not, exercise that right in respect of any particular amendment.

(6)   When, in a case where the first beneficiary has retained his right to refuse, an amendment is advised to the transferring bank, the bank must advise the first beneficiary of it and give the first beneficiary a reasonable time to instruct the bank whether it is to be advised to the second beneficiary. If the first beneficiary does not exercise his right of refusal within a reasonable time, it appears that the amendment should be advised to the second beneficiary.

10.31 Article 38.e and 38.f as drafted appear to apply to any amendments to the credit. However, it is suggested that, seen in context, the first beneficiary's right in Article 38.e to refuse to allow amendments to be advised to the second beneficiary must apply only to amendments to those terms in respect of which the transferred credit need not reflect the original credit, i.e. those terms such as amount etc. which are specified in Article 38.g.[1] There is commercial sense in a beneficiary reserving the right to refuse to pass on to his supplier, the second beneficiary, amendments to, for example, the price or shipping date. However, it would make no sense for the first beneficiary to have the ability to accept amendments to other terms, such as the quality or description of the goods, without reference to the second beneficiary. If such an amendment would not be binding on the second beneficiary, then the transferred credit would no longer reflect the terms of the original, in breach of Article 38. On the other hand, if it would be binding on the second beneficiary, then the second beneficiary might find himself unable to make a presentation of conforming documents, and thereby deprived of the benefit of the credit, without any say in the matter. It is unfortunate, however, that the scope of Article 38.e and 38.f is not more clearly expressed.

1 See para **10.14** above.

10.32 If the beneficiary exercises his right to refuse to allow an amendment to be advised to the second beneficiary, then it is up to him to decide whether to accept the amendment – either way, the second beneficiary will not know that an amendment was offered or accepted and can continue to utilise the transferred credit on the original terms. If the first beneficiary permits the amendment to be advised to the second beneficiary, then both beneficiaries must separately decide whether to accept it; depending on their decisions, the amendment may be made to one or other or both of the original and transferred credit.

10.33 What happens if, after a transfer has taken place, there is a request to amend a term of the credit other than one of those specified in Article 38.g? For example, the ultimate buyer may request a change to the quality of the goods. Such an amendment would, if the view expressed in para **10.30** above is correct, fall outside the scope of Article 38. The UCP does not specifically provide how it should be dealt with. It is suggested that Article 10.a would apply but on the basis that the agreement of the issuing bank, the confirming bank and both (or all) of the beneficiaries (first and second) would be required before the amendment could be made. In that way, the transferred credit would continue to reflect the terms of the original.

Notification of transfer to issuing bank

10.34 There is no requirement for the transferring bank to notify the issuing bank of a transfer unless the credit itself provides for it. It is suggested that it is generally undesirable if the notification consists of more than the fact of transfer because it may lead to breach of confidentiality as to the first beneficiary's supplier and the price between them.[1]

1 See *Decisions* (1975–1979) ICC No 371, Ref 57 and *Case Studies on Documentary Credits*, ICC No 459, Case 154.

Charges

10.35   Unless there is agreement otherwise, the costs of transfer are payable by the first beneficiary. Article 38.c provides:

> 'c.   Unless otherwise agreed at the time of transfer all charges (such as commissions, fees, costs or expences) incurred in respect of a transfer must be paid by the first beneficiary.'

B   ASSIGNMENT

Function

10.36   Assignment as it is considered here performs a wholly different function to transfer. The assignment referred to is an assignment of either the right to moneys which may become payable under a credit following the future presentation of documents by the beneficiary, or of the right to moneys which will become payable in accordance with the terms of the credit under a deferred payment undertaking, documents having already been presented. It is concerned with the transfer of a future debt from the one creditor, the beneficiary, to another, the assignee. It enables the assignee instead of the beneficiary to receive payment following the beneficiary's performance of the credit contract. In contrast the transfer of a credit provides for a second beneficiary to present documents pursuant to the credit and so to be paid for them; by transfer the first beneficiary hopes largely to avoid the presentation of documents himself.

10.37   UCP Article 39 provides:

> '**Article 39 Assignment of Proceeds:**
> The fact that a credit is not stated to be transferable shall not affect the right of the beneficiary to assign any proceeds to which it may be, or may become, entitled under the credit, in accordance with the provisions of applicable law. This article relates only to the assignment of proceeds and not to the assignment of the right to perform under the credit.'

Legal and equitable assignments

10.38   In English law assignments are divided into legal assignments and equitable assignments. The difference in practice is that a legal assignee can bring an action in his own name, whereas an equitable assignee must also join the assignor to the proceedings. In order to be effective in law, the assignment must comply with s 136 of the Law of Property Act 1925: it must be absolute and not by way of charge; it must be in writing; and express notice in writing must be given to the debtor (ie the issuing bank). Only an existing debt or chose in action is capable of legal assignment. If the documents have already been presented and accepted, then it is clear that a debt is already in existence even though not payable until a later date. The position is more complicated if no documents have been presented. In that case the beneficiary is not obliged to activate the credit and may choose not to, or may be unable to, present compliant documents. The proceeds should probably be treated as a future and contingent chose in action with no present existence and not therefore capable of legal assignment. The intricacies of this topic are beyond the scope of this work.[1] Note also that there can be no legal assignment of only part of the proceeds.[2] If s 136 is inapplicable for any of these reasons, the assignment will take effect in equity and when the debt becomes payable an equitable interest will at once pass to the assignee.[3]

1 Reference may be made to Oditah *Legal Aspects of Receivables Financing* (1st edn) and *Chitty on Contracts* (30th edn) paras 19-028, 19-029; See, inter alia, *Walker v Bradford Old Bank Ltd* (1884) 12 QBD 511; *Hughes v Pump House Hotel Co* [1902] 2 KB 190; *Torkington v Magee* [1902] 2 KB 427 and *G & T Earle Ltd v Hemsworth RDC* (1928) 140 LT 69. It is suggested that there is no fully satisfactory discussion of the problem in the authorities. The court seems to have treated the proceeds as a future chose in action in *Marathon Electrical Manufacturing Corp v Mashreqbank PSC* [1997] 2 BCLC 460 although the question of whether the assignment was legal or equitable did not depend on that point because the assignment was of part of the debt only.
2 *Chitty on Contracts* (30th edn) para 19-014; *Marathon Electrical Manufacturing Corpn v Mashreqbank PSC*, [1997] 2 BCLC 460.
3 *Tailby v Official Receiver* (1888) 13 App Cas 523.

Notice of assignment

10.39   Notice of the assignment, whether legal or equitable, must be given by the assignee to the paying bank (and preferably also to any other bank which has given an undertaking in respect of payment) otherwise the bank will get a good discharge by paying the assignor. Where the proceeds are assigned to more than one party – a state of affairs which normally indicates dishonesty by the beneficiary – then whoever gives notice first obtains priority.[1] One potential complication is that generally notice of assignment cannot be given until the debt is in existence which, as discussed above, is problematic if the assignment is made before presentation. However, in *Marathon Electrical Manufacturing Corpn v Mashreqbank PSC*[2] Mance J recognised a 'pragmatic exception' to this rule (if, indeed, it would otherwise apply) and held that notification to the bank was effective even though made before presentation of the documents.

1 Under the rule in *Dearle v Hall* (1823) 3 Russ 1 priority between successive assignees is determined by the order in which they give notice to the debtor.
2 [1997] 2 BCLC 460 at 467.

Assignment 'subject to equities'

10.40 Ordinarily, the position of an assignee is no better than that of the original beneficiary since the assignee takes 'subject to equities', but as a matter of principle it is open to the parties to provide by contract for the protection of assignees. So a claim by the assignee to the proceeds under the credit could be defeated by any defence (such as fraud by the beneficiary) that would have been available as against the assignor, unless the parties provided for the assignment to take free of the risk of fraud or other prior equities.[1]

1 See *Banco Santander S.A. v Bayfern Ltd* [2000] Lloyd's Rep. Bank 165 per Waller LJ at pp 168-170 and para **9.40** above. See also *Standard Bank London Ltd v Canara Bank* [2002] EWHC 1574 (Comm), per Moore-Bick J at [73] to [81].

Set-off

10.41 The assignee will take subject to any set-off arising between the bank and the assignor/beneficiary if the set-off arises prior to the date of the assignment in the case of a set-off arising out of a separate transaction. As to such set-off against the issuing bank, see para **5.102** above. Circumstances will rarely lead to a set-off between the issuing bank and beneficiary because it is unlikely that there is an existing business relationship between them. However, the assignee must be more wary of taking an assignment of an obligation of the assignor's own bank. This was the position in *Marathon Electrical Manufacturing Corp v Mashreqbank PSC* where the claimant took an assignment of the right of the beneficiary against his collecting bank to receive the proceeds of the credit. The assignment was worthless because it was subject to the bank's right of set-off. Mance J said:[1]

> 'One lesson of the present case may be that, where a creditor/supplier aims at being paid out of proceeds to which his debtor may become entitled as the beneficiary of a letter of credit, the creditor/supplier should ensure not only (a) that he acquires an outright, rather than security, interest, but also (b) that the interest acquired is in his debtor's entitlement under the letter of credit as against the issuing bank, rather than in the debtor's entitlement against the

debtor's collecting banker, to whom the debtor may also have pre-existing indebtedness. Even then, a creditor/ supplier would have to ensure that his debtor had not already granted to the collecting banker by debenture or otherwise an effective fixed charge which would embrace any entitlement of the debtor against the issuing banker and take priority over a later assignment to the creditor/ supplier.'

The importance of the assignment being outright is that an assignment by way of security made by a company must be registered and is otherwise void under s 395 of the Companies Act 1985.

1 [1997] 2 BCLC 460 at 465.

Assignment to support a second credit

10.42 Where a buyer in a string wishes to use a credit opened in his favour by one bank to support a credit opened on his instructions with a second bank, this can be achieved by the assignment of the proceeds of the first credit to the second bank. An example of this (and of the disastrous consequences brought upon itself by the second or assignee bank) is provided by *Mannesman Handel AG v Kaunlaren Shipping Corpn*.[1]

1 [1993] 1 Lloyd's Rep 89. See also para **2.31** above.

Irrevocable mandates or instructions

10.43 It appears that where a credit is not transferable and a solution is not found by opening a back-to-back credit, beneficiaries under credits sometimes seek to secure payment to their own suppliers by giving the paying bank an irrevocable mandate or instruction to pay to the supplier a sum from the proceeds of the credit, and the bank then confirms to the supplier its receipt of the instruction. According to the authority of *Brice v Bannister*,[1] this would be a good assignment in equity under English law. In that case Gough agreed to build a vessel for Bannister and later directed Bannister to pay £100 to Brice out of money due or to become due from Bannister to Gough. The majority of the court held that this was a good equitable assignment. An irrevocable instruction was also treated as an assignment in *Marathon Electrical Manufacturing Corpn v Mashreqbank PSC*.[2] It would strengthen the third party supplier's position if in addition to the instruction from the beneficiary to the bank, the beneficiary made a written assignment of the sum in question due or to become due from the bank under the credit, which it enclosed to the bank with its instruction.

1 (1878) 3 QBD 569, CA.
2 [1997] 2 BCLC 460.

Credits payable to the order of the beneficiary

10.44 Where the beneficiary foresees that he will or may wish to instruct the paying bank in the manner which has just been considered, he may feel that it will ease his way if the credit is made payable to his order rather than to him. The advising bank could not then object to acting on his instructions.

'Assignment of the credit'

10.45 It is sometimes considered whether the credit itself, that is the right to present documents under it and to receive payment, can be assigned.[1] It is suggested that transfer is the only appropriate mechanism because, first, the credit is addressed specifically to the beneficiary and it is with him and not some other party that the applicant and the banks wish to deal and, secondly, because the mechanism provided for transfer by Article 38 (if the credit is designated as transferable) taken with Article 39 shows that what would amount to a transfer by assignment is not intended. So if a credit is not designated as transferable, the only and limited mechanism which can be used to enable another party to receive the payment which the credit should provide, is an assignment of the proceeds as envisaged by Article 39, and the validity and effect of that assignment will depend upon its governing law.

1 See Gutteridge & Megrah *The Law of Bankers' Commercial Credits* (8th edn) pp 132–135.

Chapter 11

The Bank's Security

INTRODUCTION

11.1 When a bank pays on a letter of credit it looks for reimbursement to the next in the chain, namely to the issuing bank if it is a nominated bank and to the applicant if it is an issuing bank. It is only when that payment is not made that the question of security arises. A confirming bank and an issuing bank may not receive payment as they intend in two quite different situations. One is where the paying party has become insolvent. The other is where the bank has erred and paid on documents which are found not to comply with the credit and so it has no right of indemnity. In the former case any security arrangements which the bank has in relation to the paying party may be relied upon, and the bank will have the security of the documents provided it retains them and they are such as to provide security. Where the bank has paid in error, it will have only the latter, namely such security as the documents may provide. The security provided to banks by the documents was regarded historically as an important aspect of the letter of credit arrangement. Thus in *Guaranty Trust Co of New York v Hannay*[1] Scrutton LJ included in his description of a credit using time drafts the following:[2] 'The vendor thus gets his money before the purchaser would, in the ordinary course, pay; the exchange house duly presents the bill for acceptance, and has, until the bill is accepted, the security of a pledge of the documents attached and the goods they represent.' When the transport document was almost invariably a negotiable bill of lading and therefore a document of title, there was little difficulty. But today the use of other forms of transport document[3] which are not documents of title has greatly weakened the banks' security. Today banks are more likely to look to the creditworthiness of the parties with whom they deal, and to their security arrangements with them, than to the security provided by the documents to be presented under the credit.

1 [1918] 2 KB 623.
2 [1918] 2 KB 623 at 659.
3 In relation to the sea waybill, see the discussion at para **8.106** above.

SECURITIES PROVIDED BY THE PAYING PARTY

11.2   Depending on the arrangements which it has made, an issuing bank may have various securities which it can rely on in the event of the insolvency of the applicant. It may have taken a debenture over the assets of the applicant, or a charge over particular properties. It may hold guarantees from its holding companies or from its directors. These are only mentioned for the sake of completeness, and their legal attributes are not within the scope of this book. A confirming bank which finds itself to have confirmed a credit issued by a bank which then becomes insolvent may be holding deposits from the issuing bank under the terms of the arrangements whereby it agreed to act as the issuing bank's correspondent. If it holds those deposits on appropriate terms it may be able to reimburse itself from them rather than having to refund them to the liquidator and to prove in the liquidation for its entitlement and, as is then likely, to receive only a dividend.

SECURITY PROVIDED BY THE DOCUMENTS – PLEDGE

11.3   A pledge may be described as the transfer of the possession of goods by way of security whereby the ownership of the goods remains in the pledgor and the pledgee obtains a right to possession only. He has a 'special interest' in the goods, which includes a right to sell.[1] The goods must be transferred to the possession of the pledgee and actual possession is normally required. One of the exceptions to actual possession is the case where a bill of lading is transferred with the intention of pledging the goods to which the bill is title. Then the pledge is effective on the transfer of the bill alone. The special position of a bill of lading is emphasised in the judgment of the Privy Council in *Official Assignee of Madras v Mercantile Bank of India Ltd*[2] where Lord Wright stated:[3]

> 'But where goods were represented by documents the transfer of the documents did not transfer the possession of the goods, save one exception, unless the custodier (carrier, warehouseman or such) was notified of the transfer and agreed to hold in future as bailee for the pledgee. The one exception was the case of bills of lading, the transfer of which by the law merchant operated a transfer of the possession of, as well as the property in, the goods.'

The limited interest passed by the pledge of a bill of lading was considered by the House of Lords in *Sewell v Burdick*,[4] in holding on the particular facts that bankers to whom bills of lading had been delivered as security for a loan were not liable for freight.[5] Where the goods are in a warehouse at the time of the transaction and are intended to remain there, as is indicated in the passage quoted, a bank may seek to protect its interest and to obtain a pledge by getting the warehouseman to attorn to the bank. This can be achieved by the bank requiring the inclusion among the documents to be presented under the credit of warehouse receipts made out of its own order.[6] For example, the London Metal Exchange operates a system of warrants whereby goods stored in approved warehouses are delivered against production of the relevant warrant.[7]

1 *The Odessa* [1916] 1 AC 145.
2 [1935] AC 53.
3 [1935] AC 53 at 59.
4 (1884) 10 App Cas 74.
5 See (1884) 10 App Cas 74 at 92, 93 per Lord Blackburn.
6 See as an intended example of this, *Rafsanjan Pistachio Producers Co-operative v Bank Leumi (UK) plc* [1992] 1 Lloyd's Rep 513.
7 See *Niru Battery Manufacturing Co v Milestone Trading Ltd* [2002] 2 All ER (Comm) 705 at para 14.

11.4   The position of a bank as pledgee which receives documents under a documentary credit has been touched on in the reported cases rather than forming the nub of the case or part of the *ratio decidendi*. But it is clear that in the classic situation where the bank receives bills of lading made out to the order of the shipper and blank indorsed it becomes a pledgee of them. This is the case for a negotiating bank as much as for an issuing or confirming bank.[1] The position is that, when the documents are accepted by the bank as conforming to the credit, the property in the goods which has previously been retained by the seller will pass to the buyer, the intention being that the seller no longer looks to the documents for his security (or the goods) but looks to the promise of the bank. As Paull J stated in *Sale Continuation Ltd v Austin Taylor & Co Ltd*:[2]

> 'The ownership of the goods passes to the buyer but the bank has the possessory title of a pledgee as against the buyer. He has that title until the buyer puts the bank in funds and discharges his liability for interest payable in respect of the draft. If the pledgor does not do so the bank has the usual right of a pledgee to see as if he were the owner.'[3]

Where the bills of lading are drawn to the order of the bank or are indorsed to the order of the bank, the bank will obtain a pledge in the same way as where the bills are drawn to order and blank indorsed. Where they are drawn in favour of the buyer or other consignee, the bank, it is suggested, still obtains its pledge (for by setting up the credit the buyer has consented to the bank doing so). But, unless the bank can obtain the indorsement of the bills to itself, its power of sale will be ineffective because the bills themselves will not evidence any right on the part of the bank to the goods. In order to enforce its rights, the bank would probably have to bring an action for delivery of the cargo against both the named consignee or indorsee and the carrier.

1 *The Stone Gemini* [1999] 2 Lloyd's Rep 255, a case in the Federal Court of Australia.
2 [1968] 2 QB 849 at 861.
3 See also the judgments of Scrutton LJ in *Guaranty Trust Co of New York v Hannay & Co* [1918] 2 KB 623 at 659, 660; *Rosenberg v International Banking Corpn* (1923) 14 Ll L Rep 344 at 347; and *Guaranty Trust Co of New York v Van Den Berghs Ltd* (1925) 22 Ll l Rep 447 at 452.2; and *Kwei Tek Chao v British Traders and Shippers Ltd* [1954] 2 QB 459 at 487 per Devlin J. As to the retention by the seller of the property in goods prior to the operation of the credit, see *The Glenroy (No 2)* [1945] AC 124.

11.5   It is worth briefly considering what happens to the property in the goods in these circumstances. Passage of property is ultimately determined by the objectively construed intentions of the parties. There will often be an inference that the seller intends to retain title in the goods until payment, an inference which is not displaced merely because payment is to be by letter of credit.[1] On acceptance of the documents against payment by the bank, property passes to the buyer, but, so long as the bank retains the bills of lading, subject to the bank's pledge interest. If the buyer refuses to take up the documents on the ground that they do not comply with the credit, either himself or by declining to authorise the issuing bank to take them up from the errant confirming bank, then he cannot retain the property in the goods. Where a buyer rejects goods because they are found on arrival not to conform to the contract, the property in the goods – which has been described as vesting in the buyer conditionally – revests in the seller.[2] But that would be inappropriate here. For the seller has been paid, or has his right to be paid, by the bank and has no further interest in the goods. It is therefore tentatively suggested that the property should find a resting place with the bank, perhaps by way of a type of subrogation, so that although the bank may not always have a complete documentary title it will become the owner of the goods.

1 See *Mitsui & Co Ltd v Flota Mercante Grancolombiana SA* [1988] 1 WLR 1145, 1153: 'Even the most copper-bottomed letter of credit sometimes fails to produce payment for one reason or another...'
2 See *Kwei Tek Chao v British Traders and Shippers Ltd* [1954] 2 QB 459 at 487.

11.6   In the preceding paragraphs the bank's position as pledgee is considered on the basis that the pledge arises, in effect by implication, from the circumstances. In the case of an issuing bank it may well be that the pledge is expressly provided for in the terms of the application made by the buyer to the bank for the opening of the credit. The terms of the pledge and of any specific remedies should then be referred to.

Sale by pledgee

11.7   The right of sale has already been mentioned. Provided that the bank has the bills of lading and they are made out to the bank or to the seller's order and blank indorsed, the bank may take possession of the goods and sell them.[1] When there is no time fixed for payment, before a pledgee can exercise his right of sale he must give notice to the pledgor.[2] The bank, however, will have informed its customer that the documents are available for collection and will have required to be put in funds, so this will not arise. Where the bank is a confirming bank which has had documents rejected by the issuing bank on the ground of non-compliance with the credit, the documents are returnable to the confirming bank.[3]

1 Provided, of course, that the goods have not already been discharged and become unavailable.
2 *Deverges v Sandeman, Clark & Co* [1902] 1 Ch 579.
3 UCP Article 16.c.

Claim in conversion by pledgee

11.8   When the bank calls for the goods it may find that they have been released by the carrier against an indemnity and without production of the bill of lading to, for example, a sub-purchaser. Nor is it unknown for a dishonest buyer to refuse the documents on the ground of discrepancies and so avoid having to pay through the credit, while at the same time arranging to take up the goods against an indemnity so it can sell them on and itself receive payment. In such circumstances the bank will have a right to sue the carrier for misdelivery and the buyer and the party who has received the goods (and anyone else who has dealt in them) in conversion.[1]

1 *The Stone Gemini* [1999] 2 Lloyd's Rep 255; *Uzinterimpex JSC v Standard Bank plc* [2008] 2 Lloyd's Rep 456 at [27]; *Glyn, Mills Currie & Co v East and West India Dock Co* (1882) 7 App Cas 591 at 606; *Bristol and West of England Bank v Midland Rly Co* [1891] 2 QB 653; and *Ernest Scragg & Sons Ltd v Perseverance Banking and Trust Co Ltd* [1973] 2 Lloyd's Rep 101. In *Mannesman Handel AG v Kaunlaren Shipping Corpn* [1993] 1 Lloyd's Rep 89 demise charterers had settled a claim made on this basis.

Documents not including a bill of lading – lien

11.9   Where the credit calls for a transport document which is not a bill of lading, in some cases it may nonetheless be capable of argument that by modern mercantile usage the document is a negotiable document of title and so the bank has a pledge.[1] But otherwise the bank will be unable to put itself forward as a pledgee. Where the bank cannot assert a pledge, the best that it will be able to assert is a lien over the documents, namely the right of retaining the documents until its claims are satisfied. Where the problem is the insolvency of the applicant, this may enable the bank to negotiate with the liquidator or receiver of the applicant, and it can be agreed that the goods be sold on terms that the proceeds (or at least the greater part) go in reduction of the bank's claim against the applicant. Where the problem is that the bank has paid against documents which do not conform to the credit, it is in an unenviable position. Suppose – to take a clear example – that the transport document which it holds is an airway bill, being the consignor's copy, naming the buyer as the consignee.[2] In such a situation, which is now increasingly likely, one of the elements previously considered an essential part of the scheme of documentary credits is missing: the bank does not have the security of the goods by means of negotiable documents of title.[3] It may be, as suggested above,[4] that the ingenuity of the law will find a way of vesting the property in the goods in the bank in such situations, and possibly even of compelling the seller or buyer to do what may be necessary to complete the bank's documentary title where that is needed. But this is an area which has yet to be considered by the courts. No doubt where such situations have arisen, on becoming aware of the legal difficulties banks and traders have found ways of settling their differences without resort to law. The clausing of a sea waybill to provide security for a bank by way of a lien has been referred to above.[5]

1 A candidate is the 'combined transport bill of lading'.
2 See Carriage by Air Act 1961, Sch 1, art 6(2).
3 See the cases cited at para **11.4** above and the emphasis on security by Lord Wright in *Ross T Smyth & Co Ltd v T D Bailey, Son & Co* [1940] 3 All ER 60 at 68 where Lord Wright appears to be considering a pledge of goods arising on a negotiation of documents prior to presentation of them under the credit.
4 See para **11.5**.
5 See para **8.106**.

Where time drafts result in a delay in payment

11.10   Where the credit provides for immediate payment the banks involved need not lose possession of the documents, or the right to their possession, until they receive payment themselves. Thus an issuing bank is not obliged to release documents to its customer, the buyer, save against payment, and a confirming bank is entitled to have the documents returned to it where they are rejected by the issuing bank. But the position is different where time drafts are involved. Suppose that a draft is drawn on the issuing bank, or on the buyer, payable three months after sight. When the three months are up, the documents will have long since reached the buyer who will have taken possession of the goods and the bank's security will have been lost. In this situation an issuing bank can protect itself by ensuring that it has other securities from the buyer such as debentures, charges or guarantees. Or it may utilise the mechanism of a trust receipt.

Trust receipts

11.11 It was held in *North Western Bank Ltd v Poynter, Son and Macdonalds*[1] that the transfer of possession of goods by means of the return of the bill of lading by a pledgee to the pledgor for the purpose of sale on the pledgee's behalf, the pledgor undertaking to account for the proceeds of sale towards satisfaction of the debt, did not destroy the pledgee's security: the pledgee was entitled to the proceeds against the general creditors of the pledgor.[2] The ability to transfer possession for such a purpose is the foundation of trust receipts. Under a trust receipt the bank releases the bills of lading to the applicant for the credit on the applicant's undertaking that on taking possession of the goods he will hold them in trust for the bank and will sell them on behalf of the bank. He likewise undertakes to hold on trust the proceeds of sale, which will be remitted to the bank, at least up to the amount due. The document will contain other terms to protect the bank's interest such as a requirement to keep the goods and moneys separate from other goods and moneys, and to insure the goods. The document is not registrable as a bill of sale (where the applicant is an individual) nor as a charge (in the case of a company) because, among other reasons, the rights of the bank arise from the pre-existing pledge. This was established in *Re David Allester*,[3] where it was held that trust receipts were effective against a liquidator. The case involved the pledge of bills of lading to a bank to secure an overdraft and the liquidator claimed the proceeds of sale against the bank. Such a situation is to be distinguished from that where there is no pledge in advance of the transaction, as was the case in *Ladenburg & Co v Goodwin, Ferreira & Co Ltd*.[4] There the defendant merchants sold goods to customers in South America and the property in the goods passed to the customers. The merchants sent invoices to the plaintiff bankers for acceptance. The bank accepted the drafts. The merchants' letter enclosing the drafts had stated that the goods and their proceeds were hypothecated to the bank. The merchants went into liquidation and the bank claimed the proceeds of sale against the liquidator. It was held that the merchants had created a charge on their book debts, which was void as it had not been registered. The bank never had the right to possession of the goods either prior to the transaction (as is the case with a trust receipt) or as the outcome of the transaction itself.

1 [1895] AC 56.
2 See also *Official Assignee of Madras v Mercantile Bank of India Ltd* [1935] AC 53 at 63, 64, PC, per Lord Wright.
3 [1922] 2 Ch 211.
4 [1912] 3 KB 275.

11.12   A recent case has considered the effect of a trust receipt operating alongside a retention of title clause in a financing arrangement for mechanical equipment. In *Fairfax Gerrard Holdings Ltd and Others v Capital Bank plc*[1] the claimant bank had financed the purchase by its client, Dimond, of certain mechanical equipment pursuant to a contract which Dimond had entered into with Carrprint to supply such machinery. Carrprint had itself financed its purchase from Dimond by arranging a finance lease from the defendant, Capital Bank. The material clause of the finance agreement between the claimant and Dimond provided that the claimant would sell the machinery to Dimond with reservation of title and subject to the terms of the claimant's standard trust receipt, and that Dimond could sell on the machinery in the ordinary course of business, subject to holding the proceeds on trust for the claimant. In the event, following the transfer of the machinery to Carrprint and the receipt of the agreed purchase price by Dimond from Capital Bank, Dimond went into liquidation and was ultimately dissolved. The claimant issued proceedings against Capital Bank on the basis that the retention of title clause had prevented Dimond from passing title to Carrprint or Capital Bank. Thus, it was alleged that, in entering into the leasing arrangement with Carrprint and collecting rent thereunder, Capital Bank had thereby converted the machinery. At first instance[2] the court, finding in favour of the claimant, held that Dimond had no authority to transfer title in the machinery. The Court of Appeal reversed the first instance decision and held that on either basis Dimond had express authority to transfer title in the machinery. The Court of Appeal construed the retention of title clause and the trust receipt – which had been considered below to be inconsistent – as covering different situations, albeit in both cases Dimond had authority to transfer title. The retention of title clause and the requirement to advise Carrprint/Capital Bank to pay the purchase price directly to the claimant covered the situation where a direct payment was possible, whilst the trust receipt covered the alternative position where, notwithstanding the request for direct payment, Capital Bank had made payment to Dimond: the funds would then be held by Dimond on trust for the claimant. The Court of Appeal found that on the proper construction of the retention of title clause, for so long as the machinery remained in the possession of Dimond the claimant was entitled to assert title in relation to it. Once Dimond transferred possession of the machinery to Carrprint, as was envisaged under the terms of the finance agreement, the retention of title clause is given effect by the requirement either to procure direct payment from Carrprint/Capital Bank to the claimant or the effect of the trust receipt in constituting Dimond as trustee for the claimant of such sums as it received.

1 [2008] 1 All ER (Comm) 632.
2 [2007] 1 Lloyd's Rep 171.

11.13   Where the applicants for a credit who have possession of goods under a trust receipt deal in the goods dishonestly by, for example, raising fresh moneys on the security of them, their acts will bind the bank. For they are likely to be treated as mercantile agents, and the bank is the owner for the purposes of s 2(1) of the Factors Act 1889, as is shown by *Lloyds Bank Ltd v Bank of America National Trust*.[1] If the applicant for the credit after having entered into the trust receipt arrangement simply fails to account to the bank for the proceeds of sale, which are disposed of and cannot be identified, the bank will only have a claim in debt against the applicant.[2] A trust receipt is therefore efficacious where an honest applicant becomes insolvent, but it may fail to protect the bank's interest when the applicant is dishonest.

1 [1938] 2 KB 147, CA.
2 If they can be identified in the hands of a volunteer (one who did not give value) a tracing claim may be possible, and a claim could also be made against anyone who received the proceeds of sale with notice of the breach of trust: see generally Goff and Jones on Restitution (5th edn).

PLEDGE ESSENTIAL TO TRUST RECEIPT

11.14 If the documents which come into the bank's hands through the credit are not such that the bank becomes a pledgee of the goods, the release of them to the buyer under a trust receipt will not protect the bank's interest. In *Official Assignee of Madras v Mercantile Bank of India Ltd*[1] the railway receipts with which the case was concerned were documents of title under the Indian Contract Act 1872 and were to be treated in the same way as bills of lading.[2] So, if the transport documents are not bills of lading, or are not other negotiable transport documents which are to be treated in the same way as bills of lading, the device of a trust receipt cannot be used.

1 [1935] AC 53.
2 See [1935] AC 53 at 63.

TRUST RECEIPTS AND THE FAILURE OF THE BANK

11.15 If a bank which has undertaken to pay on a time draft becomes insolvent or otherwise makes it clear that it will not perform its obligation, the pledge is likely to be released. This emerges from the complicated facts in *Sale Continuation Ltd v Austin Taylor & Co Ltd*.[1] The application of the principles applied in this case to the more usual situation is considered at the end of this paragraph. Sale, the plaintiffs by their liquidator, were merchant bankers who later became insolvent. They agreed with the defendants, Austin Taylor, who were timber merchants and brokers, to open a letter of credit in favour of foreign principals of Austin Taylor named Nenasi. The credit was available by drafts drawn on the bank accompanied by usual documents. Austin Taylor undertook to the bank to indemnify it. The bank accepted a draft and handed the documents to Austin Taylor under the terms of a trust receipt so Austin Taylor could present the documents to the buyers and receive payments for which they would be accountable to the bank. After the documents had been delivered to the buyers but before they had paid, the bank was put into receivership, and then went into liquidation. The draft was returned dishonoured to Nenasi. When Austin Taylor received payment from the buyers they remitted it to their principals, Nenasi. The liquidator of the bank claimed from Austin Taylor the amount of the draft, alternatively damages for breach of the trust constituted by the receipt. It was held by Paull J that it was an implied term of the contract between the bank and Austin Taylor that the bank should honour drafts drawn on them by payment as well as by acceptance, and that Austin Taylor's obligation to provide funds to the bank only arose when it had done so. The appointment of the receiver and the company's entering into liquidation had the effect of evincing an intention by the bank not to pay on the draft even if put in funds. This released Austin Taylor from the mutual obligation to put the bank in funds. So far as the trust receipt was concerned Paull J found as follows:

> 'In this case by the terms of the contract with the buyers, entered into by their agents (the defendants), Nenasi parted with their property in the goods for all purposes when the goods were shipped except for their vendors' lien for the unpaid purchase price and when Nenasi sent the documents to the plaintiffs Nenasi retained that lien as against the buyers. Having that lien they pledged the documents to the plaintiffs who took them as security against not receiving the purchase price before they had to honour the draft, subject to the buyers' right to demand them as soon as they paid for the goods. The application states that the drafts are to be secured by the delivery of the documents of title as collateral security.
>
> Now the essence of a pledge is that it is security against either an immediate advance or against a present liability to make a future payment. The trust receipt contemplated that the defendants would part with the documents to the Belgian buyer and recover the purchase price. It was no breach of trust to do so. In my judgment the same principle applies to the money as applies to the obligation to put the plaintiffs in funds before the maturity date of the draft. Once the draft is dishonoured (or notice of intention not to honour given) Nenasi is entitled to cancel the contract of pledge by returning the draft for cancellation and claiming the purchase money from their agents, the defendants. It is as though a pawnbroker having received the pledge and given his pawn ticket to the pledgor refused to hand over the sum agreed to be lent. The pledgor can say: "Very well, here is your pawn ticket. Hand me back my goods." In this case "the goods" (being the documents of title, or rather the money received for them) were already in the hands of the pledgor.'

In the more usual situation the trust receipt is entered into by the buyer rather than by an agent for the seller. Translating the reasoning of the decision to that situation provides for it to be an implied term of the buyer's or applicant's contract with the bank that the bank shall pay the seller in due course. When the bank becomes insolvent it repudiates that undertaking and releases the applicant buyer from the contract. The foundation of the trust receipt is the pledge to the bank to secure the bank's liability to pay. So, when that liability is repudiated, the foundation is gone. As the applicant already has possession of the goods pledged under the terms of the trust receipt, he is entitled to terminate the pledge (and the trust arrangement) and to retain the goods. He may then pay the seller direct as he will be liable to do when the credit fails to pay through the insolvency of the bank – unless the credit was provided as absolute rather than conditional payment (which is unlikely).[2]

1 [1968] 2 QB 849.
2 See paras **3.47** et seq.

BILLS OF EXCHANGE DRAWN AGAINST GOODS

11.16   Bills of exchange may sometimes state that they are drawn against particular goods or against a particular cargo. Unless the holder of the bill also has the bills of lading, the fact that a draft is so drawn will not give him any rights in the cargo. As was stated by Mellish LJ in *Robey & Co's Perseverance Ironworks v Ollier*:[1] 'A mercantile man who is intended to have a lien on a cargo expects to have the bill annexed; if there is no bill of lading annexed he only expects to get the security of the bill itself.' The position will be the same where the holder of such a bill of exchange delivers the bills of lading to a bank under a letter of credit against the bank's acceptance of the bill: he loses any right in the cargo which he had through the bills of lading. Thus in *Re Suse, ex p Dever*[2] a London bank opened a letter of credit in favour of a Shanghai tea merchant on terms that bills of exchange drawn on the bank should identify the parcels of tea in respect of which they were drawn. Bills drawn on the bank were discounted together with the bills of lading with a Chinese bank, the Hongkong and Shanghai Bank whose agent in London presented the bills for acceptance to the bank. The bank accepted the bills of exchange against delivery of the bills of lading. The bank then went into liquidation. It was held that the holders of the bills of exchange had no rights in the tea.[3] The function of such a statement on a bill of exchange appears simply to be to encourage its negotiation by indicating that the bill is part of transactions relating to specific goods: it does not add to the rights given by the bill.

1 (1872) 7 Ch App 695 at 699.
2 (1884) 13 QBD 766.
3 See also *Re Barned's Banking Co, Banner and Young v Johnston* (1871) LR 5 HL 157 and *Brown, Shipley & Co v Kough* (1885) 29 Ch D 848.

Chapter 12

Standby Credits, and Demand Guarantees and Bonds

A   OVERVIEW

12.1   The documentary credits which have been considered so far have been used principally in contracts for the sale of goods or services to guarantee the payment of the purchase price by the buyer. The bank pays against stipulated documents, the most important of which is the bill of lading or other transport document evidencing shipment of the goods. The credit is the means by which the buyer/applicant performs his contract with the seller/beneficiary. This type of credit is sometimes called a commercial credit. This chapter is concerned with undertakings or instruments known as standby credits, demand guarantees or performance (or demand) bonds. Although the terminology and form differ, the usual function of the instruments is to enable one party to a contract to obtain money from a reliable source, usually a bank, when the other party has failed, or is alleged to have failed, to perform the contract or some aspect of it. They are often used in construction contracts as security for any liability of the contractor to the employer.

12.2   Two types of instrument, standby credits and independent guarantees, will be considered separately. The terms 'performance bond', 'demand bond', 'demand guarantee' and 'performance guarantee' are often used interchangeably[1] and in this chapter the term 'independent guarantee' will be used to refer to any of them.[2] The nature of standby credits and independent guarantees can be best understood by comparing them first with commercial credits and second with conditional guarantees.

1 Thus Lord Denning MR began his judgment in *Edward Owen Engineering Ltd v Barclays Bank International Ltd* [1978] QB 159 at 164: 'This case concerns a new business transaction called a performance guarantee or a performance bond.' In *RD Harbottle (Mercantile) Ltd v National Westminster Bank Ltd* [1978] QB 146 at 149 Kerr J stated 'All the contracts provided that the plaintiffs were to establish a guarantee confirmed by a bank of 5% of the price in favour of the buyers. These were in effect to be performance bonds. They were called

guarantees *simpliciter*, but their purpose was to provide security to the buyers for the fulfilment by the plaintiffs of their obligations under the contracts.'

2 The term is borrowed from the UN Convention on Independent Guarantees and Standby Letters of Credit. See para **12.93** below.

Comparison with commercial credits

12.3   In their operation standby credits and independent guarantees are similar to commercial credits in that:

(a)   The bank's obligation to pay arises on the presentation of conformant documents as specified, or as required by the UCP or other applicable rules.

(b)   The undertaking is autonomous and the bank is not concerned with the underlying contract between applicant and beneficiary, any more than the issuer of a commercial credit is concerned with whether the price is in fact payable to the seller.

However, they differ in three important respects:

(1)   The purpose of a standby credit or independent guarantee is usually to give security against the applicant's breach of contract, not to enforce his performance. Thus, in *Bachmann Pty Ltd v BHP Power New Zealand Ltd*,[1] Brooking JA stated, 'International trade is facilitated by traditional credits, which provide a mechanism for performance of contracts of sale. Standby credits are a safeguard which comes into play where there is a suggestion that contracts (whose subject-matter can vary widely) have been broken.' For example, the seller/beneficiary will call on a commercial credit whenever the goods are shipped, but an employer/beneficiary will (or should) call on a standby credit or independent guarantee only if he believes that the contractor/applicant is in breach.

(2)   The documents required for presentation are also different: no transport document is involved and often payment is made against a simple written demand by the beneficiary.

(3)   The identities of the applicant and beneficiary are often reversed. The beneficiary of a commercial credit is the party receiving payment, eg the supplier of the goods or services, whereas the beneficiary of a standby credit or independent guarantee is usually the purchaser of the goods or services.

Many of the principles discussed in the English cases on commercial letters of credit are applicable to standby credits and independent guarantees, and vice versa, and analogies have often been drawn between them. Some of the cases on independent guarantees have already been discussed, in particular in Chapter 9 relating to fraud and injunctions.

Comparison with conditional guarantees

12.4   Whatever the undertaking may be called, a distinction must be drawn between what is referred to in this chapter as an independent guarantee (encompassing demand guarantees, demand bonds etc) and a true contract of guarantee (or suretyship). Although the terminology unfortunately[1] overlaps, the legal nature is very different. As explained above, an independent guarantee is an autonomous obligation of the party giving it. A true contract of guarantee, on the other hand, is 'an accessory contract by which the promisor undertakes to be answerable to the promisee for the debt, default or miscarriage of another person, whose primary liability to the promisee must exist or be contemplated'.[2] The liability of the guarantor is conditional on the non-performance of the party who he is guaranteeing. A contract of guarantee is not, therefore, autonomous and is often described as collateral to the underlying contract. For the purpose of distinguishing them from independent guarantees, contracts of guarantee will be referred to in this chapter as 'conditional guarantees'. As will be seen, the position of the recipient of a conditional guarantee is substantially less favourable than that of a beneficiary of an independent guarantee or standby credit.

1 '... it is difficult to understand why business men persist in entering upon considerable obligations in old fashioned forms of contract which do not adequately express the true transaction ... why insurance of credits or contracts, if insurance is intended, or guarantees of the same, if guarantees are intended, should not be expressed in appropriate language, passes comprehension. It is certainly not the fault of lawyers': *Trade Indemnity Co Ltd v Workington Harbour and Dock Board* [1937] AC 1 at 17, per Lord Atkin.
2 49 *Halsbury's Laws* (5th edn 2008) para 1013.

(a)   Proof of primary liability

12.5   'Under what are sometimes called first demand bonds the obligation to pay arises without any evidence of the validity of the claim on a simple demand, or on a demand either in a specified form or accompanied by a specified document.'[1] However, in an action on a conditional guarantee the claimant must ordinarily prove the fact of the indebtedness of the party guaranteed and the amount, and the guarantor has all the defences available to the party guaranteed. So, for example, with a guarantee of a construction contract, the employer would have to prove against the guarantor of the contractor's performance the same probably detailed and complicated case which he would have to prove were he to sue the contractor himself for damages for default in the performance of the contract.[2] A judgment or an arbitration award against the principal debtor will not avoid the need for this unless the guarantee provides otherwise.[3] Thus a guarantee as described provides the party to whom it is addressed with a second, and in financial terms, hopefully more secure source of payment. But, subject to its terms, it does not otherwise improve his position. In particular he is in no better position against the guarantor in proving that the money is owed than he is against the main debtor. It is necessary to say 'subject to the terms of the guarantee' because it is not uncommon for guarantees, particularly bank guarantees, to provide that the certificate of, for example, the bank, shall be conclusive evidence of the indebtedness of the party guaranteed. Such a term is likely to be construed as covering both the legal existence of the debt and its amount: see *Dobbs v National Bank of Australasia Ltd*[4] and *Bache & Co (London) Ltd v Banque Vernes*.[5] Thus it was stated in *Dobbs*:[6]

> 'It was contended, however, for the appellant that, upon its true construction, the clause did not make the certificate conclusive of the legal existence of the debt but only of the amount. It is not easy to see how the amount can be certified unless the certifier forms some conclusion as to what items ought to be taken into account, and such conclusion goes to the existence of the indebtedness. Perhaps such a clause should not be interpreted as covering all grounds which go to the validity of the debt; for instance, illegality, a matter considered in *Swan v Blair* (1836) 6 ER 1566. But the manifest object of the clause was to provide a ready means of establishing the existence and amount of the guaranteed debt and avoiding an inquiry upon legal evidence into the debits going to make up the indebtedness. The clause means what it says, that a certificate of the balance due to the bank by the customer shall be conclusive evidence of his indebtedness to the bank.'

But note that even in that case, and unlike an independent guarantee, the guarantee is not payable against documents; the function of the certificate is purely evidential.

1 *IE Contractors Ltd v Lloyds Bank plc* [1989] 2 Lloyd's Rep 205 at 207.1, per Leggatt J. For further proceedings, see note 1 to para **12.58**.
2 For example, see *General Surety and Guarantee Co Ltd v Francis Parker Ltd* (1977) 6 BLR 16.
3 *Bruns v Colocotronis* [1979] 2 Lloyd's Rep 412; *Alfred McAlpine Construction Ltd v Unex Corpn Ltd* (1994) 38 Con LR 63, CA.
4 (1935) 53 CLR 643.
5 [1973] 2 Lloyd's Rep 437.
6 (1935) 53 CLR 643 at 651.

(b)   Other features of conditional guarantees

12.6   (i) A guarantee falling within the Statute of Frauds must be in writing and signed by the person sought to be made liable under it, or by his agent.[1]

1 The Statute of Frauds 1677. The rule is here stated in very short form, and reference should be made to another work if a fuller statement on this very technical topic is required.

12.7   (ii) Every guarantee not under seal must be supported by consideration moving from the beneficiary of the guarantee, ie the creditor. It need not benefit the guarantor directly but may consist of an advantage given to the principal debtor by the creditor at the surety's request, such as an advance of money, or a forbearance to seek to recover money due. A past or executed consideration is insufficient.[1]

1 See *Chitty on Contracts* (30th edn) vol 2, paras 44-019 et seq.

12.8   (iii) As a surety a guarantor has a favoured position in English law. A number of events may result in his discharge, which the beneficiary of the guarantee would not ordinarily intend or perhaps expect.[1] Thus, if the principal debtor is discharged, the surety is usually discharged. Any variation of the terms of the contract with the principal debtor which might prejudice the surety and which occurs without the surety's consent will discharge the surety,[2] including an agreement to give time to the debtor. These serious inconveniences can be avoided by drawing the contract of guarantee appropriately.

1 See *Chitty on Contracts* (30th edn) vol 2, paras 44-070–44-110.
2 See the argument which prevailed at first instance in *Mercers v New Hampshire Insurance* [1992] 2 Lloyd's Rep 365, appeal allowed on other grounds.

12.9   Whether a particular instrument is treated as a conditional guarantee or not is a matter of construction and is not determined by what the parties may have chosen to call it. It can be a question of some difficulty and importance.

12.10   The problem is unlikely to arise in respect of standby credits because they are issued in an easily recognisable form similar to commercial credits but there are a number of authorities relating to disputes over performance bonds and demand guarantees which are considered at paras **12.54** et seq below.

Types of documents tendered

12.11   It is illustrative to set out a range of events or documents on which guarantee obligations may become payable, moving from those most favourable to the seller or contractor to those most favourable to the buyer or employer:

Most favourable to seller/contractor
–   proof of liability under a conditional guarantee as set out at para **12.5** above
–   a judgment or arbitration award in favour of the buyer or employer against the seller or contractor
–   the certificate of an (independent) third party, such as the engineer appointed pursuant to the conditions of an engineering or construction contract
–   a formal statement or certificate by the buyer or employer that there has been a default, and/or that the amount demanded is due
–   the simple demand of the buyer or employer

Most favourable to buyer/employer
–   a draft only; this is known in the United States, for obvious reasons, as a 'suicide credit'.[1]

1 See Uniform Commercial Code (US) §5–109, official commentary, para 3 and see *Oliver v Dubai Bank Kenya Ltd* [2007] EWHC 2165 (Comm) at para 16.

Governing rules

12.12   There are several sets of rules which may be incorporated into independent guarantees and standby credits:

- The UCP apply to standby credits, 'to the extent to which they may be applicable'.[1]
- International Standby Practices 1998 (ISP98) have been designed specifically to govern standby credits.
- The ICC Uniform Rules for Demand Guarantees apply to independent guarantees.[2]
- The UN Convention on Independent Guarantees and Standby Letters of Credit as its title indicates applies to standby credits and independent guarantees, but it has not yet been widely ratified.[3]

1 Article 1.
2 See para **12.90** below. A proposed revision of these Rules is currently under consideration and, at the time of writing, is at third draft stage within the ICC.
3 See para **12.93** below.

B   STANDBY CREDITS

Outline

12.13   A standby credit has a form similar to a commercial credit. It is usually issued by a bank and contains an undertaking to pay (or to accept drafts) against stated documents. The documents will typically relate to the non-performance or performance of a contract between the applicant and beneficiary. These may range from a simple statement of demand by the beneficiary, or a statement by the beneficiary that an amount is due, or a certificate signed by a third party, to an arbitration award or judgment, possibly accompanied by other documents. The important feature is that, as under a commercial credit, the bank gives an undertaking to pay against documents, which creates a primary obligation on the bank which is independent of the underlying transaction. A standby credit has the same commercial and contractual features as a commercial credit, so a corresponding bank may be used to advise the credit to the beneficiary and to effect payment when the credit is operated by presentation of documents, and this bank may confirm the credit.

History and development

12.14   Standby letters of credit originated in the United States, and came about because of prohibitions on national banking associations from issuing bonds by way of guarantees. They are used in domestic transactions of a very wide variety.[1]

1 See *Benjamin's Sale of Goods* (8th edn) para 23-237ff.

12.15   In some cases standby credits have begun to replace the use of commercial credits as payment for goods, eg in the international oil trade. The bank undertakes that it will pay against, eg, the written certificate of the seller that documents complying with the underlying contract have been presented to the buyer but payment has not been made.[1] Alternatively, copies of some or all of the documents presented to the buyer are also required. This gives much less security to the buyer (and the bank), since an unscrupulous seller can obtain payment without physically producing a bill of lading or other negotiable document of title. However, it is suggested that there are a number of reasons for this change in practice. First, it has the slight advantage that the buyer and seller are able to deal with each other direct so far as the documents are concerned and to avoid the banking chain, while giving the seller the security of a bank's undertaking with regard to payment. Secondly, the increasing use of non-negotiable transport documents such as waybills, and the widespread misuse of bills of lading, means that the documents tendered under a commercial credit may in practice provide little security in any event. Thirdly, and of most concern, the large number of non-conformant presentations, and the uncertainties in the law on rejection has made banks and beneficiaries more reluctant to commit to presenting or examining commercial documents. The use of pro-forma certificates or written demands under a standby credit substantially reduces the room for doubt about conformance.

1 This may be compared with the intended arrangements in *Sinason-Teicher Inter-American Grain Corpn v Oilcakes and Oilseeds Trading Co Ltd* [1954] 1 WLR 935 cited in para 3.21 above. There the buyers undertook to provide through their London bank a guarantee to the sellers that documents would be taken up under the CIF contract between them. It appears that the guarantee would have required the sellers to prove that documents had not been taken up in order to establish the bank's liability.

Legal nature

12.16   At the heart of a standby credit is the bank's undertaking to the beneficiary to pay as the credit provides if documents are presented in accordance with the terms and conditions of the credit. Subject to such minor distinctions as may follow from the difference in function, and hence the differences in the type of documents to be presented, it is suggested that in law a standby credit is no different from any other type of credit. In particular a standby credit is a transaction in documents, and it is an autonomous contract in that its performance is separate from and unaffected by the contract between the applicant or account party and the beneficiary which has given rise to it.[1] Since commercial credits and standby credits have the same legal structure, whether an instrument is called a 'standby credit' is merely a matter of terminology which is indicative of the purpose for which the credit is used and the type of documents required for payment.

1 UCP Article 4.

12.17   In *Kvaerner John Brown Ltd v Midland Bank plc*,[1] Kvaerner had arranged for a standby credit to secure its performance of a contract to supply plant and materials and provide design and engineering services for the construction of a chemical plant in Java, Indonesia. On Kvaerner's application for an injunction restraining payment on grounds of fraud, Cresswell J said:[2]

> 'Standby credits issued by banks at the request of a seller or contractor in favour of a buyer or employer are sometimes used in lieu of first demand bonds in respect of major long-term sales or construction contracts...Similar principles for present purposes apply both in relation to standby credits and first demand bonds. In the case of a first demand bond or a standby credit, banks assume irrevocable obligations. It is only in exceptional cases that the courts will interfere with the machinery of irrevocable obligations assumed by banks. Such obligations are regarded as collateral to[3] the underlying rights and obligations between the businessmen at either end of the banking chain.'

However, Cresswell J found that the facts in that case were exceptional – it was effectively undisputed that the certificate presented by the beneficiary under the credit was false – and granted an injunction.

1 [1998] CLC 446.
2 [1998] CLC 446, at 449.
3 Perhaps 'independent from...' is more accurate.

12.18   Similarly, in *TTI Team Telecom International Ltd v Hutchison 3G UK Ltd*[1] Judge Thornton QC, sitting in the Technology and Construction Court said:[2]

> 'This faith in and reliance upon the integrity of standby payments is vital for international and, indeed, much national commercial activity. It is for this reason that English courts have developed a clear non-interventionist approach when an issuer making payment to a beneficiary is asked to desist by a third party, usually the other party to the underlying transaction who will also be the customer of the issuer and who will have to reimburse the issuer when the issuer claims reimbursement for its payment under the documentary demand.'

The case in fact concerned a performance bond but, as the judge observed, similar principles apply. For further discussion of the case, and the circumstances in which the court may intervene, see para **9.29**.

1 [2003] 1 All ER (Comm) 914A.
2 At para 31.

12.19   A form of standby credit is used in the Lloyd's insurance market: some Names are required to obtain the opening of credits in favour of the Society of Lloyd's to secure their underwriting obligations. This led to litigation in Canada,[1] England[2] and Australia[3] when, after controversial heavy market losses, Lloyd's called on these credits. In litigation about whether the calls were fraudulent, 'neither party suggested that there was anything in the form of the letters of credit that affected the question at issue, and all were of the view that the position would be the same whether or not the documents in question are to be regarded as more akin to performance guarantees or standby letters of credit than documentary letters of credit'.[4]

1 *Society of Lloyd's v Canadian Imperial Bank of Commerce* [1993] 2 Lloyd's Rep 579; *Bank of Montreal v Mitchell* (1997) 143 DLR (4th) 697; *Royal Bank of Canada v Darlington* (1995) 54 ACWS (3d) 738. The English court struck out the banks' defence of fraud and awarded judgment against the banks. The banks paid the judgment and then successfully claimed reimbursement from the Names.
2 See note 1 above.
3 *Commonwealth Bank of Australia v White* (22 October 1999, unreported) Supreme Court of Victoria.
4 *Society of Lloyd's v Canadian Imperial Bank* [1993] 2 Lloyd's Rep 579 at 582. The judge agreed with this position.

12.20   In *Sepoong Engineering Construction Co Ltd v Formula One Management Ltd*,[1] Korea First Bank issued, and Natwest confirmed, a standby credit in favour of Formula One intended to provide payment in the event that a grand prix did not take place in Korea. There was a dispute about whether Formula One had agreed with Sepoong not to call the credit, but consistent with principle, this issue on the underlying contract could not prevent Formula One obtaining payment. Sepoong was compelled to bring an action in England to recover its payment from Formula One (which it lost).

1 [2000] 1 Lloyd's Rep 602.

12.21   Standby credits also featured in *Offshore International SA v Banco Central SA*,[1] *HongKong and Shanghai Banking Corpn v Kloeckner & Co AG*[2] and *Energy Shipping Co Ltd v UDL Shipping (Singapore) Pte Ltd*[3] and allegations concerning the opening of one were considered in *Paclantic Financing Co Inc v Moscow Narodny Bank Ltd*.[4] Reference was also made to the origin and nature of standby credits in *Potton Homes Ltd v Coleman Contractors (Overseas) Ltd*.[5] The unusual situation in *SAFA Ltd v Banque Du Caire*,[6] where Banque du Caire opened a standby credit payable against the presentation of a guarantee in favour of itself, has already been discussed at paras **5.102** and **9.36** above. Because the bank was involved in a related transaction with the beneficiary, it was in principle entitled to set off a claim against the beneficiary in reduction of its liability on the credit.

1 [1977] 1 WLR 399.
2 [1989] 2 Lloyd's Rep 323.
3 [1995] 3 SLR 25 (Singapore).
4 [1984] 1 WLR 930.

5 (1984) 28 BLR 19 at 26, per Eveleigh LJ.
6 [2000] 1 Lloyd's Rep 600.

12.22 The United States Court of Appeals examined the nature of a particular standby credit in *Barclays Bank DCO v Mercantile National Bank*.[1] The case was atypical in at least one factor in that the credit was confirmed by a bank but issued by a firm of mortgage brokers. But apart from that feature the case demonstrated one manner in which standby credits may commonly be used. The facts were as follows. BHC in Trinidad wished to borrow money from Barclays Bank in New York to finance a property development. AMI who were mortgage brokers in Atlanta, Georgia, issued to Barclays a letter of credit in the amount of the loan made to BHC by Barclays. The credit was sent to Barclays by AMI's bankers, Mercantile National Bank, under cover of a letter confirming that it was a valid letter of credit and giving the bank's confirmation of it and undertaking to honour drafts presented in accordance with it. Payment was to be made against a draft accompanied by 'This letter of credit. A signed statement to you[2] to the effect that the amount for which the draft is due and payable by [BHC] to you on account of loans from you to it, which matured...and are past due and unpaid...' It will be seen that another means of achieving the same effect under English law (but not under United States law because of the prohibition on national banks giving guarantees) would have been for the Mercantile National Bank to have issued their guarantee to Barclays payable against Barclays' demand accompanied by their certification of the amount due. This guarantee would have been backed by a guarantee or indemnity in favour of the Mercantile National Bank from AMI, and AMI would in their turn have received a guarantee or indemnity from BHC, the property developers. Returning to the facts of the case, when AMI dishonoured a draft drawn by Barclays pursuant to the credit, Barclays presented it to the Mercantile National Bank who denied liability. The court held that the credit fell within §5.102 of the Uniform Commercial Code, and that there was no reason why a bank should not confirm a non-bank's credit. In reaching this conclusion the court looked to the intent and purpose of the Code rather than to its precise wording – which probably favoured the opposite conclusion. In dealing with an argument that the credit was a guarantee and ultra vires the bank the court stated:[3]

> 'Mercantile's relationship to this transaction has been established as that of a confirming bank. "A confirming bank by confirming a credit becomes directly obligated on the credit to the extent of its confirmation as though it were its issuer and acquires the rights of an issuer." Section 5.107(2) (emphasis added). "It may seem that a letter of credit is in the nature of a guaranty. In fact, there is a vast difference between a guaranty and a letter of credit. The issuer of a credit assumes a primary obligation to the beneficiary as opposed to a secondary obligation under a guaranty." It is clear that Mercantile's obligation here is not a guaranty.'[4]

1 [1973] 2 Lloyd's Rep 541; 481 F2d 1224 (1973).
2 Sic: 'by you' was surely intended.
3 At [1973] 2 Lloyd's Rep 548.2.

4 The second quotation is from 50 Minn L Rev 454, J Halls. The court's own footnote to the final sentence is also worth quoting: 'A letter of credit always serves as a guaranty. This does not mean that it is a guaranty. A letter of credit is an identical twin to a guaranty, but the fact that the two things look alike and may be used for the same purpose and are difficult to distinguish one from the other, does not mean that they are the same thing, and does not mean that there are not differences, which, however subtle, are of major importance.' (H. Harfield, 'Uniform Commercial Code: Symposium – Code Treatment of Letters of Credit', 48 Corn LQ 92 at 93 (1963).) The comparison with a guarantee is not, it is suggested, valid where the transaction underlying the credit is one of sale or the provision of services. It is appropriate only where the credit is a standby credit as discussed under this heading.

12.23   It follows from the nature of standby credits that the risk to the account party – that is, the applicant – can be increased or diminished by choice of the document or documents against which the bank is to pay. Thus a credit which is payable against the beneficiary's draft accompanied by the beneficiary's demand with or without the beneficiary's statement that the sum has become due will afford the greatest security to the beneficiary and creates the greatest risk for the account party. On the other hand, one that requires a judgment or arbitration award against the account party to be included with the documents to be presented is difficult for the beneficiary to utilise and creates no undue risk for the account party. The one function which by nature a standby credit cannot perform is that of a guarantee which is payable not when documents are presented to the bank but is payable upon the fact (which must be proved) of non-performance of an underlying contract by a third party – usually the account party – namely the function fulfilled by a conditional guarantee as described at para **12.4** above. The nearest that a standby credit can obtain is to include among the documents to be presented a judgment or arbitration award or a signed admission by the account party that the amount called is due.

The UCP

12.24   UCP Article 1 begins:

'The Uniform Customs... are rules that apply to any documentary credit ("credit") (including, to the extent to which they may be applicable, any standby letter of credit) when the text of the credit expressly indicates that it is subject to these rules.'

12.25   UCP Article 2 defines 'Credit' as

'any arrangement, however, named or described, that is irrevocable and thereby constitutes a definite undertaking of the issuing bank to honour a complying presentation'.

Article 2 makes no reference to the function or purpose of the instrument and covers any arrangement which takes the form outlined, 'however named or described'. The UCP do not include any provisions which are specific to standby credits. It should be noted that the effect of UCP Article 1 is that, as with a commercial credit, the UCP apply to a standby credit only if the credit incorporates them.

12.26   The reference in the UCP to standby credits was made for the first time in UCP 400, the 1983 Revision, following an inquiry in 1977 by the Foreign Exchange Dealers Association of India.[1] The Association asked whether a standby letter of credit was to be regarded as a documentary credit covered by the 1973 Revision of the UCP or as a guarantee. The explanation provided to the Commission and on which the Commission gave its opinion was that a standby credit had the function of guaranteeing the performance of a contract and was realisable on the presentation to the issuing bank of a declaration that the underlying contract had not been fulfilled, with any other specified documents. It was said that standby credits were frequently used by United States and Japanese banks which were not authorised by law to issue guarantees. The Banking Commission's view was that such a standby credit fell within the definition provided, and that it should bear the wording that it was issued subject to the UCP.

1 See *Decisions* (1975–1979) ICC No 371, Ref 1, and UCP 1974/1983 *Revisions Compared and Explained*, ICC No 411, p 10.

12.27   A standby credit which is payable against a beneficiary's draft only – a 'clean' or 'suicide' credit – arguably falls outside the definition in Article 2 because it is not payable against a complying presentation of documents. Nevertheless, if the parties have sought expressly to incorporate the UCP , the credit should be construed to give effect to the presumed intention of the parties, and not to defeat it. It is therefore suggested that the UCP should be applied to the extent that they can be.

12.28   Another problem arises where the party issuing the credit is not a bank, or it is uncertain whether it is a bank or not. 'Bank' is not defined by the UCP, and what may be a bank under one municipal law may not be one under another. Here there is every reason to give effect to the intention of the parties expressed by the incorporation of the UCP into the credit, and to treat the party whose status as a bank is uncertain, or which is not a bank, as if it were one. That is clearly what the parties intended or would have intended had they considered the specific difficulty. The approach is supported by the decision in *Barclays Bank DCO v Mercantile National Bank*[1] discussed in para **12.22** above.

1 [1973] 2 Lloyd's Rep 541 (United States Court of Appeals).

(a)   Applicable Articles

12.29   Some articles in the UCP will clearly apply to standby credits. For example, Articles 7 and 8, setting out the undertakings of the issuing bank and any confirming bank, and Articles 4 and 5 , reflecting the principle of the autonomy of the credit, will all apply. These establish that, like a commercial credit, a standby credit is generally to be operated without regard to the terms or the performance of the underlying transaction. Articles 14, 15 and 16, as to the duty of banks examining documents and as to the duty of an issuing bank in taking up or refusing documents are also important. Precision of instruction as to the document or documents which are to be presented is particularly important, because it may alter the nature of the undertaking. On the other hand, the greater part of Articles 18 to 28, which govern the contents of tendered documents, will be inapplicable. Articles 19 to 27 which cover transport documents will not apply, since a transport document is not normally a required tender under a standby credit.

12.30   Article 29 which covers expiry dates and date for presentation is applicable. As has been mentioned in para **5.39** above, Article 32 provides a trap for standby credits. It states that, if the credit provides for instalments within given periods and any instalment is not drawn or shipped within the period, then the credit ceases to be available for that and any later instalments. The Article could be read as having the effect that, where a standby credit permits instalment drawings and one is not drawn because of the performance of the underlying obligation to which the credit relates, then the credit cannot be drawn on for any later instalment. Where a standby credit permits instalment drawings, either Article 32 should be excluded, or there should be an express provision stipulating that failure to draw in one period is not to affect the beneficiary's ability to draw in subsequent periods.

(b)   Strict compliance

12.31   Although the document or documents which the credit requires will often be such as to make the requirement of strict compliance one which is easily satisfied, perhaps even a formality, the bank should reject documents which do not comply strictly with the terms of the credit.[1] Documents 'which are almost the same, or which will do just as well' are to be rejected.[2] Of course, if the credit is not worded with precision, there may be little or nothing to which to apply the principle and, in the words of UCP Article 14.f 'banks will accept such documents as presented'. In short, the applicant for the credit should state clearly the terms in which the demand under the credit should be made, and also the terms of any accompanying certificate or other documents. Then, having incorporated the instructions of the credit, the bank must ensure that the beneficiary has precisely accorded with them before paying on the credit.[3]

---

1 See *Opinions* (1989–1991) ICC No 494, Ref 184, which indicates that in the United States compliance is more strictly required with standby credits than with ordinary credits.
2 Lord Sumner's dictum from *Equitable Trust Co of New York v Dawson Partners Ltd* (1926) 27 Ll L Rep 49 at 52.
3 Reference may also be made to para **12.70** below, where the need for strict compliance is considered in connection with performance bonds and guarantees.

ISP 98

12.32 In 1998 the ICC adopted and endorsed a new code known as International Standby Practices (ISP98) developed by the Institute of International Banking Law & Practice[1] at the request of the United States Department of State and in consultation with banks and other interested parties including the ICC. ISP98 is sometimes, although certainly not invariably, used instead of the UCP in standby credits. A full and detailed commentary on the rules, is given in Byrne, *The Official Commentary on the International Standby Practices*. It is not the intention here to present a detailed review of ISP98, but rather to indicate the broad principles and to identify the areas of difference from the UCP. The ISP98 rules are contained in Appendix 6.

1 http://www.iiblp.org.

12.33 ISP98 is applicable to independent guarantees as well as undertakings in the form of a traditional standby credit. In *TTI Team Telecom International Ltd v Hutchison 3G UK Ltd*,[1] a performance bond was issued subject to ISP98; indeed, the incorporation of ISP98 was an important factor indicating that the bond was intended to take effect as an independent guarantee rather than a conditional guarantee.

1 [2003] EWHC 762 (TCC); [2003] 1 All ER (Comm) 914.

12.34 The regime created by ISP98 is in many ways similar to that contained in the UCP. As with the UCP, ISP98 is given contractual effect only if expressly incorporated. ISP98 expressly does not cover defences to payment based on 'fraud, abuse, or other similar matters' which, as under the UCP, are left to applicable law.[1] The fundamental legal nature of a standby is set out in ISP98 rule 1.06: a standby is irrevocable, independent, documentary and binding when issued. As a consequence of its independence, the enforceability of the issuer's obligations does not depend on the issuer's right or ability to obtain reimbursement, the beneficiary's right to payment from the applicant, or the issuer's knowledge of performance or breach of any reimbursement agreement or underlying transaction. The basic obligation of the issuer of a standby is to honour a presentation which 'appears on its face to comply with the terms and conditions with the standby in accordance with these Rules supplemented by standard standby practice'.[2]

1 Rule 1.05c.
2 Rule 2.01a.

12.35 The main differences from the UCP are in the requirements as to the tender of conformant documents. These have been specifically tailored to standby credits, where in general the beneficiary is not, in contrast with a commercial traditional credit, presenting negotiable documents of commercial value. There has also been an attempt to resolve some of the problems of interpretation present in UCP 500, the revision in force when ISP98 was issued.

12.36 In a number of areas, the issuer is granted a discretion to waive certain formal requirements without reference to the applicant. For example, the issuer may 'in its sole discretion' waive the requirement that documents must not post-date the time of presentation.[1] The purpose of these discretionary powers is, according to *The Official Commentary*, to 'serve as a lubricant to the standby system'[2] and it is clearly the intention that the decision of the issuer should not be open to review by a court. It remains to be seen whether an English court would allow either an applicant or a beneficiary to challenge an exercise of the discretion if it were made without reasonable grounds or in bad faith.

1 Rule 4.06.
2 Note 4 to rule 3.11 at p 126.

(a) Presentation of documents

12.37 ISP98 is much stricter in prescribing the manner of presentation. The standby should indicate the time, place, person to whom and medium in which documents should be presented. Any failure to comply allows the bank to reject the presentation, although it has a discretion to waive some of these.[1] Documents must be presented in the medium indicated in the standby or else in paper form. However, where only a demand is required, a bank or SWIFT participant may present the demand by SWIFT tested telex or other similar authenticated means. Electronic presentation is not permitted unless provided for by the standby, but ISP98 is designed to encourage this by providing suitable definitions and procedures.[2] Commercial credits require presentation of documents which, at present, are typically issued in paper form by third parties and the scope for electronic presentation is limited. However, where only a demand or statement generated by the beneficiary is required, there is no reason why it should not be presented electronically. 'Where a presentation in an electronic medium is indicated, to comply a document must be presented as an electronic record capable of being authenticated by the issuer or nominated person to whom it is presented.'[3] Issues arising out of electronic presentations are discussed further in **Chapter 14**.

1 Rules 3.04, 3.06, 3.11.
2 Rules 1.09c, 3.06d.
3 Rule 3.06d.

12.38 Rule 3.10 expressly provides that an issuer is not required to notify the applicant upon receipt of a presentation under the standby. This differs from the ICC Uniform Rules for Demand Guarantees[1] which, in their current version, provide in Article 17 that the guarantor must notify his instructing party 'without delay'. *The Official Commentary* explains that the rationale for this is that a duty to notify the applicant calls into question the neutrality of the issuer and the independence of the standby.[2] The rule does not prevent the issuer from notifying the applicant; it seems that this is left to the issuer's discretion. One can see potential problems if, eg the applicant has clear evidence that any demand would be fraudulent but loses an opportunity to demonstrate this to the issuer because it is not aware that demand has been made.[3] Presumably rule 3.10 would protect the issuer's right to reimbursement in such circumstances.

1 See para **12.90** below.
2 See p 122.
3 This might have arisen on the facts in *Kvaerner John Brown Ltd v Midland Bank plc* [1998] CLC 446, where an injunction was granted because the demand certified that a written notice of default had been given to the applicant but it was effectively undisputed that that was untrue.

(b) Examination

12.39 The issuer's duty to examine the documents is stated in rule 4.01: 'Whether a presentation appears to comply is determined by examining the presentation on its face against the terms and conditions stated in the standby as interpreted and supplemented by these Rules which are to be read in the context of standard standby practice.' A documentary demand is required in all cases, even if not specified by the standby.[1] Documents need not be signed unless the standby so requires.[2] An important difference from the UCP is that data conflict amongst documents is not a ground for rejection, an issuer is required to examine documents for inconsistency with each other only to the extent provided in the standby.[3]

1 Rule 4.08.
2 Rule 4.07.
3 Rule 4.03. Contrast Article 14.d of the UCP; see paras **8.42** et seq.

12.40 Standbys usually require a demand or statement of default in a specified form. ISP98 allows for three possibilities with increasing levels of required precision.[1] If the standby does not specify the precise wording, then the tendered document must 'appear to convey the same meaning as that required by the standby'; if the standby quotes or exhibits the wording to be used, then the same words must be used but subject to minor typographical errors or formatting variations; if the standby requires the wording to be 'exact' or 'identical' to that specified, then an exact reproduction is essential, including typographical errors in spelling, punctuation, spacing in the standby. This last mechanism should be used very rarely if at all by banks, the purpose of requiring an exact reproduction is unclear and raises a horrifying prospect of large claims turning on whether a document should have contained a semicolon rather than a comma.

1 Rules 4.16, 4.17.

12.41 As under the UCP, non-documentary conditions in the standby can be disregarded. However, a condition is not non-documentary if its fulfilment can be 'determined by the issuer from the issuer's own records or within the issuer's normal operations', eg the date of presentation of the document to the issuer or a fact which can be taken from a published index (eg if a standby provides for determining amounts of interest accruing according to published interest rates).[1]

1 Rule 4.11.

(c)   Rejection

12.42 If the issuer rejects the presentation it must give a notice of dishonour stating all discrepancies on which the dishonour is based and return the documents to the beneficiary or dispose of them on his instructions. Failure to give notice precludes the issuer from relying on a discrepancy subsequently.[1] However, unlike the UCP, a failure to state that the documents are being returned or held pending a waiver or pending further instructions from the beneficiary does not preclude a defence to payment by the issuer.[2] This reflects the fact that documents presented under standby credits normally have no intrinsic value. The ISP98 rules on giving notice of dishonour differ from those in both UCP500 and UCP600. Notice must be given within a reasonable time, but notice within three days after presentation is deemed reasonable and notice more than seven days is deemed not reasonable.[3] A particular feature of ISP98 is that if the applicant refuses to take up documents from the issuer he is obliged to give a notice of dishonour to the issuer specifying the discrepancies, failing which he is precluded from raising them. No fixed time period is given, but notification must be given 'within a time after the applicant's receipt of the documents which is not unreasonable'.[4]

1 Rules 5.01 to 5.03.
2 Rule 5.07. Contrast UCP Article 16.c.iii.
3 Rule 5.01.
4 Rule 5.09.

(d)   Reimbursement

12.43 Rule 8.01 provides for the issuer's right to reimbursement on payment against a complying presentation. The applicant must also indemnify the issuer against all claims arising out of 'the fraud, forgery or illegal action of others'.[1] *The Official Commentary* notes that the risk of fraudulent presentations is to be borne by the applicant. It is not clear whether it is intended that the applicant should still bear the risk if the fraud was apparent to the issuer at the time of presentation, presumably not.

1 Rule 8.01b.ii.

Fraudulent and abusive calls

12.44   Where the document or documents against which the credit is payable lie within the power of the beneficiary alone, as is the position where the document is the beneficiary's written demand or his demand accompanied by his own certificate or statement in terms provided by the credit, the credit is open to considerable abuse by the beneficiary. If he is without scruple, he may make a demand under the credit whether or not he has a genuine belief that the account party is at fault in the manner intended by the credit. He will nonetheless be assured of payment unless the bank is prepared to refuse payment on the ground that it can establish lack of genuine belief so the fraud exception is established.[1] As is made clear by the outcome of the cases on fraud considered in **Chapter 9**, it will be an exceptional case in which a beneficiary fails to obtain payment on this ground. Even in cases where the situation is that the applicant is only arguably at fault and there may be considerable doubt about it, unless the beneficiary wishes to preserve his relationship with the account party, he is very likely to present documents under the credit to utilise his advantage. 'In short, the consequences of a call on a standby letter of credit... can be harsh, draconian and abrupt.'[2]

1 See **Chapter 9**.
2 *Royal Bank of Canada v Darlington* (1995) 54 ACWS (3d) 738, per Blair J.

12.45   An account party who wishes to avoid being wholly at the mercy of the beneficiary may have two lines of action open to him depending on whether he is in a position to negotiate the terms of the credit or not. His best course is to arrange for the inclusion among the documents to be presented of one which depends upon a third party of integrity. Thus his position might be improved if, where the underlying contract was an engineering or construction contract, the certificate of the architect engineer or quantity surveyor appointed under the contract was required. It has to be borne in mind that such persons are appointed by the employer under the contract, namely the beneficiary of the credit, and may tend to favour the employer. This may be particularly so in situations where the protection is most badly needed because the employer is seen as likely to behave in an unscrupulous manner. Where the underlying contract is one of sale of goods, the certificate of an independent inspection agency may be required. In other situations it may be possible to utilise the certificate of a company's auditors or that of an independent firm of accountants. Even if appointed by the employer, any third party giving a certificate in those circumstances owes a duty of care to the beneficiary, since it is given for his benefit: *Niru Battery Manufacturing Co v Milestone Trading Ltd*.[1]

1 [2004] 1 Lloyd's Rep 344. See further para **8.152**.

12.46   Another means of providing some limited protection is to ensure that the credit does not become operable until an appropriate event has occurred. This will probably be the opening of the credit by which payment pursuant to the underlying contract is to be made to the account party for the standby credit. Similarly the account party may try to arrange a cut-off point at the other end. Obviously the earlier the expiry date is, the more advantageous to him. It has to be remembered that it may well happen that, as the expiry date draws near, an unscrupulous beneficiary will ask for the credit to be extended, threatening that, if it is not, he will present documents under the credit. The applicant may try to include a cancellation clause, entitling him to require the cancellation of the credit by presenting a certificate that the underlying contract has been fully and satisfactorily performed on his part.

12.47 The circumstances in which the bank can refuse payment on the grounds of fraud by the beneficiary have been considered in **Chapter 9**. The same principles apply to a standby credit as apply to an ordinary credit.[1] It may be that in the case of standby credits and performance bonds the English courts will tend to the easing of the rule in order to check at least some of the apparently blatant abuses by beneficiaries which have gone unchecked so far.[2] It must be said, however, that if parties enter into transactions which may so easily be abused, there is only a very limited role which the courts can play in preventing that abuse if they are not to rewrite the bargains into which the parties have entered.

1 *Society of Lloyd's v Canadian Imperial Bank of Commerce* [1993] 2 Lloyd's Rep 579; *Kvaerner John Brown Ltd v Midland Bank plc* [1998] CLC 446.
2 See *United Trading Corpn SA v Allied Arab Bank Ltd* [1985] 2 Lloyd's Rep 554n at 561. See also *TTI Team Telecom International Ltd v Hutchison 3G UK Ltd* [2003] 1 All ER (Comm) 914, where Judge Thornton QC held that 'lack of good faith' by the beneficiary might justify non-payment; see further para **9.29** above.

C INDEPENDENT GUARANTEES

Functions of independent guarantees

(a) Performance bonds and guarantees

12.48 These are the most common, and can be used for straightforward contracts of sale as well as for construction and other complicated projects. Thus, in the case of sale, if a buyer is in a sufficiently strong commercial position to do so, he may require the seller to open a performance bond for a proportion, perhaps 5% or 10% of the purchase price, this to be payable on first demand in the event of the seller's failure correctly to perform the sale contract. For example, the underlying contracts in the *Harbottle* case[1] were for the sale of horse tic beans and for the sale of coal. If the seller is wise, he will, if he can, procure that his bond only becomes effective after the buyer has opened his letter of credit: this will avoid the risk that there will be disputes over the credit and the buyer will call the bond.[2] Sometimes a seller will simply add the amount of the bond, or a substantial proportion of it, to the contract price because he knows that there is a strong likelihood of the bond being called whether or not he correctly performs his part of the contract.

1 *RD Harbottle (Mercantile) Ltd v National Westminster Bank Ltd* [1978] QB 146.
2 *Edward Owen Engineering Ltd v Barclays Bank International Ltd* [1978] QB 159.

(b)   Bid or tender bonds or guarantees

12.49   Where bids or tenders are called for on large contracts the buyer (or employer) may want an assurance that the tenderers are wholly serious and capable of undertaking the work and will be able to enter a contract to do so supported by the appropriate performance bond if they are selected. The tender instructions will then require that the tenderers supply a bond which will be released either if the tenderer is not selected or following the entering into of the contract and the provision of the contract performance bond within a specified period. The tender bond must almost of necessity be a demand bond.

(c)   Advance payment bonds or guarantees

12.50   If an advance payment is to be made to a contractor or seller to provide him with some immediate finance, the employer or buyer can obtain security by means of a bond providing for repayment of the advance should the seller fail to perform the contract. An example is to be found in *Howe Richardson Scale Ltd v Polimex-Cekop*.[1] The guarantee covered an advance payment of £25,000 on the contract price of £500,000 for equipment to be manufactured by the plaintiffs. The guarantee was called by the making of a demand when the plaintiffs who had completed manufacture did not ship the equipment: the defendants had failed to open a letter of credit and to give shipping instructions. Another example is *Gulf Bank KSC v Mitsubishi Heavy Industries Ltd (No 2)*[2] where Mitsubishi arranged for an advance payment guarantee to the Kuwaiti Ministry which was later called as a result of the Iraqi invasion. A more recent example is *Uzinterimpex JSC v Standard Bank plc*,[3] where the advance payment guarantee, provided in relation to consignments of cotton, was called even though the goods had been received by the buyer. The case is discussed in para **12.69** below.

1 [1978] 1 Lloyd's Rep 161.
2 [1994] 2 Lloyd's Rep 145.
3 [2008] 2 Lloyd's Rep 456.

(d)   Retention money bonds or guarantees

12.51   It is common practice for construction and engineering contracts to provide for moneys otherwise certified as payable to be retained until completion of the work, partly by way of security, and partly because although work may have been certified for payment it is possible that maintenance work will be required in respect of it under the maintenance provisions of the contract. The employer may be prepared to release all or part of the retention moneys against a bond provided by the contractor which will give the employer security of recovery should the contractor default.

(e)   Maintenance bonds or guarantees

12.52   These secure the performance of a contractor during the maintenance period of a construction contract and are commonly linked to the release of retention moneys.

Legal nature

12.53   Independent guarantees are an autonomous obligation of the guarantor to pay against stipulated documents. In *Edward Owen Engineering Ltd v Barclays Bank International Ltd*[1] Lord Denning MR stated:[2]

> 'All this leads to the conclusion that the performance guarantee stands on a similar footing to a letter of credit. A bank which gives a performance guarantee must honour that guarantee according to its terms. It is not concerned in the least with the relations between the supplier and the customer; nor with the question whether the supplier is in default or not. The bank must pay according to its guarantee, on demand, if so stipulated, without proof or conditions. They only exception is where there is a clear case of fraud of which the bank has notice.'

The position of fraud as the 'only exception' has come under challenge in recent years from the doctrines of unconscionability (see para **9.26** et seq) and illegality (see para **13.106** et seq).

1 [1978] QB 159.
2 [1978] QB 159 at 171.

Construction: independent or conditional guarantee?

12.54   As mentioned at the start of this chapter, it is often unclear from its terms whether a particular instrument was intended to act as an independent guarantee or a conditional guarantee. This is a question of the greatest importance: under an independent guarantee, payment must be made against documents, under a conditional guarantee, proof of primary liability is required which means that there will have to be an extensive investigation of the facts and possibly a lengthy trial before payment will be ordered. The analysis is often complicated by the confusing terminology but, as one might expect, the terminology used is not conclusive and the court must analyse the substance of the obligation undertaken. In *American Home Assurance Co v Hong Lam Marine Pte Ltd*,[1] the Singapore Court of Appeal stated:

> 'The term "performance bond" or "performance guarantee" is sometimes used to denote a genuine contract of guarantee or indemnity. To make matters even more confusing, a guarantee or indemnity may be given in circumstances in which one might expect to find a true performance bond. The nature of the particular contract, whether it happens to be a guarantee or an indemnity, or a performance bond, and whether the normal incidents of a contract of that class have been modified, is ultimately a question of construction in each case, and is often very difficult to resolve...'

1 [1999] 3 SLR 682.

12.55   The principal authorities in which the question has arisen are discussed below. Each case turns on the wording of the relevant instrument, but it may be concluded from the cases that, where a guarantee or bond is stated to be payable by a bank or other financial institution on demand, in the absence of clear words indicating that liability under it is conditional upon the existence of liability on the part of the account party in connection with the underlying transaction, the guarantee is to be construed as an independent guarantee entitling its beneficiary to payment simply against an appropriately worded demand accompanied by such other documents as the guarantee may require.[1] In particular, such a guarantee will not be construed as payable only if a particular event has occurred simply because the guarantee sets out, without more, the event or events following the happening of which it is intended that a demand may be made. It is possible that where the guarantee is part of an international transaction the tendency of the court to hold that all that is required is an appropriate demand together with any other documents as may be specified by the guarantee, will be stronger than in a purely domestic context.

1 The position may be somewhat different in a non-banking context, see *Marubeni Hong Kong and South China Ltd v Government of Mongolia* [2005] EWCA Civ 395; [2005] 1 WLR 2497, discussed at para **12.61** below.

12.56   *Esal Commodities Ltd v Oriental Credit Ltd*.[1] The applicant for the bond, Reltor Ltd, an associate company of Esal, went into liquidation. The bond provided 'We, hereby issue this performance bond for a sum not exceeding US$487,300... being 10 per cent of the tender value... We undertake to pay the said amount of your written demand in the event that the supplier fails to ship the agreed quantity in accordance with the terms of their contract with you and subject to the receipt of irrevocable sight letter of credit confirmed and payable in London from you in their favour.' It was contended by Oriental Credit as the bank indemnifying Wells Fargo Bank who in their turn were indemnifying the Banque du Caire who had confirmed and paid on the bond, that there was no liability under the bond unless and until there had been a breach of the underlying contract of sale and that this had never been established. The court held that the bond was not conditional, because the parties could not have intended that it should be. If it was conditional, the bank would have had to decide the merits of the dispute under the contract of sale. '. . . if the performance bond was so conditional, then unless there was clear evidence that the seller admitted that he was in breach of the contract of sale, payment could never safely be made by the bank except on a judgment of a competent court of jurisdiction and this result would be wholly inconsistent with the entire object of the transaction, namely to enable the beneficiary to obtain prompt and certain payment'.[2] The court also referred to the nature of a performance bond as established in the *Edward Owen* case,[3] in particular that the bank is not concerned with relations between the supplier and the customer and the performance of the contractual obligations between them, subject to the fraud exception.[4] It may be said that the approach of the court was to categorise the bond as a first demand performance bond and to deduce from this that it was unconditional and the bank was not concerned with liability on the underlying contract. But banks do give conditional guarantees, whose function is the perfectly valid one of providing security against the insolvency of a seller or a contractor, and which are not intended to provide payment until the default has been established. The answer provided by the Court of Appeal was almost certainly correct. But the reasoning had surely to start with the wording of the undertaking. The reasoning might have been: it is called a performance bond; it relates to an international sale of a commodity, sugar; it refers to 'paying the amount of your written demand'; it then refers to the event in which demand may be made; but that it is not expressed in a way which makes it clear, contrary to what is commonly to be expected in transactions such as this, that the demand can only be made if the event has in fact occurred; the bond is therefore to be construed as payable simply on an appropriate demand. In any event it is to be remembered that the bond was issued in Egypt and was probably subject to Egyptian law. The Banque du Caire had been held liable under the bond in proceedings before an Egyptian tribunal. So there is some unreality in discussing the nature of the undertaking as if English law applied to it.

1 [1985] 2 Lloyd's Rep 546.
2 [1985] 2 Lloyd's Rep 546 at 549.2.
3 *Edward Owen Engineering Ltd v Barclays Bank International Ltd* [1978] QB 159.
4 See [1985] 2 Lloyd's Rep 546 at 549.2.

12.57 *Siporex Trade SA v Banque Indosuez.*[1] The key words were '. . .we hereby engage and undertake to pay on your first written demand any sum or sums not exceeding US$1,071,000 in the event that, by latest 7 December 1984 no banker's irrevocable letter of credit has been issued in favour of Siporex. . . . Any claims hereunder must be supported by your declaration to that effect. . .'. Hirst J referred to the decision of the Court of Appeal in the *Esal Commodities* case[2] and commented on the similarity of the wording of the bond in that case. The judge accepted that every bond had to be construed according to its terms, but he held that he was bound by authority to construe it as an unconditional bond payable on demand without reference to the underlying events. He continued:

> 'I also consider it is extremely important that, for such a frequently adopted commercial transaction, there should be consistency of approach by the Courts, so all parties know clearly where they stand. The whole commercial purpose of a performance bond is to provide a security which is to be readily, promptly and assuredly realizable when the prescribed event occurs; a purpose reflected in the provision here that it should be payable "on first demand". The defendants' approach in this part of the case would frustrate that essential purpose.'

It is suggested that the wording was in fact clearer than in the *Esal Commodities* case,[3] because the need for a declaration to the effect that no credit had been issued. This showed that the bond was payable on a written demand accompanied by the declaration.[4] *Siporex* was applied in *Frans Maas (UK) Ltd v Habib Bank AG Zurich*[5] where it was held that the words 'we.... hereby guarantee, waiving all right of objection and defence, the payment to yourselves a sum not exceeding [£500,000] on your first demand... Your claims should be received by us in writing stating therein that the Principals have failed to pay you under their contractual obligation' were held to be entirely apt for a demand guarantee.

1 [1986] 2 Lloyd's Rep 146.
2 [1985] 2 Lloyd's Rep 546.
3 [1985] 2 Lloyd's Rep 546.
4 For reports of the subsequent proceedings brought by the buyers, Comdel, in support of their attempts to recover by arbitration the amount paid under the bond and in respect of which they had had to indemnify Banque Indosuez, see *Comdel v Siporex (No 2)* [1988] 2 Lloyd's Rep 590, Steyn J; on appeal [1989] 2 Lloyd's Rep 13, CA; affd [1991] 1 AC 148. The saga continued in *Comdel v Siporex* [1997] 1 Lloyd's Rep 424 when the Court of Appeal discharged Comdel's Mareva injunction for delay in prosecuting the claim.
5 (3 August 2000, unreported).

12.58   *IE Contractors Ltd v Lloyds Bank plc.*[1] These proceedings concerned three performance bonds which had been issued in favour of an Iraqi beneficiary by an Iraqi bank, Rafidain, in relation to the performance by the ultimate account party, IE,[2] of contracts to build three poultry slaughterhouses in Iraq. The bonds were issued by Rafidain at the request of IE's bank, Lloyds, against counter-indemnities from Lloyds who in turn received counter-indemnities from IE. The bonds were governed by the law of Iraq. In giving the leading judgment in the Court of Appeal Staughton LJ pointed out that the general nature of performance bonds had been often considered by the English courts over 12 years, and that the decisions, and the general practice of bankers, may be a guide as to what the parties are likely to have intended, and may be treated as part of the surrounding circumstances which are relevant to the construction of a bond. Nonetheless, as he emphasised, it was the task of the court to construe the particular documents. He continued:

'The first principle which the cases establish is that a performance bond, like a letter of credit, will generally be found to be conditioned upon the presentation of one or more documents, rather than upon the actual existence of facts which those documents assert. If the letter of credit or bond requires a document asserting that goods have been shipped or that a contract has been broken, and if such a document is presented, the bank must pay. It is nothing to the point that the document is untruthful, and that the goods have not been shipped or the contract not broken. The only exception is what is called established or obvious fraud. This doctrine had been laid down in recent years by cases too numerous to mention. The justification for it is said to be that bankers can check documents, but do not have the means or the inclination to check facts, at any rate for the modest commission which they charge on a letter of credit or performance bond. There has been no suggestion that the fraud exception applies in this case.

We were told, and I am quite prepared to accept, that some performance bonds are payable merely upon a demand being made, without requiring the presentation of any other document or the assertion of any fact (unless the demand itself contains an implied assertion that the money is due). It was suggested that even an oral demand would be sufficient; but I would hesitate long before construing a performance bond as having that effect.

On the other hand there is no reason why a performance bond should not depart from the usual pattern, and be conditioned upon the existence of facts rather than the production of a document asserting those facts. It might be inconvenient for the bank, but it is a perfectly lawful contract if the parties choose to make it.'

He then referred to the *Esal Commodities* case[3] and after quoting from the judgment of Ackner LJ[4] stated:

'I take this to show that there is a bias or presumption in favour of the construction which holds a performance bond to be conditioned upon documents rather than facts. But I would not hold the presumption to be irrebuttable, if the meaning is plain.'[5]

He held that on the wording of the bond it was payable on a demand being made stating that it was a claim for damages brought about by IE. It is suggested that this judgment, with which Purchase LJ agreed, correctly sets out the approach which should be adopted by an English court.[6]

1 [1990] 2 Lloyd's Rep 496; on appeal from [1989] 2 Lloyd's Rep 205, injunction proceedings at (1985) 30 BLR 48.
2 Formerly called GKN Contractors.
3 [1985] 2 Lloyd's Rep 546, see para **12.56** above.
4 [1985] 2 Lloyd's Rep 546 at 549.
5 Later in his judgment he held that two of the three counter-indemnities given by Lloyds to Rafidain were payable on an occurrence and a demand, the occurrence being that Rafidain was obliged to pay under its guarantee to the Iraqi beneficiary.
6 The short judgment of the third member of the court, Sir Denys Buckley, expressed neither agreement nor disagreement with these principles, but set out his reasoning for reaching a like conclusion to that of Staughton LJ on the particular wording of the Iraqi bonds.

12.59 *Trafalgar House Ltd v General Surety Co.*[1] The House of Lords had to construe a 'conditional bond', an instrument widely used in the construction industry. There is a longstanding practice of requiring contractors in building or construction contracts to provide a bond or guarantee from the bank or insurance company to secure the performance of their obligations. It has usually taken the form of what is known as a double or conditional bond and has two parts. The first is a promise to pay a sum of money, namely the maximum to which the obligor is to be liable. The second part is phrased as a condition to the first part and sets out the real promise, which is to the following effect. If the contractor performs the contract or, if on his default the obligor satisfies the damages thereby sustained by the employer, the promise contained in the first part shall be void. To avoid problems of consideration such a bond is always under seal. The Court of Appeal in *Trafalgar House* had held that the bond imposed an independent obligation to pay up to the amount of the bond when called upon to do so by the respondents. However, this holding was reversed in the House of Lords:[2]

'In recent years there has come into existence a creature described as an "on demand bond" in terms of which the creditor is entitled to be paid merely on making a demand for the amount of the bond. An example of such a bond is to be found *Esal (Commodities) Ltd v Oriental Credit Ltd* [1985] 2 Lloyd's Rep. 546:

"We undertake to pay the said amount on your written demand in the event that the supplier fails to execute the contract in perfect performance..."

All that was required to activate it was a demand by the creditor stated to be on the basis of the event specified in the bond...

My Lords, I have no doubt that the Court of Appeal were in error in concluding that the bond [in the present case] was not a guarantee but was akin to an on-demand bond. No distinction can, in my view, properly be drawn between the effect of this bond minus the second part of the condition and the bond considered by Lord Atkin in the *Workington* case [1937] AC 1, 17 and other bonds using this or similar wording which have for many years been generally treated as guarantees (*Hudson's Building and Engineering Contracts*, 11th ed (1995), vol 2, pp 1499–1500, para 17-007). Thus in a second action arising out of the bond in the *Workington* case, *Workington Harbour & Dock Board v Trade Indemnity Co Ltd (No 2)* [1938] 2 All ER 101, 105, Lord Atkin said:

"My Lords, both actions were brought on the money bond." – [That is the first and second actions.] – "It is well established that in such an action the plaintiff has to establish damages occasioned by the breach or breaches of the conditions, and, if he succeeds, he recovers judgment on the whole amount of the bond, but can only issue execution for the amount of the damages proved."

This dictum makes it clear beyond doubt that proof of damage and not mere assertion thereof is required before liability under such a bond arises.

I have therefore no hesitation in concluding that the Chambers bond without the second part of the condition would amount to a guarantee and that the appellants would be entitled to raise all questions of sums due and cross-claims which would have been available to Chambers in an action against them for damages.'

Therefore, the traditional form of conditional bond gives the beneficiary no advantage over a conditional guarantee. It provides another, and more secure, source of payment, but it does not make the employer's task of recovering loss any easier than against the contractor. For in the absence of a specific provision in the bond to contrary effect he has to prove the contractor's default and what it has cost him. He may also face the special defences provided under English law to protect the position of sureties.[3]

1 [1996] AC 199.
2 [1996] AC 199 at 206–207.
3 See para **12.6** above.

12.60 *Gold Coast Ltd v Caja de Ahorros del Mediterraneo*.[1] Certain Spanish banks issued a 'refund guarantee' in relation to stage payments for the purchase of a chemical tanker under construction. The issue was whether the refund guarantee was an independent (demand) or conditional guarantee. Tuckey LJ observed:[2]

> 'In the construction industry advance payment guarantees are often issued to employers who make stage payments to contractors. Similarly, refund guarantees are a common feature of the shipbuilding industry. However, as the Judge notes, there is no standard practice in relation to such guarantees; they can either be in the form of independent performance bonds (or stand-by letters of credit) or true "see to it" guarantees. The question therefore is simply what is the nature of the refund guarantees in this case. This involves construing the instrument in its factual and contractual context having regard to its commercial purpose.
>
> … the task is to decide the nature of the instrument by looking at it as a whole without any preconceptions as to what it is…'

After considering the *I.E. Contractors*, *Esal*, and *Trafalgar House* cases discussed above, as well as the statement in para **12.57** of the third edition of this book (now para **12.55** above), he concluded that the instrument was an independent guarantee:[3]

> 'The instrument has all the appearances of a first demand guarantee. It describes itself as a guarantee, but this is simply a label; it does not use the language of guarantee. Rather the obligation, which is expressed to be an "irrevocable and unconditional undertaking", is that the banks "will pay" on a first written demand. The only express condition of payment is contained in condition 1. This requires a certificate but makes no reference to arbitration or underlying liability under the shipbuilding contract. The instrument contains its own dispute resolution provisions.'

Although the refund guarantee also contained a condition that liability would not be affected by any amendment or variation of the underlying agreement, a clause more usually seen in conditional guarantees, this was not sufficient to tip the balance. There might have been a good reason for including such a clause in an independent guarantee:

> 'It might, for example, have been included to avoid any argument that variation of the shipbuilding contract by, for example, postponing a stage

payment or remitting part of it in settlement of any cross-claim would imperil recovery under the refund guarantees. It could have been inserted simply to ensure that the rule applicable to true guarantees did not apply to this instrument.'[4]

1 [2003] 1 All ER (Comm) 142.
2 Paras 11, 15. See also *ILG Capital LLC v Van der Merwe* [2008] EWCA Civ 542.
3 Para 21.
4 Para 25.

12.61   *Marubeni Hong Kong and South China Ltd v Government of Mongolia.*[1] The claimant entered into a sale contract with a Mongolian company for the supply of machinery, equipment and services for a cashmere processing plant in Mongolia. The purchase price of US$18.8 million was secured by an arrangement with the Mongolian Government through the Mongolian Central Bank. Whether the arrangement was an independent or conditional guarantee was important because there had been significant rescheduling of the instalment payments of the purchase price without any reference to the Government of Mongolia, meaning that if it were a conditional guarantee, the surety's liability had almost certainly been discharged. The Court of Appeal reiterated that the label of the arrangement was not determinative of its character. It went on, however, to draw a distinction between labels used in the banking context and those used outside it: the cases on banks entering into performance bonds and demand guarantees are not of assistance when interpreting a document which was not issued by a bank and which contained no overt indication of an intention to create a performance bond or demand guarantee. Outside the banking context, the description of an arrangement as a guarantee would be strongly presumptive of a secondary obligation. The essential terms of the arrangement in question were that the Mongolian Government 'unconditionally pledges to pay' the seller upon its 'simple demand' all amounts payable under the sale contract 'if not paid when the same become due'. The former wording is typical of the language used in first demand bonds (independent primary obligations), the latter strongly suggestive of a secondary obligation more akin to a traditional guarantee. The Court of Appeal held that on a proper construction, the obligation in this case was a secondary one.

1 [2005] EWCA Civ 395; [2005] 1 WLR 2497.

Consideration as between the issuing bank and the beneficiary

12.62   The problem of identifying the consideration to support the contractual undertaking of the issuing bank has already been addressed in relation to documentary credits.[1] It may be thought that in a commercial situation where the parties intend that their undertakings shall be enforceable between them, the need for consideration as a condition of that enforceability is an outmoded concept. But while the court will take a practical approach and will find consideration in such situations wherever it may be found,[2] where no consideration exists for a promise it is ordinarily only enforceable in English law if it is made under seal. It was suggested in **Chapter 5** that documentary credits may constitute an exception to this general rule. However, it is clearly established in the law of conditional guarantees that consideration is required if the guarantee is to be enforceable. It is also well established in that field that past consideration will not save the contract.[3] It would therefore be more difficult to argue that independent guarantees are enforceable without consideration.

1 See para **5.8**.
2 See *New Zealand Shipping Co Ltd v AM Satterthwaite & Co Ltd* [1975] AC 154 at 167, PC, per Lord Wilberforce.
3 As to consideration generally, see *Chitty on Contracts* (30th edn), ch 3; as to consideration in relation to guarantees, see *Chitty on Contracts* (30th edn), paras 44-019 et seq.

12.63   There are two aspects to the problem:[1]

(a) The more difficult aspect is to find consideration to support the bank's promise from the moment of the issue of the guarantee. This is the difficulty which arises in connection with irrevocable documentary credits.[2] If a demand guarantee is not under seal and consideration is required and cannot be found, the consequence is that it is open to the issuing bank at any time at least up to the presentation of a demand to repudiate its liability under the guarantee and in effect to withdraw the guarantee. The position in respect of irrevocable documentary credits is that it is established that they are binding in law from the moment of issue. The legal basis is unclear: it is suggested that mercantile custom has established an exception to the consideration rule.[3] The position at and after a presentation of a demand to the bank under a demand guarantee gives rise to the second aspect.

1 The problem will only arise where the relevant obligation is governed by English law or some other law which requires consideration.
2 See para **5.8** above.
3 See para **5.11** above.

12.64   (b) The second aspect is the position when and after a demand is made pursuant to the terms of the guarantee. If a demand guarantee is enforceable from the moment of issue, this does not require separate examination. But, if it is assumed that it is not, the guarantee can be treated as an offer that, if a demand according with its terms is made, payment will be made by the bank in accordance with the guarantee. The presentation of the demand is then an acceptance of this offer. The preparation of the document or documents and the delivery of them to the bank by the beneficiary can be treated as a detriment suffered by him, which provides the consideration to support the contract made by the offer and acceptance as described. This will not be artificial where the beneficiary has had to obtain a third party document such as a certificate. Where all that is required is the beneficiary's demand, the criticism of artificiality has greater weight. Nonetheless, if a guarantee is not binding for lack of consideration prior to the making of a demand and given the great need to find consideration and achieve enforceability, it may be that it can be found in this way even where all that has to be presented is a demand. If that is right, the ambit of the problem, and the risk to a beneficiary, are reduced to whether it is open to a bank which has issued a demand guarantee or bond to repudiate its obligation at any time before the beneficiary has made his demand.

12.65 When a bank issues a demand guarantee, that will often be the first contact between the bank and the beneficiary. The reason for its issue is the previously concluded underlying contract made between the account party and the beneficiary. But it is unlikely that the issuing bank will have had any involvement in the negotiations at that stage. Further, where the issuing bank is a bank instructed and to be indemnified by the account party's bank, as is usually the case, it will have no contact at all with the account party. Consideration must move from the promisee, here the beneficiary. It need not move to the promisor, the bank giving the undertaking. Nonetheless, it is difficult to see what consideration the beneficiary of a bond provides in connection with the actual issue of the guarantee, whether by way of detriment to himself, or by way of benefit to another. The problem is that the underlying contract between the account party and the beneficiary precedes the issue of the guarantee and the bank will normally have no involvement with it. It was held in a Malaysian case, *Perbadanam Kemajuan Negeri Selangor v Public Bank Bhd*,[1] that consideration was to be found in the fact that on the execution and presentation of the guarantee required under a construction contract the contractor was given the right and benefit of commencing work under the contract. But he was not given that right by the employer, the beneficiary of the guarantee, in consequence of the employer's receipt of the guarantee. It was a contractual right which he already had, and it did not lie in the hands of the employer to stop him. The position is the same as, or very similar to, that with a documentary credit. It has been suggested in **Chapter 5** that documentary credits are best seen as an exception to the rule that, if a contract is not made under seal, it must be supported by consideration to be enforceable. It may well be that first demand bonds and guarantees are to be treated in the same way. An argument which strongly supports this is that where the bond or guarantee is payable against stipulated documents it may fall within the definition of a documentary credit provided by Article 2 of the UCP.[2] That being so, the choice is either to separate standby credits from traditional credits and to hold that they are unenforceable under English law for want of consideration, or to hold that where a bond or guarantee is payable by a bank against stipulated documents (or stipulated document) it stands in the same position as regards consideration and enforceability as a documentary credit. The latter must surely be the correct choice. If a bond which is payable simply on receipt of a written demand is not to be treated as payable against a stipulated document for the purposes of the UCP, there is nonetheless no reason for such a bond to be treated differently in respect of consideration from one which is payable against stipulated documents.

1 [1980] 1 MLJ 173.
2 This is developed in para **12.88** below.

12.66   The Contracts (Rights of Third Parties) Act 1999 may provide another solution to the consideration issue. This has been addressed in the context of documentary credits at para **5.16**.

12.67   It would be surprising if a bank of any standing and reputation were prepared to repudiate its obligations under a demand guarantee on the ground that, despite the fact that the bank had happily taken its commission from the applicant (or account party), its undertaking was worth nothing because it was unsupported by consideration. It would be the more surprising if, having done so, it was prepared to face a trial and a certain place in banking journals and in the law reports. So the problems discussed under this heading may well remain unresolved. In the meantime it must be prudent for beneficiaries under bonds and guarantees which may be governed in English law, to ensure that they are made under seal. Where a bond or guarantee is not governed by English law, if it is a valid contract under its proper law despite any absence of consideration, it is enforceable in England.[1]

1 *Re Bonacina* [1912] 2 Ch 394.

Independent guarantees as an interim payment

12.68   An independent guarantee is a form of security or interim payment so that the buyer may have money in hand to meet any claim he has for damage as a result of the seller's breach. It is not, absent express wording to the contrary, a binding pre-breach determination of the amount of damages to which a beneficiary might be entitled. Therefore, if the beneficiary has obtained payment under a demand performance guarantee, it is still open to the account party to bring proceedings for the recovery of part or all of the payment on the ground that in fact the beneficiary has suffered no loss or has been overpaid. Equally, the beneficiary can pursue the account party for further damages if his loss exceeds the value of the guarantee.[1]

1 *Cargill International SA v Bangladesh Sugar & Food Industries Corpn* [1996] 2 Lloyd's Rep 524; affd on appeal at [1998] 1 WLR 461, the decision having been previously approved by a different Court of Appeal in *Comdel v Siporex* [1997] 1 Lloyd's Rep 424. See also *Uzinterimpex JSC v Standard Bank plc* [2008] 2 Lloyd's Rep 456 at para 20.

12.69   However, the issuer of the guarantee has no right of recovery against the beneficiary on the ground that the payment demanded was or has turned out to be excessive. In *Uzinterimpex JSC v Standard Bank plc*,[1] the defendant, Standard Bank, had financed advance payments on behalf of its customer, which was purchasing consignments of cotton from the claimant, Uzinterimpex. Standard Bank was the beneficiary of a demand guarantee from the National Bank of Uzbekistan (NBU) in the amount of the advance payments, with the intention that Standard Bank could recover the payments if the goods were not delivered. The advance payment guarantee was subsequently called by Standard Bank even though some of the goods had in fact been received by the purchaser and the proceeds banked with Standard Bank. Uzinterimpex pursued the purchaser on the basis that it had been overpaid, but the purchaser was insolvent. Uzinterimpex also took an assignment of NBU's position (having presumably had to reimburse NBU in respect of the guarantee) and argued that Standard Bank had an implied obligation to account to the NBU 'in circumstances where the bank had received both the proceeds of the guarantee and the proceeds of the cotton to which it related'. The Court of Appeal rejected the argument, holding that, whilst there may have been a right to recover as against the purchaser under the sale contract, no obligation to account could be implied into the demand guarantee. The demand guarantee was an autonomous contract the operation of which depended only on the presentation of conforming documents.[2]

1 [2008] 2 Lloyd's Rep 456.
2 [2008] 2 Lloyd's Rep 456 at paras 21–24.

Calling the independent guarantee: strict compliance

12.70   What has to be done by the beneficiary to entitle him to payment is a question of construing the wording of the guarantee. A well-worded guarantee will make clear what is required.[1] So, if it is intended that the beneficiary should state that the account party has defaulted in a particular way and that the beneficiary has thereby been caused loss in an amount not less than the amount of his demand, this should be set out in the guarantee with clarity and precision. But as appears from the cases which have been considered in paras **12.56–12.61** above in connection with the question whether a guarantee is a demand bond or a conditional guarantee, it is common for this not to be done.

1 See Article 3 of the ICC Uniform Rules for Demand Guarantees. A proposed revision of the Rules is currently being considered at third draft stage. See further **12.90** below.

12.71   It is suggested that the principle of strict compliance can and should be applied to demand guarantees and bonds to the extent that the wording of the guarantee or bond makes it appropriate.[1] Thus in the *Siporex* case[2] the demand was required to be accompanied by a declaration 'to that effect'.[3] It was there argued for the bank that the principle of strict compliance as established in relation to letters of credit was applicable. It was submitted on behalf of Siporex that there was a substantial difference between letters of credit and performance bonds in that with letters of credit exact compliance with documentary requirements was imperative, whereas with performance bonds precise wording was not essential, particularly where the bond required a declaration 'to that effect'. The judge accepted the buyer's argument 'subject to the rider, on this point of principle, that of course it is quite essential that there should be no ambiguity, no risk of the bank being misled, and no risk of it being confused or otherwise prejudiced'. It is to be questioned whether any such distinction is to be drawn. The only valid distinction between traditional letters of credit and bonds and guarantees in this respect lies in the fact that the documentary requirements of the former are different to those of the latter and so the scope for application of the principle may be more limited with the latter. This was the view of Leggatt J in *IE Contractors Ltd v Lloyds Bank plc*.[4] He stated:

> 'The demand must conform strictly to the terms of the bond in the same way that documents tendered under a letter of credit must conform strictly to the terms of the credit. In particular,. . ., it is important to determine whether the bond is on simple first demand, or on first demand in a specified form, or on first demand supported by a specified document. Where courts seem to have deviated from these simple principles they may have only been responding to the wording of the particular bonds under consideration.'

In the Court of Appeal, after referring to the *Siporex* case[5] Staughton LJ stated:

> 'I agree that there is less need for a doctrine of strict compliance in the case of performance bonds, since I imagine that they are used less frequently than letters of credit, and attract at a higher level in banks. They are not so much part of the day-to-day mechanism of ordinary trade. And as Hirst J pointed out, the kind of documents which they require is usually different from the kind required under a letter of credit. Nevertheless, the reasoning of Goddard LJ in *Rayner's* case (sic) at p 43 still applies:
>
> > "The question is 'What was the promise which the bank made to the beneficiary under the credit, and did the beneficiary avail himself of that promise?'"
>
> The degree of compliance required by a performance bond may be strict, or not so strict. It is a question of construction of the bond. If that view of the law is unattractive to banks, the remedy lies in their own hands.'

It is true that performance bonds (or demand guarantees) are less common than traditional documentary credits, and it may be that, because of this, they attract attention at a higher level in issuing banks. It is suggested, however, that this is not a good reason for applying any different principle of construction. The degree of leeway to be made available to the beneficiary cannot depend upon the standing of the bank official examining the documents. As Staughton LJ concluded, the application of the principle of strict compliance will depend upon the construction of the guarantee or bond. If it is loosely worded, then the wording of the demand and the content of any other documents must comply with the wording, but to say that they must comply strictly is a contradiction in terms. If, on the other hand, the guarantee or bond is precise in its requirements, they must be followed with appropriate precision. A recent example of an inadequate demand is *Frans Maas (UK) Ltd v Habib Bank AG Zurich*,[6] where the judge found that the words 'we claim the sum of £500,000, Palmier plc having failed to meet their contractual obligations to us' did not comply with the requirement of the guarantee that the claims should '[state] therein that the Principals have failed to pay you under their contractual obligation'.

1 Cf Article 19 of the ICC Uniform Rules for Demand Guarantees.
2 [1986] 2 Lloyd's Rep 146.
3 See para **12.57** above.
4 [1989] 2 Lloyd's Rep 205 at 207.
5 [1990] 2 Lloyd's Rep 496, see para **12.58** above.
6 (5 August 2000, unreported).

12.72 In *Lorne Stewart plc v Hermes Kreditversicherungs AG and Amey Asset Services Ltd*,[1] Garland J reaffirmed the requirement for strict compliance with the terms of a performance bond. The judge granted an injunction restraining the issuing bank from making payment to the beneficiary in circumstances where the demand under the bond was made out of time. It was held that a demand made out of time was no demand at all, it was a nullity. He held that the conditions of the bond were to be construed strictly and against the beneficiary; there was no room for a *de minimis* exception.

1 [2001] All ER (D) 286.

The demand: a need to state the basis of claim?

12.73 The guarantee or bond may refer to the events on which it is intended that the demand may be made without making it clear whether the demand should refer to the satisfaction of them as its basis.[1] The form which the demand must take is to be determined by considering the particular words of the bond in question, and a decision on one wording may or may not be helpful on another depending on the similarities and differences. A question arose in the *Esal Commodities* case[2] which was of this nature. The relevant wording has been set out in para **12.56** above. In the Court of Appeal Ackner LJ with whom Glidewell LJ agreed, held:[3]

> 'In addition to the beneficiary making the demand, he must also inform the bank that he does so on the basis provided in the performance bond itself. This interpretation not only gives meaning and effect to the words "in the event that the supplier fails ..." which otherwise would be mere surplusage, but it in no way imposes an extravagant demand upon the bank. A beneficiary may seek, honestly or dishonestly, to apply a performance bond to the wrong contract, and the need to inform the bank of the true basis upon which he is making his demand may be very salutary. Moreover, the desire for an extension of the performance bond may, on occasions, be due to the fact that the performance, for one reason or another, might have been justifiably delayed and the beneficiary will not yet know whether or not there will in due

course be full compliance with the contract. The requirement that he must, when making his demand for payment in order to support his request for an extension, also commit himself to claiming that the contract has not been complied with, may prevent some of the many abuses of the performance bond procedure that undoubtedly occur.'

The relevance of the reference to an extension was that Estram, the beneficiary, had asked the Banque du Caire either to extend the bond or to remit its amount. The reliance upon what may be salutary was criticised by Staughton LJ in the *IE Contractors* case[4] as an insufficient reason to adopt a particular construction of a commercial document. It may, however, be something which may be presumed to have been in the parties' minds when the bond was issued and is therefore a legitimate guide to their intentions if a bond is unclear in its wording. It is surely within the competence of the court to adopt a construction of a document of a kind which is frequently abused, which may lessen that abuse, provided of course that the document is indeed not clear in its wording. Neill LJ who otherwise agreed with the judgment of Ackner LJ preferred to leave open for decision on some future occasion the question whether it is necessary for a beneficiary to give express notice to the bank that the qualifying event has occurred. He indicated his reluctance to introduce a rule 'which provided scope for an argument that the qualifying event had not been sufficiently identified'.[5] The point did not in fact need to be decided by the court and so the view expressed by Ackner LJ was obiter, because there had been proceedings in Egypt between Estram and the Banque du Caire in which the Banque had been held liable. The Banque's submission that the demand was required to be accompanied by a statement that the supplier had failed to execute the contract had been rejected by the Egyptian tribunal. It was therefore held by the Court of Appeal that the Banque was entitled to be indemnified whether or not the Egyptian tribunal's holding was correct. It may be noted that the Court of Appeal did not consider what law was to be applied to determine the effect of the bond. This was probably Egyptian law, and, if so, the Egyptian tribunal's decision was entitled to respect for that reason.

1 Cf Article 20 of the ICC Uniform Rules for Demand Guarantees considered in para **12.90** below. This specifically requires that the breach of the underlying contract be specified. A proposed revision of the Rules is currently being considered at third draft stage.
2 [1985] 2 Lloyd's Rep 546.
3 [1985] 2 Lloyd's Rep 546 at 550.2.
4 [1990] 2 Lloyd's Rep 496.
5 [1985] 2 Lloyd's Rep 546 at 554.1.

12.74   The views expressed in the *Esal Commodities* case were considered by Leggatt J in the *IE Contractors* case[1] and were also mentioned by the Court of Appeal.[2] Leggatt J defined the approach of the court in unexceptionable terms as follows: 'First it must construe the performance bond itself, in order to see what the beneficiary has to do for the purpose of making a valid demand under it; and, secondly, it must construe the call and any associated document, in order to see whether the beneficiary has done that which for the purpose of making a valid demand is required of him.' In reliance upon the wording in the bonds 'covering damages which you claim are duly and properly owing to your organisation... under the terms of the contract...' he held that the beneficiary was required to assert a claim that the damages in respect of which a call was made were duly and properly owing to the beneficiary under the terms of the contract. In the Court of Appeal Staughton LJ held that the part of the bond from which the words quoted were taken was directed to Article 395 of the Iraqi Commercial Code, which requires a performance bond to state the purpose for which it is issued. He relied on another part, which read 'We undertake to pay you, unconditionally, the said amount on demand, being your claim for damages brought about by the above-named principle', and concluded that the demand was required to state that it was a claim for damages brought about by the contractor. The demands made asserted breaches of contract but did not in terms mention damages. He referred to the question of the degree of strict compliance required and concluded that the precise words of the part of the bond quoted were not required. He held that the demand made did say in substance, although not in express words, that what it claimed was damages for breach of contract. He and the other members of the court found that the demands were valid demands under the bonds. Leggatt J had held that they were not. It is probably not possible to draw any general conclusions from this part of the Court of Appeal's judgment, save perhaps that, with foreign language bonds governed by foreign law the English court will avoid technicality unless the need for it is plainly established. On the wording of the particular bonds the approach of Ackner LJ in the *Esal Commodities* case was not followed.

1 [1989] 2 Lloyd's Rep 205.
2 [1990] 2 Lloyd's Rep 496.

Counter-indemnities

12.75   Where there is only one bank involved the relationships are straightforward. The account party – the equivalent of the applicant for a letter of credit – approaches a bank, which is likely to be his own bank, and instructs it to provide a bond or guarantee in favour of the beneficiary in the terms in which he has contracted with the beneficiary to provide it. If it is agreeable, the bank will then issue its bond or guarantee to the beneficiary. Before doing so it will require the account party to sign an undertaking in favour of the bank agreeing to indemnify the bank in respect of any amount that it pays out under the bond to the beneficiary. The terms of the indemnity will be drafted by the bank, and will be favourable to the bank. If the account party were simply to undertake to reimburse the bank such amounts as the bank might be obliged to pay out pursuant to its undertaking to the beneficiary, this would enable the account party to question whether the bank was obliged to pay what it had in fact paid before the account party reimbursed the bank. That is not usually acceptable to banks. So the account party will usually be required to sign an indemnity which requires it to pay whatever the bank has in fact paid. For example, in *Gulf Bank KSC v Mitsubishi Heavy Industries Ltd (No 2)*,[1] Mitsubishi had entered into a counter-indemnity to bank an independent guarantee issued by Gulf Bank. The counter-indemnity provided as follows:

> 'In consideration of the agreement by the Bank to issue a Guarantee, we hereby irrevocably and unconditionally agree to pay to the Bank on its first written demand an amount equal to and in the same currency as each sum paid out by the Bank under or in connection with a Guarantee and we undertake to indemnify and keep indemnified, the Bank against any and all claims, demands, liabilities, costs, losses, damages and expenses which may be made of the Bank or which the Bank may incur or sustain under or in connection with the issue of the Guarantee...
>
> Any demand made of the Bank [under] or in connection with a Guarantee shall be sufficient authority to the Bank for the Bank's making payment of any amount so demanded and the Bank need not concern itself with the propriety of any claim made or purported to be made under or in connection with such Guarantee...
>
> Our obligations hereunder shall not be in any way discharged or diminished by reason of any extension of time or by any variation or amendment to any Guarantee or by any total or partial invalidity, illegality or un-enforceability thereof.'

Mitsubishi resisted indemnifying Gulf Bank on the ground that the guarantee had no legal effect under its governing law (Kuwaiti law). The Court of Appeal held that the intent of the clause set out above was to require the bank to make payment on the demand made 'with in effect no questions asked'.[2] Savile LJ also stated, 'as a matter of commercial common sense, it seems to me that it was a clear objective of the agreement to preclude any debate or discussion about legal effectiveness or validity of the guarantee when the question arose either of payment under the guarantee or reimbursement under the terms of the counter indemnity'.[3]

1 [1994] 2 Lloyd's Rep 145.
2 [1994] 2 Lloyd's Rep 145 at 151, per Sir Thomas Bingham MR.
3 [1994] 2 Lloyd's Rep 145 at 152.

12.76 It is more common for at least two banks to be involved, one the account party's bank in his own country and a second in the beneficiary's country which will be instructed by the first to issue the guarantee or bond to the beneficiary. The bank issuing the guarantee or bond to the beneficiary will be given an undertaking of indemnity from the account party's bank from which it receives its instructions. It may happen that a third bank is involved which acts as intermediary between the account party's bank and the bank issuing the guarantee to the beneficiary.[1] This will happen where the account party's bank does not have a correspondent in the country of the beneficiary. In such a case the bank issuing the guarantee will take an indemnity from this intermediary bank and the intermediary bank will take an indemnity in turn from the account party's bank. There is thus a chain of indemnities. Just as with the indemnity which the account party for the guarantee or bond has to provide to his own bank, the indemnities which the banks in the chain provide to one another are usually devised to ensure that, if the bank to be indemnified has paid, the indemnifying bank is bound to reimburse it without the possibility of argument, on any ground, that the former bank was not obliged to pay and should not have paid. One such provision was as follows:[2] 'In case of implementation, any claim or claims will be paid to us on first demand, despite any contestation between principals and the beneficiaries.'

1 See, eg *Esal (Commodities) Ltd v Oriental Credit Ltd* [1985] 2 Lloyd's Rep 546, discussed at para **12.56** above.
2 See *United Trading Corpn SA v Allied Arab Bank* [1985] 2 Lloyd's Rep 554n.

12.77 The difference between the counter-indemnity chain and the reimbursement process for documentary credits will be noted. Documentary credits are usually issued by the applicant's bank in the applicant's country and advised to the beneficiary by a bank in the beneficiary's country, which confirms the credit where this is required. Documents accepted by the confirming bank are passed to the issuing bank for reimbursement. This point was taken up by Parker LJ in *GKN Contractors Ltd v Lloyds Bank plc.*[1] He stated:

> 'Turning to the law, the cases clearly establish that transactions by way of performance guarantee are similar to, albeit not identical with, transactions under confirmed letters of credit. The analogy cannot, however be pressed too far, because in the case of performance guarantees there are, not merely one set of documents passing up the chain with one question arising namely, whether the documents tendered were or were not in accordance with the credit, but three different contracts. It is true that in the case of letters of credit there are also different contracts, but the difference in the case of each performance guarantees is that there are differing documents between each case.'

With a demand guarantee supported by a chain of indemnities, the bank which receives the demand does not pass on it and any accompanying documents down the line as it would with a credit: it makes its own demand in accordance with the contract of indemnity which it holds from the bank next in the line.

1 (1985) 30 BLR 48 at 62.

12.78 In addition to any express counter-indemnity, the bank issuing the guarantee may have the benefit of an implied indemnity from the account party if it can be inferred from all the circumstances that the guarantee was issued at that party's request. In *Tradigrain SA v State Trading Corporation of India,*[1] the issuing bank had required the security of a counter-indemnity from the seller's bank as a condition of issuing a performance bond. When the bond was called on, the issuing bank paid and made demand on the seller's bank pursuant to the counter-indemnity. The seller obtained an injunction (in the Indian courts) preventing its bank from indemnifying the issuing bank. In the course of an action by the seller to recover over-compensation received by the buyer under the bond, Christopher Clarke J stated, *obiter*, that whilst it was not necessary for him to determine whether the seller was liable to the issuing bank directly or indirectly (via its own bank), he was inclined to the view that, in circumstances where the seller's bank had not paid the issuing bank, the seller's obligation was to make payment to the issuing bank. This was said to be on the basis that the seller had requested the issuing bank to issue the bond and payment to it would satisfy any implied or express obligation to indemnify the issuing bank for the cost of doing so, as well as any similar obligation to the seller's own bank.

1 [2006] 1 Lloyd's Rep 216 at [35].

Calling the counter-indemnity

12.79   Just as the beneficiary must comply with the terms of the guarantee in formulating his demand, so must the issuing bank comply with the terms of its indemnity when it in its turn makes its demand. The demands of Rafidain in the *IE Contractors* case[1] were found by the Court of Appeal to comply in two instances, but not in the third, because the third counter-indemnity required Rafidain to state that they were obliged to pay the beneficiary, which the demand failed to do. Thus Rafidain succeeded in the two cases where they had to show an actual liability, but not in the third where they were entitled on their own say-so, which may be a curious outcome.

1 [1990] 2 Lloyd's Rep 496, see para **12.58** above.

12.80   If, having paid the guarantee, reimbursement under a counter-indemnity is refused, the issuing bank may wish to seek summary judgment. If the ground of refusal is that the claim by the beneficiary was fraudulent, such that the fraud exception applied, then judgment will be granted summarily unless the issuer of the counter-indemnity can demonstrate that there was a real prospect that it would be able to prove at trial both that the demand on the bond was fraudulent and that the issuing bank knew that: *Banque Saudi Fransi v Lear Siegler Services Inc.*[1]

1 [2007] 2 Lloyd's Rep 47 at [68], per Arden LJ.

No implication of terms

12.81   The corollary to the doctrine of strict compliance is that the courts are unlikely to limit the right to indemnity where there has been compliance by the implication of terms into the counter-indemnity or guarantee. In *Cauxell Ltd v Lloyds Bank plc*[1] the Iranian Meat Organisation (IMO) required a guarantee as a condition of signing a contract with Cauxell for the supply of meat. Bank Melli Iran provided a demand guarantee to IMO against a counter-guarantee from Lloyd's. The counter-guarantee provided that Lloyds would become liable on receipt by Bank Melli of a confirmation from Lloyds that the underlying contract had been signed and the associated letter of credit was satisfactory. Cresswell J rejected Bank Melli's argument that the counter-guarantee was subject to implied terms that Lloyds was obliged to take reasonable steps to fulfil this condition by inquiring into the position with regard to the contract and the letter of credit and sending an appropriate confirmation. Such a obligation would be inconsistent with the certainty necessary for the proper operation of a demand guarantee. The judge said:

> 'I do not consider that international bankers would expect Lloyds to take reasonable steps to fulfil the condition precedent and/or to take reasonable steps to ascertain the position with regard to the contract and the letter of credit. International bankers would expect Lloyds to act upon instructions from its principals before confirming that the underlying contract had been signed and that the terms and conditions of any subsequent letter of credit confirmed by a UK clearing bank in respect of the mentioned contract were acceptable to Lloyds' principals...
>
> The Courts will rarely imply terms into letters of credit or first demand guarantees. There is a need for certainty in commercial transactions and this is, as I have emphasised, particularly important in the case of obligations assumed by banks under letters of credit and first demand bonds and associated counter-undertakings.'

A further objection to the implication of terms into a counter-indemnity is that an implied term is, by its nature, non-documentary. See the discussion of non-documentary conditions in para **8.22** et seq.

1 (1995) Times, 26 December.

Claims by the account party against the issuing bank

12.82   Despite the autonomy of the issuing bank's obligation under an independent guarantee, and the rigor of counter-indemnity provisions, there may be occasions on which the account party can justifiably object to the issuing bank's decision to pay. For example, the issuing bank may have paid in breach of the terms of its undertaking to the beneficiary, or it may have paid in the face of an obvious fraud by the beneficiary. Where the guarantee is issued by the account party's own bank, there is, of course, no problem in bringing a claim: the relationship is one of a direct contract between them.[1] It is more difficult where the issuing bank is one which is instructed by the account party's bank against an indemnity from that bank. It cannot then be suggested that there is a contractual relationship between the account party and the issuing bank. The Court of Appeal so held in *United Trading Corpn SA v Allied Arab Bank*.[2] It was submitted on behalf of United Trading in that case that the issuing bank (and the other banks in the chain) would arguably be liable to them in the tort of negligence if they complied with a demand made by the beneficiary which, to the knowledge of the bank at the time of payment, was fraudulent. This was based on ordinary negligence principles relying on the fact that United Trading would ultimately have to bear the loss if payment was made against a fraudulent demand. This submission as to arguability was accepted on behalf of the Allied Arab Bank and the case therefore proceeded on that basis. The same argument was raised in *GKN Contractors Ltd v Lloyds Bank plc.*[3] Parker LJ remarked 'That cause of action is one which I have some difficulty in appreciating.' But in view of the *United Trading* case he likewise proceeded on the basis that the cause of action was arguable. More recently Rix J expressed doubts about a tortious claim in *Czarnikow-Rionda v Standard Bank.*[4] It is suggested that, were the point to be decided,[5] the decision would be that there was no such duty of care on the ground that the bank and the account party were not in such a relationship that a duty of care towards the account party should be imposed on the bank in its operation of the bond.[6]

1 The account party may also seek to restrain payment under the guarantee as happened in *Lorne Stewart plc v Hermes Kreditversicherungs AG and Amey Asset Services Ltd* [2001] All ER (D) 286, where the demand under a performance bond was out of time.
2 [1985] 2 Lloyd's Rep 554n at 559.2. There might be a contractual relationship if the guarantee was issued directly on the account party's instructions: see *Tradigrain SA v State Trading Corporation of India* [2006] 1 Lloyd's Rep 216 at para 35.
3 (1985) 30 BLR 48.
4 [1999] 2 Lloyd's Rep 187.
5 The point was not argued at the trial, perhaps because it was unnecessary: see *IE Contractors Ltd v Lloyds Bank plc* [1989] 2 Lloyd's Rep 205 (Leggatt J) and Court of Appeal [1990] 2 Lloyd's Rep 496.
6 There may also be the question of foreign law.

Confirmation

12.83   The mechanism of confirmation is sometimes used in independent guarantees in a way similar to documentary credits. In *Esal (Commodities) Ltd v Oriental Credit Ltd*[1] Reltor Ltd, an English company, made a successful bid to sell sugar to Estram, an Egyptian corporation, which was to be supported by a performance bond for 10% of the purchase price. Reltor approached their London bank, Oriental Credit, in connection with the bond. Oriental Credit instructed the London office of Wells Fargo Bank to establish the bond through their correspondents in Cairo, the Banque du Caire, and it appears that the Banque du Caire were asked to add their confirmation. The bond was therefore issued by Wells Fargo and advised through the Banque du Caire, who confirmed it. The bond as issued by Wells Fargo was made subject to the UCP, a matter which is discussed below.[2] This borrowing from the documentary credit scheme may have been due to the involvement of an American bank as the issuing bank. It demonstrates the closeness of first demand bonds to standby letters of credit. It also appears that the mechanism of confirmation may have been used in the *Harbottle* case.[3]

1 [1985] 2 Lloyd's Rep 546.
2 See para **12.88**.
3 *R D Harbottle (Mercantile) Ltd v National Westminster Bank Ltd* [1978] QB 146 at 149B/C.

Fraudulent and abusive calls

12.84   Most of the cases concerning demand guarantees or bonds which have been considered by the English courts have emphasised the autonomy of the contract between the bank issuing the guarantee or bond and the beneficiary. The analogy with documentary credits in this respect has also been strongly emphasised. As has been made clear in **Chapter 9** dealing with the topics of fraud and the granting of injunctions, the cases relating to demand guarantees and fraud are equally applicable to the position in respect of documentary credits and vice versa.

12.85   In *GKN Contractors Ltd v Lloyds Bank plc*[1] Parker LJ stated with reference to the fraud that may be committed in relation to demand guarantees[2] 'In those cases the fraud considered was a fraud on the part of the beneficiary, and in my view plainly refers to what may be called common law fraud, that is to say, a case where the named beneficiary presents a claim which he knows at the time to be an invalid claim, representing to the bank that he believes it to be a valid claim.' See also per Lord Denning MR in *State Trading Corpn of India Ltd v ED & F Man (Sugar) Ltd*[3] cited in *United Trading Corpn SA v Allied Arab Bank*:[4] 'The only term which is to be imported is that the buyer when giving notice of default, must honestly believe that there has been a default on the part of the seller. Honest belief is enough. If there is no honest belief, it may be evidence of fraud.' The representation will be made expressly in a case where the guarantee requires a statement that there has been a default. It will be one made by implication from the making of the demand where a demand is all that the bond requires. Reference should be made to **Chapter 9** for a detailed treatment of the fraud exception to the autonomy rule and the problems of obtaining an injunction to prevent payment under a guarantee or under an indemnity given by the account party's bank to the bank issuing the guarantee. Reference should also be made to **Chapter 13** for the treatment of the developing area of illegality and the discussion of *Mahonia Ltd v JP Morgan Chase Bank*.[5]

1 (1985) 30 BLR 48.
2 (1985) 30 BLR 48 at 63.
3 [1981] Com LR 235.
4 [1985] 2 Lloyd's Rep 554n at 559.
5 [2003] 2 Lloyd's Rep 911.

12.86   The same danger of abuse which has been referred to in connection with standby credits exists in connection with demand guarantees and bonds. Reference may be made to paras **12.44–12.47** above. In the *Edward Owen* case[1] Lord Denning referred to the possibility of a guarantee being called on account of a trivial breach or no breach at all. He stated:[2] 'This possibility is so real that the English supplier, if he is wise, will take it into account when quoting his price for the contract.' In the *Harbottle* case[3] Kerr J stated[4] 'In effect, the sellers rely on the probity and reputation of their buyers and on their good relations with them. But this trust is inevitably sometimes abused, and I understand that such guarantees are sometimes drawn upon, partly or wholly, without any or any apparent justification, almost as though they represented a discount in favour of the buyers.'

1 [1978] QB 159.
2 [1978] QB 159 at 170.
3 [1978] QB 146.
4 [1978] QB 146 at 150.

12.87   If the intended beneficiary of the guarantee insists on a guarantee which is payable against his demand alone, the account party can only seek to diminish his risk by endeavouring to negotiate that the guarantee does not come into effect until the payment documentary credit is in place in his favour, and that the period during which the guarantee may be called is as short as possible.[1] The account party should give careful attention to the wording of the guarantee. Thus, even if it is to include the words 'first demand', he may be able to include words which make it clear that the demand should set out the basis of the claim.[2] The account party will improve his position if he provides for the guarantee to be subject to the ICC Uniform Rules for Demand Guarantees.[3] In particular, Article 20 of the Uniform Rules requires the demand to include or to be accompanied by a statement that the account party is in breach of his obligations, and the respect in which he is in breach.

1 See para **12.46**, which is equally applicable here.
2 See paras **12.73** above.
3 See para **12.90** below.

Application of the UCP

12.88   The ICC publishes separate Uniform Rules for Demand Guarantees,[1] and it should be clear that demand guarantees are not intended to be made subject to the UCP, and that it is inappropriate to do so. Nonetheless independent guarantees payable against stipulated documents may fall within the definition of credit given by UCP Article 2, namely an 'arrangement, however named or described, that is irrevocable and thereby constitutes a definite undertaking of the issuing bank to honour a complying presentation'.

1 See paras **12.90** et seq below.

12.89   *Esal (Commodities) Ltd v Oriental Credit Ltd*[1] concerned a bond issued by the London office of Wells Fargo Bank advised to Estram in Egypt through the Banque du Caire and confirmed by that bank. One of Esal's complaints was that Wells Fargo Bank had incorporated the UCP in the bond without authority. They no doubt did so because as an American bank they treated the bond as a standby credit. It was held by the Court of Appeal that as the UCP had played no part in the reasoning of the Egyptian tribunal which had held the Banque du Caire liable, the point could not assist Esal.

1 [1985] 2 Lloyd's Rep 546. See para **12.56** above.

Uniform Rules for Demand Guarantees

12.90   In April 1992 the ICC published *Uniform Rules for Demand Guarantees* (URDG).[1] The URDG are, at the time of writing, in the process of revision with a view to publication in 2009. One important provision of the URDG, which appears both in the 1992 edition and in the draft revision is that any demand under a guarantee shall (in addition to any other document required) be supported by a written statement indicating in what respect the applicant is in breach of its obligations under the contract, tender conditions or other underlying relationship on which the guarantee may be based. Where a guarantee is made subject to the Rules, this provision applies unless it is expressly excluded.[3] So if a demand guarantee incorporating the Rules states that it is payable simply against a demand, the bank guarantor should not pay unless there is a demand complying with the express terms of the guarantee and also a statement of breach. A dishonest beneficiary has therefore to be more brazen to demand payment if not entitled: this is a psychological pressure which may curb some of the worst excesses.

1 ICC No 458. The ICC also publishes a Guide to the URDG by Professor Roy Goode, ICC No 510.

12.91   At present the URDG do not seem to be widely applied and have not been the subject of any significant analysis in the authorities.[1]

1 They were referred to by Staughton LJ in *Wahda Bank v Arab Bank plc* [1996] 1 Lloyd's Rep 470 and by Moore-Bick LJ in *Uzinterimpex JSC v Standard Bank plc* [2008] 2 Lloyd's Rep 456 at para 23.

12.92   The *Uniform Rules for Contract Guarantees*[1] were published by the ICC in 1978. Although the rules are available for incorporation into a guarantee if the parties want them, they do not seem to be in active use. The Rules seek to avoid the abuses arising in connection with first demand bonds, mainly by providing that, if a guarantee does not specify the documentation to be produced or specifies only a statement of claim by the beneficiary, in the case of a performance guarantee or a repayment guarantee there must be provided 'either a court decision or an arbitral award justifying the claim, or the approval of the principal in writing to the claim and the amount to be paid'. Their application would therefore carry a guarantee payable on demand from one end of the scale set out in para **12.11** to the other. They apply to guarantees and bonds which state that they are made subject to them.

1 ICC No 325.

UN Convention on Independent Guarantees and Standby Letters of Credit[1]

12.93   Only eight countries[2] have ratified or acceded to the Convention and so it is of limited significance at the moment. The purpose of the Convention is to provide a harmonised international set of rules, but it intended to operate alongside, rather than in replacement of, ISP98 and the Uniform Rules for Demand Guarantees.[3] The Convention applies to undertakings which come within the definition of:

> 'an independent commitment, known in international practice as an independent guarantee or as a stand-by letter of credit, given by a bank or other institution or person ('guarantor/issuer') to pay to the beneficiary a certain or determinable amount upon simple demand or upon demand accompanied by other documents, in conformity with the terms and any documentary conditions of the undertaking, indicating, or from which it is to be inferred, that payment is due because of a default in the performance of an obligation, or because of another contingency, or for money borrowed or advanced, or on account of any mature indebtedness[4] undertaken by the principal/applicant or another person.'

The Convention provides for the independence (i.e. autonomy) of the undertaking (Article 3) but its most important and interesting feature is that, unlike both ISP98 and the Uniform Rules for Demand Guarantees, it makes express provision for the effect of fraudulent or abusive drawings.[5]

1 See De Ly, 'The UN Convention on Independent Guarantees and Stand-by Letters of Credit' (1999) 3 (3) *International Lawyer* 831.
2 The Convention has been ratified by Belarus, El Salvador and Panama and acceded to by Ecuador, Gabon, Kuwait, Liberia and Tunisia. Information on accession and ratification is available at www.uncitral.org.
3 See Article 13(1) and explanatory note by the UNCITRAL Secretariat, para 5.
4 If 'mature indebtedness' includes an obligation to pay the price under a sale of goods contract then this appears to cover all possible uses of a demand guarantee or standby credit.
5 Article 19. See para **9.61** above.

Chapter 13

Conflict of Laws, Illegality and Exchange Control, Sovereign Immunity

INTRODUCTION[1]

13.1   The preceding chapters have set out the substantive principles of English law relating to documentary credits. However, because of the international nature of documentary credits the buyer, seller and banks are usually located in different countries. In any dispute which is not purely domestic two preliminary issues will always arise: first, which court can, or should, exercise jurisdiction to determine the dispute (jurisdiction); and second, what national system of law should be applied by that court (choice of governing law). The purpose of this chapter is to address how those issues are approached by the English courts. This chapter also deals with the related question of when an English court will decline to enforce one of the contracts in the documentary credit transaction[2] on the ground that the contract or its performance is illegal under foreign law, typically because of foreign exchange control regulations. Lastly the question of sovereign immunity is briefly addressed.

1 For an exhaustive treatment of the choice of law and jurisdictional rules that will be discussed in this chapter see Dicey, Morris & Collins, *The Conflict of Laws* (14th edn 2006), Briggs & Rees, *Civil Jurisdiction and Judgments* (4th edn 2005).
2 Either the obligation of a bank to make payment under the credit or the obligation of the buyer to open the credit.

A   JURISDICTION OF THE ENGLISH COURTS

13.2   Jurisdiction of courts in EU member states is subject to Council Regulation (EC) No 44/2001 on Jurisdiction and the Recognition and Enforcement of Judgments in Civil and Commercial Matters ('the Jurisdiction Regulation').[1] The Jurisdiction Regulation replaces the 1968 Brussels Convention on Civil Jurisdiction and Judgments in Civil and Commercial Matters ('the Brussels Convention') and took effect from 1 March 2002 between EU member states, including the ten new member states as from 1 May 2004. Denmark initially opted out of the Jurisdiction Regulation but, following a parallel agreement, it has been bound by the Jurisdiction Regulation since 1 July 2007.[2]

1 2001 OJ L12/1.
2 [2006] OJ L120/22: SI 2007/1655.

13.3   The 1988 Lugano Convention (which extended the Brussels Convention to EFTA countries, essentially on the same terms) was revised in 2007 and it remains the applicable jurisdictional text only in respect of the EFTA states Iceland, Norway and Switzerland.

13.4   The courts of the member states also use the Official Commentaries and Reports on the Conventions in construing the Conventions and the corresponding provisions of the Jurisdiction Regulation.[1]

1 See for example the Report signed by Mr Jenard in relation to the Brussels Convention (1979 OJ C59/1) and the Report of Professor Schlosser accompanying the Accession Convention for the United Kingdom to the Brussels Convention (1979 OJ C59/71); also Dicey, Morris & Collins 11-056.

13.5   The Jurisdiction Regulation or the Conventions apply whenever the defendant is domiciled in a contracting state[1] and, when applicable, their provisions will determine whether an English court has jurisdiction over a dispute. In other cases the rules of the English common law apply. The general principle under the Jurisdiction Regulation (which is subject to a number of exceptions) is that a defendant should be sued in the courts of the EU member state in which it is domiciled.[2]

1 The Jurisdiction Regulation applies only to 'civil and commercial matters' (Article 1(1)). Within this category, according to Article 1(2) the Jurisdiction Regulation does not apply to certain issues arising in matrimonial and probate cases; bankruptcy or proceedings relating to the winding up of insolvent companies; social security or arbitration. Due to their essentially contractual nature, it is suggested that for the most part disputes involving letters of credit are likely to fall within the terms of the Jurisdiction Regulation. The claimant's domicile is for the most part irrelevant to the application of the Jurisdiction Regulation or the Conventions in cases involving letters of credit.
2 Article 2(1).

(1)   Common law

13.6   At common law, the jurisdiction of the English court is founded primarily on service of process on a defendant. Process can be served on a defendant who is present within the jurisdiction no matter how fleeting that presence may be.[1] The assumption of jurisdiction on the basis of the defendant's presence within the jurisdiction is subject to the powers of the court to stay English proceedings on the ground that England is a *forum non conveniens*.[2] The English Courts will, however, also exercise an extraterritorial jurisdiction over a defendant who is not present within the jurisdiction by giving permission to serve out of the jurisdiction, provided a claimant can bring himself within one of the limbs of CPR Pt 6.20. In the documentary credit context at common law, the usual grounds will be that the contract was made within the jurisdiction or, by or through an agent trading or residing within the jurisdiction; that the contract was governed by English law or the dispute comes within an exclusive jurisdiction clause in favour of the English courts; or that a claim is made in respect of a breach of contract committed within the jurisdiction.[3]

1 *Carrick v Hancock* (1895) 12 TLR 59; *Colt Industries Inc v Sarlie* [1966] 1 WLR 440, CA; *HRH Maharanee Seethaderi Gaekwar of Baroda v Wildenstein* [1972] 2 QB 283, CA. With respect to service of claim forms upon overseas companies with either a place of business or branch within the jurisdiction see Companies Act 1985 ss 694A (considered in *Saab v Saudi American Bank* [1999] 1 WLR 1861, CA) and 695. See also CPR Pt 6, 6.2(2) which reduces the difference between the two provisions. The relevant provisions from the 1985 Act will be replaced by Companies Act 2006 ss1139–1142 when they come into force.
2 Under CPR Pt 11. The principles to be applied by a court in determining the appropriate forum in which to hear a dispute (also referred to as the *forum conveniens*) were authoritatively laid down in *Amin Rasheed Shipping Corp v Kuwait Insurance Co* [1984] AC 50 (per Lord Wilberforce) and *Spiliada Maritime Corpn v Cansulex Ltd* [1987] AC 460, HL (per Lord Goff) applied in *Connelly v RTZ Corpn plc* [1998] AC 854, HL and *Lubbe v Cape plc* [2000] 1 WLR 1545, HL. Contrast the rejection of the approach in *Spiliada* in Australia: *Voth v Manildra Flour Mills Pty Ltd* (1990) 171 CLR 538; *Henry v Henry* (1996) 185 CLR 571; *CSR v Cigna Assurance* [1997] AJLR 1143. In the case of letters of credit the connecting factors that are likely to be considered include the law applicable to the contract, the lex loci contractus, the place of performance of the obligation subject to dispute, the location of the performing party's place of business/central administration, the language of the contract and the currency of any payment. See also *European Asian Bank AG v Punjab and Sind Bank* [1981] 2 Lloyd's Rep 651; affd [1982] 2 Lloyd's Rep 356, CA; *Bank of Credit & Commerce Hong Kong Ltd (in liquidation) v Sonali Bank* [1995] 1 Lloyd's Rep 227.
3 Under CPR Pt 6.20(5) or 6.20(6) respectively. See *Trafigura Beheer BV v Kookmin Bank Co* [2006] EWHC 1450 (Comm) for a case on documentary credits that raised issues 'relating to tort' (by reason of the way in which the Korean defendant to the English action had put its concurrent claim in Korea under Korean law). This analysis was in reference to the law governing the issues between the parties, and not the threshold jurisdiction question under the Jurisdiction Regulation. See *PT Pan Indonesia Bank Ltd TBK v Marconi Communications International Ltd* [2007] 2 Lloyd's Rep 72 for consideration of CPR 6.20(5) and (6). See also in relation to CPR 6.20 *Habib Bank Ltd v Central Bank of Sudan* [2006] 2 Lloyd's Rep 412.

13.7 The leading case on the principles to be applied by a court when determining whether to permit service out of the jurisdiction concerned a dispute arising out of a letter of credit. In *Seaconsar Far East Limited v Bank Markazi Jomhouri Islami Iran*[1] the claimant, incorporated in Hong Kong, entered into an agreement with the Iranian Ministry of Defence for the sale of artillery shells. Bank Markazi issued an unconfirmed letter of credit in favour of the claimant, available at sight in London at the counters of Bank Melli Iran, which advised the credit to the claimant. The claimant made two shipments of the shells, but the defendant refused to make payment on the ground that the documents presented were not in conformity with the terms of the credit. Proceedings were issued and the claimant sought to serve the process on Bank Markazi out of the jurisdiction on the ground either that the contract in question was made within the jurisdiction or that the claim was made in respect of a failure to pay within the jurisdiction. Lord Goff held that for the court to grant permission to serve a party out of the jurisdiction, the claimant had to demonstrate a good arguable case that his claim fell within one of the jurisdictional heads of the predecessor in the old Rules of the

Supreme Court to CPR Pt 6.20, that there was a serious issue to be tried on the merits and that England was the *forum conveniens*.[2] In the result, the House of Lords gave the claimant permission to serve its claim form on Bank Markazi because there were serious issues to be tried regarding whether or not there had been valid rejection of the documents presented.[3]

1 *Seaconsar Far East Ltd v Bank Markazi Jomhouri Islami Iran* [1994] 1 AC 438, HL. For other cases dealing with service out of the jurisdiction in letter of credit disputes see also *Attock Cement Co Ltd v Romanian Bank for Foreign Trade* [1989] 1 WLR 1147, CA; *Bank of Baroda v Vysya Bank Ltd* [1994] 2 Lloyd's Rep 87.
2 See para **13.6** footnote 2.
3 *Seaconsar Far East Ltd v Bank Markazi Jomhouri Islami Iran* [1994] 1 AC 438 per Lord Goff at 457.

(2)   The Jurisdiction Regulation and the Conventions

13.8   The Jurisdiction Regulation is directly applicable in the United Kingdom by virtue of s2(1) of the European Communities Act 1972. The Brussels and Lugano Conventions were incorporated into English law by the Civil Jurisdiction and Judgments Act 1982 ("CJJA 1982").[1] The Jurisdiction Regulation and the Conventions provide that, as a general rule, a defendant should be sued in the state where he is domiciled unless (a) the courts of another member state have exclusive jurisdiction; (b) the parties have an agreed jurisdiction clause in the appropriate form favouring the courts of another member state; (c) the defendant has submitted to the court of another contracting state; or (d) there exists a *lis alibi pendens* in another state.[2]

1 Unlike the common law position, a claimant does not require permission to serve a claim form out of the jurisdiction if the English courts have jurisdiction according to the CJJA 1982: CPR Pt 6.19. The CJJA 1982 was amended to incorporate the Lugano Convention in 1991. For developments to the CJJA 1982 for intra-United Kingdom cases following the coming into force of the Jurisdiction Regulation see Dicey, Morris & Collins at 11-050 to 11-054 and 11-066.
2 Jurisdiction Regulation Articles 22, 23, 24, 27, and 28 (see also the corresponding provisions of the Brussels Convention at Articles 16, 17, 18, 21 and 22).

13.9   The Conventions and the Jurisdiction Regulation contain further exceptions that permit the English courts to assume 'special jurisdiction' over a defendant, even if that party is not domiciled in the UK. The following analysis is based on the provisions of the Jurisdiction Regulation though regard should be had to the corresponding provisions of the Conventions when dealing with a domiciliary of a state to which the Conventions apply.

Article 5(1) 'exception'

13.10   In respect of documentary credits, the relevant exception to the rule that the defendant should be sued in the state of its domicile is likely to arise under Article 5(1) of the Jurisdiction Regulation. Article 5(1) provides that in 'matters relating to a contract' a defendant may be sued in the courts for 'the place of performance of the obligation in question'.

13.11   Though the starting point is the same as for Article 5(1) of the Brussels Convention (ie that the matter 'relates' to a contract), Article 5(1) of the Jurisdiction Regulation differs from its Brussels Convention predecessor in one key aspect: Article 5(1)(b) contains an autonomous definition of the 'place of performance' of an obligation in relation to contracts for the sale of goods or the provision of services. In the case of a contract for the sale of goods, unless the parties otherwise agree, the place of performance shall be: 'the place in a Member State where, under the contract, the goods were delivered or should have been delivered'. In the case of a contract for the provision of services, unless the parties otherwise agree, the place of performance shall be 'the place in a Member State where, under the contract, the services were provided or should have been provided'.

13.12   Article 5(1) of the Jurisdiction Regulation does not appear to have been considered by the English Court in the context of documentary credits. The Court will be guided by the pre-Jurisdiction Regulation case of *Chailease Finance Corpn v Credit Agricole Indosuez*, in which the Court of Appeal addressed a number of points on the interpretation of Article 5(1) of the Brussels Convention.[1] The following analysis takes into account *Chailease* and later jurisprudence regarding Article 5(1) of the Jurisdiction Regulation outside the documentary credit context.

1 [2000] 1 Lloyd's Rep 348. See also *Royal Bank Of Scotland Plc v Cassa Di Risparmio Delle Provincie Lomard And Ors* [1992] 1 Bank LR 251 for a case involving Article 5(1) of the Brussels Convention and its relationship with the UCP.

'Matters relating to a Contract'

13.13   This phrase is likely to cover most claims that concern a contract under English common law. A claimant may only bring himself within this definition if the dispute concerns 'an undertaking freely entered into with another person'.[1] In *Chailease*, Potter LJ assumed, without analysis, that the contractual relationships arising out of a documentary letter of credit fell within the scope of this definition. It is suggested that this approach was correct and would be followed under the Jurisdiction Regulation; it is consistent with the broad application of Article 5(1)(a) identified by the House of Lords in *Scottish and Newcastle International v Othon Ghalanos*.[2]

1 C-26/91 *Societe Jacob Handte et Cie GmbH v TMCS* [1992] ECR I-3967; Case C-51/97 *Réunion Europeenne SA v Spliethoff's Bevrachtingskantoor BV* [1998] ECR I-6511; Case C-440/97 *GIE Groupe Concorde v Master of the Vessel Suhadiwarno Panjan* [1999] CLC 1976, ECJ. See for a discussion on this area Dicey, Morris & Collins at 11-284.
2 [2008] 1 Lloyd's Rep 462 at para 3 per Lord Bingham.

'Obligation in Question'

13.14   Identification of the obligation in question under the Brussels Convention was relatively straightforward: the obligation referred to was that upon which the claimant had founded his action.

13.15   In *Chailease* Potter LJ applied the established European jurisprudence under the Brussels Convention relating to the identification of the 'obligation in question' in respect of a documentary credit. In *Custom Made Commercial Ltd v Stawa Metallbau*[1] the European Court of Justice had held that the concept of the 'obligation in question' should be given a meaning that was autonomous of national law principles, namely the obligation 'which corresponds to the contractual right on which the plaintiff's action is based'. Potter LJ held that the obligation underlying the claim by the beneficiary against the issuing bank was 'the contractual right [of the beneficiary] to be paid, conditional on presentation of conforming documents prior to expiry of the credit.' It would appear from this conclusion that in a dispute concerning documentary credits, the 'obligation in question' will almost always involve a party's obligation to pay; whether the dispute involves a beneficiary seeking payment from a bank, a bank seeking reimbursement or the applicant seeking an injunction to restrain payment under the credit.[2]

1 [1994] ECR I-2913 and 2957 (para 23). See also Case 14/76 *Etablissements A de Bloos sprl v Société en Commandite Par Actions Bouyer* [1976] ECR 1497 at 1508 (paras 11 and 14) ('the contractual obligation forming the basis of the legal proceedings'); 266/85 *Shenavai v Kreischer* [1987] ECR 239; C-440/97 *GIE Groupe Concorde v Master of the Vessel Suhadiwarno Panjan* [1999] CLC 1976, ECJ; *Kleinwort Benson Ltd v Glasgow City Council* [1999] 1 AC 153; *Agnew v Lansförsäkringsbolagens* [2001] 1 AC 223.
2 In *Chailease* it was argued that the real obligation that underlay the action by the beneficiary against the issuing bank was not the issuing bank's obligation to make payment, but rather the issuing bank's obligation to examine and accept conforming documents. This argument was rejected on the ground that Articles 9.a and 10.b.i of the UCP 500 did not contain any obligation to accept conforming documents, but rather made the acceptance of documents a condition precedent to the issuing bank's obligation to pay. The Court of Appeal stated that, if the issuing bank did owe an obligation to accept conforming documents, this would be owed to the applicant rather than to the beneficiary. Furthermore, it was clear that the claim was for a debt and not for damages for breach of an obligation to accept documents.

13.16   However, Article 5(1)(b) of the Jurisdiction Regulation means that, for contracts that fall within its scope, it is necessary first to classify the contract and the relevant obligation that is in issue. Where a documentary credit is used as the method of payment under a contract for the sale of goods, this could *potentially* cause confusion. For example: if a sale transaction between buyer and seller fails, leading to non-delivery of the goods or non-payment in respect thereof, the Court would have to decide whether the relevant 'obligation in question' under Article 5(1)(b) was the sale of goods under the underlying sale contract, or instead whether consideration would have to be given to some or all of the contracts making up the documentary credit.

13.17   In practice, any detailed inquiry along these lines is likely to be unnecessary. Firstly because the contract upon which the claim is based should be clearly identified: where a claim is brought in respect of payment (or non-payment) in relation to any of the autonomous contractual relationships involved in a documentary credit, that autonomous contract will be the source of the contractual obligation in issue and the terms of the underlying sale of goods contract will not be determinative. Each autonomous contract could in theory give rise to a separate jurisdictional inquiry. Secondly, following the reasoning in *Chailease*, most cases relating to documentary credits are likely to be classified as involving contracts for the provision of a service for consideration, as opposed to contracts for the sale of goods.

'Place of Performance'

13.18   The 'place of performance' of the 'obligation in question' has not been given an autonomous definition under the Jurisdiction Regulation.[1] Under Article 5(1)(b), in relation to a contract for the provision of services, the Court must identify the place in which the services were provided or should have been provided. The general aim behind this revision in the Jurisdiction Regulation is said to be in order to enable a claimant 'to identify easily the court in which he may sue and the defendant reasonably to foresee before which court he may be sued.'[2]

1 Case 12/76 *Industrie Tessili Italiano Como v Dunlop AG* [1976] ECR 1473 at para 13; Case C-288/92 *Custom Made Commercial Ltd v Stawa Metallbau GmbH* [1994] ECR I-2913 at para 26; Case C-420/97 *Leathertex Divisione Sinetici SpA v Bodetex BVBA* [1999] CLC 1976 at para 33. See in a different context *Royal & Sun Alliance Insurance plc v MK Digital FZE (Cyprus) Ltd* [2006] 2 Lloyd's Rep 110 (delivery of goods); *WPP Holdings Italy SRL v Benatti* [2007] 1 WLR 2316 (employment contract).
2 *Color Drack GmbH v. Lexx International Vertriebs GmbH* (Case C–386/05) [2007] I.L.Pr. 35 paras 19, 20, 32 and 33.

13.19   In *Chailease*, Potter LJ confirmed that in the established European jurisprudence under the Conventions it was for the national court seised of the dispute to determine the place of performance of the relevant obligation by applying the law applicable under its private international law rules. The House of Lords recently confirmed this approach under Article 5.1(b) of the Jurisdiction Regulation in *Scottish and Newcastle International v Othon Ghalanos* in which it held, applying *Industrie Tessili Italiana Como v Dunlop AG*,[1] that in relation to a contract for the sale of goods governed by English law, English law would be applied to determine whether or not the goods in question were to be delivered in England.

1 *Scottish and Newcastle International v Othon Ghalanos* (2008) 1 Lloyd's Rep 462; *Industrie Tessili Italiana Como v Dunlop AG* [1976] ECR 1473.

13.20   If the documentary credit stipulates the place where a payment is to be made, this will be determinative of the issue regarding the place of performance in respect of that payment. A slightly different situation arose in *Chailease*, where the credit in issue did not indicate a specific place where payment was to be made, but instead stated that payment was to be made 'as per [the beneficiary's] instructions'. The issue before the court was whether London, as the place designated by the beneficiary, should be considered to be the place of payment. It was contended that any instructions given by the beneficiary should be ignored, otherwise a beneficiary would be entitled to designate a place for payment under the credit with the sole purpose of founding jurisdiction in that particular place.[1] Potter LJ held that there was no evidence that London had been designated as the place of payment with the sole purpose of founding jurisdiction there, but rather was 'indeed designed to determine the place where CAI was liable to perform the obligation of payment'. He stated:

> 'In the course of [determining the place of performance of the 'obligation in question'], the Court may and, in my view, should have regard to any subsidiary agreement by the parties in that respect or to the outcome of any machinery or method for the subsequent determination of the place of payment which is anticipated and/or permitted within the terms of the contract. If by those terms, the parties anticipate that the place for payment may be determined at the option of one party and subsequently communicated in instructions to the other, then there seems to me no convincing argument of principle or policy why the rule of jurisdiction in Article 5(1) should be treated as inapplicable, simply because the parties have agreed that the crystallisation of the obligation as to the place of payment be postponed in that manner. That certainly seems to me to be the position under English law.'[2]

There remains the question of where the place of performance would be when neither the terms of the credit nor the subsequent conduct of the parties indicates a place where payment is to be made.[3] In these circumstances it will first be critical to determine the law applicable to the credit since that law is likely to be used to determine the place of performance (as it was in *Scottish and Newcastle International v Othon Ghalanos*).

1 See Case C-106/95 *MSG v Les Gravières Rhénanes SARL* [1997] ECR I-911 at 946: 'The [Brussels Convention] must be interpreted as meaning that an oral agreement on the place of performance which is designed not to determine the place where the person liable is actually to perform the obligations incumbent upon him, but solely to establish that the court for a particular place have jurisdiction, is not governed by Article 5(1) of the Convention, but by Article 17, and is valid only if the requirements set out therein are complied with.'
2 *Chailease Finance Corpn v Credit Agricole Indosuez* [2000] 1 Lloyd's Rep 348 at 356.
3 Where English law applies to the contract in question, this analysis will be relevant to the common law test under CPR 6.20(6) to determine the place of payment where it is alleged that there was a breach of contract by reason of non-payment (see Dicey, Morris & Collins at 11-203).

13.21 Under English law, the general rule is that a debtor must seek out his creditor so the place of payment will be where the creditor resides or has his place of business.[1] Though this general rule has not been applied to documentary credits or demand guarantees, some commentators have suggested that it should apply as a matter of course.[2] It is suggested that the better view is that the contractual obligation to make payment in a contract under a documentary credit crystallises upon the presentation of documents and therefore that the place of payment for the purposes of Article 5(1)(b) of the Jurisdiction Regulation is the place where the documents are presented under the credit.[3] The position may be different if the credit is governed by another system of law.

1 *The Eider* [1893] P.119, 136-137 and see Dicey, Morris & Collins at 11-294 and 33-310–33-314 in the context of documentary credits. See Briggs & Rees at 2.138 for application of this general rule in other jurisdictions.
2 Brindle & Cox *Law of Bank Payments* (3rd edn 2004) at 8-107.
3 See *Offshore International SA v Banco Central SA* [1977] 1 WLR 399; *Power Curber International Ltd v National Bank of Kuwait SAK* [1981] 1 WLR 1233 at 1240D, 1242E and 1244A–B; *Britten Norman Ltd v State Ownership Fund of Romania* [2000] Lloyd's Rep Bank 315 at 318–19, per Peter Leaver QC (see criticism at Brindle & Cox at 8-110–111); *Royal Bank Of Scotland Plc v Cassa di Risparmio Delle Provincie Lombarde and ors* (Times, 23 January 1991) at first instance per Phillips J; the matter went to an appeal which was dismissed at (1992) 1 Bank LR 251. Mustill LJ made no comment on the finding below that the general rule did not apply in the international banking transaction in issue (at 255). As to this: while a distinction should be drawn between the test applied to determine jurisdiction under the Jurisdiction Regulation and the test applied to determine the governing law of a contract under the Rome Convention (see *Chailease Finance Corpn v Credit Agricole Indosuez* at 352 para 18 per Potter LJ), an analogy is appropriate in these circumstances. The overall purpose of a letter of credit transaction is to provide payment to the seller/beneficiary. With this in mind, it is suggested that from a practical and commercial standpoint, the most important factors regarding the place in which the obligations are performed in respect of the credit are (i) where the documents necessary to procure the payment are presented and checked; and (ii) where the consequent payment is to be made (see *PT Pan Indonesia Bank Ltd TBK v Marconi Communications International Ltd* [2007] 2 Lloyd's Rep 72 at 84 paras 62–63; *Power Curber* (above) at 1240F).

B CHOICE OF GOVERNING LAW

(1) General principles

13.22 Even where an English court has accepted jurisdiction over a documentary credit dispute, it does not follow that English law should be applied to determine all, or any, of the issues. Documentary credits very often involve parties from more than one country and can, by reason of the various contracting relationships that form the credit, give rise to a 'wholly undesirable multiplicity of potentially conflicting laws'.[1] Disputes over whether or not the contract in question is governed by English law often arise in the context of challenges to the jurisdiction of the English court because the fact that the governing law is English is one of the heads under which jurisdiction may be established.[2]

1 *Bank of Baroda v Vysya Bank* [1994] 2 Lloyd's Rep 87 at 93 per Mance J.
2 CPR 6.20(5).

13.23   It is possible that in a case before an English court, England may not be involved at all in the credit or its performance. The question will therefore arise as to which system of law the court should apply. It is for the parties before the court to consider whether any tactical advantage can be secured by arguing that a particular rule of foreign law applies to some or all of the issues before the court. As a general rule, the court will not involve itself in questions of foreign law unless these are raised by one of the parties. A litigant who concludes that there are such advantages to be gained must demonstrate that, according to the English conflict of laws rules, the desired foreign law governs the dispute and must prove the content of that foreign law to the satisfaction of the court by expert evidence.

13.24   The relevant statute in English conflicts of law is the Contracts (Applicable Law) Act 1990. This Act implements the 1980 Rome Convention on the Law Applicable to Contractual Obligations ('the Rome Convention'). The rules contained in the Rome Convention apply to contractual obligations in any situation involving a choice between the laws of different countries, there need be no EU connection.[1] Prior to the ratification of the Convention in English law,[2] choice of law was determined by common law rules. However, those rules will now apply only in the unlikely event of a dispute involving a documentary credit issued before April 1991.[3] For a discussion of the common law position, reference should be made to the third edition of this book.

1 Rome Convention, Article 1. For this purpose England, Scotland and Northern Ireland are different countries. Although the Convention contains no definition of the term 'contractual obligations', it is likely to have the same scope as the term 'matters relating to a contract' in the Jurisdiction Regulation, Article 5(1) and the Brussels Convention 1968, discussed above. See also in this regard Contracts (Applicable Law) Act 1990, s 3(1). In interpreting the Rome Convention, regard should also be had to the Report on the Convention by Professors Mario Giuliano and Paul Lagarde (OJ 1980 C282/1), 31.10.80 hereinafter referred to as 'the Giuliano-Lagarde Report'. The Giuliano-Lagarde Report was published with the Rome Convention and is often relied upon in interpreting the Convention.
2 By the Contracts (Applicable Law) Act 1990.
3 A recent example of such a dispute is *Habib Bank Ltd v Central Bank of Sudan* [2006] 2 Lloyd's Rep 412, which, astonishingly, involved a credit issued in 1982. Field J held (at p 418) that English law applied to letters of credit entered into between Pakistani and Sudanese banks. In reaching his conclusion the Judge drew comfort from the findings of Mance J in Bank of *Baroda v Vysya Bank*, a case under the Rome Convention in which English law was held to apply to a contract between an Indian issuing bank and an Indian confirming bank where the addition and honouring of the confirmation were all to be performed in London by the confirming bank's London branch office.

13.25   The majority of disputes over governing law in this context will arise in relation to contracts and the focus of the analysis that follows is therefore on the position in contract. However, the question of the law governing a tort claim in relation to a documentary credit has also recently been considered by the English Court.[1] The choice of law applicable to an issue in tort is determined under English conflicts of law rules by the application of Part III of the Private International Law (Miscellaneous Provisions) Act 1995 though this will be affected by the 'Rome II' Regulation, which will be directly applicable in English law.[2]

1 *Trafigura Beheer BV v Kookmin Bank Co* (2006) 2 Lloyd's Rep 455 and see related proceedings at [2005] EWHC 2350 (Comm); (2007) 1 Lloyd's Rep 669. Also Briggs 'The Further Consequences of a Choice of Law' (2007) 123 LQR 18. See below at **13.37**.
2 See generally Dicey, Morris & Collins, Ch 35 and supplement to Ch 35 in relation to the effect of the Rome II Regulation (Council Regulation (EC) 864/2007) which have direct effect in the UK.

The Role of the UCP

13.26   The UCP contain no provisions relevant to the question of what national law is to be applied to determine any particular issue which may arise in connection with a letter of credit.[1] However, given that the UCP now apply by incorporation to nearly all letters of credit, regardless of country, they provide a large degree of uniformity in the substantive rules applicable to a particular dispute. This diminishes the differences that might otherwise arise through the application of different national laws. Differences in the interpretation of the UCP and in the application of contractual principles may nevertheless persist depending upon the applicable national law. Nonetheless it is to be expected that the courts of one country should heed the decisions on similar points of the courts of other countries in the application of the UCP. Thus, whereas on general questions of contract law it may be of little interest to an English court what approach has been adopted in continental jurisdictions, decisions on particular questions involving the construction of provisions of the UCP should be given careful attention.

1 Compare Article 27 of the ICC Uniform Rules for Demand Guarantees (currently in the process of revision; see para **12.90**).

The law governing a contract

13.27   Before examining the specific contracts arising out of the documentary credit, the general principles on choice of law under the Rome Convention, will be considered.[1] There then follows an analysis of the law applicable to the different contractual relationships that arise in the context of documentary credits.

1 For a fuller treatment of these principles, see Dicey, Morris & Collins, Vol 2, ch 32 and also Plender & Wilderspin, *The European Contracts Convention* (2nd edn).

Under the Rome Convention

13.28   The characterisation of the issue in dispute determines the appropriate choice of law under the Rome Convention.[1] The majority of issues will be determined according to Articles 3 and 4, including questions relating to the material validity of the credit,[2] the interpretation of its terms and whether the documents tendered conform with the terms of the credit. The law on the need to comply with any formal requirements is determined by Article 9 whilst issues relating to the capacity of the contracting parties are, with the exception of Article 11 of the Convention, excluded from the scope of the Convention and, therefore, governed by the common law. Limitation and prescription are governed by the law of the issue in dispute.[3]

1 In *Macmillan Inc v Bishopsgate Investment Trust Plc (No 3)* [1996] 1 WLR 387 at 399 B–D Staughton LJ described this function in the following terms: 'I would regard it as plain that the rules of conflict of laws must be directed at the particular issue of law which is in dispute, rather than at the cause of action which the plaintiff relies on. We should translate *lex causae* as the law applicable to the issue, rather than the suit.'
2 See Article 8. The term 'material validity' includes questions of mistake, misrepresentation, duress and illegality. For the problems that arise when an agreement is illegal according to a law other than the *lex causae*, see para **13.91** et seq below.
3 Foreign Limitation Periods Act 1984, s 1(1); Rome Convention, Art 10(1)(d).

13.29   The primary principle is that of freedom of contract. Article 3.1 of the Rome Convention provides that a contract shall be governed by the law chosen by the parties. The choice of a particular law may be stated expressly in the contract in question and the parties may agree that a particular system of law is applicable to the whole or only part of the contract.

13.30   In the absence of a choice of law clause, the choice of law may be implied, provided that a choice is demonstrated with reasonable certainty by the terms of the contract or the circumstances of the case. Article 3.1 was considered in *Egon Oldendorff v Libera Corpn*[1] where Clarke J held that a clause providing for arbitration in London indicated an implied choice of English law to govern the agreement.[2] Nevertheless, a court must be careful not to impute a choice of law to the parties, where there is no clearly demonstrated intention to make such a choice. In that situation, the rules contained in Article 4 should be applied.

1 *Egon Oldendorff v Libera Corpn* [1996] 1 Lloyd's Rep 380. See also *Turkiye Is Bankasi AS v Bank of China* [1993] 1 Lloyd's Rep 132 (the fact that counter-guarantees had been altered so as to conform with the relevant Turkish legislation demonstrated an implied choice that Turkish law would govern the counter-guarantee); *Tryg Baltica International (UK) Ltd v Boston Compania de Seguros SA* [2004] EWHC 1186 (Comm) (the circumstances surrounding the making of reinsurance contracts, including that the contracts were made in London, agreed wordings in English on London market forms, language of contract and relevant pre-contractual documents being English, supported the inference that the parties intended English law to govern the contracts).
2 This approach accords with that suggested by the Giuliano–Lagarde Report. That Report also provides (at page 16) other important examples as to when a court should be willing to imply a choice of law: when the contract is in a standard form widely recognised to be governed or associated with a particular system of law; the contract contains a choice of court clause; the contract contains references to the legal rules of a particular system of law; a related transaction contains an express choice of law; or there is a previous course of dealing between the parties, which was itself subject to a particular choice of law. This list is not exhaustive as the analysis will be fact sensitive.

13.31   Article 4.1 of the Rome Convention provides that where no choice of law is made under Article 3, the contract shall be governed by the law of the country with which it is most closely connected. A severable part of the contract more closely connected with the law of another country may be governed by that law.

13.32   According to Article 4(2) a contract is presumed to be most closely connected with the country where the party 'who is to effect the performance which is characteristic of the contract' has, at the time of the conclusion of the contract, its habitual residence or, in the case of a company, its central administration. But where the contract is entered into in the course of that party's trade, the country shall be that where the company's place of business through which the performance is to be effected is situated.

13.33   The concept of a contract's 'characteristic performance' is drawn from Swiss law and has no equivalent in English law. As a result the Giuliano–Lagarde Report is particularly important in determining what is meant by this concept. The Report states that a contract's characteristic performance is the 'non-monetary performance', namely the performance for which payment is due.[1]

1 At page 21. Performance (for example the delivery of goods, the provision of a service, transport, banking operations etc.) is said by the authors of the Report to constitute 'the centre of gravity and the socio-economic function of the contractual transaction'.

13.34   In the particular context of banking transactions, the Giuliano–Lagarde Report states[1] that 'in a banking contract the law of the country of the banking establishment with which the transaction is made will normally govern the contract.' This passage was adopted in *Sierra Leone Telecommunications Co Ltd v Barclays Bank plc*,[2] when Cresswell J held that the characteristic performance of the contract between a bank and its customer, who held an account in credit, was the repayment of the money on deposit. The same principle is likely to apply to the relationship between the applicant for the credit and the issuing bank.[3] It is important to remember that establishing 'characteristic performance' under the contract is not the end of the inquiry. The location of the performing party's habitual residence or central administration or place of business as at the time of the contract must also be established.

1 At page 21.
2 [1998] 2 All ER 821. See also *Domicrest Ltd v Swiss Bank Corpn* [1999] QB 548, per Rix J; *Surzur Overseas Ltd v Ocean Reliance Shipping Company Ltd* (18 April, 1997 unreported), per Toulson J; *Centrax Ltd v Citibank NA*, [1999] 1 All ER (Comm) 557, CA. In this respect the position under the Rome Convention is similar to that at common law: *Libyan Arab Foreign Bank v Bankers Trust Co* [1988] 1 Lloyd's Rep 259 at 270; *Libyan Arab Foreign Bank v Manufacturers Hanover Trust Co* [1988] 2 Lloyd's Rep 494 at 502. See also *HIB Ltd v Guardian Insurance Co Inc* [1997] 1 Lloyd's Rep 412 (broker's performance is characteristic of a broking contract).
3 See the discussion at para **13.65** below.

13.35   It is important to note that Article 4(2) is no more than a presumption and remains subject to Article 4(5), which provides that Article 4(2) shall be disregarded if it appears, from the circumstances as a whole, that the contract is more closely connected with another country.[1] Logic might suggest that the court ought to determine the law with which the contract is most closely connected before applying the presumption in Article 4(2). However the intention is more probably that the presumption should be applied in most situations without the need for such an exercise, leaving Article 4(5) as the appropriate route where the application of the presumption would lead to the application of a system of law with little real connection to the dispute.[2]

1 Article 4(5) will also apply if 'the characteristic performance' of the contract cannot be determined.
2 It is submitted that the better view is that Article 4 contains a two-stage test, commencing with the application of the presumptions in Articles 4(2)–4(4) and finishing with an examination of whether the presumption should be rebutted under Article 4(5), as reflected by the Court of Appeal's approach in *PT Pan Indonesia Bank Ltd TBK v Marconi Communications International Ltd* [2007] 2 Lloyd's Rep 72. The Court of Appeal has held that the Article 4(2) presumption should only be disregarded in circumstances which demonstrate 'a preponderance of contrary connecting factors' justifying that course (see *PT Pan Indonesia Bank Ltd TBK v Marconi Communications International Ltd* per Potter LJ at 80 para 44; *Samcrete Egypt Engineers and Contractors SAE v Land Rover Exports Ltd* [2002] CLC 533 per Potter LJ at para 45; *Ennstone Building Products Ltd v Stanger Ltd* [2002] EWCA Civ 916 [2002] 1 WLR 3059 per Keene LJ at para 41)).

13.36   The weight to be attached to the presumption contained in Article 4(2) and the quality of the evidence required to rebut that presumption remains a matter of some controversy. However, it is suggested that courts will be careful to bear in mind the overriding principle that the governing law should be that of the country with which the contract in question is most closely connected. In *Credit Lyonnais v New Hampshire Insurance Co*[1] the Court of Appeal had to consider the effect of Article 4 of the Second Insurance Directive, which determines the law applicable to insurance contracts and is similarly worded to the provisions of the Rome Convention. Hobhouse LJ considered the relationship between Articles 4(2) and 4(5) and stated:[2]

'The presumption is therefore displaced if the court concludes that it is not appropriate in the circumstances of any given case. This, formally, makes the presumption very weak but it does not detract from the guidance that paragraph 2 gives as to what is meant by 'the country with which it is most closely connected' and does not detract from the need to look for a geographical connection.'

1 [1997] 2 Lloyd's Rep 1. See also *Bank of Baroda v Vysya Bank* [1994] 2 Lloyd's Rep 87 at 93 where Mance J considered there to be force in the suggestion that the presumption in Article 4(2) will be most easily rebutted in those situations where the place of performance differs from the place of business of the person whose performance is characteristic of the contract.
2 [1997] 2 Lloyd's Rep 1 at 5.

The law governing a tort

13.37   The English conflicts of law rules used to determine the law applying to a claim in contract are different to those used to determine the law applying to a claim in tort or a claim for restitution.[1] Where there is a dispute over which conflicts of law rules apply, the English court must first characterise the nature of the dispute before it.

1 See generally Dicey, Morris & Collins, Chapters 34 (restitution) and 35 (tort). Note the changes following the Rome II Regulation applicable to non-contractual obligations, as to which see Dicey, Morris & Collins, Supplement to 14th edn in relation to Chapter 35.

13.38   Claims in relation to documentary credits will ordinarily be in contract, but this need not be the case, particularly where foreign law is said to apply.

13.39   In *Trafigura Beheer BV v Kookmin Bank Co*[1] the English court dealt with a jurisdiction challenge and an antisuit injunction application filed as a result of concurrent proceedings in the Korean and English courts, the Korean court being first seised. Kookmin, a Korean bank, had issued a letter of credit to a Korean company, Huron, in relation to Huron's purchase of a cargo of oil from a Dutch company, Trafigura. When the cargo arrived at the South Korean discharge point it was discharged without production of the bills of lading. The cargo was released to Huron. Trafigura, as beneficiary, received payment under the letter of credit from a London based advising bank, ANZ Bank. Huron became insolvent and as a consequence, Kookmin, having made payment, was never reimbursed for the sums Huron owed to Kookmin.

1 The judgments were reported at [2005] EWHC 2350 (Comm); [2006] 2 Lloyd's Rep 455; [2007] 1 Lloyd's Rep 669.

13.40   To recover its losses, Kookmin issued a claim in the Korean court claiming that Trafigura had acted in breach of various obligations that Trafigura, as beneficiary, was said to owe to Kookmin, as the issuing bank. Kookmin also alleged that Trafigura acted fraudulently. The Korean proceedings involved claims said by Kookmin to be non-contractual under Korean law. As a counter to the Korean proceedings, Trafigura sued Kookmin in the English court claiming a declaration of non-liability and an anti-suit injunction. Kookmin challenged the jurisdiction of the English court in a hearing before Cooke J.[1] Kookmin accepted that the claims advanced by Trafigura fell within CPR 6.20(5)(c), as claims in relation to contracts governed by English law. The judge held that England was clearly the appropriate forum to determine questions of construction in relation to the letter of credit and a related letter of indemnity (both of which were governed by English law by reason of incorporated or express terms to that effect). Cooke J also held that Kookmin had no arguable claims against Trafigura under English law.

1 [2005] EWHC 2350 (Comm).

13.41 Following Cooke J's decision, Aikens J was asked to resolve the preliminary issue of what law applied to the question of whether or not Trafigura was liable to Kookmin on the claims advanced by Kookmin in the Korean proceedings. This question was to be determined on the basis of English conflicts of law rules and Kookmin accepted that if English law was held to apply to its claims, then Trafigura was entitled to a declaration of non-liability in the English courts. However, if Korean law applied, then in the English proceedings the English court would have to determine, as a matter of Korean law, whether or not Trafigura had committed wilful or negligent acts that were unlawful under the Korean Civil Code.

13.42 Trafigura argued as a threshold point that the law governing the claims in the Korean proceedings had to be determined under the English conflicts of law rules concerning contract and therefore that the Rome Convention applied (the dispute being a matter relating to the underlying contract for the sale of oil and also the letter of credit contracts). This point turned on the English court's characterisation of the action in Korea. Aikens J held that the Private International Law (Miscellaneous Provisions) Act 1995, Part III (PILA 1995) required the court to consider the way in which the claim had been put in Korea and as a matter of Korean law. It was inappropriate to look at the claim purely through the eyes of English law.[1] Kookmin's claim was not based on English law; rather it was based on alleged actions and omissions by Trafigura that were said by Kookmin to be outside the letter of credit and the UCP and to constitute non-contractual civil wrongs.

1 At para 74.

13.43 The general rule under PILA 1995, s 11(1) is that the law governing the tort is that of the country in which the events constituting the tort occurred. Where the elements of the tort occur in different countries (as in this case) then under PILA 1995, s 11(2)(c) the governing law is that of the country in which the 'most significant element or elements of those events occurred'. This requires that the court analyse all the elements constituting the tort as a matter of law and then make a value judgment regarding their significance, in order to identify the country in which there is either one element or several elements, which taken alone or together, outweighs or outweigh in significance any element or elements to be found in any other country. The governing law under s 11(2) will be the law of that country.[1] This general rule can be displaced under PILA 1995, s 12 if there are factors connecting the claim with a country other than that applicable under the general rule, such that it is substantially more appropriate for the law of that other country to apply.

1 At para 77, following the Court of Appeal in *Morin v Bonhams & Brooks* [2004] 1 Lloyd's Rep 702: see in particular para 16 per Mance LJ.

13.44 Applying the general rule Aikens J found that the law of Singapore governed. However, applying PILA 1995, s 12, the judge held that the general rule should be displaced in this case and that English law applied to the tort. The judge reached this conclusion by reference in particular to the fact that the letter of credit relationship, by which Kookmin was issuing bank and Trafigura was the beneficiary, was governed by English law and that English law governed all the contractual relationships between the parties.[1] Aikens J held that:

> 'when the law governing all the contractual relationships between relevant parties concerned with the Sale Contract and its financing is English law, it would seem bizarre to hold that the applicable law to determine issues arising in relation to Kookmin's tort claim against Trafigura should be the law of another country, viz. Singapore.'[2]

1 At paras 106 and 112.
2 At paras 113 and 118. Note Briggs' criticism of this approach in 'The Further Consequences of a Choice of Law' (2007) 123 LQR 18.

13.45　At a further hearing, Field J granted Trafigura an antisuit injunction restraining the Korean proceedings.[1] Field J premised his grant of the antisuit injunction on the conclusion of Aikens J in the previous hearing that English law applied to the claim in tort in the Korean proceedings and that a declaration of non-liability should be granted to Trafigura.

1 [2007] 1 Lloyd's Rep 669.

(2)　Contracts between bank and beneficiary

13.46　This section deals with the Rome Convention position on the law governing contracts between the beneficiary under a documentary credit and the banks involved in the credit. There follows a general introductory section and then consideration of the authorities.

13.47　It is unusual for a letter of credit to specify a governing law, though there is no reason why it should not do so. An issuing bank might see an advantage in specifying the law of the country where it is situated as the governing law. Where, however, the credit is payable in another country this would be undesirable from the beneficiary's point of view as in some circumstances it could undermine the security of payment which the credit is intended to provide.[1] As banking practice currently stands therefore, Article 3 of the Rome Convention is only likely to be applicable to letters of credit in situations where the terms or the circumstances of the case support a finding of an implied choice of law. To avoid the type of issues discussed in the analysis that follows, banks would be well advised to include in their contracts an express choice of law clause.

1 See the facts in *Power Curber International Ltd v National Bank of Kuwait* [1981] 1 WLR 1233.

13.48   In the absence of the application of Article 3, the governing law will, as already discussed, be determined by the application of the rules contained in Article 4. The purpose of the Rome Convention is to provide for uniformity of choice of law.[1] The choice of law rules should also enable the applicable law in the absence of choice to be predicted with a degree of certainty, but at the same time retain sufficient flexibility to deal with those situations that depart from the usual situation.

1 See the Giuliano–Lagarde Report, page 4.

13.49   Subject to this, however, it is suggested that the approach to the question of governing law in documentary credits should be to find a rule which determines the applicable law in the absence of the parties' choice and which can be easily and uniformly applied to the common situations which occur.[1] With regard to contracts between bank and beneficiary there are three main situations:

(1) Issuing bank is required to advise credit direct to beneficiary and the beneficiary is obliged to present the documents under the credit directly to the issuing bank. As such there are no other banks involved and the beneficiary is party to a single contract with the issuing bank.

(2) Issuing bank advises credit to beneficiary through an advising bank and the documents under the credit are to be presented to the advising bank which will accept or reject them on behalf of the issuing bank. As in example (1) the beneficiary is only party to a single contract with the issuing bank.

(3) This situation is the same as in example (2), save that the advising bank confirms the credit. As a result the beneficiary has two contracts, one with the issuing bank and one with the confirming bank.

Before considering the reported authorities on the law applicable to the various contractual relationships constituting the letter of credit, it is appropriate to consider the position as a matter of theory. It is suggested that in each of the above situations, in the absence of a choice of law, the applicable law should be that of the country in which the bank (or branch) is situated, which is to be the first to examine the documents and to determine acceptance or rejection.[2] The selection of the law of the place where the bank to whom presentation of documents is to be made is situated, has the advantage that in examining the documents the bank is able to apply its own law and not a foreign law. Further, that bank will usually be an advising or confirming bank which is often in the same country as the beneficiary. Where the credit is confirmed this same law should govern, irrespective of whether it is the contract between the beneficiary and the issuing bank or the contract between the beneficiary and the confirming bank which is under examination. The performance of the advising/confirming bank is central to both contracts and the application of different laws to the two contracts would create considerable difficulties.[3]

1 See *Offshore International SA v Banco Central SA* [1977] 1 WLR 399, per Ackner J.

2 See PT *Pan Indonesia Bank Ltd TBK v Marconi Communications International Ltd* [2007] 2
  Lloyd's Rep 72: Potter LJ's analysis of the common law position at 80 and factors under the
  Rome Convention at 84.
4 *PT Pan Indonesia Bank* at 83 para 55 but note para 61 at 84.

13.50   The leading authority regarding the application of Article 4 of the
Rome Convention to documentary credits is the Court of Appeal decision in
*PT Pan Indonesia Bank Ltd TBK v Marconi Communications International
Ltd*. There were a limited number of relevant decisions in the High Court
prior to this, in particular *Bank of Baroda v Vysya Bank Ltd* and *Bank of
Credit and Commerce Hong Kong Ltd v Sonali Bank*, which are also
considered here.[1]

1 *PT Pan Indonesia Bank Ltd TBK v Marconi Communications International Ltd* [2007] 2
  Lloyd's Rep 72; *Bank of Baroda v Vysya Bank Ltd* [1994] 2 Lloyd's Rep 87 approved in *Bank
  of Credit and Commerce Hong Kong Ltd v Sonali Bank* [1995] 1 Lloyd's Rep 227; *Wahda
  Bank v Arab Bank plc* [1996] 1 Lloyd's Rep 470, CA; *Bastone & Firminger Ltd v Nasima
  Enterprises (Nigeria) Ltd* [1996] CLC 1902, per Rix J.

13.51   *Bank of Baroda v Vysya Bank Ltd* involved two Indian banks. Vysya
Bank, a private bank in India, was instructed by an Indian importer, Aditya,
to issue a letter of credit in favour of Granada, an Irish incorporated company
with a London office. The underlying transaction between Aditya and
Granada related to the sale of pig iron. Vysya approached the National
Westminster Bank to advise the credit to the beneficiary. The reimbursement
instructions provided: 'Negotiating bank to claim reimbursement as per terms
of this credit Citibank, New York by debit to our international division
account with them.' The credit was confirmed by the Bank of Baroda's City of
London branch. The documents were negotiated by the Bank of Baroda,
which dispatched the documents to Vysya. Vysya informed Baroda that
reimbursement instructions had been mailed to Citibank, New York and
authorised the Bank of Baroda to claim reimbursement on the due date.
Shortly thereafter, Vysya withdrew the authorisation on the ground that one
of the bills of lading had been issued without authority. Vysya returned the
documents and the Bank of Baroda commenced proceedings against Vysya for
breach of the contract that exists between an issuing and confirming bank.
The principal issue before the court concerned the law applicable to the
relationship between Vysya Bank and the Bank of Baroda: this aspect of the
decision will be considered in a later section.[1] Mance J, however, also decided
to address the question of the law applicable to the relationship between
Vysya and Granada. In this respect he stated:[2]

> 'As between the beneficiary and Vysya, the position under Art 4(2) is that
> there is a presumption that Indian law applies. This presumption applies,
> although the performance which is characteristic of the contract is the issue of
> the letter of credit in London which was to be and was effected in London
> through National Westminster Bank, initially at least as advising bank, with
> the Bank of Baroda later adding its confirmation. Although such performance
> was to take place in London, Art 4(2) refers one back, prima facie, to India as
> the place of Vysya's central administration.'

As a result, in a situation where the issuing bank advises the credit to the beneficiary, or requests an advising bank to carry out that task on its behalf, the presumption in Article 4(2) would lead to the application of the law of the country in which the issuing bank is situated to the relationship between the issuing bank and the beneficiary. In the case before Mance J, this would have led to the application of Indian law. As the letter of credit which Mance J had to consider had also been confirmed, he also had to consider the application of the presumption in Article 4(2) to the relationship between the confirming bank. Mance J considered that the performance characteristic of the relationship between a confirming bank and a beneficiary was the addition and honouring of the confirming bank's confirmation. As the confirmation was to be added by the Bank of Baroda, the contract was governed by English law. The rigorous application of Article 4(2) to the various relationships comprising the documentary credit led to a situation where the beneficiary's rights would be determined by different laws according to whether he decided to sue the issuing bank or the confirming bank. The situation was resolved in the following way:

> 'In my judgment this is a situation where it would be quite wrong to stop at Art 4(2). The basic principle is that the governing law is that of the country with which the contract is most closely connected (Art 4(1)). Art 4(2) is, as stated in Professor Giuliano and Lagarde's report, intended to give 'specific form and objectivity' to that concept. In the present case the application of Art 4(2) would lead to an irregular and subjective position where the governing law of a letter of credit would vary according to whether one was looking at the position of the confirming bank or the issuing bank. It is of great importance to both beneficiaries and banks concerned in the issue and operation of international letters of credit that there should be clarity and simplicity in such matters. Article 4(5) provides the answer... The present situation provides in my judgment a classic demonstration of the need for and appropriateness of Art 4(5). I conclude that English law applies to the contract between Vysya and Granada.'

Mance J therefore applied Article 4(5) to ensure that the different contracts that made up the credit were governed by the same law. However, he stressed that he would have come to the same conclusion, even if the credit had been an unconfirmed credit to be advised in London by National Westminster Bank or by the Bank of Baroda's City branch. In this respect, Mance J adopted the same solution under the Rome Convention as had been adopted at common law.[3]

1 See para **13.65**.
2 *Bank of Baroda v Vysya Bank Ltd* [1994] 2 Lloyd's Rep 87 at 93.
3 See *Offshore International SA v Banco Central SA* [1977] 1 WLR 399.

13.52   The Rome Convention was also considered obiter by Cresswell J in *Bank of Credit and Commerce Hong Kong Ltd v Sonali Bank*,[1] even though choice of law fell to be determined by the common law principles as the credit had been issued before April 1991. The sale transaction to which the credit related involved the import of goods into Bangladesh. The Bangladeshi buyer applied to Sonali to open a letter of credit in favour of the seller. The Bank of Credit and Commerce Hong Kong (BCCHK) agreed to add its confirmation. The seller presented the documents to BCCHK, which subsequently negotiated the documents and presented them to Sonali. Sonali failed to reimburse BCCHK despite its having either accepted the documents or failed to reject them in a timely fashion. As a result, BCCHK commenced proceedings seeking reimbursement from Sonali. In analysing the position at common law, Cresswell J cited with approval the approach adopted by Mance J's judgment in *Bank of Baroda* above, both with respect to the characteristic performance of the relationship between confirming bank and beneficiary and also with respect to the application of Article 4(5) to ensure that the same law applied to all the contracts that the beneficiary had with the banks.

1 [1995] 1 Lloyd's Rep 227 subsequently referred to with approval by Staughton LJ in *Wahda Bank v Arab Bank plc* [1996] 1 Lloyd's Rep 470 at 473, CA.

13.53   It is suggested that there is an alternative route to this result based on an argument that the performance characteristic of the contract is that of the bank that examines the presented documents and determines whether to accept or reject them.

13.54   Where there is only one bank involved, namely example (1) in para **13.49** above, this interpretation of Article 4(2) of the Convention would result in the law of the issuing bank governing that contract.

13.55   Where the contract under examination is that between the confirming bank and the beneficiary, namely example (2) in para **13.49** above, this interpretation of Article 4(2) of the Convention would result in the law of the advising bank governing that contract.

13.56   Where there are two banks involved and the contract under examination is that between the issuing bank and the beneficiary, the presumption in Article 4(2) would only produce the suggested and desired result if the advising/confirming bank could be treated as 'a place of business other than the principal place of business'[1] of the issuing bank. Unless one is a branch of the other this will not be the case. As a result Article 4(5) would have to be applied to give the outcome desired.[2] In the Giuliano–Lagarde Report it is stated that it is 'quite natural' that, where they differ, the law of the bank's place of business shall prevail over the country of performance.[3]

1 The relevant words from Article 4(2).
2 See *Bank of Baroda v Vysya Bank* [1994] 2 Lloyd's Rep 87 at 93.1 and *Bank of Credit and Commerce Hong Kong Ltd v Sonali Bank* [1995] 1 Lloyd's Rep 227.
3 See the Giuliano–Lagarde Report page 21.

13.57   In *PT Pan Indonesia Bank Ltd TBK v Marconi Communications International Ltd* the Court of Appeal held that the factors of the most obvious significance in determining which country that has the closest connection to the contract between seller/beneficiary and issuing/confirming bank under a letter of credit were (i) the place where the documents necessary to procure payment to the seller/beneficiary are to be presented and checked; and (ii) the place where payment to the seller/beneficiary is to be made against those documents.[1] Using this test, the Court of Appeal disregarded the presumption in Article 4(2), and applied Article 4(5) to determine which law would govern the contract before it.

1 [2007] 2 Lloyd's Rep 72 at 84.

13.58   The Court of Appeal also confirmed that it was desirable that the same system of law should govern the co-existing contracts between:

(a) the issuing bank and the beneficiary;
(b) the confirming bank and the beneficiary; and
(c) the issuing bank and the confirming bank.[1]

1 [2007] 2 Lloyd's Rep 72 at 83.

13.59   Marconi entered into a contract to supply telephone equipment and services to an Indonesian company. Payment for this underlying transaction was to be by a documentary credit. The credit had been issued through an Indonesian bank, Hastin Bank, on the application of the Indonesian buyer. PT Pan Indonesia Bank ('Panin') was another Indonesian bank that acted as the confirming bank in relation to the letter of credit, under which Marconi was the beneficiary. The letter of credit was to be advised through Standard Chartered Bank in London. Standard Chartered Bank was authorised (but not obliged) to give value for Marconi's drafts drawn on Panin against compliant documents and claim reimbursement from Panin by payment of the draft upon maturity.

13.60   Both Hastin, the Indonesian issuing bank, and Panin rejected the documents presented under the letter of credit. Panin therefore refused to pay Marconi. Standard Chartered Bank rejected the alleged discrepancies as unjustified but Panin refused to pay. Hastin became insolvent. Panin admitted that it had been intended that under the letter of credit drafts would have been drawn on Panin Bank; Marconi would have negotiated such drafts with Standard Chartered Bank London and would have received payment from Standard Chartered Bank in London.

13.61   Marconi issued proceedings in England claiming damages for Panin's failure to honour its obligations as confirmer of the letter of credit. The matter came before the Court of Appeal on the Bank's challenge to the jurisdiction of the English court. Argument focused mainly upon the question of what law governed the relevant contract. In accordance with the relevant test[1] Marconi had to establish that it had a good arguable case that English law applied.

1 *Seaconsar Far East v Bank Markazi Jomhouri Islami Iran* [1994] 1 AC 438.

13.62 Potter LJ, who delivered the judgment of the Court, first stated that at common law the place with which the contract between the issuing bank and the beneficiary embodied in the credit was most closely connected was the place 'at which the documents will be presented and at which and at which authority has been given to make payments of sums due or to accept drafts drawn under the credit.' The same result was reached under the Rome Convention in *Bank of Baroda v Vysya Bank*.

13.63 At first instance in *PT Pan Indonesia Bank Ltd TBK v Marconi Communications International Ltd* David Steel J had followed *Bank of Baroda v Vysya Bank* and held that there was a good arguable case that the Article 4(2) presumption should be disregarded because the contract as a whole was more closely connected with England than Indonesia. The Court of Appeal agreed with David Steel J's approach. Potter LJ observed that it is 'misleading' to speak of a law governing a letter of credit because as a matter of fact and law a letter of credit gives rise to a number of autonomous bilateral contracts between banks and the transacting parties, each of which contracts has a separate characteristic performance and potentially a different governing law.[1] Potter LJ further stated that:[2]

'62... it is in our view important for the court to bear in mind the essential nature and commercial purpose of a letter of credit transaction in the international sale of goods, namely to provide the seller/beneficiary with the right to receive payment against compliant documents in a particular country, usually that in which the seller carries on business ...

63. In the context of the overall purpose of a letter of credit transaction, when considering the contracts arising between the seller/beneficiary and the issuing or confirming bank, the geographical location of the factors which, absent the presumption contained in Article 4(2), are of most obvious significance when considering the closest connection with a particular country, are not the location of the central administration or place of business of either of those banks but the place where the documents necessary to procure payment to the seller/beneficiary are to be presented and checked, and the place where payment to the seller/beneficiary is to be made against those documents. I would also observe that, whereas the place where the contract is made may have jurisdictional significance, in these days of electronic communication it is of little significance so far as "close connection" is concerned. While frequently the confirming bank will be the corresponding/advising bank, it is not necessarily so, as this case demonstrates. Nor does it affect the essential nature, structure and effect of the transaction as governed by the UCP. In either case, the confirming bank, by adding its confirmation, simply assumes by separate engagement, obligations to the same effect as those of the issuing bank so far as the beneficiary is concerned: see UCP Article 9(a)(iv) and 9(b)(iv).'

The place in which documents are presented and payment is made will therefore be determinative of which system of law governs the contract between the seller/beneficiary and the issuing/confirming bank. This is a practical and commercially desirable outcome.

1 [2007] 2 Lloyd's Rep 72 at 84 para 61.
2 [2007] 2 Lloyd's Rep 72 at 84 paras 62 and 63.

13.64   In *PT Pan Indonesia Bank Ltd TBK v Marconi Communications International Ltd*, the only contract that might not have justified the application of English law under Article 4(5) was that between the issuing bank (Hastin) and the confirming bank (Panin); both banks were based in Indonesia. Potter LJ remarked that the contract between issuing and confirming bank merely established the confirming bank's right to reimbursement consequential upon payment to the seller/beneficiary for whose benefit the letter of credit had been established. The court's view appears to have been that this contract is of secondary importance and the law governing it would not be permitted to override or 'infect' the question of which law governs the contract between the seller/beneficiary and the issuing/confirming banks: those contracts being the main purpose for the existence of the documentary credit.[1]

1 [2007] 2 Lloyd's Rep 72 at 85 para. 67 and see para **13.67** below.

(3)   Contracts between applicant and issuing bank

13.65   The applicant and issuing bank will normally be in the same country. It is suggested that on any analysis the contract between them must ordinarily be governed by the law of the country in which the issuing bank is situated since that is the place in which banking services would be provided by the bank to its customer (here the applicant) and in which repayment of the credit would be made to the bank by the applicant. This was certainly the position adopted by the common law. In *Libyan Arab Foreign Bank v Bankers Trust* Staughton J stated that 'as a general rule the contract between a bank and its customer is governed by the law of the place where the account is kept, in the absence of agreement to the contrary'.[1] The applicant will usually have an account with the bank that it requests to open a letter of credit. As a result the same law will govern their relations both in respect of the account and such credits as the bank is requested to open.

1 *Libyan Arab Foreign Bank v Bankers Trust* [1988] 1 Lloyd's Rep 259 at 270.

13.66   It is submitted that the same result would follow from the application of the Rome Convention. It will be the issuing bank which effects 'the performance which is characteristic of the contract'.[1] The statement in the Giuliano-Lagarde Report that 'in a banking contract the law of the country of the banking establishment with which the transaction is made will normally govern the contract' is directly applicable.[2] It is also logical that, if the issuing of the credit is the performance characteristic of the contract between the issuing bank and the beneficiary, it should also be the performance characteristic of the contract between the issuing bank and the applicant. Any other conclusion could result in the issuing bank having to apply different systems of law to its dealings with different parties to the letter of credit. This would hardly be a sensible situation. Even if Article 4(2) does not provide the desired result, Article 4(5) could be used to attain it.

1 See Article 4(2) Rome Convention.
2 Giuliano–Lagarde Report, p 21: see also the cases applying this principle to banking contracts generally at para **13.31** above.

(4) Relations between banks

13.67　If a correspondent bank is employed, it will almost certainly be in a different country to the issuing bank. The functions which it performs are carried out vis-à-vis the issuing bank as the agent of the issuing bank. Those functions, namely the advising of the credit, the examination of documents and payment functions, are all carried out by it in the country in which it is situated. It was held in *Bank of Baroda v Vysya Bank* that the 'performance which is characteristic of the contract' for the purpose of Article 4(2) of the Rome Convention is effected by the correspondent bank by adding its confirmation to the letter of credit.[1] The application of this law will result in the same law being applied as governs the relationship between the issuing/confirming bank and the beneficiary. The same conclusion would be reached under the common law rules.[2]

1 *Bank of Baroda v Vysya Bank* [1994] 2 Lloyd's Rep 87 as applied in *Bank of Credit and Commerce Hong Kong Ltd v Sonali Bank* [1995] 1 Lloyd's Rep 227. See also *Wahda Bank v Arab Bank plc* [1996] 1 Lloyd's Rep 470, per Staughton LJ: 'When one bank issues a letter of credit and instructs another bank to confirm it, once again the confirming bank will wish to be sure that its right of reimbursement is, back-to-back, the same as its liability. It will wish to ensure that it takes no risk other than the solvency of the bank that is going to reimburse it.' The performance 'characteristic' of a contract between confirming and issuing banks is not the fulfilment of the confirming bank's right to reimbursement by the issuing bank, this is merely consequential on the character of the contract and does not characterise it for the purpose of Article 4(2) (*Bank of Baroda v Vysya Bank* [1994] 2 Lloyd's Rep 87 at 91 per Mance J).
2 *Habib Bank v Central Bank of Sudan* [2006] 2 Lloyd's Rep 412.

13.68　Where the two banks are based in the same country the question of which law governs under the Rome Convention should be straightforward to answer, since all relevant events are likely to take place in that country and the law of that country will govern. This is supported by the reasoning (*obiter* as the point was not at issue) in *PT Pan Indonesia Bank Ltd TBK v Marconi Communications International Ltd* where the Court of Appeal considered this relationship between banks in the context of the Rome Convention. Potter LJ tentatively held that 'it could be said that' the contract between the issuing and confirming banks, both of whom were based in Indonesia, was governed by Indonesian law under the presumption in Article 4(2) and that overriding this by the application of Article 4(5) was unlikely to be justified.[1]

1 *PT Pan Indonesia Bank Ltd TBK v Marconi Communications International Ltd* [2007] 2 Lloyd's Rep 72 at para 67.

(5)   Negotiation credits

13.69   The credit may enable any bank to negotiate documents and to present them under the credit to the advising bank, or as the credit provides negotiation may be restricted to a class of banks (probably defined by situation) or just one bank. In each of these situations two relationships have to be considered: first, that between the negotiating bank and the banks giving undertakings under the credit; secondly, that between the beneficiary and the negotiating bank.

13.70   (a) With regard to the negotiating bank and the banks giving undertakings in respect of the credit, it is suggested that a negotiating bank is in the same position as the beneficiary himself, whom it has effectively become. Thus the same governing law must apply between the negotiating bank and the issuing and any confirming bank, and it will be the law of the place where the bank is situated to which presentation of documents is to be made by the negotiating bank. It cannot make any difference that the negotiating bank is situated in another country. Among other reasons, if that could affect the choice of proper law, it would mean that the proper law of the credit varied according to whether negotiation occurred and where the negotiating bank was situated. If the negotiation takes place in the same country as the bank to which presentation of documents is to be made under the credit, the same law will apply between the beneficiary and the negotiating bank as governs the credit. Negotiation may, however, take place in another country. For example, an issuing bank might advise a negotiable credit direct to a beneficiary in another country in which negotiation then takes place. Where the credit is available by negotiation, in the sense that the credit provides for the advising bank to negotiate the documents, the governing law of the credit will be the law of the place where the advising bank is situated.[1]

1 This statement in the third edition was approved as supporting the conclusions reached by the Court of Appeal in *PT Pan Indonesia Bank Ltd TBK v Marconi Communications International Ltd* [2007] 2 Lloyd's Rep 72 at para 65. See also Brindle & Cox at 8-115 for criticism of this view.

13.71   It is suggested in para **13.67** above that the law governing relations between an issuing bank and an advising bank which has to handle the documents is likely to be the law of the place where the advising bank is situated. This should also be the case where the credit is available by negotiation by the advising bank. If that is right, it follows that in this respect an advising bank nominated by the credit to negotiate is in a different position to a bank which negotiates under a freely negotiable credit: (i) the former's relations with the issuing bank to which it must present the documents which it has negotiated are governed by the law of the place where it is situate; while (ii) the latter's relations with the bank to which it must present the documents are governed by the law of the place where that bank is situate. This follows as a matter of logic because of the special position of a bank nominated by the credit to handle the documents.

13.72 (b) The law governing relations between the beneficiary and the bank to which it negotiates the documents need not be, and is perhaps unlikely to be, the same law as that governing the credit itself. Although that law is one factor in determining the governing law between the negotiation bank and the beneficiary, each case has to be examined on its own facts to see with which system of law the contract between them relating to the negotiation has its closest and most real connection. The law of the country where the negotiation takes place is likely to be a strong contender.

(6) Transferable credits

13.73 Where a credit is transferred to a second beneficiary, new relationships come into being with the banks giving undertakings under the credit, in that those undertakings are extended to the new beneficiary as well as remaining extended to the old. Where the place of presentation of documents remains unchanged by the transfer, it is clear that the law governing the undertakings given to the second beneficiary should be the same as the law which governs the undertakings given to the first beneficiary.

13.74 However, the credit may be transferred to another place in another country pursuant to Article 38.j of the UCP, with the object that the second beneficiary can present documents in his own country. Does this then mean that the undertakings given to him by the issuing and any confirming bank will be governed by a different law, namely the law of the second beneficiary's country? It is suggested that it does not and that there should remain one law governing the whole operation of the credit as between the undertaking banks and both beneficiaries, which should be determined, as has been discussed, as the law of the place where the bank is situated to which documents are to be presented by the first beneficiary. Anything else means that transfer of the credit to another country has the effect of partially changing the governing law.[1] By the same token, if there is one consistent governing law, it may mean that the bank to which the credit is transferred and the second beneficiary will be obliged to operate the credit in accordance with a foreign law.[2] If the bank to which the credit is transferred confirms the credit to the second beneficiary, it is suggested in this instance that the law governing the contract between that bank and the second beneficiary should be the same law that governs the contract which is being confirmed, namely the contract between the issuing bank and the second beneficiary arising from the transferred credit.

1 It may be suggested against this that, in accordance with the reasoning previously adopted, the governing law must be the law of the place where the bank to which the documents are to be presented is situated: that is, of the country of the bank at which the documents are to be presented under the transferred credit. There are here, however, other important elements to consider such as consistency and commercial certainty, which make the proposed solution preferable in relation to transferable credits.
2 A possibility to be borne in mind is that provisions of the law of the country where presentation of documents is to take place, may require to be applied to questions specifically concerning presentation.

(7)   Bills of exchange

13.75   Where there is a question of the law governing a particular issue arising in connection with the right of a claimant to be paid in reliance upon rights given by a bill of exchange, rather than by the undertakings arising in connection with the credit pursuant to which the bill has come into being, in England the applicable law is determined by s 72 of the Bills of Exchange Act 1882. Questions arising under bills of exchange and other negotiable instruments are excluded from the ambit of the Rome Convention by Article 1(2)(c). A claimant may be relying on the bill rather than on the credit when he is holder of an accepted bill either as the drawer or as a party to whom it has been negotiated, and he is claiming against the acceptor. Likewise where the claim is against the drawer of the bill (the beneficiary of the credit) and the claim is made by one to whom the bill has been negotiated with recourse. The Bills of Exchange Act 1882 does not apply to a contract that is commercially connected to a bill or note but that is not embodied within the negotiable instrument itself. Thus obligations arising from confirmed documentary credits come within the general conflicts of law rules applicable to contracts that have already been considered in this chapter.

13.76   Section 72 of the Bills of Exchange Act 1882 does not, however, provide a complete code in relation to the choice of law questions that could arise in connection with a bill of exchange.[1] Section 72 provides:

'72.   Where a bill drawn in one country is negotiated, accepted, or payable in another, the rights, duties, and liabilities of the parties thereto are determined as follows:

(1)   The validity of a bill as regards requisites in form is determined by the law of the place of issue, and the validity as regards requisites in form of the supervening contracts, such as acceptance, or indorsement, or acceptance *supra protest*, is determined by the law of the place where such contract was made. Provided that –
  (a)   Where a bill is issued out of the United Kingdom it is not invalid by reason only that it is not stamped in accordance with the law of the place of issue.
  (b)   Where a bill, issued out of the United Kingdom, conforms, as regards requisites in form, to the law of the United Kingdom, it may, for the purpose of enforcing payment thereof, be treated as valid as between all persons who negotiate, hold, or become parties to it in the United Kingdom.

(2)   Subject to the provisions of this Act, the interpretation of the drawing, indorsement, acceptance, or acceptance *supra protest* of a bill, is determined by the law of the place where such contract is made. Provided that where an inland bill is indorsed in a foreign country the indorsement shall as regards the payer be interpreted according to the law of the United Kingdom.

(3)   The duties of the holder with respect to presentment for acceptance or payment and the necessity for or sufficiency of a protest or notice of dishonour, or otherwise, are determined by the law of the place where the act is done or the bill is dishonoured.

(4) [Repealed by the Administration of Justice Act 1977, s 4(2)]
(5) Where a bill is drawn in one country and is payable in another, the due date thereof is determined according to the law of the place where it is payable.'

1 See Dicey, Morris & Collins, paras 33–330 and 33-335ff. In particular s 72 does not purport to deal with the issue of the proprietary effects of the negotiation of a bill of exchange. In this regard see *Alcock v Smith* [1892] 1 Ch 238, CA; *Embiricos v Anglo-Austrian Bank* [1904] 2 KB 870, [1905] 1 KB 677 CA; *Koechlin et Cie v Kestenbaum Bros* [1927] 1 KB 889.

(8) Independent guarantees

13.77 It is intended here to refer to unconditional performance bonds and guarantees of the first demand type.[1] In *Attock Cement Co Ltd v Romanian Bank for Foreign Trade*[2], Staughton LJ held that, as the performance bond or demand guarantee was autonomous of the underlying contract between the beneficiary of the bond and his contractor, the law applicable to that contract has no effect on the law applicable to the performance bond. An independent guarantee will commonly be issued by a bank in the same country as the beneficiary. In such cases, there will be little difficulty in determining the applicable law.

1 See **Chapter 12**.
2 [1989] 1 WLR 1147, CA.

13.78 Where the bank issuing the independent guarantee and the beneficiary are in different countries, it is submitted that the applicable law under the Rome Convention will usually be that of the country in which the bank is situated as it will be the bank that effects the performance characteristic of the contract.[1] This would accord with the common law position in the *Attock Cement* case, where it was held that a performance bond will ordinarily be governed by the law of the place where payment is made under the bond.[2] Where the Uniform Rules for Demand Guarantees are incorporated, the Rules make an express choice of law, which is again the law of the place of business of the branch issuing the guarantee.[3]

1 Article 4(2) Rome Convention. See the dictum of Mance J in *Bank of Baroda v Vysya Bank* [1994] 2 Lloyd's Rep 87 at 92 col 1.
2 See para **13.77** above. This was held to be consistent with the rule ordinarily applicable to the banker customer relationship: *Libyan Arab Foreign Bank v Manufacturers Hanover Trust Co* [1988] 2 Lloyd's Rep 494.
3 Article 27 of the Uniform Rules for Demand Guarantees 1992.

13.79 Though there is no decision on the law applicable to an independent guarantee, the English court has had to consider the law applicable to a counter-guarantee or indemnity, issued in favour of the issuing bank in connection with the independent guarantee. The bank that issues the counter-guarantee will normally be located in a different country to the issuing bank. In *Turkiye Is Bankasi SA v Bank of China*[1] (which was not a Rome Convention case) it was held that, in the absence of any choice as to the applicable law, such an indemnity or counter-guarantee would be governed by the law of the country of the bank to be indemnified on the ground that the indemnity was closely related to the independent guarantee, which was itself governed by that law.

1 *Turkiye Is Bankasi SA v Bank of China* [1993] 1 Lloyd's Rep 132.

13.80 The same conclusion was subsequently reached by the Court of Appeal in *Wahda Bank v Arab Bank plc*.[1] At common law, therefore, an English court will choose as the law to govern the indemnity that of the country of the bank issuing the independent guarantee and to be indemnified. Although no authority has yet considered the issue, it is likely that the position under the Rome Convention will be the same as the common law position. According to Article 4(2) the place of business of the party performing the obligation characteristic of the counter-guarantee will be the country where the bank providing the indemnity is situated. A strict application of Article 4(2) would lead to different laws applying to the independent guarantee and the counter-guarantee. It is likely, however, that, as with letters of credit, Article 4(5) of the Rome Convention will be applied so as to provide the same applicable law to both contracts.[2]

1 *Wahda Bank v Arab Bank plc* [1996] 1 Lloyd's Rep 470, CA.
2 See the approach adopted in *Bank of Baroda v Vysya Bank* [1994] 2 Lloyd's Rep 87; *Bank of Credit and Commerce Hong Kong Ltd v Sonali Bank* [1995] 1 Lloyd's Rep 227.

13.81 Where the Uniform Rules for Demand Guarantees are incorporated into the counter-guarantees, there will be a different result. These Rules make an express choice in favour of the law of the place where the branch issuing the counter-guarantee is situated, as the law governing the independent guarantee and counter-guarantee.[1] The Guide to the Rules[2] states that it is a logical consequence of the fact that the guarantee and counter-guarantee are independent contracts that they should be governed by different laws: it is also pointed out that it is open to the parties, if they can agree, to choose one law to govern both contracts. However in *Wahda Bank v Arab Bank plc*,[3] Staughton LJ said that this split choice of law would 'not be very attractive to bankers. I should not be surprised if they decide to adopt something which is more suitable for their needs.'

1 Uniform Rules for Demand Guarantees 1992 Article 27. Note that the Rules are currently under revision (as of May 2007 http://www.iccwbo.org/iccbdfie/index.html) but the Revised Rules are not expected before 2009.
2 By Professor Goode, ICC No 510, p 35.
3 [1996] 1 Lloyd's Rep 470. Note also that there is a similar jurisdictional split provided for by Article 28.

(9)   Proof of foreign law

13.82   The final hurdle for a litigant seeking to rely on a rule of foreign law is to prove that rule. Rules of foreign law before English courts have been referred to as 'questions of fact of a peculiar kind'.[1] As such it is the general rule that it is for the party seeking to rely on a rule of foreign law to plead and prove its contents to the satisfaction of the court. The evidence tendered will usually be in the form of expert testimony. In the absence of such proof the English court will not engage in its own research into foreign law, but rather will simply assume that the foreign law is the same as English law and determine the issue on that basis.[2] Useful guidance was provided by the Court of Appeal in *PT Pan Indonesia Bank Ltd TBK v Marconi Communications International Ltd*.[3]

1   *Parkasho v Singh* [1968] P 233 at 250 approved in *Macmillan Inc v Bishopsgate Investment Trust plc (No 4)* [1999] CLC 417. As to procedure, see CPR 33.7.
2   For a detailed discussion of the various issues relating to proof of foreign law, see Fentiman, *Foreign Law in English Courts* (Clarendon Press, Oxford 1998). Dicey, Morris & Collins at 9-013.
3   [2007] 2 Lloyd's Rep 72 at 85 and see the approach of the English court to evidence of foreign law in that case and *Trafigura Beheer BV v Kookmin Bank Co* [2006] 2 Lloyd's Rep 455 and [2007] 1 Lloyd's Rep 669.

C   ILLEGALITY IN RELATION TO THE CREDIT (EXCHANGE CONTROL)

(1)   General principles

13.83   This section addresses the problems which arise as a result of illegality in two contexts: first, where the opening of the credit is prohibited by foreign law; and second, where payment under the credit is prohibited by foreign law. In either case, there will be a question as to the liability of the buyer or bank arising from the failure to open or operate the credit. As the function of the contracts which arise in connection with documentary credits is the payment of money, the question of illegality or unenforceability is likely to arise by reason of a prohibition on the movement of money, and that will most often take the form of exchange control legislation.[1] A prohibition or restriction can also occur in the situation where an order of the courts of a country prohibits a party from performing its obligations under a credit. The question which is to be considered in connection with proceedings before an English court is whether, and sometimes to what extent, foreign exchange control legislation or a foreign court's orders will be treated as relevant to the obligations sought to be enforced before the English court.

1   There is now no exchange control existing under English law itself.

13.84   Three principles may be stated at the outset, the first two of which are of general application and the third of which is specifically related to exchange control:

(1) Where the prohibition or restriction which is relied upon is part of the governing law of the contract it will be given effect to by an English court.[1]

(2) Where the prohibition is part of the law of the place where the contract is to be performed it will be given effect to by an English court.[2]

(3) Exchange contracts involving the currency of any member of the International Monetary Fund and contrary to that member's exchange control regulations are unenforceable in England by reason of the Bretton Woods Agreement and related legislation.[3]

These are considered in turn.

1 See Dicey, Morris & Collins rr 205 and 241(a); *De Beéche v South American Stores Ltd* [1935] AC 148; *St Pierre v South American Stores Ltd* [1937] 3 All ER 349, and the commentary on these cases in Mann *The Legal Aspects of Money* (6th edn 2005) 16.24–16.26.

2 See Dicey, Morris & Collins r 205, r 241(b); *Ralli Bros v Cia Naviera Sota y Aznor* [1920] 2 KB 287; cf *Kleinwort, Sons & Co v Ungarische Baumwolle Industrie Akt* [1939] 2 KB 678, 694.

3 In *Congimex Companhia Geral di Comercia Importadora e Exportadora v Tradax Export SA* [1981] 2 Lloyd's Rep 687 at 691.1 Staughton J at first instance stated: '. . . supervening illegality is only a defence if (1) it arises by the proper law of the contract or (2) it arises by the law of the place of performance. In the case of exchange contracts, there is a third category by virtue of the Bretton Woods Order in Council.' affd [1983] 1 Lloyd's Rep 250 (CA).

(2)   Illegality by the governing law

13.85   If the making of a contract or its performance is illegal by the governing law of the contract, then an English court will not enforce the contract. This was the position at common law. It is also the position under the Rome Convention because under Articles 3 and 4 the applicable law of the contract governs questions of material validity, which includes illegality.[1]

1 See Dicey, Morris & Collins, r 241(a) and Art 8(1) Rome Convention. See also *De Beéche v South American Stores Ltd* [1935] AC 148; *St Pierre v South American Stores Ltd* [1937] 3 All ER 349; *Kahler v Midland Bank Ltd* [1950] AC 24; *Zivnostenska Banka v Frankman* [1950] AC 57; *Re Banque des Marchands de Moscou (No 2)* [1954] 1 WLR 1108; *Re Helbert Wagg & Co Ltd* [1956] Ch 323; *Rossano v Manufacturers' Life Assurance Co* [1963] 2 QB 352, and the commentary on these cases in Mann *The Legal Aspects of Money* (6th edn 2005) 16.24–16.26.

Opening the credit

13.86   The issue of illegality arises here where the contract of sale requires the buyer to open a credit, but the opening of the credit is (or becomes) illegal under the governing law of the contract, for example because of exchange control rules. Whether or not the buyer is excused from his obligation by reason of illegality depends on how the task and risk of obtaining exchange control permission is allocated under the contract. This question must be answered by reference to the governing law of the contract. But if that law were to have the same effect as English law the approach would be as follows. First, does the contract expressly deal with the obtaining of exchange control permission? For example, there might be a condition of the contract requiring that exchange control permission could be obtained. In that event the failure to obtain permission will excuse the parties from further performance.[1] Alternatively, there might be a term of the contract making it the absolute duty of the buyer to obtain such permission; hence, any failure would render him liable in damages for non-performance of the contract. If the contract does not deal with the point expressly, a term may be implied (subject to the usual principles on the implication of terms into contracts) that the buyer shall apply for permission and at least use reasonable diligence to obtain it. Or it may be implied that the duty on the buyer is absolute.

1 That is subject to the implied proviso that permission has been applied for by the buyer and due diligence used to obtain it. It is suggested that such implication is necessary to given efficacy to the contract: compare *Re Anglo-Russian Merchant Traders and John Batt & Co (London) Ltd* [1917] 2 KB 679 at 685, 689.

13.87 Further, it may be possible to infer from the express terms of the contract whether it is a duty to use due diligence or an absolute duty.[1] Where the contract does not assist, under English law the position is uncertain.[2] Where the exchange control law is only imposed after the contract is made the position may be different, as the parties may well not have had in mind the need to obtain any permission at the time they made the contract. In such circumstances it is likely to be easier for the buyer to establish that an inability on his part to obtain the required permission excuses his failure to open the credit.

1 Cf *Congimex Companhia Geral de Comercio v Tradax Export SA* [1981] 2 Lloyd's Rep 687 at 692.3; affd [1983] 1 Lloyd's Rep 250 at 253, CA.
2 See the cases cited (above) which relate to import or export licences; compare the view expressed in Sassoon *CIF and FOB Contracts* (4th edn 1995) para 624: 'In fact the formalities which the buyer may have to go through to obtain funds (including any foreign exchange permits) are normally regarded as entirely at the buyer's risk and responsibility, and absent an express stipulation which may protect him against default in the event of his failure to obtain the necessary permits, he will normally be liable for breach if payment is unaffected by his inability to obtain the necessary exchange authorisation.'

13.88 Where the governing law of the contract between buyer and seller is not the law under which the exchange control regulations are imposed, those regulations cannot be relied upon under this head. Thus in *Toprak Mahsulleri Ofisi v Finagrain Cie Commerciale*[1] the Turkish buyers alleged that they were prevented by Turkish regulations from opening the credit. But the contract was governed by English law and so the buyers had to base their argument on the law of the place of performance. They were unsuccessful.

1 [1979] 2 Lloyd's Rep 98 per Lord Denning MR at 114 col 2.

Operating the credit

13.89   Since the issue here is the obligation of the bank to make payment, it is the governing law of the relevant contract under the documentary credit which is significant and not the governing law of the underlying contract between the applicant and the beneficiary. It is to be remembered that the governing law, as suggested above,[1] is the law of the place where the bank to which documents are to be presented is situated. It is likely also to be this bank which is to make payment. So there is a probability that the law of the place of performance and the governing law of the credit will coincide. If the bank is prevented from paying by the law which governs its undertaking to the beneficiary, then an English court will not enforce payment. If the credit has been opened, the bank is unlikely to be prevented from payment by reason of exchange control regulations; that difficulty will have been surmounted by the obtaining of permission prior to it being opened. But it can happen that a court of the country providing the governing law of the contract makes an order restraining payment.

1 See para **13.46** et seq.

13.90   Thus, if the governing law of the credit in the *Power Curber* case[1] had been Kuwaiti, the English court would have given effect to the Kuwaiti court's order on the ground that the bank had a good defence under Kuwaiti law.[2] The credit may provide for presentation of documents in one country but for payment to be provided in another, as was the case in *European Asian Bank v Punjab and Sind Bank*.[3] If payment under the credit in that other country is illegal by the governing law of the credit, namely the law of the country of presentation, the bank will be excused payment. But the regulations in question, or the court order in question, are to be examined to see if they do in fact have extra-territorial effect.[4] It may well be that a court would be reluctant to construe them in that way.[5] Where, as will usually be the case, a credit is provided as conditional payment rather than in absolute payment[6] the failure of the credit to provide payment will enable the seller to sue the buyer. But he is likely to have to do so in the buyer's own country and so is likely to meet the same problems as have defeated the credit.

1 [1981] 1 WLR 1233.
2 See *Kahler v Midland Bank Ltd* [1950] AC 24.
3 [1981] 2 Lloyd's Rep 651; affd [1982] 2 Lloyd's Rep 356.
4 See *Rossano v Manufacturers Life Insurance Co Ltd* [1963] 2 QB 352 at 374.
5 See Mann *The Legal Aspect of Money* (6th edn 2005) at 16.36.
6 See para **3.47** above.

(3) Illegality by law of place of performance

13.91 Briefly, the relevance of the law of the place of performance is as follows. At common law, a contract will not be enforced:

(a) where it necessarily involves performance which is unlawful according to the place of performance (the rule in *Ralli Bros v Compania Naviera*[1]);

(b) even if it does not necessarily involve such performance, eg if there is an alternative legal manner of performance, where the real object and intention of the parties necessitates them joining in an endeavour to perform in a foreign and friendly country some act which is illegal by the law of that country (the rule in *Foster v Driscoll*[2]).

1 [1920] 2 KB 287, CA; approved in *De Beéche v South American Stores (Gath & Chaves) Ltd* [1935] AC 148 at 156, per Lord Sankey; approved in *Ispahani v Bank Melli Iran* [1998] Lloyd's Rep Bank 133. See generally Dicey, Morris & Collins, para. 32–144 et seq.
2 [1929] 1 KB 470, CA. The parties had been engaged in a scheme to smuggle whisky into the United States during Prohibition. *Foster v Driscoll* was applied in *Regazzoni v KC Sethia (1944) Ltd* [1958] AC 301 and see also *Mahonia Ltd v JP Morgan Chase Bank and ors* [2003] 2 Lloyd's Rep 911. The act must not merely be illegal by the law of the foreign country but must take place within that country: *Ispahani v Bank Melli Iran* [1998] Lloyd's Rep Bank 133. In *Toprak Mahsulleri Ofisi v Finagrain Compagnie Commerciale Agricole et Financiers* [1979] 2 Lloyd's Rep 98 at first instance Robert Goff J stated (at 107): 'No doubt it would be possible to formulate in clearer terms a wider principle which would embrace both the principle in the *Ralli Brothers* case and the principle in *Foster v Driscoll*, and indeed might also state that a principle comparable to that in the *Ralli Brothers* case is applicable in cases of existing as opposed to supervening illegality. I see, however, no need to do so; it is better, in my judgment to recognise these principles are distinct, though related in the sense that they spring from the principle of comity, a root which (as *Foster v Driscoll* itself shows) is capable of new growth from time to time.'

13.92 How these rules are affected by the Rome Convention raises some difficult and open questions.

13.93 The principle in *Foster v Driscoll* is often expressed in terms relating to English public policy, based on the comity of nations and discouraging criminal acts in foreign friendly countries, rather than in terms of the application of the law of a foreign state.[1] As such, it is certainly arguable that the same result could be achieved through the application of Article 16, which provides that the application of the governing law can be refused if it is 'manifestly incompatible with the public policy ('ordre public') of the forum'.[2]

1 *Regazzoni v KC Sethia (1944) Ltd* [1958] AC 301 at 323-324 per Lord Reid.
2 See Dicey, Morris & Collins, para 32–150 and also the concerns expressed in Cheshire & North *Private International Law* (13th edn rev 1999), p 584, which takes the view that *Foster v Driscoll* fits more readily into Art 7(1), which has not been incorporated into English law.

13.94 The status of the rule in *Ralli Brothers* is less certain. Article 10(2) of the Rome Convention provides that in relation to the 'manner of performance' a court should have regard to 'the law of the country in which performance takes place'. There are two difficulties in saying that this provision preserves the *Ralli Brothers* principle in the context of the Rome Convention. First, an English court is not required by this provision to apply the law of the place of performance, but merely to give consideration to that law. Second, it is difficult to accept that illegality in the place of performance would fall within the scope of the term 'manner of performance'. The Giuliano–Lagarde Report has made clear that this provision only concerns the minor details of the 'mechanics of performance' such as the whether performance can take place on a bank holiday.[1] There is, however, some academic support for the proposition that the 'manner of performance' does include questions of whether payment would be illegal by virtue of exchange control legislation in the place of performance.[2] If that is correct, then it is possible, at least in relation to exchange control legislation, that the effect of *Ralli Brothers* may be reflected in the terms of the Rome Convention.[3]

1 Giuliano–Lagarde Report, p 33.
2 Cheshire & North *Private International Law* (13th edn rev 1999), p 602.
3 See also the general discussion regarding whether the rule in *Ralli Brothers* survives the Rome Convention at Dicey, Morris & Collins, paras. 32-148 to 32-151.

Opening the credit

13.95   Assuming that the conclusion with respect to the *Ralli Brothers* principle in para **13.94** is correct, a buyer who is in practical difficulties in opening a credit because of exchange control restrictions but cannot rely on the governing law of his contract with the seller may seek to rely on the restrictions as to the law of the place of performance. His difficulties are illustrated by the situation of the buyers in *Toprak Mahsulleri Ofisi v Finagrain Compagnie Agricole et Financiere SA*.[1] The buyers, a Turkish state organisation, agreed to buy a large tonnage of wheat c and f named Turkish ports, payment by 'irrevocable, divisible, transferable letter of credit to be opened in Sellers' favour with and confirmed by a first class US or West European Bank covering 100% payments against presentation of shipping documents'. The contract provided that it was governed by English law and that disputes should be determined by arbitration in London. The buyers were unable to obtain foreign currency from the Turkish Ministry of Finance, no credit was opened and the sellers cancelled the contract and claimed damages by arbitration. Lord Denning MR (with whom the other members of the Court of Appeal agreed) stated:[2]

> 'I will read the particular paragraph in the case stated[3] on which the Turkish state enterprise rely. It is para 23:
>
>> 'At all times in 1974 and 1975 it would have been illegal for the buyers to have procured the opening of a letter of credit to pay a foreign seller of wheat in foreign currency without first obtaining exchange control permission from the Ministry of Finance. Furthermore, because of the tight control exercised over foreign exchange, and the number of checks and safeguards built into the routine established for the opening of letters of credit by Turkish companies it would in practice have been impossible for the buyers to have opened such a letter of credit without such permission.'

> In those circumstances, the Turkish state enterprise say that in view of that illegality by Turkish law they have a defence to this claim. They rely particularly on the well-known case *Ralli Bros v Cia Naviera Sota y Aznar*.[4] In that case under the law of Spain it was illegal to pay more than a certain price. And by the very terms of the contract the payment had to be made in Spain. It was an English contract, but it was to be performed by its very terms in Spain: and it was illegal by the law of the place of performance. It was held that this illegality was an answer.
>
> In this particular case the place of performance was not Turkey. Illegality by the law of Turkey is no answer whatever to this claim. The letter of credit had to be a confirmed letter of credit, confirmed by a first-class West European or US bank. The sellers were not concerned with the machinery by which the Turkish state enterprise provided that letter of credit at all. The place of performance was not Turkey.'

Had it been a term of the contract that the credit should be issued in Turkey as well as providing that it be confirmed by a US or West European bank as the contract in fact provided, the defence may well have succeeded.

1 [1979] 2 Lloyd's Rep 98.
2 [1979] 2 Lloyd's Rep 98 at pp 113, 114.
3 By the arbitrators for the decision of the court.
4 *Ralli Bros v Compagnia Naviera Sota y Aznar* [1920] 2 KB 287, 2 Lloyd's Rep 550.

Operating the credit

13.96   Where payment is to be made against the presentation of documents, the law of the place of payment under the credit will very often be the same as the law applicable to the various contractual relationships arising out of the credit. It is suggested that this will not be so where payment is not to be made by the bank to which documents are to be presented (the location of the latter bank being the matter which determines the applicable law[1]).

1 Discussed at para **13.46** et seq.

13.97   If documents are to be presented in a country where exchange control will prevent payment pursuant to the credit, this will provide the bank with a defence.[1] On the other hand, if documents are to be presented in Turkey where exchange control will prevent the bank from paying, but payment is to be made by a bank in New York following the presentation of documents in Turkey which are found to conform with the credit, the position in Turkey is irrelevant to payments so far as the law of the place of performance (payment) is concerned. In this example, however, as the exchange control legislation will be part of the law of the state where the documents were presented the bank may be able to rely upon the law applicable to the credit to provide it with a defence. Whether the bank has a valid defence under the applicable law will depend upon whether, on the proper construction of the exchange control regulations or the court order, they were intended to have extra-territorial effect and render illegal, according to the applicable law, activities in New York as well as Turkey.[2]

1 Compare the *Power Curber* case, had payment been due in Kuwait.
2 See *Rossano v Manufacturers Life Insurance Co Ltd* [1963] 2 QB 352.

13.98   In addition, where, as will usually be the case, a credit is provided as conditional payment rather than in absolute payment,[1] the failure to provide payment under the credit will enable the seller to sue the buyer. In the above example, however, the seller will only succeed if he can rely upon illegality by the law applicable to the contract of sale.[2] But he is likely to have to do so in the buyer's own country and so is likely to meet the same problems as have defeated the credit.

1 See para **3.47**.
2 In the above example, the seller will be unable to rely on the place of performance as this will be New York, by which law there would be no illegality.

(4)   The Bretton Woods Agreement

13.99   The International Monetary Fund Agreement, commonly known as the Bretton Woods Agreement, is made part of English law by the Bretton Woods Agreements Order in Council 1946,[1] and England is a member of the Fund.[2] Article VIII(2)(b) of the Agreement provides:

> 'Exchange contracts which involve the currency of any member and which are contrary to the exchange control regulations of any member maintained or imposed consistently with this agreement shall be unenforceable in the territories of any member.'

Pursuant to powers given by Article XVIII of the Agreement, in 1949 the Executive Directors published an interpretation of the provision, which is as follows:

> '1 Parties entering into exchange contracts involving the currency of any member of the Fund and contrary to exchange control regulations of that member which are maintained or imposed consistently with the Fund Agreement will not receive the assistance of the judicial or administrative authorities of other members in obtaining the performances of such contracts. That is to say, the obligations of such contracts will not be implemented by the judicial or administrative authorities of member countries, for example, by decreeing performance of the contracts or by awarding damages for their non-performance.
>
> 2 by accepting the Fund Agreement members have undertaken to make the principle mentioned above effectively part of their national law. This applies to all members, whether or not they have availed themselves of the transitional arrangements of Article XIV, section 2.
>
> An obvious result of the foregoing undertaking is that if a party to an exchange contract of the kind referred to in Article VIII, section 2(b) seeks to

enforce such a contract, the tribunal of the member country before which the proceedings are brought will not, on the ground that they are contrary to the public policy (ordre public) of the forum, refuse recognition of the exchange control regulations of the other member which are maintained or imposed consistently with the Fund Agreement. It also follows that such contracts will be treated as unenforceable notwithstanding that under the private international law of the forum, the law under which the foreign exchange control regulations are maintained or imposed is not the law which governs the exchange contract or its performance.

The Fund will be pleased to lend its assistance in connection with any problem which may arise in relation to the foregoing interpretation or any other aspect of Article VIII, section 2(b). In addition, the Fund is prepared to advise whether particular exchange control regulations are maintained or imposed consistently with the Fund Agreement.'

Although this statement is not binding in an English court, it will be looked to as persuasive authority.

1 SR & O 1946 No 36 made under the Bretton Woods Agreements Act 1945.
2 For the background to the Agreement see *Wilson Smithett and Cope Ltd v Terruzzi* [1976] QB 683 at 711D et seq, per Lord Denning MR.

The meaning of 'exchange contracts'

13.100   The most significant issue arising out of the operation of Article VIII(2)(b), which that provision gives no assistance with, is the meaning to be given to the expression 'exchange contract'. There are, however, a few authorities dealing with this issue.[1] Following the decision of the Court of Appeal in *Sharif v Azad*[2], there was uncertainty in English law as to the meaning of exchange contract. In that case Lord Denning expressed the view that an exchange contract was 'any contract which in any way affected the country's exchange resources', but Diplock LJ considered that this defined the term too broadly.[3] This issue was clarified in *Wilson, Smithett and Cope Ltd v Terruzzi*.[4] In that case, the claimants were brokers on the London Metal Exchange and they dealt with the defendant, a dealer and the speculator resident in Italy. The defendant entered into various contracts with the claimants for the purchase and sale of metals, which were in breach of Italian exchange control as the defendant had not obtained the appropriate ministerial authorisation. As a result of these dealings, the defendant ended up owing the brokers substantial sums of money on his account. When sued in respect of those sums, the defendant argued that the contracts were exchange contracts within the meaning of the Article VIII(2)(b) and were as a result unenforceable in the English courts. This defence was rejected. Lord Denning MR, resiling from the position that he adopted in *Sharif v Azad* stated:[5]

'The mischief being thus exposed, it seems to me that the participants at Bretton Woods inserted article VIII section 2(b) so as to stop it. They determined to make exchange contracts of that kind – for the exchange of currencies – unenforceable in the territories of any member. I do not known of any similar mischief in regard to other contracts, that is contracts for the sale or purchase of merchandise or commodities. Businessmen have to encounter fluctuations in the price of goods, but this is altogether different from the fluctuations in exchange rates. So far from there being any mischief, it seems to me that it is in the interest of international trade that there should be no restrictions on contracts for the sale and purchase of merchandise and commodities: and that they should be enforceable in the territories of the members.

The Bretton Woods Agreement itself makes provision to that end. Thus...

In conformity with those provisions, I would hold that the Bretton Woods Agreement should not do anything to hinder legitimate contracts for the sale or purchase of merchandise or commodities. The words "exchange contracts" in article VIII, section 2(b), refer only to contracts to exchange the currency of one country for the currency of another.'

He concluded that the contracts in question were legitimate contracts for the sale and purchase of metals and were not contracts for the exchange of currencies. This narrow definition of 'exchange contracts' should be contrasted with the wider definition of 'exchange contract' which had originally been accepted by Lord Denning in *Sharif v Azad*.[6] The narrow definition of 'exchange contract' has been subsequently approved by the House of Lords in *United City Merchants (Investments) Ltd v Royal Bank of Canada*[7] which is considered in the following section.

1 See *Kahler v Midland Bank* [1948] 1 All ER 811 at 819, CA; *Sharif v Azad* [1967] 1 QB 605; *Wilson Smithett & Cope v Terruzzi* [1976] QB 683; *United City Merchants (Investments) Ltd v Royal Bank of Canada* [1982] QB 208; revsd [1983] 1 AC 168; *Mansouri v Singh* [1986] 1 WLR 1393; *Ispahani v Bank Melli Iran*, [1998] 1 Lloyd's Rep Bank 133.
2 [1961] 1 QB 605.
3 See *Sharif v Azad* [1967] 1 QB 605 at 613–614 per Lord Denning and at 618, per Diplock LJ. Russell LJ confined himself at 620 to saying that the Order went no further 'than to make certain exchange contracts unenforceable'.
4 [1976] QB 683.
5 *Wilson Smithett & Cope v Terruzzi* [1976] QB 683 at 714. Ormrod and Shaw LJJ agreed with the approach adopted by Lord Denning.
6 [1967] 1 QB 605.
7 *United City Merchants (Investments) Ltd v Royal Bank of Canada* [1983] 1 AC 168. This approach was also referred to with approval in *Ispahani v Bank Melli Iran* [1998] Lloyd's Rep Bank 133.

United City Merchants (Investments) Ltd v Royal Bank of Canada[1]

13.101 In *United City Merchants*, the Peruvian buyers wished to utilise the opportunity presented by their purchase of a glass-fibre forming plant from England to transfer money from Peru to the United States, by exchanging Peruvian currency for US dollars to be available to them in Florida. They therefore arranged for the sellers to invoice them for double the price which they had quoted and to remit one half of each of the amounts which they would draw under the credit to the dollar account in Miami of an American corporation controlled by the buyers. The transfer of Peruvian currency into US dollars was contrary to the exchange control regulations of Peru, a member of the IMF. The following points emerge from the speech of Lord Diplock, with which the remainder of the House of Lords agreed:

(1) The narrow interpretation of the expression 'exchange contracts' in Article VIII(2)(b) of the Bretton Woods Agreement was considered to be correct. It was held that the meaning of 'exchange contracts' is 'confined to contracts to exchange the currency of one country for the currency of another; it does not include contracts entered into in connection with sales of goods which require the conversion by the buyer of one currency into another in order to enable him to pay the purchase price.'[2]

(2) In considering the application of the Article the court should look at the substance of the contract and not the form. As a result the court should not enforce a contract that is a 'mere monetary transaction in disguise'.[3]

(3) The effect of breach of the Article is to render the contract unenforceable rather than illegal. This has two consequences. First, the court must consider the issue of the compatibility of the contract with Article VIII(2)(b) of its own motion, even if the party to whose advantage it might work has not done so. The rationale for this approach is to avoid the court lending its aid to the enforcement of the contract. Secondly, the fact that the contract is not illegal means that a party may perform it if he wishes, but it cannot be obliged to do so by legal action.[4]

(4) 'The question whether and to what extent a contract is unenforceable under the Bretton Woods Agreement Order in Council 1946 because it is a monetary transaction in disguise is not a question of construction of the contract, but a question of the substance of the transaction to which enforcement of the contract will give effect.' Thus it is not a matter which is to be determined on the basis of whether the contract can as a matter of construction be severed into parts which are unenforceable by reason of the Order, and parts which are not. The task of the court is 'to penetrate any disguise presented by the actual words the parties have used, to identify any monetary transaction (in the narrow sense of that expression as used in the *Terruzzi* case)[5] which those words were intended to conceal and to refuse to enforce the contract to the extent that to do so would give effect to the monetary transaction.'[6]

(5) On the facts of the case:
    (a) The transaction was, as a matter of construction, simply a contract to pay currency against documents including documents of title to goods. That transaction concealed the monetary transaction to exchange Peruvian currency for dollars.
    (b) On the one hand, payment of that part of the money payable under the credit which the sellers would receive on trust for the buyers to remit to Florida, was unenforceable as an essential part of the monetary transaction or exchange contract.

(c) On the other hand, payment of that part payable under the credit, which the sellers would retain as the genuine purchase price of the goods payable by the buyers, remained enforceable.

(d) As to the first instalment of 20%, this had been paid in full and no enforcement was needed. The bank could have resisted paying one half of it had it known of the monetary transaction at the time it came to pay, but, even if it knew, there was nothing in English law to prevent it paying in full.[7]

1 [1983] 1 AC 168.
2 [1983] 1 AC 168 at 188G.
3 [1983] 1 AC 168 at 188H. In *Mahonia Ltd v JP Morgan Chase Bank and West LB* Colman J considered *United City Merchants* and described the credit therein as 'an example of a letter of credit which because of its cosmetic purpose was directly rendered unenforceable by legislation.' ([2003] 2 Lloyd's Rep 911 at 927 para.67).
4 See [1983] 1 AC 168 at 189 A–C citing *Batra v Ebrahim* noted at [1982] 2 Lloyd's Rep 11n and referred to at [1982] QB 208 at 241F–242B. As to proof of exchange control legislation see *Mansouri v Singh* [1986] 1 WLR 1393 considered at para **13.104** below.
5 *Wilson Smithett & Cope v Terruzzi* [1976] QB 683 discussed at para **13.100** above.
6 *United City Merchants (Investments) Ltd v Royal Bank of Canada* [1983] 1 AC 168 at 189G–190B.
7 [1983] 1 AC 168 at 190 B–F.

13.102   It follows from the *United City Merchants* case that where the English court can identify a monetary transaction which is an exchange contract within Article VIII(2)(b), it will refuse to enforce the transaction even though the refusal may involve the court in declining to give effect in whole or in part to an autonomous contract constituted by a letter of credit.[1]

1 See *Mansouri v Singh* [1986] 1 WLR 1393 at 1401, per Neill LJ.

13.103   In *Ispahani v Bank Melli Iran*,[1] the Court of Appeal was asked to consider the relationship between the Bretton Woods Agreement and the common law principles in *Ralli Brothers* and *Foster v Driscoll*. It was held that the Bretton Woods Agreement did not affect the common law rules recognising other foreign exchange control restrictions. As a result, the Bretton Woods Agreement and the principles set out above operate side by side. Robert Walker LJ stated his conclusions in this way:

'The purpose of the 1946 Order was to incorporate into the domestic law of England an important international agreement intended to improve international financial co-operations and stability.... One means of achieving this was by ensuring mutual recognition, by members of the IMF, of each other's restrictions on exchange contracts. It would be surprising if the 1946 Order, by incorporating that agreement into domestic law, had the effect of diminishing the recognition of other types of exchange control restrictions. That is the view of Dr FA Mann in The Legal Aspects of Money (5th edn, p 372) – 'Article VIII(2)(b) supplements the law of the member states.2 Where there is no room for its application, the contract is not necessarily valid and enforceable. On the contrary, it may well be unenforceable, for instance, because it forms part of a wider scheme involving the commission of illegal acts.'[3]

1 [1998] Lloyd's Rep Bank 133.
2 As to which see now Mann *The Legal Aspects of Money* (6th edn 2005) at 15.04ff.
3 [1998] Lloyd's Rep Bank 133. In reaching this conclusion Robert Walker LJ decided that the Court of Appeal decision in *United City Merchants* did not constitute a binding precedent with respect to the application of the 1946 Order.

Proof of exchange control regulations

13.104   It was stated in *Mansouri v Singh*[1] that the burden of proving the exchange control regulations (and presumably also the breach of them if payment were made) is on a defendant, namely the party relying on the regulations as a reason for not paying. How does this relate to the duty of the court to take a point arising under the Bretton Woods Agreements Order for itself? In the *United City Merchants* case[2] Lord Diplock referred to the court becoming aware of the unenforceability and taking the point itself in the event that it had not been pleaded by the defendant.[3]

1 *Mansouri v Singh* [1986] 1 WLR 1393 at 1404.
2 *United City Merchants (Investments) Ltd v Royal Bank of Canada* [1983] 1 AC 168.
3 [1983] 1 AC 168 at 189B.

13.105   In *Mansouri*[1] the case was remitted to the trial judge for further hearing on the ground that he had decided in favour of the defendant on inadequate evidence. The outcome is that an English court will only treat a payment obligation as unenforceable when it is proved that to enforce it would be to enforce an exchange contract contrary to the exchange control regulations of an IMF member. Proof will be required on at least the balance of probabilities. It need not be proof by a party in the sense that a party has set out to prove it: it may simply become clear during the course of the case, perhaps despite the parties' efforts to conceal it. It does not appear that once the possibility is raised by the evidence it is for the court to conduct its own enquiry.

1 *Mansouri v Singh* [1986] 1 WLR 1393.

D   ILLEGALITY IN RELATION TO THE UNDERLYING CONTRACT

13.106   The previous section considered questions of illegality relating to the opening or performance of the credit. But what if the performance of the underlying contract of sale is, or is alleged to be, illegal? Does that provide a defence to payment by the bank, or a defence to reimbursement by the applicant if payment has been made? The autonomy of the bank's obligation usually means that, subject to the fraud exception discussed in **Chapter 9**, the bank need not be concerned with the performance of the underlying contract. However, it appears that the English courts are willing to recognise a further exception to the autonomy of the documentary credit on the grounds of illegality in relation to the underlying contract or to one of the contracts involved in the letter of credit itself.

13.107 The question of whether illegality might constitute such an exception was first considered in *Group Josi Re v Walbrook Insurance Co Ltd*.[1] The claimants were reinsurance companies who had entered into reinsurance contracts with the defendants. Payment under those contracts was secured by the opening of documentary credits in favour of the defendants. Subsequently, the claimants sought injunctions preventing the defendants from drawing on the credits on the ground, inter alia, that the reinsurance contracts were illegal, unenforceable and void under English law because the claimants were not authorised to conduct insurance business under the Insurance Companies Acts. One of the issues was whether the credit could be affected by illegality of the underlying transaction. Staughton LJ stated:[2]

> 'The reinsurers put their case in this way: (i) the underlying reinsurance contracts were illegal; (ii) directly or by way of taint, this rendered the letter of credit contracts illegal or at least unenforceable; (iii) therefore it would be fraudulent for the stamp companies and Weavers to claim payment under the letters of credit.
>
> That seems to me unnecessarily complicated. Surely one can stop after stage (ii), without bringing fraud into it. I say that because, in my judgment, illegality is a separate ground for non-payment under a letter of credit.
>
> That may seem a bold assertion, when Lord Diplock in the *United City Merchants* case [1983] 1 AC 168, 183 said that there was 'one established exception.' But in that very case the House of Lords declined to enforce a letter of credit contract in part for another reason, that is to say the exchange control regulations of Peru as applied by the Bretton Woods Agreements Order in Council 1946 (SR & O 1946 No 36). I agree that the Bretton Woods point may well have been of a kind of its own, and not an indication that illegality generally is a defence under a letter of credit. But it does perhaps show that established fraud is not necessarily the only exception.
>
> It seems to me that there must be cases when illegality can affect a letter of credit. Take for example a contract for the sale of arms to Iraq, at a time when such a sale is illegal. The contract provides for the opening of a letter of credit, to operate on presentation of a bill of lading for 1,000 Kalashnikov rifles to be carried to the port of Basra. I do not suppose that a court would give judgment for the beneficiary against the bank in such a case...'

As it turned out, and after a careful analysis of the interaction between the Insurance Companies Act 1982 and the Financial Services Act 1986, the Court of Appeal held that performance of the reinsurance contracts was enforceable by the reinsured beneficiaries and, therefore, that payment could be made under the credits.

1 [1996] 1 WLR 1152. See consideration of *Group Josi* (both the decisions at first instance per Clarke J and on appeal) in *Mahonia Ltd v JP Morgan Chase Bank and West LB* [2003] 2 Lloyd's Rep 911 at 923–27; [2004] EWHC 1938 (Comm) at para 431.
2 [1996] 1 WLR 1152 at 1163.

13.108 The issue was also central to the action in *Mahonia Ltd v JP Morgan Chase Bank and West LB*, where a claim was brought by the claimant Mahonia for payment under a letter of credit issued by the defendant bank, West LB.[1] The background to the action was the collapse of the US energy giant, Enron. Mahonia was a special purpose vehicle utilised to enter into a series of swaps (as part of a 'prepay forward transaction') with Enron and JP Morgan Chase, further to which the letter of credit issued by West LB at Enron's request was a security required in relation to one of the swaps. Upon presentation to it of conforming documents, West LB refused to make payment of US$165 million under the credit. Enron was by that time in Chapter 11 bankruptcy proceedings in the US and West LB would have been unable to recover the value of the credit from Enron. West LB argued, inter alia, that the prepay forward transaction been entered into as a means of Enron obtaining a 'disguised' loan that did not need to be shown on its published accounts. This purpose was said to be contrary to US accounting standards and therefore conduct with intent to defraud in breach of US securities laws. It followed from the contention that the purpose behind the prepay forward transaction (ie the underlying contracts) was illegal under US law, that the letter of credit was consequently said to have been rendered illegal either directly or by way of taint (and/or unenforceable as a matter of English public policy).[2]

1 [2003] 2 Lloyd's Rep 911 (summary judgment application); [2004] EWHC 1938 (Comm) (trial).
2 [2003] 2 Lloyd's Rep 911 at 913–914 para 5 per Colman J. At trial West LB also advanced the argument that in obtaining the letter of credit Enron and JP Morgan had acted in concert against West LB in an unlawful means conspiracy that amounted to a criminal offence under English law ([2004] EWHC 1938 (Comm); see paras 422ff and especially 434 dismissing this argument).

13.109 Mahonia applied for summary judgment on the credit, but its application was refused by Colman J, who accepted that there was an arguable defence of illegality sufficient to go to trial. He said:[1]

> '68. [T]here is a real conflict between on the one hand the well-established principle that contracts lawful on their face which are entered into in furtherance of an illegal purpose will be unenforceable at the suit of the party having knowledge of that purpose at the time of contracting and on the other hand the policy of the law reflected in all the letter of credit cases of preserving the impregnability of the letter of credit save where the bank has clear evidence of an ex turpi causa defence such as fraud. This conflict is not, in my judgment, a matter which can be resolved simply by postulating the separate nature of the letter of credit and applying reasoning similar to that in the *Bowmakers* case. Thus, like Lord Justice Staughton in *Group Josi*, sup. at p. 362 I find it almost incredible that a party to an unlawful arms transaction would be permitted to enforce a letter of credit which was an integral part of

that transaction even if the relevant legislation did not on its proper construction render ancillary contracts illegal. To take an even more extreme example, I cannot believe that any Court would enforce a letter of credit to secure payment for the sale and purchase of heroin between foreign locations in which such underlying contracts were illegal. On the other hand, there is much to be said for the view that the public policy in superseding the impregnability of letters of credit where there is an unlawful underlying transaction defence may not be engaged where the nature of the underlying illegal purpose is relatively trivial, at least where the purpose is to be accomplished in a foreign jurisdiction. The problems which arise from attempting to reconcile conflicting considerations of public policy may well give rise to uncertain consequences, as illustrated in relation to the finality of New York Convention arbitration awards in *Westacre Investments Inc. v. Jugoimport-SDPR Holding Co.*, [1999] Q.B. 740. It would, however, be wrong in principle to invest letters of credit with a rigid inflexibility in the face of strong countervailing public policy considerations. If a beneficiary should as a matter of public policy (ex turpi causa) be precluded from utilizing a letter of credit to benefit from his own fraud, it is hard to see why he should be permitted to use the courts to enforce part of an underlying transaction which would have been unenforceable on grounds of its illegality if no letter of credit had been involved, however serious the material illegality involved. To prevent him doing so in an appropriately serious case such as one involving international crime could hardly be seen as a threat to the lifeblood of international commerce.

69. In the present case, I have therefore come to the conclusion that on the assumed facts there is at least a strongly arguable case that the letter of credit cannot be permitted to be enforced against the defendant bank. That represents at the very least a realistic prospect of success for the bank's defence based on this point. Furthermore, the conclusion as to whether enforcement is permissible at least arguably depends on the gravity of the illegality alleged. Although on the pleaded case that appears to be considerable, the uncertainty of this area of law is such that this is an issue which ought to be determined by reference to the evidence before the court at trial and not merely on assumptions derived from the pleaded defence. Moreover, I have also concluded, as I have sought to explain, that the fact that the bank did not have clear evidence of such illegality at the date when payment had to be made would not prevent it having a good defence on that basis if such clear evidence were to hand when the Court was called upon to decide the issue. For this purpose I proceed on the basis that it now has sufficiently clear evidence as expressed in the pleading.'

1 [2003] 2 Lloyd's Rep 911 at 927–928 paras. 68-69.

13.110   When the case came to trial, Cooke J found that there was no breach of the US accounting standards and therefore that the accounting of the prepay forward transaction did not constitute a breach of US securities law.[1] Due to his findings, the question of illegality did not fall to be decided in Cooke J's judgment.[2] However, the Judge considered the hypothetical case on the basis of West LB's arguments and stated that if West LB had established that there was an unlawful underlying purpose for the swap in respect of which the letter of credit had been issued (ie it constituted a disguised loan for which unlawful accounting was intended and Mahonia was a party to that unlawful purpose) then the letter of credit was directly tied to that unlawful purpose. Further, the doctrine of taint applied because the letter of credit was analogous to a form of security and the courts have refused to enforce security given for illegal contracts.[3] Cooke J essentially agreed with Colman J's earlier findings as to the operation of the law of illegality in this context so as to prevent enforcement by reason of illegality, notwithstanding the principle of the autonomy of letters of credit.[4]

1 [2004] EWHC 1938 (Comm) paras 220–236.
2 [2004] EWHC 1938 (Comm) para 423.
3 [2004] EWHC 1938 (Comm) paras 426–433 and in relation to the enforcement of security for illegal contracts see the cases cited at 428.
4 [2004] EWHC 1938 (Comm) paras 429, 432 and 433.

13.111   The extreme examples of illegality given by Staughton LJ and Colman J seem obviously correct: as a matter of public policy it is hardly likely that the courts would enforce documentary credits used to finance an unlawful conspiracy to smuggle drugs or arms. However, the scope of any proposed public policy exception based on illegality, and its relationship with the fraud exception, needs to be carefully considered.

13.112   First, the fraud exception is limited to cases where the fraud is known to the presenting party and a question arises as to whether the same limitation would apply to an illegality exception. However, testing the beneficiary's 'guilty' knowledge might be difficult because illegality is a question of law and fact.[1] Suppose, using Staughton LJ's example, a sub-seller had acquired the rifles in good faith not knowing of the prohibition on exports,[2] should he be prevented from calling the credit? Moreover, the fraud exception as a defence to payment is also limited to cases where the fraud is obvious to the bank. In this respect, Staughton LJ commented:[3]

> '...Would illegality, like fraud, have to be clearly established and known to the bank before it could operate as a defence, or a ground for restraining payment by the bank? That is not an altogether easy question, but I am inclined to think that it would. If the legality of the payment is merely doubtful, it may be that the bank would not be restrained. But whether in a *United City Merchants* type of case, if illegality were clearly proved at trial, it would be a defence that it was not clear at the time when the documents were presented for payment is even more of a problem.'

Staughton LJ went on to hold that if it were clearly established that the reinsurance contracts were illegal as alleged, and that the letters of credit were being used as a means of paying sums due under those contracts, then the court might restrain the bank from making payment or the beneficiary from demanding it because the beneficiary's claim under the credit would be founded on an illegal transaction.[4]

1 See para **9.44** and *Mahonia Ltd v JP Morgan Chase Bank and West LB* [2004] EWHC 1938 (Comm) para. 433.

2 This is not inconceivable given the complex and sometimes murky nature of UK arms export regulations.
3 [1996] 1 WLR 1152 at 1164.
4 Contrast Cooke J's analysis of the hypothetical situation had the underlying transactions in *Mahonia Ltd v JP Morgan Chase Bank and West LB* been illegal, in which event West LB could, on grounds of public policy, have resisted enforcement of the letter of credit regardless of the point at which it became aware of the illegality ([2004] EWHC 1938 (Comm) paras. 431-433). Cooke J stated (albeit *obiter*) that 'the Court ought not and will not lend its aid to enforce a contract, a security or something akin to a security for a contract, where the underlying purpose of that contract is contrary to the law of a friendly foreign state where performance is to occur and the gravity of that unlawfulness is such as to engage public policy considerations'.

13.113   Second, unlike fraud, the effect of established illegality may be unclear. For example, a statute or regulation may require some permit, licence or authorisation for the transaction underlying the credit, but the consequences of a failure to obtain one may not be spelled out. *Group Josi* illustrates the complexity of the problem: the Court had to embark on an analysis of a number of conflicting authorities on the interpretation of the statute. In the event the reinsurers' lack of authorisation meant that they could not enforce the underlying contract, but, crucially, the beneficiaries could. In *Mahonia*, Colman J further suggested that whether the exception to the autonomy principle applied might depend on the gravity of the illegality: 'there is much to be said for the view that the public policy in superseding the impregnability of letters of credit where there is an unlawful underlying transaction defence may not be engaged where the nature of the underlying illegal purpose is relatively trivial, at least where the purpose is to be accomplished in a foreign jurisdiction.'[1] This, however, creates uncertainty for the bank trying to decide whether to honour the credit.

1 *Mahonia Ltd v JP Morgan Chase Bank and West LB* [2003] 2 Lloyd's Rep 911 at 927 para. 68. See also Cooke J at [2004] EWHC 1938 at para 432.

13.114   It seems clear from these cases that illegality can, in an appropriate case, be a further exception to the autonomy rule, but the scope of the exception remains, as yet, undetermined.

E   SOVEREIGN IMMUNITY

At common law

13.115   It is a fundamental principle of the common law and of customary international law that an independent sovereign state is not subject to the jurisdiction of the English courts unless that state has previously consented to such an exercise of jurisdiction. Originally, this principle allowed for no exceptions,[1] but a more restrictive theory of immunity developed which was limited only to acts which were governmental rather than commercial in nature.[2] In *Trendtex Trading Corpn v Central Bank of Nigeria*[3] the Court of Appeal considered a claim by a beneficiary under a letter of credit issued by the Central Bank of Nigeria. It was held that the bank was not an emanation, arm, alter ego or department of the State of Nigeria and so was not entitled to immunity from suit.

1 The *locus classicus* of the doctrine of 'absolute immunity' can be found in *The Parlement Belge* (1880) 5 PD 197 at 205, per Brett CJ; *Compania Naviera Vascongada v SS Christina* [1938] 1 All ER 719 at 720; *Rahimtoola v Nizam of Hyderabad* [1958] AC 379 at 394. See generally: Fox *The Law of State Immunity* (2008; 2nd edition).
2 Acta iure imperii as opposed to acta iure gestionis.
3 [1977] QB 529.

13.116   However, two of the three members of the Court of Appeal also held that even if the bank had been a part of the Government of Nigeria, it was not immune from suit in respect of ordinary commercial transactions as distinct from acts of a governmental nature.[1] The court therefore continued an injunction ordering the Central Bank of Nigeria to retain within the jurisdiction $13,968.190 pending trial. This emphasises the two points which were relevant at common law: first, the nature of the entity claiming immunity – is it sufficiently a part of the foreign sovereign state to be accorded the immunity accorded to the state; second, if the entity is entitled to immunity, as to the nature of the transaction – is it a commercial transaction not attracting immunity, or a 'governmental' transaction attracting immunity?

1 [1977] QB 529 per Lord Denning MR at 558 and Shaw LJ at 579. This holding was approved in *Hispano Americana Mercantil SA v Central Bank of Nigeria* [1979] 2 Lloyd's Rep 277, the facts of which were close to those in the *Trendtex* case.

The State Immunity Act 1978

13.117   The position in respect of claims to immunity by a foreign state entity is governed by the State Immunity Act of 1978 in respect of matters arising after that Act came into force. This enactment places on a statutory footing the restrictive theory of state immunity adopted at common law. Section 1(1) lays down the general rule that a state is immune from the jurisdiction of the courts of the United Kingdom. This rule is, however, subject to a number of exceptions, the most important of which is contained in s 3 of the State Immunity Act 1978, which provides:

'3(1) A State is not immune as respects proceedings relating to[1] –

(a) a commercial transaction entered into by the State; or
(b) an obligation of the State which by virtue of a contract (whether a commercial transaction or not) falls to be performed wholly or partly in the United Kingdom.

(2) This section does not apply if the parties to the dispute are States or have otherwise agreed in writing; and subsection (1)(b) above does not apply if the contract (not being a commercial transaction) was made in the

territory of the State concerned and the obligation in question is governed by its administrative law.

(3) In this section 'commercial transaction' means –

(a) any contract for the supply of goods or services;

(b) any loan or other transaction for the provision of finance and any guarantee or indemnity in respect of such transaction or of any other financial obligation; and

(c) any other transaction or activity[2] (whether of a commercial, industrial, financial, professional or other similar character) into which a State enters or in which it engages otherwise than in the exercise of sovereign authority;[3]

but neither paragraph of subsection (1) above applies to a contract of employment between a State and an individual.'

Given the commercial and essentially private character of a letter of credit transaction, it is unlikely that a central bank or other monetary authority, which is part of the state's executive organs and incapable of being separately sued and which is party to a letter of credit transaction, would be able to claim immunity in proceedings arising out of that transaction.[4] The same would be true of a central bank that is considered a 'separate entity' within the meaning of s 14 of the State Immunity Act 1978.[5]

1 See *Holland v Lampen-Wolfe* [2000] 1 WLR 1573, HL. Lord Millett considered obiter whether the libel proceedings before the House of Lords would have fallen within s 3(1)(a) of the State Immunity Act 1978. He was of the view that only claims arising directly out of a contract, as opposed to tortious claims arising independently of the contract but in the course of its performance; this was applied at first instance in *Svenska Petroleum Exploration AB v Lithuania* [2006] 1 Lloyd's Rep 181 (appeal reported at [2007] QB 886).

2 See *Holland v Lampen-Wolfe* [2000] 1 WLR 1573 Lord Millett similarly considered that s 3(3)(c) of the State Immunity Act 1978 required a commercial relationship akin to, but falling short of a contract. As a result it did not cover tortious claims.

3 The phrase 'otherwise than in the exercise of sovereign authority' was considered in *Kuwait Airways Corpn v Iraqi Airways Co* [1995] 1 WLR 1147, HL which decided that the question turned upon whether the act in question was one that a private individual could perform or whether it was truly in nature a governmental act, as had been decided at common law and public international law. See also *The I Congreso del Partido* [1983] 1 AC 244; *Littrell v Government of the United States (No 2)* [1995] 1 WLR 82; *Holland v Lampen-Wolfe* [2000] 1 WLR 1573.

4 For a general discussion as to the position of central banks see Blair *The Legal Status of Central Bank Investments Under English Law* [1998] 57 CLJ 374.

5 State Immunity Act 1978, s 14 provides that a 'separate entity', viz an entity distinct from the executive organs of the government of the State and capable of suing or being sued, will only be immune if 'the proceedings relate to anything done by it in the exercise of sovereign authority'. See *Kuwait Airways Corpn v Iraqi Airways Co* [1995] 1 WLR 1147, HL where it was held that the acts of a 'separate entity' are not governmental acts simply because they are carried out at the direction of the state. See also consideration of the Act by the Court of Appeal in *Koo Golden East Mongolia v Bank of Nova Scotia and ors* [2007] EWCA Civ 1443 at paras. 40–42; and Aikens J in *AIG Capital Partners Inc and another v. Republic of Kazakhstan (National Bank of Kazakhstan intervening)* [2006] 1 WLR 1420 at para 58.

13.118   However, under ss 14(4) and 13 of the Act, the property of a State's central bank or other monetary authority shall not be regarded as in use or intended for use for commercial purposes and is absolutely immune from execution.[1] The overall effect of the State Immunity Act 1978, therefore, is that whilst a claimant will be able to obtain a judgment from the English courts against a foreign central bank or monetary authority, which is party to a letter of credit, any judgment obtained will have to be enforced against assets located in that entity's own jurisdiction.

1 See *AIG Capital Partners Inc and another v. Republic of Kazakhstan (National Bank of Kazakhstan intervening)* [2006] 1 WLR 1420 at 1439–1442. Contrast the position at common law with respect to immunity from enforcement: *Hispano Americana Mercantil SA v Central Bank of Nigeria* [1979] 2 Lloyd's Rep 277, CA. For the application of the immunity from enforcement to a foreign state entity, other than a central bank, see *Alcom Ltd v Republic of Colombia (Barclays Bank plc, garnishees)* [1984] 1 AC 580, HL. See also *A Company Ltd v Republic of X* [1990] 2 Lloyd's Rep 520, per Saville J.

Chapter 14

Electronic Credits

A INTRODUCTION

14.1 On paper at least, there has been significant progress towards implementing international documentary sales and documentary credits in pure electronic form since the third edition of this book was published in 2001. Most notably, the ICC has published its UCP Supplement for Electronic Presentation (eUCP) which resolves many of the uncertainties in the application of the UCP to purely electronic credits. In practice, however, there has been little interest from industry itself in moving away from the paper-based norm. This chapter looks at what is meant by a system of electronic credits and at the effect of the eUCP in facilitating such a system, before examining the unresolved practical and legal issues that apparently remain a barrier to its uptake.

Meaning of 'electronic credit'

14.2   Electronic credit is used here to mean a credit contract with the same function as a conventional documentary credit but where the documents tendered by the beneficiary are not in paper form but take the form of electronic messages transmitted between the parties' computers. Electronic transfer from computer to computer of commercial and administrative data is known as 'Electronic Data Interchange' or EDI. Data transmitted through EDI is generally transmitted according to agreed protocols which facilitate the electronic receiving, interpreting and processing of the information by computers at either end.

14.3   Two systems of EDI exist: open systems and closed systems. An open system is one which can be accessed by anyone without prior authorisation or arrangement. A closed system is one which is restricted to specified users or which uses dedicated communication channels (eg a secure telephone link). A closed system is simpler and also more secure since access to it is limited. However, it is not so flexible because the parties must make suitable arrangements in advance and so messages cannot easily be exchanged with non-members of the system. SWIFT, the interbank network, is an example of a closed system. Whilst it is practical and sensible for all banks to use a common system like SWIFT in their communications with each other, in a truly electronic credit more flexibility is required because the bank must accept messages from a variety of parties, with many of whom it will not have had previous contact.

14.4   The paradigm of a global open network is the Internet, where access is effectively unlimited and messages can be sent by email between any two parties anywhere in the world. Messages are routed across the Internet through a number of intermediate computers, possibly in different countries, over which the sender and recipient will have no control. There is therefore a significant security risk of the interception, accidental corruption or deliberate modification of messages en route, as well as the risk of forged messages. This risk is mitigated to an extent by the very high volume of Internet traffic which makes the detection of individual messages more difficult.

14.5   It is open to the parties to the documentary credit to provide in the contract between them (at least if it is governed by English law) for their obligations to be performed in whatever manner they choose and to make appropriate arrangements for the use of EDI. Whether an electronic message has, or can be made to have, the same legal and commercial effect as its paper equivalent, is, however, questionable.

14.6   Many of the stages in the operation of a documentary credit are already performed using electronic communications, and have been for very many years. For example, on payment of a credit funds are very often remitted electronically by the paying bank to the beneficiary's bank. Transmission of the terms of credits, and other instructions, from bank to bank is also done electronically, for example using SWIFT. There is no reason why an applicant cannot transmit his instructions to open a credit electronically, and many do.

14.7 These processes raise legal and practical issues which are inherent in all electronic communications, for example authentication and security issues. However, the novel and essential feature of a truly electronic credit would be the presentation and acceptance or rejection of documents in an entirely electronic form without the use of paper. The particular difficulty in implementing electronic commercial credits is that the documents which are to be presented have usually been issued by a range of third parties, such as carriers, inspectors, export customs authorities, etc, and may ultimately need to be passed on to a variety of different third parties, such as sub-buyers, import customs authorities, etc. The system must be acceptable to all those parties. A workable system must encompass the whole of the sale transaction, and an electronic credit cannot be developed in isolation. Where, as is usually the case, a standby credit does not require third party documentation this difficulty does not arise.

14.8 The use of electronic trade documentation and its presentation under electronic credits raises several questions:

- How does the bank know that the document is authentic?
- What does it mean to be the holder of an electronic document? How can it be transferred or indorsed?
- Can electronic documents be negotiable in law?
- How does a bank 'reject' an electronic document?
- When exactly does the bank's obligation or mandate to make payment crystallise?

The eUCP

14.9 The eUCP provides an industry code that seeks to address (if not resolve) some of these questions by amending aspects of the UCP that do not easily transfer to an electronic system of trade documentation. The eUCP is thus a supplement to rather than a replacement for the UCP. Its current version, Version 1.1, supplements UCP 600.

14.10 The most obvious amendment made by the eUCP is to extend the UCP definition of 'document' to include 'electronic record',[1] namely 'data created, generated, sent, communicated, received or stored by electronic means, that is capable of being authenticated as to the apparent identity of a sender and the apparent source of the data contained in it, and as to whether it has remained complete and unaltered, and is capable of being examined with the terms and conditions of the eUCP Credit.'[2] The definition quickly illustrates, however, the limited scope the eUCP. Whilst requiring that a credit in the form of an electronic record should be 'capable of being identified' (and indeed deeming not to have been presented an electronic record that is incapable of such authentication[3]), the eUCP does not propose any standard approach to such authorisation.

1 Article e3(a)(ii).
2 Article e3(b)(i).
3 Article e5(f).

14.11   The 'place of presentation' for an electronic record is simply defined as 'an electronic address'.[1] The technical implication of this rule is left for the parties to determine. Electronic address could, for example, mean a variety of things from a simple email address to a remotely accessed server.

1 Article e3(a)(iii).

14.12   A number of eUCP articles relate to issues of timing. The date on which an electronic record is sent by the issuer is deemed to be the date of issuance, unless the record itself contains a specific date of issuance. The time at which an electronic record is 'received' is the time when that record 'enters the information system of the applicable recipient in a form capable of being accepted by that system'[1] although this is deemed to be the date of receipt if no other date is apparent.[2] Presumably anticipating the possibility of technical problems, Article e5(e) states that where a bank's information system is 'unable to receive a transmitted electronic record' the bank is deemed to be closed until the first following banking day on which the bank's system is operative. Similarly, where the bank receives an electronic record that appears corrupted it may request the presenter to present it again and the time for examination is suspended pending re-presentation.[3]

1 Article e3(b)(v).
2 Article e9.
3 Article e11.

14.13   As to how a bank should refuse an electronic record, there are no special provisions in the eUCP, beyond a provision allowing the bank to 'dispose' of such records in any manner deemed appropriate 30 days after issuing its notice of refusal.

14.14   Finally, the eUCP includes a detailed exclusion of liability on the part of a bank checking the apparent authenticity of an electronic record for 'the identity of the sender, source of information, or its complete and unaltered character'.[1]

1 Article e12.

14.15   The eUCP has been criticised for using a model based too much on traditional documentation where real mail is replaced with email.[1] However, Article e6(a) provides that the requirement that an electronic record must enter the information system of the recipient can be satisfied by sending the recipient no more than a hyperlink to an electronic record stored on an external system. This means that the record itself does not actually need to move, whether by attachment to an email or by some form of file transfer. The eUCP is thus compatible with a registry system whereby electronic records are stored and authenticated by third party registries.

1 Todd, Bills of Lading and Bankers' Documentary Credits, 4th edn, 2007, para 8.56.

B   PRACTICAL ISSUES RELATING TO ELECTRONIC TRADE DOCUMENTATION

Authenticity

14.16   The eUCP does not purport to answer the question, How does the bank know that the document is authentic? Authenticity thus remains the primary barrier to uptake of this system. A document is authentic if it has in fact been generated by or with the authority of the apparent author. A document has integrity if it has not been modified by another person after it was generated. Together these should guarantee non-repudiation: that is, the recipient can be sure that the purported sender is bound by the contents of the document. Of course these issues arise in paper documents too. Authentication of paper documents, if required at all by the credit, is conventionally achieved by the manuscript signature of the issuer of the document. Since the bank's role is to examine the documents only for conformance on their face, no verification of signatures can be carried out and, in practice, there is no way for the bank to detect a forgery. Without a reliable system of authentication, electronic messages present a potentially higher risk than paper documents because they are easier to generate and alter undetectably. The fact that a message appears to originate from a particular location or email address proves nothing. There is also a slight risk of accidental corruption in transit. However, with a reliable system of authentication, electronic messages potentially provide a much more secure method of communication.

Dematerialisation

14.17   A related problem is that an electronic document has no physical form equivalent to that of a paper document; it is a logical, rather than a physical, construct.[1] There is no 'original' of an electronic document, and the document cannot be possessed in any meaningful sense. There is no 'guarantee of singularity',[2] that is, there is no bar to several parties having identical and indistinguishable copies of the same document at the same time and it is not possible to determine the priority of their claims by reference to the document alone. This means the familiar and important legal concepts of a party enjoying rights as the holder of an original, negotiable document, especially a bill of lading, or transferring those rights by transfer of possession are difficult to implement. The problem is recognised in the UNCITRAL Model Law on Electronic Commerce 1996 which, in respect of transport documents, states that rights can be conveyed electronically provided that 'a reliable method is used to render such data message or messages unique'.[3] Unfortunately, neither the Model Law nor the commentary gives an example of such a method. It is suggested that it is technically impossible for a guarantee of uniqueness to be manifest from the document itself, and that negotiability within a wholly electronic system will be dependent on a third party responsible for keeping an independent record or register of the transfer of rights.

1 The electronic document is represented temporarily by electrical or magnetic variations on a disk or in a computer memory.
2 UNCITRAL Model Law on Electronic Commerce 1996, Guide to Enactment, para 115.
3 UNCITRAL Model Law on Electronic Commerce 1996, art 17.

C   LEGAL ISSUES RELATING TO ELECTRONIC TRADE DOCUMENTATION

14.18   Possible legal impediments to the uptake of electronic trade documentation relate not so much to documentary credits but to associated bills of lading and bills of exchange. In general English law imposes no special requirements of form on contracts. A contract can be made by exchange of electronic messages. Similarly a bank or buyer can rely on a third party document, such as a certificate of inspection, to the same extent and with the same rights against the issuer whether electronic or on paper. However, international sale transactions are heavily dependent on the use of negotiable documents, namely bills of lading and bills of exchange. Negotiability is an attribute which is created by the general law, not just by the agreement of the parties, and applies only to certain well-defined types of document. Historically, the negotiation of documents has required physical transfer, a concept which does not easily translate into electronic commerce. It is necessary to consider whether electronic documents have, or could be made to have, the same effect as their paper equivalents.

The electronic bill of lading

14.19   Two legal features of the bill of lading are difficult to replicate electronically, namely (a) it is a negotiable document of title; (b) it gives certain rights against the carrier under the Carriage of Goods by Sea Act 1992.

(a)   As a negotiable document of title

14.20   Conventionally, the carrier should deliver the goods at the destination only to the holder of the bill of lading. Since only one person could be the holder of the bill at any one time, the holder had the security of knowing that the goods should not be released by the carrier to anyone else. The lack of physical existence and location of an electronic document means that the concept of negotiation by transfer and title by possession is not appropriate; the fact that a party has an electronic bill of lading is no evidence that he is the true holder of the bill.

(b)   Rights against the carrier

14.21   The Carriage of Goods by Sea Act 1992 gives certain rights against the carrier to the 'lawful holder of a bill of lading' and certain other transport documents.[1] It is uncertain whether an electronic bill of lading would fall within this definition. Section 1(5) empowers the Secretary of State by regulations to make provision for the application of the Act 'to cases where a telecommunication system or any other information technology is used for effecting transactions ...'. But no such regulations have yet been made.

1 Section 2(1).

Electronic bills of exchange

14.22   'A bill of exchange is an unconditional order in writing, addressed by one person to another, signed by the person giving it'.[1] An electronic message cannot, therefore, be a bill of exchange.[2] There are no proposals for implementing electronic bills of exchange, which, lacking a physical existence, would suffer from the same problem of negotiability and transfer discussed above. If anyone were in the future to devise a comparable negotiable electronic instrument for deferred payment, it seems unlikely that it would be based on the nineteenth century code for bills of exchange which is dependent on the transfer of paper from party to party and on the concept of the holder. Therefore, an electronic credit which did not provide for immediate payment would have to be structured as a deferred payment credit rather than an acceptance credit.[3] The *Banco Santander* case[4] is a salutary reminder of the fact that these two payment mechanisms can have different legal effects even though the commercial and economic intent of the parties may be the same.

1 Bills of Exchange Act 1882 s 3(1). Bills of exchange 'might be written on parchment, linen, cloth, leather, or any other convenient substitute for paper not being a metallic substance': *Byles on Bills of Exchange* (26th edn) p 11.
2 For a different view, see Gamertsfelder 'Electronic Bills of Exchange: Will the Current Law Recognise Them?' (1998) 21(2) UNSWLJ 566.
3 See para **2.17** above.
4 *Banco Santander SA v Bayfern Ltd* [1999] 2 All ER (Comm) 18: see para **9.43** above.

D   PRACTICAL SOLUTIONS

14.23   Whilst electronic signatures are increasingly trusted to authenticate the origin of email messages, it seems likely that no amount of technical reassurance will persuade industry to adopt a system where electronic credits are transferred directly from party to party. The risk of duplication, corruption or interception is simply too high. All suggested models, including some pioneering systems currently in operation, depend upon third party agencies authenticating the origin, uniqueness and ownership of key contractual documents.

Electronic signatures

14.24   The most widely used authentication method is the 'electronic signature'.[1] The message is coded in such a way that the recipient can be sure that the message was generated by the purported author and has not been altered after signature. The technique relies on public key cryptography, a system of encoding where each party has a unique 'private' electronic code key, which is kept secret, and an associated 'public' code key, which can be freely distributed. The sender uses his private key (and appropriate software) to code the message before it is sent. Anyone in possession of the public key can decode and read the message but only the private keyholder can code it in that form. Therefore anyone reading the message can be sure that the private keyholder was the author of it. In order to complete the authentication, the recipient needs to know which person is the owner of that private key so that he can be sure that the author is who he claims to be. This is achieved by using a 'trusted third party', an agency which manages the issue of keys and keeps a register of keyholders. This third party certifies, again in electronic form, the identity of keyholders. If the third party is reliable, then so is the identification. The strength of the technique is that it is very, very difficult and time-consuming to derive the private key from the public key.[2] It is not, however, impossible and unsurprisingly a great deal of time, money, effort and computing resources is being invested by those trying both to make and to break the codes. Nevertheless, in the documentary credit field this type of electronic security is far preferable to the present paper system which in practice provides no protection at all against forgery.

1 See further Warne and Elliot, *Banking Litigation*, (2nd edition) paras 7-024–7-033.
2 The process involves the factorisation of very large prime numbers.

14.25   The legal status of electronic signatures in English law is governed by the Electronic Communications Act 2000, which provides at s 7:

> '**7. Electronic signatures and related certificates**
> (1) In any legal proceedings—
>> (a)   an electronic signature incorporated into or logically associated with a particular electronic communication or particular electronic data, and
>> (b)   the certification by any person of such a signature,
>
> shall each be admissible in evidence in relation to any question as to the authenticity of the communication or data or as to the integrity of the communication or data.'

The reference to 'certification' of signatures is to certification by a third party who manages the issue of private keys for use as electronic signatures.

Secure communication networks

14.26   A number of systems are being developed to facilitate secure and reliable communications in electronic commerce. For example, TrustAct, a SWIFT[1] scheme, provides a system for the certification and logging of messages by trusted financial institutions. The system is designed to prove the identity of parties and to guarantee the non-repudiation of trade message. It uses the SWIFT network for inter-bank communications and the internet for trading parties. APACS[2] (the Association for Payment Clearing Services) is also launching a trust certification scheme.

1 http://www.swift.com
2 http://www.apacs.org.uk

Third party registries

14.27   Bolero,[1] an organisation founded by SWIFT and the Through Transport club, is intended to offer a comprehensive system for electronic trade and electronic documentation. It is a 'closed' system, accessible only to members. Users of the systems, whether buyers, sellers, carriers or banks, communicate electronically with each other through a central 'Core Messaging Platform'. The document status problem is addressed by the use of a 'Bolero Bill of Lading': this is, in substance, an entry on a secure, centrally maintained database of a shipment of goods, recording all of the information contained in a conventional bill of lading and also the identity of the holder or owner of the bill. Transfer of the bill is effected by an instruction sent by the register holder to a Central Title Registry. The Bolero Bill is said to be functionally equivalent to a conventional bill of lading, a position apparently achieved by the implementation of existing legal incidents of bills of lading as express contractual obligations in the Bolero Rulebook. Bolero has said that it is confident (on the advice of English lawyers) that the system is fully effective. As discussed above, it remains unclear under English law whether it is possible by contract alone to confer on an instrument the status of a fully negotiable document of title giving valuable proprietary rights to third parties. It is also uncertain whether an electronic bill of lading would, for example, be a document covered by the Carriage of Goods by Sea Act 1992.

1 http://www.bolero.net

14.28 An alternative approach is taken by the Comité Maritime International (CMI) Rules for Electronic Bills of Lading 1990 which make the carrier itself responsible for recording the current owner of the rights to the goods. This is much more flexible; provided that there is a suitable accepted protocol for the transmission of messages between buyers, sellers and carriers there is no need for a separate registry. The carrier will always know to whom to deliver the goods and the owner of the goods has the security of knowing that his interest is recorded with the carrier.[1] The parties are still at risk of fraud or error by the carrier, but no more so than with a conventional bill of lading.

1 Electronic signatures should make the process secure and reliable. The shipper and carrier enter into a contract of carriage. The carrier then sends to the shipper an authenticated message containing the terms of the bill of lading. When the shipper wants to 'indorse' the electronic bill of lading, he sends an authenticated message to the carrier giving an email address and public key of the indorsee. The carrier records the transfer and sends an authenticated confirmation to the indorsee. The process is then repeated for further indorsements. On arrival, the carrier can accept authenticated instructions from the current registered holder for unloading. There is no need for the carrier even to know the true identity of the holder. Since all communications are electronically signed the risk of fraud, apart from by the carrier, is slight.

E   ELECTRONIC STANDBY CREDITS

14.29 Electronic standby credits do not raise the same legal or practical problems as commercial credits because the document to be presented is most often a simple demand. Thus bills of lading and other third party documents are not normally required. ISP98[1] specifically allows for electronic presentations; rule 1.09 defines 'Document' as covering documents 'whether in paper or electronic medium' and also defines what is acceptable as electronic records, electronic signatures etc. An electronic record must be capable of being authenticated[2] but is deemed to be an 'original' for the purposes of compliance with the credit.[3]

1 See para **12.32** et seq.
2 ISP98, r 1.09(c).
3 ISP98, r 4.15(b).

Appendix 1

ICC Uniform Customs and Practice for Documentary Credits 600

INTRODUCTION

(by Gary Collyer, technical adviser to the ICC Commission on Banking Technique and Practice)

In May 2003, the International Chamber of Commerce authorized the ICC Commission on Banking Technique and Practice (Banking Commission) to begin a revision of the Uniform Customs and Practice for Documentary Credits, ICC Publication 500.

As with other revisions, the general objective was to address developments in the banking, transport and insurance industries. Additionally, there was a need to look at the language and style used in the UCP to remove wording that could lead to inconsistent application and interpretation.

When work on the revision started, a number of global surveys indicated that, because of discrepancies, approximately 70% of documents presented under letters of credit were being rejected on first presentation. This obviously had, and continues to have, a negative effect on the letter of credit being seen as a means of payment and, if unchecked, could have serious implications for maintaining or increasing its market share as a recognized means of settlement in international trade. The introduction by banks of a discrepancy fee has highlighted the importance of this issue, especially when the underlying discrepancies have been found to be dubious or unsound. Whilst the number of cases involving litigation has not grown during the lifetime of UCP 500, the introduction of the ICC's Documentary Credit Dispute Resolution Expertise Rules (DOCDEX) in October 1997 (subsequently revised in March 2002) has resulted in more than 60 cases being decided.

To address these and other concerns, the Banking Commission established a Drafting Group to revise UCP 500. It was also decided to create a second group, known as the Consulting Group, to review and advise on early drafts submitted by the Drafting Group.

The Consulting Group, made up of over 40 individuals from 26 countries, consisted of banking and transport industry experts. Ably co-chaired by John Turnbull, Deputy General Manager, Sumitomo Mitsui Banking Corporation Europe Ltd, London and Carlo Di Ninni, Adviser, Italian Bankers Association, Rome, the Consulting Group

443

provided valuable input to the Drafting Group prior to release of draft texts to ICC national committees.

The Drafting Group began the review process by analyzing the content of the official Opinions issued by the Banking Commission under UCP 500. Some 500 Opinions were reviewed to assess whether the issues involved warranted a change in, an addition to or a deletion of any UCP article. In addition, consideration was given to the content of the four Position Papers issued by the Commission in September 1994, the two Decisions issued by the Commission (concerning the introduction of the euro and the determination of what constituted an original document under UCP 500 sub-article 20(b) and the decisions issued in DOCDEX cases.

During the revision process, notice was taken of the considerable work that had been completed in creating the International Standard Banking Practice for the Examination of Documents under Documentary Credits (I SBP), ICC Publication 645. This publication has evolved into a necessary companion to the UCP for determining compliance of documents with the terms of letters of credit. It is the expectation of the Drafting Group and the Banking Commission that the application of the principles contained in the ISBP, including subsequent revisions thereof, will continue during the time UCP 600 is in force. At the time UCP 600 is implemented, there will be an updated version of the ISBP to bring its contents in line with the substance and style of the new rules.

The four Position Papers issued in September 1994 were issued subject to their application under UCP 500; therefore, they will not be applicable under UCP 600. The essence of the Decision covering the determination of an original document has been incorporated into the text of UCP 600. The outcome of the DOCDEX cases were invariably based on existing ICC Banking Commission Opinions and therefore contained no specific issues that required addressing in these rules.

One of the structural changes to the UCP is the introduction of articles covering definitions (article 2) and interpretations (article 3). In providing definitions of roles played by banks and the meaning of specific terms and events, UCP 600 avoids the necessity of repetitive text to explain their interpretation and application. Similarly, the article covering interpretations aims to take the ambiguity out of vague or unclear language that appears in letters of credit and to provide a definitive elucidation of other characteristics of the UCP or the credit.

During the course of the last three years, ICC national committees were canvassed on a range of issues to determine their preferences on alternative texts submitted by the Drafting Group. The results of this exercise and the considerable input from national committees on individual items in the text is reflected in the content of UCP 600. The Drafting Group considered, not only the current practice relative to the documentary credit, but also tried to envisage the future evolution of that practice.

This revision of the UCP represents the culmination of over three years of extensive analysis, review, debate and compromise amongst the various members of the Drafting Group, the members of the Banking Commission and the respective ICC national committees. Valuable comment has also been received from the ICC Commission on Transport and Logistics, the Commission on Commercial Law and Practice and the Committee on Insurance.

It is not appropriate for this publication to provide an explanation as to why an article has been worded in such a way or what is intended by its incorporation into the rules. For those interested in understanding the rationale and interpretation of the articles of UCP 600, this information will be found in the Commentary to the rules, ICC Publication 601, which represents the Drafting Group's views.

ARTICLE 1

Application of UCP
The *Uniform Customs and Practice for Documentary Credits, 2007 Revision*, ICC Publication No. 600 ("UCP") are rules that apply to any documentary credit ("credit") (including, to the extent to which they may be applicable, any standby letter of credit) when the text of the credit expressly indicates that it is subject to these rules. They are binding on all parties thereto unless expressly modified or excluded by the credit.

ARTICLE 2

Definitions
For the purpose of these rules:

Advising bank means the bank that advises the credit at the request of the issuing bank.

Applicant means the party on whose request the credit is issued.

Banking day means a day on which a bank is regularly open at the place at which an act subject to these rules is to be performed.

Beneficiary means the party in whose favour a credit is issued.

Complying presentation means a presentation that is in accordance with the terms and conditions of the credit, the applicable provisions of these rules and international standard banking practice.

Confirmation means a definite undertaking of the confirming bank, in addition to that of the issuing bank, to honour or negotiate a complying presentation.

Confirming bank means the bank that adds its confirmation to a credit upon the issuing bank's authorization or request.

Credit means any arrangement, however named or described, that is irrevocable and thereby constitutes a definite undertaking of the issuing bank to honour a complying presentation.

Honour means:

a.   to pay at sight if the credit is available by sight payment.
b.   to incur a deferred payment undertaking and pay at maturity if the credit is available by deferred payment.
c.   to accept a bill of exchange ("draft") drawn by the beneficiary and pay at maturity if the credit is available by acceptance.

Issuing bank means the bank that issues a credit at the request of an applicant or on its own behalf.

Negotiation means the purchase by the nominated bank of drafts (drawn on a bank other than the nominated bank) and/or documents under a complying presentation, by advancing or agreeing to advance funds to the beneficiary on or before the banking day on which reimbursement is due to the nominated bank.

Nominated bank means the bank with which the credit is available or any bank in the case of a credit available with any bank.

Presentation means either the delivery of documents under a credit to the issuing bank or nominated bank or the documents so delivered.

Presenter means a beneficiary, bank or other party that makes a presentation.

ARTICLE 3

Interpretations
For the purpose of these rules:

Where applicable, words in the singular include the plural and in the plural include the singular.

A credit is irrevocable even if there is no indication to that effect.

A document may be signed by handwriting, facsimile signature, perforated signature, stamp, symbol or any other mechanical or electronic method of authentication.

A requirement for a document to be legalized, visaed, certified or similar will be satisfied by any signature, mark, stamp or label on the document which appears to satisfy that requirement.

Branches of a bank in different countries are considered to be separate banks.

Terms such as "first class", "well known", "qualified", "independent", "official", "competent" or "local" used to describe the issuer of a document allow any issuer except the beneficiary to issue that document.

Unless required to be used in a document, words such as "prompt", "immediately" or "as soon as possible" will be disregarded.

The expression "on or about" or similar will be interpreted as a stipulation that an event is to occur during a period of five calendar days before until five calendar days after the specified date, both start and end dates included.

The words "to", "until", "till", "from" and "between" when used to determine a period of shipment include the date or dates mentioned, and the words "before" and "after" exclude the date mentioned.

The words "from" and "after" when used to determine a maturity date exclude the date mentioned.

The terms "first half " and "second half " of a month shall be construed respectively as the 1st to the 15th and the 16th to the last day of the month, all dates inclusive.

The terms "beginning", "middle" and "end" of a month shall be construed respectively as the 1st to the 10th, the 11th to the 20th and the 21st to the last day of the month, all dates inclusive.

ARTICLE 4

Credits v. Contracts
a.   A credit by its nature is a separate transaction from the sale or other contract on which it may be based. Banks are in no way concerned with or bound by such contract, even if any reference whatsoever to it is included in the credit. Consequently, the undertaking of a bank to honour, to negotiate or to fulfil any other obligation under the credit is not subject to claims or defences by the applicant resulting from its relationships with the issuing bank or the beneficiary.

   A beneficiary can in no case avail itself of the contractual relationships existing between banks or between the applicant and the issuing bank.
b.   An issuing bank should discourage any attempt by the applicant to include, as an integral part of the credit, copies of the underlying contract, proforma invoice and the like.

ARTICLE 5

Documents v. Goods, Services or Performance
Banks deal with documents and not with goods, services or performance to which the documents may relate.

ARTICLE 6

Availability, Expiry Date and Place for Presentation
a.   A credit must state the bank with which it is available or whether it is available with any bank. A credit available with a nominated bank is also available with the issuing bank.
b.   A credit must state whether it is available by sight payment, deferred payment, acceptance or negotiation.
c.   A credit must not be issued available by a draft drawn on the applicant.
d.   i.   A credit must state an expiry date for presentation. An expiry date stated for honour or negotiation will be deemed to be an expiry date for presentation.
     ii. The place of the bank with which the credit is available is the place for presentation. The place for presentation under a credit available with any bank is that of any bank. A place for presentation other than that of the issuing bank is in addition to the place of the issuing bank.
e.   Except as provided in sub-article 29 (a), a presentation by or on behalf of the beneficiary must be made on or before the expiry date.

ARTICLE 7

Issuing Bank Undertaking
a.   Provided that the stipulated documents are presented to the nominated bank or to the issuing bank and that they constitute a complying presentation, the issuing bank must honour if the credit is available by:
     i.   sight payment, deferred payment or acceptance with the issuing bank;
     ii.   sight payment with a nominated bank and that nominated bank does not pay;
     iii. deferred payment with a nominated bank and that nominated bank does not incur its deferred payment undertaking or, having incurred its deferred payment undertaking, does not pay at maturity;
     iv.   acceptance with a nominated bank and that nominated bank does not accept a draft drawn on it or, having accepted a draft drawn on it, does not pay at maturity;
     v.   negotiation with a nominated bank and that nominated bank does not negotiate.
b.   An issuing bank is irrevocably bound to honour as of the time it issues the credit.
c.   An issuing bank undertakes to reimburse a nominated bank that has honoured or negotiated a complying presentation and forwarded the documents to the issuing bank. Reimbursement for the amount of a complying presentation under a credit available by acceptance or deferred payment is due at maturity, whether or not the nominated bank prepaid or purchased before maturity. An issuing bank's undertaking to reimburse a nominated bank is independent of the issuing bank's undertaking to the beneficiary.

ARTICLE 8

Confirming Bank Undertaking
a. Provided that the stipulated documents are presented to the confirming bank or to any other nominated bank and that they constitute a complying presentation, the confirming bank must:
  i. honour, if the credit is available by
    a) sight payment, deferred payment or acceptance with the confirming bank;
    b) sight payment with another nominated bank and that nominated bank does not pay;
    c) deferred payment with another nominated bank and that nominated bank does not incur its deferred payment undertaking or, having incurred its deferred payment undertaking, does not pay at maturity; d) acceptance with another nominated bank and that nominated bank does not accept a draft drawn on it or, having accepted a draft drawn on it, does not pay at maturity;
    e) negotiation with another nominated bank and that nominated bank does not negotiate.
  ii. negotiate, without recourse, if the credit is available by negotiation with the confirming bank.
b. A confirming bank is irrevocably bound to honour or negotiate as of the time it adds its confirmation to the credit.
c. A confirming bank undertakes to reimburse another nominated bank that has honoured or negotiated a complying presentation and forwarded the documents to the confirming bank. Reimbursement for the amount of a complying presentation under a credit available by acceptance or deferred payment is due at maturity, whether or not another nominated bank prepaid or purchased before maturity. A confirming bank's undertaking to reimburse another nominated bank is independent of the confirming bank's undertaking to the beneficiary.
d. If a bank is authorized or requested by the issuing bank to confirm a credit but is not prepared to do so, it must inform the issuing bank without delay and may advise the credit without confirmation.

ARTICLE 9

Advising of Credits and Amendments
a. A credit and any amendment may be advised to a beneficiary through an advising bank. An advising bank that is not a confirming bank advises the credit and any amendment without any undertaking to honour or negotiate.
b. By advising the credit or amendment, the advising bank signifies that it has satisfied itself as to the apparent authenticity of the credit or amendment and that the advice accurately reflects the terms and conditions of the credit or amendment received.
c. An advising bank may utilize the services of another bank ("second advising bank") to advise the credit and any amendment to the beneficiary. By advising the credit or amendment, the second advising bank signifies that it has satisfied itself as to the apparent authenticity of the advice it has received and that the advice accurately reflects the terms and conditions of the credit or amendment received.
d. A bank utilizing the services of an advising bank or second advising bank to advise a credit must use the same bank to advise any amendment thereto.

e. If a bank is requested to advise a credit or amendment but elects not to do so, it must so inform, without delay, the bank from which the credit, amendment or advice has been received.

f. If a bank is requested to advise a credit or amendment but cannot satisfy itself as to the apparent authenticity of the credit, the amendment or the advice, it must so inform, without delay, the bank from which the instructions appear to have been received. If the advising bank or second advising bank elects nonetheless to advise the credit or amendment, it must inform the beneficiary or second advising bank that it has not been able to satisfy itself as to the apparent authenticity of the credit, the amendment or the advice.

ARTICLE 10

Amendments

a. Except as otherwise provided by article 38, a credit can neither be amended nor cancelled without the agreement of the issuing bank, the confirming bank, if any, and the beneficiary.

b. An issuing bank is irrevocably bound by an amendment as of the time it issues the amendment. A confirming bank may extend its confirmation to an amendment and will be irrevocably bound as of the time it advises the amendment. A confirming bank may, however, choose to advise an amendment without extending its confirmation and, if so, it must inform the issuing bank without delay and inform the beneficiary in its advice.

c. The terms and conditions of the original credit (or a credit incorporating previously accepted amendments) will remain in force for the beneficiary until the beneficiary communicates its acceptance of the amendment to the bank that advised such amendment. The beneficiary should give notification of acceptance or rejection of an amendment. If the beneficiary fails to give such notification, a presentation that complies with the credit and to any not yet accepted amendment will be deemed to be notification of acceptance by the beneficiary of such amendment. As of that moment the credit will be amended.

d. A bank that advises an amendment should inform the bank from which it received the amendment of any notification of acceptance or rejection.

e. Partial acceptance of an amendment is not allowed and will be deemed to be notification of rejection of the amendment.

f. A provision in an amendment to the effect that the amendment shall enter into force unless rejected by the beneficiary within a certain time shall be disregarded.

ARTICLE 11

Teletransmitted and Pre-Advised Credits and Amendments

a. An authenticated teletransmission of a credit or amendment will be deemed to be the operative credit or amendment, and any subsequent mail confirmation shall be disregarded.

   If a teletransmission states "full details to follow" (or words of similar effect), or states that the mail confirmation is to be the operative credit or amendment, then the teletransmission will not be deemed to be the operative credit or amendment. The issuing bank must then issue the operative credit or amendment without delay in terms not inconsistent with the teletransmission.

b. A preliminary advice of the issuance of a credit or amendment ("pre-advice") shall only be sent if the issuing bank is prepared to issue the operative credit or amendment.

449

An issuing bank that sends a pre-advice is irrevocably committed to issue the operative credit or amendment, without delay, in terms not inconsistent with the pre-advice.

ARTICLE 12

Nomination

a. Unless a nominated bank is the confirming bank, an authorization to honour or negotiate does not impose any obligation on that nominated bank to honour or negotiate, except when expressly agreed to by that nominated bank and so communicated to the beneficiary.

b. By nominating a bank to accept a draft or incur a deferred payment undertaking, an issuing bank authorizes that nominated bank to prepay or purchase a draft accepted or a deferred payment undertaking incurred by that nominated bank.

c. Receipt or examination and forwarding of documents by a nominated bank that is not a confirming bank does not make that nominated bank liable to honour or negotiate, nor does it constitute honour or negotiation.

ARTICLE 13

Bank-to-Bank Reimbursement Arrangements

a. If a credit states that reimbursement is to be obtained by a nominated bank ("claiming bank") claiming on another party ("reimbursing bank"), the credit must state if the reimbursement is subject to the ICC rules for bank-to-bank reimbursements in effect on the date of issuance of the credit.

b. If a credit does not state that reimbursement is subject to the ICC rules for bank-to-bank reimbursements, the following apply:

  i. An issuing bank must provide a reimbursing bank with a reimbursement authorization that conforms with the availability stated in the credit. The reimbursement authorization should not be subject to an expiry date.

  ii. A claiming bank shall not be required to supply a reimbursing bank with a certificate of compliance with the terms and conditions of the credit.

  iii. An issuing bank will be responsible for any loss of interest, together with any expenses incurred, if reimbursement is not provided on first demand by a reimbursing bank in accordance with the terms and conditions of the credit.

  iv. A reimbursing bank's charges are for the account of the issuing bank. However, if the charges are for the account of the beneficiary, it is the responsibility of an issuing bank to so indicate in the credit and in the reimbursement authorization. If a reimbursing bank's charges are for the account of the beneficiary, they shall be deducted from the amount due to a claiming bank when reimbursement is made. If no reimbursement is made, the reimbursing bank's charges remain the obligation of the issuing bank.

c. An issuing bank is not relieved of any of its obligations to provide reimbursement if reimbursement is not made by a reimbursing bank on first demand.

ARTICLE 14

Standard for Examination of Documents

a. A nominated bank acting on its nomination, a confirming bank, if any, and the issuing bank must examine a presentation to determine, on the basis of the documents alone, whether or not the documents appear on their face to constitute a complying presentation.

b.   A nominated bank acting on its nomination, a confirming bank, if any, and the issuing bank shall each have a maximum of five banking days following the day of presentation to determine if a presentation is complying. This period is not curtailed or otherwise affected by the occurrence on or after the date of presentation of any expiry date or last day for presentation.

c.   A presentation including one or more original transport documents subject to articles 19, 20, 21, 22, 23, 24 or 25 must be made by or on behalf of the beneficiary not later than 21 calendar days after the date of shipment as described in these rules, but in any event not later than the expiry date of the credit.

d.   Data in a document, when read in context with the credit, the document itself and international standard banking practice, need not be identical to, but must not conflict with, data in that document, any other stipulated document or the credit.

e.   In documents other than the commercial invoice, the description of the goods, services or performance, if stated, may be in general terms not conflicting with their description in the credit.

f.   If a credit requires presentation of a document other than a transport document, insurance document or commercial invoice, without stipulating by whom the document is to be issued or its data content, banks will accept the document as presented if its content appears to fulfil the function of the required document and otherwise complies with sub-article 14 (d).

g.   A document presented but not required by the credit will be disregarded and may be returned to the presenter.

h.   If a credit contains a condition without stipulating the document to indicate compliance with the condition, banks will deem such condition as not stated and will disregard it.

i.   A document may be dated prior to the issuance date of the credit, but must not be dated later than its date of presentation.

j.   When the addresses of the beneficiary and the applicant appear in any stipulated document, they need not be the same as those stated in the credit or in any other stipulated document, but must be within the same country as the respective addresses mentioned in the credit. Contact details (telefax, telephone, email and the like) stated as part of the beneficiary's and the applicant's address will be disregarded. However, when the address and contact details of the applicant appear as part of the consignee or notify party details on a transport document subject to articles 19, 20, 21, 22, 23, 24 or 25, they must be as stated in the credit.

k.   The shipper or consignor of the goods indicated on any document need not be the beneficiary of the credit.

l.   A transport document may be issued by any party other than a carrier, owner, master or charterer provided that the transport document meets the requirements of articles 19, 20, 21, 22, 23 or 24 of these rules.

ARTICLE 15

Complying Presentation

a.   When an issuing bank determines that a presentation is complying, it must honour.

b.   When a confirming bank determines that a presentation is complying, it must honour or negotiate and forward the documents to the issuing bank.

c.   When a nominated bank determines that a presentation is complying and honours or negotiates, it must forward the documents to the confirming bank or issuing bank.

ARTICLE 16

Discrepant Documents, Waiver and Notice

a. When a nominated bank acting on its nomination, a confirming bank, if any, or the issuing bank determines that a presentation does not comply, it may refuse to honour or negotiate.

b. When an issuing bank determines that a presentation does not comply, it may in its sole judgement approach the applicant for a waiver of the discrepancies. This does not, however, extend the period mentioned in sub-article 14 (b).

c. When a nominated bank acting on its nomination, a confirming bank, if any, or the issuing bank decides to refuse to honour or negotiate, it must give a single notice to that effect to the presenter.

The notice must state:

i.   that the bank is refusing to honour or negotiate; and

ii. each discrepancy in respect of which the bank refuses to honour or negotiate; and

iii. a) that the bank is holding the documents pending further instructions from the presenter; or

b) that the issuing bank is holding the documents until it receives a waiver from the applicant and agrees to accept it, or receives further instructions from the presenter prior to agreeing to accept a waiver; or

c) that the bank is returning the documents; or

d) that the bank is acting in accordance with instructions previously received from the presenter.

d. The notice required in sub-article 16 (c) must be given by telecommunication or, if that is not possible, by other expeditious means no later than the close of the fifth banking day following the day of presentation.

e. A nominated bank acting on its nomination, a confirming bank, if any, or the issuing bank may, after providing notice required by sub-article 16 (c) (iii) (a) or (b), return the documents to the presenter at any time.

f. If an issuing bank or a confirming bank fails to act in accordance with the provisions of this article, it shall be precluded from claiming that the documents do not constitute a complying presentation.

g. When an issuing bank refuses to honour or a confirming bank refuses to honour or negotiate and has given notice to that effect in accordance with this article, it shall then be entitled to claim a refund, with interest, of any reimbursement made.

ARTICLE 17

Original Documents and Copies

a. At least one original of each document stipulated in the credit must be presented.

b. A bank shall treat as an original any document bearing an apparently original signature, mark, stamp, or label of the issuer of the document, unless the document itself indicates that it is not an original.

c. Unless a document indicates otherwise, a bank will also accept a document as original if it:

i.   appears to be written, typed, perforated or stamped by the document issuer's hand; or

ii. appears to be on the document issuer's original stationery; or

iii. states that it is original, unless the statement appears not to apply to the document presented.

d. If a credit requires presentation of copies of documents, presentation of either originals or copies is permitted.

e. If a credit requires presentation of multiple documents by using terms such as "in duplicate", "in two fold" or "in two copies", this will be satisfied by the presentation of at least one original and the remaining number in copies, except when the document itself indicates otherwise.

ARTICLE 18

Commercial Invoice

a. A commercial invoice:
    i.   must appear to have been issued by the beneficiary (except as provided in article 38);
    ii. must be made out in the name of the applicant (except as provided in sub-article 38 (g));
    iii. must be made out in the same currency as the credit; and
    iv. need not be signed.
b. A nominated bank acting on its nomination, a confirming bank, if any, or the issuing bank may accept a commercial invoice issued for an amount in excess of the amount permitted by the credit, and its decision will be binding upon all parties, provided the bank in question has not honoured or negotiated for an amount in excess of that permitted by the credit.
c. The description of the goods, services or performance in a commercial invoice must correspond with that appearing in the credit.

ARTICLE 19

Transport Document Covering at Least Two Different Modes of Transport

a. A transport document covering at least two different modes of transport (multimodal or combined transport document), however named, must appear to:
    i.   indicate the name of the carrier and be signed by:
        • the carrier or a named agent for or on behalf of the carrier, or
        • the master or a named agent for or on behalf of the master.
        Any signature by the carrier, master or agent must be identified as that of the carrier, master or agent.
        Any signature by an agent must indicate whether the agent has signed for or on behalf of the carrier or for or on behalf of the master.
    ii. indicate that the goods have been dispatched, taken in charge or shipped on board at the place stated in the credit, by:
        • pre-printed wording, or
        • a stamp or notation indicating the date on which the goods have been dispatched, taken in charge or shipped on board.
        The date of issuance of the transport document will be deemed to be the date of dispatch, taking in charge or shipped on board, and the date of shipment. However, if the transport document indicates, by stamp or notation, a date of dispatch, taking in charge or shipped on board, this date will be deemed to be the date of shipment.
    iii. indicate the place of dispatch, taking in charge or shipment, and the place of final destination stated in the credit, even if:
        a) the transport document states, in addition, a different place of dispatch, taking in charge or shipment or place of final destination, or
        b) the transport document contains the indication "intended" or similar qualification in relation to the vessel, port of loading or port of discharge.

453

    iv. be the sole original transport document or, if issued in more than one original, be the full set as indicated on the transport document.

    v. contain terms and conditions of carriage or make reference to another source containing the terms and conditions of carriage (short form or blank back transport document). Contents of terms and conditions of carriage will not be examined.

    vi. contain no indication that it is subject to a charter party.

b. For the purpose of this article, transhipment means unloading from one means of conveyance and reloading to another means of conveyance (whether or not in different modes of transport) during the carriage from the place of dispatch, taking in charge or shipment to the place of final destination stated in the credit.

c. i. A transport document may indicate that the goods will or may be transhipped provided that the entire carriage is covered by one and the same transport document.

    ii. A transport document indicating that transhipment will or may take place is acceptable, even if the credit prohibits transhipment.

ARTICLE 20

Bill of Lading

a. A bill of lading, however named, must appear to:

    i. indicate the name of the carrier and be signed by:

- the carrier or a named agent for or on behalf of the carrier, or
- the master or a named agent for or on behalf of the master.

Any signature by the carrier, master or agent must be identified as that of the carrier, master or agent.

    Any signature by an agent must indicate whether the agent has signed for or on behalf of the carrier or for or on behalf of the master.

    ii. indicate that the goods have been shipped on board a named vessel at the port of loading stated in the credit by:

- pre-printed wording, or
- an on board notation indicating the date on which the goods have been shipped on board.

The date of issuance of the bill of lading will be deemed to be the date of shipment unless the bill of lading contains an on board notation indicating the date of shipment, in which case the date stated in the on board notation will be deemed to be the date of shipment.

    If the bill of lading contains the indication "intended vessel" or similar qualification in relation to the name of the vessel, an on board notation indicating the date of shipment and the name of the actual vessel is required.

    iii. indicate shipment from the port of loading to the port of discharge stated in the credit.

    If the bill of lading does not indicate the port of loading stated in the credit as the port of loading, or if it contains the indication "intended" or similar qualification in relation to the port of loading, an on board notation indicating the port of loading as stated in the credit, the date of shipment and the name of the vessel is required. This provision applies even when loading on board or shipment on a named vessel is indicated by pre-printed wording on the bill of lading.

    iv. be the sole original bill of lading or, if issued in more than one original, be the full set as indicated on the bill of lading.

    v. contain terms and conditions of carriage or make reference to another source containing the terms and conditions of carriage (short form or blank back bill of lading). Contents of terms and conditions of carriage will not be examined.

    vi. contain no indication that it is subject to a charter party.

b. For the purpose of this article, transhipment means unloading from one vessel and reloading to another vessel during the carriage from the port of loading to the port of discharge stated in the credit.

c. i. A bill of lading may indicate that the goods will or may be transhipped provided that the entire carriage is covered by one and the same bill of lading.

    ii. A bill of lading indicating that transhipment will or may take place is acceptable, even if the credit prohibits transhipment, if the goods have been shipped in a container, trailer or LASH barge as evidenced by the bill of lading.

d. Clauses in a bill of lading stating that the carrier reserves the right to tranship will be disregarded.

ARTICLE 21

Non-Negotiable Sea Waybill

a. A non-negotiable sea waybill, however named, must appear to:

    i. indicate the name of the carrier and be signed by:

- the carrier or a named agent for or on behalf of the carrier, or
- the master or a named agent for or on behalf of the master.

Any signature by the carrier, master or agent must be identified as that of the carrier, master or agent.

Any signature by an agent must indicate whether the agent has signed for or on behalf of the carrier or for or on behalf of the master.

    ii. indicate that the goods have been shipped on board a named vessel at the port of loading stated in the credit by:

- pre-printed wording, or
- an on board notation indicating the date on which the goods have been shipped on board.

The date of issuance of the non-negotiable sea waybill will be deemed to be the date of shipment unless the nonnegotiable sea waybill contains an on board notation indicating the date of shipment, in which case the date stated in the on board notation will be deemed to be the date of shipment.

If the non-negotiable sea waybill contains the indication "intended vessel" or similar qualification in relation to the name of the vessel, an on board notation indicating the date of shipment and the name of the actual vessel is required.

    iii. indicate shipment from the port of loading to the port of discharge stated in the credit.

If the non-negotiable sea waybill does not indicate the port of loading stated in the credit as the port of loading, or if it contains the indication "intended" or similar qualification in relation to the port of loading, an on board notation indicating the port of loading as stated in the credit, the date of shipment and the name of the vessel is required. This provision applies even when loading on board or shipment on a named vessel is indicated by pre-printed wording on the non-negotiable sea waybill.

    iv. be the sole original non-negotiable sea waybill or, if issued in more than one original, be the full set as indicated on the non-negotiable sea waybill.

      v.   contain terms and conditions of carriage or make reference to another source containing the terms and conditions of carriage (short form or blank back non-negotiable sea waybill). Contents of terms and conditions of carriage will not be examined.

      vi. contain no indication that it is subject to a charter party.

b.   For the purpose of this article, transhipment means unloading from one vessel and reloading to another vessel during the carriage from the port of loading to the port of discharge stated in the credit.

c.   i.   A non-negotiable sea waybill may indicate that the goods will or may be transhipped provided that the entire carriage is covered by one and the same non-negotiable sea waybill.

      ii. A non-negotiable sea waybill indicating that transhipment will or may take place is acceptable, even if the credit prohibits transhipment, if the goods have been shipped in a container, trailer or LASH barge as evidenced by the non-negotiable sea waybill.

d.   Clauses in a non-negotiable sea waybill stating that the carrier reserves the right to tranship will be disregarded.

ARTICLE 22

Charter Party Bill of Lading

a.   A bill of lading, however named, containing an indication that it is subject to a charter party (charter party bill of lading), must appear to:

      i.   be signed by:

- the master or a named agent for or on behalf of the master, or
- the owner or a named agent for or on behalf of the owner, or
- the charterer or a named agent for or on behalf of the charterer.

Any signature by the master, owner, charterer or agent must be identified as that of the master, owner, charterer or agent.

Any signature by an agent must indicate whether the agent has signed for or on behalf of the master, owner or charterer.

An agent signing for or on behalf of the owner or charterer must indicate the name of the owner or charterer.

      ii. indicate that the goods have been shipped on board a named vessel at the port of loading stated in the credit by:

- pre-printed wording, or
- an on board notation indicating the date on which the goods have been shipped on board.

The date of issuance of the charter party bill of lading will be deemed to be the date of shipment unless the charter party bill of lading contains an on board notation indicating the date of shipment, in which case the date stated in the on board notation will be deemed to be the date of shipment.

      iii. indicate shipment from the port of loading to the port of discharge stated in the credit. The port of discharge may also be shown as a range of ports or a geographical area, as stated in the credit.

      iv. be the sole original charter party bill of lading or, if issued in more than one original, be the full set as indicated on the charter party bill of lading.

b.   A bank will not examine charter party contracts, even if they are required to be presented by the terms of the credit.

ARTICLE 23

Air Transport Document
a. An air transport document, however named, must appear to:
  i.   indicate the name of the carrier and be signed by:
       - the carrier, or
       - a named agent for or on behalf of the carrier.
       Any signature by the carrier or agent must be identified as that of the carrier or agent.
         Any signature by an agent must indicate that the agent has signed for or on behalf of the carrier.
  ii. indicate that the goods have been accepted for carriage.
  iii. indicate the date of issuance. This date will be deemed to be the date of shipment unless the air transport document contains a specific notation of the actual date of shipment, in which case the date stated in the notation will be deemed to be the date of shipment.
         Any other information appearing on the air transport document relative to the flight number and date will not be considered in determining the date of shipment.
  iv. indicate the airport of departure and the airport of destination stated in the credit.
  v.   be the original for consignor or shipper, even if the credit stipulates a full set of originals.
  vi. contain terms and conditions of carriage or make reference to another source containing the terms and conditions of carriage. Contents of terms and conditions of carriage will not be examined.
b. For the purpose of this article, transhipment means unloading from one aircraft and reloading to another aircraft during the carriage from the airport of departure to the airport of destination stated in the credit.
c. i.   An air transport document may indicate that the goods will or may be transhipped, provided that the entire carriage is covered by one and the same air transport document.
  ii. An air transport document indicating that transhipment will or may take place is acceptable, even if the credit prohibits transhipment.

ARTICLE 24

Road, Rail or Inland Waterway Transport Documents
a. A road, rail or inland waterway transport document, however named, must appear to:
  i.   indicate the name of the carrier and:
       - be signed by the carrier or a named agent for or on behalf of the carrier, or
       - indicate receipt of the goods by signature, stamp or notation by the carrier or a named agent for or on behalf of the carrier.
       Any signature, stamp or notation of receipt of the goods by the carrier or agent must be identified as that of the carrier or agent.
         Any signature, stamp or notation of receipt of the goods by the agent must indicate that the agent has signed or acted for or on behalf of the carrier.
         If a rail transport document does not identify the carrier, any signature or stamp of the railway company will be accepted as evidence of the document being signed by the carrier.

    ii.   indicate the date of shipment or the date the goods have been received for shipment, dispatch or carriage at the place stated in the credit. Unless the transport document contains a dated reception stamp, an indication of the date of receipt or a date of shipment, the date of issuance of the transport document will be deemed to be the date of shipment.

    iii. indicate the place of shipment and the place of destination stated in the credit.

b. i.   A road transport document must appear to be the original for consignor or shipper or bear no marking indicating for whom the document has been prepared.

    ii. A rail transport document marked "duplicate" will be accepted as an original.

    iii. A rail or inland waterway transport document will be accepted as an original whether marked as an original or not.

c. In the absence of an indication on the transport document as to the number of originals issued, the number presented will be deemed to constitute a full set.

d. For the purpose of this article, transhipment means unloading from one means of conveyance and reloading to another means of conveyance, within the same mode of transport, during the carriage from the place of shipment, dispatch or carriage to the place of destination stated in the credit.

e. i.   A road, rail or inland waterway transport document may indicate that the goods will or may be transhipped provided that the entire carriage is covered by one and the same transport document.

    ii. A road, rail or inland waterway transport document indicating that transhipment will or may take place is acceptable, even if the credit prohibits transhipment.

ARTICLE 25

Courier Receipt, Post Receipt or Certificate of Posting

a. A courier receipt, however named, evidencing receipt of goods for transport, must appear to:

    i.   indicate the name of the courier service and be stamped or signed by the named courier service at the place from which the credit states the goods are to be shipped; and

    ii. indicate a date of pickup or of receipt or wording to this effect. This date will be deemed to be the date of shipment.

b. A requirement that courier charges are to be paid or prepaid may be satisfied by a transport document issued by a courier service evidencing that courier charges are for the account of a party other than the consignee.

c. A post receipt or certificate of posting, however named, evidencing receipt of goods for transport, must appear to be stamped or signed and dated at the place from which the credit states the goods are to be shipped. This date will be deemed to be the date of shipment.

ARTICLE 26

"On Deck", "Shipper's Load and Count", "Said by Shipper to Contain" and Charges Additional to Freight

a. A transport document must not indicate that the goods are or will be loaded on deck. A clause on a transport document stating that the goods may be loaded on deck is acceptable.

b.   A transport document bearing a clause such as "shipper's load and count" and "said by shipper to contain" is acceptable.
c.   A transport document may bear a reference, by stamp or otherwise, to charges additional to the freight.

ARTICLE 27

Clean Transport Document
A bank will only accept a clean transport document. A clean transport document is one bearing no clause or notation expressly declaring a defective condition of the goods or their packaging. The word "clean" need not appear on a transport document, even if a credit has a requirement for that transport document to be "clean on board".

ARTICLE 28

Insurance Document and Coverage
a.   An insurance document, such as an insurance policy, an insurance certificate or a declaration under an open cover, must appear to be issued and signed by an insurance company, an underwriter or their agents or their proxies.
       Any signature by an agent or proxy must indicate whether the agent or proxy has signed for or on behalf of the insurance company or underwriter.
b.   When the insurance document indicates that it has been issued in more than one original, all originals must be presented.
c.   Cover notes will not be accepted.
d.   An insurance policy is acceptable in lieu of an insurance certificate or a declaration under an open cover.
e.   The date of the insurance document must be no later than the date of shipment, unless it appears from the insurance document that the cover is effective from a date not later than the date of shipment.
f.   i.   The insurance document must indicate the amount of insurance coverage and be in the same currency as the credit.
     ii.   A requirement in the credit for insurance coverage to be for a percentage of the value of the goods, of the invoice value or similar is deemed to be the minimum amount of coverage required.
          If there is no indication in the credit of the insurance coverage required, the amount of insurance coverage must be at least 110% of the CIF or CIP value of the goods.
          When the CIF or CIP value cannot be determined from the documents, the amount of insurance coverage must be calculated on the basis of the amount for which honour or negotiation is requested or the gross value of the goods as shown on the invoice, whichever is greater.
     iii. The insurance document must indicate that risks are covered at least between the place of taking in charge or shipment and the place of discharge or final destination as stated in the credit.
g.   A credit should state the type of insurance required and, if any, the additional risks to be covered. An insurance document will be accepted without regard to any risks that are not covered if the credit uses imprecise terms such as "usual risks" or "customary risks".

459

h.   When a credit requires insurance against "all risks" and an insurance document is presented containing any "all risks" notation or clause, whether or not bearing the heading "all risks", the insurance document will be accepted without regard to any risks stated to be excluded.
i.   An insurance document may contain reference to any exclusion clause.
j.   An insurance document may indicate that the cover is subject to a franchise or excess (deductible).

ARTICLE 29

Extension of Expiry Date or Last Day for Presentation
a.   If the expiry date of a credit or the last day for presentation falls on a day when the bank to which presentation is to be made is closed for reasons other than those referred to in article 36, the expiry date or the last day for presentation, as the case may be, will be extended to the first following banking day.
b.   If presentation is made on the first following banking day, a nominated bank must provide the issuing bank or confirming bank with a statement on its covering schedule that the presentation was made within the time limits extended in accordance with sub-article 29 (a).
c.   The latest date for shipment will not be extended as a result of sub-article 29 (a).

ARTICLE 30

Tolerance in Credit Amount, Quantity and Unit Prices
a.   The words "about" or "approximately" used in connection with the amount of the credit or the quantity or the unit price stated in the credit are to be construed as allowing a tolerance not to exceed 10% more or 10% less than the amount, the quantity or the unit price to which they refer.
b.   A tolerance not to exceed 5% more or 5% less than the quantity of the goods is allowed, provided the credit does not state the quantity in terms of a stipulated number of packing units or individual items and the total amount of the drawings does not exceed the amount of the credit.
c.   Even when partial shipments are not allowed, a tolerance not to exceed 5% less than the amount of the credit is allowed, provided that the quantity of the goods, if stated in the credit, is shipped in full and a unit price, if stated in the credit, is not reduced or that sub-article 30 (b) is not applicable. This tolerance does not apply when the credit stipulates a specific tolerance or uses the expressions referred to in sub-article 30 (a).

ARTICLE 31

Partial Drawings or Shipments
a.   Partial drawings or shipments are allowed.
b.   A presentation consisting of more than one set of transport documents evidencing shipment commencing on the same means of conveyance and for the same journey, provided they indicate the same destination, will not be regarded as covering a partial shipment, even if they indicate different dates of shipment or different ports of loading, places of taking in charge or dispatch. If the presentation consists of more than one set of transport documents, the latest date

of shipment as evidenced on any of the sets of transport documents will be regarded as the date of shipment.

ARTICLE 32

Instalment Drawings or Shipments
If a drawing or shipment by instalments within given periods is stipulated in the credit and any instalment is not drawn or shipped within the period allowed for that instalment, the credit ceases to be available for that and any subsequent instalment.

ARTICLE 33

Hours of Presentation
A bank has no obligation to accept a presentation outside of its banking hours.

ARTICLE 34

Disclaimer on Effectiveness of Documents
A bank assumes no liability or responsibility for the form, sufficiency, accuracy, genuineness, falsification or legal effect of any document, or for the general or particular conditions stipulated in a document or superimposed thereon; nor does it assume any liability or responsibility for the description, quantity, weight, quality, condition, packing, delivery, value or existence of the goods, services or other performance represented by any document, or for the good faith or acts or omissions, solvency, performance or standing of the consignor, the carrier, the forwarder, the consignee or the insurer of the goods or any other person.

ARTICLE 35

Disclaimer on Transmission and Translation
A bank assumes no liability or responsibility for the consequences arising out of delay, loss in transit, mutilation or other errors arising in the transmission of any messages or delivery of letters or documents, when such messages, letters or documents are transmitted or sent according to the requirements stated in the credit, or when the bank may have taken the initiative in the choice of the delivery service in the absence of such instructions in the credit.

If a nominated bank determines that a presentation is complying and forwards the documents to the issuing bank or confirming bank, whether or not the nominated bank has honoured or negotiated, an issuing bank or confirming bank must honour or negotiate, or reimburse that nominated bank, even when the documents have been lost in transit between the nominated bank and the issuing bank or confirming bank, or between the confirming bank and the issuing bank.

A bank assumes no liability or responsibility for errors in translation or interpretation of technical terms and may transmit credit terms without translating them.

ARTICLE 36

Force Majeure
A bank assumes no liability or responsibility for the consequences arising out of the interruption of its business by Acts of God, riots, civil commotions, insurrections, wars, acts of terrorism, or by any strikes or lockouts or any other causes beyond its control.

   A bank will not, upon resumption of its business, honour or negotiate under a credit that expired during such interruption of its business.

ARTICLE 37

Disclaimer for Acts of an Instructed Party
a.   A bank utilizing the services of another bank for the purpose of giving effect to the instructions of the applicant does so for the account and at the risk of the applicant.
b.   An issuing bank or advising bank assumes no liability or responsibility should the instructions it transmits to another bank not be carried out, even if it has taken the initiative in the choice of that other bank.
c.   A bank instructing another bank to perform services is liable for any commissions, fees, costs or expenses ("charges") incurred by that bank in connection with its instructions.

   If a credit states that charges are for the account of the beneficiary and charges cannot be collected or deducted from proceeds, the issuing bank remains liable for payment of charges.

   A credit or amendment should not stipulate that the advising to a beneficiary is conditional upon the receipt by the advising bank or second advising bank of its charges.
d.   The applicant shall be bound by and liable to indemnify a bank against all obligations and responsibilities imposed by foreign laws and usages.

ARTICLE 38

Transferable Credits
a.   A bank is under no obligation to transfer a credit except to the extent and in the manner expressly consented to by that bank.
b.   For the purpose of this article: Transferable credit means a credit that specifically states it is "transferable". A transferable credit may be made available in whole or in part to another beneficiary ("second beneficiary") at the request of the beneficiary ("first beneficiary"). Transferring bank means a nominated bank that transfers the credit or, in a credit available with any bank, a bank that is specifically authorized by the issuing bank to transfer and that transfers the credit. An issuing bank may be a transferring bank.

   Transferred credit means a credit that has been made available by the transferring bank to a second beneficiary.
c.   Unless otherwise agreed at the time of transfer, all charges (such as commissions, fees, costs or expenses) incurred in respect of a transfer must be paid by the first beneficiary.

d. A credit may be transferred in part to more than one second beneficiary provided partial drawings or shipments are allowed.

    A transferred credit cannot be transferred at the request of a second beneficiary to any subsequent beneficiary. The first beneficiary is not considered to be a subsequent beneficiary.

e. Any request for transfer must indicate if and under what conditions amendments may be advised to the second beneficiary. The transferred credit must clearly indicate those conditions.

f. If a credit is transferred to more than one second beneficiary, rejection of an amendment by one or more second beneficiary does not invalidate the acceptance by any other second beneficiary, with respect to which the transferred credit will be amended accordingly. For any second beneficiary that rejected the amendment, the transferred credit will remain unamended.

g. The transferred credit must accurately reflect the terms and conditions of the credit, including confirmation, if any, with the exception of:
    - the amount of the credit,
    - any unit price stated therein,
    - the expiry date,
    - the period for presentation, or
    - the latest shipment date or given period for shipment,
    any or all of which may be reduced or curtailed.

    The percentage for which insurance cover must be effected may be increased to provide the amount of cover stipulated in the credit or these articles.

    The name of the first beneficiary may be substituted for that of the applicant in the credit.

    If the name of the applicant is specifically required by the credit to appear in any document other than the invoice, such requirement must be reflected in the transferred credit.

h. The first beneficiary has the right to substitute its own invoice and draft, if any, for those of a second beneficiary for an amount not in excess of that stipulated in the credit, and upon such substitution the first beneficiary can draw under the credit for the difference, if any, between its invoice and the invoice of a second beneficiary.

i. If the first beneficiary is to present its own invoice and draft, if any, but fails to do so on first demand, or if the invoices presented by the first beneficiary create discrepancies that did not exist in the presentation made by the second beneficiary and the first beneficiary fails to correct them on first demand, the transferring bank has the right to present the documents as received from the second beneficiary to the issuing bank, without further responsibility to the first beneficiary.

j. The first beneficiary may, in its request for transfer, indicate that honour or negotiation is to be effected to a second beneficiary at the place to which the credit has been transferred, up to and including the expiry date of the credit. This is without prejudice to the right of the first beneficiary in accordance with sub-article 38 (h).

k. Presentation of documents by or on behalf of a second beneficiary must be made to the transferring bank.

ARTICLE 39

Assignment of Proceeds

The fact that a credit is not stated to be transferable shall not affect the right of the beneficiary to assign any proceeds to which it may be or may become entitled under the credit, in accordance with the provisions of applicable law. This article relates only to the assignment of proceeds and not to the assignment of the right to perform under the credit.

ICC Uniform Customs and Practice for Documentary Credits 600E

Scope of the eUCP
a. The Supplement to the Uniform Customs and Practice for Documentary Credits for Electronic Presentation ("eUCP") supplements the Uniform Customs and Practice for Documentary Credits (2007 Revision ICC Publication No. 600) ("UCP") in order to accommodate presentation of electronic records alone or in combination with paper documents.
b. The eUCP shall apply as a supplement to the UCP where the credit indicates that it is subject to eUCP.
c. This version is Version 1.1. A credit must indicate the applicable version of the eUCP. If it does not do so, it is subject to the version in effect on the date the credit is issued or, if made subject to eUCP by an amendment accepted by the beneficiary, on the date of that amendment.

ARTICLE E2

Relationship of the eUCP to the UCP
a. A credit subject to the eUCP ("eUCP credit") is also subject to the UCP without express incorporation of the UCP.
b. Where the eUCP applies, its provisions shall prevail to the extent that they would produce a result different from the application of the UCP.
c. If an eUCP credit allows the beneficiary to choose between presentation of paper documents or electronic records and it chooses to present only paper documents, the UCP alone shall apply to that presentation. If only paper documents are permitted under an eUCP credit, the UCP alone shall apply.

ARTICLE E3

Definitions
a. Where the following terms are used in the UCP, for the purposes of applying the UCP to an electronic record presented under an eUCP credit, the term:

i.   appear on their face and the like shall apply to examination of the data content of an electronic record.

ii. document shall include an electronic record.

iii. place for presentation of electronic records means an electronic address.

iv. sign and the like shall include an electronic signature.

v.   superimposed, notation or stamped means data content whose supplementary character is apparent in an electronic record.

b. The following terms used in the eUCP shall have the following meanings:

i.   electronic record means
   • data created, generated, sent, communicated, received or stored by electronic means
   • that is capable of being authenticated as to the apparent identity of a sender and the apparent source of the data contained in it, and as to whether it has remained complete and unaltered, and
   • is capable of being examined for compliance with the terms and conditions of the eUCP credit.

ii. electronic signature means a data process attached to or logically associated with an electronic record and executed or adopted by a person in order to identify that person and to indicate that person's authentication of the electronic record.

iii. format means the data organization in which the electronic record is expressed or to which it refers.

iv. paper document means a document in a traditional paper form.

v.   received means the time when an electronic record enters the information system of the applicable recipient in a form capable of being accepted by that system. Any acknowledgement of receipt does not imply acceptance or refusal of the electronic record under an eUCP credit.

ARTICLE E4

Format

An eUCP credit must specify the formats in which electronic records are to be presented. If the format of the electronic record is not so specified, it may be presented in any format.

ARTICLE E5

Presentation

a. An eUCP credit allowing presentation of:

i.   electronic records must state a place for presentation of the electronic records.

ii. both electronic records and paper documents must also state a place for presentation of the paper documents.

b. Electronic records may be presented separately and need not be presented at the same time.

c. If an eUCP credit allows for presentation of one or more electronic records, the beneficiary is responsible for providing a notice to the bank to which presentation is made signifying when the presentation is complete. The notice of completeness may be given as an electronic record or paper document and must identify the eUCP credit to which it relates. Presentation is deemed not to have been made if the beneficiary's notice is not received.

d.   i.   Each presentation of an electronic record and the presentation of paper documents under an eUCP credit must identify the eUCP credit under which it is presented.

ii.   A presentation not so identified may be treated as not received.

e.   If the bank to which presentation is to be made is open but its system is unable to receive a transmitted electronic record on the stipulated expiry date and/or the last day of the period of time after the date of shipment for presentation, as the case may be, the bank will be deemed to be closed and the date for presentation and/or the expiry date shall be extended to the first following banking day on which such bank is able to receive an electronic record. If the only electronic record remaining to be presented is the notice of completeness, it may be given by telecommunications or by paper document and will be deemed timely, provided that it is sent before the bank is able to receive an electronic record.

f.   An electronic record that cannot be authenticated is deemed not to have been presented.

ARTICLE E6

Examination

a.   If an electronic record contains a hyperlink to an external system or a presentation indicates that the electronic record may be examined by reference to an external system, the electronic record at the hyperlink or the referenced system shall be deemed to be the electronic record to be examined. The failure of the indicated system to provide access to the required electronic record at the time of examination shall constitute a discrepancy.

b.   The forwarding of electronic records by a nominated bank pursuant to its nomination signifies that it has satisfied itself as to the apparent authenticity of the electronic records.

c.   The inability of the issuing bank, or confirming bank, if any, to examine an electronic record in a format required by the eUCP credit or, if no format is required, to examine it in the format presented is not a basis for refusal.

ARTICLE E7

Notice of Refusal

a.   i.   The time period for the examination of documents commences on the banking day following the banking day on which the beneficiary's notice of completeness is received.

ii.   If the time for presentation of documents or the notice of completeness is extended, the time for the examination of documents commences on the first following banking day on which the bank to which presentation is to be made is able to receive the notice of completeness.

b.   If an issuing bank, the confirming bank, if any, or a nominated bank acting on their behalf, provides a notice of refusal of a presentation which includes electronic records and does not receive instructions from the party to which notice of refusal is given within 30 calendar days from the date the notice of refusal is given for the disposition of the electronic records, the bank shall return any paper documents not previously returned to the presenter but may dispose of the electronic records in any manner deemed appropriate without any responsibility.

ARTICLE E8

Originals and Copies
Any requirement of the UCP or an eUCP credit for presentation of one or more originals or copies of an electronic record is satisfied by the presentation of one electronic record.

ARTICLE E9

Date of Issuance
Unless an electronic record contains a specific date of issuance, the date on which it appears to have been sent by the issuer is deemed to be the date of issuance. The date of receipt will be deemed to be the date it was sent if no other date is apparent.

ARTICLE E10

Transport
If an electronic record evidencing transport does not indicate a date of shipment or dispatch, the date of issuance of the electronic record will be deemed to be the date of shipment or dispatch. However, if the electronic record bears a notation that evidences the date of shipment or dispatch, the date of the notation will be deemed to be the date of shipment or dispatch. A notation showing additional data content need not be separately signed or otherwise authenticated.

ARTICLE E11

Corruption of an Electronic Record After Presentation
a.   If an electronic record that has been received by the issuing bank, confirming bank, or another nominated bank appears to have been corrupted, the bank may inform the presenter and may request that the electronic record be re-presented.
b.   If the bank requests that an electronic record be re-presented:
   i.   the time for examination is suspended and resumes when the presenter re-presents the electronic record; and
   ii.   if the nominated bank is not the confirming bank, it must provide the issuing bank and any confirming bank with notice of the request for re-presentation and inform it of the suspension; but
   iii.   if the same electronic record is not re-presented within thirty (30) calendar days, the bank may treat the electronic recordas not presented, and
   iv.   any deadlines are not extended.

ARTICLE E12

Additional Disclaimer of Liability for Presentation of Electronic Records under eUCP
By satisfying itself as to the apparent authenticity of an electronic record, banks assume no liability for the identity of the sender, source of the information or its complete and unaltered character other than that which is apparent in the electronic record received by the use of a commercially acceptable data process for the receipt, authentication and identification of electronic records.

Appendix 2

ICC Uniform Customs and Practice for Documentary Credits 500

A. GENERAL PROVISIONS AND DEFINITIONS

ARTICLE 1

Application of UCP
The Uniform Customs and Practice for Documentary Credits, 1993 Revision, ICC Publication N°500, shall apply to all Documentary Credits (including to the extent to which they may be applicable, Standby Letter(s) of Credit) where they are incorporated into the text of the Credit. They are binding on all parties thereto, unless otherwise expressly stipulated in the Credit.

ARTICLE 2

Meaning of Credit
For the purposes of these Articles, the expressions "Documentary Credit(s)" and "Standby Letter(s) of Credit" (hereinafter referred to as "Credit(s)"), mean any arrangement, however named or described, whereby a bank (the "Issuing Bank") acting at the request and on the instructions of a customer (the "Applicant") or on its own behalf,

  i.   is to make a payment to or to the order of a third party (the "Beneficiary"), or is to accept and pay bills of exchange (Draft(s)) drawn by the Beneficiary, or

  ii. authorises another bank to effect such payment, or to accept and pay such bills of exchange (Draft(s)), or

  iii. authorises another bank to negotiate,

against stipulated document(s),provided that the terms and conditions of the Credit are complied with.

   For the purposes of these Articles, branches of a bank in different countries are considered another bank.

a Credits, by their nature, are separate transactions from the sales or other contract(s) on which they may be based and banks are in no way concerned with or bound by such contract(s), even if any reference whatsoever to such contract(s)

469

is included in the Credit. Consequently, the undertaking of a bank to pay, accept and pay Draft(s) or negotiate and/or to fulfil any other obligation under the Credit, is not subject to claims or defences by the Applicant resulting from his relationships with the Issuing Bank or the Beneficiary.

b   A Beneficiary can in no case avail himself of the contractual relationships existing between the banks or between the Applicant and the Issuing Bank.

ARTICLE 4

Documents v. Goods/Services/Performances
In Credit operations all parties concerned deal with documents, and not with goods, services and/or other performances to which the documents may relate.

ARTICLE 5

Instructions to Issue/Amend Credits
a   Instructions for the issuance of a Credit, the Credit itself, instructions for an amendment thereto, and the amendment itself, must be complete and precise.
   In order to guard against confusion and misunderstanding, banks should discourage any attempt:
   i.   to include excessive detail in the Credit or in any amendment thereto;
   ii. to give instructions to issue, advise or confirm a Credit by reference to a Credit previously issued (similar Credit) where such previous Credit has been subject to accepted amend-ment(s), and/or unaccepted amendment(s).
b   All instructions for the issuance of a Credit and the Credit itself and, where applicable, all instructions for an amendment thereto and the amendment itself, must state precisely the document(s) against which payment, acceptance or negotiation is to be made.

B. FORM AND NOTIFICATION OF CREDITS

ARTICLE 6

Revocable v. Irrevocable Credits
a   A Credit may be either
   i.   revocable,
      or
   ii. irrevocable.
b   The Credit, therefore, should clearly indicate whether it is revocable or irrevocable.
c   In the absence of such indication the Credit shall be deemed to be irrevocable.

ARTICLE 7

Advising Bank's Liability
a   A Credit may be advised to a Beneficiary through another bank (the "Advising Bank") without engagement on the part of the Advising Bank, but that bank, if it elects to advise the Credit, shall take reasonable care to check the apparent authenticity of the Credit which it advises. If the bank elects not to advise the Credit, it must so inform the Issuing Bank without delay.

b   If the Advising Bank cannot establish such apparent authenticity it must inform, without delay, the bank from which the instructions appear to have been received that it has been unable to establish the authenticity of the Credit and if it elects nonetheless to advise the Credit it must inform the Beneficiary that it has not been able to establish the authenticity of the Credit.

ARTICLE 8

Revocation of a Credit

a   A revocable Credit may be amended or cancelled by the Issuing Bank at any moment and without prior notice to the Beneficiary.

b   However, the Issuing Bank must:
   i.   reimburse another bank with which a revocable Credit has been made available for sight payment, acceptance or negotiation - for any payment, acceptance or negotiation made by such bank - prior to receipt by it of notice of amendment or cancellation, against documents which appear on their face to be in compliance with the terms and conditions of the Credit;
   ii. reimburse another bank with which a revocable Credit has been made available for deferred payment, if such a bank has, prior to receipt by it of notice of amendment or cancellation, taken up documents which appear on their face to be in compliance with the terms and conditions of the Credit.

ARTICLE 9

Liability of Issuing and Confirming Banks

a   An irrevocable Credit constitutes a definite undertaking of the Issuing Bank, provided that the stipulated documents are presented to the Nominated Bank or to the Issuing Bank and that the terms and conditions of the Credit are complied with:
   i.   if the Credit provides for sight payment – to pay at sight;
   ii. if the Credit provides for deferred payment – to pay on the maturity date(s) determinable in accordance with the stipulations of the Credit;
   iii. if the Credit provides for acceptance:
a. by the Issuing Bank – to accept Draft(s) drawn by the Beneficiary on the Issuing Bank and pay them at maturity,
   or
b. by another drawee bank – to accept and pay at maturity Draft(s) drawn by the Beneficiary on the Issuing Bank in the event the drawee bank stipulated in the Credit does not accept Draft(s) drawn on it, or to pay Draft(s) accepted but not paid by such drawee bank at maturity;
   iv. if the Credit provides for negotiation – to pay without recourse to drawers and/or bona fide holders, Draft(s) drawn by the Beneficiary and/ or document(s) presented under the Credit. A Credit should not be issued available by Draft(s) on the Applicant. If the Credit nevertheless calls for Draft(s) on the Applicant, banks will consider such Draft(s) as an additional document(s).

b   A confirmation of an irrevocable Credit by another bank (the "Confirming Bank") upon the authorisation or request of the Issuing Bank, constitutes a definite undertaking of the Confirming Bank, in addition to that of the Issuing Bank, provided that the stipulated documents are presented to the Confirming Bank or to any other Nominated Bank and that the terms and conditions of the Credit are complied with:

      i.   if the Credit provides for sight payment – to pay at sight;

      ii.   if the Credit provides for deferred payment – to pay on the maturity date(s) determinable in accordance with the stipulations of the Credit;

     iii. if the Credit provides for acceptance:

         a. by the Confirming Bank – to accept Draft(s) drawn by the Beneficiary on the Confirming Bank and pay them at maturity,

          or

         b. by another drawee bank – to accept and pay at maturity Draft(s) drawn by the Beneficiary on the Confirming Bank, in the event the drawee bank stipulated in the Credit does not accept Draft(s) drawn on it, or to pay Draft(s) accepted but not paid by such drawee bank at maturity;

     iv. if the Credit provides for negotiation – to negotiate without recourse to drawers and/or bona fide holders, Draft(s) drawn by the Beneficiary and/or document(s) presented under the Credit. A Credit should not be issued available by Draft(s) on the Applicant. If the Credit nevertheless calls for Draft(s) on the Applicant, banks will consider such Draft(s) as an additional document(s).

c   i.   If another bank is authorised or requested by the Issuing Bank to add its confirmation to a Credit but is not prepared to do so, it must so inform the Issuing Bank without delay.

     ii.   Unless the Issuing Bank specifies otherwise in its authorisation or request to add confirmation, the Advising Bank may advise the Credit to the Beneficiary without adding its confirmation.

d   i.   Except as otherwise provided by Article 48, an irrevocable Credit can neither be amended nor cancelled without the agreement of the Issuing Bank, the Confirming Bank, if any, and the Beneficiary.

     ii.   The Issuing Bank shall be irrevocably bound by an amendment(s) issued by it from the time of the issuance of such amendment(s). A Confirming Bank may extend its confirmation to an amendment and shall be irrevocably bound

as of the time of its advice of the amendment. A Confirming Bank may, however, choose to advise an amendment to the Beneficiary without extending its confirmation and if so, must inform the Issuing Bank and the Beneficiary without delay.

     iii. The terms of the original Credit (or a Credit incorporating previously accepted amend-ment(s)) will remain in force for the Beneficiary until the Beneficiary communicates his acceptance of the amendment to the bank that advised such amendment. The Beneficiary should give notification of acceptance or rejection of amendment(s). If the Beneficiary fails to give such notification, the tender of documents to the Nominated Bank or Issuing Bank, that conform to the Credit and to not yet accepted amendment(s), will be deemed to be notification of acceptance by the Beneficiary of such amendment(s) and as of that moment the Credit will be amended.

     iv. Partial acceptance of amendments contained in one and the same advice of amendment is not allowed and consequently will not be given any effect.

ARTICLE 10

Types of Credit

a   All Credits must clearly indicate whether they are available by sight payment, by deferred payment, by acceptance or by negotiation.

b   i.   Unless the Credit stipulates that it is available only with the Issuing Bank, all Credits must nominate the bank (the "Nominated Bank") which is authorised to pay, to incur a deferred payment undertaking, to accept Draft(s) or to negotiate. In a freely negotiable Credit, any bank is a Nominated Bank.

Presentation of documents must be made to the Issuing Bank or the Confirming Bank, if any, or any other Nominated Bank.

    ii.   Negotiation means the giving of value for Draft(s) and/or document(s) by the bank authorised to negotiate. Mere examination of the documents without giving of value does not constitute a negotiation.

c   Unless the Nominated Bank is the Confirming Bank, nomination by the Issuing Bank does not constitute any undertaking by the Nominated Bank to pay, to incur a deferred payment undertaking, to accept Draft(s), or to negotiate. Except where expressly agreed to by the Nominated Bank and so communicated to the Beneficiary, the Nominated Bank's receipt of and/or examination and/or forwarding of the documents does not make that bank liable to pay, to incur a deferred payment undertaking, to accept Draft(s), or to negotiate.

d   By nominating another bank, or by allowing for negotiation by any bank, or by authorising or requesting another bank to add its confirmation, the Issuing Bank authorises such bank to pay, accept Draft(s) or negotiate as the case may be, against documents which appear on their face to be in compliance with the terms and conditions of the Credit and undertakes to reimburse such bank in accordance with the provisions of these Articles.

ARTICLE 11

Teletransmitted and Pre-Advised Credits

a   i.   When an Issuing Bank instructs an Advising Bank by an authenticated teletransmission to advise a Credit or an amendment to a Credit, the teletransmission will be deemed to be the operative Credit instrument or the operative amendment, and no mail confirmation should be sent. Should a mail confirmation nevertheless be sent, it will have no effect and the Advising Bank will have no obligation to check such mail confirmation against the operative Credit instrument or the operative amendment received by teletransmission.

    ii.   If the teletransmission states "full details to follow" (or words of similar effect) or states that the mail confirmation is to be the operative Credit instrument or the operative amendment, then the teletransmission will not be deemed to be the operative Credit instrument or the operative amendment. The Issuing Bank must forward the operative Credit instrument or the operative amendment to such Advising Bank without delay.

b   If a bank uses the services of an Advising Bank to have the Credit advised to the Beneficiary, it must also use the services of the same bank for advising an amendment(s).

c   A preliminary advice of the issuance or amendment of an irrevocable Credit (pre-advice), shall only be given by an Issuing Bank if such bank is prepared to issue the operative Credit instrument or the operative amendment thereto. Unless otherwise stated in such preliminary advice by the Issuing Bank, an Issuing Bank having given such pre-advice shall be irrevocably committed to issue or amend the Credit, in terms not inconsistent with the pre-advice, without delay.

ARTICLE 12

Incomplete or Unclear Instructions

If incomplete or unclear instructions are received to advise, confirm or amend a Credit, the bank requested to act on such instructions may give preliminary notification to the

Beneficiary for information only and without responsibility. This preliminary notification should state clearly that the notification is provided for information only and without the responsibility of the Advising Bank. In any event, the Advising Bank must inform the Issuing Bank of the action taken and request it to provide the necessary information.

The Issuing Bank must provide the necessary information without delay. The Credit will be advised, confirmed or amended, only when complete and clear instructions have been received and if the Advising Bank is then prepared to act on the instructions.

C. LIABILITIES AND RESPONSIBILITIES

ARTICLE 13

Standard for Examination of Documents

a   Banks must examine all documents stipulated in the Credit with reasonable care, to ascertain whether or not they appear, on their face, to be in compliance with the terms and conditions of the Credit. Compliance of the stipulated documents on their face with the terms and conditions of the Credit, shall be determined by international standard banking practice as reflected in these Articles. Documents which appear on their face to be inconsistent with one another will be considered as not appearing on their face to be in compliance with the terms and conditions of the Credit.

     Documents not stipulated in the Credit will not be examined by banks. If they receive such documents, they shall return them to the presenter or pass them on without responsibility.

b   The Issuing Bank, the Confirming Bank, if any, or a Nominated Bank acting on their behalf, shall each have a reasonable time, not to exceed seven banking days following the day of receipt of the documents, to examine the documents and determine whether to take up or refuse the documents and to inform the party from which it received the documents accordingly.

c   If a Credit contains conditions without stating the document(s) to be presented in compliance therewith, banks will deem such conditions as not stated and will disregard them.

ARTICLE 14

Discrepant Documents and Notice

a   When the Issuing Bank authorises another bank to pay, incur a deferred payment undertaking, accept Draft(s), or negotiate against documents which appear on their face to be in compliance with the terms and conditions of the Credit, the Issuing Bank and the Confirming Bank, if any, are bound:

     i.   to reimburse the Nominated Bank which has paid, incurred a deferred payment undertaking, accepted Draft(s), or negotiated,

     ii.   to take up the documents.

b   Upon receipt of the documents the Issuing Bank and /or Confirming Bank, if any, or a Nominated Bank acting on their behalf, must determine on the basis of the documents alone whether or not they appear on their face to be in compliance with the terms and conditions of the Credit. If the documents appear on their face not to be in compliance with the terms and conditions of the Credit, such banks may refuse to take up the documents.

c   If the Issuing Bank determines that the documents appear on their face not to be in compliance with the terms and conditions of the Credit, it may in its sole judgment approach the Applicant for a waiver of the discrepancy(ies). This does not, however, extend the period mentioned in sub-Article 13 (b).

d   i.   If the Issuing Bank and/or Confirming Bank, if any, or a Nominated Bank acting on their behalf, decides to refuse the documents, it must give notice to that effect by telecommunication or, if that is not possible, by other expeditious means, without delay but no later than the close of the seventh banking day following the day of receipt of the documents. Such notice shall be given to the bank from which it received the documents, or to the Beneficiary, if it received the documents directly from him.

    ii.   Such notice must state all discrepancies in respect of which the bank refuses the documents and must also state whether it is holding the documents at the disposal of, or is returning them to, the presenter.

    iii.   The Issuing Bank and/or Confirming Bank, if any, shall then be entitled to claim from the remitting bank refund, with interest, of any reimbursement which has been made to that bank.

e   If the Issuing Bank and/or Confirming Bank, if any, fails to act in accordance with the provisions of this Article and/or fails to hold the documents at the disposal of, or return them to the presenter, the Issuing Bank and/or Confirming Bank, if any, shall be precluded from claiming that the documents are not in compliance with the terms and conditions of the Credit.

f   If the remitting bank draws the attention of the Issuing Bank and/or Confirming Bank, if any, to any discrepancy(ies) in the document(s) or advises such banks that it has paid, incurred a deferred payment undertaking, accepted Draft(s) or negotiated under reserve or against an indemnity in respect of such discrepancy(ies), the Issuing Bank and/or Confirming Bank, if any, shall not be thereby relieved from any of their obligations under any provision of this Article. Such reserve or indemnity concerns only the relations between the remitting bank and the party towards whom the reserve was made, or from whom, or on whose behalf, the indemnity was obtained.

ARTICLE 15

Disclaimer on Effectiveness of Documents
Banks assume no liability or responsibility for the form, sufficiency, accuracy, genuineness, falsification or legal effect of any document(s), or for the general and/or particular conditions stipulated in the document(s) or superimposed thereon; nor do they assume any liability or responsibility for the description, quantity, weight, quality, condition, packing, delivery, value or existence of the goods represented by any document(s), or for the good faith or acts and/or omissions, solvency, performance or standing of the consignors, the carriers, the forwarders, the consignees or the insurers of the goods, or any other person whomsoever.

ARTICLE 16

Disclaimer on the Transmission of Messages
Banks assume no liability or responsibility for the consequences arising out of delay and/or loss in transit of any message(s), letter(s) or document(s), or for delay, mutilation or other error(s) arising in the transmission of any telecommunication. Banks assume no liability or responsibility for errors in translation and/or

interpretation of technical terms, and reserve the right to transmit Credit terms without translating them.

ARTICLE 17

Force Majeure
Banks assume no liability or responsibility for the consequences arising out of the interruption of their business by Acts of God, riots, civil commotions, insurrections, wars or any other causes beyond their control, or by any strikes or lockouts. Unless specifically authorised, banks will not, upon resumption of their business, pay, incur a deferred payment undertaking, accept Draft(s) or negotiate under Credits which expired during such interruption of their business.

ARTICLE 18

Disclaimer for Acts of an Instructed Party
a   Banks utilizing the services of another bank or other banks for the purpose of giving effect to the instructions of the Applicant do so for the account and at the risk of such Applicant.
b   Banks assume no liability or responsibility should the instructions they transmit not be carried out, even if they have themselves taken the initiative in the choice of such other bank(s).
c   i.   A party instructing another party to perform services is liable for any charges, including commissions, fees, costs or expenses incurred by the instructed party in connection with its instructions.
    ii.   Where a Credit stipulates that such charges are for the account of a party other than the instructing party, and charges cannot be collected, the instructing party remains ultimately liable for the payment thereof.
d   The Applicant shall be bound by and liable to indemnify the banks against all obligations and responsibilities imposed by foreign laws and usages.

ARTICLE 19

Bank-to-Bank Reimbursement Arrangements
a   If an Issuing Bank intends that the reimbursement to which a paying, accepting or negotiating bank is entitled, shall be obtained by such bank (the "Claiming Bank"), claiming on another party (the "Reimbursing Bank"), it shall provide such Reimbursing Bank in good time with the proper instructions or authorisation to honour such reimbursement claims.
b   Issuing Banks shall not require a Claiming Bank to supply a certificate of compliance with the terms and conditions of the Credit to the Reimbursing Bank.
c   An Issuing Bank shall not be relieved from any of its obligations to provide reimbursement if and when reimbursement is not received by the Claiming Bank from the Reimbursing Bank.
d   The Issuing Bank shall be responsible to the Claiming Bank for any loss of interest if reimbursement is not provided by the Reimbursing Bank on first demand, or as otherwise specified in the Credit, or mutually agreed, as the case may be.
e   The Reimbursing Bank's charges should be for the account of the Issuing Bank. However, in cases where the charges are for the account of another party, it is the responsibility of the Issuing Bank to so indicate in the original Credit and in the

reimbursement authorisation. In cases where the Reimbursing Bank's charges are for the account of another party they shall be collected from the Claiming Bank when the Credit is drawn under. In cases where the Credit is not drawn under, the Reimbursing Bank's charges remain the obligation of the Issuing Bank.

D. DOCUMENTS

ARTICLE 20

Ambiguity as to the Issuers of Documents
a   Terms such as "first class", "well known", "qualified", "independent", "official", "competent", "local" and the like, shall not be used to describe the issuers of any document(s) to be presented under a Credit. If such terms are incorporated in the Credit, banks will accept the relative document(s) as presented, provided that it appears on its face to be in compliance with the other terms and conditions of the Credit and not to have been issued by the Beneficiary.
b   Unless otherwise stipulated in the Credit, banks will also accept as an original document(s), a document(s) produced or appearing to have been produced:
    i.   by reprographic, automated or computerized systems;
    ii. as carbon copies;
provided that it is marked as original and, where necessary, appears to be signed.
    A document may be signed by handwriting, by facsimile signature, by perforated signature, by stamp, by symbol, or by any other mechanical or electronic method of authentication.
c   i.   Unless otherwise stipulated in the Credit, banks will accept as a copy(ies), a document(s) either
    ii. Credits that require multiple document(s) such as "duplicate", "two fold", "two copies" and the like, will be satisfied by the presentation of one original and the remaining number in copies except where the document itself indicates otherwise.
d   Unless otherwise stipulated in the Credit, a condition under a Credit calling for a document to be authenticated, validated, legalised, visaed, certified or indicating a similar requirement, will be satisfied by any signature, mark, stamp or label on such document that on its face appears to satisfy the above condition.

ARTICLE 21

Unspecified Issuers or Contents of Documents
When documents other than transport documents, insurance documents and commercial invoices are called for, the Credit should stipulate by whom such documents are to be issued and their wording or data content. If the Credit does not so stipulate, banks will accept such documents as presented, provided that their data content is not inconsistent with any other stipulated document presented.

ARTICLE 22

Issuance Date of Documents v. Credit Date
Unless otherwise stipulated in the Credit, banks will accept a document bearing a date of issuance prior to that of the Credit, subject to such document being presented within the time limits set out in the Credit and in these Articles.

ARTICLE 23

Marine/Ocean Bill of Lading

a   If a Credit calls for a bill of lading covering a port-to-port shipment, banks will, unless otherwise stipulated in the Credit, accept a document, however named, which:

    i.   appears on its face to indicate the name of the carrier and to have been signed or otherwise authenticated by:

      –   the carrier or a named agent for or on behalf of the carrier, or

      –   the master or a named agent for or on behalf of the master.

Any signature or authentication of the carrier or master must be identified as carrier or master, as the case may be. An agent signing or authenticating for the carrier or master must also indicate the name and the capacity of the party, i.e. carrier or master, on whose behalf that agent is acting,

      and

    ii.   indicates that the goods have been loaded on board, or shipped on a named vessel.

Loading on board or shipment on a named vessel may be indicated by pre-printed wording on the bill of lading that the goods have been loaded on board a named vessel or shipped on a named vessel, in which case the date of issuance of the bill of lading will be deemed to be the date of loading on board and the date of shipment.

In all other cases loading on board a named vessel must be evidenced by a notation on the bill of lading which gives the date on which the goods have been loaded on board, in which case the date of the on board notation will be deemed to be the date of shipment.

If the bill of lading contains the indication "intended vessel", or similar qualification in relation to the vessel, loading on board a named vessel must be evidenced by an on board notation on the bill of lading which, in addition to the date on which the goods have been loaded on board, also includes the name of the vessel on which the goods have been loaded, even if they have been loaded on the vessel named as the "intended vessel".

If the bill of lading indicates a place of receipt or taking in charge different from the port of loading, the on board notation must also include the port of loading stipulated in the Credit and the name of the vessel on which the goods have been loaded, even if they have been loaded on the vessel named in the bill of lading. This provision also applies whenever loading on board the vessel is indicated by pre-printed wording on the bill of lading,

      and

    iii.   indicates the port of loading and the port of discharge stipulated in the Credit, notwithstanding that it:

a.   indicates a place of taking in charge different from the port of loading, and/or a place of final destination different from the port of discharge,

    and/or

b.   contains the indication "intended" or similar qualification in relation to the port of loading and/or port of discharge, as long as the document also states the ports of loading and/or discharge stipulated in the Credit,

      and

    iv.   consists of a sole original bill of lading or, if issued in more than one original, the full set as so issued,

    v.   appears to contain all of the terms and conditions of carriage, or some of such terms and conditions by reference to a source or document other than the bill of lading (short form/ blank back bill of lading); banks will not examine the contents of such terms and conditions, and

    vi.   contains no indication that it is subject to a charter party and/or no indication that the carrying vessel is propelled by sail only,

      and

    vii. in all other respects meets the stipulations of the Credit.

b   For the purpose of this Article, transhipment means unloading and reloading from one vessel to another vessel during the course of ocean carriage from the port of loading to the port of discharge stipulated in the Credit.

c   Unless transhipment is prohibited by the terms of the Credit, banks will accept a bill of lading which indicates that the goods will be transhipped, provided that the entire ocean carriage is covered by one and the same bill of lading.

d   Even if the Credit prohibits transhipment, banks will accept a bill of lading which:

    i.   indicates that transhipment will take place as long as the relevant cargo is shipped in Container(s), Trailer(s) and/or "LASH" barge(s) as evidenced by the bill of lading, provided that the entire ocean carriage is covered by one and the same bill of lading,

    and/or

    ii.   incorporates clauses stating that the carrier reserves the right to tranship.

ARTICLE 24

Non-Negotiable Sea Waybill

a   If a Credit calls for a non-negotiable sea waybill covering a port-to-port shipment, banks will, unless otherwise stipulated in the Credit, accept a document, however named, which:

    i.   appears on its face to indicate the name of the carrier and to have been signed or otherwise authenticated by:

       –   the carrier or a named agent for or on behalf of the carrier, or

       –   the master or a named agent for or on behalf of the master,

    Any signature or authentication of the carrier or master must be identified as carrier or master, as the case may be. An agent signing or authenticating for the carrier or master must also indicate the name and the capacity of the party, i.e. carrier or master, on whose behalf that agent is acting,

    and

    ii.   indicates that the goods have been loaded on board, or shipped on a named vessel.

       Loading on board or shipment on a named vessel may be indicated by pre-printed wording on the non-negotiable sea waybill that the goods have been loaded on board a named vessel or shipped on a named vessel, in which case the date of issuance of the non-negotiable sea waybill will be deemed to be the date of loading on board and the date of shipment.

       In all other cases loading on board a named vessel must be evidenced by a notation on the non-negotiable sea waybill which gives the date on which the goods have been loaded on board, in which case the date of the on board notation will be deemed to be the date of shipment.

       If the non-negotiable sea waybill contains the indication "intended vessel", or similar qualification in relation to the vessel, loading on board a named vessel must be evidenced by an on board notation on the non-negotiable sea waybill which, in addition to the date on which the goods have been loaded on board, includes the name of the vessel on which the goods have been loaded, even if they have been loaded on the vessel named as the "intended vessel".

If the non-negotiable sea waybill indicates a place of receipt or taking in charge different from the port of loading, the on board notation must also include the port of loading stipulated in the Credit and the name of the vessel on which the goods have been loaded, even if they have been loaded on a vessel named in the non-negotiable sea waybill. This provision also applies whenever loading on board the vessel is indicated by pre-printed wording on the nonnegotiable sea waybill,
and

   iii.   indicates the port of loading and the port of discharge stipulated in the Credit, notwithstanding that it:

      a.   indicates a place of taking in charge different from the port of loading, and/or a place of final destination different from the port of discharge, and/or

      b.   contains the indication "intended" or similar qualification in relation to the port of loading and/or port of discharge, as long as the document also states the ports of loading and/or discharge stipulated in the Credit,
and

   iv.   consists of a sole original non-negotiable sea waybill, or if issued in more than one original, the full set as so issued,

   v.   appears to contain all of the terms and conditions of carriage, or some of such terms and conditions by reference to a source or document other than the non-negotiable sea waybill (short form/blank back non-negotiable sea waybill); banks will not examine the contents of such terms and conditions,
and

   vi.   contains no indication that it is subject to a charter party and/or no indication that the carrying vessel is propelled by sail only,
and

   vii.   in all other respects meets the stipulations of the Credit.

b   For the purpose of this Article, transhipment means unloading and reloading from one vessel to another vessel during the course of ocean carriage from the port of loading to the port of discharge stipulated in the Credit.

c   Unless transhipment is prohibited by the terms of the Credit, banks will accept a non-negotiable sea waybill which indicates that the goods will be transhipped, provided that the entire ocean carriage is covered by one and the same non-negotiable sea waybill.

d   Even if the Credit prohibits transhipment, banks will accept a non-negotiable sea waybill which:

   i.   indicates that transhipment will take place as long as the relevant cargo is shipped in Container(s), Trailer(s) and/or "LASH" barge(s) as evidenced by the non-negotiable sea waybill, provided that the entire ocean carriage is covered by one and the same non-negotiable sea waybill,
and/or

   ii.   incorporates clauses stating that the carrier reserves the right to tranship.

ARTICLE 25

Charter Party Bill of Lading

a   If a Credit calls for or permits a charter party bill of lading, banks will, unless otherwise stipulated in the Credit, accept a document, however named, which:

   i.   contains any indication that it is subject to a charter party,
and

   ii.   appears on its face to have been signed or otherwise authenticated by:

     – the master or a named agent for or on behalf of the master, or
     – the owner or a named agent for or on behalf of the owner.

    Any signature or authentication of the master or owner must be identified as master or owner as the case may be. An agent signing or authenticating for the master or owner must also indicate the name and the capacity of the party, i.e. master or owner, on whose behalf thatagent is acting, and

iii. does or does not indicate the name of the carrier, and

iv. indicates that the goods have been loaded on board or shipped on a named vessel.

    Loading on board or shipment on a named vessel may be indicated by pre-printed wording on the bill of lading that the goods have been loaded on board a named vessel or shipped on a named vessel, in which case the date of issuance of the bill of lading will be deemed to be the date of loading on board and the date of shipment.

    In all other cases loading on board a named vessel must be evidenced by a notation on the bill of lading which gives the date on which the goods have been loaded on board, in which case the date of the on board notation will be deemed to be the date of shipment, and

v. indicates the port of loading and the port of discharge stipulated in the Credit, and

vi. consists of a sole original bill of lading or, if issued in more than one original, the full set as so issued, and

vii. contains no indication that the carrying vessel is propelled by sail only, and

viii. in all other respects meets the stipulations of the Credit.

b Even if the Credit requires the presentation of a charter party contract in connection with a charter party bill of lading, banks will not examine such charter party contract, but will pass it on without responsibility on their part.

ARTICLE 26

Multimodal Transport Document

a If a Credit calls for a transport document covering at least two different modes of transport (multimodal transport), banks will, unless otherwise stipulated in the Credit, accept a document, however named, which:

i. appears on its face to indicate the name of the carrier or multimodal transport operator and to have been signed or otherwise authenticated by:
     – the carrier or multimodal transport operator or a named agent for or on behalf of the carrier or multimodal transport operator, or
     – the master or a named agent for or on behalf of the master.

    Any signature or authentication of the carrier, multimodal transport operator or master must be identified as carrier, multimodal transport operator or master, as the case may be. An agent signing or authenticating for the carrier, multimodal transport operator or master must also indicate the name and the capacity of the party, i.e. carrier, multimodal transport operator or master, on whose behalf that agent is acting, and

   ii. indicates that the goods have been dispatched, taken in charge or loaded on board.

        Dispatch, taking in charge or loading on board may be indicated by wording to that effect on the multimodal transport document and the date of issuance will be deemed to be the date of dispatch, taking in charge or loading on board and the date of shipment. However, if the document indicates, by stamp or otherwise, a date of dispatch, taking in charge or loading on board, such date will be deemed to be the date of shipment,
and

   iii. a. indicates the place of taking in charge stipulated in the Credit which may be different from the port, airport or place of loading, and the place of final destination stipulated in the Credit which may be different from the port, airport or place of discharge,

       and/or

       b. contains the indication "intended" or similar qualification in relation to the vessel and/or port of loading and/or port of discharge,

  and

   iv. consists of a sole original multimodal transport document or, if issued in more than one original, the full set as so issued,
and

   v. appears to contain all of the terms and conditions of carriage, or some of such terms and conditions by reference to a source or document other than the multimodal transport document (short form/blank back multimodal transport document); banks will not examine the contents of such terms and conditions,
and

   vi. contains no indication that it is subject to a charter party and/or no indication that the carrying vessel is propelled by sail only,
and

   vii. in all other respects meets the stipulations of the Credit.

b   Even if the Credit prohibits transhipment, banks will accept a multimodal transport document which indicates that transhipment will or may take place, provided that the entire carriage is covered by one and the same multimodal transport document.

ARTICLE 27

Air Transport Document

a   If a Credit calls for an air transport document, banks will, unless otherwise stipulated in the Credit, accept a document, however named, which:

   i. appears on its face to indicate the name of the carrier and to have been signed or otherwise authenticated by:

      – the carrier, or

      – a named agent for or on behalf of the carrier.

     Any signature or authentication of the carrier must be identified as carrier. An agent signing or authenticating for the carrier must also indicate the name and the capacity of the party, i.e. carrier, on whose behalf that agent is acting,
and

   ii. indicates that the goods have been accepted for carriage,
and

   iii. where the Credit calls for an actual date of dispatch, indicates a specific notation of such date, the date of dispatch so indicated on the air transport document will be deemed to be the date of shipment.

482

For the purpose of this Article, the information appearing in the box on the air transport document (marked "For Carrier Use Only" or similar expression) relative to the flight number and date will not be considered as a specific notation of such date of dispatch.

In all other cases, the date of issuance of the air transport document will be deemed to be the date of shipment,
and

    iv.   indicates the airport of departure and the airport of destination stipulated in the Credit,
and

    v.   appears to be the original for consignor/shipper even if the Credit stipulates a full set of originals, or similar expressions,
and

    vi.   appears to contain all of the terms and conditions of carriage, or some of such terms and conditions, by reference to a source or document other than the air transport document; banks will not examine the contents of such terms and conditions,
and

    vii.   in all other respects meets the stipulations of the Credit.

b   For the purpose of this Article, transhipment means unloading and reloading from one aircraft to another aircraft during the course of carriage from the airport of departure to the airport of destination stipulated in the Credit.

c   Even if the Credit prohibits transhipment, banks will accept an air transport document which indicates that transhipment will or may take place, provided that the entire carriage is covered by one and the same air transport document.

ARTICLE 28

Road, Rail or Inland Waterway Transport Documents

a   If a Credit calls for a road, rail, or inland waterway transport document, banks will, unless otherwise stipulated in the Credit, accept a document of the type called for, however named, which:

    i.   appears on its face to indicate the name of the carrier and to have been signed or otherwise authenticated by the carrier or a named agent for or on behalf of the carrier and/or to bear a reception stamp or other indication of receipt by the carrier or a named agent for or on behalf of the carrier.

Any signature, authentication, reception stamp or other indication of receipt of the carrier, must be identified on its face as that of the carrier. An agent signing or authenticating for the carrier, must also indicate the name and the capacity of the party, i.e. carrier, on whose behalf that agent is acting,
and

    ii.   indicates that the goods have been received for shipment, dispatch or carriage or wording to this effect. The date of issuance will be deemed to be the date of shipment unless the transport document contains a reception stamp, in which case the date of the reception stamp will be deemed to be the date of shipment,
and

    iii.   indicates the place of shipment and the place of destination stipulated in the Credit,
and

    iv.   in all other respects meets the stipulations of the Credit.

b   In the absence of any indication on the transport document as to the numbers issued, banks will accept the transport document(s) presented as constituting a full set. Banks will accept as original(s) the transport document(s) whether marked as original(s) or not.

c   For the purpose of this Article, transhipment means unloading and reloading from one means of conveyance to another means of conveyance, in different modes of transport, during the course of carriage from the place of shipment to the place of destination stipulated in the Credit.

d   Even if the Credit prohibits transhipment, banks will accept a road, rail, or inland waterway transport document which indicates that transhipment will or may take place, provided that the entire carriage is covered by one and the same transport document and within the same mode of transport.

ARTICLE 29

Courier and Post Receipts

a   If a Credit calls for a post receipt or certificate of posting, banks will, unless otherwise stipulated in the Credit, accept a post receipt or certificate of posting which:

   i.   appears on its face to have been stamped or otherwise authenticated and dated in the place from which the Credit stipulates the goods are to be shipped or dispatched and such date will be deemed to be the date of shipment or dispatch,
         and

   ii.   in all other respects meets the stipulations of the Credit.

b   If a Credit calls for a document issued by a courier or expedited delivery service evidencing receipt of the goods for delivery, banks will, unless otherwise stipulated in the Credit, accept a document, however named, which:

   i.   appears on its face to indicate the name of the courier/service, and to have been stamped, signed or otherwise authenticated by such named courier/service (unless the Credit specifically calls for a document issued by a named Courier/Service, banks will accept a document issued by any Courier/Service),
         and

   ii.   indicates a date of pick-up or of receipt or wording to this effect, such date being deemed to be the date of shipment or dispatch,
         and

   iii. in all other respects meets the stipulations of the Credit.

ARTICLE 30

Transport Documents issued by Freight Forwarders

Unless otherwise authorised in the Credit, banks will only accept a transport document issued by a freight forwarder if it appears on its face to indicate:

   i.   the name of the freight forwarder as a carrier or multimodal transport operator and to have been signed or otherwise authenticated by the freight or

   ii.   the name of the carrier or multimodal transport operator and to have been signed or otherwise authenticated by the freight forwarder as a named agent for or on behalf of the carrier or multimodal transport operator.

ARTICLE 31

"On Deck", "Shipper's Load and Count", Name of Consignor
Unless otherwise stipulated in the Credit, banks will accept a transport document which:

  i.   does not indicate, in the case of carriage by sea or by more than one means of conveyance including carriage by sea, that the goods are or will be loaded on deck. Nevertheless, banks will accept a transport document which contains a provision that the goods may be carried on deck, provided that it does not specifically state that they are or will be loaded on deck, and/or
  ii. bears a clause on the face thereof such as "shipper's load and count" or "said by shipper to contain" or words of similar effect, and/or
  iii. indicates as the consignor of the goods a party other than the Beneficiary of the Credit.

ARTICLE 32

Clean Transport Documents
a   A clean transport document is one which bears no clause or notation which expressly declares a defective condition of the goods and/or the packaging.
b   Banks will not accept transport documents bearing such clauses or notations unless the Credit expressly stipulates the clauses or notations which may be accepted.
c   Banks will regard a requirement in a Credit for a transport document to bear the clause "clean on board" as complied with if such transport document meets the requirements of this Article and of Articles 23, 24, 25, 26, 27, 28 or 30.

ARTICLE 33

Freight Payable/Prepaid Transport Documents
a   Unless otherwise stipulated in the Credit, or inconsistent with any of the documents presented under the Credit, banks will accept transport documents stating that freight or transportation charges (hereafter referred to as "freight") have still to be paid.
b   If a Credit stipulates that the transport document has to indicate that freight has been paid or prepaid, banks will accept a transport document on which words clearly indicating payment or prepayment of freight appear by stamp or otherwise, or on which payment or prepayment of freight is indicated by other means. If the Credit requires courier charges to be paid or prepaid banks will also accept a transport document issued by a courier or expedited delivery service evidencing that courier charges are for the account of a party other than the consignee.
c   The words "freight prepayable" or "freight to be prepaid" or words of similar effect, if appearing on transport documents, will not be accepted as constituting evidence of the payment of freight.
d   Banks will accept transport documents bearing reference by stamp or otherwise to costs additional to the freight, such as costs of, or disbursements incurred in connection with, loading, unloading or similar operations, unless the conditions of the Credit specifically prohibit such reference.

ARTICLE 34

Insurance Documents

a   Insurance documents must appear on their face to be issued and signed by insurance companies or underwriters or their agents.

b   If the insurance document indicates that it has been issued in more than one original, all the originals must be presented unless otherwise authorised in the Credit.

c   Cover notes issued by brokers will not be accepted, unless specifically authorised in the Credit.

d   Unless otherwise stipulated in the Credit, banks will accept an insurance certificate or a declaration under an open cover pre-signed by insurance companies or underwriters or their agents. If a Credit specifically calls for an insurance certificate or a declaration under an open cover, banks will accept, in lieu thereof, an insurance policy.

e   Unless otherwise stipulated in the Credit, or unless it appears from the insurance document that the cover is effective at the latest from the date of loading on board or dispatch or taking in charge of the goods, banks will not accept an insurance document which bears a date of issuance later than the date of loading on board or dispatch or taking in charge as indicated in such transport document.

f   i.   Unless otherwise stipulated in the Credit, the insurance document must be expressed in the same currency as the Credit.

   ii.   Unless otherwise stipulated in the Credit, the minimum amount for which the insurance document must indicate the insurance cover to have been effected is the CIF (cost, insurance and freight (... "named port of destination")) or CIP (carriage and insurance paid to (... "named place of destination")) value of the goods, as the case may be, plus 10%, but only when the CIF or CIP value can be determined from the documents on their face. Otherwise, banks will accept as such minimum amount 110% of the amount for which payment, acceptance or negotiation is requested under the Credit, or 110% of the gross amount of the invoice, whichever is the greater.

ARTICLE 35

Type of Insurance Cover

a   Credits should stipulate the type of insurance required and, if any, the additional risks which are to be covered. Imprecise terms such as "usual risks" or "customary risks" shall not be used; if they are used, banks will accept insurance documents as presented, without responsibility for any risks not being covered.

b   Failing specific stipulations in the Credit, banks will accept insurance documents as presented, without responsibility for any risks not being covered.

c   Unless otherwise stipulated in the Credit, banks will accept an insurance document which indicates that the cover is subject to a franchise or an excess (deductible).

ARTICLE 36

All Risks Insurance Cover

Where a Credit stipulates "insurance against all risks", banks will accept an insurance document which contains any "all risks" notation or clause, whether or not bearing the heading "all risks", even if the insurance document indicates that certain risks are excluded, without responsibility for any risk(s) not being covered.

ARTICLE 37

Commercial Invoices

a   Unless otherwise stipulated in the Credit, commercial invoices;

    i.   must appear on their face to be issued by the Beneficiary named in the Credit (except as provided in Article 48),
and

    ii. must be made out in the name of the Applicant (except as provided in sub-Article 48 (h)),
and

    iii. need not be signed.

b   Unless otherwise stipulated in the Credit, banks may refuse commercial invoices issued for amounts in excess of the amount permitted by the Credit. Nevertheless, if a bank authorised to pay, incur a deferred payment undertaking, accept Draft(s), or negotiate under a Credit accepts such invoices, its decision will be binding upon all parties, provided that such bank has not paid, incurred a deferred payment undertaking, accepted Draft(s) or negotiated for an amount in excess of that permitted by the Credit.

c   The description of the goods in the commercial invoice must correspond with the description in the Credit. In all other documents, the goods may be described in general terms not inconsistent with the description of the goods in the Credit.

ARTICLE 38

Other Documents

If a Credit calls for an attestation or certification of weight in the case of transport other than by sea, banks will accept a weight stamp or declaration of weight which appears to have been superimposed on the transport document by the carrier or his agent unless the Credit

E. MISCELLANEOUS PROVISIONS

ARTICLE 39

Allowances in Credit Amount, Quantity and Unit Price

a   The words "about", "approximately", "circa" or similar expressions used in connection with the amount of the Credit or the quantity or the unit price stated in the Credit are to be construed as allowing a difference not to exceed 10% more or 10% less than the amount or the quantity or the unit price to which they refer.

b   Unless a Credit stipulates that the quantity of the goods specified must not be exceeded or reduced, a tolerance of 5% more or 5% less will be permissible, always provided that the amount of the drawings does not exceed the amount of the Credit. This tolerance does not apply when the Credit stipulates the quantity in terms of a stated number of packing units or individual items.

c   Unless a Credit which prohibits partial shipments stipulates otherwise, or unless sub-Article (b) above is applicable, a tolerance of 5% less in the amount of the drawing will be permissible, provided that if the Credit stipulates the quantity of the goods, such quantity of goods is shipped in full, and if the Credit stipulates a unit price, such price is not reduced. This provision does not apply when expressions referred to in sub-Article (a) above are used in the Credit.

ARTICLE 40

Partial Shipments/Drawings

a   Partial drawings and/or shipments are allowed, unless the Credit stipulates otherwise.

b   Transport documents which appear on their face to indicate that shipment has been made on the same means of conveyance and for the same journey, provided they indicate the same destination, will not be regarded as covering partial shipments, even if the transport documents indicate different dates of shipment and/or different ports of loading, places of taking in charge, or despatch.

c   Shipments made by post or by courier will not be regarded as partial shipments if the post receipts or certificates of posting or courier's receipts or dispatch notes appear to have been stamped, signed or otherwise authenticated in the place from which the Credit stipulates the goods are to be dispatched, and on the same date.

ARTICLE 41

Instalment Shipments/Drawings

If drawings and/or shipments by instalments within given periods are stipulated in the Credit and any instalment is not drawn and/or shipped within the period allowed for that instalment, the Credit ceases to be available for that and any subsequent instalments, unless otherwise stipulated in the Credit.

ARTICLE 42

Expiry Date and Place for Presentation of Documents

a   All Credits must stipulate an expiry date and a place for presentation of documents for payment, acceptance, or with the exception of freely negotiable Credits, a place for presentation of documents for negotiation. An expiry date stipulated for payment, b Except as provided in sub-Article 44(a), documents must be presented on or before such expiry date.

c   If an Issuing Bank states that the Credit is to be available "for one month", "for six months", or the like, but does not specify the date from which the time is to run, the date of issuance of the Credit by the Issuing Bank will be deemed to be the first day from which such time is to run. Banks should discourage indication of the expiry date of the Credit in this manner.

ARTICLE 43

Limitation on the Expiry Date

a   In addition to stipulating an expiry date for presentation of documents, every Credit which calls for a transport document(s) should also stipulate a specified period of time after the date of shipment during which presentation must be made in compliance with the terms and conditions of the Credit. If no such period of time is stipulated, banks will not accept documents presented to them later than 21 days after the date of shipment. In any event, documents must be presented not later than the expiry date of the Credit.

b   In cases in which sub-Article 40(b) applies, the date of shipment will be considered to be the latest shipment date on any of the transport documents presented.

ARTICLE 44

Extension of Expiry Date

a   If the expiry date of the Credit and/or the last day of the period of time for presentation of documents stipulated by the Credit or applicable by virtue of Article 43 falls on a day on which the bank to which presentation has to be made is closed for reasons other than those referred to in Article 17, the stipulated expiry date and/or the last day of the period of time after the date of shipment for presentation of documents, as the case may be, shall be extended to the first following day on which such bank is open.

b   The latest date for shipment shall not be extended by reason of the extension of the expiry date and/or the period of time after the date of shipment for presentation of documents in accordance with sub-Article (a) above. If no such latest date for shipment is stipulated in the Credit or amendments thereto, banks will not accept transport documents indicating a date of shipment later than the expiry date stipulated in the Credit or amendments thereto.

c   The bank to which presentation is made on such first following business day must provide a statement that the documents were presented within the time limits extended in accordance with sub-Article 44(a) of the Uniform Customs and Practice for Documentary Credits, 1993 Revision, ICC Publication No. 500.

ARTICLE 45

Hours of Presentation

Banks are under no obligation to accept presentation of documents outside their banking hours.

ARTICLE 46

General Expressions as to Dates for Shipment

a   Unless otherwise stipulated in the Credit, the expression "shipment" used in stipulating an earliest and/or a latest date for shipment will be understood to include expressions such as, "loading on board", "dispatch", "accepted for carriage", "date of post receipt", "date of pick-up", and the like, and in the case of a Credit calling for a multimodal transport document the expression "taking in charge".

b   Expressions such as "prompt", "immediately", "as soon as possible", and the like should not be used. If they are used banks will disregard them.

c   If the expression "on or about" or similar expressions are used, banks will interpret them as a stipulation that shipment is to be made during the period from five days before to five days after the specified date, both end days included.

ARTICLE 47

Date Terminology for Periods of Shipment

a   The words "to", "until", "till", "from" and words of similar import applying to any date or period in the Credit referring to shipment will be understood to include the date mentioned.

b   The word "after" will be understood to exclude the date mentioned.

c   The terms "first half", "second half" of a month shall be construed respectively as the 1st to the 15th, and the 16th to the last day of such month, all dates inclusive.

d   The terms "beginning", "middle", or "end" of a month shall be construed respectively as the 1st to the 10th, the 11th to the 20th, and the 21st to the last day of such month, all dates inclusive.

F. TRANSFERABLE CREDIT

ARTICLE 48

Transferable Credit

a   A transferable Credit is a Credit under which the Beneficiary (First Beneficiary) may request the bank authorised to pay, incur a deferred payment undertaking, accept or negotiate (the "Transferring Bank"), or in the case of a freely negotiable Credit, the bank specifically authorised in the Credit as a Transferring Bank, to make the Credit available in whole or in part to one or more other Beneficiary(ies) (Second Beneficiary(ies)).

b   A Credit can be transferred only if it is expressly designated as "transferable" by the Issuing Bank. Terms such as "divisible", "fractionable", "assignable", and "transmissible" do not render the Credit transferable. If such terms are used they shall be disregarded.

c   The Transferring Bank shall be under no obligation to effect such transfer except to the extent and in the manner expressly consented to by such bank.

d   At the time of making a request for transfer and prior to transfer of the Credit, the First Beneficiary must irrevocably instruct the Transferring Bank whether or not he retains the right to refuse to allow the Transferring Bank to advise amendments to the Second Beneficiary(ies). If the Transferring Bank consents to the transfer under these conditions, it must, at the time of transfer, advise the Second Beneficiary(ies) of the First Beneficiary's instructions regarding amendments.

e   If a Credit is transferred to more than one Second Beneficiary(ies), refusal of an amendment by one or more Second Beneficiary(ies) does not invalidate the acceptance(s) by the other Second Bene-ficiary(ies) with respect to whom the Credit will be amended accordingly. With respect to the Second Beneficiary(ies) who rejected the amendment, the Credit will remain unamended.

f   Transferring Bank charges in respect of transfers including commissions, fees, costs or expenses are payable by the First Beneficiary, unless otherwise agreed. If the Transferring Bank agrees to transfer the Credit it shall be under no obligation to effect the transfer until such charges are paid.

g   Unless otherwise stated in the Credit, a transferable Credit can be transferred once only. Consequently, the Credit cannot be transferred at the request of the Second Beneficiary to any subsequent Third Beneficiary. For the purpose of this Article, a retransfer to the First Beneficiary does not constitute a prohibited transfer.

   Fractions of a transferable Credit (not exceeding in the aggregate the amount of the Credit) can be transferred separately, provided partial shipments/ drawings are not prohibited, and the aggregate of such transfers will be considered as constituting only one transfer of the Credit.

h   The Credit can be transferred only on the terms and conditions specified in the original Credit, with the exception of:
   – the amount of the Credit,
   – any unit price stated therein,
   – the expiry date,
   – the last date for presentation of documents in accordance with Article 43,
   – the period for shipment,
   any or all of which may be reduced or curtailed.

The percentage for which insurance cover must be effected may be increased in such a way as to provide the amount of cover stipulated in the original Credit, or these Articles.

In addition, the name of the First Beneficiary can be substituted for that of the Applicant, but if the name of the Applicant is specifically required by the original Credit to appear in any document(s) other than the invoice, such requirement must be fulfilled.

The First Beneficiary has the right to substitute his own invoice(s) (and Draft(s)) for those of the Second Beneficiary(ies), for amounts not in excess of the original amount stipulated in the Credit and for the original unit prices if stipulated in the Credit, and upon such substitution of invoice(s) (and Draft(s)) the First Beneficiary can draw under the Credit for the difference, if any, between his invoice(s) and the Second Beneficiary's(ies') invoice(s).

When a Credit has been transferred and the First Beneficiary is to supply his own invoice(s) (and Draft(s)) in exchange for the Second Beneficiary's(ies') invoice(s) (and Draft(s)) but fails to do so on first demand, the Transferring Bank has the right to deliver to the Issuing Bank the documents received under the transferred Credit, including the Second Beneficiary's(ies') invoice(s) (and Draft(s)) without further responsibility to the First Beneficiary.

j The First Beneficiary may request that payment or negotiation be effected to the Second Beneficiary(ies) at the place to which the Credit has been transferred up to and including the expiry date of the Credit, unless the original Credit expressly states that it may not be made available for payment or negotiation at a place other than that stipulated in the Credit. This is without prejudice to the First Beneficiary's right to substitute subsequently his own invoice(s) (and Draft(s)) for those of the Second Beneficiary(ies) and to claim any difference due to him.

G. ASSIGNMENT OF PROCEEDS

ARTICLE 49

Assignment of Proceeds
The fact that a Credit is not stated to be transferable shall not affect the Beneficiary's right to assign any proceeds to which he may be, or may become, entitled under such Credit, in accordance with the provisions of the applicable law. This Article relates only to the assignment of proceeds and not to the assignment of the right to perform under the Credit itself.

Appendix 3

International Standard Banking Practice 681

PRELIMINARY CONSIDERATIONS

The Application and Issuance of the Credit

1. The terms of a credit are independent of the underlying transaction even if a credit expressly refers to that transaction. To avoid unnecessary costs, delays and disputes in the examination of documents, however, the applicant and beneficiary should carefully consider which documents should be required, by whom they should be produced and the time frame for presentation.

2. The applicant bears the risk of any ambiguity in its instructions to issue or amend a credit. Unless expressly stated otherwise, a request to issue or amend a credit authorizes an issuing bank to supplement or develop the terms in a manner necessary or desirable to permit the use of the credit.

3. The applicant should be aware that UCP 600 contains articles such as 3, 14, 19, 20, 21, 23, 24, 28(i), 30 and 31 that define ter ms in a manner that may produce unexpected results unless the applicant fully acquaints itself with these provisions. For example, a credit requiring presentation of a bill of lading and containing a prohibition against transhipment will, in most cases, have to exclude UCP 600 sub article 20(c) to make the prohibition against transhipment effective.

4. A credit should not require presentation of documents that are to be issued or countersigned by the applicant. If a credit is issued including such terms, the beneficiary must either seek amendment or comply with them and bear the risk of failure to do so.

5. Many of the problems that arise at the examination stage could be avoided or resolved by careful attention to detail in the underlying transaction, the credit application and issuance of the credit as discussed.

GENERAL PRINCIPLES

Abbreviations

6. The use of generally accepted abbreviations, for example "Ltd" instead of "Limited", "Int'l" instead of "International", "Co." instead of "Company", "kgs" or "kos" instead of "kilos", "Ind" instead of "Industry", "mfr" instead of "manufacturer" or "mt" instead of "metric tons" – or vice versa – does not make a doument discrepant.

7.   Virgules (slash marks "/") may have different meanings and, unless apparent in the context used, should not be used as a substitute for a word.

Certifications and Declarations
8.   A certification, declaration or the like may either be a separate document or contained within another document as required by the credit. If the certification or declaration appears in another document which is signed and dated, any certification or declaration appearing on that document does not require a separate signature or date if the certification or declaration appears to have been given by the same entity that issued and signed the document.

Corrections and Alterations
9.   Corrections and alterations of information or data in documents, other than documents created by the beneficiary, must appear to be authenticated by the party who issued the document or by a party authorized by the issuer to do so. Corrections and alterations in documents which have been legalized, visaed, certified or similar, must appear to be authenticated by the party who legalized, visaed, certified etc., the document. The authentication must show by whom the authentication has been made and include the signature or initials of that party. If the authentication appears to have been made by a party other than the issuer of the document, the authentication must clearly show in which capacity that party has authenticated the correction or alteration.
10. Corrections and alterations in documents issued by the beneficiary itself, except drafts, which have not been legalized, visaed, certified or similar, need not be authenticated. See also "Drafts and Calculation of Maturity Date".
11. The use of multiple type styles or font sizes or handwriting in the same document does not, by itself, signify a correction or alteration.
12. Where a document contains more than one correction or alteration, either each correction must be authenticated separately or one authentication must be linked to all corrections in an appropriate way. For example, if the document shows three corrections numbered 1, 2 and 3, one statement, such as "Correction numbers 1, 2 and 3 above authorized by XXX" or similar, will satisfy the requirement for authentication.

Dates
13. Drafts, transport documents and insurance documents must be dated even if a credit does not expressly so require. A requirement that a document, other than those mentioned above, be dated may be satisfied by reference in the document to the date of another document forming part of the same presentation (e.g., where a shipping certificate is issued which states "date as per bill of lading number xxx" or similar terms). Although it is expected that a required certificate or declaration in a separate document be dated, its compliance will depend on the type of certification or declaration that has been requested, its required wording and the wording that appears within it. Whether other documents require dating will depend on the nature and content of the document in question.
14. Any document, including a certificate of analysis, inspection certificate and pre-shipment inspection certificate, may be dated after the date of shipment. However, if a credit requires a document evidencing a preshipment event (e.g., preshipment inspection certificate), the document must, either by its title or content, indicate that the event (e.g., inspection) took place prior to or on the date of shipment. A requirement for an "inspection certificate" does not constitute a requirement to evidence a preshipment event. Documents must not indicate that they were issued after the date they are presented.

15. A document indicating a date of preparation and a later date of signing is deemed to be issued on the date of signing.
16. Phrases often used to signify time on either side of a date or event:
    a. "within 2 days after" indicates a period from the date of the event until 2 days after the event.
    b. "not later than 2 days after" does not indicate a period, only a latest date. If an advice must not be dated prior to a specific date, the credit must so state.
    c. "at least 2 days before" indicates that something must take place not later than 2 days before an event. There is no limit as to how early it may take place.
    d. "within 2 days of " indicates a period 2 days prior to the event until 2 days after the event.
17. The term "within" when used in connection with a date excludes that date in the calculation of the period.
18. Dates may be expressed in different formats, e.g., the 12th of November 2007 could be expressed as 12 Nov 07, 12Nov07, 12.11.2007, 12.11.07, 2007.11.12, 11.12.07, 121107, etc. Provided that the date intended can be determined from the document or from other documents included in the presentation, any of these formats are acceptable. To avoid confusion it is recommended that the name of the month should be used instead of the number.

Documents for which the UCP 600 Transport Articles Do Not Apply
19. Some documents commonly used in relation to the transportation of goods, e.g., Delivery Order, Forwarder's Cer tificate of Receipt, Forwarder 's Cer tificate of Shipment, For warder 's Cer tificate of Transpor t, Forwarder's Cargo Receipt and Mate's Receipt, do not reflect a contract of carriage and are not transport documents as defined in UCP 600 articles 19–25. As such, UCP 600 subarticle 14(c) would not apply to these documents. Therefore, these documents will be examined in the same manner as other documents for which there are no specific provisions in UCP 600, i.e., under subarticle 14(f). In any event, documents must be presented not later than the expiry date for presentation as stated in the credit.
20. Copies of transport documents are not transport documents for the purpose of UCP 600 articles 19–25 and subarticle 14(c). The UCP 600 transport articles apply where there are original transport documents presented.
     Where a credit allows for the presentation of a copy transport document rather than an original, the credit must explicitly state the details to be shown. Where copies (nonnegotiable) are presented, they need not evidence signature, dates, etc.

Expressions Not Defined in UCP 600
21. Expressions such as "shipping documents", "stale documents acceptable", "third par ty documents acceptable" and "exporting country" should not be used as they are not defined in UCP 600. If used in a credit, their meaning should be made apparent. If not, they have the following meaning under international standard banking practice:
    a. "shipping documents" – all documents (not only transport documents), except drafts, required by the credit.
    b. "stale documents acceptable" – documents presented later than 21 calendar days after the date of shipment are acceptable as long as they are presented no later than the expir y date for presentation as stated in the credit.
    c. "third party documents acceptable" – all documents, excluding drafts but including invoices, may be issued by a party other than the beneficiary. If it is the intention of the issuing bank that the transport or other documents may show a shipper other than the beneficiary, the clause is not necessary because it is already permitted by subarticle 14(k).

    d.   "exporting country " – the country where the beneficiary is domiciled, or the country of origin of the goods, or the country of receipt by the carrier or the country from which shipment or dispatch is made.

Issuer of Documents

22.   If a credit indicates that a document is to be issued by a named person or entity, this condition is satisfied if the document appears to be issued by the named person or entity. It may appear to be issued by a named person or entity by use of its letterhead, or if there is no letterhead, the document appears to have been completed or signed by, or on behalf of the named person or entity.

Language

23.   Under international standard banking practice, it is expected that documents issued by the beneficiary will be in the language of the credit. When a credit states that documents in two or more languages are acceptable, a nominated bank may, in its advice of the credit, limit the number of acceptable languages as a condition of its engagement in the credit.

Mathematical Calculations

24.   Detailed mathematical calculations in documents will not be checked by banks. Banks are only obliged to check total values against the credit and other required documents.

Misspellings or Typing Errors

25.   A misspelling or typing error that does not affect the meaning of a word or the sentence in which it occurs does not make a document discrepant. For example, a description of the merchandise as "mashine" instead of "machine", "fountan pen" instead of "fountain pen" or "modle" instead of "model" would not make the document discrepant. However, a description as "model 123" instead of "model 321" would not be regarded as a typing error and would constitute a discrepancy.

Multiple Pages and Attachments or Riders

26.   Unless the credit or a document provides otherwise, pages which are physically bound together, sequentially numbered or contain internal cross references, however named or entitled, are to be examined as one document, even if some of the pages are regarded as an attachment. Where a document consists of more than one page, it must be possible to determine that the pages are part of the same document.

27.   If a signature or endorsement is required to be on a document consisting of more than one page, the signature is normally placed on the first or last page of the document, but unless the credit or the document itself indicates where a signature or endorsement is to appear, the signature or endorsement may appear anywhere on the document.

Originals and Copies

28.   Documents issued in more than one original may be marked "Original", "Duplicate", "Triplicate", "First Original", "Second Original", etc. None of these markings will disqualify a document as an original.

29.   The number of originals to be presented must be at least the number required by the credit, the UCP 600 or, where the document itself states how many originals have been issued, the number stated on the document.

30. It can sometimes be difficult to determine from the wording of a credit whether it requires an original or a copy, and to determine whether that requirement is satisfied by an original or a copy.

    For example, where the credit requires:
    a. "Invoice", "One Invoice" or "Invoice in 1 copy", it will be understood to be a requirement for an original invoice.
    b. "Invoice in 4 copies", it will be satisfied by the presentation of at least one original and the remaining number as copies of an invoice.
    c. "One copy of Invoice", it will be satisfied by presentation of either a copy or an original of an invoice.

31. Where an original would not be accepted in lieu of a copy, the credit must prohibit an original, e.g., "photocopy of invoice – original document not acceptable in lieu of photocopy", or the like. Where a credit calls for a copy of a transpor t document and indicates the disposal instructions for the original of that transport document, an original transport document will not be acceptable.

32. Copies of documents need not be signed.

33. In addition to UCP 600 article 17, the ICC Banking Commission Policy Statement, document 470/871(Rev), titled "The Determination of an 'Original' Document in the Context of UCP 500 subAr ticle 20(b)" is recommended for further guidance on originals and copies and remains valid under UCP 600. The content of the Policy Statement appears in the Appendix of this publication, for reference purposes.

Shipping Marks

34. The purpose of a shipping mark is to enable identification of a box, bag or package. If a credit specifies the details of a shipping mark, the documents mentioning the marks must show these details, but additional information is acceptable provided it is not in conflict with the credit terms.

35. Shipping marks contained in some documents often include information in excess of what would normally be considered "shipping marks" and could include information such as the type of goods, warnings as to the handling of fragile goods, net and/or gross weight of the goods, etc. The fact that some documents show such additional information while others do not is not a discrepancy.

36. Transport documents covering containerized goods will sometimes only show a container number under the heading "Shipping marks". Other documents that show a detailed marking will not be considered to be in conflict for that reason.

Signatures

37. Even if not stated in the credit, drafts, certificates and declarations by their nature require a signature. Transport documents and insurance documents must be signed in accordance with the provisions of UCP 600.

38. The fact that a document has a box or space for a signature does not necessarily mean that such box or space must be completed with a signature. For example, banks do not require a signature in the area titled "Signature of shipper or their agent" or similar phrases commonly found on transport documents, such as air waybills or road transport documents. If the content of a document indicates that it requires a signature to establish its validity (e.g., "This document is not valid unless signed" or similar terms), it must be signed.

39. A signature need not be handwritten. Facsimile signatures, perforated signatures, stamps, symbols (such as chops) or any electronic or mechanical means of authentication are sufficient. However, a photocopy of a signed document does

not qualify as a signed original document, nor does a signed document transmitted through a fax machine, absent an original signature. A requirement for a document to be "signed and stamped", or a similar requirement, is also fulfilled by a signature and the name of the par ty typed, or stamped, or handwritten, etc.

40. A signature on a company letterhead paper will be taken to be the signature of that company, unless otherwise stated. The company name need not be repeated next to the signature.

Title of Documents and Combined Documents

41. Documents may be titled as called for in the credit, bear a similar title or be untitled. For example, a credit requirement for a "Packing List" may also be satisfied by a document containing packing details whether titled "Packing Note", "Packing and Weight List", etc., or an untitled document. The content of a document must appear to fulfil the function of the required document.

42. Documents listed in a credit should be presented as separate documents. If a credit requires a packing list and a weight list, such requirement will be satisfied by presentation of two separate documents, or by presentation of two original copies of a combined packing and weight list, provided such document states both packing and weight details.

DRAFTS AND CALCULATION OF MATURITY DATE

Tenor

43. The tenor must be in accordance with the terms of the credit.

    a. If a draft is drawn at a tenor other than sight, or other than a certain period after sight, it must be possible to establish the maturity date from the data in the draft itself.

    b. As an example of where it is possible to establish a maturity date from the data in the draft, if a credit calls for drafts at a tenor 60 days after the bill of lading date, where the date of the bill of lading is 12 July 2007, the tenor could be indicated on the draft in one of the following ways:

        i. "60 days after bill of lading date 12 July 2007", or

        ii. "60 days after 12 July 2007", or

        iii. "60 days after bill of lading date" and elsewhere on the face of the draft state "bill of lading date 12 July 2007", or

        iv. "60 days date" on a draft dated the same day as the date of the bill of lading, or

        v. "10 September 2007", i.e., 60 days after the bill of lading date.

    c. If the tenor refers to xxx days after the bill of lading date, the on board date is deemed to be the bill of lading date even if the on board date is prior to or later than the date of issuance of the bill of lading.

    d. UCP 600 article 3 provides guidance that where the words "from" and "after" are used to determine maturity dates, the calculation of the maturity commences the day following the date of the document, shipment or other event, i.e., 10 days after or from March 1 is March 11.

    e. If a bill of lading showing more than one on board notation is presented under a credit which requires drafts to be drawn, for example, at 60 days after or from bill of lading date, and the goods according to both or all on board notations were shipped from ports within a permitted geographical area or region, the earliest of these on board dates will be used for calculation of the maturity date. Example: the credit requires shipment from European port, and the bill of lading evidences on board vessel "A" from Dublin August 16 and on board vessel "B" from Rotterdam August 18. The draft should reflect 60 days from the earliest on board date in a European port, i.e., August 16.

f.   If a credit requires drafts to be drawn, for example, at 60 days after or from bill of lading date, and more than one set of bills of lading is presented under one draft, the date of the last bill of lading will be used for the calculation of the maturity date.

44.   While the examples refer to bill of lading dates, the same principles apply to all transport documents.

Maturity Date

45.   If a draft states a maturity date by using an actual date, the date must have been calculated in accordance with the requirements of the credit.

46.   For drafts drawn "at XXX days sight", the maturity date is established as follows:

a.   in the case of complying documents, or in the case of noncomplying documents where the drawee bank has not provided a notice of refusal, the maturity date will be XXX days after the date of receipt of documents by the drawee bank.

b.   in the case of noncomplying documents where the drawee bank has provided a notice of refusal and subsequent approval, at the latest XXX days after the date of acceptance of the draft by the drawee bank. The date of acceptance of the draft must be no later than the date the issuing bank accepts the waiver of the applicant.

47.   In all cases the drawee bank must advise the maturity date to the presenter. The calculation of tenor and maturity dates, as shown above, would also apply to credits designated as being available by deferred payment, i.e., where there is no requirement for a draft to be presented by the beneficiary.

Banking Days, Grace Days, Delays in Remittance

48.   Payment must be available in immediately available funds on the due date at the place where the draft or documents are payable, provided such due date is a banking day in that place. If the due date is a nonbanking day, payment will be due on the first banking day following the due date. Delays in the remittance of funds, such as grace days, the time it takes to remit funds, etc., must not be in addition to the stated or agreed due date as defined by the draft or documents.

Endorsement

49.   The draft must be endorsed, if necessary.

Amounts

50.   The amount in words must accurately reflect the amount in figures if both are shown, and indicate the currency, as stated in the credit.

51.   The amount must agree with that of the invoice, unless as a result of UCP 600 subarticle 18(b).

How the Draft is Drawn

52.   The draft must be drawn on the party stated in the credit.

53.   The draft must be drawn by the beneficiary.

Drafts on the Applicant
54. A credit may be issued requiring a draft drawn on the applicant as one of the required documents, but must not be issued available by drafts drawn on the applicant.

Corrections and Alterations
55. Corrections and alterations on a draft, if any, must appear to have been authenticated by the drawer.
56. In some countries a draft showing corrections or alterations will not be acceptable even with the drawer's authentication. Issuing banks in such countries should make a statement in the credit to the effect that no correction or alteration must appear in the draft.

INVOICES

Definition of Invoice
57. A credit requiring an "invoice" without further definition will be satisfied by any type of invoice presented (commercial invoice, customs invoice, tax invoice, final invoice, consular invoice, etc.). However, invoices identified as "provisional", "proforma" or the like are not acceptable. When a credit requires presentation of a commercial invoice, a document titled "invoice" will be acceptable.

Description of the Goods, Services or Performance and other General Issues Related to Invoices
58. The description of the goods, services or performance in the invoice must correspond with the description in the credit. There is no requirement for a mirror image. For example, details of the goods may be stated in a number of areas within the invoice which, when collated together, represent a description of the goods corresponding to that in the credit.
59. The description of goods, services or performance in an invoice must reflect what has actually been shipped or provided. For example, where there are two types of goods shown in the credit, such as 10 trucks and 5 tractors, an invoice that reflects only shipment of 4 trucks would be acceptable provided the credit does not prohibit partial shipment. An invoice showing the entire goods description as stated in the credit, then stating what has actually been shipped, is also acceptable.
60. An invoice must evidence the value of the goods shipped or services or performance provided. Unit price(s), if any, and currency shown in the invoice must agree with that shown in the credit. The invoice must show any discounts or deductions required in the credit. The invoice may also show a deduction covering advance payment, discount, etc., not stated in the credit.
61. If a trade term is part of the goods description in the credit, or stated in connection with the amount, the invoice must state the trade term specified, and if the description provides the source of the trade term, the same source must be identified (e.g., a credit term "CIF Singapore Incoterms 2000" would not be satisfied by "CIF Singapore Incoterms"). Charges and costs must be included within the value shown against the stated trade term in the credit and invoice. Any charges and costs shown beyond this value are not allowed.
62. Unless required by the credit, an invoice need not be signed or dated.
63. The quantity of merchandise, weights and measurements shown on the invoice must not conflict with the same quantities appearing on other documents.

64. An invoice must not show:
     a. overshipment (except as provided in UCP 600 subarticle 30(b)), or
     b. merchandise not called for in the credit (including samples, advertising materials, etc.) even if stated to be free of charge.
65. The quantity of the goods required in the credit may vary within a tolerance of +/– 5%. This does not apply if a credit states that the quantity must not be exceeded or reduced, or if a credit states the quantity in terms of a stipulated number of packing units or individual items. A variance of up to +5% in the goods quantity does not allow the amount of the drawing to exceed the amount of the credit.
66. Even when partial shipments are prohibited, a tolerance of 5% less in the credit amount is acceptable, provided that the quantity is shipped in full and that any unit price, if stated in the credit, has not been reduced. If no quantity is stated in the credit, the invoice will be considered to cover the full quantity.
67. If a credit calls for instalment shipments, each shipment must be in accordance with the instalment schedule.

TRANSPORT DOCUMENT COVERING AT LEAST TWO DIFFERENT MODES OF TRANSPORT

Application of UCP 600 Article 19
68. If a credit requires presentation of a transport document covering transportation utilizing at least two modes of transpor t (multimodal or combined transpor t document), and if the transport document clearly shows that it covers a shipment from the place of taking in charge or port, airport or place of loading to the place of final destination mentioned in the credit, UCP 600 article 19 is applicable. In such circumstances, the transport document must not indicate that shipment or dispatch has been effected by only one mode of transport, but it may be silent regarding the modes of transport utilized.
69. In all places where the term "multimodal transport document" is used within this document, it also includes the term "combined transport document". A document need not be titled "multimodal transport document" or "combined transport document" to be acceptable under UCP 600 article 19, even if such expressions are used in the credit.

Full Set of Originals
70. A UCP 600 article 19 transport document must indicate the number of originals that have been issued. Transport documents marked "First Original", "Second Original", "Third Original", "Original", "Duplicate", "Triplicate", etc., or similar expressions are all originals. Multimodal transport documents need not be marked "original" to be acceptable under a credit. In addition to UCP 600 article 17, the ICC Banking Commission Policy Statement, document 470/871(Rev), titled "The Determination of an 'Original' Document in the Context of UCP 500 subArticle 20(b)" is recommended for further guidance on originals and copies and remains valid under UCP 600. The content of the Policy Statement appears in the Appendix of this publication, for reference purposes.

Signing of Multimodal Transport Documents
71. Original multimodal transport documents must be signed in the form described in UCP 600 subarticle 19(a)(i) and indicate the name of the carrier, identified as the carrier.

72. If a credit states "Freight For warder 's Multimodal transport document is acceptable" or uses a similar phrase, then the multimodal transport document may be signed by a freight forwarder in the capacity of a freight forwarder, without the need to identify itself as carrier or agent for the named carrier. In this event, it is not necessary to show the name of the carrier.

    a. If an agent signs a multimodal transport document on behalf of the carrier, the agent must be identified as agent and must identify on whose behalf it is signing, unless the carrier has been identified elsewhere on the multimodal transport document.

    b. If the master (captain) signs the multimodal transport document, the signature of the master (captain) must be identified as "master" ("captain"). In this event, the name of the master (captain) need not be stated.

    c. If an agent signs the multimodal transport document on behalf of the master (captain), the agent must be identified as agent. In this event, the name of the master (captain) need not be stated.

On Board Notations

73. The issuance date of a multimodal transport document will be deemed to be the date of dispatch, taking in charge or shipped on board unless it bears a separate dated notation evidencing dispatch, taking in charge or shipped on board from the location required by the credit, in which event the date of the notation will be deemed to be the date of shipment whether or not the date is before or after the issuance date of the document.

74. "Shipped in apparent good order", "Laden on board", "clean on board" or other phrases incorporating words such as "shipped" or "on board" have the same effect as "Shipped on board".

Place of Taking in Charge, Dispatch, Loading on Board and Destination

75. If a credit gives a geographical range for the place of taking in charge, dispatch, loading on board and destination (e.g., "Any European Port"), the multimodal transport document must indicate the actual place of taking in charge, dispatch, shipped on board and destination, which must be within the geographical area or range stated in the credit.

Consignee, Order Party, Shipper and Endorsement, Notify Party

76. If a credit requires a multimodal transport document to show that the goods are consigned to a named party, e.g., "consigned to Bank X" (a "straight" consignment), rather than "to order" or "to order of Bank X", the multimodal transport document must not contain words such as "to order" or "to order of" that precede the name of that named party, whether typed or preprinted. Likewise, if a credit requires the goods to be consigned "to order" or "to order of " a named party, the multimodal transport document must not show that the goods are consigned straight to the named party.

77. If a multimodal transport document is issued to order or to order of the shipper, it must be endorsed by the shipper. An endorsement indicating that it is made for or on behalf of the shipper is acceptable.

78. If a credit does not stipulate a notify party, the respective field on the multimodal transport document may be left blank or completed in any manner.

Transhipment and Partial Shipment

79. In a multimodal transport, transhipment will occur, i.e., unloading from one means of conveyance and reloading to another means of conveyance (whether or

not in different modes of transport) during the carriage from the place of dispatch, taking in charge or shipment to the place of final destination stated in the credit.

80. If a credit prohibits partial shipments and more than one set of original multimodal transport documents are presented covering shipment, dispatch or taking in charge from one or more points of origin (as specifically allowed, or within the geographical area or range stated in the credit), such documents are acceptable, provided that they cover the movement of goods on the same means of conveyance and same journey and are destined for the same destination. In the event that more than one set of multimodal transport documents are presented and if they incorporate different dates of shipment, dispatch or taking in charge, the latest of these dates will be taken for the calculation of any presentation period, and such date must fall on or before any latest date of shipment, dispatch or taking in charge specified in the credit.

81. Shipment on more than one means of conveyance (more than one truck (lorry), vessel, aircraft, etc.) is a partial shipment, even if such means of conveyance leave on the same day for the same destination.

Clean Multimodal Transport Documents

82. Clauses or notations on multimodal transport documents that expressly declare a defective condition of the goods or packaging are not acceptable. Clauses or notations that do not expressly declare a defective condition of the goods or packaging (e.g., "packaging may not be sufficient for the journey") do not constitute a discrepancy. A statement that the packaging "is not sufficient for the journey" would not be acceptable.

83. If the word "clean" appears on a multimodal transport document and has been deleted, the multimodal transport document will not be deemed to be claused or unclean unless it specifically bears a clause or notation declaring that the goods or packaging are defective.

Goods Description

84. A goods description in the multimodal transport document may be shown in general terms not in conflict with that stated in the credit.

Corrections and Alterations

85. Corrections and alterations on a multimodal transport document must be authenticated. Such authentication must appear to have been made by the carrier or master (captain) or any one of their agents who may be different from the agent that may have issued or signed it, provided they are identified as an agent of the carrier or master (captain).

86. Nonnegotiable copies of multimodal transport documents do not need to include any signature on, or authentication of, any alterations or corrections that may have been made on the original.

Freight and Additional Costs

87. If a credit requires that a multimodal transport document show that freight has been paid or is payable at destination, the multimodal transport document must be marked accordingly.

88. Applicants and issuing banks should be specific in stating the requirements of documents to show whether freight is to be prepaid or collected.

89. If a credit states that costs additional to freight are not acceptable, a multimodal transport document must not indicate that costs additional to the

freight have been or will be incurred. Such indication may be by express reference to additional costs or by the use of shipment terms which refer to costs associated with the loading or unloading of goods, such as Free In (FI), Free Out (FO), Free In and Out (FIO) and Free In and Out Stowed (FIOS). A reference in the transport document to costs which may be levied as a result of a delay in unloading the goods or after the goods have been unloaded, e.g., costs covering the late return of containers, is not considered to be an indication of additional costs in this context.

Goods Covered by more than One Multimodal Transport Document
90. If a multimodal transport document states that the goods in a container are covered by that multimodal transport document plus one or more other multimodal transport documents, and the document states that all multimodal transport documents must be surrendered or words of similar effect, this means that all multimodal transport documents related to that container must be presented in order for the container to be released. Such a multimodal transport document is not acceptable unless all the multimodal transport documents form part of the same presentation under the same credit.

BILL OF LADING

Application of UCP 600 Article 20
91. If a credit requires presentation of a bill of lading ("marine", "ocean" or "porttoport" or similar) covering sea shipment only, UCP 600 article 20 is applicable.
92. To comply with UCP 600 article 20, a bill of lading must appear to cover a porttoport shipment but need not be titled "marine bill of lading", "ocean bill of lading", "porttoport bill of lading" or similar.

Full Set of Originals
93. A UCP 600 article 20 transport document must indicate the number of originals that have been issued. Transport documents marked "First Original", "Second Original", "Third Original", "Original", "Duplicate", "Triplicate", etc., or similar expressions are all originals. Bills of lading need not be marked "original" to be acceptable as an original bill of lading. In addition to UCP 600 article 17, the ICC Banking Commission Policy Statement, document 470/871(Rev), titled "The Determination of an 'Original' Document in the Context of UCP 500 subArticle 20(b)" is recommended for further guidance on originals and copies and remains valid under UCP 600. The content of the Policy Statement appears in the Appendix of this publication, for reference purposes.

Signing of Bills of Lading
94. Original bills of lading must be signed in the form described in UCP 600 subarticle 20(a)(i) and indicate the name of the carrier, identified as the carrier.
95. If a credit states "Freight Forwarder's Bill of Lading is acceptable" or uses a similar phrase, then the bill of lading may be signed by a freight forwarder in the capacity of a freight forwarder, without the need to identify itself as carrier or agent for the named carrier. In this event, it is not necessary to show the name of the carrier.
    a. If an agent signs a bill of lading on behalf of the carrier, the agent must be identified as agent and must identify on whose behalf it is signing, unless the carrier has been identified elsewhere on the bill of lading.

b. If the master (captain) signs the bill of lading, the signature of the master (captain) must be identified as "master" ("captain"). In this event, the name of the master (captain) need not be stated.

c. If an agent signs the bill of lading on behalf of the master (captain), the agent must be identified as agent. In this event, the name of the master (captain) need not be stated.

On Board Notations

96. If a preprinted "Shipped on board" bill of lading is presented, its issuance date will be deemed to be the date of shipment unless it bears a separate dated on board notation, in which event the date of the on board notation will be deemed to be the date of shipment whether or not the on board date is before or after the issuance date of the bill of lading.

97. "Shipped in apparent good order", "Laden on board", "clean on board" or other phrases incorporating words such as "shipped" or "on board" have the same effect as "Shipped on board".

Ports of Loading and Ports of Discharge

98. While the named port of loading, as required by the credit, should appear in the port of loading field within the bill of lading, it may instead be stated in the field headed "Place of receipt" or the like, if it is clear that the goods were transported from that place of receipt by vessel and provided there is an on board notation evidencing that the goods were loaded on that vessel at the port stated under "Place of receipt" or like term.

99. While the named port of discharge, as required by the credit, should appear in the port of discharge field within the bill of lading, it may be stated in the field headed "Place of final destination" or the like if it is clear that the goods were to be transported to that place of final destination by vessel and provided there is a notation evidencing that the port of discharge is that stated under "Place of final destination" or like term.

100. If a credit gives a geographical area or range of ports of loading or discharge (e.g., "Any European Port"), the bill of lading must indicate the actual port of loading or discharge, which must be within the geographical area or range stated in the credit.

Consignee, Order Party, Shipper and Endorsement, Notify Party

101. If a credit requires a bill of lading to show that the goods are consigned to a named party, e.g., "consigned to Bank X" (a "straight" bill of lading), rather than "to order" or "to order of Bank X", the bill of lading must not contain words such as "to order" or "to order of " that precede the name of that named party, whether typed or preprinted. Likewise, if a credit requires the goods to be consigned "to order" or "to order of " a named party, the bill of lading must not show that the goods are consigned straight to the named party.

102. If a bill of lading is issued to order or to order of the shipper, it must be endorsed by the shipper. An endorsement indicating that it is made for or on behalf of the shipper is acceptable.

103. If a credit does not state a notify party, the respective field on the bill of lading may be left blank or completed in any manner.

Transhipment and Partial Shipment

104. Transhipment is the unloading from one vessel and reloading to another vessel during the carriage from the port of loading to the port of discharge stated in the

credit. If it does not occur between these two ports, unloading and reloading is not considered to be transhipment.

105. If a credit prohibits partial shipments and more than one set of original bills of lading are presented covering shipment from one or more por ts of loading (as specifically allowed, or within the geographical area or range stated in the credit), such documents are acceptable provided that they cover the shipment of goods on the same vessel and same journey and are destined for the same port of discharge. In the event that more than one set of bills of lading are presented and incorporate different dates of shipment, the latest of these dates of shipment will be taken for the calculation of any presentation period and must fall on or before the latest shipment date specified in the credit. Shipment on more than one vessel is a partial shipment, even if the vessels leave on the same day for the same destination.

Clean Bills of Lading

106. Clauses or notations on bills of lading which expressly declare a defective condition of the goods or packaging are not acceptable. Clauses or notations which do not expressly declare a defective condition of the goods or packaging (e.g., "packaging may not be sufficient for the sea jour ney ") do not constitute a discrepancy. A statement that the packaging "is not sufficient for the sea journey" would not be acceptable.

107. If the word "clean" appears on a bill of lading and has been deleted, the bill of lading will not be deemed to be claused or unclean unless it specifically bears a clause or notation declaring that the goods or packaging are defective.

Goods Description

108. A goods description in the bill of lading may be shown in general terms not in conflict with that stated in the credit.

Corrections and Alterations

109. Corrections and alterations on a bill of lading must be authenticated. Such authentication must appear to have been made by the carrier, master (captain) or any of their agents (who may be different from the agent that may have issued or signed it), provided they are identified as an agent of the carrier or the master (captain).

110. Nonnegotiable copies of bills of lading do not need to include any signature on, or authentication of, any alterations or corrections that may have been made on the original.

Freight and Additional Costs

111. If a credit requires that a bill of lading show that freight has been paid or is payable at destination, the bill of lading must be marked accordingly.

112. Applicants and issuing banks should be specific in stating the requirements of documents to show whether freight is to be prepaid or collected.

113. If a credit states that costs additional to freight are not acceptable, a bill of lading must not indicate that costs additional to the freight have been or will be incurred. Such indication may be by express reference to additional costs or by the use of shipment terms which refer to costs associated with the loading or unloading of goods, such as Free In (FI), Free Out (FO), Free In and Out (FIO) and Free In and Out Stowed (FIOS). A reference in the transport document to costs which may be levied as a result of a delay in unloading the goods or after the goods have been unloaded, e.g., costs covering the late return of containers, is not considered to be an indication of additional costs in this context.

Goods Covered by more than One Bill of Lading

114. If a bill of lading states that the goods in a container are covered by that bill of lading plus one or more other bills of lading, and the bill of lading states that all bills of lading must be surrendered, or words of similar effect, this means that all bills of lading related to that container must be presented in order for the container to be released. Such a bill of lading is not acceptable unless all the bills of lading form part of the same presentation under the same credit.

CHARTER PARTY BILL OF LADING

Application of UCP 600 Article 22

115. If a credit requires presentation of a charter party bill of lading or if a credit allows presentation of a charter party bill of lading and a charter party bill of lading is presented, UCP 600 article 22 is applicable.

116. A transport document containing any indication that it is subject to a charter party is a charter party bill of lading under UCP 600 article 22.

FULL SET OF ORIGINALS

117. A UCP 600 article 22 transport document must indicate the number of originals that have been issued. Transport documents marked "First Original", "Second Original", "Third Original", "Original", "Duplicate", "Triplicate", etc., or similar expressions are all originals. Charter party bills of lading need not be marked "original" to be acceptable under a credit. In addition to UCP 600 article 17, the ICC Banking Commission Policy Statement, document 470/871(Rev), titled "The Determination of an 'Original' Document in the Context of UCP 500 subArticle 20(b)" is recommended for further guidance on originals and copies and remains valid under UCP 600. The content of the Policy Statement appears in the Appendix of this publication, for reference purposes.

Signing of Charter Party Bills of Lading

118. Original charter party bills of lading must be signed in the form described in UCP 600 subarticle 22(a)(i).
    a. If the master (captain), charterer or owner signs the charter party bill of lading, the signature of the master (captain), charterer or owner must be identified as "master" ("captain"), "charterer" or "owner".
    b. If an agent signs the charter party bill of lading on behalf of the master (captain), charterer or owner, the agent must be identified as agent of the master (captain), charterer or owner. In this event, the name of the master (captain) need not be stated, but the name of the charterer or owner must appear.

On Board Notations

119. If a preprinted "Shipped on board" charter party bill of lading is presented, its issuance date will be deemed to be the date of shipment unless it bears an on board notation, in which event the date of the on board notation will be deemed to be the date of shipment whether or not the on board date is before or after the issuance date of the document.

120. "Shipped in apparent good order", "Laden on board", "clean on board" or other phrases incorporating words such as "shipped" or "on board" have the same effect as "Shipped on board".

Ports of Loading and Ports of Discharge

121. If a credit gives a geographical area or range of ports of loading or discharge (e.g., "Any European Port"), the charter party bill of lading must indicate the actual port or ports of loading, which must be within the geographical area or range indicated but may show the geographical area or range of ports as the port of discharge.

Consignee, Order Party, Shipper and Endorsement, Notify Party

122. If a credit requires a charter party bill of lading to show that the goods are consigned to a named party, e.g., "consigned to Bank X" (a "straight" bill of lading), rather than "to order" or "to order of Bank X", the charter party bill of lading must not contain words such as "to order" or "to order of " that precede the name of that named party, whether typed or preprinted. Likewise, if a credit requires the goods to be consigned "to order" or "to order of" a named party, the charter party bill of lading must not show that the goods are consigned straight to the named party.

123. If a charter party bill of lading is issued to order or to order of the shipper, it must be endorsed by the shipper. An endorsement indicating that it is made for or on behalf of the shipper is acceptable.

124. If a credit does not state a notify party, the respective field on the charter party bill of lading may be left blank or completed in any manner.

Partial Shipment

125. If a credit prohibits partial shipments, and more than one set of original charter party bills of lading are presented covering shipment from one or more ports of loading (as specifically allowed, or within the geographical area or range stated in the credit), such documents are acceptable, provided that they cover the shipment of goods on the same vessel and same journey and are destined for the same port of discharge, range of ports or geographical area. In the event that more than one set of charter party bills of lading are presented and incorporate different dates of shipment, the latest of these dates of shipment will be taken for the calculation of any presentation period and must fall on or before the latest shipment date specified in the credit. Shipment on more than one vessel is a partial shipment, even if the vessels leave on the same day for the same destination.

Clean Charter Party Bills of Lading

126. Clauses or notations on charter party bills of lading which expressly declare a defective condition of the goods or packaging are not acceptable. Clauses or notations that do not expressly declare a defective condition of the goods or packaging (e.g., "packaging may not be sufficient for the sea journey") do not constitute a discrepancy. A statement that the packaging "is not sufficient for the sea journey" would not be acceptable.

127. If the word "clean" appears on a charter party bill of lading and has been deleted, the charter party bill of lading will not be deemed to be claused or unclean unless it specifically bears a clause or notation declaring that the goods or packaging are defective.

Goods Description

128. A goods description in charter party bills of lading may be shown in general terms not in conflict with that stated in the credit.

Corrections and Alterations

129. Corrections and alterations on charter party bills of lading must be authenticated. Such authentication must appear to have been made by the owner, charterer, master (captain) or any of their agents (who may be different from the agent that may have issued or signed it), provided they are identified as an agent of the owner, charterer or the master (captain).

130. Nonnegotiable copies of charter party bills of lading do not need to include any signature on, or authentication of, any alterations or corrections that may have been made on the original.

Freight and Additional Costs

131. If a credit requires that a charter party bill of lading show that freight has been paid or is payable at destination, the charter party bill of lading must be marked accordingly.

132. Applicants and issuing banks should be specific in stating the requirements of documents to show whether freight is to be prepaid or collected.

133. If a credit states that costs additional to freight are not acceptable, a charter party bill of lading must not indicate that costs additional to the freight have been or will be incurred. Such indication may be by express reference to additional costs or by the use of shipment terms which refer to costs associated with the loading or unloading of goods, such as Free In (FI), Free Out (FO), Free In and Out (FIO) and Free In and Out Stowed (FIOS). A reference in the transport document to costs which may be levied as a result of a delay in unloading the goods or after the goods have been unloaded, is not considered to be an indication of additional costs in this context.

AIR TRANSPORT DOCUMENT

Application of UCP 600 Article 23

134. If a credit requires presentation of an air transport document covering an airporttoairport shipment, UCP 600 article 23 is applicable.

135. If a credit requires presentation of an "air waybill", "air consignment note" or similar, UCP 600 article 23 applies. To comply with UCP 600 article 23, an air transport document must appear to cover an airporttoairport shipment but need not be titled "air waybill", "air consignment note" or similar.

Original Air Transport Document

136. The air transport document must appear to be the original for consignor or shipper. A requirement for a full set of originals is satisfied by the presentation of a document indicating that it is the original for consignor or shipper.

Signing of Air Transport Documents

137. An original air transport document must be signed in the form described in UCP 600 subarticle 23(a)(i) and indicate the name of the carrier, identified as carrier. If an agent signs an air transport document on behalf of a carrier, the agent must be identified as agent and must identify on whose behalf it is signing, unless the carrier has been identified elsewhere on the air transport document.

138. If a credit states "House air waybill is acceptable" or "Freight Forwarder's air waybill is acceptable" or uses a similar phrase, then the air transport document may be signed by a freight forwarder in the capacity of a freight forwarder without the need to identify itself as a carrier or agent for a named carrier. In this event, it is not necessary to show the name of the carrier.

Goods Accepted for Carriage, Date of Shipment, and Requirement for an Actual Date of Dispatch

139. An air transport document must indicate that the goods have been accepted for carriage.

140. The date of issuance of an air transport document is deemed to be the date of shipment unless the document shows a separate notation of the flight date, in which case this will be deemed to be the date of shipment. Any other information appearing on the air transport document relative to the flight number and date will not be considered in determining the date of shipment.

Airports of Departure and Destination

141. An air transport document must indicate the airport of departure and airport of destination as stated in the credit. The identification of airports by the use of IATA codes instead of writing out the name in full (e.g., LHR instead of London Heathrow) is not a discrepancy.

142. If a credit gives a geographical area or range of airports of departure or destination (e.g., "Any European Airport"), the air transport document must indicate the actual airport of departure or destination, which must be within the geographical area or range stated in the credit.

Consignee, Order Party and Notify Party

143. An air transport document should not be issued "to order" or "to order of" a named party, because it is not a document of title. Even if a credit calls for an air transport document made out "to order" or "to order of" a named party, a document presented showing goods consigned to that party, without mention of "to order" or "to order of", is acceptable.

144. If a credit does not state a notify party, the respective field on the air transport document may be left blank or completed in any manner.

Transhipment and Partial Shipment

145. Transhipment is the unloading from one aircraft and reloading to another aircraft during the carriage from the airport of departure to the airport of destination stated in the credit. If it does not occur between these two airports, unloading and reloading is not considered to be transhipment.

146. If a credit prohibits partial shipments and more than one air transport document is presented covering dispatch from one or more airports of departure (as specifically allowed, or within the geographical area or range stated in the credit), such documents are acceptable, provided that they cover the dispatch of goods on the same aircraft and same flight and are destined for the same airport of destination. In the event that more than one air transport document is presented incorporating different dates of shipment, the latest of these dates of shipment will be taken for the calculation of any presentation period and must fall on or before the latest shipment date specified in the credit.

147. Shipment on more than one aircraft is a partial shipment, even if the aircraft leave on the same day for the same destination.

Clean Air Transport Documents

148. Clauses or notations on an air transport document which expressly declare a defective condition of the goods or packaging are not acceptable. Clauses or notations on the air transport document which do not expressly declare a defective condition of the goods or packaging (e.g., "packaging may not be sufficient for the air journey") do not constitute a discrepancy. A statement that the packaging "is not sufficient for the air journey" would not be acceptable.

149. If the word "clean" appears on an air transport document and has been deleted, the air transport document will not be deemed to be claused or unclean unless it specifically bears a clause or notation declaring that the goods or packaging are defective.

Goods Description
150. A goods description in an air transport document may be shown in general terms not in conflict with that stated in the credit.

Corrections and Alterations
151. Corrections and alterations on air transport documents must be authenticated. Such authentication must appear to have been made by the carrier or any of its agents (who may be different from the agent that may have issued or signed it), provided it is identified as an agent of the carrier.
152. Copies of air transport documents do not need to include any signature of the carrier or agent (or shipper, even if required by the credit to appear on the original air transport document), nor any authentication of any alterations or corrections that may have been made on the original.

Freight and Additional Costs
153. If a credit requires that an air transport document show that freight has been paid or is payable at destination, the air transport document must be marked accordingly.
154. Applicants and issuing banks should be specific in stating the requirements of documents to show whether freight is to be prepaid or collected.
155. If a credit states that costs additional to freight are not acceptable, an air transport document must not indicate that costs additional to the freight have been or will be incurred. Such indication may be by express reference to additional costs or by the use of shipment terms that refer to costs associated with the loading or unloading of goods. A reference in the transport document to costs which may be levied as a result of a delay in unloading the goods or after the goods have been unloaded is not considered an indication of additional costs in this context.
156. Air transport documents often have separate boxes which, by their preprinted headings, indicate that they are for freight charges "prepaid" and for freight charges "to collect", respectively. A requirement in a credit for an air transport document to show that freight has been prepaid will be fulfilled by a statement of the freight charges under the heading "Freight Prepaid" or a similar expression or indication, and a requirement that an air transport document show that freight has to be collected will be fulfilled by a statement of the freight charges under the heading "Freight to Collect" or a similar expression or indication.

ROAD, RAIL OR INLAND WATERWAY TRANSPORT DOCUMENTS

Application of UCP 600 Article 24
157. If a credit requires presentation of a transport document covering movement by road, rail or inland waterway, UCP 600 article 24 is applicable.

Original and Duplicate of Road, Rail or Inland Waterway Transport Documents
158. If a credit requires a rail or inland waterway transport document, the transport document presented will be accepted as an original whether or not it is marked

as an original. A road transport document must appear to be the original for consignor or shipper or bear no marking indicating for whom the document has been prepared. With respect to rail waybills, the practice of many railway companies is to provide the shipper or consignor with only a duplicate (often a carbon copy) duly authenticated by the railway company's stamp. Such a duplicate will be accepted as an original.

Carrier and Signing of Road, Rail or Inland Waterway Transport Documents
159. The term "carrier" need not appear at the signature line provided the transport document appears to be signed by the carrier or an agent on behalf of the carrier, if the carrier is otherwise identified as the "carrier" on the transport document. International standard banking practice is to accept a railway bill evidencing date stamp by the railway company or railway station of departure without showing the name of the carrier or a named agent signing for or on behalf of the carrier.
160. The term "carrier" used in UCP 600 article 24 includes terms in transport documents such as "issuing carrier", "actual carrier", "succeeding carrier" and "contracting carrier".
161. Any signature, stamp or notation of receipt on the transport document must appear to be made either by:
    a. the carrier, identified as the carrier, or
    b. a named agent acting or signing for or on behalf of the carrier and indicating the name and capacity of the carrier on whose behalf that agent is acting or signing.

Order Party and Notify Party
162. Transport documents which are not documents of title should not be issued "to order" or "to order of " a named party. Even if a credit calls for a transport document which is not a document of title to be made out "to order" or "to order of" a named party, such a document showing goods consigned to that party, without mention of "to order" or "to order of", is acceptable.
163. If a credit does not stipulate a notify party, the respective field on the transport document may be left blank or completed in any manner.

Partial Shipment
164. Shipment on more than one means of conveyance (more than one truck (lorry), train, vessel, etc.) is a partial shipment, even if such means of conveyance leave on the same day for the same destination.

Goods Description
165. A goods description in the transport document may be shown in general terms not in conflict with that stated in the credit.

Corrections and Alterations
166. Corrections and alterations on a UCP 600 article 24 transport document must be authenticated. Such authentication must appear to have been made by the carrier or any one of their named agents, who may be different from the agent that may have issued or signed it, provided they are identified as an agent of the carrier.
167. Copies of UCP 600 article 24 transport documents do not need to include any signature on, or authentication of, any alterations or corrections that may have been made on the original.

Freight and Additional Costs

168. If a credit requires that a UCP 600 article 24 transport document show that freight has been paid or is payable at destination, the transport document must be marked accordingly.

169. Applicants and issuing banks should be specific in stating the requirements of documents to show whether freight is to be prepaid or collected.

INSURANCE DOCUMENT AND COVERAGE

Application of UCP 600 Article 28

170. If a credit requires presentation of an insurance document such as an insurance policy, insurance certificate or declaration under an open cover, UCP 600 article 28 is applicable.

Issuers of Insurance Documents

171. Insurance documents must appear to have been issued and signed by insurance companies or underwriters or their agents or proxies. If required by the insurance document or in accordance with the credit terms, all originals must appear to have been countersigned.

172. An insurance document is acceptable if issued on an insurance broker's stationery, provided the insurance document has been signed by an insurance company or its agent or proxy, or by an underwriter or its agent or proxy. A broker may sign as agent for the named insurance company or named underwriter.

Risks to Be Covered

173. An insurance document must cover the risks defined in the credit. Even though a credit may be explicit with regard to risks to be covered, there may be reference to exclusion clauses in the document. If a credit requires "all risks" coverage, this is satisfied by the presentation of an insurance document evidencing any "all risks" clause or notation, even if it is stated that certain risks are excluded. An insurance document indicating that it covers Institute Cargo Clauses (A) satisfies a condition in a credit calling for an "all risks" clause or notation.

174. Insurance covering the same risk for the same shipment must be covered under one document unless the insurance documents for partial cover each clearly reflect, by percentage or otherwise, the value of each insurer's cover and that each insurer will bear its share of the liability severally and without preconditions relating to any other insurance cover that may have been effected for that shipment.

Dates

175. An insurance document that incorporates an expiry date must clearly indicate that such expiry date relates to the latest date that loading on board or dispatch or taking in charge of the goods (as applicable) is to occur, as opposed to an expiry date for the presentation of any claims thereunder.

Percentage and Amount

176. An insurance document must be issued in the currency of, and, as a minimum for, the amount required by the credit. The UCP does not provide for any maximum percentage of insurance coverage.

177. If a credit requires the insurance cover to be irrespective of percentage, the insurance document must not contain a clause stating that the insurance cover is subject to a franchise or an excess deductible.

178. If it is apparent from the credit or from the documents that the final invoice amount only represents a certain par t of the gross value of the goods (e.g., due to discounts, prepayments or the like, or because part of the value of the goods is to be paid at a later date), the calculation of insurance cover must be based on the full gross value of the goods.

Insured Party and Endorsement
179. An insurance document must be in the form as required by the credit and, where necessary, be endorsed by the party to whose order claims are payable. A document issued to bearer is acceptable where the credit requires an insurance document endorsed in blank and vice versa.
180. If a credit is silent as to the insured party, an insurance document evidencing that claims are payable to the order of the shipper or beneficiary would not be acceptable unless endorsed. An insurance document should be issued or endorsed so that the right to receive payment under it passes upon, or prior to, the release of the documents.

CERTIFICATES OF ORIGIN

Basic Requirement
181. A requirement for a certificate of origin will be satisfied by the presentation of a signed, dated document that certifies to the origin of the goods.

Issuers of Certificates of Origin
182. A certificate of origin must be issued by the party stated in the credit. However, if a credit requires a certificate of origin to be issued by the beneficiary, the exporter or the manufacturer, a document issued by a chamber of commerce will be deemed acceptable, provided it clearly identifies the beneficiary, the exporter or the manufacturer as the case may be. If a credit does not state who is to issue the certificate, then a document issued by any party, including the beneficiary, is acceptable.

Contents of Certificates of Origin
183. The certificate of origin must appear to relate to the invoiced goods. The goods description in the certificate of origin may be shown in general terms not in conflict with that stated in the credit or by any other reference indicating a relation to the goods in a required document.
184. Consignee information, if shown, must not be in conflict with the consignee information in the transport document. However, if a credit requires a transport document to be issued "to order", "to the order of shipper", "to order of the issuing bank" or "consigned to the issuing bank", the certificate of origin may show the applicant of the credit, or another party named therein, as consignee. If a credit has been transferred, the name of the first beneficiary as consignee would also be acceptable.
185. The certificate of origin may show the consignor or exporter as a party other than the beneficiary of the credit or the shipper on the transport document.

AFTERWORD

* The information contained in this Afterword is not part of the official ISBP publication or approved by the ICC Commission on Banking Technique and Practice. The information contained herein is intended to provide a historical perspective and is solely the work of the author.

Since the early days of letters of credit, bankers and banking groups have been collecting and documenting banking practices. The national r ules established prior to the development of the first *Uniform Customs and Practice for Documentary Credits* ("UCP") were, in fact, collections of banking practice in a number of individual countries. These national documents, created in the early 1900s established basic rules for letters of credit in Argentina, Czechoslovakia, France, Germany, Italy, Sweden and the United States. The first paragraph of the *Regulations Affecting Export Commercial Letters of Credit* created in the United States in 1920 stated: "Payments under Export Commercial Credits advised to the undersigned are made in conformity with the following regulations, which are in accord with the standard practice adopted by the New York Bankers Commercial Credit Conference of 1920". Note the reference to "standard practice".

These rules and practices, distributed by banks to their cor respondents throughout the world, were simply an articulation of how banks handled letters of credit and were intended to inform their correspondents of the practices they followed in their own countries. Ultimately, these practices were documented more formally and on a global scale in the first UCP, at the time entitled *Uniform Customs and Practice for Commercial Documentary Credits*. Even after this, it was not unusual for banks and banking groups to continue documenting banking practices in the form of checklists that were often used during the process of document examination.

After the revision of UCP 400 and the introduction of UCP 500 in 1993, banks in the United States decided to focus their attention on documenting the various banking practices in the US and Mexico to supplement those articulated in the UCP. With the introduction of UCP 500, these practices were highlighted in Article 13 in the sentence "Compliance of the stipulated documents on their face with the terms and conditions of the Credit shall be determined by international standard banking practice as reflected in these Articles." While this reference was restricted to the articles of the UCP, it was felt that standard banking practices were composed of many practices not specifically articulated in the UCP. In 1996, these practices were published in the *Standard Banking Practices for the Examination of Letter of Credit Documents* ("SBPED") by the US Council on International Banking (now the International Financial Services Association). Like the documents distributed in the early 1900s, the SBPED were distributed by banks to their correspondents worldwide.

In May 2000, a request was made for the International Chamber of Commerce to undertake a similar project on a more global scale. As a result, a working group was established to collect and document global banking practices that were not included in the UCP. The result of their work was the publication in January 2003 of the *International Standard Banking Practice for the Examination of Documents under Documentary Credits*

("ISBP"). This publication was updated in 2007 to bring it in line with the latest revision of the UCP, UCP 600.

Dan Taylor
President and CEO of the International Financial Services Association; and Vice Chairman of the ICC Commission on Banking Technique and Practice.

APPENDIX

The Determination of an "Original" Document in the Context of UCP 500 sub-Article 20(b)*

*Decision approved by the ICC Commission on Banking Technique and Practice and published on 12 July 1999

1. Background
Over a period of several years there have been a number of queries raised with the ICC Banking Commission as to the determination, by banks, of what is an "original" document under a letter of credit and the necessity, if any, for such a document to be so marked.

For ease of reference the text of subArticle 20(b) reads:

> "Unless otherwise stipulated in the Credit, banks will also accept as an original document(s), a document(s) produced or appearing to have been produced:
> i.   by reprographic, automated or computerized systems;
> ii. as carbon copies;
> provided that it is marked as original and, where necessary, appears to be signed.
>
> A document may be signed by handwriting, by facsimile signature, by perforated signature, by stamp, by symbol, or by any other mechanical or electronic method of authentication."

2. Determination of Originality
In documentary credit operations, the document checker is faced with a number of issues pertaining to originality including:

Apparent Originality
Banks undertake to determine whether a document appears on its face to be an original document, as distinguished from a copy. Except as expressly required by a letter of credit including an incorporated term – such as UCP 500 subArticles 23(a)(iv) or 34(b) – banks do not undertake to determine whether an apparent original is the sole original. Banks rely on the apparent intent of the issuer of the document that it be treated as an original rather than a copy.

In this regard, a person sending a telefax or making a photocopy on plain paper or pressing through carbon paper presumably intends to produce a copy. On the other hand, a person printing a document on plain paper from a text that that person created and electronically stored presumably intends to produce an original. Accordingly, documents bearing facsimile signatures or printed in their entirety (even including the issuer's letterhead and/or signature) from electronically stored text are presumably intended by the document issuer to be original and in practice are accepted by banks as original.

Documents that Appear to be Original But Are Not
Banks do not undertake to determine whether a document is original in fact. Under UCP 500 Article 15, banks are not responsible for the genuineness or falsification of any document. If a document appears to be original or to have been marked as original but is in fact not original, then its presentation may give rise to exceptional defences, rights, or obligations under the law applicable to forged or fraudulent presentations and is beyond the scope of UCP 500.

UCP 500 Requirements
The UCP neither requires nor permits an examination beyond the face of a document to determine how the document was in fact produced, unless the document was produced by the bank, e.g. on a telefax, telex, e-mail, or other system that prints outmessages received by the bank. The "produced or appearing to have been produced" language in subArticle 20(b) does not override UCP 500 subArticles 13(a), 13(c), or 14(b), or other practice and law that prohibit issuers and confirmers from deter mining compliance on the basis of extrinsic facts.

As indicated by inclusion of the word "also" ("... banks will also accept as original(s) ..."), sub-Ar ticle 20(b) is neither comprehensive nor exclusive in its provisions that distinguish originals from copies. For example, a document printed on plain paper from electronically stored text is acceptable, without regard to 20(b), if it appears to be an original.

SubArticle 20(b) does not apply to documents that appear to be only partially produced by reprographic, automated, or computerized systems or as carbon copies. In this regard, a photocopy ceases to be "reprographically produced" within the meaning of sub-Article 20(b) when it is also manually stamped, dated, completed, or signed by the issuer of the document.

The "marked as original" proviso in sub-Article 20(b) is satisfied by any marking on a document or any recital in the text of a document that indicates that the issuer of the document intends it to be treated as an original rather than a copy. Accordingly, a document that appears to have been printed on plain paper from electronically stored text is "marked as original" under sub-Article 20(b) if it also states that it is original or includes letterhead or is hand marked.

SubArticle 13(a) of UCP 500 refers to compliance of the presented documents being determined by international standard banking practice as defined in the articles of UCP. Inter national standard banking practice in relation to determination of "original" documents could be described as follows:

3. *Correct Interpretation of Subarticle 20(b)*

General Approach

Banks examine documents presented under a letter of credit to determine, among other things, whether on their face they appear to be original. Banks treat as original any document bearing an apparently original signature, mark, stamp, or label of the issuer of the document, unless the document itself indicates that it is not original. Accordingly, unless a document indicates otherwise, it is treated as original if it:

(A)   appears to be written, typed, perforated, or stamped by the document issuer's hand; or

(B)   appears to be on the document issuer's original stationery; or

(C)   states that it is original, unless the statement appears not to apply to the document presented (e.g. because it appears to be a photocopy of another document and the statement of originality appears to apply to that other document).

Hand Signed Documents

Consistent with subparagraph (A) above, banks treat as original any document that appears to be hand signed by the issuer of the document. For example, a hand signed draft or commercial invoice is treated as an original document, whether or not some or all other constituents of the document are preprinted, carbon copied, or produced by reprographic, automated, or computerized systems.

Facsimile Signed Documents

Banks treat a facsimile signature as the equivalent of a hand signature. Accordingly, a document that appears to bear the document issuer's facsimile signature is also treated as an original document.

Photocopies

Banks treat as nonoriginal any document that appears to be a photocopy of another document. If, however, a photocopy appears to have been completed by the document issuer's hand marking the photocopy, then, consistent with subparagraph (A) above, the resulting document is treated as an original document unless it indicates otherwise. If a document appears to have been produced by photocopying text onto original stationery rather than onto blank paper, then, consistent with subparagraph (B) above, it is treated as an original document unless it indicates otherwise.

Telefaxed Presentation of Documents
Banks treat as nonoriginal any document that is produced at the bank's telefax machine. A letter of credit that permits presentation by telefax waives any requirement for presentation of an original of any document presented by telefax.

Statements Indicating Originality
Consistent with either or both of subparagraphs (A) and (C) above, a document on which the word "original" has been stamped is treated as an original document. A statement in a document that it is a "duplicate original" or the "third of three" also indicates that it is original. Originality is also indicated by a statement in a document that it is void if another document of the same tenor and date is used.
Statements Indicating Nonoriginality
   A statement in a document that it is a true copy of another document or that another document is the sole original indicates that it is not original. A statement in a document that it is the "customer's copy" or "shipper's copy" neither disclaims nor affirms its originality.

4. What is Not an "Original"?
A document indicates that it is not an original if it
   i.   appears to be produced on a telefax machine;
   ii.   appears to be a photocopy of another document which has not otherwise been completed by hand marking the photocopy or by photocopying it on what appears to be original stationery; or
   iii. states in the document that it is a true copy of another document or that another document is the sole original.

5. Conclusion
Based upon the comments received from ICC national committees, members of the ICC Banking Commission and other interested parties, the statements in clauses 3 and 4 above reflect international standard banking practice in the correct interpretation of UCP 500 subArticle 20(b).

Appendix 4

International Standby Practices – ISP98

General provisions
Scope, Application, Definitions, and Interpretation of These Rules

1.01 Scope and application
a. These Rules are intended to be applied to standby letters of credit (including performance, financial, and direct pay standby letters of credit).
b. A standby letter of credit or other similar under-taking, however named or described, whether for domestic or international use, may be made subject to these Rules by express reference to them.
c. An undertaking subject to these Rules may expressly modify or exclude their application.
d. An undertaking subject to these Rules is here-inafter referred to as a **'standby'**.

1.02 Relationship to law and other rules
a. These Rules supplement the applicable law to the extent not prohibited by that law.
b. These Rules supersede conflicting provisions in any other rules of practice to which a standby letter of credit is also made subject.

1.03 Interpretative principles
These Rules shall be interpreted as mercantile usage with regard for:

a. integrity of standbys as reliable and efficient undertakings to pay;
b. practice and terminology of banks and businesses in day-to-day transactions;
c. consistency within the worldwide system of banking operations and commerce; and
d. worldwide uniformity in their interpretation and application.

1.04 Effect of the rules
Unless the context otherwise requires, or unless expressly modified or excluded, these Rules apply as terms and conditions incorporated into a standby, confirmation, advice, nomination, amendment, transfer, request for issuance, or other agreement of:

519

i.   the issuer;
ii. the beneficiary to the extent it uses the standby;
iii. any advisor;
iv. any confirmer;
v.   any person nominated in the standby who acts or agrees to act; and
vi. the applicant who authorises issuance of the standby or otherwise agrees to the application of these Rules.

1.05 Exclusion of matters related to due issuance and fraudulent or abusive drawing
These Rules do not define or otherwise provide for:

a. power or authority to issue a standby;
b. formal requirements for execution of a standby (eg a signed writing); or
c. defenses to honour based on fraud, abuse, or similar matters.

These matters are left to applicable law.

GENERAL PRINCIPLES

1.06 Nature of standbys
a. A standby is an irrevocable, independent, documentary and binding undertaking when issued and need not so state.
b. Because a standby is irrevocable, an issuer's obligations under a standby cannot be amended or cancelled by the issuer except as provided in the standby or as consented to by the person against whom the amendment or cancellation is asserted.
c. Because a standby is independent, the enforceability of an issuer's obligations under a standby does not depend on:
    i.   the issuer's right or ability to obtain reimbursement from the applicant;
    ii. the beneficiary's right to obtain payment from the applicant;
    iii. a reference in the standby to any reimbursement agreement or underlying transaction; or
    iv. the issuer's knowledge of performance or breach of any reimbursement agreement or underlying transaction.
d. Because a standby is documentary, an issuer's obligations depend on the presentation of documents and an examination of required documents on their face.
e. Because a standby or amendment is binding when issued, it is enforceable against an issuer whether or not the applicant authorised its issuance, the issuer received a fee, or the beneficiary received or relied on the standby or the amendment.

1.07 Independence of the issuer-beneficiary relationship
An issuer's obligations toward the beneficiary are not affected by the issuer's rights and obligations toward the applicant under any applicable agreement, practice, or law.

1.08 Limits to responsibilities
An issuer is not responsible for:

a. performance or breach of any underlying transaction;
b. accuracy, genuineness, or effect of any document presented under the standby;
c. action or omission of others even if the other person is chosen by the issuer or nominated person; or
d. observance of law or practice other than that chosen in the standby or applicable at the place of issuance.

TERMINOLOGY

1.09 Defined terms
In addition to the meanings given in standard banking practice and applicable law, the following terms have or include the meanings indicated below:

a.   Definitions

'Applicant' is a person who applies for issuance of a standby or for whose account it is issued, and includes (i) a person applying in its own name but for the account of another person or (ii) an issuer acting for its own account.

'Beneficiary' is a named person who is entitled to draw under a standby. See Rule 1.11(c)(ii).

'Business Day' means a day on which the place of business at which the relevant act is to be performed is regularly open; and **'Banking Day'** means a day on which the relevant bank is regularly open at the place at which the relevant act is to be performed.

'Confirmer' is a person who, upon an issuer's nomination to do so, adds to the issuer's undertaking its own undertaking to honour a standby. See Rule 1.11(c)(i).

'Demand' means, depending on the context, either a request to honour a standby or a document that makes such a request.

'Document' means a draft, demand, document of title, investment security, invoice, certificate of default, or any other representation of fact, law, right, or opinion, that upon presentation (whether in a paper or electronic medium), is capable of being examined for compliance with the terms and conditions of a standby.

'Drawing' means, depending on the context, either a demand presented or a demand honoured.

'Expiration Date' means the latest day for a complying presentation provided in a standby.

'Person' includes a natural person, partnership, corporation, limited liability company, government agency, bank, trustee, and any other legal or commercial association or entity.

'Presentation' means, depending on the context, either the act of delivering documents for examination under a standby or the documents so delivered.

'Presenter' is a person who makes a presentation as or on behalf of a beneficiary or nominated person.

'Signature' includes any symbol executed or adopted by a person with a present intent to authenticate a document.

b.   Cross References
'Amendment' – Rule 2.06
'Advice' – Rule 2.05
'Approximately' ('About' or 'Circa') – Rule 3.08(f)
'Assignment of Proceeds' – Rule 6.06
'Automatic Amendment' – Rule 2.06(a)
'Copy' – Rule 4.15(d)
'Cover Instructions' – Rule 5.08

'Honour' – Rule 2.01
'Issuer' – Rule 2.01
'Multiple Presentations' – Rule 3.08(b)
'Nominated Person' – Rule 2.04
'Non-documentary Conditions' – Rule 4.11
'Original' – Rule 4.15(b) & (c)
'Partial Drawing' – Rule 3.08(a)
'Standby' – Rule 1.01(d)
'Transfer' – Rule 6.01
'Transferee Beneficiary' – Rule 1.11(c)(ii)
'Transfer by Operation of Law' – Rule 6.11

c. Electronic presentations

The following terms in a standby providing for or permitting electronic presentation shall have the following meanings unless the context otherwise requires:

'Electronic record' means:

i.   a record (information that is inscribed on a tangible medium or that is stored in an electronic or other medium and is retrievable in perceivable form);
ii. communicated by electronic means to a system for receiving, storing, re-transmitting, or otherwise processing information (data, text, images, sounds, codes, computer programs, software, databases, and the like); and
iii. capable of being authenticated and then examined for compliance with the terms and conditions of the standby.

'Authenticate' means to verify an electronic record by generally accepted procedure or methodology in commercial practice:

i.   the identity of a sender or source, and
ii. the integrity of or errors in the transmission of information content.

The criteria for assessing the integrity of information in an electronic record is whether the information has remained complete and unaltered, apart from the addition of any endorsement and any change which arises in the normal course of communication, storage and display.

'Electronic signature' means letters, characters, numbers, or other symbols in electronic form, attached to or logically associated with an electronic record that are executed or adopted by a party with present intent to authenticate an electronic record.

'Receipt' occurs when:

i.   an electronic record enters in a form capable of being processed by the information system designated in the standby, or
ii. an issuer retrieves an electronic record sent to an information system other than that designated by the issuer.

1.10 Redundant or otherwise undesirable terms

a. A standby should not or need not state that it is:
   i.   unconditional or abstract (if it does, it signifies merely that payment under it is conditioned solely on presentation of specified documents);
   ii. absolute (if it does, it signifies merely that it is irrevocable);
   iii. primary (if it does, it signifies merely that it is the independent obligation of the issuer);
   iv. payable from the issuer's own funds (if it does, it signifies merely that payment under it does not depend on the availability of applicant funds and is made to satisfy the issuer's own independent obligation); or

v.   clean or payable on demand (if it does, it signifies merely that it is payable upon presentation of a written demand or other documents specified in the standby).

b. A standby should not use the term **'and/or'** (if it does it means either or both).

c. The following terms have no single accepted meaning:

    i.   and shall be disregarded:
      'callable',
      'divisible',
      'fractionable',
      'indivisible', and
      'transmissible',

    ii.   and shall be disregarded unless their context gives them meaning:
      'assignable',
      'evergreen',
      'reinstate', and
      'revolving'.

1.11 Interpretation of these rules

a. These Rules, are to be interpreted in the context of applicable standard practice.

b. In these Rules, 'standby letter of credit' refers to the type of independent undertaking for which these Rules were intended, whereas 'standby' refers to an undertaking subjected to these Rules.

c. Unless the context otherwise requires:

    i.   'Issuer' includes a 'confirmer' as if the confirmer were a separate issuer and its confirmation were a separate standby issued for the account of the issuer;

    ii.   'Beneficiary' includes a person to whom the named beneficiary has effectively transferred drawing rights ('transferee beneficiary');

    iii. 'Including' means 'including but not limited to';

    iv. 'A or B' means 'A or B or both'; 'either A or B' means 'A or B, but not both'; and 'A and B' means 'both A and B';

    v.   Words in the singular number include the plural, and in the plural include the singular; and

    vi. Words of the neuter gender include any gender.

d. i.   Use of the phrase 'unless a standby otherwise states' or the like in a rule emphasizes that the text of the standby controls over the rule;

    ii.   Absence of such a phrase in other rules does not imply that other rules have priority over the text of the standby;

    iii. Addition of the term 'expressly' or 'clearly' to the phrase 'unless a standby otherwise states' or the like emphasizes that the rule should be excluded or modified only by wording in the standby that is specific and unambiguous; and

    iv. While the effect of all of these Rules may be varied by the text of the standby, variations of the effect of some of these Rules may disqualify the standby as an independent undertaking under applicable law.

e. The phrase 'stated in the standby' or the like refers to the actual text of a standby (whether as issued or effectively amended) whereas the phrase 'provided in the standby' or the like refers to both the text of the standby and these Rules as incorporated.

RULE 2

OBLIGATIONS

2.01 Undertaking to honour by issuer and any confirmer to beneficiary
a.   An issuer undertakes to the beneficiary to honour a presentation that appears on its face to comply with the terms and conditions of the standby in accordance with these Rules supplemented by standard standby practice.
b.   An issuer honours a complying presentation made to it by paying the amount demanded of it at sight, unless the standby provides for honour:
   i.   by acceptance of a draft drawn by the beneficiary on the issuer, in which case the issuer honours by:
     (a)   timely accepting the draft; and
     (b)   thereafter paying the holder of the draft on presentation of the accepted draft on or after its maturity.
   ii.   by deferred payment of a demand made by the beneficiary on the issuer, in which case the issuer honours by:
     (a)   timely incurring a deferred payment obligation; and
     (b)   thereafter paying at maturity.
   iii.   by negotiation, in which case the issuer honours by paying the amount demanded at sight without recourse.
c.   An issuer acts in a timely manner if it pays at sight, accepts a draft, or undertakes a deferred payment obligation (or if it gives notice of dishonour) within the time permitted for examining the presentation and giving notice of dishonour.
d.   i.   A confirmer undertakes to honour a complying presentation made to it by paying the amount demanded of it at sight or, if the standby so states, by another method of honour consistent with the issuer's undertaking.
   ii.   If the confirmation permits presentation to the issuer, then the confirmer undertakes also to honour upon the issuer's wrongful dishonour by performing as if the presentation had been made to the confirmer.
   iii.   If the standby permits presentation to the confirmer, then the issuer undertakes also to honour upon the confirmer's wrongful dishonour by performing as if the presentation had been made to the issuer.
e.   An issuer honours by paying in immediately available funds in the currency designated in the standby unless the standby states it is payable by:
   i.   payment of a monetary unit of account, in which case the undertaking is to pay in that unit of account; or
   ii.   delivery of other items of value, in which case the undertaking is to deliver those items.

2.02 Obligation of different branches, agencies, or other offices
For the purposes of these Rules, an issuer's branch, agency, or other office acting or undertaking to act under a standby in a capacity other than as issuer is obligated in that capacity only and shall be treated as a different person.

2.03 Conditions to issuance
A standby is issued when it leaves an issuer's control unless it clearly specifies that it is not then 'issued' or 'enforceable'. Statements that a standby is not 'available', 'operative', 'effective', or the like do not affect its irrevocable and binding nature at the time it leaves the issuer's control.

2.04 Nomination
a.   A standby may nominate a person to advise, receive a presentation, effect a transfer, confirm, pay, negotiate, incur a deferred payment obligation, or accept a draft.

b.   Nomination does not obligate the nominated person to act except to the extent that the nominated person undertakes to act.
c.   A nominated person is not authorised to bind the person making the nomination.

2.05 Advice of standby or amendment

a.   Unless an advice states otherwise, it signifies that:
   i.   the advisor has checked the apparent authenticity of the advised message in accordance with standard letter of credit practice; and
   ii.   the advice accurately reflects what has been received.
b.   A person who is requested to advise a standby and decides not to do so should notify the requesting party.

2.06 When an amendment is authorised and binding

a.   If a standby expressly states that it is subject to 'automatic amendment' by an increase or decrease in the amount available, an extension of the expiration date, or the like, the amendment is effective automatically without any further notification or consent beyond that expressly provided for in the standby. (Such an amendment may also be referred to as becoming effective 'without amendment'.)
b.   If there is no provision for automatic amendment, an amendment binds:
   i.   the issuer when it leaves the issuer's control; and
   ii.   the confirmer when it leaves the confirmer's control, unless the confirmer indicates that it does not confirm the amendment.
c.   If there is no provision for automatic amendment:
   i.   the beneficiary must consent to the amendment for it to be binding;
   ii.   the beneficiary's consent must be made by an express communication to the person advising the amendment unless the beneficiary presents documents which comply with the standby as amended and which would not comply with the standby prior to such amendment; and
   iii.   an amendment does not require the appli-cant's consent to be binding on the issuer, the confirmer, or the beneficiary.
d.   Consent to only part of an amendment is a rejection of the entire amendment.

2.07 Routing of amendments

a.   An issuer using another person to advise a standby must advise all amendments to that person.
b.   An amendment or cancellation of a standby does not affect the issuer's obligation to a nominated person that has acted within the scope of its nomination before receipt of notice of the amendment or cancellation.
c.   Non-extension of an automatically extendable (renewable) standby does not affect an issuer's obligation to a nominated person who has acted within the scope of its nomination before receipt of a notice of non-extension.

RULE 3

PRESENTATION

3.01 Complying presentation under a standby

A standby should indicate the time, place and location within that place, person to whom, and medium in which presentation should be made. If so, presentation must be so made in order to comply. To the extent that a standby does not so indicate, presentation must be made in accordance with these Rules in order to be complying.

3.02 What constitutes a presentation

The receipt of a document required by and presented under a standby constitutes a presentation requiring examination for compliance with the terms and conditions of the standby even if not all of the required documents have been presented.

3.03 Identification of standby

a. A presentation must identify the standby under which the presentation is made.

b. A presentation may identify the standby by stating the complete reference number of the standby and the name and location of the issuer or by attaching the original or a copy of the standby.

c. If the issuer cannot determine from the face of a document received that it should be processed under a standby or cannot identify the standby to which it relates, presentation is deemed to have been made on the date of identification.

3.04 Where and to whom complying presentation made

a. To comply, a presentation must be made at the place and any location at that place indicated in the standby or provided in these Rules.

b. If no place of presentation to the issuer is indicated in the standby, presentation to the issuer must be made at the place of business from which the standby was issued.

c. If a standby is confirmed, but no place for presentation is indicated in the confirmation, presentation for the purpose of obligating the confirmer (and the issuer) must be made at the place of business of the confirmer from which the confirmation was issued or to the issuer.

d. If no location at a place of presentation is indicated (such as department, floor, room, station, mail stop, post office box, or other location), presentation may be made to:

    i. the general postal address indicated in the standby;

    ii. any location at the place designated to receive deliveries of mail or documents; or

    iii. any person at the place of presentation actually or apparently authorised to receive it.

3.05 When timely presentation made

a. A presentation is timely if made at any time after issuance and before expiry on the expiration date.

b. A presentation made after the close of business at the place of presentation is deemed to have been made on the next business day.

3.06 Complying medium of presentation

a. To comply, a document must be presented in the medium indicated in the standby.

b. Where no medium is indicated, to comply a document must be presented as a paper document, unless only a demand is required, in which case:

    i. a demand that is presented via SWIFT, tested telex, or other similar authenticated means by a beneficiary that is a SWIFT participant or a bank complies; otherwise

    ii. a demand that is not presented as a paper document does not comply unless the issuer permits, in its sole discretion, the use of that medium.

c. A document is not presented as a paper document if it is communicated by electronic means even if the issuer or nominated person receiving it generates a paper document from it.

d. Where presentation in an electronic medium is indicated, to comply a document must be presented as an electronic record capable of being authenticated by the issuer or nominated person to whom it is presented.

3.07 Separateness of each presentation

a. Making a non-complying presentation, withdrawing a presentation, or failing to make any one of a number of scheduled or permitted presentations does not waive or otherwise prejudice the right to make another timely presentation or a timely re-presentation whether or not the standby prohibits partial or multiple drawings or presentations.
b. Wrongful dishonour of a complying presentation does not constitute dishonour of any other presentation under a standby or repudiation of the standby.
c. Honour of a non-complying presentation, with or without notice of its non-compliance, does not waive requirements of a standby for other presentations.

3.08 Partial drawing and multiple presentations; amount of drawings

a. A presentation may be made for less than the full amount available ('partial drawing').
b. More than one presentation ('multiple presentations') may be made.
c. The statement 'partial drawings prohibited' or a similar expression means that a presentation must be for the full amount available.
d. The statement 'multiple drawings prohibited' or a similar expression means that only one presentation may be made and honoured but that it may be for less than the full amount available.
e. If a demand exceeds the amount available under the standby, the drawing is discrepant. Any document other than the demand stating an amount in excess of the amount demanded is not discrepant for that reason.
f. Use of 'approximately', 'about', 'circa', or a similar word permits a tolerance not to exceed 10% more or 10% less of the amount to which such word refers.

3.09 Extend or pay

A beneficiary's request to extend the expiration date of the standby or, alternatively, to pay the amount available under it:

a. is a presentation demanding payment under the standby, to be examined as such in accordance with these Rules; and
b. implies that the beneficiary:
   i. consents to the amendment to extend the expiry date to the date requested;
   ii. requests the issuer to exercise its discretion to seek the approval of the applicant and to issue that amendment;
   iii. upon issuance of that amendment, retracts its demand for payment; and
   iv. consents to the maximum time available under these Rules for examination and notice of dishonour.

3.10 No notice of receipt of presentation

An issuer is not required to notify the applicant of receipt of a presentation under the standby.

3.11 Issuer waiver and applicant consent to waiver of presentation rules

In addition to other discretionary provisions in a standby or these Rules, an issuer may, in its sole discretion, without notice to or consent of the applicant and without effect on the applicant's obligations to the issuer, waive:

a. the following Rules and any similar terms stated in the standby which are primarily for the issuer's benefit or operational convenience:
   i. treatment of documents received, at the request of the presenter, as having been presented at a later date (Rule 3.02);
   ii. identification of a presentation to the standby under which it is presented (Rule 3.03(a));

      iii. where and to whom presentation is made (Rule 3.04(b), (c), and (d)), except the country of presentation stated in the standby; or

      iv. treatment of a presentation made after the close of business as if it were made on the next business day (Rule 3.05(b)).

b. the following Rule but not similar terms stated in the standby:

      i. a required document dated after the date of its stated presentation (Rule 4.06); or

      ii. the requirement that a document issued by the beneficiary be in the language of the standby (Rule 4.04).

c. the following Rule relating to the operational integrity of the standby only in so far as the bank is in fact dealing with the true beneficiary: acceptance of a demand in an electronic medium (Rule 3.06(b)).

Waiver by the confirmer requires the consent of the issuer with respect to paragraphs (b) and (c) of this Rule.

3.12 Original standby lost, stolen, mutilated or destroyed

a. If an original standby is lost, stolen, mutilated or destroyed, the issuer need not replace it or waive any requirement that the original be presented under the standby.

b. If the issuer agrees to replace an original standby or to waive a requirement for its presentation, it may provide a replacement or copy to the beneficiary without affecting the applicant's obligations to the issuer to reimburse, but, if it does so, the issuer must mark the replacement or copy as such. The issuer may, in its sole discretion, require indemnities satisfactory to it from the beneficiary and assurances from nominated persons that no payment has been made.

Closure on Expiry Date

3.13 Expiration date on a non-business day

a. If the last day for presentation stated in a standby (whether stated to be the expiration date or the date by which documents must be received) is not a business day of the issuer or nominated person where presentation is to be made, then presentation made there on the first following business day shall be deemed timely.

b. A nominated person to whom such a presentation is made must so notify the issuer.

3.14 Closure on a business day and authorisation of another reasonable place for presentation

a. If on the last business day for presentation the place for presentation stated in a standby is for any reason closed and presentation is not timely made because of the closure, then the last day for presentation is automatically extended to the day occurring thirty calendar days after the place for presentation re-opens for business, unless the standby otherwise provides.

b. Upon, or in anticipation of, closure of the place of presentation, an issuer may authorise another reasonable place for presentation in the standby or in a communication received by the beneficiary. If it does so, then:

      i. presentation must be made at that reasonable place; and

      ii. if the communication is received fewer than thirty calendar days before the last day for presentation and for that reason presentation is not timely made, the last day for presentation is automatically extended to the day occurring thirty calendar days after the last day for presentation.

RULE 4

EXAMINATION

4.01 Examination for compliance
a. Demands for honour of a standby must comply with the terms and conditions of the standby.
b. Whether a presentation appears to comply is determined by examining the presentation on its face against the terms and conditions stated in the standby as interpreted and supplemented by these Rules which are to be read in the context of standard standby practice.

4.02 Non-examination of extraneous documents
Documents presented which are not required by the standby need not be examined and, in any event, shall be disregarded for purposes of determining compliance of the presentation. They may without responsibility be returned to the presenter or passed on with the other documents presented.

4.03 Examination for inconsistency
An issuer or nominated person is required to examine documents for inconsistency with each other only to the extent provided in the standby.

4.04 Language of documents
The language of all documents issued by the beneficiary is to be that of the standby.

4.05 Issuer of documents
Any required document must be issued by the beneficiary unless the standby indicates that the document is to be issued by a third person or the document is of a type that standard standby practice requires to be issued by a third person.

4.06 Date of documents
The issuance date of a required document may be earlier but not later than the date of its presentation.

4.07 Required signature on a document
a. A required document need not be signed unless the standby indicates that the document must be signed or the document is of a type that standard standby practice requires be signed.
b. A required signature may be made in any manner that corresponds to the medium in which the signed document is presented.
c. Unless a standby specifies:
   i.   the name of a person who must sign a document, any signature or authentication will be regarded as a complying signature.
   ii. the status of a person who must sign, no indication of status is necessary.
d. If a standby specifies that a signature must be made by:
   i.   a named natural person without requiring that the signer's status be identified, a signature complies that appears to be that of the named person;
   ii. a named legal person or government agency without identifying who is to sign on its behalf or its status, any signature complies that appears to have been made on behalf of the named legal person or government agency; or
   iii. a named natural person, legal person, or government agency requiring the status of the signer be indicated, a signature complies which appears to be that of the named natural person, legal person, or government agency and indicates its status.

4.08 Demand document implied
If a standby does not specify any required document, it will still be deemed to require a documentary demand for payment.

4.09 Identical wording and quotation marks
If a standby requires:
a. a statement without specifying precise wording, then the wording in the document presented must appear to convey the same meaning as that required by the standby;
b. specified wording by the use of quotation marks, blocked wording, or an attached exhibit or form, then typographical errors in spelling, punctuation, spacing, or the like that are apparent when read in context are not required to be duplicated and blank lines or spaces for data may be completed in any manner not inconsistent with the standby; or
c. specified wording by the use of quotation marks, blocked wording, or an attached exhibit or form, and also provides that the specified wording be 'exact' or 'identical', then the wording in the documents presented, including typographical errors in spelling, punctuation, spacing and the like, as well as blank lines and spaces for data, must be exactly reproduced.

4.10 Applicant approval
A standby should not specify that a required document be issued, signed, or counter-signed by the applicant. However, if the standby includes such a requirement, the issuer may not waive the requirement and is not responsible for the applicant's withholding of the document or signature.

4.11 Non-documentary terms or conditions
a. A standby term or condition which is non-documentary must be disregarded whether or not it affects the issuer's obligation to treat a presentation as complying or to treat the standby as issued, amended or terminated.
b. Terms or conditions are non-documentary if the standby does not require presentation of a document in which they are to be evidenced and if their fulfillment cannot be determined by the issuer from the issuer's own records or within the issuer's normal operations.
c. Determinations from the issuer's own records or within the issuer's normal operations include determinations of:
    i.   when, where, and how documents are presented or otherwise delivered to the issuer;
    ii. when, where, and how communications affecting the standby are sent or received by the issuer, beneficiary, or any nominated person;
    iii. amounts transferred into or out of accounts with the issuer; and
    iv. amounts determinable from a published index (eg, if a standby provides for determining amounts of interest accruing according to published interest rates).
d. An issuer need not re-compute a beneficiary's computations under a formula stated or referenced in a standby except to the extent that the standby so provides.

4.12 Formality of statements in documents
a. A required statement need not be accompanied by a solemnity, officialisation, or any other formality.
b. If a standby provides for the addition of a formality to a required statement by the person making it without specifying form or content, the statement complies if it indicates that it was declared, averred, warranted, attested, sworn under oath, affirmed, certified, or the like.

c.   If a standby provides for a statement to be witnessed by another person without specifying form or content, the witnessed statement complies if it appears to contain a signature of a person other than the beneficiary with an indication that the person is acting as a witness.

d.   If a standby provides for a statement to be counter-signed, legalized, visaed, or the like by a person other than the beneficiary acting in a governmental, judicial, corporate, or other representative capacity without specifying form or content, the statement complies if it contains the signature of a person other than the beneficiary and includes an indication of that person's representative capacity and the organization on whose behalf the person has acted.

4.13 No responsibility to identify beneficiary

Except to the extent that a standby requires presentation of an electronic record:

a.   a person honouring a presentation has no obligation to the applicant to ascertain the identity of any person making a presentation or any assignee of proceeds;

b.   payment to a named beneficiary, transferee, an acknowledged assignee, successor by operation of law, to an account or account number stated in the standby or in a cover instruction from the beneficiary or nominated person fulfills the obligation under the standby to effect payment.

4.14 Name of acquired or merged issuer or confirmer

If the issuer or confirmer is reorganized, merged, or changes its name, any required reference by name to the issuer or confirmer in the documents presented may be to it or its successor.

4.15 Original, copy and multiple documents

a.   A presented document must be an original.

b.   Presentation of an electronic record, where an electronic presentation is permitted or required is deemed to be an 'original'.

c.   i.   A presented document is deemed to be an 'original' unless it appears on its face to have been reproduced from an original.

    ii.   A document which appears to have been reproduced from an original is deemed to be an original if the signature or authentication appears to be original.

d.   A standby that requires presentation of a 'copy' permits presentation of either an original or copy unless the standby states that only a copy be presented or otherwise addresses the disposition of all originals.

e.   If multiples of the same document are requested, only one must be an original unless:

    i.   'duplicate originals' or 'multiple originals' are requested in which case all must be originals; or

    ii.   'two copies', 'two-fold', or the like are requested in which case either originals or copies may be presented.

Standby Document Types

4.16 Demand for payment

a.   A demand for payment need not be separate from the beneficiary's statement or other required document.

b.   If a separate demand is required, it must contain:

    i.   a demand for payment from the beneficiary directed to the issuer or nominated person;

ii.   a date indicating when the demand was issued;
iii. the amount demanded; and
iv.   the beneficiary's signature.
c.   A demand may be in the form of a draft or other instruction, order, or request to
pay. If a standby requires presentation of a 'draft' or 'bill of exchange', that draft
or bill of exchange need not be in negotiable form unless the standby so states.

4.17 Statement of default or other drawing event

If a standby requires a statement, certificate, or other recital of a default or other
drawing event and does not specify content, the document complies if it contains:
a.   a representation to the effect that payment is due because a drawing event
described in the standby has occurred;
b.   a date indicating when it was issued; and
c.   the beneficiary's signature.

4.18 Negotiable documents

If a standby requires presentation of a document that is transferable by endorsement
and delivery without stating whether, how, or to whom endorsement must be made,
then the document may be presented without endorsement, or, if endorsed, the
endorsement may be in blank and, in any event, the document may be issued or
negotiated with or without recourse.

4.19 Legal or judicial documents

If a standby requires presentation of a government-issued document, a court order, an
arbitration award, or the like, a document or a copy is deemed to comply if it appears
to be:
i.   issued by a government agency, court, tribunal, or the like;
ii. suitably titled or named;
iii. signed;
iv. dated; and
v.   originally certified or authenticated by an official of a government agency, court,
tribunal, or the like.

4.20 Other documents

a.   If a standby requires a document other than one whose content is specified in these
Rules without specifying the issuer, data content, or wording, a document
complies if it appears to be appropriately titled or to serve the function of that
type of document under standard standby practice.
b.   A document presented under a standby is to be examined in the context of
standby practice under these Rules even if the document is of a type (such as a
commercial invoice, transport documents, insurance documents or the like) for
which the Uniform Customs and Practice for Documentary Credits contains
detailed rules.

4.21 Request to issue separate undertaking

If a standby requests that the beneficiary of the standby issue its own separate
undertaking to another (whether or not the standby recites the text of that
undertaking):
a.   the beneficiary receives no rights other than its rights to draw under the standby
even if the issuer pays a fee to the beneficiary for issuing the separate undertaking;
b.   neither the separate undertaking nor any documents presented under it need be
presented to the issuer; and

c. if originals or copies of the separate undertaking or documents presented under it are received by the issuer although not required to be presented as a condition to honour of the standby:
    i.   the issuer need not examine, and, in any event, shall disregard their compliance or consistency with the standby, with the beneficiary's demand under the standby, or with the beneficiary's separate undertaking; and
    ii. the issuer may without responsibility return them to the presenter or forward them to the applicant with the presentation.

RULE 5

NOTICE, PRECLUSION, AND DISPOSITION OF DOCUMENTS

5.01 Timely notice of dishonour
a. Notice of dishonour must be given within a time after presentation of documents which is not unreasonable.
    i.   Notice given within three business days is deemed to be not unreasonable and beyond seven business days is deemed to be unreasonable.
    ii.   Whether the time within which notice is given is unreasonable does not depend upon an imminent deadline for presentation.
    iii. The time for calculating when notice of dishonour must be given begins on the business day following the business day of presentation.
    iv.   Unless a standby otherwise expressly states a shortened time within which notice of dishonour must be given, the issuer has no obligation to accelerate its examination of a presentation.
b. i.   The means by which a notice of dishonour is to be given is by telecommunication, if available, and, if not, by another available means which allows for prompt notice.
    ii.   If notice of dishonour is received within the time permitted for giving the notice, then it is deemed to have been given by prompt means.
c. Notice of dishonour must be given to the person from whom the documents were received (whether the beneficiary, nominated person, or person other than a delivery person) except as otherwise requested by the presenter.

5.02 Statement of grounds for dishonour
A notice of dishonour shall state all discrepancies upon which dishonour is based.

5.03 Failure to give timely notice of dishonour
a. Failure to give notice of a discrepancy in a notice of dishonour within the time and by the means specified in the standby or these rules precludes assertion of that discrepancy in any document containing the discrepancy that is retained or re-presented, but does not preclude assertion of that discrepancy in any different presentation under the same or a separate standby.
b. Failure to give notice of dishonour or acceptance or acknowledgment that a deferred payment undertaking has been incurred obligates the issuer to pay at maturity.

5.04 Notice of expiry
Failure to give notice that a presentation was made after the expiration date does not preclude dishonour for that reason.

5.05 Issuer request for applicant waiver without request by presenter
If the issuer decides that a presentation does not comply and if the presenter does not otherwise instruct, the issuer may, in its sole discretion, request the applicant to waive non-compliance or otherwise to authorise honour within the time available for giving notice of dishonour but without extending it. Obtaining the applicant's waiver does not obligate the issuer to waive non-compliance.

5.06 Issuer request for applicant waiver upon request of presenter
If, after receipt of notice of dishonour, a presenter requests that the presented documents be forwarded to the issuer or that the issuer seek the applicant's waiver:
a.   no person is obligated to forward the discrepant documents or seek the applicant's waiver;
b.   the presentation to the issuer remains subject to these Rules unless departure from them is expressly consented to by the presenter; and
c.   if the documents are forwarded or if a waiver is sought:
    i.   the presenter is precluded from objecting to the discrepancies notified to it by the issuer;
    ii.   the issuer is not relieved from examining the presentation under these Rules;
    iii. the issuer is not obligated to waive the discrepancy even if the applicant waives it; and
    iv.   the issuer must hold the documents until it receives a response from the applicant or is requested by the presenter to return the documents, and if the issuer receives no such response or request within ten business days of its notice of dishonour, it may return the documents to the presenter.

5.07 Disposition of documents
Dishonoured documents must be returned, held, or disposed of as reasonably instructed by the presenter. Failure to give notice of the disposition of documents in the notice of dishonour does not preclude the issuer from asserting any defense otherwise available to it against honour.

5.08 Cover instructions/transmittal letter
a.   Instructions accompanying a presentation made under a standby may be relied on to the extent that they are not contrary to the terms or conditions of the standby, the demand, or these Rules.
b.   Representations made by a nominated person accompanying a presentation may be relied upon to the extent that they are not contrary to the terms or conditions of a standby or these Rules.
c.   Notwithstanding receipt of instructions, an issuer or nominated person may pay, give notice, return the documents, or otherwise deal directly with the presenter.
d.   A statement in the cover letter that the documents are discrepant does not relieve the issuer from examining the presentation for compliance.

5.09 Applicant notice of objection
a.   An applicant must timely object to an issuer's honour of a noncomplying presentation by giving timely notice by prompt means.
b.   An applicant acts timely if it objects to discrepancies by sending a notice to the issuer stating the discrepancies on which the objection is based within a time after the applicant's receipt of the documents which is not unreasonable.
c.   Failure to give a timely notice of objection by prompt means precludes assertion by the applicant against the issuer of any discrepancy or other matter apparent on the face of the documents received by the applicant, but does not preclude assertion of that objection to any different presentation under the same or a different standby.

RULE 6

TRANSFER, ASSIGNMENT, AND TRANSFER BY OPERATION OF LAW

Transfer of Drawing Rights

6.01 *Request to transfer drawing rights*
Where a beneficiary requests that an issuer or nominated person honour a drawing from another person as if that person were the beneficiary, these Rules on transfer of drawing rights ('transfer') apply.

6.02 *When drawing rights are transferable*
a.   A standby is not transferable unless it so states.
b.   A standby that states that it is transferable without further provision means that drawing rights:
   i.   may be transferred in their entirety more than once;
   ii.   may not be partially transferred; and
   iii.   may not be transferred unless the issuer (including the confirmer) or another person specifically nominated in the standby agrees to and effects the transfer requested by the beneficiary.

6.03 *Conditions to transfer*
An issuer of a transferable standby or a nominated person need not effect a transfer unless:
a.   it is satisfied as to the existence and authenticity of the original standby; and
b.   the beneficiary submits or fulfills:
i.   a request in a form acceptable to the issuer or nominated person including the effective date of the transfer and the name and address of the transferee;
ii.   the original standby;
iii.   verification of the signature of the person signing for the beneficiary;
iv.   verification of the authority of the person signing for the beneficiary;
v.   payment of the transfer fee; and
vi.   any other reasonable requirements.

6.04 *Effect of transfer on required documents*
Where there has been a transfer of drawing rights in their entirety:
a.   a draft or demand must be signed by the transferee beneficiary; and
b.   the name of the transferee beneficiary may be used in place of the name of the transferor beneficiary in any other required document.

6.05 *Reimbursement for payment based on a transfer*
An issuer or nominated person paying under a transfer pursuant to Rule 6.03(a), (b)(i), and (b)(ii) is entitled to reimbursement as if it had made payment to the beneficiary.

Acknowledgment of Assignment of Proceeds

6.06 *Assignment of proceeds*
Where an issuer or nominated person is asked to acknowledge a beneficiary's request to pay an assignee all or part of any proceeds of the beneficiary's drawing under the standby, these Rules on acknowledgment of an assignment of proceeds apply except where applicable law otherwise requires.

6.07 Request for acknowledgment
a.   Unless applicable law otherwise requires, an issuer or nominated person
  i.   is not obligated to give effect to an assignment of proceeds which it has not acknowledged; and
  ii.   is not obligated to acknowledge the assignment.
b.   If an assignment is acknowledged:
  i.   the acknowledgment confers no rights with respect to the standby to the assignee who is only entitled to the proceeds assigned, if any, and whose rights may be affected by amendment or cancellation; and
  ii.   the rights of the assignee are subject to:
    (a) the existence of any net proceeds payable to the beneficiary by the person making the acknowledgment;
    (b) rights of nominated persons and transferee beneficiaries;
    (c) rights of other acknowledged assignees; and
    (d) any other rights or interests that may have priority under applicable law.

6.08 Conditions to acknowledgment of assignment of proceeds
An issuer or nominated person may condition its acknowledgment on receipt of:
a.   the original standby for examination or notation;
b.   verification of the signature of the person signing for the beneficiary;
c.   verification of the authority of the person signing for the beneficiary;
d.   an irrevocable request signed by the beneficiary for acknowledgment of the assignment that includes statements, covenants, indemnities, and other provisions which may be contained in the issuer's or nominated person's required form requesting acknowledgment of assignment, such as:
  i.   the identity of the affected drawings if the standby permits multiple drawings;
  ii.   the full name, legal form, location, and mailing address of the beneficiary and the assignee;
  iii. details of any request affecting the method of payment or delivery of the standby proceeds;
  iv.   limitation on partial assignments and prohibition of successive assignments;
  v.   statements regarding the legality and relative priority of the assignment; or
  vi.   right of recovery by the issuer or nominated person of any proceeds received by the assignee that are recoverable from the beneficiary;
e.   payment of a fee for the acknowledgment; and
f.   fulfillment of other reasonable requirements.

6.09 Conflicting claims to proceeds
If there are conflicting claims to proceeds, then payment to an acknowledged assignee may be suspended pending resolution of the conflict.

6.10 Reimbursement for payment based on an assignment
An issuer or nominated person paying under an acknowledged assignment pursuant to Rule 6.08(a) and (b) is entitled to reimbursement as if it had made payment to the beneficiary. If the beneficiary is a bank, the acknowledgment may be based solely upon an authenticated communication.

Transfer by operation of Law

6.11 Transferee by operation of law
Where an heir, personal representative, liquidator, trustee, receiver, successor corporation, or similar person who claims to be designated by law to succeed to the

interests of a beneficiary presents documents in its own name as if it were the authorised transferee of the beneficiary, these Rules on transfer by operation of law apply.

6.12 Additional document in event of drawing in successor's name

A claimed successor may be treated as if it were an authorized transferee of a beneficiary's drawing rights in their entirety if it presents an additional document or documents which appear to be issued by a public official or representative (including a judicial officer) and indicate:

a.   that the claimed successor is the survivor of a merger, consolidation, or similar action of a corporation, limited liability company, or other similar organisation;
b.   that the claimed successor is authorised or appointed to act on behalf of the named beneficiary or its estate because of an insolvency proceeding;
c.   that the claimed successor is authorised or appointed to act on behalf of the named beneficiary because of death or incapacity; or
d.   that the name of the named beneficiary has been changed to that of the claimed successor.

6.13 Suspension of obligations upon presentation by successor

An issuer or nominated person which receives a presentation from a claimed successor which complies in all respects except for the name of the beneficiary:

a.   may request in a manner satisfactory as to form and substance:
  i.   a legal opinion;
  ii.   an additional document referred to in Rule 6.12 (Additional Document in Event of Drawing in Successor's Name) from a public official;
  iii. statements, covenants, and indemnities regarding the status of the claimed successor as successor by operation of law;
  iv.   payment of fees reasonably related to these determinations; and
  v.   anything which may be required for a transfer under Rule 6.03 (Conditions to Transfer) or an acknowledgment of assignment of proceeds under Rule 6.08 (Conditions to Acknowledgment of Assignment of Proceeds); but such documentation shall not constitute a required document for purposes of expiry of the standby.
b.   Until the issuer or nominated person receives the requested documentation, its obligation to honour or give notice of dishonour is suspended, but any deadline for presentation of required documents is not thereby extended.

6.14 Reimbursement for payment based on a transfer by operation of law

An issuer or nominated person paying under a transfer by operation of law pursuant to Rule 6.12 (Additional Document in Event of Drawing in Successor's Name) is entitled to reimbursement as if it had made payment to the beneficiary.

RULE 7

CANCELLATION

7.01 When an irrevocable standby is cancelled or terminated

A beneficiary's rights under a standby may not be cancelled without its consent. Consent may be evidenced in writing or by an action such as return of the original standby in a manner which implies that the beneficiary consents to cancellation. A beneficiary's consent to cancellation is irrevocable when communicated to the issuer.

7.02 Issuer's discretion regarding a decision to cancel
Before acceding to a beneficiary's authorization to cancel and treating the standby as cancelled for all purposes, an issuer may require in a manner satisfactory as to form and substance:
a. the original standby;
b. verification of the signature of the person signing for the beneficiary;
c. verification of the authorization of the person signing for the beneficiary;
d. a legal opinion;
e. an irrevocable authority signed by the beneficiary for cancellation that includes statements, covenants, indemnities, and similar provisions contained in a required form;
f. satisfaction that the obligation of any confirmer has been cancelled;
g. satisfaction that there has not been a transfer or payment by any nominated person; and
h. any other reasonable measure.

RULE 8

REIMBURSEMENT OBLIGATIONS

8.01 Right to reimbursement
a. Where payment is made against a complying presentation in accordance with these Rules, reimbursement must be made by:
    i. an applicant to an issuer requested to issue a standby; and
    ii. an issuer to a person nominated to honour or otherwise give value.
b. An applicant must indemnify the issuer against all claims, obligations, and responsibilities (including attorney's fees) arising out of:
    i. the imposition of law or practice other than that chosen in the standby or applicable at the place of issuance;
    ii. the fraud, forgery, or illegal action of others; or
    iii. the issuer's performance of the obligations of a confirmer that wrongfully dishonours a confirmation.
c. This Rule supplements any applicable agreement, course of dealing, practice, custom or usage providing for reimbursement or indemnification on lesser or other grounds.

8.02 Charges for fees and costs
a. An applicant must pay the issuer's charges and reimburse the issuer for any charges that the issuer is obligated to pay to persons nominated with the applicant's consent to advise, confirm, honour, negotiate, transfer, or to issue a separate undertaking.
b. An issuer is obligated to pay the charges of other persons:
    i. if they are payable in accordance with the terms of the standby; or
    ii. if they are the reasonable and customary fees and expenses of a person requested by the issuer to advise, honour, negotiate, transfer, or to issue a separate undertaking, and they are unrecovered and unrecoverable from the beneficiary or other presenter because no demand is made under the standby.

8.03 Refund of reimbursement
A nominated person that obtains reimbursement before the issuer timely dishonours the presentation must refund the reimbursement with interest if the issuer dishonours. The refund does not preclude the nominated person's wrongful dishonour claims.

8.04 Bank-to-bank reimbursement
Any instruction or authorization to obtain reimbursement from another bank is subject to the International Chamber of Commerce standard rules for bank-to-bank reimbursements.

RULE 9

TIMING

9.01 Duration of standby
A standby must:
a.　contain an expiry date; or
b.　permit the issuer to terminate the standby upon reasonable prior notice or payment.

9.02 Effect of expiration on nominated person
The rights of a nominated person that acts within the scope of its nomination are not affected by the subsequent expiry of the standby.

9.03 Calculation of time
a.　A period of time within which an action must be taken under these Rules begins to run on the first business day following the business day when the action could have been undertaken at the place where the action should have been undertaken.
b.　An extension period starts on the calendar day following the stated expiry date even if either day falls on a day when the issuer is closed.

9.04 Time of day of expiration
If no time of day is stated for expiration, it occurs at the close of business at the place of presentation.

9.05 Retention of standby
Retention of the original standby does not preserve any rights under the standby after the right to demand payment ceases.

RULE 10

SYNDICATION / PARTICIPATION

10.01 Syndication
If a standby with more than one issuer does not state to whom presentation may be made, presentation may be made to any issuer with binding effect on all issuers.

10.02 Participation
a.　Unless otherwise agreed between an applicant and an issuer, the issuer may sell participations in the issuer's rights against the applicant and any presenter and may disclose relevant applicant information in confidence to potential participants.
b.　An issuer's sale of participations does not affect the obligations of the issuer under the standby or create any rights or obligations between the beneficiary and any participant.

Appendix 5

Issue of documentary credit on SWIFT form MT700

To Institution	TPBKTWTPXXX
	TAIPEIBANK LIMITED
	HEAD OFFICE, 50 SEC.2
	CHUNGSHAN NORTH ROAD, P O BOX 1646
	TAIPEI
Priority N	
27:	Sequence of total
	1/1
40A:	Form of Documentary Credit
	IRREVOCABLE
20:	Documentary Credit number
	IMP70003208
31C:	Date of Issue
	090127
40E:	Applicable Rules
	UCP LATEST VERSION
31D:	Date and Place of Expiry
	090327
50:	Applicant
	VISION PHOTOGRAPHY PLC
59:	Beneficiary
	THE WOODWARE ENTERPRISE CO LTD
	TAIPEI HSEIN TAIWAN
32B:	Currency Code, amount
	USD 100383.00
39A:	Percentage Credit Amount Tolerance
	05/05
41D:	Available with ... By ...
	Any bank in Taiwan
	BY NEGOTIATION
43P:	Partial Shipments
	NOT ALLOWED
43T:	Transhipment
	NOT ALLOWED

44E:	Port of Loading/Airport of Departure
	ANY TAIWAN PORT
44F:	Port of Discharge/Airport of Destination
	FELIXSTOWE
44D:	Shipment Period
	GOODS TO BE SHIPPED IN TWO CONSIGNMENTS
	1ST SHIPMENT NO LATER THAN 20/02/2009
	2ND SHIPMENT NO LATER THAN 06/03/2009
45A:	Description of goods and/or Services
	WOOD PHOTO FRAMES AS PER PURCHASE ORDER NO
	HK00/11
	FOB TAIWAN PORT
46A:	Documents Required
	+ ORIGINAL AND TWO COPIES COMMERCIAL INVOICE
	+ ORIGINAL AND TWO COPIES PACKING LIST SHOWING

CONTENT

OF EACH CONTAINER BY SKU NOS AND BRIEF DESCRIPTION OF
GOODS.
+ ORIGINAL CERTIFICATE OF ORIGIN PLUS ONE COPY
+FULL SET ON BOARD MARINE BILLS OF LADING COVERING PORT
TO PORT SHIPMENT ISSUED TO ORDER AND BLANK ENDORSED,
MARKED FREIGHT COLLECT AND NOTIFY APPLICANT.
+ INSPECTION CERTIFICATE
+ COPY OF BENEFICIARY'S FAX ADVISING INVOICE VALUE NAME
OF CARRYING VESSEL AND QTY OF GOODS BEING SHIPPED
DATED AT LEAST 7 DAYS PRIOR TO SHIPMENT DATE.

47A:	Additional Conditions
	+ WE RESERVE THE RIGHT TO MAKE A CHARGE OF GBP 40.00,
	IN ADDITION TO COSTS WHICH ARISE, WHERE DOCUMENTS DO
	NOT COMPLY WITH THE TERMS AND CONDITIONS OF THE
	LETTER OF CREDIT.
71B:	Charges
	ALL BANK CHARGES OTHER THAN THOSE OF THE ISSUING BANK
	ARE FOR ACCOUNT OF THE BENEFICIARY.
48:	Period for Presentation
	DOCUMENTS MUST BE PRESENTED WITHIN 21 DAYS FROM THE
	DATE OF THE SHIPPING DOCUMENT.
49:	Confirmation Instructions
	WITHOUT
78:	Instructions to the Paying/Accepting/Negotiating Bank
	+ UPON RECEIPT OF DOCUMENTS IN COMPLIANCE WITH THE
	TERMS AND CONDITIONS OF THIS DOCUMENTARY CREDIT,
	PAYMENT WILL BE EFFECTED AT SIGHT IN THE CURRENCY OF
	THE DOCUMENTARY CREDIT.
	+ DOCUMENTS SHOULD BE SENT TO US IN TWO SEPARATE
	COURIERS.
57D:	Advise Through bank
	TAIPEIBANK, TAIPEI WORLD TRADE
	CENTRE BRANCH, 13F NO 333 SEC 1
	KEELUNG ROAD, TAIPEI, TAIWAN
	ROC SWIFT TPBKTWTP

Index

All references are to paragraph numbers